PLEASURE and DANGER

PLEASURE
and DANGER:
exploring female
sexuality

Edited by
Carole S. Vance

Routledge & Kegan Paul
Boston, London, Melbourne and Henley

First published in 1984 by Routledge & Kegan Paul plc
9 Park Street, Boston, Mass. 02108, USA
14 Leicester Square, London WC2H 7PH, England
464 St Kilda Road, Melbourne, Victoria 3004, Australia and
Broadway House, Newtown Road, Henley-on-Thames, Oxon RG9 1EN, England
Printed in The United States of America
Library of Congress Cataloging in Publication Data
Main entry under title:
Pleasure and danger.
Papers presented at the Scholar and the feminist IX conference, held Apr. 24,
1982 at Barnard College, New York City.
Bibliography: p.
Includes index.
1. Women – Sexual behavior – Congresses. 2. Feminism – Congresses. I. Vance,
Carole S.
HQ29.P54 1984   306.7'088042   84-8402

British Library CIP Data available

ISBN 0-7100-9974-6 (c)
ISBN 0-7102-0248-2 (p)

To the memory of my father, William
T. Vance, and to my mother, Madlyn
L. Vance

Contents

vii

viii   *Contents*

Notes on contributors

Dorothy Allison was an editor for *Quest: A Feminist Quarterly* from 1976 until 1980. Since 1981 she has been a member of the editorial collective of *Conditions*. Her first book, *The Women Who Hate Me*, was recently published by Long Haul Press (P.O. Box 592, Van Brunt Station, Brooklyn, NY 11215). She has been a regular columnist for the *New York Native* for the past few years. Her short stories have appeared in *Conditions* and in the *Lesbian Fiction Anthology* published in 1981 by Persephone Press. A known trouble-maker, she intends to concentrate on writing fiction for a while.

Meryl Altman is a graduate student in American Literature at Columbia University, where she also teaches writing. Her dissertation, *Mythologies of Influence: Four Modernist American Poets*, is a feminist examination of the works of and relationships between H.D., Ezra Pound, William Carlos Williams, and Marianne Moore. She is a graduate of Swarthmore College, and was a member of the planning committee for the Scholar and the Feminist IX conference

Mary S. Calderone, MD, MPH, was Medical Director, Planned Parenthood Federation of America, 1953–64, and Co-founder, Executive Director, and President of SIECUS (Sex Information and Education Council of the US), 1964-82. She is Adjunct Professor, Program in Human Sexuality in New York University's Department of Health Education. Her books include *The Family Book About Sexuality* and *Talking With Your Child About Sex*.

Muriel Dimen is an anthropologist, psychoanalyst, and writer on sexuality, feminism, women, and psychoanalytic and social theory. An Associate Professor of Anthropology at Lehman College, she is the author of *The Anthropological Imagination* (New York, McGraw-Hill, 1977) and is currently writing *Sexual Contradictions* (New York, Macmillan, forthcoming). She is a founding member of CARASA (Committee for Abortion Rights and Against Sterilization Abuse) and of GRHS (Group for a Radical Human Science). She received her Ph.D. in anthropology from Columbia in 1970 and her Certificate from the New York University Postdoctoral Program in Psychotherapy and Psychoanalysis in 1983.

Ellen Carol DuBois teaches history and American Studies at SUNY/Buffalo, where she is also coordinator of Women's Studies. She is the author of *Feminism and Suffrage: The Emergence of an Independent Women's Movement in America, 1848-1869* (Ithaca, NY, Cornell) and *Elizabeth Cady Stanton, Susan B. Anthony: Correspondence, Writings, Speeches* (New York, Schocken). She is currently completing a book on Harriot Stanton Blatch and the woman suffrage movement in New York in the Progressive Era.

Alice Echols teaches women's studies at the University of Michigan. She is currently completing a dissertation on radical feminist theory and praxis which covers the period 1967-78 and which analyzes the supplantation of radical feminism by cultural feminism. Her most recent articles appeared in *Social Text* and *Powers of Desire: The Politics of Sexuality*.

Oliva M. Espín teaches at Boston University, in the graduate Program in Counseling Psychology. She also practices psychotherapy and consultation. She chaired the Hispanic Task Force, Division 35, American Psychological Association. She is active in other professional organizations, including the National Hispanic Psychological Association.

She was NIMH fellow at Harvard University for two years, while doing a study of Hispanic women healers. She has published widely and is presently editing a book on psychotherapy with women from different cultural backgrounds.

Roberta Galler is a psychoanalyst and psychotherapist in private practice in New York City. She was trained at and is on the staff of the Post-Graduate Center for Mental Health. A long-time social activist, she is currently involved in issues of feminism and disability. She is a founding board member of the Association of Mental Health Practitioners with Physical Disabilities. A frequent speaker, she has authored several articles on various aspects of women and disability.

Faye Ginsburg is a doctoral candidate in anthropology at the Graduate Center, CUNY where she is completing her dissertation on grassroots abortion activists in the Upper Midwest. Her abiding interests in religion, sex and politics led her to research and author a paper on menstrual rituals in a Syrian Jewish community to be published in *Sex Roles in Jewish Communities*, R. Berger-Sofer and Y. Katzir (eds). Faye has produced a number of documentaries including "In Her Hands: Women and Ritual," funded by the NEH and distributed by Women Make Movies; and "Prairie Storm" for WCCO-TV, Minneapolis.

Bette Gordon is a New York City filmmaker whose works include *Empty Suitcases, Exchanges,* and other short films. Her most recent feature film, *Variety*, was funded by West German television, British television, and the New York State Council for the Arts. Ms Gordon is an Assistant Professor of Film at Hofstra University and a board member of the Collective for Living Cinema in New York. Her work has been exhibited extensively in the United States as well as in international festivals (including Berlin, Edinburgh, Rotterdam and Toronto) and reviewed in *The Village Voice, Camera Obscura,* and *Screen.* Gordon has received several awards for her films, including a prize at the 1975 Chicago International Film Festival.

Linda Gordon is Professor of women's history at the University of Massachusetts/Boston. She is the author of several books including a history of birth control (*Woman's Body, Woman's Right: A Social History of Birth Control in the U.S.*, Viking/Penguin, 1976) and is now writing a book on the history of family violence. She is an editor of *Radical America.* She has been discussing feminism, women's history and sex with Ellen DuBois (with whom she co-authored an article for this book) for over a decade.

hattie gossett. work herstory; babysitter asst playground attendant cook paid companion waitress secy cleaning person. presented here is part of her own collection of writings titled *presenting sister noblues & the original wild & free wimmins jazz & blues desert caravan* for which she is currently seeking an insightful and venturesome publisher.

Brett Harvey is a freelance writer who lives in Brooklyn, New York. She was publicity director at The Feminist Press from 1974 to 1980. Prior to that, she produced women's programming and was co-director of the Drama and Literature department at WBAI-FM in New York. Her work has appeared in the *Christian Science Monitor, Ms. Magazine, Village Voice, In These Times* and *Nation.*

Amber Hollibaugh is a writer and activist now living in New York City. She was a founding member of the San Francisco Lesbian and Gay History Project and is an editor of *Socialist Review.* She has been writing and speaking about sexuality and politics for many years. She is currently at work on a book about butch/femme with her lover, Esther Newton, called *They Are Connected Underneath: A Book of Butch/Femme Explorations.*

Barbara Kruger works as an artist, a critic, and a curator. Her recent one-person exhibitions include the ICA in London, the Nouveau Musée in Lyon, and the Annina Nosei Gallery in New York. Group exhibitions include the 1983 Whitney Biennial, Documenta 7 in Kassel, Germany, and the 1982 Venice Biennale, the Mary Boone Gallery, New York, and "The Revolutionary Power of Women's Laughter" at Protech McNeil. She is currently collaborating with Jane Weinstock on a feature film, "Next to Nothing," and writing film criticism for *Artforum*.

Kate Millett is the author of *Sexual Politics, Flying, Sita*, and *The Basement*. Her degrees are from Oxford and Columbia. A sculptor, painter, and filmmaker as well as a writer, she is founding an art colony for women at her farm in Poughkeepsie. Millett has worked in many areas of civil rights for blacks, women and gays.

Cherríe Moraga is a Los Angeles-born Chicana. She is the author of *Loving in the War Years, Lo Que Nunca Pasó Por Sus Labios* and the co-editor of *Cuentos: Stories by Latinas* and *This Bridge Called My Back: Writings by Radical Women of Color*. She is currently living in New York where she is a founding and active member of Kitchen Table: Women of Color Press.

Carol Munter is a psychotherapist in private practice in New York City. She has worked extensively with women with compulsive eating problems and currently has developed, with Janice La Rouche, a theme-centered workshop for women on the use of assertive techniques in male/female relationships.

Joan Nestle is a co-founder of the Lesbian Herstory Archives and The Lesbian Herstory Educational Foundation, Inc. She also teaches in the SEEK Program at Queens College, CUNY.

Esther Newton is associate professor of anthropology and women's studies at SUNY/Purchase. She is the author of *Mother Camp* (University of Chicago Press) and, with Shirley Walton, of *Womenfriends*. She was a member of the Scholar and the Feminist IX planning committee, and has remained interested in issues of gender and sexuality. Currently, she is editing a book on butch/femme identities with Amber Hollibaugh, called *Connected Underneath*.

Sharon Olds's first book of poems, *Satan Says* (University of Pittsburgh Press, 1980), received the San Francisco Poetry Center Award for 1981. Her second book, *The Dead and the Living* (New

York, Alfred A. Knopf, 1983) has been named the Lamont Selection for 1984 by the Academy of American Poets.

Patricia Murphy Robinson is a clinical social worker, in private practice for twenty years, author of several essays on poor black women and their culture; editorial consultant for *Lessons from the Damned*, a book written by black people from a decaying neighborhood in Westchester County, New York; and presently co-editor for *My Soul Looks Back in Wonder: Presenting Sister No-Blues*, a collection of writing by hattie gossett, forthcoming.

Gayle Rubin is an anthropologist, feminist, sex radical, and world-class procrastinator who is currently living in San Francisco. She is working on a dissertation on the history and culture of the gay male leather community.

Kaja Silverman is associate professor of film and women's studies at Simon Fraser University. She is the author of *The Subject of Semiotics* (Oxford University Press, 1983) and numerous articles on film and post-structuralist theory. She is currently writing *Women In Cinema: Body and Voice*.

Hortense J. Spillers is an associate professor of English at Haverford College, Haverford, Pa. She has written numerous pieces of criticism and fiction and with Marjorie Pryse is presently co-editing a collection of essays on black women writers in the United States, to be published by Indiana University Press. She is at work herself on a critical theory of black women's writing, a critical perspective on the rhetoric of the African-American sermon, and a long piece of fiction.

Sharon Thompson has been an activist in the reproductive rights movement. Her stories and articles have appeared in a number of publications, including *Feminist Studies* and *Heresies*, and she co-edited, with Ann Snitow and Christine Stansell, *Powers of Desire: The Politics of Sexuality*.

Carole S. Vance is an anthropologist and epidemiologist at Columbia University and is co-director of the Institute for the Study of Sex in Society and History in New York. She writes about the intersection of sexuality, gender, and disease, with her most recent work about female genital surgery. She was the Academic Coordinator of the Scholar and the Feminist IX conference.

Shirley Walton is a journalist covering New York City for the *Toronto Star*, co-author with Esther Newton of *Womenfriends:*

Our Journal, as well as author of several sports books, most recently *The Hockey Encyclopedia*. After gaining access for women to the Madison Square Garden pressbox, Ms Walton edited a sport magazine, moderated a radio show, was the first woman TV color commentator for hockey games and was for six years co-owner of Djuna Books, a women's bookstore in Manhattan's Greenwich Village.

Paula Webster is an anthropologist and writer, co-author of *Bound by Love: The Sweet Trap of Daughterhood* and member of the *Heresies Sex Issue* collective. She is currently working on a book about the development of the psychoanalytic discourse on female sexual repression.

The photographs in "*Variety:* The Pleasure in Looking" are by **Nan Goldin**, who, for the last ten years, has been exploring the themes of gender identification, sexuality, relationships, and alienation through photography. She approaches these issues in a diaristic format through intimate portraits of her friends, lovers, and herself, through images of men, women, drag queens, children, skin heads, motherhood, prostitution, fetishism, cars, drinking, onanism, eroticism, and sexual encounters. She has been influenced by movie imagery, press photos, and the work of Larry Clark, Weegee, Brassaï, and August Sanders.

Preface

The papers, images, and poetry collected in this volume originated at the Scholar and the Feminist IX conference, "Towards a Politics of Sexuality," held on April 24, 1982 at Barnard College in New York City. The conference, the ninth in an annual series which explores the relationship between feminist scholarship and practice, was sponsored by the Barnard College Women's Center and funded by the Helena Rubinstein Foundation. Over 800 women attended the conference, and their comments and questions during formal presentations and workshop sessions were incorporated by authors as they revised their papers for publication. The views expressed in each paper, of course, are solely those of its author.

Organized by a planning committee of twenty-five diverse women over a nine-month period of study and discussion, the conference explored the tension between sexual danger and sexual pleasure in feminist theory and in women's lives during the past hundred years in Euro-America. The book, like the conference, does not attempt to provide definitive answers but suggests frameworks within which feminist thought may proceed, and represents an opportunity for readers to question some of their understandings and consider anew the complexity of women's sexual situation.

Acknowledgments

The birth of an edited book originating in a conference calls for many thanks. It is my pleasure to acknowledge the many individuals whose encouragement and help over several years made this book possible.

My first debt is to the members of the Scholar and the Feminist IX planning committee which met during 1981-2 in order to organize the conference: Julie Abraham, Hannah Alderfer, Meryl Altman, Jan Boney, Frances Doughty, Ellen DuBois, Kate Ellis, Judith Friedlander, Julie German, Faye Ginsburg, Diane Harriford, Beth Jaker, Mary Clare Lennon, Sherry Manasse, Nancy K. Miller, Marybeth Nelson, Esther Newton, Claire Riley, Susan R. Sacks, Ann Snitow, Quandra P. Stadler, Judith Walkowitz, Ellen Willis, and Patsy Yaeger. Members were extraordinarily generous with their time and energy, and the richness of the conference derived from their complex and varied understandings of women's situation. Called by one member a "postgraduate seminar in sexuality," the planning committee represented women's diversity and individuality. Their fast-moving discussions were a steady source of insight, humor, and delight. Thanks to Diarists Hannah Alderfer, Beth Jaker, and Marybeth Nelson for their work in producing the *Diary of a Conference on Sexuality*, an attempt to share the planning process with a larger audience.

I am grateful to Jane Gould, Director of the Barnard College Women's Center since its inception, for her efforts on behalf of women and her willingness to explore new questions and topics. Thanks to Janie Kritzman for her support and organizational contributions to the conference, and to Maria LaSala for her efficiency and patience. The conference was funded by the Helena Rubinstein Foundation and sponsored by the Barnard College Women's Center. Special thanks to the women – too legion to name individually – who contributed advice, suggestions, and encouragement at every stage of conference planning.

My second debt is to the members of the Scholar and the Feminist IX study group, an offspring of the planning committee which has continued to meet during 1982-3 and 1983-4: Julie Abraham, Hannah Alderfer, Jan Boney, Frances Doughty, Kate Ellis, Faye Ginsburg, Diane Harriford, Beth Jaker, Barbara Kerr, Mary Clare Lennon, Marybeth Nelson, Ann Snitow, Paula Webster, and Ellen Willis. The members of this group continue to prefer hard questions to easy answers, and I have benefited enormously from their discussions. I am also indebted to them for their steady encouragement, practical assistance, and warm friendship in completing the book.

Thanks also to the many women who have been thinking and talking sex during the past several years. Although often holding diverse opinions, they constitute a community of feminists engaged in friendly conversation with each other, and I have learned much from their discussions. The members of my New York sex and history study group, John D'Emilio, Jonathan Katz, Ann Snitow, Paula Webster, and Jeffrey Weinstein, have also provided intellectual nourishment over many years.

I am grateful to Lawrence Krasnoff and Lou McDonald for their patience, love and support during their close, if often involuntary, relationship to both the conference and the book. Special thanks are due to Ann Snitow for her generous intelligence and unfailingly good-humored counsel on many topics, large and small. Thanks to Pat Califfifia for advice, encouragement, and most reliable assistance, and to Jonathan Miller, David Schwartz, Robert Roth and Madlyn Vance for warm support.

I especially want to acknowledge Frances Doughty and Paula Webster, since the book would not have been completed without their loving help. Thanks to Frances for her intuition and enthusiasm, unyielding support, generous sharing of her ideas, and her friendship. Thanks to Paula for rare imagination, many hours of concrete help, years of stimulating discussion, and loyal affection.

Although personal and professional obligations prevented some conference participants from meeting the publication deadline, I am grateful to all for their contributions to the program. Thanks to authors in this volume for their cooperation and patience through the course of the editorial process. Thanks to my agent, Frances Goldin, for her good advice and energetic efforts on my behalf, and to Philippa Brewster, editor at Routledge & Kegan Paul.

The authors and publisher are also grateful to Audre Lorde and W.W. Norton for their permission to reproduce "Who Said It Was Simple?" from *Chosen Poems*, 1982; to Judith Levine and Laura Liben for their song, "Sex Cops"; to Pauline Réage and Grove Press for permission to use material from *Story of O*, 1965; International Creative Management for "Despisals" from *Breaking Open*, copyright © 1973 Muriel Rukeyser; Alfred A. Knopf, Inc. for Sharon Olds, "Sex Without Love" from *The Dead and the Living*; University of Pittsburgh Press for "The Sisters of Sexual Treasure" from Satan Says © 1980 by Sharon Olds; *Missouri Review*, for "The Partisans and the SS" by Sharon Olds; Dr David Reuben for material from *Everything You Always Wanted to*

Know About Sex, Bantam Books, 1969; and to Faber & Faber and Harcourt Brace Jovanovich Inc. for three lines from "Gerontion" by T.S. Eliot; to Nan Goldin for the illustrations in "*Variety*: The Pleasure in Looking". The illustrations on pp. 211-6 are copyright © Barbara Kruger, and those on pp. 281-2 are copyright © Gayle Rubin.

Despisals

Muriel Rukeyser

In the human cities, never again to
despise the backside of the city, the ghetto,
or build it again as we build the despised
backsides of houses.   Look at your own building.
You are the city.

Among our secrecies, not to despise our Jews
(that is, ourselves) or our darkness, our blacks,
or in our sexuality   wherever it takes us
and we now know we are productive
too productive, too reproductive
for our present invention – never to despise
the homosexual who goes building another

with touch   with touch   (not to despise any touch)
each like himself, like herself each.
You are this.

            In the body's ghetto
never to go despising the asshole
nor the useful shit that is our clean clue
to what we need.   Never to despise
the clitoris in her least speech.

Never to despise in myself what I have been taught
to despise.   Nor to despise the other.
Not to despise the *it*.   To make this relation
with the it : to know that I am it.

Pleasure and Danger: Toward a Politics of Sexuality

Carole S. Vance

The tension between sexual danger and sexual pleasure is a powerful one in women's lives. Sexuality is simultaneously a domain of restriction, repression, and danger as well as a domain of exploration, pleasure, and agency. To focus only on pleasure and gratification ignores the patriarchal structure in which women act, yet to speak only of sexual violence and oppression ignores women's experience with sexual agency and choice and unwittingly increases the sexual terror and despair in which women live.

The juxtaposition of pleasure and danger has engaged the attention of feminist theorists and activists in both the nineteenth and twentieth centuries, just as it has been an ongoing subject in the lives of individual women who must weigh the pleasures of sexuality against its cost in their daily calculations, choices, and acts. For some, the dangers of sexuality – violence, brutality, and coercion, in the form of rape, forcible incest, and exploitation, as well as everyday cruelty and humiliation – make the pleasures pale by comparison. For others, the positive possibilities of sexuality – explorations of the body, curiosity, intimacy, sensuality, adventure, excitement, human connection, basking in the infantile and non-rational – are not only worthwhile but provide sustaining energy. Nor are these positions fixed, since a woman might chose one perspective or the other at different points in her life in response to external and internal events.

Since the nineteenth century, feminist theorists have disagreed on how to improve women's sexual situation and, even more basically, on what women want sexually. Some have been broadly protectionist, attempting to secure some measure of safety from male lust and aggression, assuming either that women's sexuality is intrinsically muted or at least that it cannot flower until greater safety is established. Others, more often in the twentieth century than the nineteenth, have been expansionist and exploratory, believing that women could venture to be sexual in more visible and daring ways, especially as material changes which favored women's autonomy in general (wage labor, urbanization, contraception, and abortion) also supported sexual

1

autonomy.[1] Throughout one hundred years of intermittent but intense dialogue among theorists, organizers, and activists run a host of questions to which we do not fully know the answers, despite the progress we have made:

- Are male and female sexual natures essentially different, or the product of specific historical and cultural conditions?
- Has women's sexuality been muted by repression, or is it wholly different from men's?
- Does the source of sexual danger to women lie in an intrinsically aggressive or violent male nature, or in the patriarchal conditions that socialize male sexuality to aggression and female sexuality to compliance and submission?
- How can male sexual violence be reduced or eliminated?
- How does the procreative possibility of sex enter into women's experience of sexuality?
- Should feminism be promoting maximum or minimum differentiation in the sexual sphere, and what shape should either vision take?

Behind these questions are changes in material conditions and social organization wrought by capitalist transformations and the women's movement itself, most notably in the weakening of the traditional bargain women were forced to make with men: if women were "good" (sexually circumspect), men would protect them; if they were not, men could violate and punish them. As parties to this system, "good" women had an interest in restraining male sexual impulses, a source of danger to women, as well as their own sexuality which might incite men to act. Nineteenth-century feminists elaborated asexuality as an option for respectable women, using female passionlessness and male sexual restraint to challenge male sexual prerogatives. The second wave of feminism demanded and won increased sexual autonomy for women and decreasing male "protection," still within a patriarchal framework. Amid this flux, many women have come to feel more visible and sexually vulnerable. Despite the breakdown in the old bargain, which placed sexual safety and sexual freedom in opposition, women's fear of reprisal and punishment for sexual activity has not abated.

This sense of vulnerability has been played on by the Right. The conservative attack on feminist gains has taken the form of a moral crusade. In its campaign against the evils of abortion, lesbian and gay rights, contraceptive education and services, and women's economic independence, the Right is attempting to reinstate traditional sexual arrangements and the formerly inexorable link between reproduction and sexuality. In this, the Right offers a comprehensive plan for sexual practice which resonates in part with women's apprehension about immorality and sexual danger.[2] To respond convincingly as feminists, we cannot abandon our radical insights into sexual theory and practice. Instead, we must deepen and expand them, so that more women are encouraged to identify and act in their sexual self-interest.

The papers, poems, and images collected in this book are a move in this direction. They originated at the Scholar and the Feminist IX conference, "Towards a Politics of Sexuality," held at Barnard College on April 24, 1982. The conference attempted to explore the ambiguous and complex relationship between sexual pleasure and danger in women's lives and in feminist theory. The intent of conference planners was not to weaken the critique of danger. Rather, we wished to expand the analysis of pleasure, and to draw on women's energy to create a movement that speaks as powerfully in favor of sexual pleasure as it does against sexual danger. As feminists, we need to draw on women's experience of pleasure in imagining the textures and contours that would unfurl and proliferate in a safer space. What we want is not a mystery, not a blank. The clues to it are found in our daily experience already.

One clue lies in an obvious form of danger – the sexual violence committed by men against women: rape, sexual harassment, incest. As women began to speak out, it became clear that these apparently taboo acts were far from uncommon, and their damage to women was great. Beyond the actual physical or psychological harm done to victims of sexual violence, the threat of sexual attack served as a powerful reminder of male privilege, constraining women's movement and behavior. The cultural mythology surrounding sexual violence provided a unique and powerful route for it to work its way into the heart of female desire. A rag-bag of myths and folk knowledge that the contemporary feminist movement opposed depicted male lust as intrinsic, uncontrollable, and easily aroused by any show of female sexuality and desire. The main features of this ideology have been roundly critiqued by feminists, primarily for blaming the female victim while letting men off the hook, but its corollaries are equally pernicious. If female sexual desire triggers male attack, it cannot be freely or spontaneously shown, either in public or in private.

Instead, female desire should be restricted to zones protected and privileged in the culture: traditional marriage and the nuclear family. Although the boundaries of the safe zone have been somewhat renegotiated since the nineteenth century to include relatively respectable forms of unmarried and non-procreative heterosexuality, gross and public departures from "good" woman status, such as lesbianism, promiscuity, or non-traditional heterosexuality, still invite – and are thought to justify – violation.

Many women think that this ideology is unjust, illogical, and misogynous. Nevertheless, they believe it is widespread and potent, although to what degree can never be known with certainty. Better safe than sorry is still a dominant caution. Women – socialized by mothers to keep their dresses down, their pants up, and their bodies away from strangers – come to experience their own sexual impulses as dangerous, causing them to venture outside the protected sphere. Sexual abandon and impulsiveness acquire a high price, since women must think not only about the consequences of their sexual actions for themselves, but also about the consequences for men, whose sexual "natures" are supposedly lustful, aggressive, and unpredictable. Through a culturally dictated chain of reasoning, women become the moral custodians of male behavior, which they are perceived as instigating and eliciting. Women inherit a substantial task: the management of their own sexual desire and its public expression. Self-control and watchfulness become major and necessary female virtues. As a result, female desire is suspect from its first tingle, questionable until proven safe, and frequently too expensive when evaluated within the larger cultural framework which poses the question: is it really worth it? When unwanted pregnancy, street harassment, stigma, unemployment, queer-bashing, rape, and arrest are arrayed on the side of caution and inaction, passion often doesn't have a chance.

The second wave of feminism mounted a major critique of male sexual violence, indicting the complicity of state institutions and the cultural ideologies that justify it. However, feminism is newly beginning to appreciate the intra-psychic effects of a gender system that places pleasure and safety in opposition for women. Sexual constriction, invisibility, timidity, and uncuriosity are less the signs of an intrinsic and specific female sexual nature and more the signs of thoroughgoing damage. The resulting polarization of male and female sexuality is a likely product of the prevailing gender system, which is used to justify women's need for a restricted, but supposedly safe space and highly controlled sexual expression. The horrific effects of gender inequality may include not only brute violence, but the internalized control of women's impulses, poisoning desire at its very root with self-doubt and anxiety. The subtle connection between how patriarchy interferes with female desire and how women experience their own passion as dangerous is emerging as a critical issue to be explored.

The threat of male violence is, however, not the only source of sexual danger. Sexuality activates a host of intra-psychic anxieties: fear of merging with another, the blurring of body boundaries and the sense of self that occurs in the tangle of parts and sensations, with attendant fears of dissolution and self-annihilation. In sex, people experience earlier substrates, irrational connections, infantile memories, and a range of rich sensations.[3] We fear dependency and possible loss of control, as well as our own greedy aggression, our wishes to incorporate body parts, even entire persons. Having been told that pleasure threatens civilization, we wonder: what if there is no end to desire?

Sexuality also raises the fear of competition, as we recognize our own wishes to compete for attention and for loved objects. Whether women are lesbian or heterosexual, the competitors are other women, an unsisterly prospect. Finally, to the extent that women's experience of desire signals the giving up of vigilance and control – the responsibility of a proper woman – it causes profound unease about violating the bounds of traditional femininity.[4] Trangressing gender raises the specter of separation from other women – both the mother and literal and metaphorical sisters – leaving one isolated and vulnerable to attack. These subterranean pulls on women are no less powerful by remaining unnamed. Our unspoken fears are added to the sum of sexual terror. Without a better language to excavate and delineate these other sources of danger, everything is attributed to men, thereby inflating male power and impoverishing ourselves. Moreover, we leave the irrationality and volatility of sex open to manipulation by others, easily mobilized in campaigns against sexual deviance, degeneration, and pollution.

The hallmark of sexuality is its complexity: its multiple meanings, sensations, and connections. It is all too easy to cast sexual experience as either wholly pleasurable or dangerous; our culture encourages us to do so. Women are encouraged to assent that all male sexuality done to them is pleasurable and liberatory: women really enjoy being raped but can't admit it, and the often horrid cartoons in *Hustler* are just a lighthearted joke. In a counter-move, the feminist critique emphasized the ubiquity of sexual danger and humiliation in a patriarchal surround. Initially useful as an ideological interruption, this critique now shares the same undialectical and simplistic focus as its opposition. Women's actual sexual experience is more complicated, more difficult to grasp, more unsettling. Just as agreeing not to mention danger requires that one's sexual autobiography be recast, agreeing not to speak about pleasure requires a similar dishonest alchemy, the transmutation of sexuality into unmitigated danger and unremitting victimization.

The truth is that the rich brew of our experience contains elements of pleasure and oppression, happiness and humiliation. Rather than regard this ambiguity as confusion or false consciousness, we should use it as a source-book to examine how women experience sexual desire, fantasy, and action. We need to sort out individually and together what the elements of our pleasure and displeasure are. What, for instance, is powerful, enlivening, interesting in our experience? Our task is to identify what is pleasurable and under what conditions, and to control experience so that it occurs more frequently. To begin, we need to know our sexual histories, which are surely greater than our own individual experience, surely more diverse than we know, both incredible and instructive. To learn these histories, we must speak about them to each other. And for speech to flourish, there must be tolerance for diversity and curiosity, which Joan Nestle calls "the respect that one life pays to another."[5] Without women's speech, we fall back on texts and myths, prescriptive and overgeneralized.

Even some feminist analysis runs the risk of overemphasizing sexual danger, following the lead of the larger culture. The anti-pornography movement in a sense restates the main premises of the old gender system: the dominant cultural ideology elaborates the threat of sexual danger, so the anti-pornography movement responds by pushing for sexual safety via the control of public expression of male sexuality.[6] Although this would seem in certain respects a decisive break with an oppressive system – sexual danger is being directly challenged – in other respects the focus continues unchanged in that sexual pleasure for women is still minimized and the exploration of women's pleasurable experience remains slight. Feminism has succeeded in making public previously unmentionable activities like rape and incest. But the anti-pornography movement often interprets this as an indicator of rising violence against women and a sign of backlash against feminism. The net effect has been to suggest that women are less sexually safe than ever and that discussions and explorations of pleasure are better deferred to a safer time.

Women are vulnerable to being shamed about sex, and the anti-pornography ideology makes new forms of shaming possible. Traditional objections that women's concern with sex is unimportant are restated in suggestions that sexuality is trivial, diversionary, or not political. If sexual desire is coded as male, women begin to wonder if they are really ever sexual. Do we distrust our passion, thinking it perhaps not our own, but the construction of patriarchal culture? Can women be sexual actors? Can we act on our own behalf? Or are we purely victims, whose efforts must be directed at resisting male depredations in a patriarchal culture? Must our passion await expression for a safer time? When will that time come? Will any of us remember what her passion was? Does exceeding the bounds of femininity – passivity, helplessness, and victimization – make us deeply uncomfortable? Do we fear that if we act on our most deeply felt sexual passion that we will no longer be women? Do we wish, instead, to bind ourselves together into a sisterhood which seeks to curb male lust but does little to promote female pleasure? Sex is always guilty before proven innocent, an expensive undertaking considering the negative sanctions it easily evokes.

The overemphasis on danger runs the risk of making speech about sexual pleasure taboo. Feminists are easily intimidated by the charge that their own pleasure is selfish, as in political rhetoric which suggests that no woman is entitled to talk about sexual pleasure while any woman remains in danger – that is – never. Some also believe that sexuality is a privileged topic, important only to affluent groups, so to talk of it betrays bad manners and bad politics on the part of sexual betters toward the deprived, who reputedly are only interested in issues that are concrete, material, and life-saving, as if sexuality were not all of these. The result is that sexual pleasure in whatever form has become a great guilty secret among feminists.

Hiding pleasure and its sources in feminist discussion does not make the world safe for women, any more than women's acceding to the system of male protection made the world safe for them. When pleasure occupies a smaller and smaller public space and a more guilty private space, individuals do not become empowered; they are merely cut off from the source of their own strength and energy. If women increasingly view themselves entirely as victims through the lens of the oppressor and allow themselves to be viewed that way by others, they become enfeebled and miserable. The taboo on investigating pleasure led to an abstract sexual theory which bears little relationship to daily life. If theory is to have any valid relationship to experience, we need to acknowledge that sexuality is worth talking about seriously. We cannot create a body of knowledge that is true to women's lives, if sexual pleasure cannot be spoken about safely, honestly, and completely.

Much feminist work on sexuality starts from the premise that sex is a social construction, articulated at many points with the economic, social, and political structures of the material world. Sex is not simply a "natural" fact, as earlier, essentialist theories would suggest. Although sexuality, like all human cultural activity, is grounded in the body, the body's structure, physiology, and functioning do not directly or simply determine the configuration or meaning of sexuality; were this so, we would expect to find great uniformity across the world's cultures. Yet the sexual diversity we see is startling: activities condemned in one society are encouraged in another, and ideas about what is attractive or erotic or sexually satisfying or even sexually possible vary a great deal.

Nor is the role of culture confined to choosing some sexual acts (by praise, encouragement, or reward) and rejecting others (by scorn, ridicule, or condemnation), as if selecting from a sexual buffet. The social construction of sexuality is far more thorough-going, encompassing the very way sex is conceptualized, defined, labeled, and described from time to time and from culture to culture.[7] Although we can name specific physical actions like anal sex, heterosexual intercourse, kissing, fellatio, or masturbation, it is clear that the social and personal meanings attached to each of these acts in terms of sexual identity and sexual community have varied historically. Without denying the body, we note that the body and its actions are understood according to prevailing codes of meaning. Recent work on the history of male homosexuality shows, for instance, that although sodomy occurred and was punished in earlier periods in Europe and America, it was viewed as the result of carnal lust to which any mortal could fall prey, not as an act committed by a particular type of individual, the "homosexual." The classification of sexual types awaited the late nineteenth century, when capitalism and urban development made it possible for individuals to exist beyond the sphere of the extended family as a productive and reproductive unit.[8] Historians have also traced the outlines of changing definitions of women's intimacy. In the nineteenth century, two women who shared the same household and bed were usually perceived as close friends; by the twentieth century, such women were increasingly viewed as lesbians.[9] Doubtless, modern forms of heterosexuality have a history to be written as well.[10]

One might expect that feminists would be especially receptive to a social construction approach to sexuality, since in many ways it is analogous to social construction theories about gender: that the body is the agent of human activity, but the body's configuration does not literally determine it. Scientific "know-ledge" or folklore suggesting that the dominant cultural arrange-ments are the result of biology – and therefore intrinsic, eternal, and unchanging – are usually ideologies supporting prevailing power relations. Deeply felt personal identities – for example, masculinity/femininity or heterosexuality/homosexuality – are not private or solely the product of biology, but are created through the intersection of political, social, and economic forces, which vary over time.

Yet social construction theory remains a radical view of sexuality which poses a range of unsettling questions for feminists and other thinkers brought up on an essentialist view of sexuality. What is the nature of the relationship between the arbitrariness of social construction and the immediacy of our bodily sensations and functions? Is sexuality not a unitary, ongoing phenomenon with an essential core, but something created differently at each time and place? If sexuality is not a transhistorical, transcultural essence whose manifestations are mildly shaped by cultural factors, must we then consider the possibility that desire is not intrinsic but itself constituted or constructed, and if so, by what mechanisms?

Social construction theory has run into some misguided interpretations. Some suggest that if sexuality is constructed at the cultural level, then it can be easily reconstructed or deconstructed at the social or personal level. Not necessarily. The cultural analogue is useful here, for although human cultures are arbitrary in that behavior is learned and not intrinsic, anthropologists do not believe that entire cultures can transform themselves overnight, or that individuals socialized in one cultural tradition can acculturate at whim. The mutability of sexuality in an individual lifetime is an interesting and important question, however. Clearly, there are examples of both persistence and fluidity in sexual desire: for example, individuals who "knew" they were gay at an early age and remained so despite aversion therapy and incarceration, and others who "become" gay or lesbian at different stages in the life cycle in a manner suggesting internal change, rather than belated expression of "repressed" desire. Although questions about fluidity of sexuality often focus on sexual orientation and object choice, there are many other areas where similar questions could be asked: fantasy, masturbation, or non-monogamy. The question of the stability and flexibility of sexual behavior within and across individuals remains intriguing and poorly understood.

The parallels between social constructionist approaches to gender (the cultural marking of biological sex) and sexuality (desire and erotic pleasure) make it possible to see that although both may be socially constructed, sexuality and gender are separate but overlapping domains or, as Gayle Rubin calls them, "vectors of oppression." Of particular interest is the articulation between specific features of each system, namely how the configurations of the sexual system bear on the experience of being female and, conversely, how the definitions of gender resonate with and are reflected in sexuality. Despite the many interrelationships of sexuality and gender, sexuality is not a residual category, a subcategory of gender; nor are theories of gender fully adequate to account for sexuality.[11] The task is to describe and analyze how cultural connections are made between female bodies and what comes to be understood as "women" and "female sexuality."

Social construction, then, requires a more detailed investigation of how categories acquire meaning and change over time, how objects and acts become eroticized, how external symbols acquire internal, psychic meaning. If sexuality is constructed, what is the site of the construction? Recent work has attended not only to the larger social formations that organize sexuality – the political economy, religion, the educational system, the criminal code, public and mental health systems – but also to how these forces are mediated through "private" life: marriage, the family, child nurturing, the household, intimacy, and effect.

Information about sexuality comes from multiple sources, as well as from many disciplines. A survey of the literature reveals information, partial though it may be, on sexual behavior and acts, along with their physiological and biological dimensions; fantasy and inner, psychological experience; the public presentation of our sexual selves; visual images and representations available in the culture; sexual styles; the place of sexuality in the discourse of the political community to which we belong; sexual ideologies, both scientific and religious. Yet when we examine a specific group of women, we often find that a full range of information covering all these realms is not available. Nevertheless, rather than restrict our comments to the domains for which we have information, we often formulate large-scale generalizations, with varying degrees of plausibility. Unfortunately, one of the most interesting questions – the relationship between these sexual domains – are they consistent, or inconsistent? – can never be examined as long as data are lacking and, worse, we have a dulled sense of what is missing. These informational gaps have several consequences.

First, understudied groups are often victims of the most far-flung generalizations, spun on the basis of some lyric, poem, or piece of art. One cannot, for instance, assume to be knowledgeable about lesbianism in the twentieth century simply because one has read Colette's *The Pure and the Impure*. Second, it remains impossible to compare sexual domains among groups of women – to ask, for example, what is the content of fantasy for white, black, and Hispanic women? Third, attempts to gauge the overall situation of specific groups usually end up relying on not only incomplete but usually non-comparable domains: for example, images of women's sexuality in the oral literature of an

ethnic minority may be held up against Kinsey's data on the
incidence of premarital sex among white, college-educated
females in the 1950s. When we compare the sexual situation
between and within groups of women, it is important to
remember that no conclusions can be drawn by looking at only
one layer of sexual information without considering the others.

The information we have – social science surveys, literary
analyses, fiction, poetry, visual art, biomedical observations,
biographies and autobiographies – raises serious questions of
interpretation. None is the straightforward report about women's
sexual reality that we wish, and sometimes imagine, we had. If
sex is a cultural product, all the representations, descriptions, and
depictions of that sexuality are too. Just as our own bodily
experience is mediated through culture, so reports or descriptions of others' experience are mediated through cultural forms,
conventions, and codes of meaning.[12] We understand more
readily that visual representations – movies, paintings, even
photographs – are not literal or realistic; they betray a style, an
emphasis, a perspective, raising questions for the viewer about
the relationship between what is depicted and what is. The
presence of the artist destroys the illusion of objectivity. Scientific
reports, fiction, diaries, letters, social science surveys, humanistic
accounts are also, to varying degrees, cultural products. Even the
most empirically oriented form requires a cultural frame of
organization, a code of meaning, a language that classifies
feelings and the body. Since the 1890s, for example, sex
researchers' attempts to define female pleasure and sexual
gratification have undergone dramatic shifts, from vague euphemisms about marital harmony to Masters and Johnson's measurement of the strength and number of vaginal contractions during
orgasm. For the viewer or reader, the question remains the same:
what is the relationship between what is written in the text or
shown in the image, and what *is*? We are most aware of
embedded assumptions when reading material from another time
or place, which may appear incongruous or disjunctive. Yet we
must admit that contemporary work by both men and women has
embedded meanings too. These embedded assumptions are
especially significant, because so much of the literature on female
sexuality has been written by men, suggesting the need for
critical reading.

Whether scientific, religious, or political, prescriptive texts that
aim to tell people what to do or what is normal pose a number of
questions. Are they a self-assured restatement of prevailing
norms, safely read as literal indicators of behavior? Or are they
anxious attempts to resocialize renegade readers to norms they
are flouting? To what degree do prescriptive texts reach a mass

audience, and did they in the past, and with what effect? Historical examination of even the most seemingly objective "scientific" prescriptive material reveals that its messages have not been homogeneous and static, but have changed over time. These fluctuations are traceable to the emergence of different scientific groups; changes in theories about workable solutions to social problems; battles and competition for ideology, professional turf, patients, and money; and the rise and fall of particular scientific paradigms.

Similar questions can be raised about depictions of women's sexuality in the dominant culture, both in the privileged forms of high culture and in popular culture. Although different in formal intent from the prescriptive text and so nominally differentiated from it, mainstream representations of sexuality may perform a similar educative or socializing function. Such representations are complex, to varying degrees both depicting and distorting actual behavior, as well as influencing it. Yet the material being analyzed – for example, popular fiction in women's magazines, 1950s movies, or radio jingles – suggests that dominant culture is not cranked out by an unseen hand, but that each cultural product bears a relationship to a particular genre and its conventions, as well as to other objects of its kind, and to the creator's purpose and intended audience. Thus, within the dominant culture, there is inconsistency, contradiction, and tension, especially in relation to social change, as well as uniformity and pattern.

How do we understand such popular sexual images and representations? Are they overt restatements of conservative ideology; conspiratorial attempts to prevent cultural change; efforts to smooth over cultural contradictions and tensions; or a mixed bag containing both interruptions as well as continuities? For example, the proliferation of information about clitoral orgasm and oral sex in contemporary women's magazines and popular sex manuals can be read in a variety of ways. It can be seen as a liberating expansion beyond the bounds of procreative heterosexuality, enabling women to learn about and experience a type of pleasure not connected to reproduction or even to the penis. Male concern that their partners experience orgasm may signal the development of more egalitarian and reciprocal sexual standards. On the other hand, the anxious question, "Did you come?" may demarcate a new area of women's behavior men are expected to master and control – female orgasm. In this light, the marital literature may be seen as an attempt to capture and contain the potentially radical implications of clitoral orgasm, which challenges both the form that heterosexual practice usually takes and the notion that heterosexuality is superior.

The dominant culture and its symbolic system reflect the class arrangements of that society, and are not mirror reflections of ongoing social reality. The cultural assumptions of higher-status groups receive a privileged position, with lower status groups consigned to varying degrees of cultural invisibility. Mainstream culture is white, male, heterosexual, upper and middle class in its point of view and assumptions. Appearing in mainstream culture either rarely (literal invisibility) or inaccurately through caricature or other distortion, members of lower-status groups become culturally invisible. Dominant culture often does not reflect the lived social reality of subordinate groups, although these groups by necessity must be familiar with it. Members of dominant groups not only participate freely and comfortably in mainstream culture, which reflects their own world-view, but they are also allowed the conceit that lower-status groups share their assumptions and that other perspectives or points of view don't exist.[13]

It is clear that non-dominant groups, to the extent that their social lives are different from those in the mainstream, have different sensibilities and consciousness which are expressed in a variety of cultural forms – lyrics and music, oral tradition, humor as well as in fiction and art. Because the printed word is often the enclave of dominant culture, used to enforce cultural invisibility, the voices of lower-status groups are relatively absent from dominant texts. But these groups have not been silent; they have created rival cultural and symbolic systems, requiring methods which tap oral tradition in order to describe them. Thus, the minimal appearance of black women in dominant cultural forms is no guide to the way women's sexuality was represented by black people to each other. Such an investigation requires examination of jokes, songs, and oral narratives, important as sources of information, socialization, and transmission of knowledge across generations within the black community.[14] Lesbian subcultures are similarly absent from the written record, although they vigorously responded to a partial and distorting depiction of lesbians in dominant culture, which found the acknowledgment of love between women at once ridiculous and threatening. Although mainstream culture has a vested interest in keeping alternative cultures out of the printed record and invisible, stigmatized groups also have their own motives for keeping their cultural products and conventions hidden: for self-protection, to prevent cooptation, and to create a safe cultural space, a world over which they have some control. The description of alternative cultures makes it possible to entertain important questions: How powerful and vigorous are alternative cultural forms regarding sexuality? What competition do they offer to dominant forms, or what contradictions do they mediate or resolve?

Another interesting issue is the way in which political and

social movements position sexuality in theory, discourse, and action. For participants in social movements, whether ethnic, racial, or religious, the conventions of sexual discourse may not mirror literal behavior. Nevertheless, they constitute an important arena in which topics are consigned to importance or oblivion. The nineteenth-century feminist discourse about women's sexuality and sexual reform, for instance, remained largely heterosexual and marital, despite evidence of women's actual experience with romantic female friendships that offered physical and emotional intensity. The public, political discussions did not introduce "lesbians" or "lesbianism" as named categories for women's choices and experiences. Such a historical contrast between lived experience and constructed social reality is obvious to feminists now, raising questions about what other unnamed realms lurk silently in our own discussions.

We also need to look at how sexual information, instruction, and experience are transmitted across and between generations. Our understanding of the development of sexuality in infancy and childhood is only beginning.[15] The family, obviously important for infants and children, may remain an important socializing site for adult sexuality as well. Large social shifts often appear as generational contrasts that are observable within families. The shift, for example, from the nineteenth-century pattern of separate spheres for the sexes and female passionlessness to the modern pattern of companionate marriage with a modicum of female sexual pleasure is reflected in generational contrasts between mothers and daughters. Although some age cohorts provide a sharp contrast between old and new, other transitional ones provide clues to how, through what processes, and at what cost large-scale social change moved through individual lives. The notion of sexual transformation and change occurring within an individual lifetime is a crucial one, because it forces us to give up the static picture of an unchanging sexual order depending on infant and child socialization that is impermeable and rigid. It suggests that childhood experience, though perhaps not totally mutable, may be later shaped in various directions, and raises questions about individual perception of and reactions to sexual change and the degree to which individuals feel that their sexual expression is an intrinsic given or a choice. Examples include "frigid" women who did not reach orgasm in heterosexual penetration during the 1950s who became merely "preorgasmic" by the 1960s or "multiply orgasmic" in the face of a modern technological advance, the vibrator; and women whose close and lifelong intimacy with other women might have caused them to be labeled celibates or spinsters who are now called, or call themselves, lesbians.

In examining these domains in which women's sexuality is described or represented – and these are only a few – the observer, interpreter, or scholar is striving to understand what the various representations mean – that is, what their relationship is to women's thought and experience at the time of their creation. To answer this question, the analyst applies an interpretive frame, through which meaning can be detected and inferred. Do we assume that all women share this interpretive frame? That it is universal? This assumption may be especially risky if there is a social disjunction between the observer and the observed, if the interpretive frame of mainstream culture is applied to invisible groups, or if the analysis concentrates on implicit meanings and deep structure written at the level of the unconscious. In each case, the assumption about the universality of sexual meaning obscures one of the other questions we should be asking: how does the audience perceive sexual representations? The assumption of a universal meaning is economical and efficient, but it may be mistaken.

If we want to study sexuality, we need more information about individual responses to symbol and image. We need to know what the viewer brings with her to make an interpretation: a cultural frame, resonances, connections, and personal experience. The question of context is important too, since viewers read symbols differently depending on the material they are embedded in and the relationship they have to other symbols, as well as individual interpretive frames which are somewhat idiosyncratic.

To assume that symbols have a unitary meaning, the one dominant culture assigns them, is to fail to investigate the individuals' experience and cognition of symbols, as well as individual ability to transform and manipulate symbols in a complex way which draws on play, creativity, humor, and intelligence. This assumption grants mainstream culture a hegemony it claims, but rarely achieves. To ignore the potential for variation is to inadvertently place women outside of culture except as passive recipients of official symbol systems. It continues to deny what mainstream culture has always tried to make invisible – the complex struggles of disenfranchised groups to grapple with oppression using symbolic, as well as economic and political, resistance. Mainstream symbols may be used to both reveal and mock dominant culture.

The symbolic transformations presented by some butch/femme couples as they manipulate gender symbols, for example, are stunning.[16] To the dominant, heterosexual culture, the butch/ femme couple appears to be a pitiful imitation by inferiors, who mimic the semiotics of gender distinctions while violating ındamental rules of gender: that women do not have access to women, do not take sexual initiative, and cannot be sexual without men. Lesbians, depending on their historical and political positioning, may interpret the butch/femme couple as presenting a defiant statement to dominant culture about female power, visibility, and resistance, a refusal to be invisible and conform, or as replicating heterosexual patterns for want of a more original model or for lack of feminist consciousness. The relevance of context and individual aptitude at cultural transformation and play points to the speed and subtlety with which symbolic slippage occurs, and calls for much more intensive attempts to describe and understand the history and meaning of sexual symbols to both actors and viewers.

It is no accident that recent feminist sexual controversies about pornography, S/M, and butch/femme all demonstrate a need for a more developed analysis of symbolic context and transformation, especially difficult in regard to visual material where our education, vocabulary, and sophistication are far less developed than in regard to literary texts. Our visual illiteracy renders the image overpowering. The emotion aroused by an image is easily attached to rhetorical arguments, overwhelming more subtle analysis and response, and the audience as well, by manipulative imagery, as in polemical slide shows mounted by Right to Life groups or some feminist anti-pornography groups. In each case, the shock induced by the image of a fetus in a bottle or a woman in chains is effectively used to propel viewers to the desired conclusion.

Sexuality poses a challenge to feminist inquiry, since it is an intersection of the political, social, economic, historical, personal, and experiential, linking behavior and thought, fantasy and action. That these domains intersect does not mean that they are identical. Feminists need sophisticated methodologies and analyses that permit the recognition of each discrete domain as well as their multiple intersections. Recognizing these layers of sexual information, we form and adopt generalizations about even one apparently homogeneous group, white middle-class women, for example, more cautiously. Popular sex manuals, content analysis of women's fiction magazines, vibrator sales, number of contraceptive prescriptions registered, clothing styles – each provides a clue, but even for well-studied groups there are many lacunae. We recognize these lacunae only if we stop extrapolating from one domain to the other. This recognition spurs inquiry into missing areas, and ultimately makes possible the comparison of one domain to another.

A sophisticated analysis of sexual symbols requires that we

look beyond easy generalization. Feminist scholarship has delivered a scathing critique of an androcentric and falsely universalizing history in which the historical Everyman, like his authors, was male, white, heterosexual, and affluent. Such accounts omitted women as both subjects of inquiry and as self-conscious historical actors. Corrective research indicates that social characteristics modify the perception and experience of historical events, with gender a significant social marker. Despite its critique of false universals, feminist scholarship and inquiry has not escaped the same sin. Until recently challenged, feminist descriptions and analyses have often assumed that women are white, middle- or upper-class, heterosexual, able-bodied, and moderately youthful, or that the experiences and perspectives of these women are shared by all. The term "woman" used in feminist discourse often substituted part of women's experience for the whole, a "deadly metonymy" in Hortense Spillers's words, relegating the experience of some women to silence.[17] The experience of those standing outside both mainstream culture and "women's culture" has been excluded from the feminist canon as well. Self-criticism of feminist parochialism has proliferated in recent years[18] and has been persuasive in showing why feminist analysis must attempt to include the experience of diverse groups of women, with conclusions specific to particular groups identified as such.[19]

This development, when applied to female sexuality, suggests that sexuality may be thought about, experienced, and acted on differently according to age, class, ethnicity, physical ability, sexual orientation and preference, religion, and region. Confrontation with the complex intersection of social identities leads us away from simple dichotomies (black/white, lesbian/heterosexual, working-class/middle-class) toward recognizing the multiple intersection of categories and the resulting complexity of women's lived experience.[20]

This insight leads to a scholarship increasingly self-conscious about omissions, gaps, and silences, which is willing to qualify and specify findings, if they apply to particular groups only, and to take more aggressive efforts in researching areas and topics up to now ignored. The simple recognition that little is known about Asian lesbians, Jewish working-class prostitutes, or Catholic women who patronize singles bars does not in itself produce the needed information, although it is certainly a necessary step in its production. Additional steps include: better use of available material, which requires more funding, freer access to papers and diaries held in private collections, and a willingness to ask more imaginative questions about the sexual aspects of women's lives; further work by scholars who are members of the groups under study as those most attentive to and attuned to nuances in the material; and an effort to generate more data, especially about contemporary life. A great deal of interesting research is being conducted outside the formal boundaries of academe by community projects and groups that have been imaginative and resourceful in locating and developing unusual kinds of material.[21]

But if careless overgeneralization about women's experience is dangerous and mystifying, so too is the avoidance of generalization in the belief that each woman's experience is so unique and conditioned by multiple social intersections that larger patterns are impossible to discern, and that to attempt generalization is to do violence to individual experience: the anarchy of sexual idiosyncrasy. Feminist work on sexuality must confront the dialectic between specificity and generalization, and endure its ongoing tension. Theory can only be developed through reference to an ever-expanding body of information, made possible through more intensive use of historical material and through eliciting women's current experience in a comfortable climate.[22] Specific data about one group of women may then acquire more meaning through comparison and contrast with those for other groups. It is important to simultaneously examine women's similarities and differences, questioning whether the acquisition of femininity and the conditions for its reproduction affect all women in similar ways, cutting across sexual preference, sexual object, and specific behavior. Since feminism, for political even more than intellectual reasons, is unlikely to abandon using the term "woman" until all of women's experience has been adequately described, its provocative overgeneralizations might be most positively viewed as an invitation to test the hypotheses proposed: to object, qualify, and correct.

Although a portion of feminist reluctance to acknowledge differences among women derives from arrogance on the part of mainstream feminists, a significant part derives from another source: the fear of difference among women. If women organize around their oppression by and through differentiation from men, should they not maintain a united front, stressing their shared and unifying characteristic, femaleness? Does the admission of women's cross-cutting allegiances and links to groups containing men weaken the universal sisterhood? Once differences are admitted, what is to prevent them from becoming bitter and divisive, fracturing the base for shared political action? In a society that structures and maintains group antagonisms, what model do we have for acknowledging difference and working together? Exploration of differences has, in fact, been a painful experience, beginning with lesbian and heterosexual differences in the early stages of the women's movement and continuing in recent years to differences involving class, religion, ethnicity, and race. Although some have retreated to doctrines which emphasize women's commonality on the one hand, or women's total separation by factors of race and class on the other, many feminists see the importance of dealing with difference, while they remain wary and uncertain of how to do so.

Our discomfort with difference is especially evident around questions of sexual variation, which have expanded beyond the topic of lesbian and heterosexual difference to include all the ways women can obtain pleasure. Sexual orientation is not the only, and may not be the most significant, sexual difference among women.[23] Our ability to think about sexual difference is limited, however, by a cultural system that organizes sexual differences in a hierarchy in which some acts and partners are privileged and others are punished. Privileged forms of sexuality, for example, heterosexuality, marriage, and procreation, are protected and rewarded by the state and subsidized through social and economic incentives. Those engaging in privileged acts, or pretending to do so, enjoy good name and good fortune. Less privileged forms of sexuality are regulated and interdicted by the state, religion, medicine, and public opinion. Those practicing less privileged forms of sexuality – what Rubin calls members of the sexual "lower orders" – suffer from stigma and invisibility, although they also resist.[24]

The system of sexual hierarchy functions smoothly only if sexual nonconformity is kept invisible, hence the interpersonal tension when sexual difference surfaces. For dominant sexual groups, the appearance of the sexual lower orders produces anxiety, discomfort, the threat of pollution, and a challenge to their hegemony. Sexual liberals are caught between a reluctance to lose the privileges attendant upon being members of the majority and a fear of losing their claims to political savvy if they do not side with the newly vocal, emerging minorities. The women's movement has already experienced a similar scenario with the "lavender menace" panic – a consequence of more visible lesbian participation in the movement. Some feminists may still feel that it would be easier to attain their goals without the liability of perceived "sexual deviance" of any sort. In the current sex debates, some fear that the women's movement will come to be identified with issues even more stigmatized and threatening than female homosexuality. Thus, feminists' fear of sexual difference manifests itself as a concern with public relations, an attempt to keep the women's movement respectable and free of pollution.

The appearance of any sexual difference thus raises a question about its positioning in the sexual hierarchy: Is it normal? Sinful?

Deranged? Given this backdrop, feminists, like all members of the culture, find it difficult to think about sexual difference with equanimity. The concept of benign sexual variation is a relatively new one, as Rubin suggests, and for most of us, differences in sexual taste carry great significance, whether explained in terms of sin, pathology, or bad politics. Our relative ignorance about the actual range of sexual behavior and fantasy makes us into latter-day sexual ethnocentrists; the observer is convinced that her own sex life is normal, understandable, and tasteful, while the observed's preferences may be frightening, strange, and disgusting. The external system of sexual hierarchy is replicated within each of us, and herein lies its power. Internalized cultural norms enforce the status quo. As each of us hesitates to admit deviations from the system of sexual hierarchy, nonconformity remains hidden, invisible, and apparently rare. The prevailing system retains hegemony and power, appearing to be descriptive as well as prescriptive, a statement of what *is* as well as what should be. Individuals who deviate appear to themselves to be few and isolated; they resolve anew to hide their nonconformity.

Underlying reactions of shock, disgust, and startle lurk other, more complex reactions. Our own insecurity and sexual deprivation make us wonder about what other women are doing.[25] Could I do that too? Is it better? Are they getting more pleasure? Do I come out unfavorably in the sexual sweepstakes? Are they pathetic and sick? Am I? Our state of sexual insecurity, fueled by ignorance and mystification, turns any meeting with sexual difference into an occasion for passing harsh judgment on ourselves as well as others. Stigmatized acts or preferences are devalued according to the rules of sexual hierarchy, yet paradoxically we judge our own behavior second-rate and unsatisfying, resenting those whose mere existence makes us doubtful and deprived. Thus, the presentation of sexual difference, whether intended or not, is often interpreted as a chauvinistic statement of superiority, if not an exhortation to experiment or an attempt to prescribe a new sexual norm.

An enduring slogan in the women's movement has been "the personal is the political," born from the initial discovery that personal life as lived and experienced is not totally private and individual, devoid of cultural and social shaping. Discussing personal life in consciousness-raising groups provided a way for women who participated to see commonalities in their lives, to realize that they were not crazy or alone in their dissatisfaction, and to begin to trace the economic, political, and social forces that articulated with domains previously thought of as private: the family, relationships, the self. Examination of women's lives also affirmed that they were important and instructive, in fact, in Joan

Nestle's words, "our deepest text" in a society which marginal-
ized and ignored female experience.[26] Not only did personal life
have social and political dimensions, but personal pain and
unhappiness often suggested possible targets for political action
and organizing.

The ubiquity of the slogan, however, led toward unintended
and problematic extremes which proved particularly damaging
for sexuality. If personal life had a political dimension, did that
mean that sexual life was singularly and entirely political? If so, it
was perhaps logical to expect that feminists who shared the same
politics should have identical or highly similar sexual lives, and
that there should be a close conformity between political goals
and personal behavior. If the personal was political, then perhaps
the political was personal, converting efforts to change and
reform sexual life and ·relations into substitutes for political action
and organizing. If so, scrutiny, criticism, and policing of peers'
sexual lives, if not fantasies, may become a necessary political
obligation.[27]

The quest for politically appropriate sexual behavior has led to
what Alice Echols calls prescriptivism, the tendency to transform
broad, general principles like equality, autonomy, and self-
determination into fairly specific and rigid standards to which all
feminists are expected to conform. There is a very fine line
between talking about sex and setting norms; we err very easily
given our ignorance of diversity, our fear of difference, and our
naive expectation that all like the same sexual food as we.
Although we need open discussion to expand theory, we are
especially vulnerable to transforming statements of personal
preference that inevitably appear in honest discussion ("I like
oral sex") into statements that may be probabalistically true
("Women like clitoral stimulation more than penetration") into
statements that are truly prescriptive ("Women should avoid
penetration"). Certainly, there are intentional efforts at chauvinism. But even mere statements of individual, personal preference
are often heard as statements of superiority, criticisms of the
listener's practice, or an exhortation to try something new.
Women's insecurity, deprivation, and guilt make it difficult to hear
a description of personal practice as anything but a prescription.

All political movements, feminism included, espouse social and
ethical ideals as they articulate their vision of the good life or
more just society. Such movements attempt to analyze and
change current behavior, as well as the prevailing social
institutions that shape such behavior. Beginning as radical
renegades, visionaries, and outsiders, their political success
exposes them to the danger of becoming the orthodoxy, if only to
their own members, with their own structure of deadening

conformity. The dangers of political analysis transmuted from illuminating vision to stale dogma loom especially large in regard to sexuality. Our vast ignorance, our reliance on overgeneralization, and the invisibility of so many groups suggest that we are in a particularly resourceless position to determine which sexual paths will lead to heaven. Although declaring opposition to patriarchal culture, some recent feminist pronouncements about politically desirable and undesirable forms of sexuality bear a striking resemblance to those of the dominant culture, with one possible exception: the repositioning of certain varieties of lesbianism. Within feminism, lesbianism has been rehabilitated, undergoing a transition from the realm of bad sex to the realm of good sex, and within some sectors of the movement, given a privileged position as the most egalitarian and feminist sexual identity. With this exception, new feminist punishments are still meted out to the denizens of the same old sexual lower orders.

Quite apart from our ignorance and prejudice, sexuality may be a particularly unpromising domain for regulation. As Muriel Dimen argues, sexuality remains fluid and everchanging, evolving through adult life in response to internal and external vicissitudes: flexible, anarchic, ambiguous, layered with multiple meanings, offering doors that open to unexpected experience. The connection of both sexual behavior and fantasy to infancy, the irrational, the unconscious is a source of both surprise and pleasure. We impose simplistic and literal standards congruent with political goals at our own peril, ultimately undermining the search for pleasure and expansiveness that motivates visions of political change and human connection.[28]

A serious effort to examine the relationship between sexual fantasy and behavior and agendas for social change is circumvented by the enormity of what we do not know: silences, oppressions, repressions, invisibility, denials, omissions, lies. Paradoxically, the effort to rein in sexual behavior and fantasy according to political dogma guarantees that the silence will continue and that information challenging it is unlikely to emerge.

Following the path of older political movements, the prevailing feminist ideology has the power to punish non-conformists by exclusion and personal attack. If adult sexuality is not so mutable – an interesting question that remains to be answered – how do we regard someone whose sexual practice or thought falls short of current standards: the detritus of patriarchy whose sexual acts are stigmata of oppression; a fossil, soon to be replaced by a younger generation free of such taint; or a victim, entitled to special consideration as long as she laments her unhappy state? If patriarchal socialization makes the achievement of the sexual ideal impossible, we may charitably continue to love the sinner, while hating the sin.

Like religious orthodoxy, political ideology about sexual behavior contrasts lofty goals with gritty, or fleshy, reality, exhorting individuals to strive against the odds for perfection. Falls from grace may be tolerated for those who continue to believe; thus, actual practice can become quite discrepant from theoretically desired behavior, without posing any challenge to the empirical or logical foundations of sexual ideology. The ideology functions to set up new social categories and maintain strict boundaries between them: the good and the bad, believers and infidels.

In its first stage, this wave of feminism moved women by speaking about what lay below the surface of daily convention and acknowledged social reality. The excitement of feminism, its ability to propel women into extraordinary changes in their lives which were as joyful and exhilarating as they were unexpected and terrifying came from breaking silence and from naming the unspoken. This revelation, along with the thought and analysis it inspired, was radical and revolutionary: it changed women's lives.

In the course of any social movement, the passage of time and its very success renders the radical insight routine, as formerly exciting discoveries become natural and familiar features of the landscape. At this point, feminism needs to excavate new levels of women's experience. The fear and hesitation we feel are akin to what we felt fifteen years ago: where will this take us? This is a terrifying undertaking. To overcome our anxiety, we need to remind ourselves of what excited us: pleasure in discovery, the enjoyment of complexity, delight in each other.

What directions might a feminist politics on sex take in the future? Above all, feminism must be a movement that speaks to sexuality, that does not forfeit the field to reactionary groups who are more than willing to speak. We cannot be cowardly, pretending that feminism is not sexually radical. Being a sex radical at this time, as at most, is less a matter of what you do, and more a matter of what you are willing to think, entertain, and question.

Feminism must, of course, continue to work for material changes that support women's autonomy, including social justice, economic equality, and reproductive choice. At the same time, feminism must speak to sexuality as a site of oppression, not only the oppression of male violence, brutality, and coercion which it has already spoken about eloquently and effectively, but also the repression of female desire that comes from ignorance, invisibility, and fear. Feminism must put forward a politics that resists deprivation and supports pleasure. It must understand pleasure as life-affirming, empowering, desirous of human connection and the future, and not fear it as destructive, enfeebling, or corrupt. Feminism must speak to sexual pleasure as a fundamental right, which cannot be put off to a better or easier time. It must understand that the women to whom it speaks, and those it hopes to reach, care deeply about sexual pleasure and displeasure in their daily lives; that sexuality is a site of struggle – visceral, engaging, riveting – and not a domain of interest only to a narrow, small, and privileged group.

Feminism should encourage women to resist not only coercion and victimization, but also sexual ignorance, deprivation and fear of difference. Feminism should support women's experiments and analyses, encouraging the acquisition of knowledge. We can begin by examining our own experience, sharing it with each other, knowing that in sexuality as in the rest of social life, our adventures, risks, impulses, and terrors provide clues to the future. Feminism must insist that women are sexual subjects, sexual actors, sexual agents; that our histories are complex and instructive; that our experience is not a blank, nor a mere repetition of what has been said about us, and that the pleasure we have experienced is as much a guide to future action as the brutality.

In doing so, we admit that it is not safe to be a woman, and it never has been. Female attempts to claim pleasure are especially dangerous, attacked not only by men, but by women as well. But to wait until a zone of safety is established to begin to explore and organize for pleasure is to cede it as an arena, to give it up, and to admit that we are weaker and more frightened than our enemies ever imagined.

Social movements, feminism included, move toward a vision; they cannot operate solely on fear. It is not enough to move women away from danger and oppression; it is necessary to move toward something: toward pleasure, agency, self-definition. Feminism must increase women's pleasure and joy, not just decrease our misery. It is difficult for political movements to speak for any extended time to the ambiguities, ambivalences, and complexities that underscore human experience. Yet movements remain vital and vigorous to the extent that they are able to tap this wellspring of human experience. Without it, they become dogmatic, dry, compulsive, and ineffective. To persist amid frustrations and obstacles, feminism must reach deeply into women's pleasure and draw on this energy.

Acknowledgments

My thinking about sex has been very much influenced by ongoing discussions with members of the Scholar and the Feminist IX study group: Julie Abraham, Hannah Alderfer, Jan Boney, Frances Doughty, Kate Ellis, Faye Ginsburg, Diane Harriford, Beth Jakcr, Barbara Kerr, Mary Clare Lennon, Marybeth Nelson, Ann Snitow, Paula Webster, and Ellen Willis. I know that the many refinements and insights proposed during two years of discussion have become part of my own thinking, but their density and number make specific acknowledgment a daunting task. My admiration for members' intelligence, ability, and wit is exceeded only by gratitude for their intellectual generosity and friendship.

I am indebted to Frances Doughty and Paula Webster who read tender, early drafts with care, patience, and tact. Thanks to Frances Doughty for unstinting encouragement, feisty counsel against the demons, innumerable conversations from which I learned much, and "suddenly possible shifts of meaning."[29] Thanks to Paula Webster for rich discussions spanning many years, loyal and steady support, a haven in a hard time, and her generosity and friendship.

I am also indebted to conversations with many other individuals. Though despairing of thanking all by name, I am particularly grateful to Dorothy Allison, Pat Califia, Deborah Edel, Amber Hollibaugh, Joan Nestle, Esther Newton, and Gayle Rubin. Thanks also to members of my sex and history study group for conversations, questions, and encouragement over the years: John D'Emilio, Jonathan Katz, Ann Snitow, Paula Webster, and Jeffrey Weinstein.

I am grateful to Julie Abraham, Meryl Altman, Jan Boney, Pat Califia, Frances Doughty, Faye Ginsburg, Jonathan Katz, Barbara Kerr, Ann Snitow, Paula Webster, and Jeffrey Weinstein for reading and commenting on intermediate drafts of this essay, though infelicities and errors remain mine.

Notes

1 Ellen Carol DuBois and Linda Gordon, "Seeking Ecstasy on the Battlefield: Danger and Pleasure in Nineteenth-century Feminist Sexual Thought", in this volume.

2 Faye Ginsburg, "The Body Politic: The Defense of Sexual Restriction by Anti-Abortion Activists", in this volume.

3 Muriel Dimen, "Politically Correct, Politically Incorrect?", in this volume.

4 Lucy Gilbert and Paula Webster, *Bound By Love*, Boston, Beacon, 1982.

5 Joan Nestle, "The Fem Question", in this volume, p. 234.

6 Alice Echols, "The Taming of the Id: Feminist Sexual Politics, 1968-1983", in this volume.

7 Social construction texts include: Michel Foucault, *A History of Sexuality, vol. 1, An Introduction*, trans. Robert Hurley, New York, Pantheon, 1978; Jeffrey Weeks, *Coming Out: Homosexual Politics in Britain*, London, Quartet, 1977; Jonathan Katz, *Gay/Lesbian Almanac: A New Documentary*, New York, Harper & Row, 1983, pp. 138-74.

8 Jonathan Katz, *Gay American History: Lesbians and Gay Men in the USA*, New York, Crowell, 1976.

9 Lillian Faderman, *Surpassing the Love of Men*, New York, Morrow, 1981; Nancy Sahli, "Smashing: Women's Relationships Before the Fall", *Chrysalis*, no. 8, 1979, pp. 17-27.

10 Jonathan Katz, "The Invention of Heterosexuality", unpublished manuscript, 1983.

11 See Gayle Rubin, "Thinking Sex", in this volume, for a fuller development of this argument.

12 For varied approaches to the question of representation, see: Meryl Altman, "Everything They Always Wanted You to Know: The Ideology of Popular Sex Literature"; Bette Gordon, "*Variety*: The Pleasure in Looking"; Barbara Kruger, "No Progress in Pleasure"; and Kaja Silverman, "*Histoire d'O*: The Construction of a Female Subject", all in this volume.

13 I am indebted to Frances Doughty for many conversations about representation and the question of invisibility. See Francis Doughty, "Lesbian Biography, Biography of Lesbians" in Margaret Cruikshank (ed.), *Lesbian Studies*, Old Westbury, Feminist Press, 1982, pp. 122-7.

14 Hortense J. Spillers, "Interstices: A Small Drama of Words", in this volume, pp. 73-100.

15 Mary Calderone, "Above and Beyond Politics: The Sexual Socialization of Children"; Kate Millett, "Beyond Politics? Children and Sexuality"; and Sharon Thompson, "Search for Tomorrow: On Feminism and the Reconstruction of Teen Romance", all in this volume.

16 See Joan Nestle, op. cit.; Esther Newton and Shirley Walton, "The Misunderstanding: Toward a More Precise Sexual Vocabulary", in this volume.

17 Spillers, op. cit.

18 See, for example, Margaret Cruikshank (ed.), *Lesbian Studies*, op. cit.; Lorraine Bethel and Barbara Smith (eds), *Conditions Five*: "The Black Women's Issue", 1979; Cherríe Moraga and Gloria Anzaldúa (eds), *This Bridge Called My Back*, Massachusetts, Persephone Press, 1981; Gloria T. Hull, Patricia Bell Scott, and Barbara Smith (eds), *But Some of Us Are Brave*, New York, Feminist Press, 1982.

19 Self-consciousness about the limitations of one's data and the specific category of women to whom conclusions apply raise interesting questions of style. How and when should such qualifications be made? At the beginning of a report or article, after which one resumes the word "women" in describing one's subjects? Or should the article doggedly and probably awkwardly continue to specify the subjects, for example, "white, middle-class, heterosexual Bohemians

in the 1920s" or "urban, working-class Hispanic single mothers"? Although the awkwardness in the second form is evident, use of the first results in unintended illogical statements. Consider, for example, an article noting that post-World War I feminist thinkers on sexuality included both heterosexual and lesbian women. It then goes on, a mere paragraph later, to characterize these women's thought:

> Even when it contradicted their own experience, they continued to accept a male and heterosexual definition of the "sex act." They were, so to speak, upwardly mobile, and they wanted integration into the sexual world as defined by men. The man's orgasm remained the central event, although now it was preferable if a woman had one at the same time. (Ellen Carol DuBois and Linda Gordon, op. cit., p. 99.)

It seems unlikely, without further evidence, that lesbians of the time defined sex in this way. Yet the problem is linguistic, as well as conceptual and political: do we have the words or an available apparatus that can simply and elegantly specify the subjects of study?

This essay in no way escaped a struggle with the use of words like "women," "feminists," and even "we," reminiscent of the issues raised by Lorraine Bethel in her poem, "What Chou Mean *We*, White Girl?" in Lorraine Bethel and Barbara Smith (eds), op. cit., pp. 86-92.

20 Frances Doughty, "Introduction: The Daily Life of Lesbian Sexuality", unpublished paper, National Women's Studies Association, Columbus, Ohio, June 1983; and Oliva M. Espín, "Cultural and Historical Influences on Sexuality in Hispanic/Latin Women: Implications for Psychotherapy"; Roberta Galler, "The Myth of the Perfect Body"; Carol Munter, "Fat and the Fantasy of Perfection", in this volume.

21 For example, the Buffalo Lesbian Oral History Project (Liz Kenneday and Madeline Davis) and the San Francisco Lesbian and Gay Men's History Project.

22 Frances Doughty, "Introduction", op. cit.

23 Pat Califia, "Doing It Together: Gay Men, Lesbians, and Sex", *Advocate*, July 7, 1983, pp. 24-7.

24 Rubin, op. cit.

25 Paula Webster, "The Forbidden: Eroticism and Taboo", in this volume.

26 Joan Nestle, op. cit.

27 See Alice Echols, op. cit., for a fuller discussion.

28 Dimen, op. cit.

29 Olga Broumas, "Artemis", in *Beginning with O*, New Haven, Yale University Press, 1977, p. 24.

MORNING PAPERS

Seeking Ecstasy on the Battlefield: Danger and Pleasure in Nineteenth-century Feminist Sexual Thought

Ellen Carol DuBois and Linda Gordon

It is often alleged that female sexuality is a more complex matter than men's, and, if so, a major reason is that sex spells potential danger as well as pleasure for women. A feminist politics about sex, therefore, if it is to be credible as well as hopeful, must seek both to protect women from sexual danger and to encourage their pursuit of sexual pleasure.

This complex understanding of female sexuality has not always characterized the feminist movement. In general feminists inherit two conflicting traditions in their approach to sex. The strongest tradition, virtually unchallenged in the mainstream women's rights movement of the nineteenth century, addressed primarily the dangers and few of the possibilities of sex. Another perspective, much less developed despite some eloquent spokeswomen by the early twentieth century, encouraged women to leap, adventurous and carefree, into sexual liaisons, but it failed to offer a critique of the male construction of the sexual experience available to most women. It is no use to label one side feminist and the other antifeminist, to argue by name-calling. We cannot move ahead unless we grasp that both traditions are part of our feminism.

Neither feminist tradition is adequate to our needs today. Both were thoroughly heterosexist in their assumptions of what sex is. Even the nineteenth-century women who experienced intense emotional and physical relationships with each other did not incorporate these into their definition of what was sexual. Certainly women had relationships with other women that included powerful sexual components, but the feminists who are the subject of this paper did not theorize these relationships as sexual.[1] Furthermore, both feminist lines of thought – that emphasizing danger and that emphasizing pleasure – were often

31

moralistic. They condemned those whose sexual behavior deviated from their standards, not only sexually exploitive men but also women who did not conform.

Still, without an appreciation of these legacies and the processes of thought and experience that produced them, we cannot have much historical insight into our own concerns. Without a history, political movements like ours swing back and forth endlessly, reacting to earlier mistakes and overreacting in compensation, unable to incorporate previous insights or transcend previous limitations. Today we observe some of that pendulum-like motion. In reaction to the profound disappointments of what has passed for "sexual liberation," some feminists are replicating an earlier tradition, focusing exclusively on danger and advocating what we believe to be a conservative sexual politics.

We use a label like "conservative" cautiously. Such terms, like "left" and "right," come to us from class politics. When applied to sex and gender, they fit less comfortably. The oppressions of women, the repressions of sex, are so many and so complex by virtue of their location in the most intimate corners of life, coexisting even with love, that it is not always obvious in which direction a better world lies. We use the term "conservatism" to characterize strategies that accept existing power relations. We are suggesting that even feminist reform programs can be conservative in some respects if they accept male dominance while trying to elevate women's "status" within it. In this case, we believe that the nineteenth-century feminist mainstream accepted women's sexual powerlessness with men as inevitable, even as it sought to protect women from its worst consequences. Its appraisal of women's sexual victimization was not, on balance, offset by recognition of women's potential for sexual activity and enjoyment. We think our judgment will be justified by the historical description which follows. Through that description we hope to show, too, that despite the stubborn continuities of women's sexual oppression, there have also been momentous changes in the last 150 years, changes that require different strategies today.

The feminist movement has played an important role in organizing and even creating women's sense of sexual danger in the last 150 years. In that movement, two themes more than others have encapsulated and symbolized women's fears: prostitution and rape. There is a certain parallel construction between the nineteenth-century focus on prostitution and the modern emphasis on rape as the quintessential sexual terror. It is remarkable, in fact, how little emphasis nineteenth-century feminists placed on rape per se. It is as if the norms of legal sexual intercourse were in themselves so objectionable that rape did not seem that much worse! Instead feminists used prostitution as the leading symbol of male sexual coercion. While rape is an episode, prostitution suggests a condition that takes hold of a woman for a long time – possibly for life – and is difficult to escape. The symbolic emphasis in prostitution is on ownership, possession, purchase by men, while in rape it is on pure violence. Rape can happen to any woman, while prostitution involves the separation of women into the good and the bad, a division with class implications, as we shall see, even when the division is blamed on men.

Lest it seem trivializing to the real sufferings of women as prostitutes or rape victims to treat experiences as symbols or metaphors, let us emphasize again our subject: we are looking at how feminists conceptualized different sexual dangers, as a means of organizing *resistance* to sexual oppression. We want to look at how these feminist strategies changed, so that we can examine historically how we conduct feminist campaigns around sexual issues today.

In different periods, feminists emphasized different aspects of prostitution. In the 1860s and 1870s, for example, they focused on the economic pressures forcing women into sexual commerce, while in the Progressive Era their primary theme was "white slavery," the physical coercion of women into the trade. Despite these shifts, however, aspects of their approach to prostitution were consistent. First, they exaggerated its magnitude.[2] They did so because their definition of prostitute included virtually all women who engaged in casual sex, whether or not they were paid. Second, feminists consistently exaggerated the coerciveness of prostitution. In their eagerness to identify the social structural forces encouraging prostitution, they denied the prostitute any role other than that of passive victim. They insisted that the women involved were sexual innocents, helpless young women who "fell" into illicit sex. They assumed that prostitution was so degrading that no woman could freely choose it, not even with the relative degree of freedom with which she could choose to be a wife or a wage earner. Thus the "fallen woman" was always viewed as a direct victim, not only of male dominance in general, but of kidnapping, sexual imprisonment, starvation, and/or seduction in particular.[3] These attitudes toward prostitution were not exclusive to feminists, but were also part of the ideological outlook of many male reformers, including some antifeminists. Our point here, however, is that feminists not only failed to challenge this oversimplified and condescending explanation of prostitution, but also made it central to their understanding of women's oppression.

The feminists' exclusive emphasis on the victimization of the prostitute ultimately prevented transcending a sexual morality dividing women into the good and the bad.[4] They wanted to rescue women from prostitution, and to admit prostitution's victims into the salvation of good womanhood; but they clung fast to the idea that some kinds of sex were inherently criminal, and they were confounded by the existence of unrepentant whores. Furthermore, the equation of prostitution with any illicit sex indicates that a crucial element of their fear was loss of respectability. The power of prostitution rested on the common understanding that once a woman had sex outside of marriage she was "ruined," and would become a prostitute sooner or later. This potential loss of respectability was not imaginary, but a real, material process with sanctions that varied by culture and class. For middle-class and many white working-class women, the loss of purity – we would call it getting a bad reputation – damaged prospects for marriage. It led to a total loss of control over one's own sexuality, since once "used" by a man, a woman became free game for that entire sex.

Maintaining respectability was an especially severe problem for black women, fighting to free their entire race from a slave heritage that tended to place them at the disposal of white men's sexual demands. Thus the black women's movement conducted a particularly militant campaign for respectability, often making black feminists spokespeople for prudery in their communities.[5] White feminists assimilated the horror of black slavery to their fears of prostitution. They understood the sexual tyranny of slavery as central, and as a form of prostitution; among their most powerful antislavery writings were images of beautiful, pure black womanhood defiled; and white feminist abolitionists found it difficult to accept the possibility of willing sex between black women and white men.[6]

The fear of prostitution represented also a fear of direct physical violence, but in a displaced manner. In the nineteenth century, as today, women encountered sexual and nonsexual violence most often at home. Rape in marriage was no crime, not even generally disapproved; wifebeating was only marginally criminal. Incest was common enough to require skepticism about the idea that it was tabooed. Although feminists occasionally organized against domestic violence, they did not make it the object of a sustained campaign, largely because they were unable to challenge the family politically.[7] The focus on prostitution was a focus on extrafamilial violence. Nineteenth-century feminists came closer to intrafamily matters in the temperance campaign. Their criticisms of drinking were laced through with imagery of the bestial, violent quality of male sexuality, but blaming alcohol also allowed a displacement of focus, an avoidance of criticizing men and marriage directly.[8]

Certain dangers in marriage had to be faced. One was venereal disease, and this too was assimilated to the central imagery of prostitution, for men who patronized prostitutes could then transmit disease to their wives. In keeping with the division of women between good and bad, feminists implicitly considered prostitution as the source of venereal disease. The communicability and incurability of these diseases proved to them that absolute monogamy was women's only source of safety amid the sexual dangers.[9] (One is reminded of conservative response to herpes today.) Feminists also opposed the sexual demands of the self-centered husbands on their wives, which law and convention obligated women to meet. But instead of protesting "marital rape," as we do, they criticized what they called "legalized prostitution" in marriage.[10]

Sex posed another serious danger in marriage – unwanted conception. Given the equation of sex with intercourse, and the lack of access to reliable contraception, desire to control conception often resulted in the antisexual attitudes of women.[11] Despite a great reverence for motherhood, an unexpected pregnancy was often threatening. For poor women, for virtually all black women, having children meant introducing them into social and economic circumstances where their safety and well-being could not be guaranteed. Even for prosperous women, mothers' economic dependence on men was extreme. Single motherhood was an extremely difficult situation in the absence of any regular welfare or childcare provisions. Mothers were frequently forced to remain with abusive men for fear of losing their children. Indeed, prostitution was sometimes seen as an option for a single mother, for at least she could do it while she remained at home with her children![12] A bitter irony surrounds the place of motherhood in the sexual system of nineteenth-century feminism: clearly it was women's greatest joy and source of dignity; for many women it was what made sexual intercourse acceptable. But at the same time motherhood was the last straw in enforcing women's subordination to men, the factor that finally prevented many from seeking independence. What was conceived as women's greatest virtue, their passionate and self-sacrificing commitment to their children, their capacity for love itself, was a leading factor in their victimization.

Of the many factors constructing the feminist fear of prostitution perhaps none is so hard for contemporary feminists to understand as religion. But we would miss the dilemma that these women faced in dealing with sex if we did not thoroughly appreciate their religious culture. Those actively rebelling against established religion were as influenced by it as the dutiful church members or Christian reform activists. All had been raised on the concept of sin, especially sexual sin. They all shared the view that there could be high and low pleasures, and the guilt they felt about indulging in the low was not just psychological self-doubt. It was a sense of self-violation, violation of the source of their dignity.[13]

We are arguing here that the feminist understanding of sexual danger, expressed so poignantly in the fear of prostitution, must be seen as part of a sexual system in which they were participants, sometimes willing and sometimes unwilling, sometimes conscious and sometimes unaware.[14] Their very resistance often drew them into accommodation with aspects of this oppressive system. What is surprising is the extent of resistance that actually challenged this sexual system. Some women labeled "loose," who might or might not have been prostitutes, rejected the notion that their disreputable sexual behavior was something to be ashamed of or something that had been forced upon them.[15] There were young sexual "delinquents" who took pleasure and pride in their rebellion.[16] There were women who passed as men in order to seize male sexual (and other) prerogatives, and to take other women as wives.[17] Even respectable, middle-class married women had orgasms more than they were supposed to. One survey had 40 percent of women reporting orgasms occasionally, 20 percent frequently, and 40 percent never, proportions which may not be so different than those among women today.[18] About the present, it is angering that so many women do not experience orgasm; about the past, it is impressive – and analytically important – that so many women did. In other words, our nineteenth-century legacy is one of resistance to sexual repression as well as victimization by it.

Despite resistance, the weight of the nineteenth-century feminist concern was with protection from danger. This approach, usually known as "social purity," reflected an experienced reality and was overwhelmingly protectionist in its emphasis.

The major target of the feminist social purity advocates was the double standard. Their attack on it had, in turn, two aspects: seeking greater safety for women and more penalties for men. Their object was to achieve a set of controls over sexuality, structured through the family, enforced through law and/or social morality, which would render sex, if not safe, at least a decent, calculable risk for women. Social purity feminists railed against male sexual privileges, against the vileness of male drunkenness and lust, and they sought with every means at their disposal to increase the costs attached to such indulgences.[19]

The most positive achievements of social purity feminism were in the homes and communities of the middle-class women most likely to be its advocates. Here, efforts to make marriage laws more egalitarian, upgrade women's property rights, and improve women's educational and professional opportunities altered the balance of power between wife and husband. Social purity thought emphasized the importance of consensual sex for women, and insisted that even married women should not be coerced into any sexual activities they did not choose freely; inasmuch as they believed that sexual drive and initiative were primarily male, they understood this was women's right to say no. Through organizations like the Women's Christian Temperance Union, feminists propagandized for these standards with tirades against the threat to civilization caused by immorality and with energetic moral and sex education programs.[20] And they succeeded in changing culture and consciousness. Without knowing precisely how much people's lives conformed to this new standard, we can say that the ideal of marital mutuality and a woman's right to say no were absorbed into middle-class culture by the turn of the century. There is mounting evidence that, for reasons not yet clear, immigrant and poor women did not establish the same standards of marital mutuality, but fought for power within their families differently, by accepting certain patriarchal prerogatives while asserting their power as mothers and housewives.[21]

The negative consequences of social purity's single-minded focus on sexual danger come into focus when we look at their vigorous campaign against prostitution. Over time the repressive tendencies of this campaign overwhelmed its liberatory aspects and threw a pall over feminism's approach to sexuality. The beginning of women's reform work on prostitution in the early nineteenth century was a big step forward in the development of feminism. That "respectable" women took the risk of reaching out, across a veritable gulf of sexual sin, to women stigmatized as whores, was a declaration of female collectivity that transcended class and moralistic divisions. The reformers visited and talked with prostitutes, conducted public discussion of the issue, and established homes into which prostitutes could "escape." In doing so they were opening a crack in the wall of sexual "innocence" that would eventually widen into an escape route for women of their class as well. The attitudes that we today perceive as a patronizing desire to "help," were initially a challenge to the punitive and woman-hating morality that made sexual "ruin" a permanent and irredeemable condition for women.[22]

In the 1860s and 1870s feminists reactivated themselves into a militant and successful campaign to halt government regulation of prostitution. The system of regulation, already in existence in France and parts of England, forced women alleged to be prostitutes to submit to vaginal examinations and licensing; its purpose was to allow men to have sex with prostitutes without the risk of venereal disease. Feminist opposition drew not only on their anger at men who bought female flesh, but also reaffirmed their identification with prostitutes' victimization. Feminists asserted that all women, even prostitutes, had a right to the integrity of their own bodies.[23]

But, after a relatively easy victory over government regulation, social purity feminists began to press for the abolition of prostitution itself. They sponsored legislation to increase the criminal penalties for men clients, while continuing to express sympathy with the "victimized" women. The catch was that the prostitutes had to agree that they were victims. The "white slavery" interpretation of prostitution – that prostitutes had been forced into the business – allowed feminists to see themselves as rescuers of slaves.[24] But if the prostitutes were not contrite, or denied the immorality of their actions, they lost their claim to the aid and sympathy of the reformers. "The big sisters of the world [want the] chance to protect the little and weaker sisters, by surrounding them with the right laws for them to obey for their own good," one feminist explained, unwittingly capturing the repressive character of this "sisterhood."[25] The class nature of American society encouraged these middle-class feminists to conduct their challenge to the double standard through other women's lives, and to focus their anger on men other than their own husbands and fathers.

Another attack on prostitution which sometimes turned into an attack on women was the campaign to raise the age of sexual consent.[26] In many states in the nineteenth century this had been as low as nine or ten years for girls. The feminist goals were to deny the white slavers their younger victims, to extend sexual protection to girls, and to provide punishments for male assailants. Like most of these feminist sexual causes, this one had a radical moment: it communicated an accurate critique of the limitations of "consent" by women in a male-dominated society. Yet by late in the century, when urban life and the presence of millions of young working girls changed the shape of family and generational relations, age-of-consent legislation explicitly denied women the right to heterosexual activity until they were adults, or – and note that this qualification applied at any age – married. In fostering this hostility to girls' sexual activity, the feminists colluded in the labeling of a new class of female offenders: teenage sex delinquents. Sex delinquency was soon the largest category within which young women were sent to reformatories.[27] These moralistic reformers, some of them feminists, allowed the criminal justice system to take over the task of disciplining teenage girls to conform to respectable morality.

This inability to see anything in prostitution but male tyranny and/or economic oppression affected not only "bad" women, but the "good" ones as well. Feminists' refusal to engage in a concrete examination of the actuality of prostitution was of a piece with their inability to look without panic at any form of sexual nonconformity. We do not suggest that prostitutes were necessarily freer than other women sexually. Our point is that feminists remained committed to the containment of female sexuality within heterosexual marriage, despite the relative sexual repressiveness that marriage meant for women at that time.[28] "Are our girls to be [as] free to please themselves by indulging in the loveless gratification of every instinct . . . and passion as our boys?" the social purity feminist Frances Willard asked her audience in 1891; and we can imagine that they answered with a resounding "No!"[29]

Feminist politics about sex became more conservative in the period up to World War I because women's aspirations and possibilities outstripped the feminist orthodoxy. Growing feminist organizational strength and the ability to influence legislation, combined with the class and racial elitism of the world in which the feminists moved, further strengthened their conservative political tendencies. Social purity feminists not only accepted a confining sexual morality for women, but they also excluded from their sisterhood women who did not or could not go along. The prostitute remained, for all their sympathy for her, the leading symbol of the woman excluded, not only from male-bestowed privilege, but also from the women's community.[30]

Yet, just as there was behavioral resistance to the sexually repressive culture of the nineteenth century, so too there was political resistance within the women's movement. Although a decidedly minority viewpoint, a thin but continuous stream of feminists insisted that increased sexual activity was not incompatible with women's dignity and might even be in women's interests. We refer to this as the "pro-sex" tendency within the feminist tradition. It began with the free love and utopian movements of the 1820s through the 1840s. These radicals challenged the identification of sexual desire as masculine; and even though they remained for the most part advocates of the strictest monogamy, they challenged the coercive family and legal marriage as the channels for sexuality.[31] In the 1870s the free lover Victoria Woodhull appeared as a spokesperson from within the women's movement, idealizing as "true love" sex that involved mutual desire and orgasms for both parties.[32] At the same time Elizabeth Cady Stanton, a revered, if maverick, heroine, also asserted women's sexual desires.[33] In the 1880s and 1890s a few extremely visionary free love feminists began to formulate the outlines of a sexuality not organized around the male orgasm. Alice Stockham, a physician and suffragist, condemned the "ordinary, hasty and spasmodic mode of cohabitation . . . in which the wife is a passive party" and envisioned instead a union in which "the desires and pleasure of the wife calls forth the desire and pleasure of the husband."[34] Still, on the whole these nineteenth-century feminists were only relatively "pro-sex," and most of them shared with social purity advocates a belief in the need to control, contain, and harness physiological sex expression to "higher" ends. Furthermore, even this limited sex-radical tradition was so marginal to American feminism that when the twentieth-century feminist Margaret Sanger searched for a more positive attitude to sex, she had to go to Europe to find it.

The only issue within mainstream nineteenth-century feminism where "pro-sex" ideas had a significant impact was divorce. Led by Cady Stanton, some feminists argued that the right to divorce and *then to remarry* – for that was the crucial element, the right to another sexual relationship after leaving a first – was a freedom important enough for women to risk granting it to men as well. Still, most feminists took a strict social purity line and opposed divorce for fear it would weaken marriage and expose women to even greater sexual danger.[35]

Ironically, one sexual reform strongly supported by social purity advocates became the vehicle by which a new generation of feminists began to break with the social purity tradition. This was birth control.[36] Nineteenth-century feminists had argued this as "voluntary motherhood," the right of women to refuse intercourse with their husbands if they did not want to conceive. Voluntary motherhood was a brilliant tactic because it insinuated a rejection of men's sexual domination into a politics of defending and improving motherhood. Consistent with its social purity orientation, voluntary motherhood advocates rejected contraception as a form of birth control for fear it would allow men to force even more sex upon their wives and to indulge in extramarital sex with even greater impunity. In the early twentieth century, by contrast, an insurgent feminist support for contraception arose, insisting that sexual abstinence was an unnecessary price for women to pay for reproductive self-determination, and that sexual indulgence in the pursuit of pleasure was good for women.

That this new generation of feminists could break with social purity was possible in part because they were no longer controlled by their fear of becoming, or being labeled, prostitutes. They no longer saw the prostitute as only a victim; they began to break the association between sexual desire and prostitution. Indeed they embraced and romanticized sexual daring of all sorts.[37] The specter of the white slaver no longer haunted them, and they were willing to take risks. They ventured unchaperoned into theaters and bars, lived without families in big cities, and moved about the city to discover the lives of those across class and race boundaries where their mothers would not have gone. Some of their names you recognize – Emma Goldman, Margaret Sanger, Crystal Eastman, Elizabeth Gurley Flynn, even Louise Bryant – but there were many many more. Above all they asserted a woman's right to be sexual. They slept with men without marrying. They took multiple lovers. They became single mothers. Some of them had explicitly sexual relationships with other women, although a subsequent repression of evidence, along with their own silences about homosexuality, make it hard for us to uncover this aspect of their sexual lives.[38]

In many ways these women were beginning to explore a sexual world which we are determined to occupy. But as pioneers they could explore only part of it and they did not imagine changing its overall boundaries. Even when it contradicted their own experience, they continued to accept a male and heterosexual definition of the "sex act." They were, so to speak, upwardly mobile, and they wanted integration into the sexual world as defined by men. The man's orgasm remained the central event, although now it was preferable if a woman had one at the same time; stimulation other than intercourse was considered foreplay; masturbation was unhealthy. And sex, all the more desirable now because of the transcendent possibilities they attributed to it, remained bound up with the structure of gender; it could only happen between a man and a woman.[39] These feminists criticized male dominance in the labor force and in the public arena, but they did not seem to notice how it shaped sex. They fought for women's freedom, but they rarely criticized men.

Once the organized women's rights movement began to fade, women who advocated this "pro-sex" politics were more and more alienated from a larger community of women; they seemed to feel that, to enter the world of sex, they had to travel alone and leave other women behind. This rejection of women occurred both because the dominant tradition of feminism was so antisexual, and because their own understanding of sex was so heterosexual. They were part of a generation that branded intense female friendships as adolescent.[40] The tragedy was that in rejecting a community of women which they experienced as constricting and repressive, they left behind their feminist heritage.

At the same time these pioneering sex radicals offer us a positive legacy in their willingness to take risks. It would be easier if we could progress toward sexual liberation without sufferings, if we could resolve the tension between seeking pleasure and avoiding danger by some simple policy; but we cannot. We must conduct our sexual politics in the real world. For women this is like advancing across a mined field. Looking only to your feet to avoid the mines means missing the horizon and the vision of why the advance is worthwhile; but if you only see the future possibilities, you may blow yourself up.

This warlike imagery is not bravado. The dangers are substantial, women are assaulted and killed. But each act of violence against women would be multiplied in its effect if it prevented us from seeing where we have won victories, and if it induced us to resign ourselves to restriction of our sexual lives and constriction of our public activities.

Seen in this light, the contemporary focus on rape and other sexual violence against women represents an advance over the earlier campaign against prostitution. Through this new conceptualization of the problem of sexual danger, feminists have rejected the victim-blaming that was inherent in the notion of the "fallen woman"; we know that any of us can be raped. Our critique of sexual violence offers an analysis of the institution of male supremacy which attempts to show the commonalities of women, as potential agents as well as victims. Thus the campaign against rape comes out of our strength as well as our victimization. Whether the actual incidence of rape has increased or decreased, the feminist offensive against it represents an escalation of our demands for freedom. We have redefined rape to include many sexual encounters that nineteenth-century feminists would have considered mere seduction, and for which they might have held the woman responsible; we have included in our definition of rape what was once normal .marital intercourse. We have denied impunity to all men: we will bring charges against boyfriends, fathers, and teachers; we will label as sexual harassment what was once the ordinary banter of males asserting their dominance. We declare our right – still contested, viciously – to safety not only in our homes but in the streets. We *all* intend to be streetwalkers.

It is vital to strategy building to know when we are winning and when we are losing, and where. Failing to claim and take pride in our victories leads to the false conclusion that nothing has changed. When the campaign against rape is fought as if we were the eternal, unchanged victims of male sexuality, we run the risk of reentering the kind of social purity world view that so limited the nineteenth-century feminist vision.[41] It is important to offer our comprehensive critique of misogyny, violence, and male dominance without ceding the arena of sexuality itself to men, as the nineteenth-century feminists did.

We have tried to show that social purity politics, although an understandable reaction to women's nineteenth-century experience, was a limited and limiting vision for women. Thus we called it conservative. Today, there seems to be a revival of social purity politics within feminism, and it is concern about this tendency that motivates us in recalling its history. As in the nineteenth century, there is today a feminist attack on pornography and sexual "perversion" in our time, which fails to distinguish its politics from a conservative and antifeminist version of social purity, the Moral Majority and "family protection movement." The increasing tendency to focus almost exclusively on sex as the primary arena of women's exploitation, and to attribute women's sexual victimization to some violent essence labeled "male sexuality" is even more conservative today because our situation as women has changed so radically. Modern social purists point to one set of changes. The rise of sexual consumerism, and the growing power of the mass media to enforce conformity to sexual norms are debilitating for women's sexual freedom. As feminists, we are learning to be suspicious of a sexual politics that simply calls for "doing your own thing," and to ask whether women's desires are represented in these visions of sexual "freedom." We must not make the same mistake as the early twentieth-century sexual libertarians who believed that ending sexual inhibition in itself could save women. Instead, we have to continue to analyze how male supremacy and other forms of domination shape what we think of as "free" sexuality.

But there have been liberating developments as well, that we can ill afford to ignore. Women have possibilities for sexual subjectivity and self-creation today that did not exist in the past. We have a vision of sexuality that is not exclusively heterosexual, nor tied to reproduction. We have a much better physiological understanding of sexual response, and a vision of ungendered parenting. We have several strong intellectual traditions for understanding the psychological and social formation of sexuality. Perhaps most important, we have today at least a chance at economic independence, the necessary material condition for women's sexual liberation. Finally, we have something women have never enjoyed before – a feminist past, 150 years of feminist theory and praxis in the area of sexuality. This is a resource too precious to squander by not learning it, in all its complexity.

Notes

Since this paper grew out of material we have been thinking about for years, our intellectual debts are innumerable. For specific critical comments on this paper, we want to thank Ann Ferguson, Vivian Gornick, Amber Hollibaugh, Jill Lewis, Cora Kaplan, Esther Newton, Ann Snitow, Carole S. Vance, Judith R. Walkowitz, and Marilyn B. Young. About this paper we need to add, more than ever, that we alone are responsible for our conclusions.

This paper first appeared in *Feminist Studies* 9, no. 1, spring 1983.

1 These "homosocial" relationships are documented and analyzed in Lillian S. Faderman, *Surpassing the Love of Men: Romantic Friendship and Love Between Women from the Renaissance to the Present*, New York, William Morrow, 1981; Carroll Smith Rosenberg, "The Female World of Love and Ritual: Relations Between Women in Nineteenth-Century America", *Signs*, vol. 1, no. 1, Autumn 1975, pp. 1-35; Blanche Wiesen Cook, "Female Support Networks and Political Activism: Lillian Wald, Crystal Eastman, Emma Goldman", *Chrysalis*, vol. 3, 1977, pp. 43-61.

We distinguish here between behavior recognized as sexual by its actors and behavior not so recognized, aware that some historians will not agree. Furthermore, we are also emphasizing the importance of conscious sexual politics, theorizing and politicizing for the feminist effort to transform women's sexual experience. We do so, aware that, in the past decade, in an exciting renaissance of feminist historical scholarship, women's historians have chosen to focus more on behavior and culture than on political ideology. In the history of American feminism, for reasons that are undoubtedly important to explore, the initial focus for explicitly sexual politics was on the relations between women and men. The history and chronology of feminist conceptualization of what we today call lesbianism is different and we do not address it here, but Carroll Smith Rosenberg and Esther Newton do so in their unpublished paper, "The Mythic Lesbian and the New Woman: Power, Sexuality, and Legitimacy", delivered at the Fifth Berkshire Conference on the History of Women, June 1981, Poughkeepsie, New York.

2 For instance, in 1913, a suffrage newspaper estimated that there were 15,000 to 20,000 prostitutes in New York City, who serviced 150,000 to 225,000 male customers daily; this would work out to roughly one out of every 100 female persons in all five boroughs and one out of every ten males (*Women's Political World*, June 2, 1913, p. 7). Using a more precise definition of prostitution, for example, women who supported themselves solely by commercial sex, a member of New York City's Vice Commission estimated less than one-half that number (Frederick Whitten to Mary Sumner Boyd, March 17, 1916, National American Women's Suffrage Association Collection, New York Public Library).

3 The historical literature on nineteenth-century and early twentieth-century reformers' views of prostitution is extensive. The best recent study is Judith R. Walkowitz, *Prostitution and Victorian Society:*

Women, Class, and the State, Cambridge, Cambridge University Press, 1980; although he is much less aware of issues concerning gender, see Mark Connelly, *Response to Prostitution in the Progressive Era*, Chapel Hill, University of North Carolina Press, 1980.
4 Marian S. Goldman, *Gold Diggers and Silver Miners: Prostitution and Social Life on the Comstock Lode*, Ann Arbor, University of Michigan Press, 1981, chap. 7. Also see Elizabeth Jameson, "Imperfect Unions: Class and Gender in Cripple Creek, 1894-1904", in Milton Cantor and Bruce Laurie (eds), *Class, Sex and the Woman Worker*, Westport, Greenwood, 1977.
5 Gerda Lerner (ed.), *Black Women in White America: A Documentary History*, New York, Pantheon, 1972, pp. 150-72; Cynthia Neverdon-Morton, "The Black Woman's Struggle for Equality in the South, 1895-1925", in Sharon Harley and Rosalyn Terborg-Penn (eds), *The Afro-American Woman: Struggle and Images*, Port Washington, Kennikat, 1978, pp. 55-6.
    After attending the 1914 convention of the National Association of Colored Women, white feminist Zona Gale wrote of black women's efforts to work "against the traffic in women (which I hope I shall never again call the 'white slave' traffic)." ("National Association of Colored Women's Biennial", *Life and Labor*, 4, September 1914, p. 264).
6 For examples of feminist abolitionists' focus on sexual abuse in their attacks on slavery, see Lydia Maria Child, "Appeal in Favor of that Class of Americans Called Africans", in Mary R. Beard (ed.), *America Through Women's Eyes*, New York, Macmillan, 1933, p. 164; and Elizabeth Cady Stanton, "Speech to the [1860] Anniversary of the American Anti-Slavery Society", in Ellen C. DuBois (ed.), *Elizabeth Cady Stanton-Susan B. Anthony: Correspondence, Writings, Speeches*, New York, Schocken, 1981, p. 84.
    The reluctance of white feminist abolitionists to acknowledge the possibility of affection and/or voluntary sex between black women and white men can be seen in the initial response of Angelina and Sarah Grimké to the discovery that their brother had fathered a child by a slave woman. They assumed that Thomas Grimké had raped the woman, but their nephew Archibald, who had been raised as a slave, objected that this was untrue and cast his parents and the circumstances of his birth in a sordid light.
7 Linda Gordon, *Woman's Body, Woman's Right: A Social History of Birth Control in America*, New York, Viking/Penguin, 1976, chaps 5 and 6; William L. O'Neill, *Everyone Was Brave: A History of Feminism in America*, Chicago, Quadrangle, 1971.
8 Barbara Leslie Epstein, *The Politics of Domesticity: Women, Evangelism, and Temperance in Nineteenth-Century America*, Middletown, Wesleyan University Press, 1981, pp. 100-14; Ruth Bordin, *Woman and Temperance: The Quest for Power and Liberty, 1873-1900*, Philadelphia, Temple University Press, 1981, pp. 7, 26.
9 Walkowitz, *Prostitution and Victorian Society*, op. cit., chap. 3; Gordon, *Woman's Body, Woman's Right*, op. cit., p. 106; E. M. Sigsworth and T. J. Wyke, "A Study in Victorian Prostitution and

Venereal Disease", in Martha Vicinus (ed.), *Suffer and Be Still: Women in the Victorian Age*, Bloomington, Indiana University Press, 1972; Connelly, *Response to Prostitution*, op. cit., chap. 4.

10 For example, see Elizabeth Cady Stanton, "Speech to the McFarland-Richardson Protest Meeting", 1869, in DuBois, *Elizabeth Cady Stanton-Susan B. Anthony*, op. cit., p. 129; Clara Cleghorne Hoffman, "Social Purity" and Lucinda B. Chandler, "Marriage Reform", in *Report of the International Council of Women*, Washington, DC, R. H. Darby, 1888, pp. 283, 285.

11 Gordon, *Woman's Body, Woman's Right*, op. cit., chap. 5, "Voluntary Motherhood".

12 Evidence of these problems abounds in case records of social service agencies used by Linda Gordon in her research on family violence, and in her unpublished paper, "Child-saving and the Single Mother: A View from the Perspective of the Massachusetts Society for the Prevention of Cruelty to Children, 1880-1920".

13 For an exceptionally good account of the religious culture of nineteenth-century women and the conflicts it generated, see Kathryn Kish Sklar, *Catherine Beecher: A Study in American Domesticity*, New Haven, Yale University Press, 1973; the major nineteenth-century feminist opponent of women's religious traditions was Elizabeth Cady Stanton; see DuBois, *Elizabeth Cady Stanton-Susan B. Anthony*, op. cit., part 3.

14 In taking this approach, we are drawing on two recent schools of historical interpretation: feminist historians, for instance, Nancy Cott, Gerda Lerner, and Ann Douglas, who emphasize the role of women as active agents of cultural change, but who have concentrated on domesticity rather than sexuality; and male theorists of sexuality, notably Michel Foucault, who regard sexuality as a socially constructed, historically specific cultural system, but leave women out of their accounts.

15 Ruth Rosen and Sue Davison (eds), *The Maimie Papers*, Old Westbury, Feminist Press, 1977.

16 Estelle B. Freedman, *Their Sisters' Keepers: Women's Prison Reform in America, 1830-1930*, Ann Arbor, University of Michigan Press, 1981; Rosalind Rosenberg, *Beyond Separate Spheres: Intellectual Roots of Modern Feminism*, New Haven, Yale University Press, 1982, chap. 5 and p. 228; Sheldon Glueck and Eleanor T. Glueck, *Five Hundred Delinquent Women*, New York, Alfred A. Knopf, 1934, chap. 5; Mabel Ruth Fernald et el., *A Study of Women Delinquents in New York State*, New York, Century, 1920, chap. 12.

17 Jonathan Katz, *Gay American History: Lesbians and Gay Men in American History*, New York, Crowell, 1976, part 3; Erna O. Hellerstein et. al. (eds), *Victorian Women: A Documentary Account of Women's Lives in Nineteenth-Century England, France, and the United States*, Stanford, Stanford University Press, 1981, pp. 185-9.

18 Carl Degler, *At Odds: Women and the Family in America from the Revolution to the Present*, New York, Oxford, 1980, pp. 262-3; Beatrice Campbell, "Feminist Sexual Politics: Now You See It, Now You Don't", *Feminist Review*, no. 5, 1981, pp. 1-18. For a contemporary

assessment of women's orgasms, see Shere Hite, *The Hite Report: A Nationwide Study on Female Sexuality*, New York, Macmillan, 1976. Despite conceptual problems, Hite's study points to women's continuing problems with having orgasms, at least in partnered sex.

19 David J. Pivar, *Purity Crusade: Sexual Morality and Social Control, 1868-1900*, Westport, Greenwood, 1973; Degler, *At Odds*, op. cit., chap. 12; Walkowitz, *Prostitution and Victorian Society*, op. cit., chap. 12; Gordon, *Woman's Body, Woman's Right*, op. cit., chap. 6; "Social Purity Session", *Report of the International Council of Women*, op. cit., pp. 251-84.

20 Epstein, *Politics of Domesticity*, op. cit., pp. 125-37; Bordin, *Woman and Temperance*, op. cit., chap. 6.

21 For a good summary of black and immigrant family life, in contrast to middle-class families, see Degler, *At Odds*, op. cit., chap. 4 and passim. For specific evidence of poor women's weaker marital positions *vis-à-vis* their husbands' sexual demands, see Eli S. Zaretsky, "Female Sexuality and the Catholic Confessional", *Signs*, vol. 6, no. 1, Autumn 1980, pp. 176-84; and Ruth Hall (ed.), *Dear Dr. Stopes: Sex in the 1920s*, New York, Penguin, 1978, chaps 1 ("The Lower Classes") and 2 ("The Upper Classes"). Note that we deliberately avoid expressing this difference as a contrast between middle- and working-class families. We suspect that greater male sexual dominance is not so much a matter of proletarian experience as it is of peasant authoritarian background and women's extreme economic dependence.

22 Carroll Smith Rosenberg, "Beauty, the Beast, and the Militant Woman: A Case Study in Sex Roles and Social Stress in Jacksonian America", *American Quarterly*, vol. 23, 1971, pp. 562-84; Mary P. Ryan, "Power of Women's Networks: A Case Study of Female Moral Reform in Antebellum America", *Feminist Studies*, vol. 5, Spring 1979, pp. 66-89; Barbara Berg, *The Remembered Gate: Origins of American Feminism*, New York, Oxford, 1978.

23 Walkowitz, *Prostitution and Victorian Society*, op. cit., part 2; Pivar, *Purity Crusade*, op. cit., chap. 2; Degler, *At Odds*, op. cit., pp. 284-9; John Burnham, "Medical Inspection of Prostitutes in America in the Nineteenth Century: St. Louis Experiment and its Sequel", *Bulletin of the History of Medicine*, vol. 45, May-June 1971, pp. 203-18.

24 Connelly, *Response to Prostitution*, op. cit., chap. 6; Pivar, *Purity Crusade*, op. cit., pp. 135-9; Walkowitz, *Prostitution and Victorian Society*, op. cit., epilogue; Deborah Gorham, " 'The Maiden Tribute of Modern Babylon' Re-examined: Child Prostitution and the Idea of Childhood in Late Victorian England", *Victorian Studies*, vol. 21, Spring 1978, pp. 353-79; Mari Jo Buhle, *Women and American Socialism, 1870-1920*, Urbana, University of Illinois Press, 1981, pp. 253-6.

25 Jeanette Young Norton, "Women Builders of Civilization", *Women's Political World*, September 1, 1913, p. 5.

26 On efforts to raise the age of consent, see Pivar, *Purity Crusade*, op. cit., pp. 139-46; Degler, *At Odds*, op. cit., pp.288-9; Gorham, " 'The Maiden Tribute' ", op. cit.; Michael Pearson, *The Age of Consent:*

Victorian Prostitution and its Enemies, Newton Abbot, David & Charles, 1972.

27 Steven Schlossman and Stephanie Wallach, "The Crime of Precocious Sexuality: Female Juvenile Delinquency in the Progressive Era", *Harvard Educational Review*, vol. 48, no. 1, February 1978, pp. 65-94; Steven Schlossman, *Love and the American Delinquent*, Chicago, University of Chicago Press, 1977; William I. Thomas, *The Unadjusted Girl, with Cases and Standpoint for Behavior Analysis*, Boston, Little, Brown, 1923.

28 Leslie Fishbein, "Harlot or Heroine? Changing Views of Prostitution, 1870-1920", *Historian*, vol. 43, December 1980, pp. 23-35.

29 Quoted in Pivar, *Purity Crusade*, op. cit., p. 157.

30 This is one of the themes in *The Maimie Papers*. Wrote sometime prostitute, Maimie Pinzer, "I would like to have women friends – but I can't have. . . . I dreaded [they] would find out, perhaps inadvertently, something about me, and perhaps cut me, and I couldn't stand that." (p. 10)

31 On the free love movement in general, see Taylor Stoehr, *Free Love in America: A Documentary History*, New York, AMS Press, 1979; Hal D. Sears, *The Sex Radicals: Free Love in High Victorian America*, Lawrence, Regents Press of Kansas, 1977; Gordon, *Woman's Body, Woman's Right*, op. cit., chaps 5 and 6; Mary S. Marsh, *Anarchist Women, 1870-1920*, Philadelphia, Temple University Press, 1981, chap. 4; William Leach, *True Love and Perfect Union: Feminist Reform of Sex and Society*, New York, Basic Books, 1981, pp. 82-3 and passim. We use the term "pro-sex" provisionally, in lieu of a more precise term which is yet to emerge.

32 Victoria C. Woodhull, *Tried as by Fire: or, The True and the False Socially: An Oration*, New York, Woodhull & Claflin, 1874.

33 DuBois, *Elizabeth Cady Stanton-Susan B. Anthony*, op. cit., pp. 94-8 and 185-7.

34 Alice Stockham, *Karezza: Ethics of Marriage*, Chicago, Alice B. Stockham, 1897, p. 22.

35 William L. O'Neill, *Divorce in the Progressive Era*, New York, Franklin Watts, 1973; DuBois, *Elizabeth Cady Stanton-Susan B. Anthony*, op. cit., passim; Leach, *True Love and Perfect Union*, op. cit., passim.

36 Gordon, *Woman's Body Woman's Right*, op. cit., chap. 5; James Reed, *From Private Vice to Public Virtue: The Birth Control Movement and American Society Since 1830*, New York, Basic Books, 1978.

37 Caroline Ware, *Greenwich Village, 1920-1930*, Boston, Houghton Mifflin, 1935; Floyd Dell, *Love in Greenwich Village*, New York, George H. Doran, 1926; Rheta Childe Dorr, *A Woman of Fifty*, New York, Funk & Wagnalls, 1924; Judith Schwarz, *Radical Feminists of Heterodoxy, Greenwich Village, 1912-1940*, Lebanon, New Victoria, 1982; Buhle, *Women and American Socialism*, op. cit., pp. 257-268; Gordon, *Woman's Body, Woman's Right*, op. cit., pp. 189-99.

38 For lesbianism among the Greenwich Village feminists, see Schwarz, *Radical Feminists of Heterodoxy*, op. cit., pp. 30-1 and 67-72. Also see Marion K. Sanders, *Dorothy Thompson: A Legend in Her Time*,

Boston, Houghton Mifflin, 1973. Emma Goldman's relationship with Almeda Sperry is discussed in Katz, *Gay American History*, op. cit., pp. 523-9. Elizabeth Gurley Flynn's long relationship with the pioneering lesbian, Marie Equi, is traced in Rosalyn F. Baxandall, "Introduction", *Selected Writings of Elizabeth Gurley Flynn*, unpublished manuscript. There is also some suggestion that Flynn gave lesbianism a positive treatment in her original draft of *The Alderson Story: My Life as a Political Prisoner*, New York, International, 1972, but that Communist party officials insisted that she rewrite the material and make her portrait more judgmental and negative (Baxandall, private communication to authors, 1982). The large issue of repression of evidence of lesbianism is considered in Blanche Wiesen Cook, "The Historical Denial of Lesbianism", *Radical History Review*, vol. 5, no. 20, Spring/Summer 1979, pp. 55-60.

39 Gordon, *Woman's Body, Woman's Right*, op. cit., pp. 359-80; note the *new* insistence on the importance of the vagina, replacing an older recognition of the role of the clitoris in women's experience of orgasm.

40 Faderman, *Surpassing the Love of Men*, op. cit., parts 2 and 3; Christina Simmons, "Companionate Marriage and the Lesbian Threat", *Frontiers*, vol. 4, no. 3, Fall 1979, pp. 54-9; Nancy Sahli, "Smashing: Women's Friendships Before the Fall", *Chrysalis*, 8, Summer 1979, pp. 17-27.

41 For a major modern feminist study of rape which is extremely important to our movement but marred by its ahistorical assumptions, see Susan Brownmiller, *Against Our Will: Men, Women, and Rape*, New York, Simon & Schuster, 1975.

The Taming of the Id: Feminist Sexual Politics, 1968-83

Alice Echols

In reviewing the last fifteen years of radical feminist sexual politics, it seems that one element has remained constant – sex is as difficult and contested an area for feminists in 1983 as it was in the earliest days of the movement. Although it often seems as though we have been engaged in one long, seamless debate all these years, radical feminist sexual politics have changed in very fundamental ways over the decade. For instance, while early radical feminists were hardly disinterested in identifying particular sexual expressions as feminist and others patriarchal, today's radical feminists have developed a more highly prescriptive understanding of sexuality – one which in some crucial respects is antithetical to early radical feminist sexual politics. In the following pages, I will explore the permutations in radical feminist sexual politics since the late 1960s so that we might better appreciate the theoretical distance we have traveled.

However, it is impossible to understand current feminist views on sexuality without first analyzing broader shifts in feminist thinking on gender over the past decade. In fact, our understanding of gender really informs our anlaysis of sexuality. Early radical feminists believed that women's oppression derived from the very construction of gender and sought its elimination as a meaningful social category. Today's radical feminists, by contrast, claim that our oppression stems from the repression of female values and treat gender differences as though they reflect deep truths about the intractability of maleness and femaleness. For instance, in 1972 Bonnie Kreps argued that women's oppression "is based on the corrupt notion of 'maleness vs. femaleness,'" yet in 1979 Janice Raymond asks ominously what feminists "can hope to agree on ... if [we] cannot agree on the boundaries of what constitutes femaleness?"[1]

For any oppressed group it is tempting to seek solace in the reclaiming of that identity which the larger culture has systematically denigrated. This approach becomes especially compelling when the possibilities for radical change seem remote, and the only alternative seems to be assimilation into an oppressive and inegalitarian system. Unfortunately, as recent feminism has become synonymous with the rehabilitation of female values, it has come to reflect and reproduce dominant cultural assumptions about women. For instance, anti-pornography feminists suggest that women's sexual inhibition is further confirmation of women's superiority rather than emblematic of our oppression. And, in contradiction to early radical feminists who maintained that the identification of women with nature is a patriarchal construct, many eco-feminists and pacifist feminists claim not only that women are closer to nature, but that our "bond with the natural order" makes us uniquely qualified to save the planet from nuclear holocaust and ecological ruination.[2]

I believe that what we have come to identify as radical feminism represents such a fundamental departure from its radical feminist roots that it requires renaming. To this end, I will refer to this more recent strain of feminism as cultural feminism, because it equates women's liberation with the nurturance of a female counter culture which it is hoped will supersede the dominant culture.[3] Cultural feminism's polarization of male and female sexuality and its demonization of the former and idealization of the latter has its political incarnation in the anti-pornography movement. By the end of the 1970s, cultural feminism had achieved hegemony within the movement and its celebration of femaleness, which has led some to label it "femininism," not only informs the anti-pornography campaign, but eco-feminism and the feminist peace movement as well. Like its French counterpart, *néo-féminité*, cultural feminism is "an ideal bound up through symmetrical opposition in the very ideological system feminists want to destroy."[4] Of course, to propose that there exists a theoretical coherence to cultural feminism is not to suggest that it is monolithic.

While cultural feminists are committed to preserving rather than challenging gender differences, some demonstrate a cavalier disinterest in whether these differences are biological or cultural in origin. In *The Transsexual Empire*, Janice Raymond argues:

Yet there are differences, and some feminists have come to realize that those differences are important whether they spring from socialization, from biology, or from the total history of existing as a woman in a patriarchal society.

Raymond considers the source of these differences irrelevant, because she reasons that, as women, "we know who *we* are."(her italics)[5]

Even more troubling than equivocation of this sort is the

growing tendency among other cultural feminists to invoke biological explanations of gender differences. This is a particularly ironic development, given radical feminists' opposition to pre-cultural explanations of gender asymmetry.[6] These cultural feminists generally attribute male dominance to the rapaciousness or barrenness of male biology. Thus Susan Brownmiller accepts that rape is a function of male biology, while Mary Daly argues that the "emptiness" of male biology explains male supremacy. As though it proves her point, Daly cites arch-conservative George Gilder's view that "while the female body is full of internal potentiality, the male is internally barren."[7] While Daly suggests that men are "mutants [who may like other mutations] manage to kill themselves off eventually," Sally Gearhart insists that the preservation of the planet requires that the "proportion of men must be reduced to and maintained at approximately 10% of the human race."[8]

Although radical feminists viewed female biology as a liability and thus in some cases mirrored the culture's devaluation of the female body, cultural feminists have over-reacted to this earlier position in arguing that female biology is a powerful resource.[9] While Jane Alpert's 1973 article, "Mother-Right," is the earliest articulation of this revisionism, Adrienne Rich is its most eloquent exponent:

I have come to believe, as will be clear throughout this book, that female biology . . . has far more radical implications than we have yet come to appreciate. Patriarchal thought has limited female biology to its own narrow specifications. The feminist vision has recoiled from female biology for these reasons; it will, I believe, come to view our physicality as a resource, rather than a destiny. In order to live a truly human life we require not only *control* of our bodies . . . we must touch the unity and resonance of our physicality, our bond with the natural order, the corporeal ground of our intelligence. (her italics)[10]

Although Rich fails to acknowledge that feminist biological determinsim might reproduce dominant cultural assumptions about women, Gearhart admits that it does:

But if by believing that women are by nature less violent we reinforce the sex roles that have held women down for so long, then perhaps it is time to dare to admit that some of the sex-role mythology is in fact true and to insist that the qualities attributed to women (specifically empathy, nurturance and cooperativeness) be affirmed as human qualities capable of cultivation by men even if denied them by nature.[11]

Not all cultural feminists are enthusiastic supporters of biologically-based explanations of gender. Both Florence Rush and Andrea Dworkin have criticized biological determinism. However, for others, like Robin Morgan, the danger lies less in the concept itself than in the control of its application. Morgan has advised feminists against accepting "biological-determination theories . . . until we have enough feminists to right the current imbalance and bias and to create a genuinely value-free science."[12]

This new feminist biological determinism, like its anti-feminist counterpart, is fraught with contradictions. For instance, cultural feminists distinguish between patriarchally-conditioned femininity which they associate with passivity and submissiveness, and female nature which they assume to be nurturant, tender, and egalitarian. However, no such distinction is made between patriarchally-conditioned masculinity and biologically-determined maleness. So while female passivity is believed to be socially constructed, male violence is seen as intrinsic and the crystallization of maleness.

Although radical feminists often stressed the psychological dimension of women's oppression, they understood the importance of analyzing and challenging the material basis of patriarchy. By contrast, cultural feminists have demonstrated less interest in effecting structural change than in nurturing an alternative female consciousness, or what Mary Daly terms "the spring into free space."[13] Cultural feminists believe that the struggle against male supremacy begins with women exorcizing the male within us and maximizing our femaleness. And while radical feminists were generally careful to distinguish between individual and political solutions, cultural feminists typically believe that individual solutions are political solutions. Cultural feminism's validation of individual solutions not only encouraged the scrutiny of personal behavior rather than ideas, but moreover, contributed to the development of standards of "liberated" behavior. It has also fostered a blamatory and elitist attitude among those who consider themselves "woman-identified." In one of the most egregious examples of this, Daly has suggested that heterosexual women could get themselves "off the hook of the . . . contraceptive dilemma" were they to follow the example of "Spinsters" – "women who choose to be agents of be-ing" – and elect "Misterectomy."[14]

Finally, whereas radical feminists like Shulamith Firestone believed that a "sexual revolution much larger than – inclusive of – a socialist one [was needed] to truly eradicate all class systems," cultural feminists see capitalism and socialism as equally injurious to women.[15] While radical feminists "criticized the left *from the left* for refusing to broaden its analysis to account for women's oppression," cultural feminists insist that feminism and the left are intrinsically incompatible.[16] For cultural feminists, the left, like pornography, is an intrusive and contaminating force which prevents us from fully "dispossessing ourselves" of our patriarchal past.[17] In fact, cultural feminism began to emerge as philosophically distinct from radical feminism in early 1975 with the creation of the Circle of Support for Jane Alpert. Rather than deny the charge that Alpert had supplied the FBI with information about fellow members of the underground, the Circle rejoiced in her defection from the left and her conversion to feminism.[18]

But, it was in the mid-1970s phenomenon of feminist capitalism that cultural feminism really took shape. These early cultural feminists treated capitalism as a relatively benign system which could be enlisted in the struggle to defeat patriarchy.[19] Some even embraced capitalism while repudiating democratic process and rationalized this position by invoking women's superiority and commonality of interests.[20] Those feminists who criticized their attempt to wed capitalism with feminism were characterized as "aping" the "correct-line politics" and "trashing" style of the male left.[21] Anti-pornography feminists have tried to silence their intra-movement critics with the same red-baiting tactics used against critics of feminist capitalism. Recently, Kathy Barry characterized the feminist opposition to the anti-pornography movement as a cabal of leftist lesbian and heterosexual women who want to destroy the movement so that "male leftists can continue their sexual abuse of women without fear of censure."[22]

Cultural feminists vilify the left because its analysis so completely contravenes their belief system, especially their faith that truly radical change will be achieved only when the culture "returns" to female values and that race and class are merely ancillary to gender hierarchy. Just as some socialists argue that socialism will eliminate women's oppression, cultural feminists maintain that feminism will eradicate race and class oppression. Cultural feminist faith in women's superiority and commonality not only encourages them to label dissent "unsisterly" or left-inspired, but it promotes political expediency as well.[23]

Given this theoretical incompatibility, how did radical feminism devolve into cultural feminism? In part the fragmentation within our ranks and the erosion of feminist gains in the recent past have made cultural feminism, with its promise of female unity, especially attractive. More specifically, the debate around the relationship of lesbianism to feminism was, to a great extent, responsible for promoting the assumptions which underlie cultural feminism. The struggle for lesbian visibility and recognition in the 1970s was extremely important because it forced feminists to acknowledge that sexuality is socially conditioned and that heterosexuality is culturally, rather than biologically, mandated. But the homophobia, and, to a lesser extent, the anti-sex attitudes within certain elements of the movement precluded lesbian feminists from promoting lesbianism as a sexual rather than a political choice. Initially, some heterosexual feminists, reflecting dominant cultural assumptions, defined and dismissed lesbianism as a solely sexual experience. And for Ti-Grace Atkinson, founder of the New York group, The Feminists, and Abby Rockefeller of the Boston group, Cell 16, who believed that sex is the foundation of women's oppression, lesbianism was particularly threatening. For instance, Atkinson cautioned:

a case could be made that lesbianism, in fact *all* sex, is reactionary, and that feminism is revolutionary.... Because lesbianism involves role-playing and more important, because it is based on the primary assumption of male oppression, that is, sex, lesbianism reinforces the sex class system. (her italics)[24]

And Rockefeller argued that lesbianism "muddles what is the real issue for women by making it appear that women really like sex as much as men – that they just don't like sex *with* men." (her italics)[25] Even Anne Koedt whose politics could hardly be characterized as erotophobic, hedged her approval of lesbianism:

two lesbians who have chosen not to fall into imitative roles, but are instead exploring the positive aspects of both "masculine" and "feminine" behavior beyond roles – forming something new and equal in the process – would in my opinion probably be healthy.[26]

Given this context, it is understandable that many lesbian feminists found it easier to justify their sexuality on exclusively political grounds.

Lesbian recognition was achieved by locating the discourse within the already established framework of separatism. The conviction that feminism is conditional upon separation from men predated lesbian separatism. For example, The Feminists established a quota system at the time of their founding in 1969 to limit women living with men to one-third of the group's membership.[27] Lesbian separatists, like the Washington, DC Furies collective, argued further that heterosexual women were impeding the movement's progress. Furies member, Rita Mae Brown, opined:

Straight women are confused by men, don't put women first. They betray lesbians and in its deepest form, they betray their own selves. You can't build a strong movement if your sisters are out there fucking with the oppressor.[28]

By defining lesbianism as a political choice and encouraging an idealization of female sexuality, lesbian feminists deprived heterosexual feminists of one of their favorite charges against lesbianism – that it was male-identified.[29] However, this assumption that sexual relationships with men are inevitably debilitating while those with women are automatically liberating has had, as we shall see, serious consequences for lesbian sexuality. Furthermore, in establishing lesbianism as a true measure of one's commitment to feminism, lesbian separatists distorted the meaning of "the personal is political," giving it a prescriptive rather than a descriptive meaning. Of course, the tendency to judge a woman on the basis of her sexual preference, marital status or hair length did not originate with lesbian separatism, but it was further legitimated by it.[30]

Lesbian separatism's open hostility to heterosexual feminists guaranteed that it would remain a minority view. However, in its reincarnation as cultural feminism, lesbian separatism has been modified and refined in such a way as to make it more acceptable to a wider audience. Whereas lesbian separatists advocated separation from men, cultural feminists advocate separation from male values. And rather than promote lesbianism, cultural feminists encourage woman-bonding and thus avoid estranging heterosexual feminists.

With the rise of cultural feminism, relations between lesbian and heterosexual feminists have become more cordial. However, the very terms of this reconciliation have ensured that suspicion and acrimony would be preserved, though often below the surface. First, lesbian recognition has been achieved by further abstracting it from the realm of sexuality – cloaking it as female bonding. And lesbian acceptance is contingent upon the extent to which our relationships conform to standards of egalitarianism. Second, although they are more likely to be defined now as victims rather than traitors, heterosexual feminists remain objects of suspicion, for their acceptance depends upon how completely they conceal or renounce heterosexual desire. Ironically, heterosexual feminists are still made to feel like the movement's backsliders by virtue of their proximity to contaminating maleness. Occasionally hostility surfaces, as it did at the 1979 Women Against Pornography conference when a lesbian separatist denounced Susan Brownmiller as a "cocksucker." Brownmiller retaliated by pointing out that her critic "even dresses like a man."[31] But, with the anti-pornography movement, cultural feminism has succeeded in mobilizing feminists regardless of sexual preference, however fragile the alliance.

Radical feminists embraced a dualistic approach to sexuality – one which acknowledged both the danger and the pleasure associated with sexual exploration for women in this culture. For instance, the popularity of feminist sex manuals was not believed to undermine the effectiveness of the anti-rape movement. While radical feminists recognized that the ideology of the sexual revolution discriminated against women, they did not conclude from this, as have cultural feminists, that sexual liberation and women's liberation are mutually exclusive. For instance, in *The Dialectic of Sex*, Shulamith Firestone argued that "in our new society, humanity could finally revert to its natural polymorphous sexuality – all forms of sexuality would be allowed and indulged."[32] In a 1971 article, "Thoughts on Promiscuity," Karen Lindsey claimed that men's continued acceptance of the sexual double standard had sabotaged the sexual revolution. Moreover, she warned that:

unless we understand, very exactly, what is at the heart of the failure in our sexual experimenting, we are, in fact, in danger of reverting to a rejection of sex without love – with all the self-denial, smugness, guilt, and dishonesty that goes with such a rejection.[33]

Radical feminists did not idealize women's sexual conservatism, but rather would have agreed with Muriel Dimen that "female sexual turf and male emotional range need expansion."[34] For instance, Karen Durbin contended that rock music encouraged female sexual assertion:

Rock music . . . provided me and a lot of women with a channel for saying, "I want," for asserting our sexuality without apologies and without having to pretty up every passion with the traditionally "feminine" desire for true love and marriage, and that was a useful step toward liberation.[35]

Radical feminists understood that women's sexual inhibition is related in large part to the absence of safe, accessible, and effective contraception which renders women sexually vulnerable. They attributed women's attachment to traditional morality not to the innately spiritual quality of women's sexuality, but rather to our socialization which encourages sexual alienation and guilt. This consciousness informed the radical feminist struggle for reproductive rights. Radical feminists understood, as does the New Right, that the fight for reproductive freedom is the struggle for sexual self-determination.

Of course, from the earliest days of the women's movement there were those radical feminists whose views on sexuality anticipated cultural feminist sexual politics. Ti-Grace Atkinson declared that "*all* sex is reactionary." Dana Densmore suggested that celibacy is preferable to "making love to a man who despises you."[36] And Abby Rockefeller claimed that "women *don't* like [sex] either with the same frequency or in the same way as men." (her italics)[37] But these views represented a minority opinion within the ranks of radical feminists.

However, in some crucial respects radical feminist thinking on sexuality did contribute to the development of cultural feminist sexual politics. Radical feminists' skepticism towards individual solutions disinclined them from defining "the personal is political" prescriptively. However, this same wariness encouraged them to trivialize individual attempts towards sexual empowerment. For instance, two reporters for the feminist newspaper, *Off Our Backs*, criticized NOW's 1974 Conference on Sexuality for focusing upon sexual technique rather than political analysis:

Viewing [the conference] from ... a strictly radical feminist perspective ... we react with anger and disappointment. We went hoping to hear some feminist analyses of women's sexuality. Instead, we were inundated with tales of organic masturbation parties, bisexual chic, and why whips can be fun.[38]

While radical feminists disparaged personal solutions, they none the less believed that one's sexuality should mirror one's politics – a conviction that promoted prescriptivism. In their desire to develop a genuinely feminist sexuality, radical feminists subordinated sexuality to politics in what Deirdre English has suggested is a feminist version of "sexuality in service to society."[39] Most importantly, by envisioning feminist sexuality as requiring the elimination of power, radical feminism encouraged us to renounce our sexuality as it is now. In assuming that a liberated sexuality demanded the disentanglement of power and sexuality, radical feminists, quite unintentionally, contributed to our alienation from psychological and social sources of sexual power.

On the whole, however, cultural feminist thinking on sexuality represents a significant deviation from radical feminist sexual politics. In the cultural feminist analysis, sexual danger so defines women's lives that it precludes a consideration of sexual pleasure. Unlike radical feminists, who generally located the source of women's oppression in the nuclear family, cultural feminists agree with Andrea Dworkin that "the heart of sex oppression [is] the use of women as pornography, pornography as what women *are*."[40] The argument that "pornography is the theory, rape the practice," represents cultural feminism's contribution to the domino theory of sexuality.[41] It identifies pornography as the scourge which leads inexorably to violence against women. More recently, anti-pornography feminists have extended their critique to encompass fantasy, which they claim is dangerous because it entails the substitution of an illusion for the "social-sexual reality" of another person. In rejecting as so much "male-identified mind-body dualism" the belief that fantasy is the repository of our ambivalent and conflictual feelings, cultural feminists have developed a highly mechanistic, behaviorist analysis that conflates fantasy with reality and pornography with violence. "Integrity," their answer to patriarchy's dangerous dualism, entails the transformation of all aspects of our lives into one seamless, unambiguous reflection of our politics.[42] Such a view assumes that we can and should be held accountable for our desires. And if we fail to banish those tainted fantasies, we can console ourselves with Julia Penelope's suggestion that fantasy may be another "phallocentric 'need' from which we are not yet free."[43]

Cultural feminists define male and female sexuality as though they were polar opposites. Male sexuality is driven, irresponsible, genitally oriented, and potentially lethal. Female sexuality is muted, diffuse, interpersonally-oriented, and benign. Men crave power and orgasm, while women seek reciprocity and intimacy. Although cultural feminists often assume the immutability of male and female sexuality, the prescriptivism which permeates their writing reflects an underlying fear about their mutability. For instance, in her 1973 West Coast Lesbian Feminist Conference address, Robin Morgan warned that lesbian feminists who advocated non-monogamy, accepted transvestites, and listened to the Rolling Stones had adopted a "male style [which] could be a destroyer from within" the women's movement.[44] By defining the pursuit of relationships as female and the pursuit of sex as male, Morgan tried to intimidate her lesbian audience back into the familiar terrain of romantic love:

Every woman here knows in her gut the vast differences between her sexuality and that of any patriarchally trained male's – gay or straight ... that the emphasis on genital sexuality, objectification, promiscuity, emotional noninvolvement, and coarse invulnerability was the *male style*, and that we, as women, placed greater trust in love, sensuality, humor, tenderness, commitment. (her italics)[45]

Unlike radical feminists who attacked romantic love, cultural feminists apotheosize it.[46]

For cultural feminists, male sexuality is not only compulsive, but, as Dworkin has described it, "the stuff of murder, not love."[47] Thus, for men, sexuality and violence are inextricably linked and find their cultural expression in pornography. Cultural feminists are so convinced that male sexuality is, at its core, lethal, that they reduce it to its most alienated and violent expressions. The actions of de Sade or Son of Sam come to symbolize the murderousness of male sexuality, and sexual intercourse becomes a mere euphemism for rape.[48] Liberal and leftist men who oppose censorship are characterized as having a prurient interest in pornography. And men's growing interest in their partner's sexual satisfaction is said simply to demonstrate men's obsession with sexual performance. Everything, no matter how contradictory, confirms the premise that male sexuality is selfish, violent, and woman-hating. Their characterization of male sexuality is so uniformly unflattering and overwhelmingly bleak that one wonders what would be accomplished by the restriction or elimination of pornography.[49]

By contrast, women's sexuality is assumed to be more spiritual than sexual, and considerably less central to their lives than is sexuality to men's. For instance, Adrienne Rich describes female sexuality as an "energy which is unconfined to any single part of the body or solely to the body itself."[50] And Ethel Person maintains that "many women have the capacity to abstain from sex without negative psychological consequences." For Person, women's more highly developed "capacity for abstinence, repression, or suppression [has] adaptive advantages" over male hypersexuality.[51] Person fails to understand that women's apparent mental health in the face of anorgasmia or abstention testifies to women's conditioning to subordinate and repress sexual drive. Unfortunately, sexual repression may very well become adaptive for women once again if the Human Life Amendment and Family Protection Act are enacted into law.[52] In fact, cultural feminism feeds what one feminist has described as "our society's treasured illusion that male sexuality is like a bludgeon or a speeding train," and its equally cherished corollary that women seek affection rather than orgasm in their sexual encounters.[53]

It follows from this that cultural feminists would see heterosexuality as a metaphor for male rapaciousness and female victimization. In contrast to lesbian feminists for whom heterosexuality generally represented collaboration with the enemy, cultural feminists appear to take a more sympathetic position towards heterosexual women. They understand women's participation in heterosexuality as more apparent than real, and suggest that women are coerced and bribed into compliance with heterosexual norms. For instance, Adrienne Rich cites Barry's *Female Sexual Slavery* as evidence that "for women heterosexuality may not be a 'preference' at all but something that has to be imposed, managed, organized, propagandized, and maintained by force."[54] Although specific explanations vary, cultural feminists believe that for women heterosexuality is neither fully chosen nor truly pleasurable. It is worth noting that heterosexual cultural feminists seem to accept this understanding of their sexuality, although to do so would appear to involve guilt and self-deprecation, if not self-flagellation.

If the cultural feminist view of heterosexuality is over-determined, their position on sexual minorities is myopic. Janice Raymond maintains that "all transsexuals rape women's bodies by reducing the real female form to an artifact, appropriating this body for themselves."[55] The contradiction of transsexualism is that it both undermines and reinforces gender as a significant category. However, cultural feminists, especially those who favor biological determinism, find transsexualism troubling, because it confounds the boundaries between maleness and femaleness. But cultural feminists' real contempt is reserved for male-to-female lesbian-feminist transsexuals who seduce lesbians, they argue, by appealing to their vestigial heterosexuality. Mary Daly complains that their "whole presence becomes a 'member' invading women's presence and dividing us once more from each other."[56]

Cultural feminists believe that the centrality of public and anonymous sex to the gay male sexual landscape merely demonstrates that heterosexual men have no monopoly on sexual callousness. They maintain that the gay male subculture of s/m and cross-generational sex is further evidence of male rapacity.[57] NOW endorsed this view at its 1980 convention which adopted the infamous resolution designed to ensure that NOW does not work with any groups which might misconstrue pornography, s/m, cross-generational sex and public sex as "Lesbian Rights issues."[58] Ironically, the resolution was introduced by the chair of NOW's Sexual Preference Task Force.[59]

How has it come to pass that some lesbians are in the forefront of a movement which has resurrected terms like "sexual deviance" and "perversion" – terms which one would have thought the feminist movement made anachronistic a decade ago? Lesbian cultural feminists would, however, explain, as does Adrienne Rich, that lesbianism is a "profoundly female experience" which needs to be dissociated from "male homosexual values and allegiances."[60] Lesbian cultural feminists' insistence that lesbianism is an issue of "radical female friendship" rather than sexual preference reflects an unwillingness to admit that within the larger culture lesbianism is viewed as a "perversion."[61] For instance, Sally Gearhart suggests that lesbian sexuality is wholesome:

In being part of the word "gay" weary lesbians have spent untold hours explaining to Middle America that lesbians do not worry about venereal disease, do not have sex in public bathrooms . . . and do not want to go to the barricades fighting for the lowering of the age of consent.[62]

Even more, this hostility towards other sexual minorities reflects their fear that male sexuality as it is symbolized to them in s/m, cross-generational sex, transsexualism and pornography is polluting the "women's community." Adrienne Rich maintains that pornography impairs the "potential of loving and being loved by women in mutuality and integrity."[63] Raymond cautions us against accepting lesbian-feminist male-to-female transsexuals into our communities for she fears they might "seduce" us back into heterosexuality.[64] And Gearhart complains:

I am frustrated and angry that ... many gay men remain totally oblivious to the effect on women of their objectification of each other, their obsession with youth and beauty, their camped-up consumerism, and their demand for freer sexual expression.[65]

Statements like these betray an apprehension that women's sexuality may not be innately ethereal and that lesbianism may not offer the uncomplicated refuge from what Rita Mae Brown in 1972 termed the "silly, stupid, harmful games that men and women play."[66] But rather than acknowledge that the quest for completely egalitarian relationships and politically-correct sex has proved difficult at best, lesbian cultural feminists have retreated from the ambiguities of sexuality and have used ideological justifications to de-emphasize sex. The growing number of lesbian feminists experimenting with s/m, butch-femme roles, and bisexuality only demonstrates to lesbian cultural feminists that we must be more vigilant in the struggle against the residual heterosexuality which they believe informs these "deviations." They see in the growth of the lesbian-feminist sexual fringe the corrupting influence of male-identified sexuality rather than a rebellion against the ever-narrowing standard for politically permissible sexuality.[67]

This admonition that our sexuality mirror our politics may have originated with radical feminists, but for lesbian cultural feminists it has become the justification for a destructive sexual prescriptivism. The sexual repressiveness of the lesbian cultural feminist orthodoxy has contributed to the heterophobia which is in turn vented in the anti-pornography movement. Perhaps the movement's success in enlisting the support of certain sectors of the lesbian community reflects the extent to which the movement validates lesbianism through its demonization of maleness and heterosexuality.

For cultural feminists the proliferation of pornography, the apparent increase in rape and incest, and the growing assertiveness of the sexual fringe testify to the evils of sexual permissiveness. They indict pornography for eroding the traditional boundary separating the virgin from the whore. Morgan argues that pornography has contributed to a "new 'all women are really whores' attitude, thus erasing the last vestige of (even corrupted) respect for women."[68] Although pornography is obviously the focus of their struggle, cultural feminists believe that the real villain is the sexual revolution rather than its "propaganda" tool, pornography. Cultural feminists never seem to consider that the apparent growth in violence against women might demonstrate the effectiveness of the feminist movement in challenging the heretofore closeted and uncontested nature of rape, battery and incest rather than the success of the sexual revolution in promoting these crimes.[69] Instead they maintain that the sexual revolution allowed men to choose "swinging" over commitment, pornographic images over real people, and violence over love.

More importantly, cultural feminists argue that the sexual revolution's affirmation of male sexual values encouraged women to abandon female sexual values in a misguided quest for assimilation. According to Barry, who here sounds disturbingly like Phyllis Schlafly, many women have rejected intimacy only to discover that "new problems arose as they escaped from male power into self-centeredness, and as they tried to depersonalize their sexual being."[70] Cultural feminists also accuse rampant individualism of discouraging intimacy by encouraging us to become selfishly absorbed in meeting our own needs. Barry has even vilified democracy for breeding a "pluralistic notion of cultural diversity" which in turn encourages a perilous tolerance towards "sexual perversion."[71] For cultural feminists sexual freedom is a reactionary, rather than a subversive, force which secures social order by numbing us into political apathy.[72]

This analysis fails to explain why the Reagan administration is more intent upon ushering us back into the sexual repressiveness of the 1950s than in promoting sexual liberation. This equation of sexual freedom with irresponsibility, selfishness and dehumanization has, in fact, already been used by the New Right in its struggle against feminism, abortion, and gay rights. This analysis further denies the extent to which early radical feminism was a rebellion against traditional sexual morality. The sexual revolution's failure to challenge gender asymmetry hardly justifies cultural feminists' promotion of a traditional sexual standard – albeit modified to include those lesbians and gay men whose sexuality appears to be orthodox. And by fingering individualism as the enemy, cultural feminism ignores the role individualism played in the emergence of the women's movement. Individualism may be bourgeois, but it is precisely the breakdown of a familial orientation and the development of individualism which gave birth to feminism.[73]

To curb the promiscuity and rapacity spawned by the sexual revolution, cultural feminists propose that we impose upon the culture a female sexual standard – a standard which seems to correspond to their understanding of their mothers' sexual values. Thus Morgan argues that in repudiating sexual liberation she is affirming her identification with her mother.[74] And Barry suggests:

In going back into new sexual values we are really going back to the values women have always attached to sexuality, values that have been robbed from us, and destroyed as we have been colonized through both sexual violence and so-called liberation.[75]

Cultural feminist sexual politics really offer us nothing more than women's traditional sexual values disguised as radical feminist sexual values. Moreover, these values derive not from our biology, as Barry suggests, but from our powerlessness. In promoting romantic love as an authentically female and thus feminist sexuality, cultural feminists endorse the same constraining sexuality to which our mothers were condemned. Rather than develop a feminist understanding of sexual liberation, cultural feminists reject it as inherently anti-feminist and instead endorse a sexual code which drastically circumscribes the sorts of sexual expressions considered acceptable. And, in demanding "respect," rather than challenging the terms upon which women are granted "respect," cultural feminists reinforce the distinction between the virgin and the whore.

In fact their solution to violence against women is nothing more than a return to the spurious "respect" traditionally reserved for women. This analysis confuses "respect" for liberation and fails to recognize that "respect" is merely the flip side of violation. More importantly, this view suggests that sexual repression is a satisfactory solution to violence against women. Anti-pornography feminist Diana Russell has admitted that censorship would only push pornography underground, but she reasons this is preferable to seeing it "flourish as an accepted part of the culture."[76]

Cultural feminists seem nostalgic for the old days when men "respected" some women, women acknowledged that love was female and sex was male, and pornography was kept behind the counter. Although cultural feminists blame the sexual revolution for destroying the old sexual order, radical feminists' attack on marriage, romantic love, puritan morality, and respect certainly hastened its downfall. In fact, the cultural feminist analysis of sexuality constitutes an unacknowledged repudiation of radical feminist sexual politics. The radical feminist critiques of the nuclear family, sexual repression, the State and religion have disappeared from the cultural feminist analysis which focuses instead upon the "pornographic mind" and sexual permissiveness. And as we have seen, cultural feminists are in the process of rehabilitating much of what radical feminists found most oppressive to women.

Why do cultural feminists, while recognizing that they cannot eliminate pornography, continue to define it as the overriding feminist issue? On one level the anti-pornography campaign represents a calculated attempt to unify and fortify a movement seriously divided by the issues of race, class and sexual preference and badly demoralized by the anti-feminist backlash. In their desperate efforts to construct a mass women's movement to combat male lust, anti-pornographpy feminists abandon feminism for female moral outrage.[77] For instance, anti-pornography activist Judith Bat-Ada insists that a "coalition of all women . . . regardless of race, color, creed, religion, or *political persuasion*" should be formed to fight pornography (emphasis mine).[78] Unfortunately, in advocating sexual repression as a solution to violence against women, cultural feminists resort to mobilizing women around their fears rather than their visions.[79]

On a less obvious level, the anti-pornography movement's insistence upon the incorrigibility of male sexuality suggests that it is concerned with something other than its reformation. This movement is as much an attempt to regulate female sexuality as it is an effort to curb men's sexuality. The movement's mono-maniacal concern with sexual danger, epitomized by Barry's claim that "sexual slavery lurks in the corners of every woman's life," and its disinterest in developing strategies for sexual empowerment discourage women from struggling towards sexual self-definition.[80] It has become a vehicle to establish the proper parameters of lesbian sexuality so as to diminish the possibility that lesbians will defect to "male-identified" sexual expressions, whether these be s/m, roles, or heterosexuality. Perhaps anti-pornography feminists prefer to foreclose on sexuality rather than to explore it and to risk discovering the disjuncture between their desires and their politics.

Although the movement's villainization of heterosexuality seems to offer heterosexual feminists very little but self-denial and guilt, it should be understood that they do achieve a measure of political legitimacy by virtue of their status as victims of male lust. For lesbian and heterosexual feminists alike, the anti-pornography crusade functions as the feminist equivalent to the anti-abortion movement – reinforcing and validating women's sexual alienation and manipulating women's sense of themselves as the culture's victims as well as its moral guardians. The anti-pornography movement, like the anti-abortion movement, represents a rebellion against the new sexual order. In acknow-ledging women's right to sexual pleasure while ignoring the risks associated with sexual exploration for women, the sexual revolution has heightened women's sense of sexual vulnera-bility.[81] But do we really want to return to the old sexual order whereby women were accorded male protection in exchange for sexual circumspection?

On a more profound level, I suspect that sexual problematic is related to the mother-daughter problematic. The cultural feminist injunction against "going too far" sexually may also be an injunction against going too far, or becoming too differentiated, from our mothers. Whereas radical feminism represented a rebellion against the mother in which identification with the mother was suppressed, cultural feminism represents fusion with the mother in which differences between mother and daughter are suppressed. Perhaps cultural feminists advise us to embrace our mother's putative sexual values because they fear that the sexual empowerment and self-definition implicit in radical feminism involve a betrayal of our mothers?[82]

In conclusion, I suggest that we reclaim the radical feminist vision that joined sexual liberation with women's liberation. The struggle for sexual pleasure is legitimate and need not imply a callous disregard of sexual danger. In order to develp a truly transformative sexual politics we must once again resist the familiarity of sexual repression and the platitudes about male and female sexuality. But we must also break with the radical feminist tradition which encourages us to subordinate sexuality to politics in an effort to make our sexuality conform to our political ideology, treating our sexuality as an ugly blemish which with vigilance and time might be overcome. We must abandon the belief so deeply entrenched in the feminist community that particular sexual expressions are intrinsically liberated or intrinsically degraded. Inequality can exist in relationships where the love-making is assiduously egalitarian as well as in relationships where the polarized roles of top and bottom are carefully cultivated.[83] We should acknowledge the possibility that power inheres in sexuality rather than assume that power simply withers away in egalitarian relationships. Perhaps we might achieve more equality were we to negotiate rather than deny power. The solution is not to reprivatize sexuality or eschew a critical analysis of sexuality. Nor is our sexuality so hopelessly conditioned that our efforts to transform it are misguided and futile. Instead we need to develop a feminist understanding of sexuality which is not predicated upon denial and repression, but which acknowledges the complexities and ambiguities of sexuality. Above all, we should admit that we know far too little about sexuality to embark upon a crusade to circumscribe it. Rather than foreclose on sexuality we should identify what conditions will best afford women sexual autonomy, safety, and pleasure and work towards their realization.

Notes

Many people have made constructive criticisms of this piece. I would especially like to thank Kate Ellis, Constance Samaras, Sandra Silberstein, Bette Skandalis, Ann Snitow, Carole S. Vance, and Ellen Willis.

1 Bonnie Kreps "Radical Feminism 1", in Anne Koedt, Ellen Levine, and Anita Rapone (eds), *Radical Feminism*, New York, New York Times Book Co., 1973, p. 239; Janice Raymond, *The Transsexual Empire*, Boston, Beacon Press, 1979, p. 114.

2 Adrienne Rich, Susan Griffin, and Mary Daly are the best known proponents of this view. The belief that women's more extensive experience with nurturance inclines them towards peace and ecology is widespread among cultural feminists. See *Off Our Backs (OOB)*, January 1981, on the Women's Pentagon Action and Ynestra King, "Feminism and the Revolt of Nature", *Heresies #13*, for an introduction to eco-feminism. For more sophisticated versions of this argument, see Jean Bethke Elshtain, "Women, War and Feminism", *Nation*, June 14, 1980, and Sara Ruddick, "Maternal Thinking", *Feminist Studies*, vol. 6, no. 2, Summer 1980.

3 The *reconstituted* Redstockings first termed this theoretical tendency "cultural feminism" in their 1975 publication, *Feminist Revolution* (reissued by Random House in 1978). Although their critique did identify some of the problems with cultural feminism, it was seriously marred by paranoia and homophobia. More recently, Ellen Willis has analyzed cultural feminism especially as it informs the anti-pornography movement and eco-feminism. See her fine collection of essays, *Beginning to See the Light*, New York, Knopf, 1981, and "Betty Friedan's 'Second Stage': A Step Backward", *Nation*, November 14, 1981. Major cultural feminist texts include: Adrienne Rich, *Of Woman Born*, New York, Norton, 1976; Mary Daly, *Gyn-Ecology*, Boston, Beacon, 1978; Raymond, op. cit.; Kathleen Barry *Female Sexual Slavery*, Englewood Cliffs, Prentice Hall, 1979; Susan Griffin, *Woman and Nature: The Roaring Inside Her*, New York, Harper & Row, 1978. The now-defunct Los Angeles-based magazine, *Chrysalis*, also served as a major outlet for cultural feminist work since its founding by Susan Rennie and Kirsten Grimstad in 1977. The best single radical feminist anthology is Koedt, Levine, Rapone, op. cit. Also see Shulamith Firestone, *The Dialectic of Sex*, New York, Morrow, 1970.

4 Ann Rosalind Jones, "Writing the Body: Toward an Understanding of *L'Ecriture Feminine*", *Feminist Studies*, vol. 7, no. 2, Summer 1981, p. 255.

5 Raymond, op. cit., p. 114.

6 Anne Koedt, "Lesbianism and Feminism", in Koedt, Levine, Rapone, op. cit., p. 249.

7 Susan Brownmiller, *Against Our Will*, New York, Simon & Schuster, 1975, p. 16; Daly, op. cit., p. 360. For an especially incisive analysis of Gilder, see Michael Walzer, "Gilderism", *The New York Review of Books*, April 2, 1981, p. 3.

8 Mary Daly, quoted in *OOB*, May 1979; Sally Gearhart, "The Future – If There Is One – Is Female", in Pam McAllister (ed.), *Reweaving the*

Web, Philadelphia, New Society, 1982, p. 271.

9 Firestone's *The Dialectic of Sex*, op. cit., illustrates the problem with the radical feminist view of female biology.

10 Jane Alpert, "Mother-Right", *Ms.*, August 1973; and Rich, *Of Woman Born*, op. cit., p. 39.

11 Gearhart, in McAllister, op. cit., p. 271.

12 Robin Morgan, *Going Too Far*, New York, Random House, 1978, p. 164.

13 Daly, *Gyn-Ecology*, op. cit., p. 12.

14 Ibid., p. 239.

15 Firestone, op. cit., p. 12.

16 Personal communication from Ellen Willis, 1980. For the cultural feminist view of the left, see Kathy Barry, "Did I Ever Really Have A Chance? Patriarchal Judgement of Patricia Hearst", *Chrysalis 1*, 1977; Morgan, *Going Too Far*, op. cit.; Rich, *Of Woman Born*, op. cit., p. 285; Alpert, "Mother Right", op. cit.; Kathleen Barry, " 'Sadomasochism': The New Blacklash to Feminism", *Trivia*, Fall 1982.

17 Barbara Deming, "To Fear Jane Alpert is to Fear Ourselves", *OOB*, May-June 1975.

18 Rennie and Grimstad of *Chrysalis* were instrumental in establishing the Circle of Support. It is worth noting that upon Alpert's surrender her lawyer stressed her "renunciation of radical activities and her conversion to the feminist movement." This prompted *OOB* reporter Madeleine Janover to ask, "What does this mean for radical feminism?" See *OOB*, December 1974, p. 5.

19 See Jennifer Woodul, "What's This About Feminist Businesses?", *OOB*, June 1976.

20 It was this view which informed the ill-fated and short-lived Feminist Economic Network (FEN) founded in Detroit in 1975 and dissolved less than one year later. FEN was the brainchild of the Oakland Feminist Women's Health Center, the Detroit Feminist Federal Credit Union, and Diana Press. For detailed accounts see: Belita Cowan and Cheryl Peck, "The Controversy at FEN", *Her-Self*, May 1976; Jackie St Joan, "Feminist Economic Seeds Split", in *Big Mama Rag*, vol. 4, no. 1; Martha Shelley, "What is FEN?", circulated by author; Janis Kelly et. al., "Money on the Line", in *OOB*, March 1976; Alice Echols, "Cultural Feminism: Feminist Capitalism and the Anti-Pornography Movement", *Social Text*, no. 7, Spring-Summer 1983. See Kathy Barry's apologia for FEN in *OOB*, January 1977. This piece was originally submitted to the Bay Area feminist newspaper, *Plexus*. However, Barry admitted to reporter Nancy Stockwell of *Plexus* that the article was a collaborative effort involving three of the major principals in FEN – Laura Brown, Joanne Parrent, and Barbara Hoke. Barry reasoned that an exoneration of FEN would be better received were it to "come from a community source," rather than from those responsible for its creation. *Plexus* refused to publish the article. See Shelley, op. cit.

21 Barry (Brown, Parrent, Hoke), *OOB*, op. cit.

22 Barry, " 'Sadomasochism': The New Backlash to Feminism", op. cit., pp. 83-4. Incredibly, Barry argues " 'lesbian sadomasochism' is the latest, and so far the most effective leftist strategy for isolating radical

feminism, invalidating it, and attempting to annihilate it." (p. 89).

23 Their faith in women's moral superiority and commonality of interests allows them to assume that feminism can be reconciled with capitalism, sexual repression, and possibly biological determinism. Cultural feminism can easily degenerate into the view so cynically articulated by feminist entrepreneur Laura Brown that "feminism is anything we say it is." Quoted in Cowan and Peck, op. cit.

24 Ti-Grace Atkinson, "Lesbianism and Feminism", *Amazon Odyssey*, New York, Links, 1974, p. 86.

25 Abby Rockefeller, "Sex: The Basis of Sexism", *No More Fun and Games: A Journal of Female Liberation*, no. 6, May 1973, p. 31.

26 Anne Koedt, "Lesbianism and Feminism", in Koedt, Levine, Rapone, op. cit., p. 250.

27 See "The Feminists: A Political Organization to Annihilate Sex Roles", in Koedt, Levine, Rapone, op. cit., p. 374.

28 Rita Mae Brown, "The Shape of Things to Come", *Plain Brown Rapper*, Baltimore, Diana, 1976, p. 114. In a recent interview, Rita Mae Brown remarked, "Out of that outburst [of anger at homophobia within the women's movement] on my part developed the whole ideology of the lesbian as the ultimate feminist and superior human being which I would like to say, many years later, is pure horseshit." Chris Bearchell, "Interview with Rita Mae Brown", *The Body Politic*, no. 95, July-August 1983, p. 36.

29 See Brown, ibid.; Charlotte Bunch and Nancy Myron (eds), *Lesbianism and the Women's Movement*, Baltimore, Diana, 1975; Martha Shelley, "Notes of a Radical Lesbian", in Robin Morgan (ed.), *Sisterhood is Powerful*, New York, Random House, 1970, p. 309.

30 Koedt, op. cit. in Koedt, Levine, Rapone, p. 255.

31 Susan Chute, "Backroom with the Feminist Heroes: Conference for Women Against Pornography", *Sinister Wisdom*, Fall 1980, p. 2.

32 Firestone, op. cit., p. 209.

33 Karen Lindsey, "Thoughts on Promiscuity", *The Second Wave*, vol. 1, no. 3, 1971, p. 3.

34 Muriel Dimen, "Variety is the Spice of Life", *Heresies #12*, 1981, p. 70.

35 Karen Durbin, "Can a Feminist Love the World's Greatest Rock and Roll Band?", *Ms.*, October 1974, p. 26.

36 Dana Densmore, "On Celibacy", Leslie Tanner (ed.), *Voices from Women's Liberation*, New York, New American Library, 1970, p. 264. Although Atkinson's anti-sex perspective anticipated and contributed to the development of cultural feminism, she should be recognized for her incisive and prescient analysis of certain aspects of cultural feminism, or what she termed "female nationalism." See Judy Antonelli, "Atkinson Re-evaluates Feminism", *OOB*, vol. 5, no. 5, May-June 1975, p. 19 for a regrettably hostile account of Atkinson's gloomy assessment of feminism.

37 Abby Rockefeller, op. cit., p. 25.

38 Roni and Vickie Leonard, "NOW Sexuality Conference", *OOB*, vol. 4, no. 11, November 1974, p. 3.

39 Deirdre English, Amber Hollibaugh, and Gayle Rubin, "Talking Sex: A Conversation on Sexuality and Feminism", *Socialist Review*, no. 58,

July-August 1981, p. 44.

40 Andrea Dworkin, *Right-Wing Women*, New York, Perigree, 1983, p. 237.

41 This slogan originated with Robin Morgan's 1974 article, "Theory and Practice: Pornography and Rape", reprinted in *Going Too Far*, op. cit.

42 The earliest discussion of "integrity" is probably in Janice Raymond, "The Illusion of Androgyny", *Quest*, vol. 2, no. 1, Summer 1975. See Rich's critique of "male-identified" dualism in *Of Woman Born*, op. cit., pp. 56-83; Susan Griffin, *Pornography and Silence*, New York, Harper & Row, 1981. For a pithy critique of Griffin's analysis of dualism, see Robert Christgau's review in *Village Voice*, vol. 26, no. 29, July 15-21, 1981.

43 Julia Penelope, "And Now For the Hard Questions", *Sinister Wisdom*, 1980, p. 103. Cultural feminists use a double standard when analyzing fantasy – women's masochistic fantasies reflect their socialization, while men's sadistic fantasies reveal their fundamentally murderous nature. Interestingly, in *Homosexuality in Perspective*, Boston, Little, Brown, 1979, Masters and Johnson report that in their heterosexual sample men's second most frequently reported fantasy entailed forced sex. However, they reported fantasies of being forced to have sex slightly more frequently than fantasies of forcing another. See pp. 188-9.

44 Morgan, *Going Too Far*, op. cit., p. 171.

45 Ibid., p. 181.

46 For the radical feminist view, see Firestone, op. cit.

47 Andrea Dworkin, "Why So-Called Radical Men Love and Need Pornography", in Laura Lederer (ed.), *Take Back the Night: Women on Pornography*, New York, William Morrow, 1980, p. 152.

48 Adrienne Rich, "Compulsive Heterosexuality and Lesbian Existence" in Catharine R. Stimpson and Ethel Spector Person (eds), *Women: Sex and Sexuality*, Chicago, University of Chicago Press, 1980, p. 73. Rich praises Catharine MacKinnon, author of *Sexual Harassment of Working Women*, for criticizing Susan Brownmiller's "unexamined premise that 'rape is violence, intercourse is sexuality' ", or, in other words, for differentiating between rape and intercourse.

49 The movement luminaries interviewed in the anti-pornography documentary, *Not A Love Story*, avoided their usual polemics against male sexuality and heterosexuality and instead displayed a newly-discovered concern for the ways in which pornography victimizes men. Of course, a humanist facade is not only more compatible with the movement's stated aim of eliminating pornography, but more likely to elicit support and sympathetic coverage. For a review of *Not A Love Story*, see B. Ruby Rich, "Anti-Porn: Soft Issue, Hard World", *Village Voice*, July 30, 1982.

50 Rich, "Compulsory Heterosexuality and Lesbian Existence", in Stimpson and Person, op. cit., p. 81.

51 Ethel Person, "Sexuality as the Mainstay of Identity: Psychoanalytic Perspectives", in Stimpson and Person, op. cit., p. 57.

52 See Larry Bush and Richard Goldstein, "The Anti-Gay Backlash", *Village Voice*, April 8-14, 1981; Deirdre English, "The War Against

Choice", *Mother Jones*, February/March 1981.

53 Ann Snitow, "The Front-Line: Notes on Sex in Novels by Women, 1969-1979", in Stimpson and Person, op. cit., p. 165.

54 Rich, "Compulsory Heterosexuality and Lesbian Existence", in Stimpson and Person, op. cit., p. 79.

55 Raymond, *The Transsexual Empire*, op. cit., p. 104.

56 Raymond worries that male-to-female lesbian-feminist transsexuals might be used to transform "lesbian-feminist space [into a] harem." See ibid., pp. 104-13. Daly is quoted on p. 104.

57 Dworkin, "Pornography and Grief", in Lederer, op. cit., p. 289; Rich, "Compulsory Heterosexuality and Lesbian Existence", in Stimpson and Person, op. cit., p. 80; Jill Clark, "Interview with Robin Morgan", *Gay Community News*, January 20, 1979.

58 *Heresies #12*, 1981, published both the NOW resolution and two separate letters of protest, pp. 92-3; Scott Tucker, "The Counter-revolution", *Gay Community News*, February 21, 1981.

59 Some gay men, like lesbian cultural feminists, are committed to maximizing gender differences – a course likely to have calamitous consequences for the already fractured "gay movement." For an introduction to this masculinist ethic, see John Preston, "Goodbye Sally Gearhart: Gay Men and Feminists Have Reached a Fork in the Road", *Christopher Street*, no. 59; Eric Rofes, "The Revolution of the Clones/Talking with John Preston", *Gay Community News*, March 27, 1982, p. 8.

60 Rich, "Compulsory Heterosexuality and Lesbian Existence", in Stimpson and Person, op. cit., p. 81.

61 Daly, *Gyn-Ecology*, op. cit., p. 373.

62 Quoted in Richard Goldstein, "I Left My Scalp in San Francisco", *Village Voice*, October 1, 1979.

63 Rich, "Compulsory Heterosexuality and Lesbian Existence", in Stimpson and Person, op. cit., p. 72.

64 Raymond, *The Transsexual Empire*, op. cit., p. 113.

65 Quoted in Goldstein, op. cit.

66 Brown, *Plain Brown Rapper*, op. cit., p. 112.

67 Barry, " 'Sadomasochism': The New Backlash to Feminism", op. cit., p. 82; Rich, "Compulsory Heterosexuality and Lesbian Existence", in Stimpson and Person, op. cit., p. 72; Penelope, op. cit., p. 103; Daly, *Gyn-Ecology*, op. cit., p. 20.

68 Morgan, *Going Too Far*, op. cit., p. 168.

69 See Ellen DuBois and Linda Gordon, "Seeking Ecstasy on the Battlefield: Danger and Pleasure in Nineteenth-century Feminist Sexual Thought", this volume, pp. 31-49.

70 Barry, *Female Sexual Slavery*, op. cit., p. 228.

71 Ibid., p. 211

72 Person, in Stimpson and Person, op. cit., pp. 50-1; Irene Diamond, "Pornography and Repression", in Lederer, op. cit., p. 202; Florence Rush, *The Best Kept Secret*, Engelwood Cliffs, Prentice Hall, 1980, pp. 190-1.

73 See Willis, *Beginning to See the Light*, op. cit., for a good analysis of the relationship between feminism and individualism.

74 Morgan, *Going Too Far*, op. cit., p. 16.

75 Barry, *Female Sexual Slavery*, op. cit., p. 227.

76 Diana Russell and Laura Lederer, "Questions We Get Asked Most Often", in Lederer, op. cit., p. 29.

77 Willis, *Beginning to See the Light*, op. cit., p. 225.

78 Judith Bat-Ada, "Playboy Isn't Playing", in Lederer, op. cit., p. 132.

79 The parallel development within the left is the pro-family ideology promoted by cultural conservatives like Christopher Lasch, Michael Lerner, and Tom Hayden. See Michael Lerner, "Recapturing the Family Issue", *Nation*, February 2, 1982, and Barbara Ehrenreich's response, "Family Feud on the Left", *Nation*, March 13, 1982.

80 Barry, *Female Sexual Slavery*, op. cit., p. 103. For an elaboration of this point, see Paula Webster, "Pornography and Pleasure", *Heresies #12*, 1981, p. 50.

81 See Carole S. Vance, conference concept paper, "Towards a Politics of Sexuality", this volume, pp. 443-6.

82 For a discussion of cultural feminism's idealization of the mother-daughter bond, see Echols, op. cit., p. 39. For another view of the mother-daughter problematic, see Susan Contratto and Nancy Chodorow, "The Fantasy of the Perfect Mother", in Barrie Thorne (ed.), *Rethinking the Family: Some Feminist Questions*, New York, Longman, 1982.

83 Some s/m lesbian-feminists suggest that s/m sex is more egalitarian and less solipsistic than "vanilla" sex. Like lesbian chauvinism of the early 1970s, s/m chauvinism is an understandable response to the near-unanimous vilification of s/m within the feminist community. Fortunately, it is improbable that s/m will be venerated as *the* feminist sexuality, because, unlike lesbianism, it so fundamentally contradicts movement orthodoxy. However, the distinction between personal preference and prescriptivism is often confounded in a movement such as ours which requires that we justify our sexual impulses in political terms and which encourages us to generalize and theorize from our own experience. For example, at a recent Boston forum on s/m a woman in the audience – not a practitioner of s/m – suggested that "s/m may be the *only* way to lessen power imbalances that are rooted in our culture." (reporter's italics) Jil Clark, "Lesbian S/M Forum", *Gay Community News*, vol. 10, no. 50, July 9, 1983, p. 6. By contrast, Pat Califia maintains that s/m is neither intrinsically feminist nor anti-feminist. See Pat Califia, "The Advisor", *Advocate*, no. 375, October 13, 1983, p. 38.

Interstices: A Small Drama of Words

Hortense J. Spillers

Who Said It Was Simple?

There are so many roots to the tree of anger
that sometimes the branches shatter
before they bear.

Sitting in Nedicks
the women rally before they march
discussing the problematic girls
they hire to make them free.
An almost white counterman passes
a waiting brother to serve them first
and the ladies neither notice nor reject
the slighter pleasures of their slavery.
But I who am bound by my mirror
as well as my bed
see causes in Colour
as well as sex

and sit here wondering
which me will survive
all these liberations.[1]

When I told a friend of mine that I was going to address the issue
of sexuality as discourse during a spring conference at Barnard
College, she laughed: "Is that what you talk about when you
make love?" Silence. "Well?" Well, I hadn't thought of that, but
now that she had raised the question, what about it? There
probably is at least one book to be written on erotic exclamations
that would likely enrich our understanding of cultural forms in
their sexual dress, but this meeting of terms is both my point and
beside it. I am interested here primarily in what we might call
discursive and iconic fortunes and misfortunes, facilities, abuses,
or plain absences that tend to travel from one generation of
kinswomen to another, not unlike love and luck, or money and
real estate. Just so, the elders pass on their voice, their tongue,
their language, and it might even surprise us that they said the
same words, or none at all, in the vaunted coital embrace, or the
celebrated post-orgasmic fall-out. Every child in us dreams, we
might supppose, of knowing just what "they" said and did in
"there" and do they still?

73

At any rate, sexuality is the locus of great drama – perhaps the fundamental one – and, as we know, wherever there are actors, there are scripts, scenes, gestures, and reenactments, both enunciated and tacit. Across the terrain of feminist thought, the drama of sexuality is a dialectic with at least one missing configuration of terms. Whatever my mother, niece, and I might say and do about our sexuality (the terms of kinship are also meant collectively) remains an unarticulated nuance in various forms of public discourse as though we were figments of the great invisible empire of womankind. In a very real sense, black American women are invisible to various public discourse, and the state of invisibility for them has its precedent in an analogy on any patriarchal symbolic mode that we might wish to name. However we try not to call up men in this discussion we know full well, whether we like it or not, that these "they" do constitute an element of woman-scenery. For instance, in my attempt to lay hold of non-fictional texts – of any discursively rendered experience concerning the sexuality of black women in the United States, authored by themselves, for themselves – I encountered a disturbing silence that acquires, paradoxically, the status of contradiction. With the virtually sole exception of Calvin Hernton's *Sex and Racism in America* and less than a handful of very recent texts by black feminist and lesbian writers,[2] black women are the beached whales of the sexual universe, unvoiced, misseen, not doing, awaiting *their* verb. Their sexual experiences are depicted, but not often by them, and if and when by the subject herself, often in the guise of vocal music, often in the self-contained accent and sheer romance of the blues.

My survey, however, is mostly limited to some of the non-fictional texts on sexuality because I wish to examine those rhetorical features of an intellectual/symbolic structure of ideas that purport to describe, illuminate, reveal, and valorize the *truth* about its subject. Fictional texts, which transport us to another world of symbols altogether, are much beyond the scope of this essay and the central tenets of its argument. The non-fictional feminist work along a range of issues is the privileged mode of feminist expression at the moment, and its chief practitioners and revisionists are Anglo-American women/feminists in the academy. The relative absence of African-American women/feminists, in and out of the academic community, from this visionary company, is itself an example of the radically divergent historical situations that intersect with feminism. Such absence quite deliberately constitutes the hidden and implicit critique of this essay. The non-fictional feminist text is, to my mind, the empowered text – not fiction – and I would know how power works in the guise of feminist exposition when "sexuality" is its theme. If the African-American women's community is relatively "word-poor" in the critical/argumentative displays of symbolic power, then the silence surrounding their sexuality is most evident in the structure of values I am tracing. It is, then, ironical that some of the words that tend to break silence here are, for whatever their purpose, male-authored.

Hernton's *Sex and Racism in America* proposes to examine the psychological make-up of America's great sexual quartet – the black female, the black male, the white female, the white male – and the historical contexts in which these overlapping complexities work. Each of his chapters provides a study of collective aspects of psyche as Hernton seeks insight into the deep structure of sexual fantasies that operate at the subterranean level of being. The chapter on the black female interlards anonymous personal witness with the author's historical survey of the black female's social and political situation in the United States. We can call Hernton's text a dialectical/discursive analysis of the question and compare it with words from aspects of oral tradition.

As an example of a spate of discourse that portrays black women as a sexual reality, we turn to the world of "toasts," or the extended and elaborate male oratorical display under the ruse of ballad verse. This form of oral narrative projects a female figure most usually poised in an antipathetic, customarily unflattering, sexual relationship to the male.[3] These long oral narratives, which black men often learn in their youth and commit to memory, vary from place to place and time to time, describing contests of the male sexual will to power. Several versions of "The Titanic,"[4] for instance, project a leading character named "Shine" as the great race/sex man, who not only escapes from the ill-fated maiden voyage of the celebrated ship, but also ends up in a Harlem nightclub, after the disaster, drinking Seagram's Seven and boasting his exploits. Within this community of male-authored texts, the female is appropriately grotesque, tendentiously heterosexual, and olympically comparable in verbal prowess to the male, whom she must sexually best in the paradigmatic battle of the ages – that between the sexes. Relevant to the hyperbolic tall tale, comedian Rudy Moore's version of the battle of the sexes depicts evenly-matched opponents, with the world "making book" on one side of the contest, or the other. The agents literally "screw" for days in language far bolder than mine. But we already know beforehand, according to the wisdom of Chaucer's Wife of Bath, the outcome of the tale that the lion did not write. The woman in the "toasts" is properly subdued, or, more exactly in the latter-day versions of phallic dominance, "tooled" into oblivion.

So, here are two textual instances – Hernton's sympathetic

account of the black female and the subject from the point of view of the people's oral poetry. Both instances insinuate quite different, though gratuitously related, versions of female sexuality. The correspondences are crucial. In the world of "toasts," "roasts," and "boasts," in the universe of unreality and exaggeration, the black female is, if anything, a creature of sex, but *sexuality* touches her nowhere. In the universe of "clean" discourse and muted analysis, to which we relegate Hernton's book, the black woman is reified into a status of non-being. In any comparison with white women in the sexual fantasies of black men, black women flunk – in truth, they barely register as fantastic impressibility – because of the ravages of the "Peculiar Institution." The latter was not the ideal workshop for refining the feminine sensibilities, Hernton argues. We infer from his reading that the black woman disappears as a legitimate subject of female sexuality. In all fairness to Hernton, however, we are obligated to point out his own acknowledgment of the silence that has been imposed on black American women:

Out of the dark annals of man's inhumanity to woman, the epic of the black woman's ordeal in America is yet to be written.... But the change is just beginning, and the beginning is fraught with hazards.[5]

My own interpretation of the historical narrative concerning the lives of black American women is in accord with Hernton's: Their enslavement relegated them to the marketplace of the flesh, an act of commodifying so thoroughgoing that the daughters labor even now under the outcome.[6] Slavery did not transform the black female into an embodiment of carnality at all, as the myth of the black woman would tend to convince us, nor, alone, the primary receptacle of a highly-rewarding generative act. She became instead the principal point of passage between the human and the non-human world. Her issue became the focus of a cunning difference – visually, psychologically, ontologically – as the route by which the dominant male decided the distinction between humanity and "other." At this level of radical discontinuity in the "great chain of being," black is vestibular to culture. In other words, the black person mirrored for the society around her and him what a human being was *not*. Through this stage of the bestial, the act of copulating travels eons before culture incorporates it, before the concept of sexuality can reclaim and "humanize" it.[7] Neither the picture I am drawing here, nor its symbolic interpretation, is unheard of to our understanding of American and New-World history. If, however, it is a stunning idea in its ritual repetition, none the less, then that is because the black female remains exotic, her history transformed into a pathology turned back on the subject in tenacious blindness.

That this unthinkably vast and criminal fraud created its own contradictions and evasions within the creating brain ultimately does not concern us. The point is that neither we, nor Hernton, can easily approach the subtleties of a descriptive apparatus that would adequately account for the nexus *dis-effected* in this case between female gender and color. The rift translates into unthinkable acts, unspeakable practices. I am not identifying here the black female as the focal point of cultural and political inferiority. I do not mean to pose the black female as an object of the primitive, uxoricidal nightmares, or interrupted nocturnal emissions (elevated to the status of form) as in a Henry Miller or Norman Mailer. The structure of unreality that the black woman must confront originates in the historical moment when language ceases to speak, the historical moment at which hierarchies of power (even the ones to which *some* women belong) simply run out of terms because the empowered meets in the black female the veritable nemesis of degree and difference. Having encountered what they understand as chaos, the empowered need not name further, since chaos is sufficient naming within itself. I am not addressing the black female in her historical apprenticeship as inferior being, but, rather, the paradox of non-being. Under the sign of this particular historical order, black female and black male are absolutely equal. We note with quiet dismay, for instance, the descriptive language of affirmative-action advertisements, or even certain feminist analyses, and sense once again the historic evocation of chaos: The collective and individual "I" lapses into a cul-de-sac, falls into the great black hole of meaning, wherein there are only "women," and "minorities," "blacks" and "other."

I wish to suggest that the lexical gaps I am describing here are manifest along a range of symbolic behavior in reference to black women and that the absence of sexuality as a structure of distinguishing terms is solidly grounded in the negative aspects of symbol-making. The latter, in turn, are wed to the abuses and uses of history, and how it is perceived. The missing word – the interstice – both as that which allows us to speak about and that which enables us to speak at all – shares, in this case, a common border with another country of symbols – the iconographic. Judy Chicago's exhibit, "Dinner Party," for example, in the artist's tribute to women, had a place set at table for the black female. Sojourner Truth is their representative symbol, and as the female figures around her are imagined through ingenious variations on the vagina, *she* is inscribed by three faces. As Alice Walker comments: "There is of course a case to be made for being 'personified' by a face rather than by a vagina, but that is not what this show [was] about."[8]

The point of the example is self-evident. The excision of the female genitalia here is a symbolic castration. By effacing the genitals, Chicago not only abrogates the disturbing sexuality of her subject, but also hopes to suggest that her sexual being did not exist to be denied in the first place. Truth's "femaleness," then, sustains an element of drag. In fact, she is merged here with a notion of sexual neutrality whose features, because they have not yet been defined, could assume any form, or none at all – in either case, the absence of articulation. Ironically, Sojourner Truth's piercing, rhetorical, now-famous question on the floor of the second annual Convention of Women's Rights in Akron, 1852 – "Ain't I a woman?" – anticipates the "atmosphere" of the artist's deepest assumptions.[9] The displacement of a vagina by a face invites protracted psychological inquiry,[10] but it is enough to guess, almost too much to bear guessing, that if Sojourner, in the female artist's mind, does not have the necessary female equipment, then its absence might be expressed in a face whose orifices are still searching for a *proper* role in relationship to the female body.

While there are numerous references to the black woman in the universe of signs, many of them perverted, the prerogatives of sexuality are refused her because the concept of sexuality originates in, stays, with, the dominative mode of culture and its elaborate strategies of thought and expression. As a substitute term for "race" and "racism," I would borrow Edward Said's "dominative mode"[11] because the latter, not unlike "patriarchy," moves us closer to the heart of the lion's den. We would discover the ways and means of power in its intellectual and contemplative fulfillment – those places where most of us do not think to look because the intellectual enterprise, the lie goes, is so "objective" and so "disinterested" that it has little to do with what impresses the brain and the heart, to say nothing of what the legs straddle. If we are "intellectualizing" the issue away, which feminists used to say we ought not do, yet, interestingly enough, have done most of the time, then we mean to "intellectualize" exactly, since the questions about woman-sex and the practices of exclusion that demarcate it are among the more impressive intellectual stunts of our time.

We would argue that sexuality as a term of power belongs to the empowered. Feminist thinking often appropriates the term in its own will to discursive power in a sweeping, patriarchist, symbolic gesture that reduces the human universe of women to its own image. The process might be understood as a kind of deadly metonymic playfulness – a part of the universe of women speaks for the whole of it. The structure of values, the spectacle of symbols under which we presently live and have our being –

in short, the theme of domination and subordination – is practiced, even pursued, in many of the leading feminist documents of scholarship this past decade or so. We can, then, affiliate sexuality – that term that flirts with the concealment of the activity of sex by way of an exquisite dance of textual priorities and successions, revisions and corrections – with the very project and destiny of power.

Through the institutionalization of sexual reference in the academy, in certain public forums; in the extensive responses to Freud and Lacan; in the eloquent textual discontinuities with the Marquis de Sade and D.H. Lawrence, sexual meaning in the feminist universe of academic discourse threatens to lose its living and palpable connection to training in the feelings and to become, rather, a mode of theatre for the dominating myth-ologies. The discourse of sexuality seems another way, in its present practices, that the world divides decisively between the haves/have-nots, those who may speak and those who may not, those who, by choice or the accident of birth, benefit from the dominative mode, and those who do not. Sexuality describes another type of discourse that splits the world between the "West and the Rest of Us."

Black American women in the public/critical discourse of feminist thought have no acknowledged sexuality because they enter the historical stage from quite another angle of entrance from that of Anglo-American women. Even though my remarks are addressed specifically to feminists, I do not doubt that the different historical occasions implicated here have dictated sharp patterns of divergence not only in living styles, but also ways of speaking between black and white American women, without modification. We must have refinement in the picture at the same time that we recognize that *history* has divided the empire of women against itself. As a result, black American women project in their thinking about the female circumstance and their own discourse concerning it an apparently divergent view from feminist thinking on the issues. I am not comfortable with the "black-woman/feminist" opposition that this argument apparently cannot avoid. I am also not cheered by what seems a little noticed elision of meaning – when we say "feminist" without an adjective in front of it, we mean, of course, white women, who, as a category of social and cultural agents, fully occupy the territory of feminism. Other communities of women, overlapping feminist aims, are noted, therefore, by some qualifying term. Alice Walker's "Coming Apart" addresses this linguistic and cultural issue forthrightly and proposes the term, "womanist" for black women and as a way to dissolve these apparently unavoidable locutions.[12] The disparities that we observe in this case are *symptomatic* of the problem and are a *part* of the problem. Because black American women do not participate, as a category of social and cultural agents, in the legacies of symbolic power, they maintain no allegiances to a strategic formation of texts, or ways of talking about sexual experience, that even remotely resemble the paradigm of symbolic domination, except that such paradigm has been their concrete disaster.

We hope to show in time how African-American women's peculiar American encounter, in the specific symbolic formation we mean, differs in both degree and kind from Anglo-American women's. We should not be at all surprised that difference among women is the case, but I am suggesting that in order to anticipate a more definitive social criticism, feminist thinkers, whom African-American women must confront in greater number on the issues, must begin to take on the dialectical challenge of determining *in the discourse* the actual realities of American women in their pluralistic ways of being. By "actual," I do not intend to mean, or even deny, some superior truth about life outside books, but, rather, to say that feminist discourse can risk greater truth by examining its profoundest symbolic assumptions, by inquiring into the herstory of American women with a sharpened integrity of thought and feeling. We are, after all, talking about words, as we realize that by their efficacy we are damned or released. Furthermore, by talking about words as we have seen them marshalled in the discussion, we hope to provide more clues to the duplicitous involvement of much of feminist thinking with the mythological fortunes (words and images) of patriarchal power. By doing so, I believe that we understand more completely the seductive means of power at whatever point it involves women.

While my analysis here is focused primarily on Shulamith Firestone's *Dialectic of Sex*,[13] one of the earlier documents of the contemporary women's movement, I should point out that the kind of silence and exclusion I am describing is by no means limited to any one particular text. Firestone's work serves a vivid analytical purpose because its "narrative voice," to my mind, replicates the basic flaws of the patriarchal word-game in its swift "objectifying" of women and men of color. Firestone addresses black women's issues in a single chapter, and everywhere else in the book, "woman" – a universal and unmodified noun – does not mean *them*. "Woman/women" belong to that cluster of nominatives that includes "feminist," "lesbian," even "man," that purport to define the essence of what they name, and such essence is inherently paradigmatic, or the standard from which deviation and variation are measured. As simple and familiar as the point is, the symbolic behavior is not often checked in our various discourses. An anthropology of women's language would perhaps reveal the conditions in time and space that generate the colonization of words. I do not think that I exaggerate when claiming that there are few exceptions to this general linguistic rule. The exceptions are, of course, dramatic in their isolation: two examples – Adrienne Rich's "Disloyal to Civilization," with its solid evoking of an enlightened feminist critique, and Catharine A. MacKinnon's "Feminism, Marxism, Method and the State."[14] MacKinnon's attempt to understand her own appropriation of "woman" in her essay invites pause:

Throughout this essay, I have tried to see if women's condition is shared, even when contexts and magnitudes differer.... I aspire to include all women in the term "women" in some way, without violating the particularity of any woman's experience. Whenever this fails, the statement is simply wrong and will have to be qualified or the aspiration (or the theory) abandoned.[15]

Neither of these essays focuses on the theme of sexuality, but I make use of them in order to point, by inference, to a particular terministic program whose doggedness is symptomatic of the very problems of power and its arrangements that feminists of all descriptions say they would correct.

Besides Firestone's, many of the other premier texts on the entangling issues of female sexuality argue the black woman's case by negation; moving along points of contact: Kate Millett's early classic, *Sexual Politics*, conflates the black woman under the entitlement of "blacks," and Susan Brownmiller's *Against Our Will* is so intent on pursuing the black-man-as-rapist icon that her notes on black women's sexual experience, static and reified in "Two Studies in American History: Slavery," strike the reader as a rather perverse and exotic exercise.[16] Stimpson and Person's *Women: Sex and Sexuality* is an elegant metonymic elaboration in its range of inquiry that converges on the theme of sexuality and without any particular nuance or articulation that sounds black female sexual experience.[17] The works of Dorothy Dinnerstein, Nancy Chodorow, and Mary Daly[18] overlap questions of sexuality in drawing out other feminist interrogation, but that we read these texts – and might include along with them an impressive number of gynocritical[19] works in women's literature – as though their emblems, their figures of thought, the purposes and motivations that precede and accompany their execution, the living condi-tions out of which their search comes and the shape it takes speak monolithically across the empire of women – reminds me of the period of symbolic oppression we believe we're leaving. The assumptions of symbolic power (or gestures toward it) and the ways in which we are governed by them occur in such rapid sequence that we observe no apparent break or disjuncture in the patterns of succession; in short, this *undifferentiated* spatial progression of texts is experienced as an "environment" whose air we quite "naturally" breathe. I make no attempt here to be definitive in these bibliographical notes and queries inasmuch as the library of books on women concerning various aspects of experience proliferates with the rapidity of light-years, it seems. But the texts I have seen point to a center of gravity, a tendency of the field toward a certain word-behavior. It is that apparent centrality that I address here.

A Dialectic of Sex has a noble purpose – to propose a program for the liberation of women from the tyranny of reproductive biology. The "master" and precursor texts to which Firestone directly speaks include Marx's. In fact, we could say that *A Dialectic* is a post-modernist and feminist invocation to the Marxian canon in its hot pursuit of a solidly materialist theme – the site of the child and who shall tend it and what that means to woman-freedom. To my ears, however, Firestone's chapter on the black female in this projected configuration of social change is not only stridently critical of the Black Nationalist Movement (the only place the book "locates" black women), but also incredibly ominous in its pronouncements on black women's past and future. A patriarch is not speaking, we have every reason to suppose, but there It is, hustled in under the skirts of Mama in the chapter, "Racism: The Sexism of the Family of Man." In this account, black and white American women are locked in a deadly familial struggle in the House of the White Father. With fathers and sons, they engage in a ferocious Oedipal/Electra contest to the death. Is this woman doing comedy here, or have we widely misfired our "close reading" of her text? The object of All-love is of course the white mom-dad duo, and the children – black female and black male – share their first "sympathetic identification" with the white mother.

This titillating riff on Freud calibrates through more thematic layers of American myth-making sleight-of-hand than one has the goodwill to endure, but what strikes this reader most forcefully about Firestone's overlapping typologies is the narcissistic arrogance of the creating feminist narrator so persistently and ingenuously deployed that the parental possibility does not even exist for her black characters, is not even imaginable. These children – black female and male – spring into being, into time, the spontaneous gagline of an obscene national joke, at best its ambiguous by-blow, spawned in some Harlem *estaminet*.[20] Since the line of legitimate descent that Firestone is limning here can be generated only by virtue of a *real* domestic pair (which black mothers and fathers most certainly are not), then these children are dirty little bastards, who manage, somehow to grow up. When we finally discover a black female character on the ruins of this cultural debris, she is nothing other than bastard daughter, turned "whore," who belongs to a "pimp," the black bastard's only possible legacy. By 1970, however, Firestone's black whore is on her way to another and more creditable transformation – "Reverend-Black-Queen-Mother-of-my-Children" – in one of the most disdainfully sustained anti-lyrics on the American Black Nationalist Movement that I've seen.

To Firestone, the Movement was not only the last picture show of phallic domination, but also an inefficacious imitation of it. In short, black Americans in this chapter have no human right to aspire to the nuclear family, political and economic freedom, or any of the affective postures since they can only ape WASPs in doing so. Firestone goes on to tell us that the Movement's attempted revision and correction of the historic identity of the black woman that she is imagining is not really possible since its success is based on fantasy:

for as long as the white man is still in power, he has the privilege to define the black community as he chooses – they are dependent on him for their very survival – and the psychosexual consequences of this inferior definition must continue to operate. Thus the concept of the Dignified Black Family rarely penetrates beyond the circles of the copycat Bourgeoisie or the True Believer Revolutionaries.[21]

Of course the Black Revolutionary in this book – female and male – is not a serious person, but only a parody.

Backing up a moment, we see that the black family in the United States is a recent invention of the late twentieth century: "Attempts are now being made to institute the family in the black community, to transform the black community from Whorehouse for the White Family to Black Family."[22] For those of us who grew up in black families across the country, observations like the foregoing are simply astonishing. Some of the readers with whom I have shared this paper have complained that my remarks are based on a book that is by now "old" and that the women's movement has gone way beyond Firestone's opinions. The criticism is to say, of course, that there is Progress and that feminists have "gotten their act together" on the question of race, but the complaint about the lament is itself frightening since it would suggest that we are not always properly attuned to the deep chords of deception that sound through the language and the structures of thought in which it fixes us. The version of anomie that Firestone is fabricating in this chapter stretches back through the last 500 years of human history, and it is not my fault that the jaundice is still with us.

Perhaps the genuine culprit here is the "Family" and Firestone is warning her reader against its entrapments, but it is difficult to tell whether we are in the midst of an ironical display, or being forced to reengage an all-too-familiar configuration of imposed meanings. At any rate, Firestone manages, by a complicated series of grammatical maneuvers and with enviable journalistic verve, to convoke the entire structure of dominating symbolic moves as it operates against the dispossessed. The values, the emblems, the modes of perception, their patterns of discourse, and quasi-religious feelings that choreograph male and female, black and white not only into a precisely Manichean frieze, but also, consequently, out of history, are so brazenly mobilized in Firestone's drama that with feminist interpretations like this, who in the world needs patriarchs? It is clear: If the Anglo-American father (and by genetic association his woman) is God, then he is also the Devil, which status would assign his household the customary omnipotence that we believe, we say, is a lie. If Firestone is urging us in this discussion to put afoot God-terms in their hint of first and last things, of the elected and the damned, then we are no longer in *this* world. We have slipped and slid, shuffled and bucked and winged into Paradise. I would go so far as to say that Firestone reconstitutes the white female as the "gyneolatrous"[23] object of desire, who willingly trades her body for a little piece of the patriarchal soul. In short, Firestone's "Family of Man" is a mysterious essence, drooping down from an ahistorical source, and I am not at all so sure that the reading is ambiguously intended.

A replacement of this psychosexual drama into history would attempt, first of all, a dismantling of the God-terms. For example, "as long as the white man [read white person] is still in power, he has the privilege to define the black community as he chooses" proffers a dose of "necessity" that we might as well refuse, since it gives the white male unlimited potence. The fact of domination *is* alterable only to the extent that the dominated subject recognizes the potential power of its own "double-consciousness".[24] The subject is certainly seen, but she or he certainly sees. It is this latter seeing that negotiates at every point a space for living, and it is the latter, though an armed force will help, that we must willingly name the counter-power, the counter-mythology.

Firestone, however, is so busy making a case against the patriarchal bogey-man, so passionate in gathering allies against him, and so intent on throwing out the bath water of the nuclear family, babies and all, that she actually reinforces the very notions of victimization that she claims she would undo, and in overstating, misstating the black female "condition," assumes herself the negating posture that will not liberate either black or white female into the possibilities of her own history. Once the agents are replaced onto a material/historical scene, wherein they recover their collective and individual and differentiated human status, then we can begin to talk about power in its human and negotiable limit. We do not recognize human agency in Firestone's farce. In fact, one entire group of characters drops out of sight. Dangled by her "pimp," handled by White Daddy, who gets to fondle everybody, held in contempt by White Mother, and uncreated, unimagined, in an existential reality by a biological mother and father, whom she in turn cannot now recreate, Firestone's black woman can only throw the reflection of an imposed pathology.

We know how myths work – through the impoverishment of history – and Firestone's chapter is, for the black woman, an exemplary killing myth. In this account, she is not touched by sexuality either, as we have seen in the toasts, in Calvin Hernton's text, in Judy Chicago's imagistic absences, and in the endless and other-named litanies of symbolic negation on which bases Firestone's work is ignorantly raised.

The black-female-as-whore forms an iconographic equation with black-female-vagina-less, but in different clothes, we might say. From the point of view of the dominant mythology, it seems that sexual experience among black people (or sex between black and any other) is so boundlessly imagined that it loses meaning and becomes, quite simply, a medium through which the individual is suspended. From this angle, the act of sex has no occasional moments of inauguration, transition, and termination; it does not belong to human process, embedded in time, pledged to time and to notions of mortality. It is, on the contrary, a state, of vicious, routinized entanglement, whose passions are pure, direct, and untrammeled by consciousness. Under this condition of seeing, we lose all nuance, subjects are divested of their names, and, oddly enough, the female has so much sexual potential that she has none at all that anybody is ready and able to recognize at the *level of culture*. Thus, the unsexed black female and the supersexed black female embody the very same vice, cast the very same shadow, inasmuch as both are an exaggeration – at either pole – of the uses to which sex might be put.

Michel Foucault argues that the whore in European history was a demarcation of banishment, an embodied point at which institutional Europe in the eighteenth century fixed its sundry perversions, as the latter will reenter the mainstream culture under the rule of psychiatric medicine.[25] According to him,

European bourgeois culture and the career of sexuality are co-terminously linked by the newly-empowered as a strategy to assure their dominance. Those outside the circle of culture, i.e., the whore, the pimp, were robbed of legitimate sexual being and, to that degree, defined the point of passage between inner and outer; the brothel, for instance, became an "insularized form of reality," a place where sex reigned uninterrupted. Consequently, the banished place and the banished person acquire an element of secrecy, and discourse about them is circumscribed and coded.[26] The black American female, whether whore or asexed, serves an analogous function for the symbolically empowered on the American scene in fixing the frontier of "woman" with her own being. If life as the black person – female or male – leads it is the imagined site of an illegitimate sexuality, then it is also, paradoxically enough, the affirmation of asexuality. ("Sidney Poitier," an idea that might be appropriated by female gender in this case, never gets to kiss the bride, we remember, in "Guess Who's Coming to Dinner?") The fiction of this symbolic act does not impress us with its awful tenacity nearly so much as when we witness its repetitions under a feminist auspice.

To find another and truer sexual self-image the black woman must turn to the domain of music and America's black female vocalists, who suggest a composite figure of ironical grace. The singer is likely closer to the poetry of black female sexual experience than we might think, not so much, interestingly enough, in the words of her music, but in the sense of dramatic confrontation between ego and world that the vocalist herself embodies. We must be careful here not to romanticize the singer, with her sometimes unlovely self-destructive life, as a lame reading of the content of Sojourner's life turns it into an idea that Truth herself would probably not recognize. I do not intend to take the vocalist out of history, but to try and see her firmly within it.

The Burkean pentad of fiction[27] – act, agency, scene, agent, and purpose as the principal elements involved in the human drama – is compressed in the singer into a living body, insinuating itself through a material scene, and in that dance of motives, in which the motor behavior, the changes of countenance, the vocal dynamics, the calibration of gesture and nuance in relationship to a formal object – the song itself – is a precise demonstration of the subject turning in fully conscious knowledge of her own resources toward her object. In this instance of being-for-self, it does not matter that the vocalist is "entertaining" under Amerikkan skies because the woman, in her particular and vivid thereness, is an unalterable and discrete moment of self-knowledge. The singer is a good example of "double consciousness" in action. We lay hold of a metaphor of commanding female sexuality with the singer who celebrates, chides, embraces, inquires into, controls her womanhood through the eloquence of form that she both makes use of and brings into being. Black women have learned as much (probably more) that is positive about their sexuality through the practicing activity of the singer as they have from the polemicist. Bessie Smith, for instance,

in a deliberate inversion of the Puritanism of the Protestant ethic ... articulated, as clearly as anyone before or since, how fundamental sexuality was to survival. Where work was often death to us, sex brought us back to life. It was better than food, and sometimes a necessary substitute.

With her, Black women in American culture could no longer just be regarded as sexual objects. She made us sexual subjects, the first step in taking control. She transformed our collective shame at being rape victims, treated like dogs, or worse, the meat dogs eat, by emphasizing the value of our allure. In so doing, she humanized sexuality for black women.[28]

My aim in quoting Michele Russell's valorization of the singer is to trace her proposal that the dancing voice embodied is the chief teaching model for black women of what *their* femaleness is and to highlight Russell's discussion of the implied praxis in some of the Smith discography. The attention that the vocalist pays to building a relationship of equality in the woman's own house with her male lovers is quite explicit in "Get It, Bring It, and Put It Right Here":

He's got to get it, bring it, and put it right here
Or else he's gonna keep it out there.
He can steal it, beg it, borrow it somewhere
Long as he gets it, chile, I don't care.[29]

We can perform various exegeses on this text, for example, the modulations through which the singer runs "it" so that the ambiguity of phrasing is a point of humor. To that extent, hyperbolean phallic status is restored to quite normal size, and the man himself, inverted in the display as the dispenser of gifts. Whatever we might ultimately think of the message of Smith's inversions and its quite explicit heterosexual leanings, as in most of the discography of black female vocalists, we are interested in the singer's *attitude* toward her material, her audience, and, ultimately, her own ego status in the world as it is interpreted through form. If we can draw out the emphasis on the female vocalist's art, rather than her biographies – a work for volumes – then we gather from the singer that power and control maintain an ontological edge. Whatever luck or misfortune the Player has dealt to her, she is in the moment of performance the primary subject of her own being. Her sexuality is precisely the physical expression of the highest self-regard and, often, the sheer pleasure she takes in her own powers.

The difference and distance between the way black women are seen in their sexual experience and the way that they see themselves are considerable, as Russell's notes on blues tradition attest. We would argue that the black female's sexuality in feminist and patriarchist discourse is paradigmatic of her status in the universe of symbol-making so that our grasp of one complements clarity in the other: The words that would make her the subject of sexual inquiry are analogous to the enabling postulates that would give her the right action in history. To state the problem metaphorically, the black woman must translate the female vocalist's gestures into an apposite structure of terms that will articulate both her kinship to other women and the particualar nuances of her own experience.

It is perhaps not useless to repeat an observation that we made earlier in different terms: feminist discourse has achieved over the last decade or so a logological dimension, or words that talk about other words,[30] in a response to prior texts – male- and female-authored. A *Dialectic of Sex* and Dorothy Dinnerstein's *Mermaid and Minotaur*, for instance, are as much a reading on Freud and/or Marx as they are an attempt to establish women at the center of the theoretical enterprise. Firestone's text is in fact enabled by the prior symbolic acts so that her book and Engels's *Origin of the Family, Private Property and the State*, as a specific precedent, now belong to a category of alignment that establishes a perspective between prior statements and counter- and successive statements.[31] That the feminist writer challenges certain symbolic formations of the past in correcting and revising them does not destroy the previous authority, but extends its possibilities. By opening up the borders of a prior closure, feminist writers at once define a new position of attack and lay claim to a site of ancestral imperative. Do feminist revisionary acts become, therefore, futile? This question that a reader put to me about the last few sentences could not possibly have "yes" for an answer. My point is that the feminist analytical discourse that women engage in different ways and for different reasons must not only ascertain vigil over its procedures, but must also know its hidden and impermissible origins. I am remembering a folk-say from my childhood, and to introduce it seems relevant to what I am driving at: "Mama's baby, papa's maybe." In other words, to know the seductions of the father and *who*, in fact, the father is might also help to set us free, or to know wherein we occasionally speak when we have least suspected it.

Whether we are talking about sexuality, or some other theme, we would identify this process of categorical aligning with prior acts of the text as the subtle component of power that bars black women, indeed, women of color, as a proper subject of inquiry from the various topics of contemporary feminist discourse. Such exclusion is neither deliberate, perhaps, nor inevitable, for sure, but moves through phases of symbolic value that conform precisely to equations of political power: the first order of symbolic "business" within a community is the articulation of what we would call a first-order naming, words that express the experience of the community in diachronic time, in daily social relationships, in economic well-being, in the identity of a self. A second order of naming, or words about the first order, would articulate another level of symbolic responses. I would be careful not to say a "higher," but "another" in order to get at differences of function. The literature of African-Americans and the criticism of it, for example, constitute a second and third order of naming, with the potential power to become a first order, to the degree that the community and the writer sustain a mutual engagement that leads to seeing anew in both. Since the content concerning the actual life experiences of black women is barely articulated, to say nothing of exhausted,[32] we are in the incredible position of having either to create a first-order discourse on black women's community and/or speak immediately into the void left by its absence and the next phase of meaning, that stage at which we would locate contemporary feminist discourse. The relationship in orders of naming that I suggest here is not as static as the explanation sounds since orders and degrees of naming are simultaneously active and dynamic and can travel among each other with great ease in the life of a community. I do insist on identifying, however, careers of words that do different things with regard to a common point of reference. Essentially, the distinction that I mean here is quite similar to the one that the editors of *New French Feminisms* imply about analyses that "relate discourse to discourse and divorce it from experience."[33] The discourse of sexuality has declared a logological status, on the pre-eminence of Freud, wherein the writer produces discourse in response to other discourse. In the case of French feminists, we are told that the father-text is Lacan. (We note with great interest, by the way, that the term "sexuality" did not enter the English lexis until c. 1800, according to the *OED*.) It is no use trying to decide whether or not discourse about discourse, or the impure good of theory, is "good" or "bad." The apparent reality is that it *is*, as the prose disciplines seem fated, for good or ill, to reflect the paucity or affluence of a cultural GNP. Symbolic power, like the genetic parent, begets power, takes pleasure in proliferating itself. Feminist discourse, to extend the figure, keeps talking, or reproducing itself, tending to do so in its own image, on the bases of initiating symbolic gestures, against which it might struggle,[34] or with which it tacitly seeks alignment by way of various strategies.

The "Sex and Work" chapter of John Gwaltney's *Drylongso*[35] is an anthropologist's account of a contemporary cross-sectional view of black Americans addressing their life-experiences in the post-Black Nationalist era. Gwaltney's procedure is the interview, here a seamlessly woven fabric of conversations, about a wealth of subjects, whose interlocutors appear to speak effortlessly and gracefully into the void. Gwaltney is so skilled an interviewer/ worker that the questions that precede the responses, in fact, orchestrate them with masterful direction, are never explicit. We leave the text having heard a concert of voices – male, female, the elderly, the younger, with varying grades of education and involvement in dominant American culture with no sense that Gwaltney himself has been an intrusive presence. The interviews took place during the mid-1970s and in an unidentified urban community of the northeastern United States. Some of the models for the work might have been reminiscence narratives of the progeny of formerly enslaved persons and Studs Terkel's *Working*.[36] Gwaltney's text, however, is an attempt to represent the coeval patterns of thinking among African-Americans – those without particular intellectual bias, specified political allegiance, or academic and institutional connection of any sort. In other words, Gwaltney's interviewees are just "drylongso," the ordinary people of the family and what they think about money, love, sex, white folk, war, the presidency, pollution, the economy, the future of human society.

The women that Gwaltney interviewed in the "Sex and Work" chapter express what I would call a first-order naming concerning their sexual reality. I would call their words first-order because they speak "naturally," in which case words seem to come off the human tongue and need not be referred back to a dictionary in order to be understood. The sense that Gwaltney manages to convey is that he has entered these lives without noise and the lives have gone on, as if he were not there, and with the conversation that the actors were having when he arrived. To say that the book makes us comfortable, gives us feelings of coziness and charm is not to speak pejoratively, but to describe what we mean by first-order naming here; that the speaking is written makes the conversations a naming since we recognize that we talk all the time, and most of it is not naming, has no significance or record beyond the transitory business of our daily lives. The trick, though, to reading these intriguing witnesses is that, first of all, they are a *translation* through the medium of a male voice. I personally trust Gwaltney's project and its outcome since I think I know what some black Americans think sometimes about some things. At the same time, I realize that the reader in us has no way of knowing under what constraints and mandates the women felt compelled to speak, nor whether they reported the truth of their feelings to the interviewer. Second, the women interviewed are not academically affiliated, and while their status does not disqualify them to have an opinion about anything, their views are not consonant in their shape to the argument I am pursuing here, nor the discourse of sexuality as we engage it in and out of books. I must observe, then, a disparity of interest, which this essay has already anticipated, and know not entirely where to fit these women's words about their bodies, or the status of their report. We proceed, though, on a sort of poetic faith that Gwaltney's partially fictionalized women provide clues to the kind of discursive differences that prevail among American women in their sounding the depths of individual and collective sexual differences. Gwaltney's interviewees are also heterosexual female, as far as I can see, and I am not prepared to call him heterosexist/homophobic because of it. The experiences of lesbians of color is as recent a chapter of public discourse (if not the actual experience itself) as are the experiences of lesbians of non-color. At any rate, we believe that the sexual realities of black American women across the spectrum of sexual preference and widened sexual styles tend to be a missing dialectical feature of the entire discussion. In any event, Gwaltney's interlocutors take us to another universe of symbol-making, intimate different ways of saying sexuality, and express *one* of the vocabularies of feeling among black American women on the meeting place between biology and survival.

For them sexual experience is overwhelmingly related to the thematics of work. Among the older women, the loss of jobs, because the subject often defended herself against the sexual aggressions of another is a major focus for feminist inquiry: "Sexual harassment of working women has been one of the most pervasive but carefully ignored features of our national life."[31] The kind of sexual harassment that Gwaltney's interlocutors describe, however, is occasionally lost to feminist discussion because it is often entangled with notions of domestic work and intimacy and inhabits, therefore, a vast domain of silence. That the care of Anglo-American families in certain communities has been entrusted over time to black women largely remains unspoken in feminist discourse. Its articulation would alter considerably feminist thinking about women's social history and the problems evoked by economic and social inequities. But the writing of a new feminist project will require the critic's commitment to a thorough exploration of patterns of domination in its racist, as well as gender and sexual-preferential, manifestations.

Seventy-three-old Mrs Nancy White, one of the fictitiously-named women of Gwaltney's work, talks about her own sexual menace this way:

"I've had to ask some hands off me and I've had to give up some jobs if they got too hot behind me. Now, I have lost some money that way, but that's all right. When you lose control of your body, you have just about lost all you have in this world."[38]

Nancy White's metaphors of the body are scarcely negotiable through layers of abstraction. In this case, tenor and vehicle are virtually useless distinctions, as in the following observation: "My mother used to say that the black woman is the white man's mule and the white woman is his dog."[39] According to her conclusions,

"white women are not free either, but most of them think they are and that is because that white man pats them wherever he feels like patting them and throws all that moonlight boogie-joogie on them and they eat it up! It's killing them, but they eat it up and beg the doctor for a prescription so they can get more."[40]

At seventy-three years, which would date her birth near the turn of the century, Mrs White expresses a culture of feeling different from our own, but she touches none the less, the origins of a central vein of disaffection in African-American women, not only from the major tenets of the historic feminist movement, but also from the community of Anglo-American women in general. Bell Hook's *Aint't I A Woman*[41] rehearses the corruptive tendencies of racist ideology to filter through the cracks of America's earlier women's movement of the late-nineteenth and early-twentieth century. Mrs White registers an attitude that the black woman has difficulty overcoming for good reason, and that is her sense of being embattled at once by patriarchal culture and white women complicitous with it. This perceived connection, whether real or imagined, is the "covering cherub" that feminist criticism must entirely disarm.

That no love was lost in Mrs White's career between herself and white women will not surprise and is complemented by her classic understanding of "male nature." Twice-married, she knows quite well that "boogie-joogie," her play-word that shimmers across the borders of magic, is just so much garbage. Gwaltney's glossary of terms defines the word as "non-sense, trickery." The truth for Mrs White is that:

"Men don't need women and women don't need men for nothing but getting children. Now, most of these men out here are not on strike. They will be evermore glad to give you just as much nature as you need. . . . I listened to all the moonlight boogie-joogie [from black men] and before a hoecake could make a crust, there I was with two children. Well, I promised God that if he would help me through that little tight, that I was going to think about what I did a long time before I done it. Now, that's what I did."[42]

Not only does Mrs White think "a long time" before trusting the premises of romantic love again, but she also achieves a perspective on the matter that does not allow any confusion in her own mind between sexual indulgence and the mandates of survival: "Hard work don't have a thing between its legs. I know there ain't nothing I don't know about real hard work."[43]

The leisure that Mrs White does not perceive that she has had to contemplate her sexuality as an isolated ontological detail bespeaks a classically schismatic feature between African-American and Anglo-American historical reality. I observe a tendency, if not a law. A mediation in this case between a first-order expression of sexual reality and the discourse of sexuality would try to elicit the hierarchies of value that the respective terms stand for. "Body," for example, is not a polyvalent or ambiguous referent for a Mrs White. At the level of analysis and experience, we witness no arbitrary bonding between a signifier and a signified so that for Mrs White the word, the gesture that fulfills it, and the actual consequences of both converge on a literal moment of time. To lose control of the body is to be hostage to insufferable circumstances; it is also in the historical outline of black American women often enough the loss of life. In either case, we are exposed immediately to fatal implications of changes in the state of nature. The threatened return of the metaphors of experience to their original ground of tangible and material meaning demonstrates the distance we must travel between the status of the protected and that of the unprotected, or the difference between *sex* and *sexuality*.

Gwaltney's May Anna Madison is nearly a generation younger than Nancy White, but the complicated equation that she draws betwen her own life in relationship to white women, the tenets of feminist social analysis, and sexual experience is comparable:

"The t.v. is full of people talking about women's lib. Well, I can handle black men; what I can't handle is this prejudice. White women have done more bad things to me than black men ever thought of doing. . . . It was a female chauvinist sow that worked me a full day for seventy-five cents. When I was nothing but a child myself, white women looked the other way when their fresh little male chauvinist pigs were trying to make a fool out of me! That's why I don't pay any attention to all that stuff! A black man can't do any more to me than I will let him do because I can and have taken care of myself. But I do have to work to be able to do that and that means that I have to be able to deal with white people."[44]

Madison's solution to inequities is radically democratic:

"These white people are not really running things right, and that's the fault of the white men mostly and the white women go along with that. I would get color out of it altogether. I just wouldn't let nobody get but so rich and I wouldn't let nobody get but so poor."[45]

In these instances that the text brings to light, Gwaltney's interlocutors perceive their sexual being in so poignant a connection with the requirements of survival that we lose the theme of relationship in its isolated emphasis. The fusion, however, might be useful to the feminist critic in suggesting that a contrastive historical order engenders a different slope of consciousness and at least one structure of first-order terms *to be interpreted*. Gwaltney has already provided one interpretive instrument – transcribed interviews edited into a text with the voices speaking to us as in an imagined spontaneity of responses. A third order of naming would attempt to discover, layer by layer, the symptoms of culture that engender this order of things. From whatever angle of history and temperament the feminist addresses cultural issues, she ignores historical particularities as symbol-making refracts them at peril to the program of action that would free the universe of women from the seductions and betrayals of patriarchal dominance.

To return in conclusion to Kenneth Burke's grammar of motives and the pentad of terms on which it is built refocuses quite deliberately the dramatic character of sexuality as human potential and discursive possibility. In order to supply the missing words in the discourse of sexuality, we would try to encounter agent, agency, act, scene, and purpose in ways that the dominative mode certainly forbids. Its division of the kingdoms of women along various lines of stress is the superior talisman that has worked across the centuries. To dissipate its energies requires that the feminist critic/historian actively imagine women in their living and pluralistic confrontation with experience (at least, the way they report it), and perhaps the best guarantee of such commitment is the critic's heightened self-consciousness with regard to the conceptual tools with which we operate.

The dominative symbolic mode proceeds through a sequence of violent acts to attenuate historical particularities, whereas the agents in question become items in the store of mythical signifiers. The image of the "whore" and the "female eunuch," for example, has been invested with semiological and ideological values whose origins are concealed by the image itself. The latter acquires mystical attribution doing overtime, divested of specific reference and dispersed over time and space in blind disregard for the particular agents and scenes on which it lands. The reified image can be imposed at any moment on any individual "I." This sort of symbol-making is analogous to an act of mugging that catches the agent not only off guard, but also, most effectively, in the dark. A feminist critique in the specific instance of sexuality would, then, encourage a counter thrust, a kind of karate chop, in the relentless pursuit of the provenience and career of word- and image-structures in order that agent, agency, act, scene, and purpose regain their differentiated responsiveness. The aim, though obvious, might be restated: to restore to the historical movement of women its plenitude of issues and supply the right verb to the subject searching for it, feminists are called upon to initiate a corrected and revised view of women of color on the frontiers of symbolic action.

Because black women have had long experience with the brutalizations of male power, are subject to rape, know their womanhood and sexual being as crucially related and decisively timed moments in the creation and nurture of human life; because they experience their biological and human destiny by way of women and must sooner or later face their mirror and catch their own reflection of imagination in it, they do not live out their destiny on the periphery of American race and gender magic, but in the center of its Manichean darkness. But the foregoing configuration is only part of the picture. There is at least one other. Because they love their fathers, sons, and brothers, yet must be free of them as a willed act of the mind and the heart; because they witness no lapse in this narrative because they have seen their fathers, sons, and brothers cut down in war and even in peace for the very same reason that they have been; their daughters debased and humiliated and invisible often enough in the company of other women; because other women have helped to foster the myth of their "superotherness" on either end of the scale of being; and after two closely contiguous women's movements in this country, parallel and related to the historical movements of black people, have yet to come to grips with the irremediable meeting of race and gender in the subject, black women do not live out their destiny on the borders of femaleness, but in the heart of its terrain. We are, then, urged to raise this energetic scheme of conflicting tensions, allegiances, affirmations, and denials to an act of discursive form that confronts the image of the woman of color with other world women, with other dominated communities. We would try to do so in order that this generation of women ("this" as on-going) may lay hold at last of a *comparative* human order, whose primary noun Person has been modified to points of a detailed refinement. The discourse of sexuality might provide an example of how such refinement can be accomplished.

In putting afoot a new woman, we delight in remembering that half the world is female. We are challenged, though, when we recall that more than half the globe's female half is yellow, brown, black, and red. I do not mean to suggest that "white" in this ethnic and political calculus is an addendum, but, rather, only an angle on a thematic vision whose agents in gaining authenticity have the radical chance now, which patriarchy passed up, to help orchestrate the dialectics of a world-wide new-woman sense of being. As I see it, the goal is not an articulating of sexuality so much as it is a global restoration and dispersal of power. In such an act of restoration, sexuality is rendered one of several active predicates. So much depends on it.

Notes

1 Audre Lorde, *Chosen Poems: Old and New*, New York, W. W. Norton, 1982, pp. 49-50.

2 Calvin C. Hernton, *Sex and Racism in America*, New York, Grove, 1965, pp. 121-68. I should point out that while the following texts actually do not specifically address the question of black female sexuality, many of their concerns intersect the issues, especially the three essays under "Sexuality and Sexual Attitudes" in Gloria I. Joseph and Jill Lewis (eds), *Common Differences: Conflicts in Black and White Feminist Perspectives*, New York, Anchor, 1981, pp. 151-274. Other points of reference touching sex-related questions in the African-American women's community include Tracey A. Gardner's "Racism in Pornography and the Women's Movement" and Luisah Teish's "Quiet Subversion" in Laura Lederer (ed.), *Take Back the Night: Women on Pornography*, New York, William Morrow, 1980; Lorraine Bethel and Barbara Smith (eds), *Conditions Five – The Black Women's Issue*, 1979.

3 Dennis Wepman, Ronald B. Newman, and Murray B. Binderman (eds), *The Life: The Lore and Folk Poetry of the Black Hustler* in The Folklore and Folklife Series, gen. ed. Kenneth S. Goldstein, Philadelphia, University of Pennsylvania Press, 1976, pp. 20-150. The Wepman text provides mostly a collection of narratives in the tradition. A more comprehensive and useful perspective on the meanings and transformations of this type of oral narrative is supplied by Roger D. Abrahams in his important study, *Deep Down in the Jungle: Negro Narrative Folklore from the Streets of Philadelphia*, Hatboro, Pennsylvania, Folklore Associates, 1964.

4 Ibid., pp. 111-23. Different versions of "The Titanic" are given by Abrahams in demonstration of the "oikotype," the local variations that an oral narrative achieves when it reaches a specific area (pp. 10ff).

The expurgated version of the narrative, reprinted in the Hughes collection, *The Book of Negro Folklore*, might be advantageously compared with Abrahams's. Langston Hughes and Arna Bontemps (eds), New York, Dodd, Mead, 1958, pp. 366-7.

5 Hernton, *Sex and Racism in America*, op. cit., p. 166.

6 Two recent additions to the women's studies library inquire into the black female's economic exploitation and its political and historical significance: Angela Y. Davis, *Women, Race, and Class*, New York, Random House, 1981; Bell Hooks, *Ain't I A Woman: Black Women and Feminism*, Boston, South End Press, 1981.

7 Winthrop Jordan's *White Over Black: American Attitudes Toward the Negro, 1550-1812* (Baltimore, Penguin, 1969) is virtually unique in its systematic exploration of the concept of race in its European symbolic and geopolitical origins. An analysis of cultural vestibularity in its symbolic contours is the aim of Henry Louis Gates's "Binary Oppositions" in chap. 1 of *Narrative of the Life of Frederick Douglass, An American Slave Written by Himself*, in Dexter Fisher and Robert B. Stepto (eds), *Afro-American Literature: The Reconstruction of Instruction*, New York, Modern Language Association, 1979, pp. 212-32.

8 Alice Walker, "One Child of One's Own: A Meaningful Digression Within the Work(s) – An Excerpt", Gloria T. Hull, Patricia Bell Scott, and Barbara Smith (eds), *All the Women Are White, All the Blacks Are Men, But Some of Us Are Brave: Black Women's Studies*, Old Westbury, New York, Feminist Press, 1981, pp. 42-3.

9 For a recent account of this famous story from the annals of the historic women's movement, the reader might consult chap. 5 of Hooks's *Ain't I A Woman*, op. cit., pp. 159-60.

10 Freud's notes on the "frequency with which sexual repression makes use of transpositions from a lower to an upper part of the body" were for me a surprising find in connection with this point. He specifically names the replacement of the genitals by the face as a dynamic "in the symbolism of unconscious thinking," "The Dream Work", *The Interpretation of Dreams*, trans. James Strachey, New York, Avon, 1966, p. 422. I do not claim to know the artist's mind and might guess that she was thinking of a Freudian "reading" of her subjects, giving her viewers the benefit of the doubt, or that they knew their Freud. But beyond this exhibit, we might wonder, on the other hand, if the entire culture is involved in an intricate calculus of sexual repressions that both identifies the black person with "wild" sex and at the same time suppresses the name in reference to her and him.

11 Edward Said, *Orientalism*, New York, Vintage, 1979, p. 28. Said adopts the term from Raymond Williams in *Culture and Society, 1780-1950*, London, Chatto & Windus, 1958, p. 376.

12 Alice Walker in Lederer, *Take Back the Night*, op. cit., p. 100.

13 Shulamith Firestone, *The Dialectic of Sex: The Case for Feminist Revolution*, New York, Bantam, rev. ed 1971, pp. 105-26.

14 Adrienne Rich, *On Lies, Secrets and Silence: Selected Prose, 1966-1978*, New York, W. W. Norton, 1979, pp. 275-310; Catharine A. MacKinnon in *Feminist Theory: A Critique of Ideology*, Chicago,

98   *Hortense J. Spillers*

University of Chicago Press, 1982, pp. 1-30.

15 MacKinnon, *Feminist Theory*, op. cit., p. 6, n. 7.

16 Kate Millett, *Sexual Politics*, New York, Ballantine, 1970; Susan Brownmiller, *Against Our Will: Men, Women and Rape*, New York, Bantam, 1975.

17 Catharine R. Stimpson and Ethel Spector Person (eds), *Women: Sex and Sexuality*, Chicago, University of Chicago Press, 1980.

18 Dorothy Dinnerstein, *The Mermaid and the Minotaur: Sexual Arrangements and Human Malaise*, New York, Harper Colophon, 1976; Nancy Chodorow, *The Reproduction of Mothering: Psycho-analysis and the Sociology of Gender*, Berkeley, University of California Press, 1978; Mary Daly, *Gyn/Ecology: The Metaethics of Radical Feminism*, Boston, Beacon, 1978. Audre Lorde's "Open Letter to Mary Daly" specifically addresses those aspects of African women's culture that Lorde believes Daly has either missed altogether or misinterpreted in Cherríe Moraga and Gloria Anzaldúa (eds), *This Bridge Called My Back: Writings by Radical Women of Color*, Watertown, Massachusetts, Persephone, 1981, pp. 94-8.

19 The various positions within the gynocritical spectrum of procedure – women critics and writers at the center of the critical enterprise with women's culture as their theme – is the subject of this striking essay by Elaine Showalter, "Feminist Criticism in the Wilderness", in Elizabeth Abel (ed.), *Writing and Sexual Difference*, Chicago, University of Chicago Press, 1982, pp. 9-37. It is noteworthy that this interesting volume of essays on points of intersection between writing culture and female gender does not have a single item in it on black American women's writings. The absence is stunning to my mind in that it demonstrates precisely the sort of symbolic lapse of nerve I am identifying in the associating women of color with the intellectual and artistic project.

20 A café (where smoking is permitted!). The resonance of the line in the text is borrowed directly from T.S. Eliot's "Gerontion": "My house is a decayed house,/And the Jew squats on the window sill, the owner,/Spawned in some estaminet of Antwerp" I intrude the image to make plain the bad taste that Firestone's emblem-making leaves in my mouth as certain aspects of Eliot's poem might do for certain other American communities, though I'd assume quite a lot in thinking so and would ignore, for the sake of the point, the poem's "aesthetic surface." That would vulgarly *wrench* meaning, but the poet occasionally and the scholar more often compel a sort of resistance of reading in this case. *The Complete Poems and Plays, 1909-1950*, New York, Harcourt Brace, 1971, p. 21.

21 Firestone, *The Dialectic of Sex*, op. cit., pp. 119-20.

22 Ibid., p. 118.

23 The term is taken from W.J. Cash's *Mind of the South*, New York, Vintage, 1941.

24 The condition of the "double-consciousness" in a specific reference to the black American is first explored by W.E.B. DuBois in this early twentieth-century classic, "Of Our Spiritual Strivings", *The Souls of Black Folk: Essays and Sketches*, New York, Fawcett Premier, 1961,

pp. 15-22.

25 Michel Foucault, *The History of Sexuality, Vol. I: An Introduction*, trans. Robert Hurley, New York, Pantheon, 1978, pp. 1-15.

26 Ibid., pp. 4-5.

27 Kenneth Burke, *A Grammar of Motives*, New York, Prentice-Hall, 1952, pp. 3-15. This important study by a distinguished American critic is crucial to many of the ideas in this article. Though a specific reference to the literature of the stage, Burke's notion of the "five key terms of dramatism" is applicable to any human situation that involves a structure of motives to be read and interpreted. The *act* names what has occurred; the *scene* is the background of the act; the *agent* is the actor or performer; the *agency* is the instrument by which the act is performed; and the *purpose* is the goal of the act.

28 Michele Russell, "Slave Codes and Liner Notes", in Hull, Scott, and Smith, *But Some of Us Are Brave*, op. cit., pp. 129-40.

29 Ibid., p. 133.

30 Kenneth Burke, "On Words and the Word", *The Rhetoric of Religion: Studies in Logology*, Berkeley, University of California Press, 1970, pp. 14-15. Burke proposes that of the four realms to which words may refer, the third realm – words about words – "is the realm of dictionaries, grammar, etymology, philology, literary criticism, rhetoric, poetics, dialectics."

31 Michel Foucault, *The Archaeology of Knowledge and the Discourse of Language*, trans. A. M. Sheridan Smith, New York, Harper Colophon, 1972. Foucault's discussion of fields of discourse, or the "enunciative field" is very useful in explaining continuities and discontinuities among concepts that share a common familial identity; concepts within an "enunciative field" may be related in three ways: (1) by way of a "field of presence," (2) a "field of concomitance," and (3) a "field of memory." (pp. 57-8ff.)

32 In an address at Wellesley College a few years ago, writer Toni Morrison provided a moving testimony to the textual silence concerning black American women. She could find on the library shelves books about virtually every community of women in the world, but precious few about her own. One of Morrison's ambitions as a writer, she said, is to supply some of the missing narrative.

33 Elaine Marks and Isabelle de Courtivron (eds), "Introduction I: Discourses of Anti-Feminism and Feminism", *New French Feminisms: An Anthology*, New York, Schocken, 1981.

34 Foucault, *The Archaeology of Knowledge*; cf. n. 15.

35 John Langston Gwaltney, *Drylongso: A Self-Portrait of Black America*, New York, Vintage, 1981, pp. 142-76.

36 An example of reminiscence narratives is Julius Lester's *To Be A Slave*, New York, Dell, 1968; Studs Terkel, *Working*, New York, Avon, 1972.

37 Catharine A. MacKinnon, *Sexual Harassment of Working Women: A Case of Sex Discrimination*, with foreword by Thomas I. Emerson, New Haven, Yale University Press, 1979, p. 1.

38 Gwaltney, *Drylongso*, op. cit., pp. 146-7.

39 Ibid., p. 148.

40 Ibid., p. 143.
41 See Hooks, *Ain't I A Woman*, op. cit.
42 Gwaltney, *Drylongso*, op. cit., p. 149.
43 Ibid., p. 150.
44 Ibid., p. 171.
45 Ibid., p. 175.

WORKSHOP PAPERS

Public Silence, Private Terror

Dorothy Allison

> I urge each one of us to reach down into that deep place of knowledge inside herself and touch that terror and loathing of any difference that lives there.
>
> Audre Lorde[1]

> What drew me to politics was my love of women, that agony I felt in observing the straight-jackets of poverty and repression I saw people in my family in. But the deepest political tragedy I have experienced is how with such grace, such blind faith, this commitment to women in the feminist movement grew to be exclusive and reactionary.
>
> Cherríe Moraga[2]

Her voice on the phone was a surprise, not only because the call had come so late in the evening or even that she was so hesitant to identify herself. She had never been a friend – only an acquaintance, another lesbian whose writing I had admired but whom I'd spoken to less than half a dozen times in all the years we'd been aware of each other's existence. There was also the too present memory of the last time I'd seen her, the way her eyes had registered, stared and then avoided mine. I'd seen in her face the same look I'd been seeing in other women's faces for all the months since the Barnard sex scandal – a look of fascination, contempt, and extreme discomfort. She'd gotten away as quickly as possible, and at the time I had reminded myself again that it really wasn't any different from the way straight women use to avoid me back in 1971.

"I didn't wake you, did I?" Her voice almost trembled with anxiety and automatically I told her, "No, I don't go to bed this early." I started to make a joke, to try to put her a little more at ease, but I stopped myself. After all she was the one who had called me; she had to know what she wanted.

But it didn't seem that way. She rambled, made small talk, her voice so soft and hesitant that I couldn't bring myself to grab hold of the conversation, to say "Just why was it you called anyway?" I don't remember now just how we steered through it, her fear so palpable that gradually I figured out that whatever else she wanted, some part of it had to be about sex. When she finally said, "Well I thought I could talk to *you* anyway," I was so

103

relieved that she was going to get around to the point that it almost overcame my sudden, tired anger at her for being one more person to put it that way.

"Yeah, you should be able to say anything to me," I thought but did not say, and she finally got around to it. Sex, and her terror, her disgust with herself. I listened to her voice and felt my anger melt to grief. It was that same old tone I'd heard before, choked with shame and desperation. She had been doing these things – no, she couldn't say what exactly – but there was no one she could talk to about it. She had tried to stop herself, stop the fantasies, masturbation, stray thoughts. But it didn't go away, either her fear or her desire, and finally she had tried to talk to another woman she thought she was close to, someone she had thought would understand. That woman had stared at her, hesitated and then told her she was sick.

"Sick," she said in a very small voice.

I put my head down onto my arm and cradled the phone close to my shoulder. I didn't know her well enough to be having this conversation. I didn't know what to say. I didn't even know exactly what she'd been doing, or imagining doing. I remembered an old lover whose terror had been so great, who liked to imagine herself held down, unable to reach the mouth that hovered over hers until she had to beg for it – that mouth, that release. I started to tell the voice on the phone that story, of how I noticed that when we made love, my lover's mouth worked and worked but never made a sound, of how gradually I'd teased her and comforted her and reassured her until finally she let go and shouted and roared her passion.

"She was so afraid," I said, "so certain that she was a terrible, sick person but when it all came out, there was so little to it, nothing to match all those years of knotted up silent grief. It's usually like that, you know. We're very rarely as terrible as we believe ourselves to be."

Silence answered me and stretched out. I pushed my hair back, waiting, wondering if I was saying the absolutely wrong thing. Maybe she really was terrible, maybe she was even a little bit sick? What did I know? Maybe her desire was to slice little pieces of herself off and feed them to her cat. What good was it for me to tell her about someone she didn't know, who after all had a desire that was relatively easy to accomplish, that didn't really demand much of anyone else or herself except the strength to put it out. What lover would refuse to pin her down and tease her? What friend would call her sick for that?

"I'm not an expert," I finally said, "not a sex therapist. Sometimes I think the only thing I understand is myself, and that not very well – just a few of the ways I've fucked myself over, let myself be fucked over, invited it or cooperated with it." Talk to me, I wanted to say, I can't say anything if you don't give a little.

"I've been putting stuff inside me," she whispered. I just about dropped the phone in relief. OK, what was she putting inside her, and inside her where? But she wouldn't give me that. Quickly, it became clear that she would never be able to stand having said that little bit, and I knew that after this phone call she would never speak to me again. She would always feel vulnerable to me, imagine I knew more than I did – all her secret thoughts, what she did alone in her bed in the dark – and she would always feel that I had betrayed her or would when the chance came.

I grabbed onto that phone like a lifeline. Did she know there was a group – a lesbian group she could go talk to? No, but as I repeated the address I knew she wasn't writing it down. I could hear her urge to run and hide, knew certainly that whatever she did, she wasn't ready to talk to people – not about this tender stuff. Well, did she have any books about sex? "I'm sure you've seen *Sapphistry*," I said, "but I could loan you some others, or you could buy them if you wanted." Probably she wouldn't want to see me, but if she had the titles she could get them herself in some store where no one knew her. But there was so little to recommend. How few feminists write about sex, I thought for perhaps the hundredth time.

"Seen what? *Sapphistry*?"

I made myself talk quietly, slowly, though all I really wanted was to start yelling, not really at her but at anything, kicking furniture, and screaming in frustration.

"That's Pat Califia's book from Naiad Press.[3] It's good, very good with lots of practical information, especially about what's dangerous and what's not."

"Oh." I could hear it in her voice. She'd heard that name before, read some review that had growled indignation about all that s/m stuff and probably reinforced all her own sexual terrors. It didn't matter that, if she really was pushing something into her cunt or ass, *Sapphistry* would be one of the few books that would tell her what was involved in plain and simple terms, that wouldn't play into all the guilt and self-hatred she was carrying. Odds were, the same *friend* who had told her she was sick told her all about Pat Califia.

Suddenly she had to get off the phone. Her cat was getting into the garbage. She thought she heard someone at the door. It was an excuse, and we both knew it, and the phone went silent. I sat holding the receiver until the hum broke into a howl. Then I put it down and went to wrap myself around my lover, so angry I couldn't even speak, couldn't even say, "It was just another one of those terrible phone calls."

On the wall over my desk, I hang pictures, clippings and notes to myself. It is crowded with fantasy images, lists, and ideas, even love letters several years old. The picture of the young woman in a black lace dress and feathered hat has been up there almost as long as the samurai woman sweeping her long sword into the sunlight. Each inspires me, though in very different ways. Some days I want to become one or the other. Some days I want to write the story of how they became lovers. Other days I can't stand to look at them at all and turn instead to notecards pinned up between the pictures, reading the words over and over to myself, knowing I have not yet exhausted all I need to learn from them.

The quote from Adrienne Rich's introduction to the reprint of her *Compulsory Heterosexuality and Lesbian Existence* is pinned next to the paragraphs I copied from Barbara Smith's short story, "Home," so that the words follow each other and echo an idea that has been worrying me for months.

There has recently been an intensified debate on Female sexuality among feminists and lesbians, with lines often furiously drawn, with sado-masochism and pornography as key words which are variously defined according to who is talking. The depth of women's rage and fear regarding sexuality and its relation to power and pain is real, even when the dialogue sounds simplistic, self-righteous, or like parallel monologues.

Adrienne Rich[4]

I knew when I first met her that it would be all right to love her, that whatever happened we would emerge from this not broken. It would not be about betrayal. Loving doesn't terrify me. Loss does. The women I need literally disappearing from the face of the earth. It has already happened.

Barbara Smith[5]

I keep wanting to take down the card that holds Adrienne Rich's words and file them away, not to have to think any more about the fact that it is certainly fear that has dominated the debate on female sexuality, that it is fear that has provoked the shouting, name-calling, and rejection. I am tired of trying to understand why people fall into self-righteous hatred, but I keep the card up for just that reason, to remember the human dimensions of the debate. The quote from "Home" serves the same purpose, but it also reaches my own fear and goes deeper still to a level of desire I have known since I first realized just what it would mean to my life to be queer. *Home* is what I want, what I have always wanted – the trust that my life, my love does not betray those I need most, that they will not betray me.

You confuse the two, a friend once told me. When we talk

about love, we are not necessarily speaking of sex. When we talk about sex, love is not at issue. Is that true? I ask myself and read the cards over again.

Underneath those two, held by the same pin that positions a picture of my younger sister with her two children, is a line I have written for myself, the beginning to an article I know I must someday finish: "The terrors of sex are real," it reads, "the awful vulnerability of the individual exposed physically and emotionally – and we are too often betrayed by our own desires or the failures of our lovers." Betrayal again, I notice, and this time failure. It does not appear that I am so very much different from the woman who called me that night. We are both stumbling over our private fears, worrying at desire from the downhill side, not speaking to the trust and joy I know we both are seeking.

When we speak of sex, grief should not be where we have to start. But the idea of a life in which rage, physical fear or emotional terror prevents even the impetus of desire – that is the image that haunts the discussion for me now. The thought that we could all be forced to live isolated in our own bodies, never safe enough to risk ourselves in naked intimacy with others rides me now like an old nightmare from my childhood: a dream of silence, cold hands, and suspicious eyes. It was a nightmare I used to believe was common to all lesbians but one I thought had grown less powerful in our everyday lives. It was the fear behind our politics, a unifying and radicalizing perception that we did not need to voice since we all knew it so well. The experience of having the meaning of our love and desire for women twisted, misused, or denied totally seemed to me central and basic to feminism in the same way that our politics itself was supposed to rest in the actual lived experience of women who must name for themselves their needs, hopes, and desires. But I never wanted fear to be the only impulse behind political action. As deeply as I wanted safety or freedom, I wanted desire, hope, and joy. What after all was the worth of one without the other?

All those notes hang on my wall and stare back at me as piteously as the pictures of my lovers, sisters, and fantasy figures. I can neither answer them, tear them down nor ignore them because, in trying to write about sex, I am always faced with the fear that any conclusion I make will betray someone. If I outline, even if only for myself, a new understanding of how our desire for sex is used against us, some face always stares back at me unsatisfied. If I demand my right as a lesbian to examine and explore my relationships with other women, both as sources of passion and grief, I am flat up against it again. I imagine not only faceless heterosexual feminists who cannot understand any human relationship not rooted in the dynamics of male-female interaction; but also the lesbians who will tell me I am betraying them by putting such information out for the perusal and possible use of "boys" or non-feminists; or even the lesbians who will dismiss me, because my life is nothing like theirs, the sources of my passions strange or frightening to them.

In fact, it is difficult to frame questions about sex without getting caught up in endless considerations of the *meaning* of the acts, sometimes quite astonishing philosophical, political, and spiritual treatments of meaning that I cannot quite bring back down to the level of my everyday life. In all questions about sex, it is the everyday life that interests me most. All the impassioned rhetoric serves no purpose but greater obscurity, if it does not originate and flow from an examination of the specific – how we all actually live out our sexuality. Without that detail, I have concluded that there are *no* valid generalizations to be made about sex and women's lives except for the central fact that we are all hungry for the power of desire and we are all terribly deeply afraid.

The hardest lesson I have learned in the last few years is how powerful is my own desire to hang on to a shared sense of feminist community where it is safe to talk about dangerous subjects like sex, and also – how hopeless is that desire. Even within what I have thought of as my own community, and, worse, even within the community of my friends and lovers, I have never felt safe. I have never *been* safe and that is only partly because everyone else is just as fearful as I am. None of us is safe, because we have never made each other safe. We have never even recognized the fearfulness of the territory. We have addressed violence and exploitation and heterosexual assumption without establishing first the understanding that for each of us desire is unique and necessary and simply terrifying. Without that understanding, and the compassion and empathy that must be part of it, I do not know how to avoid those acts of betrayal. But it is one thing for me to confront my own fear of those different from me – whether they are women of color, middle-class women or heterosexuals – and another entirely to demand of feminists that we begin again with this understanding. Yet that is exactly what I want to do. I want to begin again by saying that as women we don't know enough about each other, our fears, our desires or the many ways that this society has acted upon us. Nor do I want to give ground and allow sex to be exempted from the discussion.

As feminists we have committed our whole lives to struggling to change what most people in this society don't even question, and sometimes the intensity of our struggle has persuaded us that the only way to accomplish change is to make hard bargains, to give up some points and compromise on others; in the end what that has always meant is trading some people for some others.

I don't want to do that.

I don't want to require any other woman to do that.

I don't want to claim a safe or comfortable life for myself that is purchased at the cost of some other woman's needs or desires. But over and over again I see us being pushed to do just that. I know for myself how easily I used to dismiss heterosexual desire. I was kind about it, and even gently patient, but I used to look at heterosexual feminists with a kind of superior disdain, wondering how long it would take them to realize the hopelessness of their position. Crawling head first through the eye of a needle didn't seem to me half as difficult as dragging a man through your life. I took as whole cloth the notion that, yes, feminism is the theory while lesbianism is the practice, and only a childhood of forced politeness kept me from preaching that conviction to the less enlightened. I made no connection then between such expectations and the kind of pressure to "reform" myself that had hurt me so badly for so many years.

I can't pinpoint the act that changed all that for me, that made me see the absurdity of such a theory. I know that a piece of it was my relationship with my sisters. I could imagine some theoretical stranger deciding that rational lesbianism was the solution. I could not face my baby sister with her children, her half-tamed boyfriend and her hard won self-respect and try to tell her that she'd be better off in a lesbian collective. I know that once when we had stayed up talking almost all night, and she'd told me how her husband was sleeping around, and I'd admitted that yes, that women I'd told her about had hurt me almost more than I could stand, she had put her hand on mine, squeezed and said, "I know. I know that pain." I knew she was right, that she understood, and I knew too that all the things wrong in her life wouldn't be solved by her trying to be something she was not.

My understanding of what feminism meant changed even more from reading and listening to the many women who contributed to *This Bridge Called My Back*.[6] It was not then only a matter of looking at the personal racism that blights all our lives but also examining the institutional racism that shapes our convictions of who is or can be "right," and what it is that we really know as feminists. In a very real sense, *Bridge* gave me a new way to look at my life because it was so full of the lives of women who, while they were very different from me, voiced the same hopes, the same desperate desire to change what any of us is allowed. Throughout, while addressing the very real ways racism tears at all of us, the writers spoke again and again of joy, of love, of power, of lives shared and things accomplished. Most of all it offered a vision that struggle between white women and women of color did not have to be framed in terms of betrayal, that just as Barbara Smith had put it we might "emerge from this not broken."[7] If we could hope for this across the barriers of color and class, why not across sexuality and gender?

Bridge raised also the question of the difference between politics and personal style – a complicated, critical, and painful issue that no one has addressed sufficiently. Part of the power of the writers' voices lay in how different they were from what I had come to think of as the same old, slightly distant and carefully respectable aura of feminist theory. Here were all kinds of voices speaking of their real lives, not abstract generalities, not shielding or obscuring anger or impatience. I thought of all the meetings I had attended and papers I had read where the dominant tone was academic, polite, and distant, while the undercurrent was personal and vicious: the desire I had always had to say, "Can we stop a minute and talk about what is *really* going on here?"

When Cherríe Moraga spoke of how "with such grace, such blind faith, this commitment to women in the feminist movement grew to be exclusive and reactionary," she was speaking specifically about racism, and the tendency to ignore or misinterpret the lives of women of color.[8] But her words not only made me look at my own fears, avoidance, and racism but they made me also see that I had the same criticisms of the movement around the issues of class and sex. Moreover, just as I was terrified of addressing my own racism, so too other women were afraid of stepping into the deep and messy waters of class and sexual desire. If we get into this, what might we lose? If we expose this, what might our enemies do with it? And what might it mean? Will we have to throw out all that theory we have built with such pain and struggle? Will we have to start over? How are we going to make each other safe, while we work through all it means?

My first response to these questions was that it was all too hard, too deep, too terrible. It was only when I took my second breath and let go a little that I began to think in terms of going ahead anyway. We learn prejudice and hatred at the same time as we learn who we are and what the world is about, at the same time as we learn all our convictions about sex. The choice of our lives is whether we will simply swallow all we are handed or whether we will risk our whole lives shaking down and changing just those bottle-fed convictions.

Essential political decisions are made not once but again and again in all kinds of situations, always against that pressure to compromise, to bargain. I have found that in my own slow reassessment of my own politics, the most telling factor has been the gap between the rhetoric of lesbian feminism and the reality of my own life. It didn't matter how many times I was told that I was oppressed as a woman, I found that that fact did not answer all the contradictions of my life. Simple answers do not satisfy, and I rarely find that only one dynamic is going on in any given situation – a fact that makes me sharply suspicious of reductionist politics. Such politics are the most prone to compromise, to say we're addressing *the* essential contradiction and all that other stuff can slide. It is people who slide.

All my life I have been subject to the fact that somebody is always trying to set the boundaries of who and what I will be allowed to be – if queer, an acceptable queer, not too forward about the details of one's sexual practice; if working-class, an intellectual, upwardly mobile type who knows her place or at least the virtues of gratitude; if a writer, a humble, consciously female one who understands her relationship to "real" writers and who is willing to listen to her editor. What is common to all these boundary lines is that their true power lies in what I can be persuaded to do to myself – the walls of fear, shame, and guilt I am encouraged to build in my own mind. I have learned, in fact, that all systems of oppression feed on public silence and private terror, but few do so more forcefully than the system of sexual oppression.

Within the feminist movement we have developed a major analysis around the issue of silence – the impact on all our lives of all the things that must not be said. Nor has this been an analysis contained only within lesbian feminism. When I have spoken as a lesbian about my own struggles to understand and publicly acknowledge the full meaning of my love for women, I have watched straight women nod back at me, heard them speak of their own terrible secrets, their own impossible desires. For all women it is the public expression of desire that is impossible, any vestige of deviation from what we are supposed to want and how we are suppposed to behave. The myth prevails that "good girls" – even modern, enlightened, liberal or radical varieties – don't really have such desires.

For ten years now I have been sharing with other women the rage with which I began my work as a feminist organizer – outrage at anybody telling us what we will be allowed to do with our lives, and what we will not. And always for me this struggle has been about sex and class; shattering the silence that has been imposed on us not only around our terrifying sexual desires, but also around the powerful details of all the different ways we approach the world. When in 1981, I helped to organize the Lesbian Sex Mafia, I felt very much in that tradition. It was to be a

CR support group whose whole concern would be the subject of sex. To be sure that we would begin focused on our outrageousness, we chose our deliberately provocative name and concentrated on attracting members whose primary sexual orientation was s/m, butch/femme, fetishes, or otherwise "politically incorrect." We drew more women from the bars than the movement, but we brought back the principles of CR in our organization and insisted that within the group we would make no assumptions, no judgments, and no conclusions. We began by asking each other: what would it be like to organize for our sexual desire as strongly as we have tried to organize for our sexual defense?

The failings of LSM were largely the failings of early CR groups. With the concentration on sharing stories, it was hard to move on to taking any action as a group or to any kind of public, political identity. Some members felt frustrated with this, while others wanted the group to concentrate only on meeting the needs of members. In fact, there were limits on how the latter could be achieved. Integrating new people was extremely difficult and in fact the membership has always been concentrated on individuals who had already come to some state of self-acceptance. The kind of hesitant, fearful young woman who called me might never have come back after an initial orientation, and women who came expecting that LSM was going to provide them with an instant source of sex and adventure could get bored with all the talk and business. But the worst failure of the organization was that none of us really expected the kind of attacks that took place at the time of the Barnard conference and the organization's only public event – a speak-out on politically incorrect sex. Concentrating on supporting each other, we had put no work into confronting critics who were horrified at our behavior as lesbians, never mind "queer" queers. None the less, the group – both before and after April 24, 1982 – fulfilled its function as a forum to talk about our pleasure, rage, and fear about sex.

Even for those of us with backgrounds as political activists who had thought we had some handle on sex and its variations in this society, the revelation of shame, fear, and guilt that we produced was overwhelming. Women talked about years of celibacy, self-hatred, rejection, and abandonment by lovers, helplessness after rape or incest, social censure and street violence, family ostracism and constantly – the fear of what our desires might mean. Even though we had set up the group to avoid judgments we would still depressingly ask: "Do you think I'm sick?" The great strength of the group was the emphasis placed on how to turn those fears and experiences to a source of insight rather than confusion. That we could feel safe while being so vulnerable to each other was a constant source of energy and power. Every forbidden thought that was spoken enriched us. Every terrible desire that we shared suddenly assumed human dimensions, and our meetings were full of warmth and laughter.

How might our lives be different, I began to ask, if we were not being constantly subjected to this fear of ourselves and each other? What kind of women might we be if we did not have to worry about being too sexual, or not sexual enough, or the wrong kind of sexual for the company we kept? More and more I have grown impatient with the limitations placed on bringing this kind of discussion out of the closed group and into the public debate that continues among feminists. Not addressing these issues reinforces the rage and fear we all hide, while supporting the status quo of sexual oppression.

Instead of speaking out in favor of sex, most feminists seem to avoid this discussion in any way possible. It is too dangerous, too painful, too hopeless – like racism, class, anti-semitism, and all the important issues that require so much of us. Everyone is afraid of what might be revealed about our personal fears and desires. It is easier to dismiss any discussion of sexuality as irrelevant or divisive than to have to look at all the different ways we have denied and dismissed each other.

But we have no choice about this issue. We cannot continue to be circumspect in how we challenge this system of sexual oppression. We cannot continue to be willing to allow each other to deny ourselves, to be so quick to make those bad bargains that look so good at the time. I think for example of all those times we have pandered to this sex-hating society: as lesbians by pretending that we're really no different from heterosexuals and by placing such a strong emphasis on monogamy; as feminists by speaking for "reproductive freedom" rather than abortion, talking about our right to control our bodies but never going on to demand all that might mean; and by talking of morality as if that word didn't stick in our mouths with the memory of every lesbian ever attacked for the "immoral" acts we all commit. Our enemies are not confused about this issue. The preachers, psychologists, and politicians who want us to be silent, frightened women they can control – they are not avoiding the issue of sex. Sex is their favorite subject for attack, because they know how vulnerable we are to it.

I know from my own life that none of us wants to go on with this fear, this sense of loss, betrayal, risk. I know that I want most what Barbara Smith described in her short story – the ability to love without fear of betrayal, the confidence that we can expose ourselves and not have the women we love literally disappear from our lives. I know too that we will not get that safe ground easily. If we are not to sacrifice some part of ourselves or our community, we will have to go through all the grief of exposure and struggle, with only a thin line of trust that we will emerge whole and unbroken. The only way I know to begin this is to start by saying, "I will give up nothing. I will give up no one."

For my lovers, my sisters, the women who are now afraid to speak to or be seen with me, I have only one promise to make. I promise someday to provide a gathering place where in the center of the room will stand a huge, open book, a book where women will write out their fearful secrets and sign them or not as they choose. The only requirement will be that they should not feel they have to lie.

Notes

1 Audre Lorde, "The Master's Tools Will Never Dismantle The Master's House", in Cherríe Moraga and Gloria Anzaldúa (eds), *This Bridge Called My Back*, New York, Kitchen Table Women of Color Press, 1981, 1983, p. 105.
2 Cherríe Moraga, "Preface", in Moraga and Anzaldúa, op. cit., p. xiv.
3 Pat Califia, *Sapphistry*, Tallahassee, Fla, Naiad, 1981.
4 Adrienne Rich, *Compulsory Heterosexuality and Lesbian Existence*, San Francisco, Calif., Antelope, 1983.
5 Barbara Smith, "Home", *Conditions*, no. 8, Fall 1982, p. 105.
6 Moraga and Anzaldúa, op. cit.
7 Smith, op. cit., p. 100.
8 Moraga, in Moraga and Anzaldúa, op. cit., p. xiv.

Everything They Always Wanted You To Know: The Ideology of Popular Sex Literature

Meryl Altman

The feminist investigation of sexuality begins with the knowledge that sex as we learn it and live it is not simply "natural," not simply a matter of biological needs and responses. The way a woman experiences her sexuality, the ways we represent our sexuality to ourselves and enact that representation, are almost impossible to separate from the representations our culture makes available to us. Our awareness of this has made it possible to talk historically about changes in sexuality, based on changes in what sexual behaviors and forms are in the cultural repertory, which are valued, which are silenced, and what women's power relationship to such representation is. Thus, one way to attack the large question of what the so-called sexual revolution of the late 1960s and early 1970s meant for women and for female sexuality is to examine a new form of representation that then emerged into popular culture: the sex manual, brought out of its plain brown wrapper onto the mass-market shelf.

Of course, instructional and/or prescriptive books about sex were nothing new. Social historians have explored an extensive nineteenth-century moral and medical literature aimed at social-izing sexuality; in this century, Dr Th. H. Van de Velde's *Ideal Marriage: Its Physiology and Technique*, the quintessential "marriage manual" first published in 1926, enjoyed a wide circulation in successive reprintings and revisions for forty years, and was frequently imitated.[1] My workshop, however, sought to address a particular explosion of "information" about sex, more accessible, packaged in a new way, and playing on a different set of cultural assumptions. No longer just a thoughtful wedding gift, the "how-to" book about sex was openly advertised for everybody; its visibility and its popularity were widely inter-preted as a sign of cultural liberalization.[2] In what ways was this new form of literature normative as well as informative? What was the ideology of these books, and how was it produced?

I began by looking at the opening paragraph of the book from

115

which the title of my workshop was adapted: *Everything You Always Wanted to Know About Sex* (*But Were Afraid to Ask)*, by Dr David Reuben (1969).

As a psychiatrist, I am constantly impressed with one outstanding paradox presented to me constantly. In virtually every patient, I see a person living in the Space Age who has left his (or her) sexual organs in the Stone Age. The cumulative effect of thousands of years of education, culture, and refinement have not had much impact on our knowledge about the genitals. Despite all the frank, "for adults only," films and books today, most people still are abysmally ignorant about sex. A jet pilot propels his airliner through space at 600 miles an hour – he cannot propel his own penis seven inches into a vagina. During the day, a woman physicist explores the mysteries of nuclear particles. At night she is left to ponder the mystery of her own homosexuality. Most of us are in the uncomfortable position of knowing more about what occurs 238,000 miles away on the surface of the moon than what happens six inches below our own navels.[3]

Reuben's book had the earliest and perhaps the widest circulation of this wave of sex manuals, for which it was paradigmatic in many ways. This paragraph, from the opening chapter entitled "Beyond the Birds and the Bees," sounds most of his characteristic themes. First, it contains sexual stereotyping of the crudest sort (for example, any woman who could be a physicist must be sexually "abnormal"), involving "cases" or examples drawn from cultural mythology rather than reality. Second, it takes a flippant, condescending attitude toward sexual difficulties. Third, Reuben assumes the stance of the psychiatrist as all-knowing expert confronted by a population of "abysmally ignorant," bewildered children, eager to become his patients and proselytes.[4] Finally, Reuben characterizes the information his book is about to divulge as a secret, by alluding to past repression and present ignorance. This functions in two ways: it enhances his authority as high priest about to initiate the reader into the mysteries; and it validates and reinforces the "truth" value of the information itself. If we believe that the truth about sex is repressed and hidden, sexual secrets become by definition sexual truths. If we have been afraid to ask, we must want – need – to know.

Michel Foucault (another expert) has outlined a characteristic trope of modern discussion of sex: the claim that such discussion breaks the sound barrier of repression is made again and again with no cumulative gain, in order to validate and create a discourse that may or may not be equally repressive:

There may be another reason that makes it so gratifying for us to define the relationship between sex and power in terms of repression:

something that one might call the speaker's benefit. If sex is repressed, that is, condemned to prohibition, nonexistence, and silence, then the mere fact that one is speaking about it has the appearance of a deliberate transgression. A person who holds forth in such language places himself to a certain extent outside the reach of power; he upsets established law; he somehow anticipates the coming freedom.[5]

Foucault builds his wider analysis of how ideology operates within culture upon an investigation of who or what, beyond individual speakers or writers, the repeated claim to challenge repression serves:

Did the critical discourse that addresses itself to repression come to act as a roadblock to a power mechanism that had operated unchallenged up to that point, or is it not in fact part of the thing it denounces (and doubtless misrepresents) by calling it "repression"? Was there really a historical rupture between the age of repression and the critical analysis of repression?[6]

I found this characteristic figure in nearly all of the 1970s sex manuals I looked into: the affirmation of a new frankness, of a break with the repression of the past. This affirmation is always completely anachronistic, if not ahistorical. Reuben attacks Anthony Comstock and the Reverend Bowdler; *The Joy of Sex* and *The Sensuous Woman* make disparaging remarks about "puritanism"; others blame "Victorian prudery" or "taboos." By locating repression in 1850 (or 1650) rather than 1950, the authors avoid any historical analysis of repression, avoid situating themselves within a process of historical change. Both repression itself and the act of denouncing and removing repression are thus curiously depoliticized. Pushing repression into some distant, murky, non-historical past, these writers create the fiction of a value-free space – the present – where discussion of sexuality is invulnerable to challenges that it is repressive or partisan. Information (which could be true or false) is transformed into a kind of mythology or folk wisdom, a process aided by the disappearance of identifiable, historically locatable authors behind pseudonyms or even hieroglyphic initials ("J," "M"), where even the gender of the writer and the distinction between individual and collective authorship are blurred.[7] In short, past repression is invoked in such a way as to make the information given appear "new," and to prevent the reader from testing it against experienced reality.

Of course, there is one sense in which the information offered by these books was in fact new information: much of the "factual" material is based on the findings of Masters and Johnson, and all these books refer to their work explicitly, implicitly, or by anecdote. However, if we owe Masters and Johnson certain important clarifications, notably new understanding of the nature of female orgasm and increased data about human sexual capacities, we (and the popular sex literature of our time) owe them certain biases as well. Paul Robinson has cogently analyzed the ideological bases of that research in *The Modernization of Sex*. He concludes, among other things, that their focus on the couple – the married heterosexual couple – as the "unit of therapy," research, and analysis, gave their work, compared with Kinsey's, an unmistakably conservative cast.[8]

We can see most easily what effect this direction had on advice literature by looking at *The Pleasure Bond: A New Look at Sexuality and Commitment* (1970), written by Masters and Johnson in association with Robert J. Levin. This book, whose title alone provides material for reflection, consists of a number of "transcripts" of group therapy sessions led by Masters and Johnson, interspersed with their commentary and analysis. A glance at the book's table of contents should lay bare its ideological agenda:

Sexual Responsibility. An Introduction.

One   The Marriage Theme.
1 Young Marriages. The Search for Sexual Pleasure.
2 How Conciliation Becomes Another Word for Marriage.
3 Young Marriages. How the Double Standard Influences Sexual Pleasure.
4 What Men Stand to Gain from Women's Liberation.
5 Why "Working" at Sex Won't Work.

Two   Variations on the Marriage Theme.
6 Extramarital Sex. Who Gambles – And Why?
7 Swinging Sex. Is There a Price to Pay?
8 What Sexual Fidelity Means in a Marriage.

Three   The Marriage Theme Restated.
9 Second Marriages. When Communication Really Counts.
10 Touching. How Intimacy is Born.
11 How Pretending Makes Sexual Pleasure Impossible.
12 Commitment. The Pleasure Bond.[9]

Sex as taught by Masters and Johnson is sex within marriage; *The Pleasure Bond* is a marriage manual in the most unironic sense. Alternatives to heterosexual marriage are "explored" in the second section only to be proven unworkable and damaging. And the glorification of the "marriage theme" goes hand in hand with the stance of the expert. As Carole Vance has explained, in discussing the ideological bases of recent research on sexuality: "as sex is isolated and privatized within the couple, the study of sexuality is encapsulated within 'sexology.'"[10]

Here the couple – Masters and Johnson themselves – become the unit of authority and knowledge as well. Apparent challenges to the success or centrality of the marriage theme are defused through expert testimony, followed by a happy ending – the heterosexual couple goes off into the sunset, reunited, cured, and "committed." The very structure of the book has facilitated what Gayle Rubin has called the "gender system ideology" of conservative culture.[11]

Rather than simply provide lists of the misinformation that the 1970s sex manuals disseminated under the guise of authoritative demystification (such a list would fill a long and very dull book), I'd like to discuss the rhetorical strategies that make such misinformation and the reaffirmation of conservative moral standards possible, indeed inevitable. The structure of Reuben's books appears on the surface quite different from that of *The Pleasure Bond*: they are set up as a long series of questions and answers. The unnamed person asking all of these questions, it is implied, is the reader. *I* am immediately psychologically implicated in the discussion and thus in the ideology. After all, I'm the one who "wants to know"; Dr Reuben is simply being obliging.

Another part of his strategy involves extensive use of the "case study" method. Aping medical and psychiatric practice, he illustrates his points by the presentation of capsule life histories, the authenticity of which is never established. Here is one, from the chapter on "Frigidity."

The emotional blunting which is so obvious and dramatic in the sexual sphere permeates most of the other aspects of the woman's personality as well. Emily is a good example; her sister Hilda can describe her best:

"Emily is only thirty-four but you wouldn't think so if you saw her, doctor. She teaches history at the junior college and most of her students think she's at least forty. It's a shame, too, because she's such a nice girl. I mean she took care of father for ten years until he died last May, and he wasn't the easiest man in the world to get along with. But she doesn't have the slightest interest in men and because of the way she acts, there aren't many men who are interested in her. And the clothes she wears – she doesn't have to wear miniskirts, but no one else in the whole college wears skirts below the knee. And I can't even get her to wear lipstick. The worst thing about it is that Emily is basically such a nice girl."

"What are her other activities besides school?"

"None, really. Since father passed away she spends even more time by herself. Occasionally a fellow will still ask her out, but she's just not interested. The thing I can't understand is how she changed so much. When she was younger she was cute as a button and I was sure she'd be married before she got out of high school."

Emily finally came for a psychiatric interview, primarily, as she said, "to please my sister," the only person with whom she still maintained emotional contact.

"I don't know what Hilda told you, doctor, but I just don't care about sex. I don't even want to talk about it. If you want to discuss something else, I'm willing to listen. But sex, no."

Hilda was right. Although Emily was attractive, her dowdy hair style and dress made her look much older.

"We don't have to talk about sex if you don't want to. How come you're so unhappy?"

Emily gave a gasp. "I didn't know it was that obvious!" She started to talk, but started crying. After a dozen pieces of Kleenex and a cup of tea she started to talk again.

"I can't explain it. For the past fifteen years I've just been drying up. At first I tried to fight it off – you know, I'd try to go out on dates and find new interests but nothing worked out. Every man seemed to be after one thing – sex, and that just scared me."

"I thought you didn't want to talk about sex."

"Oh, I don't care. I'm so miserable now it won't make any difference."

Emily entered psychiatric treatment for her basic problem: depression and anxiety, with a big burden of guilt. Gradually she recognized how she had been unconsciously trying to reproduce in her present life the dreariness and disappointment of her youth. Her interest in clothes and her own appearance increased and she began to go out on dates. She stopped picking men who were experts at disappointing her and began to look and act her age – or younger. After six months of treatment. Emily eloped with the assistant dean of the college. After her honeymoon, she stopped in to see her psychiatrist.

"I'm happy to say, doctor, this is just a social call. I wanted to tell you how happy I am. I don't know what it's done for other people but psychiatry did what Mother Nature couldn't do – it made a woman out of me."[12]

The length of that quotation is at least partly excused by its typicality: *Everything You Always Wanted to Know* contains many such cases, and Reuben's later book, *Any Woman Can* (1971) consists of very little else. The situation is always the same: a woman is unhappy because she is frigid, or because she is promiscuous, or because she is lonely; she cries in the office of the understanding male therapist; he takes care of her; she undergoes treatment; she makes a successful adjustment – and marries. This is propaganda for psychiatry, propaganda for marriage, and propaganda for female dependency on male authority. Through short fables or parables, female sexuality is represented in terms of disease for which proper re-socialization is the cure.

A similar strategy draws the (female) reader into *The Sensuous Woman* (1969). Jacket copy for this book reads, "the author of this book is not especially pretty," and she introduces herself as follows:

For the last five years, men have been telling me the most delicious things – that I'm sexy, all woman, that perfect combination of a lady in the living room and a marvelous bitch in bed, sensual, beautiful, a modern Aphrodite, maddeningly exciting, the epitome of the Sensuous Woman.

Some of the most interesting men in America have fallen in love with me. I have received marriage proposals from such diverse personalities as a concert pianist, a best-selling author, the producer of two of America's most popular television shows, a bomb expert for the CIA, a trial attorney, an apple grower, a TV and radio star and a tax expert.

Yet you'd never believe it if we came face to face on the street, for I'm not particularly pretty. I have heavy thighs, lumpy hips, protruding teeth, a ski-jump nose, poor posture, flat feet and uneven ears.

I never wear tight skirts, low-cut dresses or bikinis.

I am not brilliant and I don't have a magnetic personality. In fact, I'm shy.

Mothers, wives and girl friends think of me as the wholesome, apple pie, girl-next-door type (which, translated, means non-sexy).

But while these mothers, wives and girl friends are burning up over that spectacular-looking blonde undulating provocatively in the peek-aboo leopard print, I'm the one that's having the wonderful time – and getting and *keeping* men.

For, through intelligence and hard work, I have become a Sensuous Woman.

And that's what every man wants
More than beauty
More than brilliance
More than great housekeeping abilities
More than a model mother to his children
He wants a Sensuous Woman
Because she makes him *know* that he is the most remarkable man that ever lived.

. . . Even if you are knock-kneed, flat-chested, cross-eyed and balding, you can learn to make him feel that way and, in doing so, reap wonderful benefits for yourself.[13]

The Pleasure Bond could be thought of as a novel, and *Everything You Always Wanted to Know* as a collection of short stories, in which docile heroines are led through a therapeutic process to a resolution of conflict and are rewarded with a happy ending – a good marriage. *The Sensuous Woman* also fits this pattern. It is a classic *Bildungsroman* of a young girl from the provinces who makes good: not especially pretty, not especially intelligent, she uses a talent for social manipulation (as well as her own innocence) to attain her reward. This is also the plot of mass-market formula romances such as Harlequin and Silhouette; the first twentieth-century advice book I found that made use of it was *Sex and The Single Girl* by Helen Gurley Brown, which purports to describe an autobiographical transformation from "mouseburger" to glamour queen. It's interesting to note that *The*

Sensuous Man (1971) begins and ends with a similar narrative, with complementary gender-stereotyping: the hero, short, somewhat pudgy, and initially worried about his penis size and inability to compete with the locker-room stories of his buddies, learns to get all the women he wants. Literary critic Nancy Miller has written that

> the fictions of desire behind the desiderata of fiction are masculine and not universal constructs...the maxims that pass for the truth of human experience, and the encoding of that experience in literature, are organizations, when they are not fantasies, of the dominant culture.[14]

She and other critics have discussed the ways narrative functions in novels to encode ideology, the way certain plots, for example, the marriage plot, operate to present certain options for women as plausible and to silence alternatives. Plot helps a novel, ostensibly a pure fiction, to become a "conduct book" or manual for living, by rewarding certain behaviors and punishing others. The reader identifies, usually with the heroine, and so becomes emotionally part of the fantasy being enacted, which then becomes part of her socialization into the values of the "dominant culture." Under the guise of reading her own story, she is taught a story by and about men.[15]

In the sexual advice books, novelistic use of plot blends, often almost imperceptibly, into a pseudo-medical use of the case history. Carole Vance has described this phenomenon in her discussion of professional sexology:

> The same researchers who investigated large samples with elaborate methodologies derogated this information as "just statistics" and turned instead to highly idiosyncratic and individual examples of behavior. Perhaps the medical preference, whether in physical or psychiatric medicine, for the case history and clinical anecdote accounts for some of this behavior.[16]

While it would seem impossible to write about sex without some recourse to case histories, no rhetorical distinction is made in these books between cases and anecdotes, between clinical data and locker-room stories. They thus combine two of the most sophisticated strategies for inscribing ideology our culture has developed: the fiction which elicits identification and self-modeling, and the discourse of the expert. Moreover, each of these strategies functions to mask the other. The doctor unbends, talks about "getting some," tells a few bathroom jokes, and hides his medical authority behind the authority of the storyteller; meanwhile the reader is not conscious of reading a fiction because the book is labeled "information." The technique is doubly insidious.

The Joy of Sex might at first appear not to inscribe ideology in this way, since it is structured rather differently: it is a "cookbook," with entries arranged alphabetically within certain categories. Theoretically, an alphabetical arrangement is an impartial, non-hierarchical one. However, in the original *Joy* it's not unimportant or random that "Penis" and "Vulva," like "Beds," are under "Starters"; that "Little Death" is under "Main Course"; "Anal Sex" is under "Sauces and Pickles"; and "Bisexuality" and "Transvestism" are under "Problems," placed at the end. Moreover, the authors, a "discussing couple," are continuously present as personae, and various branches of "expert" knowledge (anthropology, sociology, animal behavior, sexological research, medicine) are frequently invoked, implicitly and explicitly. The ostensibly open discussion in *The Joy of Sex* does involve a continuing static situation, an underlying hierarchy of control.

We could discuss in a much more concrete way the unerringly male-based perspective of these books. Reuben for example assumes that the first thing I want to know about sex is "How big is the normal penis?", which he calls the "question of the century"; one of his recurring extended metaphors describes sexual intercourse as the launching of a missile from a launching pad.[17] The chapter in *The Sensuous Woman* which instructs the reader in great detail how to fake an orgasm convincingly is typical of that book and of the genre; after all, says J, "No woman of any sensitivity would refuse to make love to a man she cared for just because she 'doesn't really feel like it.'"[18] Reuben makes a similar recommendation in *Any Woman Can*. Clearly, the new liberated woman is "sensuous" and sexy – but is she sexual, on her own behalf? *The Joy of Sex* is much less overt in this respect, but occasional lapses – "put your partner on the bed in such a way so that she..."[19] – raise the question of who the implied reader and the implied speaker really are.

Also interesting is the emphasis in these books on disease, or (as it's called) dysfunction; Reuben is particularly preoccupied with this. Within the first twenty-five pages he mentions in a flippant and unsympathetic way the following things that can go wrong with the penis: bent-nail syndrome, priapism, four kinds of impotence including premature ejaculation (this gets its own chapter), the loss of the testicles (with a protracted meditation on the vulnerability of the testes to accident), undescended testicles, elephantiasis of the testes, hypospadias (a hole in the underside of the penis which causes semen and urine to drip out), valinitis (an infection of the foreskin), and cancer of the penis. There is also a chapter on frigidity and a corresponding list of potential defects in the female anatomy, including an extra set of breasts, a vagina that is too large, a vagina that is too small, no vagina at all, a tough hymen, a hymeneal carbuncle, vaginismus, dyspareunia, and the famous anecdote of the "stuck couple" – the vagina that locked. This is one of the most disturbing aspects of Reuben's book, not just because it turns a discussion of anatomy into a freak show, but because, to the uneducated or simply inexperienced reader, it can be literally terrifying. Venereal disease is also discussed here, as is usual for these books, but the emphasis is not on diseases you can catch from having sex, but on dysfunctions which can prevent you from having it at all.

A preoccupation with getting rid of "problems" which can get in the way of "normal" sexuality also informs the way homosexuality and lesbianism are discussed. *The Joy of Sex*, whose title presumes that it is all-encompassing (it is not, after all, called "The Joy of Heterosexual Sex") contains not a single mention of homosexuality, and only one reference to bisexuality; this is under "Problems," and includes the following:

Straight man-woman sex is the real thing for most people – others need something different, but their scope is usually reduced, not widened, by such needs. ... It may sound brutal, but don't, repeat don't, take on a partner with a major sex problem such as homosexuality or compulsive ritualism in order to "cure him by love." You won't.[20]

And while *The Joy of Sex* and *More Joy* both emphasize the pleasures of "swinging" or group sex, and the beneficial effects this can have on the primary relationship, they also stress that a casual lesbian or homosexual contact in the course of a "swinging scene" does not mean that the participant is GAY. *The Sensuous Woman* mentions lesbianism only to advise the acolyte rather sweetly that if she intends to participate in "swinging sex" she should be aware that many women who do so are lesbians, and so she should be prepared to discourage their advances gracefully.[21]

Everything You Always Wanted To Know includes a whole chapter on male homosexuality, which begins with an anecdote about a man picking up another man in the bathroom of a bowling alley, and goes on to repeat conventional stereotypes: all homosexuals are promiscuous, engage in s/m, are unhappy, etc. The centerpiece of this chapter is approximately ten pages of anecdotes told by doctors about objects they have found in the anuses of male patients, including flashlights and lightbulbs; locker-room sniggering is as far as Reuben's analysis gets. Lesbians are given only a few pages, interestingly located in the chapter on prostitution; Reuben repeats the old myth of the extra-long lesbian clitoris and says that lesbian sex is more romantic than gay male sex, but equally promiscuous and unsatisfying.

Like their male counterparts, lesbians are handicapped by having only half the pieces of the anatomical jigsaw puzzle. Just as one penis plus one penis equals nothing, one vagina plus another vagina still equals zero. ... basically all homosexuals are alike – looking for love where there can be no love and looking for sexual satisfaction where there can be no lasting satisfaction.[22]

Feminist social historians, in studying popular representations of sexuality in the 1920s, have shown that, at a time when heterosexuality was becoming more widely talked about and increasingly promoted, when books on such topics as companionate marriage stressed the importance of sexuality, there was a corresponding repression of lesbianism. This contrasts with the relative freedom women who loved women were given in the nineteenth century, when there was widespread silence about female sexual desire.[23] Perhaps these conclusions can be applied to popular representations of sexuality in the early 1970s: heterosexual "liberation" was accompanied by a repression of all tendencies that didn't bear out the model. The normalization of relations between men and women was contingent upon marginalizing relations that didn't fit this norm – not by calling them wrong or immoral, but simply by explaining that they weren't any fun.

The best sign of this is the centrality given to sexual intercourse amid all the apparent multiplicity of sexual possibility. *The Joy of Sex*, for example, which describes a wide variety of things people can do with their bodies, concludes by saying that the most satisfying position of all the hundreds they describe is what they call the "matrimonial position" – that is to say, the missionary position.[24] Not the most moral, or the most correct (that would be puritanism); simply the most satisfying. Reuben is even more explicit.

Is there anything wrong with fellatio and cunnilingus?
As a form of heterosexual activity incidental to penis-vagina intercourse, mouth-genital stimulation is not only perfectly all right to practice, but in many situations desirable. . . .
If fellatio and cunnilingus are so gratifying, why shouldn't they take the place of penis-vagina intercourse?
If that would happen, the birth rate would quickly fall to zero, and there would be no one around to do it with. But the most important reason that oral intercourse will not replace penis-vagina activity is that regular copulation is even more enjoyable than fellatio or cunnilingus. The most desirable use of both stimulations is to make the final stage of intercourse as exciting and rewarding as possible.[25]

Another narrative is being prescribed: from touching to oral sex to intercourse, ending if possible with simultaneous orgasm. All dysfunctions, difficulties *and alternatives* must be eliminated or silenced in order to make this happy ending possible. And this narrative is manifestly connected with the earlier one (the marriage plot). Reuben in *Any Woman Can!* gives a number of suggestions to women who want to get married, including withholding sexual favors until after the wedding. When the book opens, the reader may be under the impression that the title means "Any Woman Can Be Sexual" or "Any Woman Can Have An Orgasm." By the end, all doubt has evaporated: it means "Any Woman Can Find A Husband." And once she's found him:

> The only way for a wife to find true sexual fulfillment in marriage is to make it the primary goal. She must be willing to cast aside everything else in life that might come between herself and her husband. She must constantly dedicate herself to him as completely as she did on the day of her wedding. If she does – and if *he* does – they will be rewarded with the greatest gift any human being can ever receive. In those spectacular fleeting moments of orgasm, their souls and spirits will fuse – and just for an instant husband and wife will become one. And that, after all, is the true meaning of love between a man and a woman.[26]

This is Reuben's final paragraph, and again he sums up the genre. What is privileged is not simply "normal" intercourse between the heterosexual married couple, but LOVE. While every book I read included a denunciation of those terrible mechanical books which tell you all about "technique" but say nothing about love and "relating," I found no such books. Even *The Sensuous Man* finishes by quoting Elizabeth Barrett Browning's "How do I love thee? Let me count the ways." The appearance of romantic love in these books is, I would argue, inevitable; it represents and covers over the struggle of the narrative to reconcile an "opening" of discourse about sex with a cultural ideology that focuses on normality and reproduction.

The understanding that our sexuality is culturally constructed has led feminists to examine both popular and "high culture" representations of women for clues about our own development and about historical change. We have barely begun, however, to ask certain difficult but crucial questions about the very nature of representation within culture. If, as we assume, the ideology of a dominant, repressive culture is in some way present in "popular" images and texts, how does it get there? How do we account for the fact that such repression is less than total, and that alternate, conflicting sets of representations coexist at the same time, in the same place, under the same political system? How can we acknowledge and analyze the diversity with which women respond to such representation? And finally, what is the relationship between ideology, as we can analyze it through representation, and actual behavior?

While I cannot pretend to answer any of these questions, or even to suggest an adequate methodology for discovering their answers, their persistence indicates both a direction for further investigation and the absolute centrality of the investigation of representation to the feminist analysis of women's oppression. Within my own scope of inquiry, some related questions still remain: why were these how-to books so popular? why did people read them? and why did they emerge at this time?[27]

About the last question, we can only speculate that perhaps the first stirrings of a desire for genuine sexual liberation and openness, conditioned by the beginnings of the second wave of American feminism and of gay liberation, created tremendous anxiety in the culture and called forth a new genre that could rechannel these energies into the mainstream – the middle-class family – hiding its repression of contradictory possibilities behind the rhetoric of emancipation. Perhaps the genuinely sexually liberated woman, who as yet only potentially existed, posed such a threat to "American values" that she was immediately coopted and transformed into the Sensuous Woman, yet another sex object. It would be hard to overstate the anxiety over sexual choices and roles which was created for women by this superimposition of cultural closure upon a rhetoric of openness.

The answer to my first question – why were these books so popular? – lies somewhere between the answers to the other two, in the intersection between the need of the culture to maintain itself ideologically and the needs or anxieties of particular readers within that culture. From my analysis of the rhetoric of these books, it is possible to deduce that people read them for three reasons: for information, for titillation, and for reassurance.

In practice, these categories are seldom distinct. For many, but particularly for young women who came of age sexually during the "sexual revolution," these books could often substitute for experience or for less irrational kinds of sex education, or could even supersede other available information because they were packaged as demystifying and "new." While readers who are genuinely ignorant, or genuinely looking for new information, are perhaps most vulnerable to the strategies for transmitting ideology outlined above, other motives also operate in a powerful way. People also read these books because they definitively answer the overwhelming question, "Am I Normal?", thus ideally allaying (but in practice perhaps intensifying) anxiety, and providing guidelines for socially acceptable behavior. In other words, the books can function in a normative way because they play on widespread fears of being "abnormal."

Finally, people read and buy these books, consciously or unconsciously, because they are explicitly about sex and therefore sexually arousing. But this function reinforces, rather than conflicts with, the normative function: sexual arousal by a text occurs by means of the reader's identification with the "characters" in the text, and such identification, as I've said above, facilitates the acceptance of norms. Stephen Marcus has distinguished "pornography" from "literature" on the grounds that "pornography" is obsessively repetitive, plays the same scenes over and over, so that its readers can feel aroused without feeling threatened; it is thus ideologically conservative. The popular sex instruction literature of the late 1960s and early 1970s functions in much this way. It is a medium through which the dominant culture, under the guise of breaking taboos, reinforces those taboos, unceasingly telling itself and its initiates what it, and they, already know.

Notes

1 See, for example, Michael Gordon and M. C. Bernstein, "Mate Choice and Domestic Life in the 19th Century", *Journal of Marriage and the Family*, vol. 32, pp. 665-74; Peter Gay, "Victorian Sexuality: Old Texts and New Insights", *American Scholar*, Autumn 1980, pp. 372-8. See also Th. H. Van de Velde, MD, *Ideal Marriage: Its Physiology and Technique*, revised edn, translated by Stella Browne, New York, Random House, 1965, and Edward Brecher, "He Taught a Generation to Copulate: Theodor Hendrik Van de Velde (1873-1937)", *The Sex Researchers*, Boston, Little, Brown, 1969, pp. 82-103.

  Any attempt at an exhaustive study of instructional writing about sex during the 1960s and 1970s would, I quickly discovered, be more suited to a full-length study. I have therefore chosen to look at a few of the most widely influential manuals of the "sexual revolution," to sketch the ideological outlines of the successful product. The paradigm developed here should, of course, be tested by further application.

2 For easier reference, the books discussed are: Dr David Reuben, MD, *Everything You Always Wanted to Know About Sex** (**But Were Afraid to Ask*), New York, Bantam, 1969; and *Any Woman Can! Love and Sexual Fulfillment For the Single, Widowed, Divorced . . . And Married*, New York, David McKay, 1971; "J," *The Sensuous Woman*, New York, Dell, 1969; "M," *The Sensuous Man*, New York, Dell, 1971; Alex Comfort, MB, PhD, *The Joy of Sex: A Gourmet Guide to Lovemaking*, New York, Simon & Schuster, 1972; *More Joy of Sex*, New York, Simon & Schuster, 1972; and William H. Masters and Virginia E. Johnson in association with Robert J. Levin, *The Pleasure Bond: A New Look at Sexuality and Commitment*, Boston, Little, Brown, 1970.

3 Reuben, *Everything You Always Wanted to Know about Sex**, op. cit., p. 1.

4 See also Barbara Ehrenreich and Deirdre English, *For Her Own Good: 150 Years of the Experts' Advice to Women*, Garden City, New York, Anchor/Doubleday, 1978, for some historical perspective on this issue.

5 Michel Foucault, *The History of Sexuality. Volume I: An Introduction*, translated from the French by Robert Hurley, New York, Vintage, 1980, p. 6.

6 Ibid., p. 10.

7 Who is/are "J" and "M"? Who are the "discussing couple" who Alex Comfort claims are the real authors of *The Joy of Sex* and *More Joy*? For a related discussion of how sexual discourse creates a place outside of history, see Stephen Marcus, *The Other Victorians*, New York, Bantam, 1966.

8 Paul Robinson, *The Modernization of Sex*, New York, Harper & Row, 1976.

9 Masters and Johnson, op. cit., pp. xiii-xiv.

10 Carole S. Vance, "Gender Systems, Ideology, and Sex Research", in Ann Snitow, Christine Stansell, and Sharon Thompson (eds), *Powers of Desire*, New York, Monthly Review Press, 1983, p. 377.

11 Gayle Rubin, "The Traffic in Women: Notes on the 'Political Economy' of Sex", in Rayna R. Reiter (ed.), *Toward an Anthropology of Women*, New York, Monthly Review Press, 1975, pp. 157-210.

12 Reuben, *Everything You Always Wanted to Know About Sex**, op. cit., pp. 127-9.

13 "J," *The Sensuous Woman*, op. cit., pp. 9-11.

14 Nancy Miller, "Emphasis Added: Plots and Plausibilities in Women's Fiction", *PMLA*, vol. 96, no. 1, January 1981, p. 46.

15 See Nancy Miller, *The Heroine's Text*, New York, Columbia University Press, 1980. See also Rachel Brownstein, *Becoming a Heroine*, New York, Viking, 1982; and Julie L. Abraham, "Marriage, Desire and Deviance: The Heterosexual Plot in Virginia Woolf's *Between the Acts*", unpublished manuscript.

16 Carole S. Vance, op. cit., pp. 378-9.

17 Reuben, *Everything You Always Wanted to Know About Sex**, op. cit., p. 5-10.

18 "J," *The Sensuous Woman*, op. cit., p. 179.

19 Comfort, *The Joy of Sex*, op. cit., p. 50.

20 Ibid., pp. 225 and 235.

21 "J," *The Sensuous Woman*, op. cit., p. 160.

22 Reuben, *Everything You Always Wanted to Know About Sex**, op. cit., pp. 269, 272. See also "Sexuality and Sex Roles" in Del Martin and Phyllis Lyon, *Lesbian/Woman*, New York, Bantam, 1972.

23 See, for example, Christina Simmons, "Companionate Marriage and the Lesbian Threat", *Frontiers*, vol. IV, no. 3, Fall 1979, pp. 54-9; Lisa Duggan, "The Social Enforcement of Heterosexuality and Lesbian Resistance in the 1920's", in Amy Swerdlow and Hanna Lessinger (eds), *Class, Race, and Sex: The Dynamics of Control*, Boston G. K. Hall, 1983, pp. 75-92.

24 Comfort, *The Joy of Sex*, op. cit., p. 124.

25 Reuben, *Everything You Always Wanted to Know About Sex**, op. cit., pp. 64-5.

26 Reuben, *Any Woman Can!*, op. cit., pp. 363-4.
27 It would be equally fascinating to know, but extremely difficult to ascertain, *who* read them: how readership and response differed according to gender, social class, ethnicity, sexual preference, age, etc. The methodological difficulties of determining by whom a book was bought and read, and with what degree of attention, respect, and belief it was read, are legendary within the field of literary history, and parallel the difficulties of tracing connections between the consumption of ideological representation and an effect on actual perception and behavior. A statistically meaningful survey of reader attitudes would be invaluable.

Above and Beyond Politics: The Sexual Socialization of Children

Mary S. Calderone

Over the past fifteen years enough knowledge about human sexuality in its many-faceted aspects has accumulated to facilitate services for sexual health. Thus, a new sub-specialty has emerged in the health field, consisting of three areas: sex research, sex therapy, and education for sexuality. It is now clear to workers in this field that the latter term is not necessarily limited to sex education in the schools. Even in the absence of any formal program, education for sexuality *happens* to every infant and child in every home, with or without the conscious intervention of the adults there. Depending on a variety of factors, it may be negative or positive in its impact – the first more often than the second, to judge from the results.

The health arena now requires concerted effort by professionals in many disciplines aimed at prevention of the sexual disease so evident in various forms. Because of my background in pediatrics, public health, and preventive medicine, for many years I have chosen to concentrate my efforts regarding preventive education about human sexuality primarily on adults, particularly parents of infants and young children and those who deal with them in a health or educational capacity. Much sexual distress is identifiable in disabilities such as male impotence or premature ejaculation, and orgasmic difficulties in women. It has been estimated that perhaps 50 percent of marriages are adversely affected by these or by related conditions such as sexual apathy or distaste in one or both partners.

During their growing years all children are socialized by their families in ways characteristic for each culture. This process varies according to what is being socialized: food or living patterns, family relationships, hunting or work patterns, dress, housing, recreation, religious beliefs and rituals, moral values, government, laws – these and many other aspects of life may be subjected to quite rigid social structuring. Cultures socialize their children in three specific ways which relate to sexuality: gender identity, gender role, and eroticism.

First, in every culture the child inevitably receives liminal and

131

subliminal messages as to its gender identity, so that even before language, by eighteen months to two years, the child knows indelibly that "I'm a boy like my father" or "I'm a girl like my mother."

Second, parents and other adults continually provide clues to the developing child that certain behaviors or feelings are appropriate for its gender, that is, what kind of boy and what kind of girl is wanted by that society (gender role). Parents are generally unaware how early in their child's life they communicate such attitudes and expectations in subtle and not-so-subtle ways. Studies have shown that fathers handle their infant daughters quite differently from their infant sons, for example, when toddlers run to their mothers for comfort or reassurance at the playground, the mothers tend to push their boys away much earlier than they do their girls. It is important to emphasize that in the last fifteen years, attitudes about and understanding of gender roles in the United States have shifted enormously, particularly as women have reevaluated their own capacities and entered the paid labor force in increasing numbers.

Third, the framework for sexuality is the basis for the uniqueness in each and every person. Of sexuality's three components – gender identity, gender role, and eroticism – it is the erotic that gives trouble, especially in America. The American admixture of differing value systems in continuous confrontation with each other results from our massive immigration from different societies and ethnic backgrounds. Because this mix is overlaid with more than a few remnants of the puritan ethic, it is almost impossible for many people to contemplate the erotic and its role in human life with composure and rationality. The difficulty is compounded by the relative scientific illiteracy that presently appears to be characteristic of the population of the United States today. Just when science is exploding with knowledge about sexuality, there appears to exist a growing body of persons who knowingly and deliberately resist any findings that appear to them to go against "revealed" truth. Where the erotic is recognized as an important component of life, it is usually primarily among well-educated and trained professionals. However, those who for commercial purposes exploit the erotic in one way or another add to the confusion and misery, delaying development of social change that might alleviate the situation. Consideration of the actualities of the erotic side of human development might well help society discover and validate non-destructive ways of socializing it in the young before they reach adolescence, and should be placed high on the agenda of professionals dealing with developmental processes in infants and children.

A normal baby is born after a gestation during which every body system but one has from the earliest weeks been actively functional. The single exception is the reproductive system which remains on "hold" until puberty. As in the entire animal world, reproduction must await physiological maturation, and the mean age for this in the human mammal world is around 12.5 years. But a separate, if closely related, system has been found to begin its functioning early in fetal life, and is being spoken of as the *sexual response system*. This is composed of organs, innervation and a brain center that serve purposes quite different from the single purpose of the reproductive system, though in both sexes the two systems share some organs in common. For example, in reproduction the vagina serves passively as way of entry for sperm and of exit for menstrual fluids and for the baby. But in sexual response the vagina is active from birth in cyclic lubrication,[1] and in lubrication resulting from sexual stimulation, as shown by Masters and Johnson.[2] In the male, recent ultrasound pictures of the fetus[3] reveal that even earlier than the twenty-ninth week of gestation, the penis is seen in the rhythmic, cyclic erection that adult males display during sleep. This provides support for the hypothesis that the clitoris in the female fetus may also erect, perhaps with a periodicity coinciding with that of the vaginal lubrication observed postnatally by Langfeldt. Published observation of such periodic, postnatal clitoral erection would complete the analogy with penile erection and serve to signify existence of the female fetal sexual response system.

It is sobering to realize that now while we have facts about pre- and postnatal sexual function, we are in a position reminiscent of Galileo's when he affirmed that the earth revolved around the sun rather than the reverse. It is even more sobering to recall the 200 years it took for the Roman Catholic Church to acknowledge that truth, although, once recognized, understanding of the universe as well as of the solar system developed exponentially. The newly reported facts of fetal and infant sexuality are experiencing surprisingly similar resistance even among physicians. But concern for the welfare of children and adults alike requires careful stock-taking before honoring such objections. My thesis continues to be that the sexual response system merits the understanding, acceptance, conservation, and socialization for developmentally appropriate use that we accord to the other human body systems. What science and society might ultimately agree on as "appropriate use" should then become a matter for broad and careful discussion.

Just as acceptance of Galileo's facts required revision of everyone's perception of the solar system, so now the acceptance of the validity of the sexuality of infants and young children requires us to conceive of and to perceive them with a vision entirely new. This constitutes a paradigm shift of first importance. Clearly they have needs with respect to how we might deal with their eroticism, one of their major human endowments. We shall have to discover the nature of these needs and how, once we take them seriously, we might show them the same enlightened concern that we show their other body systems. For the musculoskeletal system we provide children with age-appropriate outdoor toys and games; for the mind we send them to school and are beginning to provide each class with at least one computer; for the metabolic system we teach children about and provide them with foods vital for their growth and well-being; and for their moral and spiritual value systems we teach them by sharing and living out with them our own religious and moral beliefs.

Seeing our children as beings-in-process of sexual develop-ment would make it possible to discriminate between what is essential for everyone to know about sexuality and what might be more a matter of manners and appropriateness depending on person, place, and time. It will also aid us to recognize, acknowledge, and deal with the often desperate and sometimes even dangerous efforts made by all young children to learn about and deal constructively with the spontaneous and normal sexual functioning that they experience almost daily. Certainly they are completely aware of and enjoy this functioning far earlier than most parents are comfortable with.

To deny the sensual nature of children places them in a precarious position of intensely experiencing something that their own loved adults deny or, even worse, punish. It has been pointed out that to deny something that an intelligent child knows full well exists can have schizoid effects. Blackman's research[4] with four- and five-year-olds demonstrated this, for between the navel and the knees was an area that they seemed convinced was "not me." This is because they had not been accorded possession of it by their parents, who had not even known how to provide correct names for the organs in that important and active area, much less their functions about which most children have been granted only the barest glimmer of knowledge. In a word, we have not learned how to trust the intelligence and rationality of our prepubertal children, and so generations of them perennially arrive at puberty as unprepared for the feelings and urges that will overwhelm them as their parents were.

An excellently designed and conducted study, *Children's Sexual Thinking*, examined the capacity of children from five to fifteen years to think logically, to reason about such sex information as they might have.[5] Of the 854 children interviewed for at least ninety minutes each, the authors found that the North Americans were about two years behind the British and Australian children in this capacity. However, all the English-speaking children were about five years behind the Swedish children, who begin sex education at school when they are eight and who learn, because it is expected of them, how to be thoughtful, practical, and responsible in their sexual attitudes and behavior as well as in their thinking. Sweden is now into the second and third generations of children brought up by parents who themselves had sex education courses in school.

Mothers and fathers need preparation for possible conflicting feelings over sexual reactions in their babies. After birth, the genital responsiveness described earlier was noted by Kinsey[6] to develop to a point where some babies only a few weeks old managed by thigh pressure to produce for themselves reactions closely resembling orgasm. As the months pass, babies explore their own bodies as they do everything within their reach; as their hands develop more and more control, it is normal for them to find their genitals, repeating the pleasurable feelings they experience during this exploration. Parents need to be prepared for the sexual feelings that can sometimes be aroused in themselves when they observe these or other sexual reactions in their babies.

Because all pleasure feels good, a baby cannot discriminate between sources of pleasure as "bad" or "good." In any case, the nerve pathways between brain and genitals which transmit sexual feelings were established during the months before birth. Frowns, scolding, or punishment about sex will only confuse the child, be associated with sex, then lead to fear of the parent who inflicts them. In an awkward social situation, the best thing to do until the baby reaches eighteen months to two years is to smile, even when company is present, pick up the baby and distract its attention. If this doesn't work then, still smiling, gently take the baby out of the room and place him/her in its crib with the diaper off. I ask parents which is more important to them – the opinion of the uninformed or the future well-being of their child? Parents can rejoice in the emerging sexuality of their newborns in the same way they rejoice over the emerging intelligence within the growing body.

Genital pleasure in babies and young children is closely linked to the pleasure derived from skin contact. This is universal to mammals, in all of which we see bonding behavior like licking and grooming between mothers and offspring, and in some apes between older males and the young. With us, bonding generally goes on from birth in gazing, murmuring, kissing, tickling, and stroking. It is a vital part of our human heritage and, in the case of malnourished babies dying from emotional neglect, the attachment and understanding generated even by the touch and stroking of strangers can be life-saving. Old people who have no one to share touching with have been found to brighten and revive interest in life when a pet is acquired with which they can share caring touch. It has also been shown that the lusty, well-cared-about infant almost always masturbates, whereas the infant depressed by lack of love rarely pleasures itself.

Until age two, then, self-pleasuring by the child should not be interfered with, except by gentle introduction to the appropriateness of privacy and the closed door. Thereafter, constant reinforcement of what the family has worked out as appropriate can be continued throughout childhood. The goal is for the child to feel secure in the ownership of its own body, all of whose products and feelings are viewed as good and subject only to the child's growing sense of appropriateness and responsibility about person, place, and time. The child should reach school age with a sense of competence and of being in charge, secure in knowing how to make the decision of who may and may not touch her/his body. The capacity to say "no" and make it stick can be built into the awareness of every child by about three on its emergence from the famous "no" period – if the noes have been listened to by the parents and dealt with intelligently and respectfully.

Conversations about sexual matters can go on between parents and children from earliest times right into and through puberty, in an atmosphere of mutual respect for the privacy of all concerned. Above all, nothing should ever pass from parent to child that is not based on solid truth. "Do you have to be married to have a baby?" "No, you don't. BUT our values for you are. . . . And I hope that when you reach adolescence, you will. . . ." That BUT leads right to where parents can state their values and beliefs loud and clear. When a parent does not have all the facts, he/she should say so and get them, perhaps from some of the many excellent parent-child sex books now available which family members of all ages can have free access to and discuss together. To wait until adolescence is too late; the child will already have gone elsewhere for knowledge that, in too many cases, is inaccurate or downright destructive. It cannot be overemphasized that schools can never replace what parents have failed to do in the previous years, but parents with school-aged children can still provide education for sexuality if they will just face their own shortcomings honestly with their children. Moreover, child psychologists generally agree that schools can back up parental efforts with well-researched and well-presented information. Solnit and Peltz have stated that the best ages for such information-giving lie between seven and twelve when children want to learn about *everything* to take back to their parents for checking.[7] "I'll ask my Mom and Dad, they always tell me the truth," is the greatest compliment any parent could wish for.

Notes

1 T. Langfeldt, "Aspects of Sexual Development, Problems and Therapy in Children", in J. M. Samson (ed.), *Proceedings of the International Symposium on Childhood and Sexuality*, Montreal, Etudes Vivantes, 1980.
2 W. H. Masters and V. Johnson, *Human Sexual Response*, Boston, Little, Brown, 1966.
3 M. S. Calderone, "Fetal Erection and Its Message to Us", *SIECUS Report*, vol. X, no. 5/6, May-July 1983.
4 N. Blackman, "Pleasure and Touching: Their Significance in the Development of the Pre-school Child", in J. M. Samson, op. cit.
5 R. Goldman and J. Goldman, *Children's Sexual Thinking*, Boston and London, Routledge & Kegan Paul, 1982.
6 A. C. Kinsey, W. B. Pomeroy, C. E. Martin, and P. Gebhard, *Sexual Behavior in the Human Female*, Philadelphia, W. B. Saunders, 1953.
7 A. Solnit, "Sexual and Gender Development in the Context of the Family, School, and Society", and M. Peltz, "Sexual and Gender Development in the Latency Years", both in E. K. Oremland and J. D. Oremland (eds), *The Sexual and Gender Development of Young Children: The Role of the Educator*, Cambridge, Ballinger, 1977.

Politically Correct?
Politically Incorrect?

Muriel Dimen

Drink in hand, he leaned against the wall with an air of teasing, self-mocking arrogance, eyes soft from intoxication. His sensual anticipation was all-enveloping. "When we get home, I want to fuck you," he said lovingly. "I'm going to put it in you, and go in and out, in and out, real slow, for a long time." He jerked his hips slightly. "That's how I'll fuck you," he said softly. "And when I'm done, you'll look a lot better. It'll perk things up here," lightly touching her breasts, "and make things smaller here," patting her waist, "and smooth things out here," caressing her hips.

An ancient ache cramped her thoughts and all she could do was laugh. She wished he were taller and looser. Knowing he was sensitive about his miniature body, she consciously fed his vanity, telling him of the lean precision of his proportions, the beauty of his classic face, the grace of his genitals. Indeed, his body awed her, even as his insecurity stimulated in her a luxuriant contempt.

Their love-making was wonderful that night – as always. He did all the work – as always. He was hurt that she was not more grateful.

Which of the following shall we say to the preceding story?

Because men can abuse women in one way or another, women should sleep only with women.

Or, women should educate men not to hurt women.

Or, women should discuss their sexuality in their CR groups in order to understand why they engage in masochistic behavior and get support for not doing it anymore.

Or, if pornography is the theory and rape is the practice, then women should not write stories like the one above, which just encourage rape and are therefcre anti-feminist.

This story, and others like it, bring up the question "What is to be done?" It thereby evokes judgments about politics, sexuality and "politically correct" behavior. We may put five questions to the issue of politically correct/incorrect behavior:

Question 1: How do you define politically correct?

Answer: Politically correct is an idea that emerges from the well-meaning attempt in social movements to bring the unsatisfactory present into line with the utopian future, in fact, to make the "revolution" happen. Although ideas about what is acceptable behavior develop in any political organization, left or right, the express phrase, politically correct, seems to be associated with the left. The phrase is charged, because the left, in its conception of itself, stands for freedom, yet finds itself in a contradictory situation: in order to realize its goal, it finds itself telling people how to behave and therefore interfering with their freedom.

Politically correct behavior, including invisible language and ideas as well as observable action, is that which adheres to a movement's morality and hastens its goals. The idea of politically correct grows naturally from moral judgments (which any political ideology or philosophy contains) that deem certain aspects of the present way of living bad. It is this moral evaluation that fuels visions of better ways of living and energizes attempts to realize them. In the light of the resulting politico-moral principles, certain behaviors and attitudes can come to seem not only "bad," because they are harmful to society or to people, but "wrong," because they hinder social transformation.

Question 2: What is politically correct?

Answer. I don't know: anything, including seeming opposites, can be correct in different groups, movements, or societies. The Talmud requires intercourse; the Shakers prohibited sexual activity; Marx, Engels and Freud celebrated (but did not practice) monogamy; Bohemianism advocates promiscuity and multiple sexualities, but disdains fidelity.

The ideology of political correctness emerges in all sorts of movements, applying to behavior, social institutions, and systems of thought and value. For example, various socialist and utopian movements have identified the nuclear family as a breeding ground for a socially destructive individualism, and propose communal living because it would promote a collectivist spirit. At various periods in Western history, then, social movements have instituted communes as a desirable first step in creating the good society they envisioned for the future. In the 1960s (which spilled into the 1970s), certain sectors of the left found the nuclear family and its bedrock, monogamous heterosexual marriage, to be both bad and wrong, i.e., politically incorrect, while communes and non-monogamy (for which no positive term ever developed) came to seem good and right, that is, "left," in other words, politically correct.

The appearance of political correctness in feminism creates a contradiction. One of feminism's tenets is an individualism (sometimes bourgeois, sometimes anarchistic) that proclaims self-determination for women, translating into "every woman for herself." However, feminism is also a mass movement based on collective struggles against the state in such areas as reproductive rights and the workplace. Such a political movement can be successful only if it is founded on shared moral and political principles. In some sense, it is this movement that constitutes the social context which makes feminism's individualistic principles possible. It is not feasible, however, for both these tendencies, one towards the individual, the other towards the social web, to be simultaneous guides to politically correct behavior.

Feminists have made judgments about political correctness particularly in the area of sexual behavior. This is because of the special cultural tension between sexuality and feminism: desire, of which sexuality is one very privileged instance, pushes and pulls at all people. Yet because it is in the domain of the subjective, desire tends to be associated with things female in the patriarchy of the twentieth-century nation-state where women, subjectivity, and sexuality share the same symbolic space. This shared symbolic space creates a second contradiction for feminists. On the one hand, since women have been traditionally defined as sex objects, feminism demands that society no longer focus on their erotic attributes, which, in turn, feminism downplays. In this way it becomes politically correct not to engage in any stereotypically feminine behavior, such as putting on make-up, wearing high heels, shaving legs and arms, or coming on to men. On the other hand, because women have been traditionally defined as being uninterested in sex, they have been deprived of pleasure and a sense of autonomous at-one-ness, both of which are necessary to self-esteem. Feminism therefore demands sexual freedom for women. In this way it becomes politically correct for women to be sexual explorers, visiting, if not settling down in, homosexuality or polysexuality; experimenting with cock-sucking or anal intercourse or tantric sex; trying out orgies or, perhaps, even celibacy. In consequence, these judgments about the correct path are as contradictory as the situation which gave rise to the feminist critique in the first place.

Question 3: Why do people want to say and do politically correct things?

Answer: Politically correct ideology and behavior are attractive, because they proceed from acute and visionary perceptions of political oppression. If people create visions of what is good, it seems sensible and self-respectful to try to live them out. Politically correct ideology and behavior attempt to escape the manifestly harmful, and to avoid things that damage, even if they feel good. In addition to these rational reasons, there are irrational forces which motivate political correctness, springing, for example, from the fear of separateness that makes conformity compelling. Conformism, present in any social group, can have an important role in making members of out-groups feel self-righteously stronger.

Question 4: What is good about politically correct ideology and behavior?

Answer. It is empowering; by psychological and ideological means, it creates the space for people to organize politically. It becomes a basis for organization and communication between people so that political structure may thrive. It also disrupts the identification with the aggressor, dispelling an individual and collective sense of victimization and providing a shared vision that guides behavior. Finally, it taps into a deeply rooted wish to belong to a collectivity in which what one desires to be is also moral to be.

Question 5: What is bad about politically correct ideology and behavior?

Answer: When the radical becomes correct, it becomes conservative. The politically correct comes to resemble what it tries to change. For it plays on the seductiveness of accustomed ways of living, the attractiveness of orthodoxy. Its social armoring can lead the person away from self-knowing authenticity and the group towards totalitarian control. It makes a misleadingly clean cut between personal experience and old, but still powerful, social practices, and draws a misleadingly neat circle around experience and a new set of supposedly completely acceptable practices.

The application of politically correct ideology and behavior to sexuality therefore founders on a double contradiction, the first in the relation between person and society, and the second in the relation between conscious and unconscious forces. The discovery/creation of sexual pleasure is very much an individual journey, even as your craft pushes off from received notions of gender, and is sped on or becalmed by concurrently developing notions of what is possible and permissible. No matter how carefully charted by conscious intentionality, the journey's course is determined finally by a complex mix of conscious and unconscious, rational and irrational currents that represent a swirling together of personal desire and cultural force.

Her tongue slid along the soft involuted folds of her labia. Her tongue slid along the soft involuted folds of her labia. She licked her clitoris; she licked her clitoris. They came together, not knowing who was who.

"Your name came up," she said, later, "but I told them I didn't want you in the group." "Why not?" she asked. "Because I want to keep my personal life and my public life clearly differentiated."

Sexuality is simultaneously highly individualized and highly socially constructed, subject to will and at the mercy of compulsion. Erotic sensation, like any feeling, is experienced personally. It is as idiosyncratic as any aspect of character, perhaps seeming even more so because spoken language, the means of adult communication, is so poor a vehicle for sharing bodily experience and its meaning. Yet sexuality, like character, is socially contextualized. The overt rules that shape sexual possibility, form, and feeling are common knowledge, but they are made more compelling by almost invisible, nearly insensible politico-moral judgments. For example, the incest prohibition is familiar enough, yet it is less commonly recognized that the heterosexual, Oedipal taboo presumes a prior, unspoken one on homosexuality.

The 1960s produced a critique of the privatization of sexual experience, which our society portrayed as both unique and unmentionable. Privatization isolated people from each other, leaving them to feel alone in the confusion that arose in the space between what they wanted and what they were supposed to want. Privatization prevented change, it was thought, because it encouraged people to act individually on what seemed to be their own idiosyncratic, personal problems originating in specific family histories. The critique examined the social construction of personal sexuality, and envisioned one more open, including openness to multiple desires in oneself and to others' experimentation, open public discussions of sexuality, and open relationships (non-monogamy, swapping, group sex).

For sexuality is by its nature an experience that benefits from a stance that anything goes, that any avenue may (but not "must") be explored. Erotic pleasure mushrooms when there are no musts. But this accessibility means that sexual experience can be affected by anything. Sexual intimacy is too generous an experience to exclude anything, including the forces of the unconscious and the forces of hierarchy. When you get into bed with someone, you bring all of you: your past, remembered or forgotten; your present, including parts of it which you think your rational mind can keep out; your hopes for the future. Sexual intimacy is therefore particularly resistant to rules of political correctness, or, rather, when it succumbs to rules, passion disappears. Its very non-rationality allows the politically incorrect to enter.

The sexual explorations of the 1960s ventured often into homosexual desires. Lesbianism, spurred on by the radical and feminist critiques of sexuality, emerged as a public, empowering, and passionate option for many, despite overt and covert homophobia in major branches of the bourgeois women's movement. The judgment that patriarchy contaminates hetero-sexual relations suggested that homosexuality was the safest and most enhancing form of erotic experience (a form that, for the previous generation, represented the most frightening, yet most intriguing, variety of bad and wrong sexuality). Indeed, by contrast with the pain and anger infusing most straight relation-ships, lesbian ones came to seem idyllic, promising the realization of honesty, equality, mutuality, and love, in the midst of a dishonest, disloyal, hierarchical, and hate-filled culture of death. To have believed this promise, however, that any relationship could be Edenic in a hellish culture, was to have forgotten what the 1960s said: the personal is political. Since social rules, structure, and language shape not only social interaction but personal experience, which accumulates as people mature, rational conscious will .nay not be their best adversary. What may be required as an effective adversary is the force of irrational passion, sexual and otherwise, unearthed from the repression/oppression of past and present.

She is 8. Her father, 41, and her brother, 5, are about to take a shower together. "Me, too," she cries, eager to see her father's genitals. "No, no, dear, little girls don't take showers with their fathers," says her mother, 40. Since when? she wonders. She knows what she wants. They know too. Do they know that she knows that they know that she knows?

In seventh grade, if you wear green on Thursday, they call you a dyke. If you wear a black sweater any day, they call you a whore. Somehow, she forgets and wears green on Thursdays and black sweaters when she likes. At a party in a suburban basement rec-room, she finds herself suddenly alone, the only girl in the room, when the lights go out and all the boys jump her and feel her up everywhere you can imagine. The girls giggle in the laundryroom.

A girl from another crowd tells her she looks nice in her black sweater. They become friends, sort of. She sleeps over at her friend's house one night. They bake chocolate chip cookies and listen to opera. Later her friend invites her into her bed to do what her friend's crowd has been doing for a while. She feels nothing, is frightened, and goes back to her own bed.

She starts kissing boys on the mouth at 11 and likes it a lot. She doesn't pet above the waist with boys until 15; she doesn't like it but does it anyway to be grown up. She won't pet below the waist until 17; then she doesn't want to admit that she likes the orgasms. She starts masturbating at 18. At 23 she has intercourse for the first time; she likes the fact that she's doing it; it takes her 15 years to like doing it.

e crisis of self vs society explodes in sexual experience.
xual arrangments provide an important set of terms by which
we negotiate, as we mature, the relation between who we are and
want to be, and who we are told and allowed to be. The
negotiation is complex and long, indeed unending, because
sexuality is multi-faceted and changes with age. Notions of
political correctness therefore constitute psychological foot-
binding.

As a married woman, she is monogamous and heterosexual for 15
years.
   She and a woman friend have a seemingly endless series of
seemingly emergency discussions about whether the two of them
should sleep together.
   She keeps wondering why she is so scared to have an affair.
   She has a one-night stand with a man and feels liberated.
   Her marriage ends.
   She becomes promiscuous.
   She imagines that every affair will end in marriage and
children.
   She loves men even when they hurt her.
   "I love to fuck with you," she says to her. "We don't call it
fucking, my dear," the other one answers.
   Gender should not exist and everyone should sleep with
everyone and everything.
   Commitment is possible and necessary.

Erotic experience is extraordinary, lying somewhere between
dream and daily life. Although sex is not amenable to mechanistic
tinkering, it is not as safely private as dream (which, fortunately,
cannot be controlled by political fiat). When you try to change
passion piece by piece, it dissipates. Sexuality therefore differs
from those domains, for example, politics or housework, in which
it may make sense to pull behavior into line with ideology. Part of
what makes sex tick is its very irrationality. It brings the crazy
passions of infancy into adult experience, a welcome relief, much
like that brought by dreams from ordinary, rational, waking
control.
   Sexuality lies between things; it borders psyche and society,
culture and nature, conscious and unconscious, self and other. It
is intrinsically ambiguous. Ambiguity confers on sexuality an
inherent novelty, creativity, discovery, and these give it its
excitement, its pleasure, its fearsomeness. Sexual experience
entails loss of self-other boundaries, the endless opening of doors
to more unknown inner spaces, confusions about what to do next,
or who the other person is, or what part of the body is being

touched, or what part of the body is doing the touching, or where one person begins and the other ends. This is sometimes pleasurable, sometimes painful, always unsettling.

Ambiguity makes sex difficult to deal with. Take, for example, part and whole relations with which we play in sex, sometimes being or relating to a part – a breast, penis, buttock – sometimes being or relating to wholeness. Parts and wholes come in bodies and in social roles. Infants have no conception of another human as a whole being. Mother, for example, is solely the nurturer, not the scientist or secretary or dreamer or lover she may be to the adults whom she knows. Were an adult to treat her in terms of only one part, it would be cruel, thoughtless. Adulthood, in our society, ideally entails seeing the other's multi-dimensionality. Adulthood also includes being receptive to one's own multi-dimensionality which paradoxically includes the parts left from infancy, such as the interest in and the ability to relate to parts. Therefore could not adulthood include in some enriched way this lost aspect of the self?

Women are taught to relate to sexuality as whole beings in a society that celebrates parts, for example, measuring women by their breasts and men by their penises. "Women are so nice," my analyst once observed, "they never say, 'You call *that* a penis?'" Whereas men can and do ask for better breasts, hips, thighs. Now, this expectation of thoughtful, feminine wholism may have hampered women's exploration of their own and others' parts, as well as their feelings about them. To the degree that this expectation becomes politically correct for feminists, it may limit each woman's exploration of herself.

More: perhaps the ability to make part-objects of others, to take the part for the whole, can be helpful in coming to know and manage the world. For example, my friend Peggy says that the best way to get rid of a flasher is to say, "Oh, that looks just like a penis, only smaller."

Still more: perhaps this ability can be fun. For example, what does it feel like to make part-objects of men? Here is a preliminary classification from years of crotch-watching:

1 A slight bulge just to one side of and two-thirds of the way down the the fly

2 A long, skinny cylinder slanting across the fly almost to the other thigh

3 A loose dangle way down the inner thigh

4 A horizontal ridge straight across the bottom of the fly

5 A faded spot right next to the bottom of the fly

6 A little bump centered on a little hump

7 A big bump centered on a big hump

8 Gay fourth button bulge

9 Tight with no bulge at all

10 Preppy-loose, denying everything

11 Packed so full, with so little differentiation, you wonder if it's real

12 A neat round wet spot which dries quickly after he returns from the bathroom

13 Huge balls stretching the pants on the thigh; you can see this as he sits with his legs spread on the subway.

Here are some feelings I had watching these crotches: Curiosity: what exactly lay beneath the blue denim, the chinos, the wool? Excitement: what might be the relation between surface, contents, and performance? Empathic discomfort: do they feel as ambivalent about being observed as we do? Shame: you are not supposed to poke into people's private business.

The whole is greater than the sum of the parts. But the more we know of the parts, the more we know of the whole. The clitoral orgasm became public knowledge in 1969 because feminism made it so. But then the clitoral orgasm became the only politically correct orgasm to have, consequently foreshortening exploration and, at best, confusing, at worst, marginalizing, those who had a different experience. Now the news of the G-spot makes it seem like there is some truth to reports of the vaginal orgasm after all.

Within the movement, it is easy for the socially correct – monogamy or nuclear families or vaginal orgasms – to be denounced as politically incorrect; for the socially incorrect – promiscuity or polysexuality or clitoral orgasms – to become politically correct; and for the once-correct, now-incorrect to disappear from politically correct history. To take another example: the conference offered no workshops on sex in a long-term relationship, perhaps suggesting its political incorrectness. Long-term monogamous relationships are sometimes taken as models of wholeness, which they most assuredly are not. But an awful lot of people live in them even while wanting out, and an awful lot of people who are out want in, even when they know better.

Indeed, sexual ambiguity may be responsible for the sexual boredom that sometimes emerges in long-term relationships. This boredom is born of the fright we feel when we reach the end of the routine pathways to intimacy, and the unknown looms before us. In thus confronting the problem of creation and of the new, we become anxious and then, to calm ourselves, bored. It is hard for us to go off into the emotional wilds with another person, because we are socially and psychologically stunted in ways, and due to forces, too complex to go into here. However, given that it is difficult to connect with anyone at all, it is not unreasonable that, rather than tolerate the uncertain provocation of sharing ever more intense inner experience with another person we seek the seductive comfort of the monogamous routine, or the familiar excitement of one-night stands.

Where does this leave us? In an ambiguous, uncertain spot. The idea of political correctness masquerades as eternal truth which we would all like to believe is possible, because it makes us feel much more secure. But everything changes – except the existence of contradictions. With social transformation come new ones. I do not believe that an eternally true consciousness of what is politically correct in sexuality, or in anything, is possible. Or, to say the same thing in other words, the road to false consciousness, no matter how you wish to define it, is paved with politically correct intentions.

Sexuality is not the route to revolution. But sexuality is a prime shaper of desire, and constraint of desire leads directly to self-betrayal and social bad faith. We suffer not from too much desire, but from too little. One reason we fail to rebel, or have incomplete revolutions, is because our hopes have been truncated, particularly by sexism whose core is sexual oppression. Sexual oppression resembles other kinds of domination, like class or race. Yet it is different, because it goes for the jugular of all social relatedness and psychological integration – desire.

We wish, we want, we are in a state of longing – this is the experience of desire, the unconscious fount of activity, creativity, and subjectivity. It is not confined to the sexual passion that arises from and speeds it. Born in the space between wish and possible satisfaction, desire is potentiated by social experience, which also gives it form. Our infant souls absorb, through our skins, its social shapes that cradling adult hands transmit. It may mean power or weakness, purity or evil, hope or despair; we learn to want to want, or not to want.

But desire always rushes beyond its psychocultural channels. It is what moves us, in our personal uniqueness, toward both intimacy and collectivity, and back to self, and again toward society. Since sexuality is the sculptor of desire, since gender organizes sexuality and shapes part of desire into the self, since gender as we know it is born of sexual oppression, then feminism, for me, must be a struggle for sexual emancipation. For we must make sure that we desire all we can so that we will be able to create, and therefore get, all we desire.

Note

Some of the material contained in this paper will receive fuller treatment in the author's forthcoming *Sexual Contradictions*, New York, Macmillan.

Suggested Reading

Kathy Acker, *Kathy Goes to Haiti*, Toronto, Rumour, 1978.

John Berger, *G.*, New York, Pantheon, 1972.

Angela Carter, *The Bloody Chamber*, Harmondsworth, Penguin, 1981.

Janine Chasseguet-Smirgel (ed.), *Female Sexuality*, Ann Arbor, University of Michigan Press, 1970.

Colette, *Earthly Paradise*, New York, Farrar Strauss, 1966.

Muriel Dimen, "Notes Toward the Reconstruction of Sexuality", *Social Text*, vol. 6, 1982, pp. 22-31.

Deirdre English, Amber Hollibaugh, and Gayle Rubin, "Talking Sex", *Socialist Review*, vol. 58, 1981, pp. 43-62.

Susan Griffin, *Women and Nature*, New York, Harper & Row, 1980.

Heresies, *The Sex Issue #12*, vol. 3, no. 4, 1981.

 Masud Khan, *Alienation in Perversions*, New York, International Universities Press, 1979.

Joel Kovel, *The Age of Desire*, New York, Pantheon, 1981.

Gayle Rubin, "The Traffic in Women: Notes on the 'Political Economy' of Sex", in Rayna Reiter (ed.), *Toward an Anthropology of Women*, New York, Monthly Review Press, 1975, pp. 157-210.

Robert Stoller, *Sexual Excitement*, New York, Simon & Schuster/ Touchstone, 1979.

Cultural and Historical Influences on Sexuality in Hispanic/Latin Women: Implications for Psychotherapy

Oliva M. Espín

The purpose of this paper is to present some ideas on the development of sexuality in Hispanic women and their implications for a psychotherapeutic relationship. This paper will examine four major factors which affect the development of sexuality in Latin women in the United States: historical influences, immigration, language, and the psychological effects of oppression.

Despite shared features of history and culture, attitudes towards sex-roles are extremely diverse among Hispanic women. For instance, some Latin women are willing to endorse "modern" and "liberated" sex-roles concerning education and employment, while maintaining very "traditional," "conservative" positions concerning sexual behaviors or personal relationships. Others are traditional in all respects and still others reject all traditional beliefs concerning the roles of women. Consequently, it is very difficult to discuss the sexuality or sexual behavior of Latin women without the danger of making some sweeping generalizations. The experiental and emotional distance between an immigrant worker of peasant extraction who barely knows how to write her name in Spanish and a "Latin princess" who comes to the United States to study at a private educational institution with all expenses paid by her parents is enormous. If these two women met each other, they probably would not acknowledge any commonalities between them. And yet, as their therapist, I can recognize a common thread and a historical background to their lives, a thread shared with daughters of immigrants born and raised in the streets of New York and in the rural areas of the Southwest.

What are the commonalities among Hispanic women in the United States that manifest themselves in spite of the enormous differences among them? *Historical influences* have left their mark in cultural processes and in class and race differentiation.

149

Other commonalities have to do with the experience of separation implied in *immigration*; with the cognitive and affective effects of sharing a common *language*; and with the experience of *oppression*.

The enormous differences between the Spanish and British conquest of Latin America and North America set these two cultures apart.[1] On the one hand, the British came with their families, escaping persecution; North America became a dumping ground for religious dissidents. The Puritans and many of those who followed turned away from England with no desire to return to the homeland, seeking a place where they could remain separated and independent from all those who were different or held different beliefs. The Spaniards, on the other hand, came to America as a male army for the specific purpose of conquering new land for their king. They landed anticipating territory full of gold, silver, and abundance where land was fertile all year long. These resources, plus the centralization of power already achieved by the native Indian empires, provided an environment profoundly different from that encountered by the Pilgrims.

Most "conquistadores" were men without fortune, nobility, or other resources. The majority of them did not come with their wives or with any female relatives; marrying women of Spanish descent was practically impossible. They initially intended to return to Spain full of honors and riches in order to marry Spanish women of a higher class. Difficult communications and the hardships of an enterprise that did not produce "gold at first sight" as they had expected delayed their return to Spain indefinitely. Many of them never returned and, instead, stayed in the Americas for the rest of their lives.

Thus, the conquerors' temporary sexual use of Indian women developed into more enduring relationships. They set up homes with the native women who were originally taken only as concubines. These relationships – some temporary, some stable – created the Mestizo population of Latin America. In spite of their known cruelties, many of the Spanish conquerors were willing to legally marry Indian or black women and to recognize, support, and pass their inheritance on to their children by those marriages. A similar behavior would have been unthinkable not only to the Puritans, but to most white gentlemen in the United States to this day. It is well known that even Thomas Jefferson had children by a black woman. However, those children were never called Jefferson and that slave woman was never freed by him.

While Calvinist theology, with its emphasis on predestination, encouraged the separation of the races in North America, the Spanish Catholic clergy battled in Europe and America for the human rights of the Amerindians, following Catholic theological

tenets which give the right to salvation to anyone who is baptized
and fulfills appropriate duties as a Christian. Once the Indians
were declared to be human by the pope, they had the right to be
Catholic and, thus, children of God.[2]

The Catholic church's proclamation of the importance of
virginity for all women, regardless of their race or social status,
became a challenge to a social system that otherwise could have
been even more oppressive to non-white women. By emphasizing
that all women, regardless of race and social class, hold the duty
and the right to remain virgins until marriage, and that all men
were responsible to women whose honor they had "stained," the
church discouraged consensual union and illegitimacy.[3] However, by upholding the standard of virginity as the proof of a
woman's honorability, the church, and later the culture in general,
further lowered the status of women who cannot or will not
maintain virginity. This also fostered the perspective that once an
unmarried woman is not a virgin, she is automatically promiscuous. These standards fell in a disproportionately harsh way
on native and Mestizo women, who were less likely to be virgins
because of the social and economic conditions in which they
lived.

Historical circumstances combined to shape gender and race
relations in Latin America in a very distinctive way. This is not to
say that racial inequality or prejudice do not exist in Latin
America, but that it differs from the forms found in North
America. There is a fluidity in racial relationships among Latins
that is difficult to understand in the United States. In Latin
America, social status is affected more profoundly by factors
other than race. Social class and income prevail over color.[4]
Different shades of color among members of the same family are
not denied. The number of political figures and upper-class Latin
Americans who are "non-white" by North American standards
attests to the difference in perspective. On the other hand,
European ancestry and "whiteness" are highly respected. "Color"
makes doors harder to open. People of color are overrepre-
sented in the lower socio-economic classes, and many a
descendant of an interracial marriage would carefully avoid such
a marriage now. The non-white woman may still be seen as not
deserving the same respect as the white woman. And, if a white
man fathers her children, she may not find the same protection as
her white counterpart. Moreover, precisely because many of the
conqueror's wives were not white, the lower status of all women
was further compounded by racial factors.

Trends created centuries ago in the relationships between men
and women of different races, cultures and political status persist
today in Hispanic cultures. Historical influences have been

modified, amplified to give a certain character and tone to the lives of Hispanic women. In addition to their shared cultural, historical and religious heritage described above, Hispanic women living in the United States today share many characteristics as a function of immigration, language, and the shared experience of oppression.

Although some Hispanic women are not immigrants, many of them come from immigrant families. A discussion of the psychological implications of *immigration* is relevant even if not applicable to all Hispanic women. Immigration or any other form of separation from cultural roots involves a process of grieving. Women seem to be affected by this process in a manner that is different from that of men. Successful adaptation after immigration involves resolution of feelings of loss, the development of decision-making skills, ego strength and the ability to tolerate ambiguities, including sex-role ambiguities. Factors pertaining to the psychological make-up of the individual woman as well as specifics of the home culture and class interplay in unique ways with the characteristics of the host culture. Newly-encountered patterns of sex-roles combine with greater access to paid employment for women and may create an imbalance in the traditional power structure of the family.

One of the most prevalent myths encountered by immigrant Hispanic women is that all American women are very free with sex. For the parents and the young women alike, "to become Americanized" is equated with becoming sexually promiscuous. Thus, in some cases, sexuality may become the focus of the parents' fears and the girl's desires during the acculturation process.

Language is another important factor in the experience of Hispanic women. To discuss the affective and cognitive implications of bilingualism and language use will take us beyond the scope of this paper. However, it is important to keep in mind that even for those Hispanic women who are fluent in English, Spanish may remain as the language of emotions because it was usually the first language heard and learned and thus it is full of deep affective meaning.[5]

The preference of one language over another, or the shift from one language to another might be an indication of more subtle processes than even the choice of words.[6] For example, in a recent study of Cuban women in Miami,[7] fluency in English appears as the single most important determinant of attitudes towards the role of women in society. Shifts between languages and the preference for one language or the other may be a means to achieve either distancing or intimacy. When the topic at hand is sexuality, the second language might be an effective tool to express what one does not dare to verbalize in the first language. Conversely, certain emotions and experiences will never be addressed appropriately unless they are discussed in the first language.[8] "The emotional significance of a specific word for a particular individual generally depends on the individual personal values and his [sic] developmental history."[9]

The emotional arousal evoked by saying taboo words decreases when they are pronounced in a foreign language.[10] Presumably, erotic language is experienced differently when uttered or heard in either English or Spanish.

The condition of *oppression* under which most Hispanics live in the United States creates certain psychological effects for both men and women, although Latin women, oppressed both as women and as Hispanics, suffer from physical and psychological consequences of oppression in a profound way. The conditions of oppression originating in the economic, political and social structures of the world become psychological as the effects of these external circumstances become internalized.[11] The external oppression of Hispanic women is expressed in political, educational, economic and social discrimination. Psychologically, the oppression of Hispanic women develops through internalized attitudes that designate women as inferior to men, including Hispanic men, while designating all Hispanics as inferior to the white mainstream of North American society. Oppressive beliefs that affect all women and all Hispanics influence the lives and the sexuality of Hispanic women.

There are specific forms in which the psychology of oppression affects women from all ethnic minority groups. One involves the importance placed on physical beauty for women, and, particularly, on standards of beauty inappropriate for non-white women. Women, regardless of ethnic group, are taught to derive their primary validation from their looks and physical attractiveness. The inability of most non-white women to achieve prescribed standards of beauty may be devastating for self-esteem.

Another psychological effect of oppression for Hispanic women is to further increase their subordination to men. As a reaction towards the oppression suffered by minority men in the larger society, minority women may subordinate their needs even further to those of men. Women and children may be suitable recipients for the displaced anger of an oppressed man. Violence takes many forms: incest, rape, wife-beating. Violence against women is produced and sustained by societal messages about women. The prevalent virgin/whore dichotomy in images of women fosters and condones the violence. It is not unusual to hear supposedly "enlightened" persons defending the violent behavior of men in oppressed groups on the grounds that their only outlet is to get drunk and beat their wives. Even if the displacement can be understood in the case of each individual, to accept and justify it is to condone injustice and another form of violence against women under the guise of understanding.

In addition, women from oppressed groups may be seen as an "easy prey" for white men or as "sexier" than their white counterparts. Their sexual behavior is supposed to be freer and less restrained when, in fact, the opposite might be true. On the other hand, a young woman's sexuality might be the only asset she has in her efforts to break away from oppressive conditions.

Contemporary sexuality and the Hispanic woman

If the role of women is currently beset with contradictions in the mainstream of American society,[12] this is probably still more true for women in Hispanic groups. The honor of Latin families is strongly tied to the sexual purity of women. And the concept of honor and dignity is one of the essential distinctive marks of Hispanic culture. For example, classical Hispanic literature gives us a clue to the importance attributed to honor and to female sexual purity in the culture. La Celestina, the protagonist of an early Spanish medieval novel, illustrates the value attached to virginity and its preservation. Celestina was an old woman who earned her living in two ways: by putting young men in touch with young maidens so they could have the sexual contact that parents would never allow, and by "sewing up" ex-virgins, so that they would be considered virgins at marriage. Celestina thus made her living out of making and unmaking virgins. The fact that she ends by being punished with death further emphasizes the gravity of what she does. In the words of a famous Spanish playwright of the seventeenth century, "al Rey la hacienda y la vida se han de dar, mas no el honor; porque el honor es patrimonio del alma y el alma solo es de Dios."[13] This quotation translates literally, "To the king you give money and life, but not your honor, because honor is part of the soul, and your soul belongs only to God."

Different penalties and sanctions for the violation of cultural norms related to female sexuality are very much associated with social class. The upper classes or those seeking an improved social status tend to be more rigid about sexuality. This of course is related to the transmission of property. In the upper classes, a man needs to know that his children are in fact his before they inherit his property. The only guarantee of his paternity is that his wife does not have sexual contact with any other man. Virginity is tremendously important in that context. However, even when property is not an issue, the only thing left to a family may be the honor of its women and as such it may be guarded jealously by both males and females. Although Hispanics in the twentieth century may not hold the same strict values – and many of them certainly cannot afford the luxury to do so – women's sexual behavior is still the expression of the family's honor. The tradition of maintaining virginity until marriage that had been emphasized among women continues to be a cultural imperative. The Virgin Mary – who was a virgin and a mother, but never a sexual being – is presented as an important role model for all Hispanic women, although Hispanic unwed mothers, who have clearly overstepped the boundaries of culturally-prescribed virginity for women, usually are accepted by their families. Married women or those living in common-law marriages are supposed to accept a double standard for sexual behavior, by which their husbands may have affairs with other women, while they themselves are expected to remain faithful to one man all of their lives. However, it is not uncommon for a Hispanic woman to have the power to decide whether or not a man is going to live with her, and she may also choose to put him out if he drinks too much or is not a good provider.[14]

In fact, Latin women experience a unique combination of power and powerlessness which is characteristic of the culture. The idea that personal problems are best discussed with women is very much part of the Hispanic culture. Women in Hispanic neighborhoods and families tend to rely on other women for their important personal and practical needs. There is a widespread belief among Latin women of all social classes that most men are undependable and are not to be trusted. At the same time, many of these women will put up with a man's abuses because having a man around is an important source of a woman's sense of self-worth. Middle-aged and elderly Hispanic women retain important roles in their families even after their sons and daughters are married. Grandmothers are ever present and highly vocal in family affairs. Older women have much more status and power than their white American counterparts, who at this age may be suffering from depression due to what has been called the "empty-nest syndrome." Many Hispanic women are providers of mental health services (which sometimes include advice about sexual problems) in an unofficial way as "curanderas," "espiritistas," or "santeras," for those people who believe in these alternative approaches to health care.[15] Some of these women play a powerful role in their communities, thanks to their reputation for being able to heal mind and body.

However, at the same time that Latin women have the opportunity to exercise their power in the areas mentioned above, they also receive constant cultural messages that they should be submissive and subservient to males in order to be seen as "good women." To suffer and be a martyr is also a characteristic of a "good woman." This emphasis on self-renunciation, combined with the importance given to sexual purity for women, has a direct bearing on the development of sexuality in Latin women. To enjoy sexual pleasure, even in marriage, may indicate lack of virtue. To shun sexual pleasure and to regard sexual behavior exclusively as an unwelcome obligation toward her husband and a necessary evil in order to have children may be seen as a manifestation of virtue. In fact, some women even express pride at their own lack of sexual pleasure or desire. Their negative attitudes toward sex are frequently reinforced by the inconsiderate behavior and demands of men.

Body image and related issues are deeply connected with sexuality for all women. Even when body-related problems may not have direct implications for sexuality, the body remains for women the main vehicle for expressing their needs. The high incidence of somatic complaints presented by low-income Hispanic women in psychotherapy might be a consequence of the emphasis on "martyrdom" and self-sacrifice, or it might be a somatic expression of needs and anxieties. More directly related to sexuality are issues of birth control, pregnancy, abortion, menopause, hysterectomy and other gynecological problems. Many of these have traditionally been discussed among women only. To be brought to the attention of a male doctor may be enormously embarrassing and distressing for some of these women. Younger Hispanic women may find themselves challenging traditional sexual mores while struggling with their own conflicts about beauty and their own embarrassment about visiting male doctors.

One of the most common and pervasive stereotypes held about Hispanics is the image of the "macho" man – an image which generally conjures up the rough, tough, swaggering men who are abusive and oppressive towards women, who in turn are seen as being exclusively submissive and long-suffering.[16]

Some authors[17] recognize that "machismo" – which is nothing but the Hispanic version of the myth of male superiority supported by most cultures – is still in existence in the Latin culture, especially among those individuals who subscribe more strongly to traditional Hispanic values. Following this tradition, Latin females are expected to be subordinated to males and to the family. Males are expected to show their manhood by behaving in a strong fashion, by demonstrating sexual prowess and by asserting their authority over women. In many cases, these traditional values may not be enacted behaviorally, but are still supported as valued assumptions concerning male and female "good" behavior. According to Aramoni,[18] himself a Mexican psychologist, "machismo" may be a reaction of Latin males to a series of social conditions, including the effort to exercise control over their ever-present, powerfully demanding, and suffering mothers and to identify with their absent fathers. Adult males continue to respect and revere their mothers, even when they may not show much respect for their wives or other women. As adolescents they may have protected their mothers from fathers' abuse or indifference. As adults they accord their mothers a respect that no other woman deserves, thus following their fathers' steps. The mother herself teaches her sons to be dominant and independent in relations with other women. Other psychological and social factors may be influential in the development of "machismo." It is important to remember that not all Latin males exhibit the negative behaviors implied in the "macho" stereotype, and that even when certain individuals do, these behaviors might be a reaction to oppressive social conditions by which Hispanic men too are victimized.

Sexually, "machismo" is expressed through an emphasis on multiple, uncommitted sexual contacts which start in adolescence. In a study of adolescent rituals in Latin America, Espín[19] found that many males celebrated their adolescence by visiting prostitutes. The money to pay for this sexual initiation was usually provided by fathers, uncles or older brothers. Adolescent females, on the other hand, were offered coming-out parties, the rituals of which emphasize their virginal qualities. Somehow, a man is more "macho" if he manages to have sexual relations with a virgin; thus, fathers and brothers watch over young women for fear that other men may make them their sexual prey. These same men, however, will not hesitate to take advantage of the young women in other families. Women, in turn, are seen as capable of surrendering to men's advances, without much awareness of their own decisions on the matter. "Good women" should always say no to a sexual advance. Those who say yes are automatically assumed to be less virtuous by everyone, including the same man with whom they consent to have sex.

Needless to say, sexual understanding and communication between the sexes is practically rendered impossible by these attitudes generated by "machismo." However, not all Hispanics subscribe to this perspective and some reject it outright. In a review of the literature on studies of decision-making patterns in Mexican and Chicano families the authors concluded that "Hispanic males may behave differently from non-Hispanic men in their family and marital lives, but not in the inappropriate fashion suggested by the myth with its strong connotations of social deviance."[20] This article reviews only research on the decision-making process in married couples and, thus, other aspects of male-female relationships in the Hispanic culture are not discussed.

In the context of culturally appropriate sex-roles, mothers train their daughters to remain virgins at all cost, to cater to men's sexual needs and to play "little wives" to their fathers and brothers from a very early age. If a mother is sick or working outside the home and there are no adult females around, the oldest daughter, no matter how young, will be in charge of caring not only for the younger siblings, but also for the father, who would continue to expect his meals to be cooked and his clothes to be washed.

Training for appropriate heterosexuality, however, is not always assimilated by all Latin women. A seldom-mentioned fact is that, as in all cultures, there are lesbians among Hispanic women. Although emotional and physical closeness among women is encouraged by the culture, overt acknowledgment of lesbianism is even more restricted than in mainstream American society. In a study about lesbians in the Puerto Rican community, Hidalgo and Hidalgo-Christensen found that "rejection of homosexuals appears to be the dominant attitude in the Puerto Rican community."[21] Although this attitude may not seem different from that of the dominant culture, there are some important differences experienced by Latin lesbian women which are directly related to Hispanic cultural patterns. Frequent contact and a strong interdependence among family members, even in adulthood, are essential features of Hispanic family life. Leading a double life becomes more of a strain in this context. "Coming out" may jeopardize not only these strong family ties, but also the possibility of serving the Hispanic community in which the talents of all members are such an important asset. Because most lesbian women are single and self-supporting, and not encumbered by the demands of husbands and children, it can be assumed that the professional experience and educational level of Hispanic lesbians will tend to be relatively high. If this is true, professional experience and education will frequently place Hispanic lesbian women in positions of leadership or advocacy in their community. Their status and prestige, and, thus, the ability to serve their community, are threatened by the possibility of being "found out."

Most "politically aware" Latins show a remarkable lack of understanding of gay-related issues. In a recent meeting of Hispanic women in a major US city, one participant expressed the opinion that "lesbianism is a sickness we get from American

women and American culture". This is, obviously, another version
of the myth about the free sexuality of American women so
prevalent among Hispanics. But it is also an expression of the
common belief that homosexuality is chosen behavior, acquired
through the bad influence of others, like drug addiction.
Socialist attitudes in this respect are extremely traditional, as the
attitudes of the Cuban revolution towards homosexuality clearly
manifest. Thus, Hispanics who consider themselves radical and
committed to civil rights remain extremely traditional when it
comes to gay rights. These attitudes clearly add further stress to
the lives of Latin women who have a homosexual orientation and
who are invested in enhancing the lives of members of their
communities.

They experience oppression in three ways: as women, as
Hispanics and as lesbians. This last form of oppression is in fact
experienced most powerfully from inside their own culture. Most
Latin women who are lesbians have to remain "closeted" among
their families, their colleagues and society at large. To be "out of
the closet" only in an Anglo context deprives them of essential
supports from their communities and families, and, in turn,
increases their invisibility in the Hispanic culture, where only the
openly "butch" types are recognized as lesbians.

Issues of sexuality in psychotherapy with Hispanic women

What does therapy have to offer Hispanic women, especially in
relation to sexuality? Unfortunately, psychotherapy could be, and
in fact has been in many instances, another instrument for the
oppression of all women. By helping people tolerate and adapt to
established sex-roles and other structures of oppression, psychotherapy can perpetuate the status quo. On the other hand, by
increasing the individual's self-awareness and allowing a better
perspective on the forces that impinge on the self, psychotherapy
can become an instrument of liberation. If psychotherapy is to
become an effective mode of growth for the individual rather
than just another instrument of society, it can do so only by taking
some risks.

Good psychotherapy for Hispanic women should free the
client's energy from the entanglement of emotional conflicts in
order to enable her to make better and freer choices. Since the
personal is political, these choices may entail engaging in
activities which in the long run will benefit the status of women –
and men – in the Hispanic community. An awareness of the
reality of women's lives and the consequent understanding that
their conflicts are not exclusively intrapsychic is essential. In fact,
an exclusive intrapsychic emphasis indicates a lack of under-

standing of the client's reality and a lack in the therapist's training. For good therapy to occur it is essential to help women distinguish between conflicts and suffering which have their source in socialization and oppression and conflicts arising from intrapsychic, individual sources. This distinction is not always neat and simple. But, contrary to partisans of an exclusively intrapsychic or an exclusively social perspective, each woman who comes to therapy carries her own particular internalized combination of externally determined and intrapsychic conflicts. Good therapy, thus, necessitates attending to both categories of factors affecting her mental health and well-being.

This form of therapy implies a political commitment to the goal of making actual changes in the life situation of Hispanic women who are in therapy, rather than simply attending to the alleviation of individual psychological symptoms. The political commitment implied in this mode of therapy, however, does not in any way detract from the therapist's professional seriousness and psycho-therapeutic expertise.[22] The therapist remains, as always, a professional with a given expertise. The desired outcome of this approach to therapy is the self-empowerment of Hispanic women. But, precisely because of this perspective, therapy may be perceived as threatening by immediate members of the woman's family, who may not be ready to cope with changes she may make as the result of the therapy.

When the therapy touches specifically on issues of sexuality, an understanding of the delicate balance among all the forces described above as manifested in the life history of each individual Latin woman becomes more important than ever. Sexuality is that point where the full self-realization of a human being intersects vividly with her vulnerability. As discussed beautifully by Carole Vance in her introduction to this volume, sexuality is about pleasure and about danger.[23] Because there is pleasure and danger in sexuality, there are problems and possibilities in every aspect of sexuality. Sexual behavior may become both liberating and enslaving. Sexual choices, although deeply personal, may also be of far-reaching political consequences.

For women undergoing a process of acculturation, as many Hispanic women are, choices about sexual behavior may become important expressions of a multitude of different experiences and values. Sexuality and sex-roles within a culture tend to remain the last bastion of tradition. Rebellion against the culture of origin or loyalty to it can, in many instances, be expressed through sexual behavior. The relative degrees of guilt or joy that may be associated with choices about sexual behavior are frequently entangled with considerations which are not fully or exclusively personal, but, rather, determined by external factors and considerations.

Sexual issues tend to be at the core of much family conflict concerning women and adolescent girls in immigrant families. The adoption of new ways of life or sexual behaviors, although satisfactory in many respects, may be associated with intense guilt and feelings of betrayal. In addition, because of the myths associating free sexuality with "Americanization", there is actual danger that young women may become promiscuous or self-destructive through sex. They may attribute their discomfort with their own behavior to parental influence or lack of adequate acculturation, when, in fact, they may be carrying themselves to behaviors considered "extreme" by most American women.

Each culture allows women a different range of accepted sexual behavior. This range goes from what is fully approved and expected – the ideals and values of the culture – to what is accepted or tolerated, even if it is not in conformity with the ideal. Some cultures allow a very narrow range of sexual expression to women, while others tolerate greater degrees of variation. There is a different cost in each culture for women who overstep the boundaries of allowed or tolerable sexual behavior. Knowledge about values concerning female sexuality in a given culture is not sufficient in itself to understand individual women. Each woman, in fact, positions herself at some point along the range of behaviors allowed by the culture. Each woman's choice expresses something about who she is as an individual as well as what her cultural values are. Superficial knowledge of a culture may lead the therapist to accept as a cultural norm what might only be the client's expression of her individuality. Conversely, a behavior that conforms to strict cultural norms or violates them at a high personal cost can be interpreted by an unknowing therapist as a strictly individual choice with no cultural implications. For example, cultural norms can be invoked by the client or assumed, inaccurately, by the therapist to explain a woman's restricted sexual behavior, thus preventing the exploration of other causes which may be in the individual's life history. Or, culturally appropriate reactions to the violation of sexual norms can be interpreted as inappropriate dependency or manifestations of personal neuroticism, thus increasing the client's guilt and confusion. To accept as "cultural" some behaviors or attitudes that might be self-defeating can be as damaging as being totally insensitive to cultural differences. There is danger of being male-centered in the name of cultural values. Precisely because sex-roles and female sexuality tend to be the last bastion of traditional cultural values while all other norms may be changing under acculturative pressures, it is possible to support these values without considering their negative effects on women. This danger is present in therapy with Latin women for non-Hispanic and Hispanic therapists alike. Paradoxically, there might be a danger of compromising essential feminist values – namely, a woman's right to her own choices – because of an insistence on a "politically correct" feminist point of view that may run contrary to the client's perspective at the time. In other words, by trying to make a "liberated" woman out of each Hispanic female client, the choices of each woman may not be appropriately respected. Being totally out of pace with the culture of origin and with the rest of the family may be extremely alienating and painful for a Hispanic woman, no matter how "liberated".

In therapy, sexuality and choices about sexual behavior have to be discussed and understood on the basis of each woman's needs and wants. Male-centered cultural values as well as mainstream or feminist beliefs about women have to be addressed and explored for what they are. Validation for each woman's sexuality and experience is provided through the expansion of feeling states and encouragement to understand their meaning. The clarification of relationships and autonomy struggles provides a recognition of her legitimate rights beyond prescribed roles and expectations. An exploration of options with their ramifications and realities expands the range of possibilities and increases her sense of empowerment.

Although some aspects of the relationship between language and sexuality in bilingual individuals has already been briefly discussed, psychotherapy relies too heavily on language to ignore the psychological implications of language in the thera- peutic process, especially for persons who constantly change between two languages or who are participating in therapy in a second language.[24]

Obviously, selecting reliable sources concerning every aspect of therapy with Latin women is imperative. Finding a competent supervisor, knowledgeable about the culture and experienced in working with this population, is ideal. Although Hispanic therapists, especially women therapists, may not need these admonitions, the reality is that most therapists working with Hispanic women are not Latin themselves. For those who are Latin, their own loyalties to and/or conflicts with their background are, inevitably, part of what they bring to the psychotherapeutic relationship with Hispanic women. As always, it is important to keep in mind that, for each woman, validation and empowerment are always achieved against the backdrop of specific cultural circumstances as well as her life history. Good psychotherapy can be an instrument for positive growth and a vehicle for integrating a responsible and creative sexuality into their lives.

Notes

1 For further information about this period, see C. A. Beard and M. R. Beard, *The Beards' New Basic History of the United States*, New York, Doubleday, 1968; and W. H. Prescott, *History of the Conquest of Mexico* and *History of the Conquest of Peru*, New York, Modern Library, no date (originally published in 1843 and 1847).

2 D. V. Kurtz, "The Virgin of Guadalupe and the Politics of Becoming Human", *Journal of Anthropological Research*, vol. 38, no. 2, 1982, pp. 194-210.

3 V. Martínez-Alier, *Marriage, Class and Colour in Nineteenth Century Cuba*, London, Cambridge University Press, 1974.

4 Ibid.

5 O. M. Espín, "Issues of Psychotherapy with Fluently Bilingual Clients", unpublished paper presented at the Stone Center for Developmental Studies, Wellesley College, Wellesley, Mass, 1982.

6 L. R. Marcos and L. Urcuyo, "Dynamic Psychotherapy with the Bilingual Patient", *American Journal of Psychotherapy*, vol. 33, no. 3, 1979, pp. 331-8.

7 O. M. Espín and B. Warner, "Attitudes towards the Role of Women in Cuban Women Attending a Community College", *International Journal of Social Psychiatry*, vol. 28, no. 3, 1982, pp. 233-9.

8 Espín, "Issues of Psychotherapy with Fluently Bilingual Clients", op. cit.

9 F. González-Reigosa, "The Anxiety-Arousing Effect of Taboo Words in Bilinguals", in C. D. Spielberger and R. Díaz-Guerrero (eds), *Cross-Cultural Anxiety*, Washington, DC, Hemisphere, 1976, p. 325.

10 Ibid.

11 P. Freire, *Pedagogy of the Oppressed*, New York, Salisbury, 1970.

12 J. B. Miller, *Toward a New Psychology of Women*, Boston, Beacon, 1976.

13 Calderón de la Barca, *El Alcalde de Zalamea*.

14 S. Brown, "Love Unites Them and Hunger Separates Them: Poor Women in the Dominican Republic", in Rayna Reiter (ed.), *Toward an Anthropology of Women*, New York, Monthly Review Press, 1975, p. 322.

15 O. M. Espín, "Hispanic Female Healers in Urban Centers in the United States", unpublished manuscript, 1983.

16 V. Abad, J. Ramos, and E. Boyce, "A Model for Delivery of Mental Health Services to Spanish-Speaking Minorities", *American Journal of Orthopsychiatry*, vol. 44, no. 4, 1974, pp.584-95.

17 E. S. Le Vine and A. M. Padilla, *Crossing Cultures in Therapy: Pluralistic Counseling for the Hispanic*, Monterey, California, Brooks/Cole, 1980.

18 A. Aramoni, "Machismo", *Psychology Today*, vol. 5, no. 8, 1982, pp. 69-72.

19 O. M. Espín, "The 'Quinceañeras': A Latin American Expression of

Women's Roles", unpublished paper presented at the national meeting of the Latin American Studies Association, Atlanta, 1975.

20 R. E. Cromwell and R. A. Ruiz, "The Myth of 'Macho' Dominance in Decision Making within Mexican and Chicano Families", *Hispanic Journal of Behavioral Sciences*, vol. 1, no. 4, 1979, p. 371.

21 H. Hidalgo and E. Hidalgo-Christensen, "The Puerto Rican Cultural Response to Female Homosexuality", in E. Acosta-Belén (ed.), *The Puerto Rican Woman*, New York, Praeger, 1979, p. 118.

22 E. I. Rawlins and D. K. Carter, *Psychotherapy for Women: Treatment toward Equality*, Springfield, Ill, Charles C. Thomas, 1977.

23 Carole S. Vance, Introduction to this volume.

24 See, for example, L. R. Marcos and M. Alpert, "Strategies and Risks in Psychotherapy with Bilingual Patients: The Phenomenon of Language Independence", *American Journal of Psychiatry*, vol. 33, no. 11, 1976, pp. 1275-8; E. E. Krapf, "The Choice of Language in Polyglot Psychoanalysis", *Psychoanalytic Quarterly*, vol. 24, 1955, pp. 343-57; Marcos and Urcuyo, op. cit.; and Espín, "Issues of Psychotherapy with Fluently Bilingual Clients", op. cit.

The Myth of the Perfect Body

Roberta Galler

A woman was experiencing severe abdominal pain. She was rushed to the emergency room and examined, then taken to the operating room, where an appendectomy was performed. After surgery, doctors concluded that her appendix was fine but that she had VD. It never occurred to them that this woman had a sexual life at all, because she was in a wheelchair.

I saw a woman who had cerebral palsy at a neuro-muscular clinic. She was covered with bruises. After talking with her, it became clear that she was a battered wife. I brought her case to the attention of the medical director and social worker, both progressive practitioners who are knowledgeable about resources for battered women. They said, "But he supports her. Who else will take care of her? And besides, if she complains, the court might take custody of her children."

As a feminist and psychotherapist I am politically and profession-ally interested in the impact of body image on a woman's self-esteem and sense of sexuality. However, it is as a woman with a disability that I am personally involved with these issues. I had polio when I was 10 years old, and now with arthritis and some new aches and pains I feel in a rather exaggerated fashion the effects of aging, a progressive disability we all share to some degree.

Although I've been disabled since childhood, until the past few years I didn't know anyone else with a disability and in fact *avoided* knowing anyone with a disability. I had many of the same fears and anxieties which many of you who are currently able-bodied might feel about close association with anyone with a disability. I had not opted for, but in fact rebelled against the prescribed role of dependence expected of women growing up when I did and which is still expected of disabled women. I became the "exceptional" woman, the "super-crip," noted for her indepen-dence. I refused to let my identity be shaped by my disability. I wanted to be known for *who* I am and not just by what I physically cannot do.

Although I was not particularly conscious of it at the time, I was additionally burdened with extensive conflicts about dependency and feelings of shame over my own imperfections and realistic

165

limitations. So much of my image and definition of myself had been rooted in a denial of the impact of my disability. Unfortunately, my values and emphasis on independence involved an assumption that any form of help implied dependence and was therefore humiliating.

As the aging process accelerated the impact of my disability, it became more difficult to be stoic or heroic or ignore my increased need for help at times. This personal crisis coincided in time with the growing national political organization of disabled persons who were asserting their rights, demanding changes in public consciousness and social policy, and working to remove environmental and attitudinal barriers to the potential viability of their lives.[1]

Disabled women also began a dialogue within the feminist community. On a personal level it has been through a slow process of disability consciousness-raising aided by newly-found "sisters in disability," as well as through profoundly moving discussions with close, non-disabled friends that we, through mutual support and self-disclosure, began to explore our feelings and to shed the shame and humiliation associated with needing help. We began to understand that to need help did not imply helplessness nor was it the opposite of independence. This increased appreciation of mutual interdependence as part of the human condition caused us to reexamine the feminist idea of autonomy versus dependence.

Feminists have long attacked the media image of "the Body Beautiful" as oppressive, exploitative, and objectifying. Even in our attempts to create alternatives, however, we develop standards which oppress some of us. The feminist ideal of autonomy does not take into account the realistic needs for help that disabled, aging – and, in fact, most – women have. The image of the physically strong "superwoman" is also out of reach for most of us.

As we began to develop disability consciousness, we recognized significant parallels to feminist consciousness. For example, it is clear that just as society creates an ideal of beauty which is oppressive for us all, it creates an ideal model of the physically perfect person who is not beset with weakness, loss, or pain. It is toward these distorted ideals of perfection in form and function that we all strive and with which we identify.

The disabled (and aging) woman poses a symbolic threat by reminding us how tenuous that model, "the myth of the perfect body," really is, and we might want to run from this thought. The disabled woman's body may not meet the standard of "perfection" in either image, form, or function. On the one hand, disabled women share the social stereotype of women in general as being weak and passive, and in fact are depicted as the epitome of the incompetent female. On the other hand, disabled women are not viewed as women at all, but portrayed as helpless, dependent children in need of protection. She is not seen as the sexy, but the sexless object, asexual, neutered, unbeautiful and unable to find a lover. This stigmatized view of the disabled woman reflects a perception of assumed inadequacy on the part of the non-disabled.

For instance, disabled women are often advised by professionals not to bear children, and are (within race and class groupings) more likely to be threatened by or be victims of involuntary sterilization. Concerns for reproductive freedom and child custody, as well as rape and domestic violence often exclude the disabled woman by assuming her to be an asexual creature. The perception that a disabled woman couldn't possibly get a man to care for or take care of her underlies the instances where professionals have urged disabled women who have been victims of brutal battery to stay with abusive males. Members of the helping professions often assume that no other men would want them.

Disability is often associated with sin, stigma and a kind of "untouchability." Anxiety, as well as a sense of vulnerability and dread, may cause others to respond to the "imperfections" of a disabled woman's body with terror, avoidance, pity and/or guilt. In a special *Off Our Backs* issue on disabled women, Jill Lessing postulated that it is "through fear and denial that attitudes of repulsion and oppression are acted out on disabled people in ways ranging from our solicitous good intentions to total invisibility and isolation."[2]

Even when the disabled woman is idealized for surmounting all obstacles, she is the recipient of a distancing admiration, which assumes her achievement to be necessary compensation for a lack of sexuality, intimacy, and love. The stereotype of the independent "super-crip," although embodying images of strength and courage, involves avoidance and denial of the realities of disability for both the observer and the disabled woman herself.

These discomforts may evoke a wish that disabled women remain invisible and that their sexuality be a hidden secret. However, disabled (and aging) women are coming out; we are beginning to examine our issues publicly, forcing other women to address not only the issues of disability but to reexamine their attitudes toward their own limitations and lack of perfection, toward oppressive myths, standards, and social conditions which affect us all. Jill Lessing urges that we move away from this kind of thinking, the ideology which upholds an ideal type of human body and which regards anyone less than perfect as not fully human, "with a political commitment as strong as our responsibility to fight racism, classism and sexism in ourselves as well as others."[3]

In more direct and personal terms, to be a feminist with disability consciousness, or to be a friend or lover of a woman with a disability, you need to be aware of and include the limitations that disability places on her and on you. You must honor the reality of her oppression in the able-bodied world. You must join with her in the fight against external constraints and social injustice in the fields of employment, housing, and transportation accessibility. Feminist events should be accessible, and feminist issues expanded to include the specific concerns of disabled women.[4]

Assumptions of asexuality, personal undesirability, and physical impossibility are perpetuated through the absence of sexual information, guidance, encouragement or social opportunity provided to disabled females growing up. Parents, educators, and health professionals remain generally silent on the subject but the message is loud and clear. *The lack of "perfection" is equated with the lack of entitlement to sexual life.* Because some disabilities limit mobility, increase levels of fatigue and/or pain, cause loss of sensation or sensory impairment, or create a need for assistance, disabled women may require special awareness, sensitivity, and creative alternatives to enable them to enjoy their sexuality. Finally, after pressure from the disabled community, sex therapists, educators, rehabilitation workers and providers of birth control have begun to specifically direct their services to the needs of the disabled woman and make them accessible to her. Beyond overcoming the realities of physical limitations, however, attitudinal barriers must be made conscious and confronted, if sexual fulfillment is to be a possibility for disabled women.

Even in the changing political climate of women challenging traditional options, if a disabled woman should decide to opt for a nontraditional or independent lifestyle, such as single motherhood, a professional career, or lesbianism, she is often not regarded as having made a choice but is perceived as not having a choice. For disabled women, "lifestyle, sexual preference and personal decisions are viewed as consequences of the disability rather than as choices."[5]

By emphasizing the external restraints, social stereotypes and perceptions of others, I do not mean to minimize the significance of the internal world of the disabled woman or her own sense of self-esteem and personal worth. Parallel to women's feelings about their fatness, as described in Carol Munter's presentation, disabled women also often have a tendency to blame themselves, or imagine that if only they were different, better, and perfect, they would be good enough to do the impossible.[6] Sometimes, like fat, disability can stand for everything a disabled woman feels to be bad about herself and is the focus of low self-esteem, embodying feelings of being damaged, inadequate, unworthy and unlovable.

As women, we all know that constantly running into external barriers reduces a sense of self-worth. The expectations of others become part of the self-concept and self-expectation. This may perpetuate a psychological sense of invisibility, self-estrangement, powerlessness, worthlessness, and lack of sexual entitlement among disabled women.

Society's standards of beauty and acceptability are embedded in our initial interactions with parents, caretakers, and health practitioners as they look at, comment about, and handle our bodies. In this way, external standards become internal realities. Too frequently our own bodies become our enemies. This is as true for non-disabled as it is for disabled women. If we are to be capable of seeing a disabled woman as a person instead of her disability, we must confront these feelings in ourselves. It is not easy to face our own limitations honestly, but to the extent that we are able to accept and make peace with the loss, pain, and vulnerability associated with our own lack of perfection, the freer we will be of myths which oppress us and with which we may oppress others.

Perhaps it is time for us all to "come out" and express our feelings about our bodily "defects." Together as women, all with imperfections, limitations, vulnerabilities, strengths and weaknesses, desires, fears and passions, we need to accept and embrace the human condition and move in the direction of being able to live and love in our imperfect bodies.

Notes

1 Disabled women bear the disproportionate economic, social, and psychological burden of what it means to be disabled. Data and an excellent discussion of disabled women's extensive oppression (as compared to non-disabled women and disabled men) are provided in Michelle Fine and Adrienne Asch, "Disabled Women: Sexism without the Pedestal", *Journal of Sociology and Social Welfare*, July 1981. Their studies reveal that disabled women are more likely than disabled men to be without work: between 65 percent and 76 percent of disabled women are unemployed. Disabled women also earn substantially less than disabled men. For vocationally-rehabilitated men and women, the mean annual incomes are $4188 and $2744, respectively.

Disabled women generally receive inadequate training for personal and professional self-sufficiency and suffer the brunt of labor-force discrimination. Disabled men are more likely than women to be referred to vocational schools or on-the-job training and are somewhat more likely to be college-educated. As a result, women are less likely to find a job post-disability. Those women who do are more likely to absorb a cut in pay than disabled men and are more likely to live in families with incomes at or below the poverty level.

Disabled women are less likely to be married: they marry later and are more likely to be divorced. A greater percentage of female heads of households than male heads of households are disabled. There is a general social neglect of the sexual and reproductive roles of disabled women, because public opinion assumes disabled women to be inappropriate as mothers or sexual beings.

Asch and Fine explore how these stark social and economic realities, the impact of a hostile economy and a discriminatory society bears heavily on the disabled woman's self-image. They cite research indicating that disabled women are significantly more likely to have negative self-perceptions and to be viewed negatively by the general public than are disabled men.

While Asch and Fine substantiate the double discrimination which disabled women face, they portray the disabled woman as neither helpless nor hopeless victim. Their perspective is that virtually all of the difficulties imposed by disability which is often painful, frustrating and degrading, stems from the cruelty, discrimination, ignorance of others and the neglect of disabled people by major economic and social institutions not from the disability per se.

While they certainly acknowledge that much remains to be done to insure that disabled women can live with independence and dignity, they also stress the strides individuals have made to challenge disability-specific constraints and cite the collective struggle of disabled women (and men) who are organizing and fighting against unjust economic and social conditions.

2 Jill Lessing, "Denial and Disability", *Off Our Backs*, vol. xi, no. 5, May 1981, p. 21.

3 Ibid.

4 The workshop utilized experiential exercises to sensitize participants to disability issues.

Exercise 1: As the workshop participants entered the room, they were asked to fill out blank index cards listing what they did and didn't like about their bodies. Throughout the workshop, someone was writing these bodily characteristics on the blackboard in front of the room so that everyone faced a list of what they and other women either liked or did not like about their bodies.

Exercise 2: After a moment of relaxation and deep breathing, the participants were asked to close their eyes and imagine themselves in bodies with disabilities other than their own. For example, imagine that you are 50 pounds heavier, or 25 years older. Imagine that you have a mobility disability; perhaps you walk with a cane or crutches, or use a wheelchair. Imagine that you have difficulty or are unable to move or use your hands and arms. Perhaps you have a speech impediment causing difficulties in communication. Perhaps you have involuntary muscular spasms, gestures, or facial expressions. Imagine that you have a sensory impairment and are unable to see or hear, or do so only with difficulty. Or perhaps you have a hidden disability or illness like a heart condition, or have had a mastectomy, or must wear a catheter or ostomy bag. These body images are more or less uncomfortable to imagine having. Choose the image you are able to entertain.

Once they assumed their imaginary bodies, a series of questions guided the participants through a variety of situations. For example, "Now that you are in that body, when you woke up this morning and were preparing to come to this conference, what kind of clothes would you choose to wear? How does that differ from what you are actually wearing?" "How did you get out of your house? How did you come to the conference? What kind of transportation were you able to use in your imaginary body?" "How might you feel when you come into this room full of strangers?" "What if you were invited to a party after the conference? Could you go? How would you feel at the party?" "What if you visited or had to return to your family with these changes in your body? How would they react to you?" "What if you were invited to the beach by friends and you had to choose a new bathing suit? Could you go to the beach? Could you let your body show?" "Suppose you met someone you were attracted to, and he/she wanted to sleep with you. How would you respond in your imaginary body?" "Imagine yourself in the bedroom. How would you feel about undressing in front of them? Now imagine yourself in bed. How would you relate to them sexually?"

5 Adrienne Asch and Michelle Fine, "Disabled Women: Sexism without the Pedestal", op. cit.

6 Carol Munter, "Fat and the Fantasy of Perfection", this volume, pp. 225-31.

Bibliography

Prepared by Harilyn Roussu, Disabilities Unlimited, 3 E. 10th St, New York, New York, NY 10003.

A. Asch and M. Fine, "Disabled Women: Sexism Without the Pedestal", *Journal of Sociology and Social Welfare*, July 1981. (The whole issue of the journal deals with disabled women.)

Elle F. Becker, *Female Sexuality Following Spinal Cord Injury*, Bloomington, Ill., Accent Special Publication, Cheever, 1978.

Sue Bregman, *Sexuality and the Spinal Cord Injured Woman*, Minneapolis, Minn., Sister Kenny Institute, 1975.

D. Bullard and S. Knight, *Sexuality and Physical Disabilty: Personal Perspectives*, St Louis, C. V. Mosby, 1981.

Pat Califia, *Sapphistry, The Book of Lesbian Sexuality*, Tallahessee, Naiad, 1980. (This book includes a chapter on disabled lesbians.)

Jo Campling, *Better Lives for Disabled Women*, London, Virago, 1979.

Jo Campling (ed.), *Images of Ourselves: Women with Disabilities Talking*, Boston and London, Routledge & Kegan Paul, 1981.

172   *Roberta Galler*

"Disabled Women Fight a Double Stereotype", *Women's Agenda*, vol. 4, no. 3, May-June 1979, pp. 8-9.

Y. Duffy, *All Things are Possible*, Ann Arbor, A. J. Garvin, 1981.

John Gliedman and William Roth, *The Unexpected Minority: Handicapped Children in America*, New York, Harcourt Brace Jovanovich, 1980. (Good discussion of disability issues.)

Marjori Inana, "You and Your Body: Self-Help Health Class for Blind Women", *Visual Impairment and Blindness*, December 1978, pp. 399-403.

S. Kelley-Linton, "Learning to Survive", *Journal of Current Social Issues*, vol. 15, no. 1, Spring 1978.

S. Kelley-Linton and M. Carrera, "The Right to a Sexual Life", *Multiple Sclerosis Quarterly*, vol. 2, no. 3, July 1979.

Carney Landis and M. Marjorie Bolles, *Personality and Sexuality of the Physically Handicapped Woman*, New York, Paul B. Hoeber, 1942.

Mary Romano, "Sexuality and the Disabled Female", *Accent on Living Reprint Series #1* (originally printed in *Accent on Living Magazine*, Winter 1973), P. O. Box 700, Bloomington, IL 61701.

H. Rousso, "Disabled People Are Sexual, Too", *Exceptional Parent*, December 1981.

H. Rousso, "Taking on the Social Scene", *Exceptional Parent*, February 1982.

H. Rousso, "Special Considerations in Counseling People with Cerebral Palsy", *Sexuality and Disability*, Summer 1982.

Sex and Disability Project, *Who Cares? A Handbook on Sex Education and Counseling Services for Disabled People*, Washington, DC, George Washington University, 1979. (Good resource on sexuality and disability.)

Sexuality and Disability: A journal devoted to the study of sex in physical and mental illness, vol. 1, no. 1, Spring 1978. (Includes several articles on disabled women.)

"Special Issue: Women with Disabilities", *Off Our Backs*, vol. XI, no. 5, May 1981. (Whole issue devoted to disabled women.)

Task Force on Concerns of Physically Disabled Women, *Toward Intimacy: Family Planning and Sexuality Concerns of Physically Disabled Women*, New York, Human Sciences, 1978.

Task Force on Concerns of Physically Disabled Women, *Within Reach: Providing Family Planning Services to Physically Disabled Women*, New York, Human Sciences, 1978.

"Women and Disability: Special Problems of Disabled Women", *International Rehabilitation Review*, February 1977, New York, Rehabilitation International.

Women's Educational Equity Communications Network, *What Happens After School? A Study of Disabled Women and Education*, San Francisco, WEECN, 1978.

The Body Politic:
The Defense of Sexual
Restriction by Anti-Abortion
Activists

Faye Ginsburg

In the tradition of Mark Twain on the Mississippi, I am exploring a great rift on the American social landscape – the controversy over abortion rights – to gain some insight into current divisions regarding the social organization of gender in the United States. How is it that women living in what appears to be the same society have come to such radically opposing views concerning the shape and control of reproduction and sexuality? What motivates some to move beyond a personal rejection of abortion and actively support its prohibition for all American women?

Grassroots abortion activists on both sides of the issue are primarily white, middle-class, and female.[1] Most recent studies of the conflict bypass the grassroots-level activist and focus instead on the political organization and leadership of the New Right.[2] Implicitly, such work assumes that motivation for action is generated at the top and thus leaves unexamined the popular base on which a large-scale initiative like the Right-to-Life movement has built its support. New political symbols can mobilize people only in so far as they provide imagery and language that give shape to a world view felt to be under attack by its adherents. It is important then to study the controversy from the bottom up, to understand the motivations of women fighting abortion on the local level in a community fresh to the debate.

The setting I chose was River City,[3] a small city in the Upper Midwest where conflict erupted full force in the fall of 1981 when the first clinic to offer abortion services in the state opened its doors there. My concern was to find an order of explanation that recognizes agency and intentionality of activists on both sides of the issue. On the one hand, many feminists assume that anti-abortion activists are dupes of organized religion or conservative politicians, thus denying pro-life women the possibility of being active, rational members of society.[4] On the other hand, some anti-abortion activists are convinced that pro-choice women are selfish and promiscuous, devoid of any moral concern.[5] Each

173

side, in viewing the other as the personification of evil, renews itself through its vision of the opposition. A more fruitful approach recognizes women on both sides as social actors who respond to and reshape the ideological and material circumstances of their lives. This is not to deny the fact that women face conditions of sexual inequality in political, economic and social arenas. The goal of such analysis is to comprehend how women confront and evaluate their situation in a particular time and place and then act to serve what they see as their own best interests.

As I began to consider activism on the abortion issue as, at least in some measure, strategic rather than reactionary – the efforts of certain women to enhance their place in the world as they see it – the landscape became clearer. The abortion controversy is not simply a battleground for skirmishes over fetal life and women's rights, or between "good" and "bad" girls. The conflict also provides an arena for a confrontation of world views whose root differences lie in opposing interpretations of the social consequences of sexual activity. Most pro-choice activists see safe and legal abortion as an essential safeguard which guarantees that a sexually active woman will have the power to control whether, when, and with whom she will have children. Pro-life activists, on the other hand, see abortion as a condensed symbol for the decline in the moral authority of motherhood and the attributes assigned to it in this culture. In Right-to-Life rhetoric, abortion epitomizes: diminution in the control parents exert over their children; devaluation of motherhood and caretaking; loss of social guarantees that a woman with dependents will be supported; and, perhaps at a more unconscious level, fear that ways of life no longer considered valuable will be annihilated, a terror which the image of abortion perfectly captures. In short, for most pro-lifers, abortion symbolizes what they see as the negative effects emerging from the increasing separation of sexual pleasure from reproduction, marriage, and traditional family life in our society. The work of pro-life activists to stop abortions is thus a movement for social reform grounded both literally and figuratively in the defense of sexual restriction.

"Right here in River City"

The River City Women's Clinic, run by a local abortion rights activist, is one of ten such facilities set up in small metropolitan areas by the Reproductive Health Association, a business headquartered in New York City. In the last ten years, 480 free-standing clinics providing first trimester abortions have been established throughout America. Each clinic has its own history, unique to its setting but part of a more general process of social change taking place across the United States.

The opening of the clinic in River City in October 1981 had a tremendous impact on the area. For the local residents, it was the source of a full-scale controversy that went on unremittingly for over six months. For women in the Upper Midwest, the clinic greatly increased their access to abortion services. Statistics on abortion rates in the area support earlier research which shows that geographic availability of abortion services is the single most powerful determinant influencing a woman's ability to obtain a safe, legal abortion.[6] In the first year of the clinic's existence, abortions in the state rose from 2554 to 3076, an increase of 32 percent. While three private doctors had been performing abortions in other cities in the state since or even prior to 1973, information about such services was not well known; in addition, the quality of their medical care was questioned by pro-choice and pro-life activists alike. By contrast, the staff of the River City Women's Clinic is committed to providing high-quality care that includes careful counseling and screening of patients as well as post-abortion check-ups, services that the physicians mentioned above do not offer.

River City, with a population of 61,000, is small enough to provide a coherent social universe. Yet, as the largest city in the state with a sister city of 30,000 across the river, it encompasses some diversity. Settled by Germans and Scandinavians who followed the railroads west, River City is now the major crossroads on east-west trucking routes, serving as a distribution and service center for the 3000 farmers in the surrounding 50-mile radius. Eighty-one manufacturing firms employ 3500 people, and 300 businesses and industrial companies have their offices in town. Most of those employed in non-agricultural salaried jobs work in service industries: education (with three universities and five technical schools in the area); health (including five hospitals and a variety of smaller facilities); and in the numerous motels and fast-food restaurants that have mushroomed alongside the new interstate highway. With women comprising just under 50 percent of the city's salaried workers, the local economy appears to be changing in step with the rest of America. Between 1975 and 1979, over 40 percent of the new jobs in this country were in fast-food, clerical, and health services.[7] Such figures indicate that services such as food preparation, laundry, and care for dependents traditionally performed by women in unpaid household labor are increasingly being provided by a low-wage service industry. These changes, identified with an expanding female labor force, reflect an overall shift in the composition and function of households and wage work.

River City residents view themselves as politically conservative, for the most part. A 1972 state referendum to liberalize abortion was defeated by 72 percent of voters in the state and 64 percent in River City. None the less, the area is also known for its tradition of progressive populism and defense of individual rights. The discovery of oil in the western prairies and the legalization of gambling in the state in 1977 have brought new wealth to the area but also contribute to fears of long-time residents that undesirable social change is being imposed on them. A blackjack pit boss in a posh casino in River City put it epigrammatically: "My mother can't understand what's going on. She says, 'Kyle, how can there be gambling going on in the state where Lawrence Welk was born?' "[8]

River City has fifty-five churches serving 30,000 adult members, over one-third of whom are Lutheran and just under one-third are Catholic. The balance belongs to non-Lutheran Protestant denominations, with Fundamentalist and Evangelical congregations growing faster than any other in the area; or to the small Jewish community. The city boasts the highest regular church attendance of any standard metropolitan area. The fact takes on significance in light of survey research which shows that regular participation in church is one of the most significant sociological variables associated with anti-abortion attitudes.[9]

That correlation was borne out in the reaction of River City residents to rumors that abortion services were going to be offered in town. The first word of the clinic's opening was met with anger and bewilderment. The transformation of a white clapboard house into a "convenience store for abortion," as opponents called it, provided the perfect image of evil imposed on innocence for people unwilling to believe that abortion and all that it represents for them could be present in their quiet city. The clinic's location, just at the edge of a residential district, is close enough to a commercial strip to be regulated as a business. Thus, it embodies for some in its physical structure and placement a disturbing image: the world of home and hearth slipping over the boundary of domesticity into the public arena.

The sentiments of one pro-life activist – nurse, mother of six, widow of a well-known River City professional and past president of Birthright, a national organization which helps women with unwanted pregnancies find alternatives to abortion – were typical of many. "It's just a little house, a little paint, a little plumbing and it's a business. I truthfully don't think there are many people in this nice rural community who would start it on their own." The feeling of "we" and "they" was exacerbated by the fact that the clinic is run by a national organization headquartered in New York. This activist, along with others, spoke as if the very need for abortion were being imported from River City's structural opposite on the East Coast.

"They've got money behind it and they just railroaded it in. And the laws are on their side. All we can do is pedal on. I'd like it to happen that they stay here and they lose money and they have to shut down because people just don't need abortions in River City."

The possibilities of pluralism are, apparently, shaky in a world of moral absolutes. It is one thing to acknowledge (regretfully) the local presence of "bad girls" who are unwilling to view marriage as the price of sex, with motherhood as the inevitable outcome. It is quite another to tolerate an institution that implicitly and publicly condones the separation of sexual pleasure from childbearing, marriage, and domesticity. Like the guardians of virtue depicted in the musical comedy *The Music Man* who, in singing their protest to a pool hall, affirmed their opposition to impending social change, the pro-life forces in River City dramatized their resistance to the alternative view of female sexuality represented by the public presence of an abortion clinic.

About a month before the clinic was scheduled to open, a variety of local people opposed to abortion banded together to form a coalition called LIFE – Life is For Everyone – led by Linda Anderson. Born and raised on a Midwestern farm, Linda is now the wife of a farmer and part-time salesman, a man she met in college where they were both involved in pro-life issues. As a devout Catholic, Linda believes the taking of any innocent human life is wrong, but she sees abortion as a special case linked to broader concerns. Like most of the other pro-life activists, she takes the legalization of abortion as a sign of growing narcissism in American society, symbolized by the unwillingness of women to carry an unwanted pregnancy to term.

"I think it says a lot about our society, an awful lot. You know, when we hear about the 'me-ism' concept, this is typical of the abortion issue. Sure it may not be easy to carry a pregnancy through nine months, but here again, are you thinking only of yourself or are you thinking of your unborn child? The decision whether or not to have that child should be made before the woman is pregnant. If she does not want to have a child, then she should take steps so that she does not have a child. If she does get pregnant, then she better be able to accept the responsibility of carrying that child to term and not taking that child's life."

Linda taught home economics and then served as banquet director at a local hotel until the birth of her first child. Now, with two children and a third on the way, her time is filled with childcare, running the farm with her husband, and serving as president of LIFE which includes supervising office staff and volunteers and speaking to the public.

In late August, the LIFE Coalition petitioned the City Commission to revoke the yet-to-be-opened clinic's building permit on the grounds that it had not listed abortion as one of its services. In the absence of the mayor and the city attorney, the four-member Commission voted two to one, with one abstention, to revoke the permit. When the mayor returned from out of town the next day, he was outraged at the Commission's action and immediately reinstated the clinic's permit, declaring that it was fully legal under federal and state law. Discriminatory enforcement of local regulations, he argued, would simply involve the city in a costly, dead-end lawsuit.

The members of LIFE Coalition were stymied by the actions of their first-term mayor – a Presbyterian from rural Iowa who is now an economics professor and father of two – and predicted his defeat in the mayoral elections six months away. In the meantime, a second pro-life force emerged. A team of two called Partners In Vision published a full-page ad in a biweekly shopper that denounced abortion and asked for contributions and a city-wide vote. The Partners had only shallow roots in the community and were looked on with some suspicion by the more established residents of River City who made up the ranks of LIFE. One Partner, a resident of the area since 1974, is a salaried special assistant to Jerry Falwell; the other, a self-styled born-again Evangelist, had only recently settled in town.

To follow up on their ad, the two sent letters to 5700 businesspeople and professionals which asked them to send money and cast a vote on the abortion issue on a ballot enclosed in the mailing. The last sentence of their letter, with its implication that votes would be made public, did them in with the citizens of River City: "Your failure to respond may be considered as unconcern and a vote in favor of the abortion clinic by the general public." The editorial run by the River City daily newspaper summed up the generally angry response to such tactics.

Our paper has traditionally been opposed to abortion on demand and we continue that policy strongly. But we are opposed to this effort to force a certain segment of our community to express personal views on a moral subject which has nothing to do with their professions or business.

All persons have a right to their private views and should not be penalized for exercising that right.

By dramatizing the mailing as a violation of privacy in the sacred sphere of commerce, the editorial helped crystallize opposition to Partners In Vision and prevented a coalition between them and the more mainstream LIFE membership.

If the activities of Partners In Vision rallied anyone, it was, ironically, their pro-choice opponents. A group calling itself Citizens for a Real Choice took out a full-page ad in the newspaper with over 2000 signatures supporting the clinic and a woman's right to choose an abortion. The spokesperson for the group was Sally Johnson, a professional woman active in state and local politics who took a considerable career risk in embracing a public pro-choice stand. Sally grew up in the area and a year after completing Catholic high school, married her "steady," a man who now works as an accountant. When she became pregnant, Sally dropped out of college to raise her first and then second daughter. Ten years ago, with her interest in politics growing, Sally went back to school and eventually earned her law degree. Her position on the abortion issue reflects almost a complete reversal of the norms she held as a young woman.

"I was raised a Catholic and was much opposed to abortion and somehow between 1968 and 1971 . . . I came to realize that women were going to have abortions whether they're legal or not. And unless they're legal, women will die in the process. My change in attitude, my personal feeling about abortion grew out of a sensitivity to the place of women in this society."

As activists on both sides escalated their campaigns in River City, abortion became the topic of countless Sunday sermons and service club luncheons. A LIFE rally of 400 people around City Hall was matched the following Sunday by a worship service, featuring Gloria Steinem, sponsored by Citizens for a Real Choice. The local newspaper was so deluged with letters to the editor that they finally put a moratorium on publishing them.

Despite all the controversy, the clinic's opening day on October 1 was uneventful, with only a silent prayer vigil outside, a protest that LIFE members maintained faithfully, even through the coldest winter on record in the state. In mid-October, a last effort was made by Partners in Vision to stop the clinic's activities. A petition with eight signatures was presented to the City Commission by an attorney hired by Partners, requesting that the clinic be closed until public hearings could be held to establish rules for its operation. Just before Thanksgiving, in front of an expectant and divided crowd, the City Commission voted unanimously to deny the petition. Their voice affirmed the position of the mayor and, in a sense, presaged his re-election in April 1982. Despite their best efforts, pro-life forces were unable to find a candidate to run against the incumbent.

The national director of the Reproductive Health Association considers the events that took place in River City to be similar to those that she has encountered in setting up other facilities.

"Opening a clinic in a non-metropolitan area is about like getting on a roller-coaster ride. You have to take the ups and downs before you come to the end and that's usually when the community begins to accept you. A tremendous amount of emotion surfaces over these votes and reversals, as if people have to show that the clinic was established over their protest. I've seen it over and over again."

The silent protests have continued outside the River City Women's Clinic, while inside approximately twenty abortions are performed every week. About 50 percent of the women who come there are from the immediate vicinity; the rest come from outlying areas, neighboring states, and Canada.

The conflicts and change catalyzed by the opening of the abortion clinic in River City show at close range how the 1973 Supreme Court decision on abortion is being woven into the social fabric. In a sense, the Roe vs Wade ruling was a pro-choice victory that outpaced the formation of public opinion on elective abortion, as the rise of organized pro-life activity over the last decade indicates. In retrospect, some consider that from a political point of view the judicial success of abortion rights was premature. As one National Abortion Rights Action League activist reflected, "Had we made more gains through the legislative and referendum processes and taken a little longer at it, the public would have moved with us."[10] Others suggest that the ruling failed to recognize that the abortion question has an emotional and symbolic valence that extends far beyond the Court's (and some activists') focus on legal questions of privacy and rights of individuals and that, inevitably, "such an atomistic view of society conflicts with the way most people see the world."[11]

You've come a long way?

While the citizens of River City may have agreed to disagree, the conflict over the clinic revealed previously unvoiced social and cultural divisions. LIFE Coalition remains active, claiming over a thousand members. The organization focuses on educational efforts in churches and classrooms and alternative counseling and aid for women with problem pregnancies. These women activists (and they are mostly women) speak with the conviction of people engaged in a fight for survival. Linda Anderson explained:

"There should be a lot of emotion in this because you're talking about life and death. That's why you have people who are dedicated to the movement to the point where their lives are completely tied up in it."

In such a battle, what are the stakes and who is the enemy?

If one looks to the leadership of the New Right, one finds individuals like Richard Viguerie using explicitly military rhetoric to describe a war in defense of an endangered ideology and lifestyle. One of the aggressors is, in his view, liberal feminism which he maintains encouraged American women to feel like failures if they want to be wives and mothers.[12] According to George Gilder's house-of-cards scheme for a more productive society, spelled out in *Wealth and Poverty*, marriage is necessary to domesticate male aggression. It links the "short-term sexuality of men" to the "extended maternal horizons of women," spurring husbands on to greater productivity in the workforce.[13] Phyllis Schlafly – who differs from Gilder in her belief that there is nothing wrong with women working for wages outside of the home if it does not conflict with childrearing – is none the less famous for her denunciations of "women's lib." The movement is, to Schlafly, responsible for advocating sexual freedoms which she sees as dismantling our social bonds. She seizes in particular upon premarital sex as depriving women of their means for ensuring their support from husbands.[14] Are these views of a gender-segregated society voiced by the New Right leadership the same as those of grassroots activists such as the pro-lifers in River City?

The LIFE Coalition has remained self-consciously local and non-partisan with little interest in the general work of the New Right, although many of its members have ties to the more liberal National Right to Life committee. Many are also active Democrats who espouse liberal positions on a range of other social issues from welfare to nuclear disarmament. While the group receives financial and organizational support from the Catholic Church, it cannot be reduced to a reflection of that institution. While approximately 50 percent of LIFE members are Catholic, 25 percent are Lutheran and 25 percent are Evangelicals, a distribution of religious affiliation close to that of River City in general.

How representative are LIFE Coalition's members in River City of local Right-to-Life supporters around the country? The results of a 1980 survey of a random sample of members of the pro-life National Right to Life Committee (NRLC) showed NRLC membership as 70 percent Catholic and 20 percent Protestant, with Baptists and Lutherans comprising the predominant Protestant affiliations. By contrast, the US population is approximately 28 percent Catholic and 60 percent Protestant.[15] The survey also indicated that a conservative approach to morality, even more than religious affiliation and church attendance, correlates consistently with active opposition to abortion.[16]

A closer examination of the survey data reveals important ideological distinctions. Of Right-to-Life members who responded, 80 percent feel it is too easy to get a divorce in America; 75 percent oppose giving birth control information to teens without parental consent (and one-third of those object even with parental consent); and 87 percent disapprove of pre-marital sex.[17] Contrary to popular stereotypes of pro-life activists, however, respondents are not anti-feminist on many issues. Ninety percent do not agree that women "should leave running the country up to men" and 83 percent approve of women working regardless of marital status and husband's income. The responses indicate support for women's economic and political power but reflect concern over loss of two of the major bargaining strategies women have traditionally used to gain power: the individual woman's refusal to engage in sex without marriage, which implicitly links female sexuality to procreation and domesticity; and the social and legal pressure on men to get and stay married. Judith Blake and Jorge del Pinal, in their comprehensive study of abortion attitudes in the US, offer the following explanation of such findings.

To have total discretion over abortion may trivialize the cosmic importance of motherhood for women who wish to use pregnancy as an instrumentality in their relations with their husbands or their lovers. [In this view] easy access to abortion lessens rather than increases feminine power. A pregnancy that has been embarked upon for the purpose of precipitating a marriage or holding one together no longer has the clout that it once did.[18]

For most pro-life women in River City, opposition to abortion is linked less to a defense of motherhood and more to a critique of the moral failure of the culture in general. "I think there is a general breakdown of sorts in moral values and I don't say abortion has caused it all," explained one activist, a grandmother several times over and a feisty organizer in the state Democratic Party. "The idea that we can say somebody can live and somebody can die for just any reason – I think is kind of all tied up with what kind of thinking there is going on today." These fears of increasing selfishness and materialism shape many pro-lifers' assumptions about their opposition, a vision from which moral identity is drawn by contrast. One young woman – past secretary of the local Right-to-Life chapter, oldest girl of nine children in a poor farm family, divorced, remarried and now a mother of three – was, like many of her colleagues, moved to a display of hostility when she considered her imagined enemy.

"These women make me so angry because they are saying if you don't have a choice to have a baby then you have no freedom. Liberationists. They're very selfish. I wouldn't want to get in their way because they'll get rid of me if I'm in their way. They're so set on 'me first'. . . *I* want to get what *I* want out of life no matter who gets in the way."

The comments of another LIFE member reflected an awareness that such images of the "liberated woman" are fabricated on Madison Avenue. Her recognition, however, did not assuage a sense that her most cherished values are no longer in vogue.

"We went through about 50 magazines to find baby pictures to decorate donation cans (for a pro-life fundraiser) and we couldn't find any. Babies aren't in style today anymore. Babies are trouble. They cry, they have to get up in the middle of the night. They get sick and they interrupt a lot of things. Babies used to sell products, but not anymore. Now it's the nice luscious young gals."

Testimony to such perception is provided by the array of women's magazines at the corner drugstore. The covers of *Savvy*, *Working Woman*, *Glamour*, and *Self* all feature beautiful young women for whom the care of infants and children seems a minor concern at best. Barbara Ehrenreich describes the media portrayal of "liberated women" in the image of upwardly-mobile corporate men (and big consumers) as "feminine machisma."[19] The effect of such mass-media imagery is insidious but none the less substantial, as journalist Ellen Goodman, for one, has pointed out.

As working mothers receive the praise of society, the women at home keenly feel a loss of status and self esteem. Housewives are on the defensive. . . . The insecurity of the role and the image reflected back to them from society fosters feelings of loss, even betrayal.[20]

If women perceive legal abortion as a threat, it is because it represents public acceptance of the possibility that female sexuality need not be tied inevitably to motherhood. In so doing, abortion also serves to weaken social pressure on men to take responsibility for the reproductive consequences of intercourse. The anxiety generated by the disengaging of sexuality from reproduction and domesticity highlights the lack of recognized social forms other than marriage that can reliably ensure emotional and material support of women with children.

Such concern on the part of American women is hardly new. The nineteenth-century ideology of "domestic feminism"[21] offers an instructive parallel to the views of contemporary anti-abortion activists. The phrase refers to the social and material separation of male and female spheres of activity that took root in America with industrialization. The differentiation of home from workplace that ensued was accompanied by the elaboration of housework, childrearing, and family care as an exclusively female domain.[22] In this arrangement, women were considered morally superior to men and more interested in motherhood and the welfare of others than in their own needs, sexual and otherwise.[23] Despite the obvious drawbacks of a system based on a double standard, to some extent women were able to use it to call upon the support of men and social institutions in their assigned spheres of marriage, family, and religion at a time when most lacked reliable contraception, yet depended on men for material support. Sexual continence until or even within marriage, justified by fear of pregnancy, gave women a significant leverage point in enforcing male responsibility for the care of mothers and children. Abortion and birth control were considered immoral in so far as they were thought to promote promiscuity and undermine the support of households in which the vocation of motherhood was embedded.[24]

Life in America has changed irreversibly in the last 150 years. None the less, one might ask how much the construction of female gender linked to reproduction and its social conse-quences has really changed for the majority of American women. As Deirdre English pointed out in her 1981 article, "The War Against Choice":

Most women who want to have children still cannot make it without a man.... Giving up children for a glamorous career may be one thing (although this is an either/or choice that men rarely face), but it may not be a decent trade for a dead-end job in the pink-collar ghetto. If men can no longer support families on a single paycheck, women sure can't. To the less than ardent feminist who is not prepared to pay any price at all for independence, the future looks bleak.[25]

Women who want to be supported by men as traditional wives and mothers have increasing cause to worry. Nearly 50 percent of American marriages end in divorce, more than double the number reported in 1965, while the number of single-parent families (90 percent of which are headed by women) increased by 100 percent.[26] Within one year of divorce, 50 percent of men default on child support payments.[27] Of women with children under the age of six, almost half work outside the home. The wages they and other women receive are, on average, 58¢ to every dollar made by men, and that wage gap seems to be widening.[28]

An interesting perspective on this situation is offered by Kristin Luker who did research with women who have repeated abortions. Luker argues that the subjects of her study, like many American women, are caught in an "option squeeze" between the disappearing world of ascribed motherhood and the unfulfilled promise of achievement in wage labor and the professions. The women who aborted repeatedly did so when pregnancy failed to transform an uncommitted lover into a husband. According to the author, the failure of conception to compel a marriage is due to a range of social factors, including

the decline in the value of childbearing, the increased availability of wifely goods and services in more specialized sectors of the service economy and the increased availability of sexual intercourse outside of marriage. . . .

In the open market of contemporary courtship, women as a class are bargaining with deflated currency.[29]

These changes in the "sexual economy" are as much the cause as the result of the increasing separation of sexual activity from procreation and heterosexual monogamy in contemporary American life. None the less, for those who see that trend as threatening, abortion has become a symbolic focus representing what is perceived as negative social change. In the view of a local obstetrician and long-time pro-life activist, abortion is a symptom of a deeper need for full-scale social reform:

"I think it is due to a decline in sexual morals, the prevalence of situational ethics, what people see on TV. You know, if it feels good, do it. Why aren't they using contraception? When I was growing up, it was unusual for things to go that far. I'm idealistic, I know. Society has to be reeducated, the spiritual training of people has to be changed. The sanctity of human life has to be understood. That comes from families, churches and to some extent through schools. You can't legislate morality. But you can make it illegal to destroy other people's lives."

Opposition to public approval of abortion summarizes a pervasive fear that a society increasingly based on individual achievement, single-minded upward mobility and a cash-based service economy no longer values or rewards those who nurture or care for dependents. Abortion represents for some the triumph of self-interest – for example, sexual pleasure separated from its procreative possibilities – over self-sacrificing traits traditionally identified as "natural" characteristics of mothers, and, by extension, women.

That such fear could motivate a full-scale social movement suggests that for many Americans, gender identity is deeply bound to a social system which supports the linking of female sexuality to pregnancy, marriage, childrearing and homemaking. When a woman can safely and legally choose to terminate a pregnancy because she does not want to be a mother, the insistent motivation to connect female sexual activity to this cultural chain of events is undone. The links are exposed as social constructions – i.e. not inevitable – and the imperative of motherhood as a condition beyond human control is dismantled.

The current head of River City Birthright interprets valuing sexual pleasure for its own sake as a kind of incomplete knowledge.

"We need to stress responsibility in sexual activity. Planned Parenthood's whole emphasis is it's something you do for fun. That's contrary to reality. Irresponsible sex is a tragedy, but a social reality. Intercourse results in a child, and a child needs two parents, and kids don't have any idea about that. Planned Parenthood has pushed contraceptives, yet there is more sexual promiscuity and unwanted pregnancy. The whole answer is in good education of kids. But people don't want to talk about sex."

The pro-life emphasis on the "unborn child" ripped from the womb invokes abortion as a perversion of the natural order. Thus women who abort can be considered as unnatural, amoral or at least psychologically unbalanced. A young woman active in LIFE Coalition whose ambition is to finish her degree in counseling and run a home for unwed mothers explained her understanding of women who abort.

"It is the weak woman who has the abortion. She is unable to deal with sexuality. She has unresolved relations with her family or her boyfriend. Even though she blames others, abortion is proof of a loss of control. . . . Society needs to accept women pregnant out of wedlock and offer them support."

The desire of pro-life activists to see their position gain exclusive social legitimacy is an effort to insist on the "naturalness" of a system in which the linking of sex to pregnancy and marriage is the linchpin for material security of women with children. In writing off the pro-life response as simply reactionary or "anti-sex", pro-choice activists fail to recognize the degree to which women in this country – by choice and by circumstance – are still invested in a system which connects their sexuality to heterosexuality, childbearing, and the support of a husband.

The danger of the current stalemate is that it masks the reality of "the option squeeze" faced by women on both sides of the issue. In so doing, the abortion polarization diverts energy from the imagination and construction of a new social landscape in which women and men no longer find that enjoying reproductive and sexual autonomy, engaging in meaningful (or at least remunerative) work, and bearing and raising children in an environment of emotional and material support are mutually exclusive choices.

Notes

I conducted much of the research on which this paper is based while working with the documentary unit of WCCO-TV Minneapolis. The final one-hour production based on the controversy over the clinic was broadcast April 25, 1982 with the title *Prairie Storm*. It is available from WCCO-TV, 90 S. 11th St, Minneapolis, Minn, 55403.

My thanks to Greg Pratt, Jan Olsen and Ben McCoy with whom I worked on the documentary; to members of LIFE, CRC, the North Dakota Women's Health Organization and others who so kindly cooperated in the work.

For financial assistance, I would like to thank Joan Arnow, the George Gund Foundation, Michael Meyer, the Money for Women Fund and the Playboy Foundation. I would also like to thank the Woodrow Wilson National Fellowship Foundation whose award of a Charlotte Newcombe Doctoral Dissertation Fellowship for 1982-3 has enabled me to continue research.

1 Daniel Granberg, "The Abortion Activists", *Family Planning Perspectives*, vol. 13, no. 4, 1981, pp. 157-63.
2 Alan Crawford, *Thunder On the Right*, New York, Pantheon, 1980; Zillah Eisenstein, "The Sexual Politics of the New Right: Understanding the Crisis of Liberalism for the 1980s", *Signs*, vol. 7, no. 3, 1982, pp. 567-88; Carol Felsenthal, *The Sweetheart of the Silent Majority*, New York, Doubleday, 1981; Andrew H. Merton, *Enemies of Choice: The Right-to-Life Movement And Its Threat to Abortion*, Boston, Beacon, 1981.
3 The identities of people and places have been altered to protect the confidentiality of those who participated in this project.
4 For example, see Stacey Oliker, "Abortion and the Left: The Limits of Pro-Family Politics", *Socialist Review*, vol. II, no. 56, March-April 1981.
5 For example, see the report on the interaction of pro-choice and pro-life women at a conference on abortion by Joy Dryfoos, "Light Into the Gathering Darkness", *Family Planning Perspectives*, vol. 13, no. 4, July-August 1981.
6 J.A. Borders and P. Cutright, "Community Determinants of U.S. Legal Abortion Rates", *Family Planning Perspectives*, vol. 11, 1979, pp. 117-33.
7 Emma Rothschild, "Reagan and the Real America", *New York Review of Books*, December 5, 1981.
8 William Schmidt, "Overnight Boom From Gambling", *New York Times*, March 4, 1982.
9 Judith Blake and Jorge del Pinal, "Predicting Polar Attitudes Toward Abortion in the U.S.", in J. Burtchaell, *Abortion Parley*, Kansas City, Andrews & McMeel, 1980.
10 Roger Williams, "The Power of Fetal Politics", *Saturday Review*, June 1, 1979.
11 Skerry, Peter, "The Class Conflict Over Abortion", *The Public Interest*, Summer 1978.
12 Richard Viguerie, *The New Right: We're Ready to Lead*, Falls Church, Va, Viguerie, 1980.

13 George Gilder, *Wealth And Poverty*, New York, Basic, 1981.
14 Phyllis Schlafly, *The Power of the Positive Woman*, New York, Jove, 1978.
15 Daniel Granberg, op. cit., p. 159.
16 Ibid., p. 158.
17 Ibid., p. 162.
18 Judith Blake and Jorge del Pinal, op. cit., p. 49.
19 Barbara Ehrenreich, "Combat In the Media Zone", *Seven Days*, March 10, 1978.
20 Ellen Goodman, "The Changing World of the Full-Time Housewife", *McCalls Magazine*, February 1979.
21 Daniel Scott Smith, "Family Limitation, Sexual Control and Domestic Feminism in Victorian America", *Feminist Studies*, Winter-Spring 1973.
22 Nancy Cott and Elizabeth Pleck, "Introduction", in N. Cott and E. Pleck, *A Heritage of Her Own: A New Social History of American Women*, New York, Simon & Schuster, 1979.
23 Barbara Epstein, *The Politics of Domesticity: Temperance in Nineteenth Century America*, Wesleyan University Press, 1981; Mary P. Ryan, "The Power of Women's Networks: A Case Study of Female Moral Reform in Antebellum America", *Feminist Studies*, vol. 5, no. 1, 1979.
24 Linda Gordon, *Woman's Body, Woman's Right*, New York, Penguin, 1976.
25 Deirdre English, "The War Against Choice", *Mother Jones*, vol. VI, no. 11, February-March 1981, pp. 567-88.
26 Merrill Sheils, "A Portrait of America", *Newsweek*, January 17, 1983.
27 US Bureau of the Census, Department of Commerce, "Divorce, Child Custody and Child Support", *Current Population Reports*, series p-23, no. 84, 1979.
28 Sheils, op. cit., p. 31.
29 Kristin Luker, *Taking Chances: Abortion and the Decision Not to Contracept*, Berkeley, University of California Press, 1975.

Variety: The Pleasure in Looking

Bette Gordon

All photos in this chapter by Nan Goldin.

The appeal of the cinema lies in its visibility, its "being-there-to-be-looked-at" quality. The pleasure of looking has been much discussed in film theory: not what we see, but how we see, how pleasure is structured by the film's text. Film plays on voyeuristic fantasy, portraying a hermetically sealed world that unfolds magically, indifferent to the presence of the audience.

Although film is produced to be seen, the conditions of screening, for example, the darkened theatre, and other narrative conventions give the spectator an illusion of looking in on a private world. The pleasurable structures of looking in the cinema arise from multiple sources: the pleasure of using another

person as an object through sight and subjecting their image to a curious and controlling gaze, and also through narcissism and identification with the image seen, for example, with the images of perfect Hollywood stars.[1]

From a feminist perspective, the pleasure of looking in the cinema has been connected with the centrality of the image of the female figure. This has involved an exploration of the way in which sexual difference is constructed in cinema, the way in which the gaze is split (men look, women are looked at), and the representation of female pleasure. It is this notion of female pleasure which interested me when making my film, *Variety*. Pornography becomes a site of feminist exploration into what it has to say about desire, what kind of fantasies it mobilizes, and how it structures diverse sexualities.

In focusing on female pleasure, I am not interested in uncovering a "feminist visual erotica," but in attending to the relation between desire and representation. Feminists have been suspicious of pleasure promoted in the cinema, dependent as it is upon the objectification of the female body. Consequently, we have avoided dealing with sexual pleasure in film. The insertion of the questions posed by fantasy provides a point from which to begin, and a challenge to the notion of sexuality as a fixed identity. In fact, it is precisely the gap between sexual fantasy and sexual identity that provides a place for exploring a number of issues which surface at the intersection of feminism and film. As I am concerned with the processes of construction in cinema, it is worth the risk of exploring female fantasy and pleasure.[2]

The film is concerned with watching at all levels, as the fictional narrative of the young woman's voyeurism becomes a metaphor for the way that men watch women not only in pornography but in all cinema. Christine works in a pornographic movie theater as a ticket-seller and becomes obsessed with watching one particular male client. Gradually succumbing to her curiosity, she begins to follow him. Her obsession is voyeuristic, and in this sense can be seen as pornographic. But in this case, the traditional male role (male as voyeur, woman as object) is reversed, positing the woman as voyeur, in an attempt to locate female desire within a patriarchal culture.

Working inside the ticket-seller's booth, Christine watches and listens to the activities of 42nd Street. As the images and sounds of the area and of her job increasingly affect her, she is less able to discern between actuality and fantasy. Indeed, she begins to construct an elaborate fantasy about the man she has chosen to follow, and that fantasy parallels her detailed descriptions of the movies she watches more and more frequently in the theater. Similarly, the organization and structure of the sex industry is

made to parallel the organization and structure of another, more
commercially respectable industry – one she discovers by
following that man. He leads her to the Fulton Fish Market,
Yankee Stadium, the Staten Island Ferry and the Jersey Shore. His
activities seem clandestine, but the narrative never reveals the
nature of his involvements.

Christine would like to be a writer, but takes a job as a ticket-
taker in a pornographic movie theater. She chooses what is easy
and illegitimate rather than what she most wants to do, since she
can't imagine supporting herself through her writing.

194   *Bette Gordon*

The ticket booth is a central image in the film: it is a transitional place, in between the theater and the streets. She is not completely involved in the sex industry, since she is not a dancer or a porno movie actress; she is a ticket-taker and could either leave the sex industry or move more deeply into it. I did not want her to be perceived as a victim. The ticket booth also provides her with a vantage point: she views men and their sexual desire as they enter the theater. She observes many, not just a few; they become commonplace and demystified.

In *Variety*, pornographic films become extreme examples of mainstream Hollywood cinema. Both employ the voyeuristic mode to exploit women as objects of male fantasy and male desire. Rather than make a film that uses explicit sex to explore these issues, I am interested in raising various questions: How does the cinema produce and construct certain prescribed sexualities and marginalize others? Since pornography doesn't tie women's sexuality to reproduction, to domesticated couples, or exclusively to men, does it offer other possibilities for women?

Pornography is not a monolithic construction but consists of a variety of practices operating across various institutions, places, and times and therefore is open to intervention. The codes and conventions which characterize particular pornographic representations, construct sexual difference, and order ways of seeing can be analyzed. I am interested in interrupting the conventions of dominant culture by twisting them around. This calls attention to the process of construction by making the viewer aware of ideas, images, and representations – where meaning comes from. The point is that the prevailing representation is not a given, not a natural phenomenon. Interruption of dominant forms leads the viewer to more active interaction with the material rather than passive consumption.

I try to intervene with the way in which the dominant culture presents ideas. My work is in the mainstream, but I insert questions and discomfort into images, narratives, and stories. Other filmmakers are interested in creating a separate or alternative feminist erotica. I am not, since that alternative suggests marginality – the "other place" outside of culture that women have already been assigned. I don't want to maintain that outsideness.

In addition, dominant forms are expert at incorporating and coopting marginal forms, so working from a place outside of male culture is no guarantee of autonomy. I prefer to work within and through the existing culture by challenging it, especially its constructions of sexuality which pervade not just representation but many other domains, for example, the family and law. Pornography provides one more place to investigate how sexuality is constructed.

Recent film writing and theory have suggested that the basic condition of cinema is voyeurism – an exchange of seeing and being seen – so that the cinema manages to be both exhibitionist and secretive. These active and passive components of voyeurism, which are part of the cinema in general, are the focus of *Variety*.

I am interested in investigating fantasy and pleasure, especially how they are constructed in culture and therefore in cinema.

Christine's boyfriend is an investigative reporter. He is researching an article about the Fulton Street Fish Market. He talks about his work, and as usual, she only listens. Then *she* begins to speak, and her speech takes the form of describing the movies she sees and eventually her fantasies. At first, he expresses his discomfort, because men become anxious when they hear women speak of their sexual desires. He is more threatened by her sexuality than her possible competition with him in investigating the story. (The man she is following appears to have some connection to the Fish Market.) Later, she tells her boyfriend her fantasy about a woman who takes a hitchhiker home with her. The hitchhiker observes her having sex with a snake and then with a tiger. He wants to join in. . . . Her boyfriend becomes mute. He doesn't speak any more; her speech takes over his, reversing the dominance of male speech.

We never see the pornographic movies; we hear only Christine's description. This is an approach opposite to the one used by *Not A Love Story*, which utilizes pornographic images and the same lure that pornography uses: "This film contains graphic material which may be objectionable." Moreover, the focus on Christine's description of and reaction to porno films raises the question of individual subjectivity: the viewer interprets and gives meaning to representations, which are far from uniform despite the conventions of culture.

Christine's fantasies become more elaborated the longer she works in the movie theater, as she is surrounded and confronted by new sexual images. Speaking of fantasies is taboo in our culture, even to those close to you, for example, a lover. Although the language of desire may be male, Christine's articulation of sexual fantasy represents a new and radical activity. The film suggests that women, even in patriarchal culture, are active agents who interpret and utilize cultural symbols on their own behalf.

There is no representation of Christine having sex in the film. She has sex by speaking it and by voyeuristically following the patron. She describes what she sees on the screen at first, but goes on to describe what she wants to see, constructed from her own desire. There is a power struggle going on between Christine and her boyfriend and the male patrons at the theater. She speaks her fantasies, which silence men: they can't deal with her desire being spoken.

She follows the anonymous client into a porno bookstore, losing sight of him momentarily, and begins to browse through the magazines. An elaborate exchange of looks takes place: men look at her; she looks at them, looking at women, looking. . . . She is out of place in the porn store, a male space. Men often leave when a woman enters an adult bookstore because they are caught in the act of looking.

Three looks operate in mainstream cinema: (1) characters in the film look at each other; (2) the camera looks at what it films; (3) the viewer looks at the screen. Paul Willemen suggests that pornography contains a fourth look: an observer looks at the viewer of pornography, catching him in a taboo act. The fourth look could be the superego or the threat of censorship, directed at the pornography's illicit place in the culture. A woman in a porn store represents the fourth look and so makes men uncomfortable. Other men are complicit, but a woman is not. She is supposed to be the object of their gaze.[3]

Christine is a viewer of men and male activities througout the film: at the fish market, at a baseball game, at a porn store. She stands out as a viewer of male space and terrain.

She dresses up for herself in a costume worn in one of the porn

films. Instead of displaying herself on the stage or screen, she looks at herself in the mirror, like a child experimenting with her mother's lipstick. She relates to her own image in the mirror, looking up close and turning around.

Christine follows him by train to Asbury Park, New Jersey, taking a room at the motel at which he stays. She waits for him to leave his room, which she enters via the shared balcony. She searches through his suitcase – the most sexual and pornographic

act in the movie – and finds only shaving cream, a shirt, an address book, and a porn magazine. By collecting these bits of information, she attempts to construct who he is. Suddenly, she hears a car pulling up and escapes back into her own room.

After following him, she returns to work and watches a film. She imagines a different image on the screen: her own in the motel room. The man enters the room and approaches her as she sits on the bed; he comes closer; she looks; he looks; he takes out his wallet. It's all in slow motion, since it is not real.

He remains unaware that she is following him. Finally, she calls
him on the telephone and confesses, "I've been watching you."
We do not hear his side of the conversation, but he appears to
express doubt, since she says, "I followed you into the store on
Broadway. *You* know which store. No, it's not a matter of money."
They agree to meet at the corner of Fulton and South Streets: the
final scene shows a dark, rainy corner. She doesn't show up; he
doesn't show up.

Heterosexual pornography substitutes a look for a touch. It
maintains a desire for gratification while never allowing direct
gratification. The viewer cannot have the man or woman on the
screen. The viewer remains unfulfilled.

The narrative enigma of my film is never completely explained,
thereby suggesting a relationship with unfulfilled pornographic
desire – for pornography offers fantasy and sustains desire for
ever-promised, but never-found gratification. It guarantees that
no representation will ever satisfy desire while maintaining a
desire for the representation itself.[4]

Notes

1 Laura Mulvey, "Visual Pleasure in Narrative Cinema", *Screen*, vol. 16,
  no. 3, Autumn 1975.
2 Leslie Stern, "The Body as Evidence", *Screen*, vol. 23, no. 5, Nov.-Dec.
  1982.
3 Paul Willemen, "Letter to John", *Screen*, vol. 21, no. 2, Summer 1980.
4 Ibid.

No More Nice Girls

Brett Harvey

In 1970 a group of New York area feminists distributed a copy of a "model abortion law": a blank piece of paper. Their position was unequivocal: a woman's right to abortion must be absolute, because her very personhood depends on her ability to control her own reproductive system. The 1973 Supreme Court decision, though ruling that abortion was a constitutional right, stopped short of endorsing the principle that the *only* person qualified to make a decison about abortion is the woman herself. Though radical feminists warned that the limited nature of the victory made it vulnerable to erosion and even reversal, most of us assumed in 1973 that the battle was over – that our right to abortion was virtually assured.

The Cassandras were right, of course. By 1977, a scant four years after *Roe* v. *Wade*, the Supreme Court allowed states to withhold Medicaid funds from poor women for abortions – the opening salvo in an all-out attack on abortion rights for all women. By 1980 Ronald Reagan had been elected on an anti-abortion platform, and ultra-conservatism had become the dominant force in the Congress. By the end of January 1981, an avalanche of bills outlawing abortion had been introduced in Congress. And in April of that year the Congress was suddenly debating a Human Life Statute which declared a fetus a person and defined abortion as murder.

The response of the women's movement to this onslaught took a number of different forms – indeed, as many forms as there were explanations for what had gone wrong. Some felt the original Supreme Court decision had been tainted from the beginning by the interests of population control groups. Others thought the women's health movement had drained energy away from the issue of abortion by broadening their focus to include every aspect of women's health care. Liberal pro-choice groups believed the political clout of the anti-abortion forces had been underestimated, and insufficient energy devoted to lobbying against them in Congress. Left groups maintained that what was needed was a mass, community-based movement in which abortion was linked with a wide range of economic and social issues.

To some extent all these explanations were accurate. But what was more important was that the New Right had changed the terms of the debate. Their attack on abortion rights had all the earmarks of a Holy War, because it focused on abortion as a moral issue: the fetus has a right to life which is paramount and sacred. Abortion is murder, pure and simple. In this context, it was easy to paint women who want abortions as selfish hedonists seeking pleasure without responsibility. This dovetailed neatly with a mounting unease among liberals about the evils of "self-fulfillment" and the supposed resulting disintegration of the family. Feminists and pro-abortion activists were not in a position to frame the debate in their own terms as they had in the early 1970s, but were forced into a defensive posture.

The strategy of liberal mainstream organizations like Planned Parenthood and NARAL (National Abortion Rights Action League) was to focus on abortion as a personal *choice*. "Abortion is something personal. Not political." ran the headline in a Planned Parenthood ad in the *New York Times* on April 26, 1981. The same Sunday NARAL ran a full-page ad which bannered, "The real issue is not abortion. The issue is the right of individuals to live free of government intrusion." Both ads emphasized the criminalization of women which would result, if the Human Life Amendment were passed.

Reproductive rights groups on the left, such as CARASA (Coalition for Abortion Rights and Against Sterilization Abuse) tied abortion rights with sterilization abuse, focused on the very real dangers of illegal abortion, and embedded abortion rights in a package of related issues like day care, health care, unemployment, education and housing.

Against this backdrop, a group of feminists came together in New York in April, 1981 to talk about what wasn't being talked about: abortion rights as the key to women's sexual freedom. The New Right, we felt, had guilt-tripped the abortion rights movement into soft-pedaling the most radical element of the abortion issue: that women's autonomy *must* include the right to express ourselves as sexual beings. That women cannot control our own destinies unless we can control our own reproductive function. At the heart of the New Right's attack on abortion rights was a traditional definition of women as childbearers – victims of nature – rather than autonomous human beings with the fundamental right to define our own sexuality. It was, in effect, a cruelly anti-woman campaign which was being combated with ladylike euphemisms like "choice" and "reproductive rights" on the one hand; or, on the other, by warnings of the dire consequences to women of a return to illegal abortions: coathangers, teenage pregancies, pregnancies as the result of rape and incest. No one was talking about women's right to *enjoy* sex without fear of pregnancy. The reasons for this, we felt, went deeper than the strategic need to reach a broad constituency. The New Right was tapping into a deep vein of puritanism and sexual guilt that seemed to lie below the surface of even the most seemingly liberal among us. We were being intimidated into apologizing for our own sexuality.

It seemed essential to reinject the abortion rights movement with the radical ideas and spirit of the early 1970s; to remind people that abortion was, after all, about sex. Our aim was not to undercut or discredit the liberal or left abortion rights organizations – we recognized that the battle must be fought on every front – but to provide another element: a bold, unequivocal demand for sexual freedom.

Our goal determined both the style and structure of the group. We wanted to create a vivid, outrageous and highly visible presence; to revive the "zap action" tactics of the early women's liberation days.[1] This dictated a small action group, unencumbered by the need to raise funds or please a large constituency. The name, "No More Nice Girls," arrived at during the course of an evening of brainstorming, seemed to us to express exactly the right note of brazen defiance.

We were fortunate in that several members of the group were political artists who were experienced in creating strong visual images to dramatize ideas. With their help, we tried out our first action at the "Sex and Language" conference at the Plaza Hotel. Barefoot, chained together, and wearing voluminous black maternity garments under which we were padded to look pregnant, six of us walked through the conference. We were accompanied by other members of the group wearing black jumpsuits and shocking pink headbands ("commandettes"), carrying a huge pink banner which read, "Forced childbearing is a form of slavery," and distributing our leaflets.

We repeated this action several times over the course of the summer, adding refinements like white-face and pink gags to dramatize the silent anonymity of the pregnant women. When we appeared at abortion rights rallies, the delighted reponse of the women around us made it clear that we were having the effect we had hoped for. We were successful in attracting a good deal of media attention as well. The November 1981 issue of *Life Magazine* used a dramatic photograph of No More Nice Girls to illustrate their feature story on abortion.[2]

When we began to do these actions in public, I had a private revelation of my own. To my surprise, the very *act* of stepping out in public wearing a sign saying "No More Nice Girls" required a certain amount of courage. Though trained as an actress, and in spite of years of demonstrations, I nevertheless had to nerve myself each time I did it. Everything in my middle-class Catholic background and upbringing recoiled at the idea of publicly identifying myself as a "not nice girl" – as a woman who admitted that she had sex, liked sex, and believed she had a *right* to be sexual. Other women in the group expressed similar feelings. Said one, "I felt a kind of drop in the pit of my stomach every time we did it, but at the same time it was exhilarating. The name itself externalized the issue in a way that made me feel defiant and 'bad.'" Some women were more comfortable in the role of "commandette" than "pregnant woman." For them, the image of a chained, pregnant woman was too potent and threatening to enact, even in the context of street theater.

By the Fall of 1981, an array of new legislation had been introduced in the Congress which made it clear that the New Right was zeroing in on sexuality itself – particularly women's sexuality. A new Human Life Amendment threatened to outlaw most forms of birth control; the Adolescent Family Life Bill aimed at preventing teenage pregnancy by encouraging abstinence, withholding contraceptive information, and penalizing programs which performed abortions or even gave abortion referrals; the Family Protection Act would penalize single parents, unmarried couples and homosexuals, and abolish child and wife abuse laws as well as programs for the victims.

In reponse to this legislation, No More Nice Girls created a skit called "Sex Cops" – a slapstick comedy in which a woman is arrested in her own bedroom by three officers, Hyde, Helms, and Hatch,[3] and tried for "a lifetime of sex crimes." She is accused of being fitted for a diaphragm at the age of 16; for obtaining venereal disease treatment without her parents' permission at 17; for falling in love with her college roommate ("a GIRL!") at 20; for having a spontaneous miscarriage at 22 and an abortion at 24; and finally, for wearing an IUD, "thereby committing possible manslaughter against innumerable pre-born citizens of the United States of America." The court's refrain, "You had the fun, so you pay the price," is also the refrain of a song, "Sex Cops," written for us by Judy Levine and Laura Liben, which we had recorded by a female punk rock group.

SEX COPS/ The sex cops know
SEX COPS/ When you take off your clothes
SEX COPS/ Don't let it show
that you're having fun
or you'll pay the price

Be a mom, be a wife
and if you can't dig that, you've got no right to life.

What's the big deal if they rape and beat us?
you're life's worth shit compared to a fetus.

SEX COPS/ You're a virgin or a whore
SEX COPS/ Don't try for nothing more
SEX COPS/ You know what's in store
You had the fun
so you pay the price.

Calvin Klein tells us to pull down our pants
but if we get knocked up, then it's out of their hands.

Wear a gold lamé mini and fuck-me shoes
but if you really get fucked, you pay the dues.

SEX COPS/ They got a chastity law
SEX COPS/ You know what it's for
SEX COPS/ To make it like it was before
When you had the fun
then you paid the price.

Teenage sex is such a thrill
pay a fine for the seed you spill.

Teenage sex is so much fun
get your parents' consent before you come.

SEX COPS/ Gay love is a crime
SEX COPS/ They're here to remind
SEX COPS/ Do it straight or do the time
You have the fun
and you'll pay the price.

SEX COPS/ They're the President and the Pope
SEX COPS/ They're your teachers and your shrink
SEX COPS/ So you better stop and think
If you have the fun
Then you'll pay the price.

© 1981 Levine/Liben

We performed "Sex Cops" in front of Right to Life Headquarters
and at several conferences and rallies in the New York area.

As of this writing (July 1983) the Supreme Court has reaffirmed
women's constitutional right to abortion, and the Senate has
defeated the so-called Human Life Federalism Amendment which
would have permitted the states themselves to pass legislation
curbing abortions. Although conservatives can be expected to
continue to chip away at women's access to abortion by
attempting to limit Medicaid funding, insurance coverage and
abortions for teenaged women, feminists have raised a consciousness in the country that cannot be reversed – a consciousness that at the very least insists on choice. As Ellen Willis
recently wrote, "many people, men as well as women, feel
entitled to reject an unwanted pregnancy; even the moral
ambivalence that many express arises in a taken-for-granted

context of choice."[4] Still, we are far away from that blank piece of paper – the guarantee of total sexual freedom and autonomy for women. The notions that underlie "free abortion on demand" – that women are not slaves to their reproductive systems; that women have the right to choose when, how, and with whom they wish to be sexual – these ideas, the bedrock of radical feminism, are still not truly accepted. As long as women who choose not to have children, or to live alone or with other women, or to have a variety of sexual partners – as long as such women are stigmatized as "selfish" or "narcissistic," "irresponsible" or "perverted," no woman is really free.

Notes

1 One such "zap action" had, in fact, already taken place. A group called the "Women's Liberation Zap Action Brigade," which included members of the Reproductive Rights National Network and CARASA, disrupted a congressional subcommittee hearing on the Human Life Statute by shouting "A woman's life is a human life!" Six of the women were arrested and fined $100 each.
2 *Life Magazine*, November 1981, pp. 45-54.
3 Representative Henry Hyde, Senator Jessie Helms, and Senator Orrin Hatch, architects of the bulk of anti-abortion and anti-sex legislation in the US Congress.
4 Ellen Willis, "The Politics of Abortion", *In These Times*, June 15, 1983, p. 12.

No Progress in Pleasure

Barbara Kruger

Photography has saturated us as spectators from its inception amidst a mingling of laboratorial pursuits and magic acts to its current status as propagator of convention, informational directive, and cultural commodity. Images are made palpable, ironed flat by technology, and, in turn, dictate the seemingly real through the representative. And it is this representative, both its appearance and distribution within culture, which detonates issues and raises questions. Is it possible to construct a way of looking which is pleasured by use value and escapes the oppressions of exchange? How do I as a woman and an artist work against the marketplace of the spectacle while residing within it? Is women's marginality oppositional or a compliance with the seemingly critical voices who are comforted by our absence? I see my work as a series of attempts to ruin certain representations, to construct an altered subjectivity and to welcome a female spectator into the audience of men. If my work is considered "incorrect," all the better, for my attempts aim to undermine that phallocentric univocality, that singular, pontificating male voice-over which "correctly" instructs our pleasures and histories or lack of them. I am wary of the phallic seriousness of certain theories, of their confidence of knowledge. I find any critical discourse which does not take considerations of gender into account to be complicit. I am concerned with who speaks and who is silent. I think about works which address the material conditions of our lives and the oppression of social relations on a global level; about work which recognizes the law of the father as the calculator of capital. I want to speak and hear outlandish questions and comments. I want to be on the side of surprise and against the certainties of pictures and property.

You thrive on

mistaken

identity

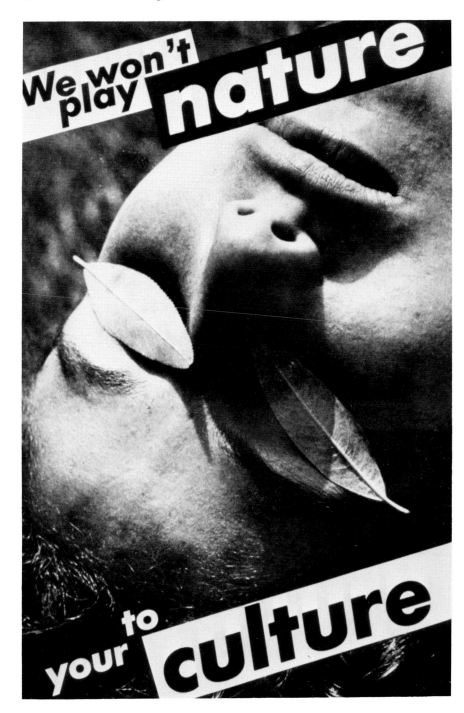

Beyond Politics? Children and Sexuality

Kate Millett

Sexuality as it is experienced by women and children in this society is by no means beyond politics. We live in a patriarchy which is in and of itself a political relationship involving male dominance, power, and control over a submerged group, women. This is built into every aspect of society: law, religion, education, economics, and state power. It is built into the family itself.

The sexual exploitation of children as we've come to discover it is a phenomenon so varied and protected by taboo that it has been virtually unmentionable until recent years. Investigators report that sexual abuse primarily involves the victimization of female children by adult males. Often the aggressors are fathers or friends of the family, whom the family protects to an astonishing degree. It is too embarrassing to deal with, so we say the child made it up. We don't report it, for fear the man might lose his job or his wife might leave him. We may see to it that the child doesn't meet him any more or that the man doesn't get his hands on her again, but in an enormous number of cases the problem is avoided, because it is too difficult to face the actual interpersonal, social, and economic circumstances that arise. Victimization of male children by adult males occurs also, but there appear to be no reports of females who aggress upon children of either sex. This is unlikely to be true, but we need to give some thought to the possible reasons for this "fact." Are adult females afraid to abuse children sexually? Does female abuse not come to attention? Is it regarded as unimportant? Does it have no harmful effects, if it does take place? It remains unclear why transgression is so one-sided.

In the case of father/daughter incest, the adult male acts with full authority of the parent, one of the complications of sexuality between generations within patriarchal society. The authority of the parent is very great indeed, being the strongest claim that we recognize in our society apart from that of the state. Adults have the edge on children in countless ways, principally through their social authority, but also through the economic dependency of children, who have no status but also no resources. The most important thing you can say about childhood is that children have no money. If your father rapes you, he also feeds you. And society scarcely permits you to disclose the liaison between you. Though one might think that disclosure would lead to instant help, it does not. In fact society will condemn you for it; society will refuse to believe you and fail to acknowledge your perhaps hardly coherent view of the relationship, because at the age of 12 or 13 it is enormously complex to be in love with your father – a matter of course, in fact, a familial injunction, a predictable situation. He has loved and protected you all your life, and you have responded with rapt admiration for all he is. That he has transgressed against the interdiction laid down forbidding him to sexualize his love has, at the moment of your adolescent sexual curiosity, led you into a whole kingdom of confusion. The world has put him over you and made him your master. He has now made you his slave as well, his partner in a guilt at once overwhelming, perplexing, nebulous, there and not there. A blanket and mist, yours and not yours, but still finally yours, your fault, the more so because all fault is ascribed to you already. You hardly even know what you are talking about. You hardly know what the adults are talking about, when they talk of their mysteries. Never mind that it was someone else's idea, perhaps even forced upon you, brought to you by adult intelligence, their standards and crimes and laws; it is done now, and you have done it. So the crime, whatever it is – and it is always unclear – is on your head. "Do this," and you do, and then you are condemned to an infamy. The conundrum of the body, the discovery of it. You try to guess between their sentences, the intakes of breath, the indirection.

Sex itself is presented as a crime to children. It is how adults control children, how they forbid them sexuality; this has been going on for ages and is infinitely important to adults. It is a control with very widespread effects. Adults absolutely proscribe and forbid, and police to be sure there is no sexual activity among children. Despite the degree of sexual activity that actually goes on among children, I think adults have been all too effective, not only in poisoning sexuality but also in preventing children from understanding or experiencing it. Adults succeed in preventing children from being a sexual group unto themselves: the logical thing is not child/adult sexuality but child/child sexuality. Their own peers are people with the same interests and vocabulary, the people they spend time with, the people they regard as attractive, though not in the more complicated ways in which they may regard adults. Adults can turn around and hit you at any moment. They can send you off to bed. Who wants a relationship with a lover who has this sort of authority?

The logical behavior is child/child sexuality, for sexuality to play itself out among children who are always in love with each other, always curious, and sometimes in their one traditional ritual, playing doctor, caught and judged. But the rhetoric and practice that surrounds children has abjured them since infancy to chastity. "Don't touch yourself there, that's nasty." Of course, even if one was going to put in a good word for chastity, which I hadn't really meant to do, it is something one might practice willingly while comprehending sex. Whereas here is a little person who has been told that one whole section of the body has a crime attached to it. Imagine, "Never, never look at your left hand." It seems silly to children, of course, but power and force is conveyed by the phrase, "that's awful," principally because it is not explained. And the explanation that "it's dirty"? Well, thinks the child, obviously it isn't; I've taken a bath. What do they mean, it's dirty?

So the taboo, because of its irrationality and mysterious quality, is yet more harmful. It attacks the whole system of mental confidence and reason itself. "Don't touch yourself there." The root and ultimate source of human understanding about sexual stimulation is autoeroticism. We would know nothing about sexuality, I suppose, if left on a desert island, or if our hands were perpetually tied. We learn about sexuality necessarily from ourselves; in some instances and upbringings, this is the only source to rely on.

If we did not have the great power of autoeroticism, we would never come to any conclusions, form any tastes, or find many sources of energy, not only erotic but creative – the self, the psyche, or the mind as it reaches out to the world in works, ideas, or things made by the hands in art or craft. But all too often autoeroticism goes under the nasty name of masturbation in the patriarchal family. Thus named, masturbation is practiced for the rest of a lifetime in secret guilt and shame, or is "rehabilitated" by those providing therapy. To shed either outcome is a miracle; the shame is pervasive. I think that now, in what we like to describe as the sexual revolution, we are so busy shedding ourselves of the shame that we do not acknowledge the full weight of its effects in shaping ourselves and society.

Even discussions about sex are not permitted to children. In households of the modern type where the little boy chatters about his penis and his sister about her vagina, real conversation about sex is still the one distinction between adult and child worlds: the final vow, the topic never discussed in front of "them." Children are not supposed to know either about money or sex; sex is often more disturbing. Shame, invented by adults and laid upon the children, is still pervasive and continues to color adolescence, particularly that of female children. Their lives are a continual apology for something that they probably haven't done and do not really understand. But they might. They might. And the possibility of sexual activity is what adults guard against relentlessly.

Parental policing of young females is the one great, unexamined oppression, not only in their lives but in our own as adult women. Women in general are controlled, I think, through shame, through being shamed, and through shaming. The effects of the ascription of nameless guilt attend us all our lives and do very much harm, most of it unexamined. Women are both wrong and apologetic as a result, and any group in that position is easy to control socially and politically.

Adults form the young into a pack deprived of autoerotic sexual activity; then peers are policed and friendships are supervised as well. Guilt over autoeroticism and sexuality itself, over the body and its shames, over the knowledge of sexual excitement is forbidden open expression, one you are afraid to confess. How could you know it except through "self-abuse" or "jerking off"? Although boys are permitted more latitude than girls, jerking off remains a term of derision. How can you admit to your friends that you engage in something universally regarded as dirty? And if you do, how can it be spoken about in any depth?

When together, children's curiosity and desire is astonishingly and successfully curtailed. Considering its possibilities, sexuality has been very effectively policed. Control works in stopping the behavior; where it doesn't work, it succeeds still because there is so much guilt; so much shame for whatever sexual activity does take place; so much fear of discovery that when sexually active children are discovered, squelched, and separated, control succeeds. Even now, with more teenage pregnancies than ever, the sexual prohibition is still in effect. Since sexuality was forbidden knowledge, contraception is also forbidden, unfortunately; the culprits can become victims as well. Examples! Pregnant teenagers are exploited in two ways: they were forbidden sexuality, but they seized their right; they were forbidden to prevent pregnancy, and now they are saddled with children they do not want and punished for that fact as well. The sadism of this predicament is extraordinary. Their lives are eaten up by being forced to bear unwanted children without the economic resources to provide for them. Further confusion, added punishment, more fear and hatred of sex accrues. It becomes tragic and terrible: you get "caught." Not a right, not a pleasure, not a natural concomitant of life, but a species of disaster.

Adults create this pool of ignorance – and that is what it is: ignorance forced upon a group of young people, not innocence. Ignorant and inexperienced, they have no outlet. Youthful energy and frustration are dreadful to behold: the vandalism of young men, the self-destructive passivity of young women. One sex turns aggression toward the world as permitted, or even prescribed; the other turns aggression against itself, punished, apologetic, and aware of its lower status. The adults who create or perpetuate this pool of youthful ignorance generation after generation then in certain cases become predators as well.

True, the injunction is that no adult may have sex with the young who are innocent. But as investigators discover, there is also an unofficial line as old as the Bible about maidens, youth, and the blush of the virgin: they are fair game. There is a predatory energy even in courting, when what is courted is youth – the helplessness, the vulnerability, the innocence, the ignorance. The prey can be tripped, caught, seduced, tricked, talked into it, and beguiled, like a pocket picked by a thief. There is an exercise of power linked with what used to be called gallantry. (As gallantry is something our literature and much of our past social relationships were built upon, it is present with us to a degree we do not quite appreciate.)

But the main point about children and relationships between adults and children is that children have no rights. They have no money. Because they have no money, no status, and no place to go, their dependence becomes emotional and psychological as well. Few relationships equaling the dependency of childhood can be found in human society. There is no other sanctioned relationship in human society where one may casually strike others, prepare them for formal sadistic beatings, and deprive them of food; yet you may mutilate children, beat them to death slowly or quickly depending upon your whim, leave them on a thin string of life at a hospital and, if detected (and detection is by no means easy and never certain), you may get them back two weeks later in child court. This sort of power exercised by one human being over another no longer exists elsewhere, although it did in slavery and servitude. It is difficult to treat even women this way any more.

Even the victim of father/daughter incest, objecting to the painful and boring penetration by a large adult male (an experience she might have found interesting once, though disturbingly forbidden, since the outside world poisoned whatever affection or curiosity was satisfied) remains this person's creature. Even telling leads to another predicament: the girl is treated and "helped" in incest clinics run by the state. Together with daddy, the whole family is brought in to make peace and renew their official bond, the family being sacred to the state as well as to the psychologists it employs. The girl will have to go on living with this situation and with this daddy, who, we're told, will stop; she must go on living at home. She has no rights at all; she has no money; there isn't any other place for her to go. Home is where abused children are fed. There is no other place that will feed them. The state claims to be without resources here, whatever its expenditures on armaments; it will invest virtually nothing in housing and feeding children. There are few shelters for children, and they are always full. And where else can a chld go? In our society, no one feeds anyone else's child. Even foster parents get paid. We sentimentalize children, yet we also accept that they are treated as property and therefore are subject, as any property, to mistreatment – which is typically regarded, as it was under slavery and serfdom, as an excess – only excess or aberration, rather than an organic part of the system itself.

Where do children get justice? Where do they get sex, as much a right for the young as for anyone else? Wilhelm Reich pointed out that a society is free to the degree that it permits freedom to its youth: sexual freedom and sexual expression. Reich was the first to address the sexuality of the young in an age when Freud was analyzing and curing young persons with sexual disorders on order and payment from their parents. Freud often dealt with children, especially females, who had been sexually abused; he resolved the entire problem by deciding that it was an Oedipal fantasy on their part. So female children were not only sexually abused, they had to assent that they imagined it. This process undermines sanity, since if what takes place isn't real but imaginary, then you are at fault: you are illogical, as well as naughty, to have imagined an unimaginable act: incest. You ascribed guilt to your father, and you are also a very guilty, sexy little creature yourself. So much for you.

Treatment may take months and years, and finally you give in. You did imagine it; you are cured, then, and in a certain sense made insane. Reich understood the child's compliance with the parents as another form of adult invasion, for it was adults who forbade sexuality in the young to start with. Despite Reich's work, we do not hear enough about the sexual rights of children. We hear excellent things about sexual education, which could probably lead to sexual expression in children's peer groups. But the preconditions for the complete sexual emancipation of children are simply not developed.

Intergenerational sex could perhaps in the future be a wonderful opportunity for understanding between human beings. But conditions between adults and children preclude any sexual relationship that is not in some sense exploitative. This is not actually the fault of the adults involved, but of the entire social structure. To succeed, a relationship needs an egalitarian space and a balance between the two partners which it cannot by virtue of society have. The adult has money, status, citizenship, and autonomy. The child has no money; the child's economic dependence is total and absolute; minor status resembles that of an incompetent, with no standing before the law, no rights, and therefore no citizenship. This is the bar to any kind of humanistic incest. I don't see any point in saying that incest is evil in and of itself. I don't think that would be the case at all, for example, between sisters and brothers, or sisters and sisters, or brothers and brothers. Siblings already have love relationships. They are finding out how sex works; they are playing. It is even difficult to say absolutely and as a matter of course that all sexual relationships between parents and children are completely wrong. I do not think one can say that; I can think of thousands which might be delicate and interesting.

However, the situation we are in because of our social organization and its patriarchal structure is what militates against intergenerational sexual relationships developing in a way that is not clearly destructive, particularly to children, the parties without rights. I think that the natural realm of sexual expression of children and youth is with each other, where they can avoid the already hated imbalance they have with adults. Adults belong to a class that dominates children. We fool ourselves if we do not acknowledge the political relationships between adults and children. Adults, however well-intentioned, can hardly refrain from exploitation.

As is the case with so many reforms, we come to speak of the rights of children after we've already spoken of their broken little bones in hospitals. We give parents absolute *carte blanche*, actual ownership of people much smaller than themselves, beings they may abuse in mind and body who are also dependent upon them for their very crust of bread, sustenance about which parents can be very controlling and petty as well – and then we say, "My, my, every now and then one of them loses their temper . . . surely they need therapy." We fail to examine the essential relationship.

It is difficult therefore to imagine the sexual emancipation of children without coming to understand how necessary are other forms of emancipation as well, all parts of progressive social change in years to come. That children have autonomy – that they do not belong to their biological parents, that they have a right to money, to a choice in where they live, that they are not property, that they are not slaves, that they belong to themselves – is a most revolutionary idea. Our emancipation is involved as well as theirs, since exploitation corrupts the abuser as well as the abused.

The guilt and shame imposed on us as adults, though first imposed on all of us as children, is imposed on us again as we reimpose it upon a new generation, perpetuating the sins of the past and its concept of sin. Spanking, for example – because we were spanked. Don't we remember how we hated it? Don't we remember how we were terrorized? How much adult behavior can be traced back to this trauma? That short, hideous experience of torture? Perhaps it helps to perpetuate torture itself, which is much on the increase throughout the world. Torture is in fact the method by which some hundred countries are run now, an acknowledged form of policy. It is very close to our gates. In fact much of it emanates from our gates, from the CIA and the interrogators we train for South America so that certain nasty little dictatorships can be held together for American economic interests.

But that, you may say, is a terrible thing – human beings being tortured. Children are just as vulnerable before adults as anyone is before the powers of the state. Are the origins of torture not in our individual psychic histories, are they not in those beatings and spankings, those expressions of overwhelming force we learned of first as children? Nightmare terror before deliberate and self-righteous cruelty. All of that was imposed on us against our will and is with us still. The wounds of childhood are a long, slow cancer eating us throughout our lives. There is no end to it unless we make one. Not until the nineteenth century was there ever any outcry about the brutalization of children; one man, Charles Dickens, made it a cause for which not only half but all of humanity may thank him. But we are not finished with the politics of childhood yet. We are just starting at last, rather tardily. You and I will live to see all this discussed for the first time in human history. Considering that we were all children once, and if we are any good at all, we are children still, we have a stake in this. The emancipation of children is our own emancipation in retrospect, but it unleashes the future as well.

Fat and the Fantasy of Perfection

Carol Munter

I Don't Like[1]

my fat tummy
or my fat behind
flab, arms, legs
thighs, abdomen (round stomach)
hips
oily skin
big hips
stubby, fat fingers
protruding stomach, like a small pot
my weight
my varicose veins
being judged by my weight and age

my hair (at times)
my hips (at the moment)
flabby bottom
wattles under my chin
my stomach
my appetite
my flat chest
my fat ass
my nose

fat around waist
thick thighs
wrinkles on neck
signs of age around mouth and eyes
narrow feet look like skis
being too pale
long toes
hairy

my thighs
my hips
the way my body makes me feel like a mistake in general
thighs
stomach
mastectomy scars

fat behind
large breasts

my hands
my thighs
my breasts
my waist
my crotch

At the beginning of the women's movement, I felt out of it in my women's group. I was fat. Everyone was busy rejecting what was being called objectification. Guiltily, I longed for the day when I could call forth the response that others seemed to be condemning. It seemed that once again I wasn't supposed to want what before feminism I always thought I wasn't supposed to want. Secretly, of course, I always wanted to be admired physically. I wanted to be looked at and desired sexually – in the way I responded to others but didn't believe they responded to me.

After all, I was fat. Didn't the right body size and shape determine sexual desirability?

My father was a professional photographer and always talked about how beautiful the brides were when he photographed them. What did he think of me? And of my mother? I was forever in a quandary about this.

My mother was fat and seemed filled with disgust about her body. She never had clothes to wear. She went to "special" ladies who made "special" all-in-ones. Her pubic hair was visible beneath these girdles. They seemed to cover a dark, strange, frightening place. She seemed happiest freed of her restraints, walking around without clothes. Not proudly, just released. Her breasts were large and sagging; the result, she thought, of being too tightly corseted too young. I should continue to wear undershirts, she said, so my muscles wouldn't break and I would keep warm. *I* felt I'd better conceal my desire to develop. I desperately wanted to, despite her self-disgust. Her body must have been desirable to me once – full, warm, and soft. And desirable to him, I assume. I remember only the later part – her distress, her diets, and my feeling that she didn't want me to be like her, to be female. Because it was awful, or because there was only enough room for one?

So I watched him taking pictures of brides and wanted to be like them. But what about her, my mother?

At thirteen, I started gaining weight. I spent the next fifteen years completely preoccupied by hatred for my body and endless resolutions to improve its degraded condition.

Food solved and salved many problems. It provided the link between home and the world; it bridged the separation. As a representative of earlier comfort, food was the medicine I used in an attempt to heal various injuries and hurts with which I was ill-equipped to deal realistically. My increasing overweight identified me more and more with my mother, a state I must have both wanted and hated. But overweight made it difficult for me to get the responses and experience necessary for the adolescent working-through of sexual development. I felt imprisoned by my body, somewhere between childhood and adulthood, living mostly in a fantasy about how life could be if only my body were improved. Little experience, much fantasy – fantasy about being attractive, looked at, sought after and admired. Did adolescent girls ever imagine a sexual exchange, or was being looked at always a means to reassurance and proof of our acceptability?

I recall this story because I hope it resonates with other stories about the difficulties we have in coming to terms with our female bodies. I tell it because it is one example of the path to the ubiquitous fantasy of self-realization through the perfection of the body, one all fat women – and, I think, all women – share. If only I were thin, or if only my body were different in whatever way, then everything would be fine.

My story is not particularly unusual. But I feel fortunate that, in 1970, because it was the height of the women's movement, it was possible for me and a few others to ask some unusual questions. For example: what is wrong with being fat? Why should I diet? If dieting has never worked, maybe there's something wrong with the concept rather than with my "willpower." The story of that early work is recorded in *Fat is a Feminist Issue.*[2]

What surprises me in thinking about the myth of the perfect body is the reawakening of my rage. I remember how angry we were in 1970 when we realized the utter misery we had lived out, the enslavement to the cultural view of our complete unacceptability as fat women. The endless years we had spent punishing ourselves, like criminals, for the crime of what? Of eating? Of seeking some way to help ourselves with profoundly difficult, if not impossible, internal and external realities? For example, how is any woman supposed to be a sexy virgin or a dependent caretaker? The contradictions are staggering. But we didn't know that then. We thought we simply failed at controlling ourselves. Yet *before* we learned anything different, some of us made a decision: that no matter what happened – if no more pounds were ever shed – we would never deprive ourselves of any food whatsoever again. No more diets, no more punishment, no more contempt. We were no longer going to hide out in the shadows. We were going to grow into ourselves, dress ourselves *as we liked* without waiting to be different tomorrow.

As long as we say "When I get thin, then . . . ," we are saying that who we are is unacceptable, unworthy of admiration, unable to be loved, unsuitable as a sexual partner. We were tired of all that. No one was ever again going to tell us what to eat or what to look like. I wore long flowing pants, long flowing tops, and long flowing hair. I made friends with the mirror; I became an accepting friend, not admiring, not criticizing, just accepting. "Oh, this is a thigh. Interesting."

I've learned a lot since then. I know a great deal about how we – those of us who struggle with compulsive eating – use food as an attempt to deal with a multitude of very complex realities. For example, when I have a sexual feeling about which I'm in conflict, I eat. And then I yell about how fat I am, how disgusting I am for eating. I imagine that if I go on a diet, everything will be all right. How? What will I do about the fact that I'm conflicted about a sexual impulse or interest? It's as if we think that when we lose weight, our conflicts will disappear.

Why do we want our conflicts to disappear? What's wrong with them? What do we mean when we say, "If only I were thin, if only I could change this or that about my body, everything would be okay"? What's okay? And what is so wrong with us in the first place that we must see ourselves as always in transit? Not how we are – fat – but always about to be redeemed.

From what do we think we need redemption? I fear that we are in search of redemption from our female bodies. From their smells, from their needs, from their contours, from their difference and variation. After all, they are the closest to us. They represent us, reveal us; they carry us about. How we feel about our bodies has much to do with how we feel about ourselves. And how we feel about ourselves has everything to do with being unempowered, with being unresponded to – except in the domain we are assigned, our bodies – and with feeling that our survival rests on pleasing them, the others. As long as our options are restricted, no woman will experience her body as her home, but rather as her meal ticket. As long as we remain unempowered, we will need our conflicts to disappear magically through the loss of a pound of flesh, because we have no access to other modes of action. We are assigned to the realm of fantasy and to magic, not to life.

We are taught early that we are not to have real power or real choice. Instead, we are told, if we look a certain way – and a different way next year and a still different way the year after that – we will be responded to, we will be "attractive," we will be looked at, we will be taken care of, we will be chosen. And then what? Besides the fact that we end up alienated from each other – mothers, daughters, grandmothers, friends – in the competitive quest for the highest pedestal, then what? Just what will all this perfection do for us?

Our attempts to conform to a cultural ideal of the sexy or beautiful woman first appear to relate to sex, but in reality we change our bodies in the hope of being acceptable and being chosen. Our desperate wish to be selected has little connection with the pursuit of our own sexual satisfaction and pleasure. In exchange for being chosen and protected, we engage in sexual relationships, but the conditions governing women's action rapidly convert reciprocal sexual exchange into sexual service.

As my thinking returned to my body and turned away from my concern about eating *per se*, I became more and more enraged. My outrage had become quiescent while I became accustomed to viewing fat as the outward manifestation of a woman's attempt to use food to cope with other issues. The rage returned when Roberta and I planned this workshop.[3] We went through a difficult time, which is relevant to describe.

In trying to talk about how disability, aging, and weight are similar and yet dissimilar realities, the concept of transformation became key. Fat, in this society, is a vehicle for fantasies of transformation and perfection. In other words, if I'm fat, I can keep imagining that I could be different. I can imagine that if I lose weight, not only me but my life will take on a new shape. In our discussions, I had to look at the fact that disability and aging are quite different experiences from obesity, at least from the vantage point of the fantasy of ultimate perfection. Nevertheless, when I imagined myself experiencing either of these conditions, I was profoundly uncomfortable.

"You mean something could be 'wrong' with me from which I couldn't magically recover? You mean it's permanent? I can't hide it? Can't change it? I'll have to ask for help? Who, me? Never."

"You mean I'll never *ever* be the twelve-year-old anorectic on the cover of *Vogue*? You mean I'll *never* have my mother's tits that my father seemed to like?"

"Oh, no, not me. I'm *always* in transit, always 'improving,' always on the way to. When that stops, I stop."

But where am I going? On the way to where, and away from what?

I think that fat women – or all women – are always on the way from an awareness of limitation and imperfection, an awareness of many different needs and feelings which have been impossible to come to terms with in our position as women. The impossibility derives from the fact that women are not given an arena in which to struggle and learn. We're taught to shape our bodies and not the world. If one feels powerless, imperfections and limitations loom enormous. Needs in search of fulfillment must be renounced.

Where do we think we're going in our fantasies of transformation? Toward perfection, of course. Toward an overcoming, a surmounting of all that has not found resolution.

We feel that we're awful, and we work toward redemption. We must, however, learn that we are confined and work toward liberation.

Let me elaborate. Every time a woman reaches for food when she has no physiological need to do so, she is making an attempt to help herself. She is attempting to deal with some bit of external or internal reality which has made her uncomfortable: a sexual longing or fantasy, a feeling of envy or rejection, the impulse to violate a sexual taboo – the list is endless. After eating or after gaining weight, the problem is relabeled as a food or body problem, and the fantasy begins. A child of her culture, she believes that for women changing the body will solve the problem. Food and bodies – that's our turf. What else are we supposed to do about a problem? We binge and then go on a diet. The problem is that we have lots of conflicts and anxieties, and we don't know what to do with them. We can't imagine real acceptance or real resolution to conflict, internal or external. Our needs and ourselves have met with so little response, we have such restricted experience of the world that we are continuously forced back into our bodies. We can imagine *them* being different, not us. We will be admired for our bodies, though for nothing else. Except perhaps for not making any demands.

To the extent that we are unable to develop conviction in our capacity to act, we must rely on the false hope offered to us daily in the power of bodily perfection. If we are unable to see ourselves as shapers of the world or our lives, we must believe that altering our physique will change the shape of reality. As long as we are the chosen and not the choosers, the sexually acted-upon and not the actors, we will blame ourselves for what does not go well and believe that when we make the correction, *they* will smile upon us.

And then what? They smile. If the fantasy of transformation starts from a sense of powerlessness, if we eat because there are so many needs and feelings we shouldn't have, so many imagined flaws we don't know how to deal with, what will smiles do for us? My father will look at me like a bride. Or I'll be a bride. Then what? Is that power? Is that equality? I arrive on the cover of *Vogue*. And then?

Pursued to its final degree, this fantasy of the perfection of the body is a fantasy about the rejection of the self and of overcoming every need that wants expression and response. It is a fantasy of stasis, of being finished and complete. On a pedestal, perhaps. Admired, perhaps. But with no needs, no desires, no voice, no sex. What looked like perfection and power turns out to be the ultimate in subjugation: the eradication of the female self.

If I'm thin, I'll be popular. If I'm thin, I'll turn people on. If I'm thin, I'll have great sex. If I'm thin, I'll be rich. If I'm thin, I'll be admired. If I'm thin, I'll be sexually free. If I'm thin, I'll be tall. If I'm thin, I'll come more easily. If I'm thin, I'll have power. If I'm thin, I'll be loved. If I'm thin, I'll be envied. But if I'm thin *I* won't be.

Notes

1 Women attending the workshop participated in an experiential exercise, listing physical characteristics in response to the statement: "I don't like these traits about my body."
2 Susie Orbach, *Fat is a Feminist Issue: The Anti-Diet Guide to Permanent Weight Loss*, New York, Berkeley, 1979 (orig. 1978).
3 Roberta Galler and Carol Munter, "The Myth of the Perfect Body: Weight, Aging, and Disability."

Suggested reading

Kim Chernin, *The Obsession: Reflections on the Tyranny of Slenderness*, New York, Harper & Row, 1981.

Susie Orbach, *Fat Is a Feminist Issue: The Anti-Diet Guide to Permanent Weight Loss*, New York, Berkeley, 1979.

Susie Orbach, *Fat Is a Feminist Issue II*, London, Hamlyn, 1982.

The Fem Question

Joan Nestle

For many years now, I have been trying to figure out how to explain the special nature of butch-fem relationships to feminists and lesbian feminists who consider butch-fem a reproduction of heterosexual models, and therefore dismiss both lesbian communities of the past and of the present that assert this style. Before I continue, my editor wants me to define the term butch-fem, and I am overwhelmed at the complexity of the task. Living a butch-fem life was not an intellectual exercise; it was not a set of theories. Deep in my gut I know what being a fem has meant to me, but it is very hard to articulate this identity in a way that does justice to its fullest nature and yet answers the questions of a curious reader. In the most basic terms, butch-fem means a way of looking, loving, and living that can be expressed by individuals, couples or a community. In the past, the butch has been labeled too simplistically the masculine partner and the fem her feminine counterpart. This labeling forgets two women who have developed their styles for specific erotic, emotional, and social reasons. Butch-fem relationships, as I experienced them, were complex erotic and social statements, not phony heterosexual replicas. They were filled with a deeply lesbian language of stance, dress, gesture, love, courage, and autonomy. In the 1950s particularly, butch-fem couples were the front-line warriors against sexual bigotry. Because they were so visibly obvious, they suffered the brunt of street violence. The irony of social change has made a radical, sexual, political statement of the 1950s appear today as a reactionary, non-feminist experience. My own roots lie deep in the earth of this lesbian custom and what follows is one lesbian's understanding of her own experience.[1]

I am a fem and have been for over twenty-five years. I know the reaction this statement gets now: many lesbians dismiss me as a victim, a woman who could do nothing else because she didn't know any better, but the truth of my life tells a different story. We fems helped hold our lesbian world together in an unsafe time. We poured out more love and wetness on our barstools and in our homes than women were supposed to have. I have no theories to explain how the love came, why the crushes on the lean dark women exploded in my guts, made me so shy that all I could do was look so hard that they had to move away. But I wasn't a piece of fluff and neither were the other fems I knew.

232

We knew what we wanted and that was no mean feat for young women of the 1950s, a time when the need for conformity, marriage and babies was being trumpeted at us by the government's policy makers. Oh, we had our styles – our outfits, our perfumes, our performances – and we could lose ourselves under the chins of our dancing partners who held us close enough to make the world safe; but we walked the night streets to get to our bars, and we came out bleary-eyed into the deserted early morning, facing a long week of dreary passing at the office or the beauty parlor or the telephone company. I always knew our lives were a bewildering combination of romance and realism. I could tell you stories . . .

about the twenty-year-old fem who carried her favorite dildo in a pink satin purse to the bar every Saturday night so her partner for the evening would understand exactly what she wanted . . .

or how at seventeen I hung out at Pam Pam's on Sixth Avenue and Eighth Street in Greenwich Village with all the other fems who were too young to get into the bars and too inexperienced to know how to forge an ID. We used this bare, tired coffee shop as a training ground, a meeting place to plan the night's forays. Not just fems – young butches were there too, from all the boroughs, taking time to comb their hair just the right way in the mirror beside the doorway . . .

or how I finally entered my world, a bar on Abingdon Square, where I learned that women had been finding each other for years, and how as young fems we took on the Vice Squad, the plainclothes police women, the bathroom line with its allotted amount of toilet paper, the Johns trying to hustle a woman for the night and the staring straights who saw us as entertaining freaks. My passion had taken me home and not all the hating voices of the McCarthy 1950s could keep me away from my community.

Every time I speak at a lesbian-feminist gathering, I introduce myself as a fem who came out in the 1950s. I do this, because it is the truth and therefore allows me to pay historical homage to my lesbian time and place, to the women who have slipped away, yet whose voices I still hear and whose V-necked sweaters and shiny loafers I still see. I do it to call up the women I would see shopping with their lovers in the Lower East Side supermarkets, the fem partners of the butch women who worked as waiters in the Club 82. I remember how unflinchingly the fem absorbed the stares of the other customers as she gently held onto the arm of her partner. Butches were known by their appearances, fems by their choices. I do it in the name of the wives of passing women[2] whose faces look up at me from old newspaper clippings, the women whom reporters described as the deceived ones and yet whose histories suggest much more complicated choices. And if fems seemed to be "wives" of passing women, the feminine protectors of the couple's propriety, it was so easy to lose curiosity about what made them sexual heretics, because they looked like women. Thus fems became the victims of a double dismissal: in the past they did not appear culturally different enough from heterosexual women to be seen as breaking gender taboos and today they do not appear feminist enough, even in their historical context, to merit attention or respect for being ground-breaking women.

If we are to piece together a profound feminist and lesbian history,[3] we must begin asking questions about the lives of these women that we have not asked before, and to do this we will have to elevate curiosity to a much more exalted position than concepts of politically correct sexuality would ever allow us to do.[4] Politically correct sexuality is a paradoxical concept. One of the most deeply held opinions in feminism is that women should be autonomous and self-directed in defining their sexual desire, yet when a woman says, "This is my desire," feminists rush in to say, "No, no, it is the prick in your head; women should not desire that act." But we do not yet know enough at all about what women – any women – desire. The real problem here is that we stopped asking questions so early in the lesbian and feminist movement, that we rushed to erect what appeared to be answers into the formidable and rigid edifice that it is now. Our contemporary lack of curiosity also affects our view of the past. We don't ask butch-fem women who they are; we tell them. We don't explore the social life of working-class lesbian bars in the 1940s and 1950s; we simply assert that all those women were victims.[5] Our supposed answers closed our ears and stopped our analysis. Questions and answers about lesbian lives that deviate from the feminist model of the 1970s strike like a shock wave against the movement's foundation, yet this new wave of questioning is an authentic one, coming from women who have helped create the feminist and lesbian movement that they are now challenging into the new growth. If we close down exploration, we will be forcing some women once again to live their sexual lives in a land of shame and guilt; only this time they will be haunted by the realization that it was not the patriarchal code they have failed, but the creed of their own sisters who said they came in love. Curiosity builds bridges between women and between the present and the past; judgment builds the power of some over others. Curiosity is not trivial; it is the respect one life pays to another. It is a largeness of mind and heart that refuses to be bounded by decorum or by desperation. It is hardest to keep alive in the times it is most needed, the times of hatred, of instability, of attack. Surely these are such times.

When I stand before a new generation of lesbians and use this word "fem." I sometimes feel very old, like a relic from a long-buried past that has burst through the earth, shaken the dust off its mouth and started to speak. The first reaction is usually shock and then laughter and then confusion, when my audience must confront their stereotyped understanding of this word and yet face the fact that I am a powerful woman who has done some good in this brave new world of lesbian feminism. But the audience is not the only one who is going through waves of reactions. I too wonder how will I be perceived through these layers of history. A 1980s lesbian activist who defines herself as a fem poses the problem of our plight as an oppressed people in a most vivid way.

Colonization and the battle against it always poses a contradiction between appearances and deeper survivals.[6] There is a need to reflect the colonizer's image back at him yet at the same time to keep alive what is a deep part of one's culture, even if it can be misunderstood by the oppressor, who omnipotently thinks he knows what he is seeing. Butch-fem carries all this cultural warfare with it. It appears to incorporate elements of the heterosexual culture in power; it is disowned by some who want to make a statement against the pervasiveness of this power, yet it is a valid style, matured in years of struggle and harboring some of our bravest women. The colonizer's power enforces not only a daily cultural devaluing but also sets up a memory trap, forcing us to devalue what was resistance in the past in a desperate battle to be different from what they say we are.[7]

Both butches and fems have a history of ingenuity in the creation of personal style,[8] but since the elements of this style – the clothing, the stance – come from the heterosexually defined culture, it is easy to confuse an innovative or resisting style with a mere replica of the prevailing custom. But a butch lesbian wearing men's clothes in the 1950s was not a man wearing men's clothes; she was a woman who created an original style to signal to other women what she was capable of doing – taking erotic responsibility. In the feminist decades, the fem is the lesbian who poses this problem of misinterpreted choice in the deepest way. If we dress to please ourselves and the other women to whom we want to announce our desire, we are called traitors by many of our own community, because we seem to be wearing the clothes of the enemy. Make-up, high heels, skirts, revealing clothes, even certain ways of holding the body are read as capitulation to patriarchal control of women's bodies. An accurate critique, if a woman feels uncomfortable or forced to present herself this way, but this is not what I am doing when I feel sexually powerful and want to share it with other women. Fems are women who have made choices, but we need to be able to read between the cultural lines to appreciate their strength. Lesbians should be mistresses of discrepancies, knowing that resistance lies in the change of context.

The message to fems throughout the 1970s was that we were the Uncle Toms of the movement. If I wore the acceptable movement clothes of sturdy shoes, dungarees, work shirt and back pack, then I was to be trusted, but that is not always how I feel strongest. If I wear these clothes, because I am afraid of the judgment of my own people, then I am a different kind of traitor, this time to my own fem sense of personal style, since this style represents what I have chosen to do with my womanness. I cannot hide it or exchange it without losing my passion or my strength. The saddest irony of all behind this misjudgment of fems is that for many of us it has been a life-long journey to take pleasure in our bodies. Butch lovers, reassuring and kind, passionate and taking, were for many of us a bridge back to acceptance of what the society around us told us to scorn: big-hipped, wide-assed women's bodies. My idiosyncratic sexual history leads me to express my feminist victories in my own way; other women, straight or gay, carry these victories of personal style within, hesitant to publicly display them, because they fear the judgment of the women's community. Our understanding of resistance is thus deeply diminished.

In the 1970s and 1980s, the fem is also charged with the crime of passing, of trying to disassociate herself from the androgynous lesbian. In the earlier decades, many fems used their appearance to secure jobs that would allow their butch lovers to dress and live the way they both wanted her to. Her fem appearance allowed her to pass over into enemy lines to make economic survival possible. But when butches and fems of this style went out together, no one could accuse the fem of passing. In fact, the more extremely fem she was, the more obvious was their lesbianism and the more street danger they faced. Now lesbian style occurs in the context of a more and more androgynous appearing society, and fem dress becomes even more problematic. A fem is often seen as a lesbian acting like a straight woman who is not a feminist – a terrible misreading of self-presentation which turns a language of liberated desire into the silence of collaboration. An erotic conversation between two women is completely unheard, not by men this time but by other women, many in the name of lesbian-feminism.

When one carries the fem identity into the arena of political activism, the layers of confusion grow. In the Spring of 1982,

Deborah, my lover, and I did the Lesbian Herstory Archives slide show at the Stony Brook campus of SUNY.[9] We were speaking to fifty women health workers, four of whom identified themselves as lesbians. I wore a long lavender dress that made my body feel good and high, black boots that made me feel powerful. Deb was dressed in pants, shirt, vest and leather jacket. I led a two-hour discussion working with the women's honest expressions of homophobia, their fears of seeing their own bodies sexually, and the different forms of tyranny they faced as women. Finally one of the straight women said how much easier it was to talk to me rather than to Deb, who was sitting at the side of the room. "I look more like you," she said pointing to me. She too was wearing a long dress and boots. Here my appearance, which was really an erotic conversation between Deb and myself, was transformed into a boundary line between us. I walked over to Deb, put my arm around her and drew her head into my breasts. "Yes," I said, "but it is the two of us together that make everything perfectly clear," Then I returned to the center of the room and lied. "I wore this dress so you would listen to me but our real freedom is the day when I can wear a three-piece suit and tie and you will still hear my words." I found myself faced with the paradox of having to fight for one freedom at the price of another. The audience felt more comfortable with me because I could pass, yet their misunderstanding of my femness was betraying its deepest meaning.

Because I am on the defensive many times in raising these issues, it is tempting to gloss over the difficulties that did exist in the past and do now. Being a fem was never a simple experience, not in the old lesbian bars of the 1950s and not now. Fems were deeply cherished and yet devalued as well. There were always fem put-down jokes going around the bar, while at the same time tremendous energy and caring was spent courting the fem women. We were not always trusted and often seen as the more flighty members of the lesbian world, a contradiction to our actual lives where we all knew fems who had stood by their butch lovers through years of struggle. We were mysterious and practical, made homes and broke them up, were glamorous and boring all at the same time. Butches and fems had an internal dialogue to work out, but when the police invaded our bars, when we were threatened with physical violence, when taunts and jeers followed us down the streets, this more subtle discussion was transformed into a monolithic front where both butch and fem struggled fiercely to protect each other against the attackers. Feminists need to know much more about how fems perceived themselves and how they were seen by those who loved them. Certainly the erotic clarity that was for me and many other fems at the heart of our style has never been clearly understood by sexologists or by feminists.

Since the butch-fem tradition is one of the oldest in lesbian culture, it came under investigation along with everything else when the sexologists began their study of sexual deviance. The feminine invert, as fems were called then, was viewed as the imperfect deviant. The sexology literature from 1909 stated that the "pure female invert feels like a man."[10] A few years later, the fem is described as an "effeminate tribadist."[11] In the 1950s, our pathology was explained this way:

> The feminine type of Lesbian is one who seeks mother love, who enjoys being a recipient of much attention and affection. She is often preoccupied with personal beauty and is somewhat narcissistic. . . . She is the clinging vine type who is often thought and spoken of by her elders as a little fool without any realization of the warped sexuality which is prompting her actions.[12]

And then the doctor adds the final blow: "She is more apt to be bisexual and also apt to respond favorably to treatment." Here the fem lesbian is stripped of all power, made into a foolish woman who can easily be beckoned over into the right camp. Historically, we have been left disinherited, seen neither as true inverts nor as grown women.

An example from early twentieth-century lesbian literature also shows the complexity of the fem tradition. In *The Well of Loneliness*, published in 1928, two major fem characters embody some of the mythic characteristics of fems.[13] One is an unhappy wife who seduces Stephen Gordon, the butch heroine, but then betrays her, choosing the security of a safe life. The other is Beth, the lover Stephen turns over to a future husband at the end of the novel so she may have a chance at a "normal" life, thus enabling the author to make a plea for greater understanding of the deviant's plight. The reality of the author's life, however, gives a different portrait of a fem woman. Lady Una Troubridge, the partner of Radclyffe Hall, who saw herself as Hall's wife, was a major force in getting *The Well of Loneliness* published, even though she knew it would open their lives to turmoil and worse.

> she [Radclyffe Hall] came to me, telling me that in her view the time was ripe, and that although the publication of such a book might mean the shipwreck of her whole career, she was fully prepared to make any sacrifice except – the sacrifice of my peace of mind.
> She pointed out that in view of our union and of all the years that we had shared a home, what affected her must also affect me and that I would be included in any condemnation. Therefore she placed the decision in my hands and would write or refrain as I should decide. I am glad to remember that my reply was made without so much as an

instant's hesistation: I told her to write what was in her heart, that so far as any effect upon myself was concerned, I was sick to death of ambiguities, and only wished to be known for what I was and to dwell with her in the palace of truth.[14]

Why Radclyffe Hall with this steadfast fem woman by her side could not portray the same type of woman in her lesbian novel is a topic that needs further exploration. Troubridge's cry, "I am sick of ambiguities," could become a fem's motto.

What this very brief examination of examples from sexology and literature point out, I hope, is how much more we need to know, to question, to explore. Fems have been seen as a problem through the decades both by those who never pretended to be our friends and now by those who say they are our comrades. The outcry over the inclusion of a discussion of butch-fem relationships in the Barnard sexuality conference was a shock to me; I had waited for over ten years for this part of my life to be taken seriously by a feminist gathering. I marched, demonstrated, conferenced, leafleted, CRed my way through the 1970s, carrying this past and the women who had lived it deep within me, believing that when we had some safe territory, we could begin to explore what our lives had really meant. Yet even raising the issue, even entertaining the possibility that we were not complete victims but had some sense of what we were doing, was enough to encourage a call for silence by feminists who feared our voices. Those of us who want to begin talking again are not the reactionary backlash against feminism, as some would call us. We are an outgrowth of the best of feminism in a new time, trying to ask questions about taboo territories, trying to understand how women in the past and now have had the strength and the courage to express desire and resistance. We ask these questions in the service of the belief that women's lives are our deepest text, even the life of a fem.

Notes

1 For more discussion of the butch-fem experience, see the following sources: Rita La Porte, "The Butch/Femme Question", *Ladder*, vol. 15, June-July 1971, pp. 4-11; Victoria Brounworth, "Butch Femme – Myth or Reality or More of the Same", *WICCE*, Summer 1975, p. 7; Merril Mushroom, "How to Engage in Courting Rituals 1950 Butch Style in the Bar: An Essay", *Common Lives/Lesbian Lives*, no. 4, Summer 1982, pp. 6-10; Lee Lynch, "Swashbuckler", *Sinister Wisdom*, vol. 24, Fall 1983, and *Toothpick House*, Tallahassee, Fl., Naiad, 1983; Amber Hollibaugh and Cherríe Moraga, "What We're Rollin Around in Bed With: Sexual Silences in Feminism – A Conversation", *Heresies Sex Issue #12*, vol. 3, no. 4, 1981, pp. 58-62; "An Old Dyke's Tale: An Interview with Doris Lunden", *Conditions*, vol. 6, 1980, pp. 26-44; Joan

Nestle, "Butch-Fem Relationships: Sexual Courage in the Fifties", *Heresies Sex Issue #12*, vol. 3, no. 4, 1981, pp. 21-4; "The Bathroom Line", *Gay Community News*, October 4, 1980; "Stone Butch, Drag Butch, Baby Butch" (poem), *Big Apple Dyke News*, August 1981; and "Esther's Story", *Common Lives/Lesbian Lives*, vol. 1, Fall 1981, pp. 5-9. Two books that are now in progress will be important new resources: the work by Liz Kennedy and Madeline Davis based on the oral histories of the pre-1970 Buffalo lesbian community and a proposed anthology by Amber Hollibaugh and Esther Newton. For a more detailed bibliography, please write to the Lesbian Herstory Educational Foundation/Lesbian Herstory Archives, P. O. Box 1258, New York, New York 10116.

2 The word "passing" is used here for lesbians who looked like men to the straight world. They wore men's clothes, took men's names and worked at jobs that were then considered men's occupations such as driving taxis and clerking in stock rooms. An excellent slide show on the historical passing women of San Francisco called "She Drank, She Swore, She Courted Girls . . . She Even Chewed Tobacco" has been prepared by the San Francisco Lesbian and Gay Men's History Project. It is available from Iris Films, Box 5353, Berkeley, California 94705. Passing women are not just an historical phenomenon; they are still very much a part of lesbian life, but they are seldom part of the organized lesbian-feminist community. They have received very little encouragement to be so.

3 For more resources on lesbian history, see Judith Schwarz (ed.), *Frontiers: A Journal of Women's Studies*, vol. 4, no. 3, Fall 1979, which contains a bibliography on "Lesbianism and American History" by Lisa Duggan. An updated version of this bibliography can be obtained from the Lesbian Herstory Archives. The works of John D'Emilio and Jonathan Katz are also vital sources in this field. See John D'Emilio, *Sexual Politics, Sexual Communities: The Making of a Homosexual Minority in the United States, 1940-1970*, Chicago, University of Chicago Press, 1983 and Jonathan Katz, *Gay American History: Lesbians and Gay Men in the USA*, New York, Crowell, 1976 and *Gay/Lesbian Almanac: A New Documentary*, New York, Harper & Row, 1983.

4 See Muriel Dimen, "Politically Correct? Politically Uncorrect?", pp. 138-48 for a discussion of the origin and development of standards of political correctness and incorrectness, particularly in regard to sexuality.

5 The work of Madeline Davis and Liz Kennedy documenting the Buffalo lesbian community pre-1970 will be a major breakthrough in ending this silence.

6 Albert Memmi's *The Colonizer and the Colonized*, New York, Orion, 1965, is an especially helpful text in clarifying cultural struggle in a pre-revolutionary period.

7 This is analogous to blacks not eating fried chicken (because that is what whites think all blacks do) when one loves eating it, both for the taste and the memories of home it evokes. One way of resisting this forced disinheritance is to make the cultural activity an in-house

affair, where only members of the family share the pleasure. Many butch-fem individuals and communities have adopted this form of resistance. They exist on the edges of the women's and lesbian-feminist movement, or some members of the community cross over, helping to build organizations and feminist projects, but return at night to butch-fem relationships.

8 I want to make clear that butch-fem style differed from community to community and over time. I have written elsewhere of butch-fem couples who appeared similar both with short hair and in trousers; see *Heresies Sex Issue #12*. Photographs of this style can be seen on many *Ladder* covers. The way straight people viewed these couples walking hand in hand in the 1950s was often hostile, with the added taunt of "which one of you is the man" for the less visibly defined couple. I think any of us from that time would be able to distinguish the butch from the fem by subtle differences in walk, how the shoulders were held, or how the heads bent during conversation.

9 Two slide shows have been developed by the Lesbian Herstory Archives, the first showing the concept and history of the Archives and the second illustrating lesbian life of the 1950s.

10 Katherine Bement Davis, *Factors in the Sex Life of Twenty-Two Hundred Women*, New York, Harper & Brothers, 1929. Davis here is citing August Forel, *The Sexual Question*, New York, Rebman, 1908.

11 Frank Caprio, MD, *Female Homosexuality*, New York, Grove, 1954, p. 18.

12 Ibid., p. 19. Caprio supports his characterization by a quotation from Dr Winifred Richmond, *The Adolescent Girl*, New York, Macmillan, 1925.

13 Radclyffe Hall, *The Well of Loneliness*, London, Jonathan Cape, 1928.

14 Lady Una Troubridge, *The Life and Death of Radclyffe Hall*, London, Hammond & Hammond, 1961, pp. 81-2.

The Misunderstanding: Toward a More Precise Sexual Vocabulary

Esther Newton and Shirley Walton

A sexual incident from our shared past suggested the topic for our workshop at the Barnard Conference. We are both committed feminists. We have written a book about our twenty-five year friendship (*Womenfriends*[1]) in which we *thought* we explored our differences as a lesbian and a heterosexual. Yet we recently discovered that we had completely misunderstood each other in 1966.

We were both between relationships and wound up spending the summer together at the beach. At night we were hitting gay and straight bars. In this unstructured, experimental phase – in our middle twenties – Shirley propositioned Esther. Though officially straight, Shirley was titillated by lesbianism in general and Esther in particular. Shirley is attracted to men and to masculine women, and she likes them to be dark. Besides, she loved danger and risk.

Esther felt little sexual attraction, even though Shirley is a type – blonde, outgoing and feminine – she is often drawn to. She couldn't explain this apathy to herself. But she felt used, and she also feared damaging or even destroying their friendship. In fact Esther had already deflected several previous passes. But this time, in a spirit of experimentation, she accepted.

We got into bed and began "heavy necking." Shirley remembers being queasy about Esther's genitals, because Esther was menstruating. Knowing that Esther was chary about having her breasts fondled, Shirley avoided that. Esther remembers that she tried to stimulate Shirley's genitals and that Shirley was unresponsive. Neither of us can remember exactly how, but the episode faltered into nothingness.

The next morning, Shirley felt like a failure. She recalls Esther implying that she (Shirley) less than a hot lover. For her part, Esther remembers feeling exposed as a lesbian, assuming Shirley hadn't responded because she was "normal." Both of us were frightened about the possible disruption of our friendship. With virtually no discussion, the matter was dropped.

242

In the early 1970s, energized by feminism, we began keeping the journals which became *Womenfriends*. If lesbianism really boiled down to women-loving, why hadn't sexuality worked between us dedicated friends? Though we rehashed the episode briefly, we had no new insights. It was re-established that Shirley was straight and that Esther hadn't been all that terribly attracted.

Then in the spring of 1982, we presented a workshop for "The Scholar and the Feminist IX Conference." Why were we interested in sexuality? For the very good reason that we were both frustrated.

Shirley, now long married, avoided intercourse because she was bored, irritated and/or afraid of contraceptive devices. She preferred to have intercourse only when she initiated it and directed it. But to make these desires explicit would have made her an unacceptable wife in conventional terms. Cunnilingus was satisfying, but since fellatio had been implicity condemned by feminism, Shirley had almost no sex life.

Esther had taken a parallel course. She had tried conscientiously to have the "egalitarian sex" demanded by feminism, without much success. "Egalitarian sex" is not easy to describe; it is fundamentally defined by what it isn't: any sexual interaction based on power such as the power men have over women. "Egalitarian sex" assumes functionally interchangeable partners and acts. But Esther kept wanting to control the sexual interchange. It was easy for her to fuck her lovers, not easy to be fucked. Sexual relationships weren't working, and just as Shirley was beginning to question her own sexual constriction, Esther found herself at a sexual dead end.

At this point, Esther read "What We're Rolling Around in Bed With."[2] She began to take another look at the question of butch and femme "roles." She also met some s/m lesbians and became familiar with their terminology.[3] One day, as she was struggling to describe a nascent idea she had about the difference between "erotic identity" and "erotic role," the light began to dawn in Shirley's mind:

"You know, I've always assumed – we've assumed – I'm a straight 'femme,' by definition, since I'm with a man. You know how I used to love dresses and make-up, before I made myself so drab to be politically correct."

"Right. . . ."

"But Esther, in bed I always want to be dominant."

"You do?" Esther was stunned. Over the years as we discussed good and bad sex, we always assumed we knew what each other meant. "That means . . . you're a top!" Esther exclaimed.

Shirley said, "You are, too. No wonder we couldn't figure out what to do when we tried to sleep together. No wonder it was such an impasse! We're both tops – we both want to start, orchestrate and complete the sexual event. We never had a chance."

"I just assumed," Esther replied. "If you are straight, you're femme. We just buried the whole thing under those labels."

Once we reached this insight we had to discuss the incident specifically and concretely, step by step, without our old assumptions. We found we needed at least four concepts to communicate with each other about sex, only one of which was familiar.

1 Sexual preference

We started with the most easily defined concept: sexual preference indicates from which gender you usually select your sexual partners.

2 Erotic identity

Each human being's erotic identity – how one images oneself as erotic object – is unique. But the unique combination is necessarily modeled on public, i.e. culturally shared, symbols (as are all aspects of mental life). Erotic identities are presented to Americans by the media (for example, Bette Midler and Brooke Shields) and, on a primary level, by our family and peer group.

Class is a crucial component of these images. Typically, working-class women are portrayed as trampish (Marilyn Monroe, Ava Gardner), middle-class as sexually neutralized (Doris Day, Jane Wyman), and upper-class as icy but desirable (Grace Kelly). But there are also "good" poor girls and "bad" rich ones. Erotic identities have strong racial and ethnic aspects, too. And male identities are equally altered by class (Marlon Brando versus James Mason). Some people may model themslves almost wholly on these cultural icons. Others have extremely complicated and idiosyncratic erotic identities.

Another crucial variable is where and how much each of us actually manifests our erotic identity. Some individuals and some groups wear their fantasies on their sleeves, so to speak. S/m gays have elaborated a symbolic code to communicate aspects of erotic identity. Erotic identity may be manifest in some contexts (the private party) and not in others (the office party). Many people's public persona may be nothing more than a mask of conventionality, designed to hide their erotic identity.

Obviously, the gender system is a key element in erotic identity. What is so confusing about (and for) straight people is that the conventional gender categories – "man" and "woman" –

are supposed to constitute erotic identities in and of themselves. Like ritually demanded grief at a funeral, these culturally prescribed categories bear a deceptive relation to the real thing, that is, how a person really images her/himself as an erotic being.

Because of the severe restrictions on straight women's eroticism, their opportunity to consider erotic identity apart from rigid gender stereotypes was virtually nil. And if a heterosexual woman perceived her erotic identity as being somehow "unfeminine," for example domineering, clumsy or fat, she was, almost by cultural definition, supposed to be a lesbian.

In the gay world, erotic identities polarized around gender appear arbitrary. The gay male drag queen is obviously "impersonating" Mae West, while we do not think of Mae West as impersonating herself. Yet a drag queen's erotic identity might be more organically tied to the image of Mae West than Mae West's was. Gender categories are learned by all, and are "natural" to none. The terms "butch" and "femme" refer to gay erotic identities, derived historically from dominant gender categories but now distinct. Thus "butch" is a gay erotic identity in which symbols from the male gender category play a significant part, and "femme" is the complementary gay identity, drawing on feminine gender symbols. The current predominance of the "clone" erotic identity among gay men, which is a stylized butch image, masks the fact that many men did and do play out erotic identities along gender differentials.

Gender, however, may not be a strong element in all erotic identities. Some people may be very fluid in relation to gender symbols, their erotic identities centering on their ability to slide through them. Others may see themselves as animals or objects or entities which are not gendered at all.

3 Erotic role

In the straight world, and to a lesser extent in the gay one, how you look is supposed to signal what you do once the sexual episode begins. Too much suffering has been caused by this assumption. Your sexy persona (your erotic identity) does not necessarily indicate what you imagine this sexy being doing in partnered sex, which is what we mean by "erotic role." Nor does it dictate who you are attracted to. It is entirely possible that you see yourself as an Ava Gardner who, when she gets Humphrey Bogart in bed, orders him to lie back and submit. More subtly, she may allow him to be very active, all the while confident she is controlling him and the entire sexual episode.

The conventional way of contrasting erotic roles – "active" and "passive" – is misleading and inaccurate. We need to describe interactions, not physical activities. The terms that best describe the most common and inclusive interpersonal polarity derive loosely from the terminology of s/m gays, "top" and "bottom." We use these terms in a general sense, distinct from the terms sadist/masochist, which center on eroticized pain and cruelty, or dominant/submissive, which, though closer to our meaning, still refer to an exchange in which power is eroticized for its own sake. We regard both pairs as specialized types of the more global categories, top/bottom.

In any given sexual exchange, the top is the person who conducts and orchestrates the episode, the one who "runs the fuck." The bottom is the one who responds, acts out, makes visible or interprets the sexual initiatives and language of the top. *How* this exchange takes place is not a given. The top might not move much, only issuing verbal or subtle kinetic instructions. The bottom might be very expressive and physically active, rather than the inert being conjured up by the word "passive."

Some people may have very fluid erotic roles. They can be top or bottom, depending on the partner and the episode, or both in the same episode. Others are very rooted in a particular erotic role, always preferring to be either bottom or top. The common feminist assumption that everyone should be fluid and change-able seems entirely inappropriate to us. In sex, what works, what brings mutual pleasure, should be the criterion of "good." The problematic issue is consent, not whether my desire is better than yours.

The erotic roles of top and bottom transcend the gay/straight dichotomy underlying the idea of sexual preference, and the gender dichotomy so often a part of erotic identity. That is, many gay and straight men and women have strong affinities for top and bottom erotic roles. Knowing a person's gender or sexual preference does not indicate whether a person usually is top or bottom. Biological males are not necessarily tops, nor are those who use male gender symbols. This applies to butch lesbians and gay men and, thousands of years of cultural mythology notwith-standing, to straight men.

4 Erotic acts

These are particular acts that obsess, please, turn you on, either to do or have done, to watch or hear. While erotic roles describe process and relation, erotic acts refer to content, such as body zones (anus, feet, penis), objects (shoes, leather, perfume) or specific scenes (rape, capture, schoolroom).

These concepts emerged from our dissection of our past sexual episode and helped us understand it. Once we realized we were both tops, we understood much more about why "nothing happened." Given that women are so sexually ignorant and restricted, it is not surprising we had so many unhelpful stereotypes and so little precision in communicating, even between best friends. What is more surprising, and very saddening, is that feminism, which purports to offer liberating concepts of gender and sexuality, didn't help us either. Rather, as feminists, we experienced a new kind of social pressure which limited exploration and understanding of our sexuality. Within the women's movement, the "politically correct" have had to believe in and practice "egalitarian sexuality," which we define as sexual partnering involving the functional (if not literal) interchangeability of partners and acts. Logically, there could only be one look and one role for all, which partly explains why lesbianism is assumed to be intrinsically more egalitarian than heterosexuality, and why lesbian feminists tend to look alike.

The underlying reasoning goes like this: men have power, women don't. Heterosexuality involves a man and a woman, hence an oppressor and a victim. Masculinity equals sexual power, femininity equals sexual powerlessness. Do away with heterosexuality and you do away with sexual oppression. Do away with masculinity and femininity and the residuum is egalitarian sexuality: open, honest, caring and non-oppressive.

Unfortunately for this program, things are not so simple. Power and sexual desire are deeply, perhaps intrinsically connected in ways we do not fully understand and just can't abolish. Masculinity and femininity are entrenched, enduring aspects of personality, not just changeable styles. Rather than encouraging an open exploration of the meaning of sex and gender in women's lives, the movement intimidated women into silence and superficial compliance. Lesbian feminists have toned down their butch or femme characteristics, and just don't talk about what they do in bed. Straight women are afraid to be sexy or attractive, on pain of displaying false consciousness and wanting to be oppressed as sex objects. They don't talk about what they do either; heterosexuality is by definition oppressive, so why bother?

It is true that men have more power than women in the sexual domain. But one cannot proceed directly from this fact to explain how sexuality works, any more than male domination of the art world, for example, explains aesthetic experience. Is "eliminating power" from sex a meaningful or realizable way of increasing women's sexual autonomy and pleasure? Or has it led instead to a new version of "moral purity" based on our sexual conservatism and ignorance? In the fight against sexual oppression, the movement – to borrow an expression from the Chinese revolution

– has "swept the floor out the door." Class prejudice and lesbian feminism have reinforced this trend.

The modern feminist movement has been dominated by white middle-class values, with its most visible manifestation in liberal, reformist organizations. But cultural feminism is also rooted in middle-class values. The sexual significance of middle-class predominance in the movement is that, historically, the middle class and the upwardly mobile working class have tended to be anti-sexual and anti-difference. De Tocqueville observed that Americans loved equality more than liberty, and for the middle class, "equality" has too often meant uniformity. Difference, whether of race, ethnic group, class or gender, has been a barrier to opportunity and mobility. At the same time, the middle class has attributed hypersexuality to both the rich and poor.

An old sociological "saw" expresses these ideas nicely. The joke in graduate school was that Americans betrayed their class by their automobile seating patterns. Working-class husbands ride together in front, wives in back (gender differences emphasized). In the middle class, couple A rides in front, couple B in back (gender difference is minimized, and sexuality is contained in the married couple). In the upper class, husband A rides in front with wife B, husband B in back with wife A (sexuality is emphasized).

While the reformist women's movement of the 1960s was predominantly middle-class, the old lesbian community was dominated (and stereotyped) by working- and upper-class images of hypersexuality and gender polarity manifested most dramatically in butch and femme roles. The founders of Daughters of Bilitis urged lesbians to minimize roles to be more respectable and acceptable, in part for class reasons, but prior to 1969, DOB was a small part of lesbian life.

The old lesbian community was defined by a sexual difference. Lesbians were stereotyped as *only* sexual. It is understandable that many lesbians have reacted by counter-defining lesbianism as a political conviction. Nevertheless, sexual liberation was an important goal of early radical feminism. As the 1970s progressed, however, sexual liberation came to mean affection and tenderness with sex distilled out. As middle-class straight women joined up with those lesbians who hated the more extravagant and stigmatized aspects of lesbianism, lesbian feminism and political lesbianism were born and invented a sexual "iron maiden" with which every dedicated feminist has had to live.

The "role playing" of the working and upper class was anathema to the new feminism. Working-class women, black, brown and white, gay and straight, had "low consciousness" unless they "cleaned up their act", i.e. became more middle-class. Unfortunately, these were largely old class putdowns, clothed in new political sanctity. The working class is too sexual and/or ignorant. The upper class is sexually decadent and elite. In reaction, most working-class women, gay and straight, have shied away from the movement. Working-class lesbians stayed in the bars and on softball teams. Working-class straight women went into occupational feminism (trade unions, neighborhood associations) or, we speculate, the New Right. The upper class was and is insulated from movement judgments.

The result of "sweeping the floor out the door" has been a very narrow sexual ideal, which can be schematized as follows:

Sexual preference

Lesbianism is seen as superior to heterosexuality or bisexuality, because the biological and presumed psychological/social sameness of the partners guarantees equality.

Erotic identity

Gone (from the movement) are the "trashy" butch and femme of yesteryear. The lesbian/feminist is a "dyke", interchangeable with all other "dykes." The dyke look is supposed to be androgynous, but leans toward masculine gender symbols: short hair, short nails, work boots, running shoes, overalls and jeans, flannel shirts. The dyke erotic identity is a modified butch look, we speculate, because femininity is the mark of difference and inferiority which must be eliminated. Paradoxically, the look is downwardly mobile. As for straight women, we are mystified as to what erotic identity they could adopt. Shirley suggests one option was to pattern oneself on the look of 1960s male radicals.

Erotic roles

Needless to say, the idea of top and bottom erotic roles are only acceptable if they are completely and immediately interchangeable. Most descriptions imply a kind of side-by-side or sibling sexual interaction for lesbians. An alternative is a nurturant, mother/child model, as long as these roles can be enacted by either partner. Straight women's role possibilities are rarely discussed in feminist circles. They should be assertive, but should they be dominant? Certainly they should never be on the bottom.

Erotic acts

Any form of fetishism or sado-masochism is a male-defined no-no, as is any sex with too much emphasis on orgasm. Sexual interaction should not be genitally focused. More specifically, lesbians should not engage in any form of "hetero" sex. This includes both penetration, either by fingers or dildoes, and tribadism (rubbing the cunt against the partner's body) which can resemble the heterosexual missionary position.

If heterosexual women are not actually urged to refrain from penetration, the insistence that the clitoris is the only center of female sexual response implies that penetration is a superfluous "male trip." Certainly all acts which could be interpreted as submissive should be eliminated, such as cock-sucking.

By limiting discussion and imposing "standards," we have stifled diversity and exploration. The new feminist sexuality is too tied to old models of good-girl behavior and to old class prejudices. But to create a vision of sexual liberation, we need to know more about sex. We can't assume we are all the same, or that we all mean the same thing by "good sex," "perversion," "attraction" or any other sexual concept. We need a more precise vocabulary to take us out of Victorian romanticism in sexual matters and toward a new understanding of women's sexual diversity and possibility. We suspect that when we know more, we will find that power exchange is a central part of sexuality. If so, women will not be freed by flattening sexual experience in the name of equality. Redistribution of power should be our goal, in sex as in society. But when old friends misunderstand one another, how can we overcome ignorance and dissension to build a strong, diverse feminist movement?

Notes

1 Esther Newton and Shirley Walton, *Womenfriends*, New York, Friends Press, 1976.
2 Amber Hollibaugh and Cherríe Moraga, "What We're Rollin Around in Bed With", *Heresies Sex Issue #12*, vol. 3, no. 4, 1981, pp. 58-62.
3 Samois (ed.), *Coming to Power*, Berkeley, Samois, 1981. Second edition from Boston, Alyson, 1983.

The Historical Repression of Women's Sexuality

Patricia Murphy Robinson

How we think about sexuality is conditioned and inhibited by a complicated history and, to make our problems worse, that history is in the power of those who have necessarily been antagonistic to women for a very long time. Males generally have been economically and socially superior to women since they became the primary producers and possessors of private property. From this position they assumed magical powers previously the possession of women. Established in their claims to power, the men originated the patriarchy, a European word rooted in the idea of lineage from the father, chief of the tribe and family head, socially and emotionally, the attitude of male supremacy.

This social relationship over a long period generated and affected hierarchical social and economic structures, contributed to the geographic movements of peoples and the eventual subordination of women. It is important to us to understand that male power over women meant the depletion of women's previous force as primary producers of the central human unit, mother and child, and from the need to care for the offspring, the producers of dwellings, clothing, tools, food and industry.

The maturation of the hierarchical structure of male power and eventual class power is protracted, extremely varied and our understanding of its history still incomplete. The enormous and bitter controvery existing around how we all began is intensified not only by the absence of direct and fundamental knowledge of the past, but also by the limitation of bourgeois thought patterns and the ascent of another class, in addition to women, out of the decaying capitalist relations and the efforts to establish new ways of producing and relating.

The nineteenth century was a historical moment of wrenching world changes and the coming to power of the bourgeois class of traders and financiers, a group of people who *did not* produce products but bought cheap and sold dear. In other words, people who took products from one group, sold to another and made a profit on the transaction. They had developed to the economic and scientific stage where they needed more awareness of the world's people to launch themselves into the ruling class of the

251

twentieth century. They had emerged from the struggle with previous classes whose invasions and explorations of then unknown countries had begun the opening of the world. It would be their historical responsibility to exploit and unify the entire earth, its natural resources and peoples. In order to achieve this they instituted laws and governments, strategic military forces and certain social strata of the conquered people to control the always recalcitrant poor people. Adam Smith, an esteemed and early spokesman for the bourgeois class, addressed this issue in a speech on jurisprudence in the 1760s:

Laws and governments may be considered in this and indeed in every case as a combination of the rich to oppress the poor, and to preserve to themselves the inequality of goods which would otherwise be soon destroyed by the attacks of the poor, who if not hindered by the government would soon reduce the others to an equality with themselves by open violence.[1]

The rapid innovations in all fields initiated by the bourgeoisie to bring everyone under their aegis and control continue today and increase geometrically. The exploitation of people to produce wealth for this class was deepened and expanded beyond what previous classes were able to do. Peoples bodies were crucial to production in the past and force was the means to extract labor. The production of wealth now rested on modern industry and technology. During this period and up to the present, it has been necessary to condition the minds of people in order to unite their labor to machinery. Even the act of conditioning evolves into a source of profit as it becomes a commodity-service to sell. Working people were molded by seduction, persuasion, mystification; distortion and obfuscation of history blended with rationalizations and apologias for duplicitous bourgeois behavior, and finally, with working people's emotional acceptance of patriarchal social and economic relationships.

Inside this reality woman's strength as a sexual being is a constant threat. We have to face the biological fact that she is the sex that harbors and brings forth the very human beings the ruling class must have to create wealth. She is still the main sustaining force who cares for what she births. This is the one ingredient in this present mode of production the bourgeoisie has been unable to replace. Our sexuality in all its facets, important as it is subjectively, is interpenetrated by the reproduction of the species and through this the reproduction of the world. The control of our minds, as a sex, is an economic necessity. We think we produce children for ourselves just as we think we work for ourselves. The essence of the matter is that we work for and in the interests of the bourgeoisie and we bear children for that class to use. Embarrassingly, our minds belong to this class also and we reproduce this class's ideas in our children. The possibility that we might develop our own minds in opposition to bourgeois conditioning is ever-present. The ramifications this has for continued bourgeois and male rule can only be speculated upon now.

This conference is a small symbolic activity of bursting the bonds of our conditioning and inhibitions to go beyond bourgeois information and its control over our minds. We are beginning to realize that their continued ownership and control of the world might not be in our interests as women. It is an opportunity to share our longing for sexual pleasure without the responsibility of bearing children to be exploited by males and the bourgeoisie. We can reveal to each other the truth of the sexual practices among ourselves as women, the fantasies so long kept secret. There has been a wealth of research on women done by many of us that we want to share. The commonalities exist among us overshadowing the differences. Part of our new consciousness is realizing the universality of one's own personal situation. For centuries the area of our sexual feelings has been hidden from ourselves as it had to be hidden from those who disallowed them. But the sexual instinct is as elastic as it is powerful. That is why it is a force that insists on finding a way to break through despite all the inner repression that results from outer oppression.

We are meeting in a moment of a great conjunction of forces, usually called a crisis by those in power. For those of us who are often invisible, women of color and women of the world underdeveloped by Europeans and North Americans, it is an expansive, mind-opening time. As our societies revolt against exploitation and old ideas, there is a sense of release from a very long bondage of mind and body.

Our histories were stopped, not just as women, but as a people. Our original strong bodies have become truncated and our muscles tightened with repressed fear and rage. We know we were once hunters. We lifted and carried heavy burdens beside our men. Stooping and bending to plant food and building our homes, walking miles for medicinal herbs and nutritional berries developed women's skeletons and musculature. We experienced the cutting away of our most sacred organs, for we were a sacred sex at one time and magic and religion began with us. Our art, industry and science arose from our tool-making and medicinal skills which healed our offspring and kin.

This great reemergence of our peoples gives us the possibility to renew our history before we were conquered by colonialists. The oppression by patriarchal forces in our societies is being studied and research into the past is revealing data challenging accepted tenets of the bourgeois class. We are freer to contribute to historical change.

I have formed three postulates from which to begin this history. We are human primates, the most sophisticated of all the animals and a branch of primates which can think, remember and change the world. Secondly, women originated the art of sexual love; and lastly, all human life rests, if it is to be sustained, on securing food, clothing and shelter and we must have them before we can have ideas.

Primates have a notoriously unrefined sexual discrimination. Homosexuality, heterosexuality, bisexuality, incest and promiscuity have been documented even when these realities disturbed the sensibilities of "great and civilized" men and women. Sexual energy exists in all animals but historical, religious, economic and social relationships have twisted, repressed and diminished human primates' sexual instincts to a condition approaching entropy.

Overall, Nelson's [Rockefeller] character illustrates Richard Sennett's thesis in THE FALL OF PUBLIC MAN; the growing pathological confusion of public persons and private personality produced by the decay of late capitalist culture. The intimate pokes itself inappropriately into the public, and the public crowds out true intimacy. Goatish, apparently to the very end of his life, Nelson enjoyed revealing details of his sexual conquests in public. According to a highly placed New York City labor leader, he turned these revelations to good political account in winning over local labor chiefs. "We were once having a Central Labor Council meeting," this union official recalls, "and all through the cocktail party that preceded it, the guys were standing around talking about 'Nelson', about what a cocksman he was and all that. They were getting a terrific thrill out of the fact that here was one of the richest guys in the world and encouraged THEM to call him by his first name and allowed them to get in on his sexual exploits."

While the labor chieftains were regaled with supposedly intimate stories of the adventure of the Rockefeller genitalia, the man himself seemed to lack the normal capacity for emotional connection where it would appear to be most called for. How sad, for example, to have delivered a staff-prepared, staff-researched eulogy on the occasion of his brother Winthrop's funeral in Arkansas.[2]

Entropy is energy degraded to an ultimate state of inert uniformity – a kind of motionless death. We exist in a time of bewildering sexuality. We live deadening lives, emotionally separated from ourselves as a human species and each other as a community of living, working people.

Women originated the art of sexual love long before the birth of Christ in a time when it is said we all knew our mother but not our father. It simply was not necessary in many ancient societies to control women's mating. The stage of society had not yet been reached where food, clothing and shelter were privately owned. Further, there was a lack of surplus production to be fought over and then claimed by the victor. In other words, women were not yet the private property of males and inheritance of wealth, the surplus, had not been firmly established. Transient cohabitation and the lack of conjugal affection in early times is a controversial subject but there is abundant evidence to support that the most important thing was from which sex did we emerge. Matrilineal descent with its ideological concepts and social forms is quite a problem for professional theorists today, conditioned and circumscribed as their thinking has to be under patriarchal and bourgeois social relations.

The lack of substantive data for the previous periods of human history and the absence of a systematic pattern tracing its development has forced us to study ancient religions and forms of worship to gain insight into women's pivotal position and the ramifications this may have had for sexuality. These are, after all, projections of peoples' emotions and partial clues to their daily lives. Bourgeois researchers have given the name, mythology, to these remote beliefs. The name connotes opposition to fact and reveals the chauvinism of those who have the power to make ideas that we have unquestioningly absorbed.

The plethora of women deities is overwhelming, steeped as we are in male-oriented religions with their omnipotent, stern, punishing and repressive gods. But then these gods also reflect the societies within which we live. The African goddess of Dahomey (now Benin), Mawu, built the mountains and the valleys, put the sun in the sky and began life on earth. Coatlicue in Mexico dwelled on a high mountain covered by clouds, giving birth to the moon, the sun and all the other gods. Nurkwa, the Chinese tell us, brought harmony back to earth which had been broken apart, and returned balance to the universe. Changing woman is the American Indian name for nature which is godlike in that culture. In Europe Stone Age religious ceremonies honored the moon goddess who demanded men should pay women spiritual and sexual homage. The moon has also been associated with fertility. In rural areas of the United States women can still be found who plant their gardens and figure their monthly cycles according to the phases of the moon. In the *Art of the Bedchamber*, manuals of feudal China from the first century AD, female homosexuality and masturbation are elaborately described with sophisticated techniques indicating the acceptance of these acts. They clearly show woman as the principal initiator of lovemaking. Her skill and techniques are supported by what is described as magic but which, in fact, was woman's knowledge of the human body and nature. At the same time her right to satisfaction by the male was incontestable.

We create ideas in the vital daily act of cooperating with others to secure, produce and distribute food, clothing and shelter, the very necessities of life the bourgeois class appropriates to itself as a commodity to sell for profit, but which working people labor to produce and to buy back from the capitalists. Those of us who are poor are continually denied these bare necessities if we refuse or are unable to work. This influences our preoccupation with them which can generate a radical perspective on capitalism and its exploitative class system where we live at the bottom. It is a possible response that must be prevented by the ruling class at all costs.

All societies develop through social relationships which produce these life-sustaining systems and reproduce societies' members. As rich and complex as this society is, it does not insure to any of its members these basic elements. Anyone can fall into the abyss of unemployment and poverty, even the bourgeois rulers and their professional intelligentsia. Their fear is a potent emotion that keeps them conforming to the system as well as praising it.

The majority of us in this country can ignore the social relations that make life possible. We profit from bourgeois control and exploitation of the rest of the world. Even poor people receive the crumbs that fall from the rich masters' tables. Thus we fail to get to the root of our conditions as women. Without these basic life systems, sexuality would be impossible.

We are objectively connected as women but we are joined antagonistically and collectively, antagonistically through the differences in our race and culture and our class position, and collectively through our long, world-wide victimization by men who own and control everything we need to live. We, as women, therefore carry both a universal and a particular past. The focus of this history is influenced by my specific past as a Black woman in the United States, whose people are only a little over a hundred years out of slavery. As an educated woman and a psycho-therapist, I have had to struggle to urge all the unnecessary intellectual deformations of the bourgeoisie I, and all of us, absorb, plus the emotional malformations that invade all our psyches. As a therapist it is my responsibility to reveal what lay behind the mystifications of the ruling-class, white bourgeois male, that make all women appear weak and inferior and men strong and superior. In other words, it is this appearance, not the essence, that keeps us fearful and conforming and represses healthy sexuality.

Males' control of our sexuality forms clearly when ancient peoples settled in one place to produce food, clothing and shelter – ushering in centuries of agricultural development. It is at this time that what we know today as father-right brings with it the patriarchal family. Children now have dual origins and fathers replace mothers as the source of all social ties. Since only women could be sure from whom the child came, women's sexuality now required severe surveillance by the males to insure their place as owners of the child and, through it, control of private property beyond one generation, inheritance. Women and children sank to lower positions of prestige and power and became the property of men along with the products they produced as surplus, the family.

Control of women's sexuality is a problem even today for men, since women can mate with several men during the menstrual cycle, making it impossible for even them to know who the father is. The problem of women's promiscuity combined with inheritance now established through the father becomes more acute in those societies where wealth is owned and controlled by a class of men who must control it beyond their own individual mortality to continue the rule of their class. The very sexual reproduction of the workforce is dependent on controlling women's bodies and minds where patriarchy and class society exist. The concerns over infanticide, abortion, birth control and homosexuality, indicating the right to free, unfettered sexuality, are mystified and made plausible through moral and religious excuses and sophisms, when in essence their effects are economic. Decreased reproduction of the species means less exploited workers to labor intensively to bring forth the wealth of surplus production so absolutely necessary to capitalism. Today the ruling bourgeois struggles to avoid this contradiction by substituting machinery for workers and finding ways to change women's reproductive practices to coincide with this problem which is deeply embedded in nature and biology. This change is theoretically possible within a society producing new scientific discoveries yearly, which, if they can be produced profitably, are put to use by the capitalist to accumulate more wealth and increase his dominance over other capitalists. But he is limited by his very perspective from the top of the class hierarchy. He must have consumers, a market, to absorb the commodities he appropriates from modern industry and cybernation in order to make profits he can turn back into increased production and even more wealth. Ridding himself of workers simultaneously rids him of his market – an irresolvable contradiction.

The root of patriarchal society is the God-King who is offered the surplus in rituals that symbolize that He is the fantastic originator of the surplus – a surplus which is possible within the division of labor between male and female, on the one hand, and new divisions and associations of labor on the other. The stratification and formation of classes becomes more complex as more is produced. Scribes-clerks, warriors-soldiers, medicine men-priests, chiefs-lords organize and dominate those who create the products as well as women whose workspace is more limited now. The actual producers and women sink to the bottom of the hierarchy and are unconscious of this gross inversion of reality. Male supremacy and class society obscures who really creates the wealth of society and crystalizes a false reality, one turned upside down. Those who create the wealth become the scorned sex and the contemptuous lower classes, and those who live on the wealth and come to control it become the prestigious sex and the powerful class, instead of the parasites they really are.

Men assumed power over other men as well as over women and children, and created an atmosphere through magic and religion that reinforced the myth of their godliness. They believed themselves to be sacred and omnipotent. It was easy then to despise those below. Correspondingly, agricultural peoples developed an estrangement from themselves as the actual originators of the wealth; if anyone was god it was certainly them. Alienation really means to transfer ownership to another and in alienation lies the main root of capitalist relations.

The above dynamic operates in our time. Dominating others, as males and ruling-class women and men do, causes a distortion of their vision and consciousness as to where real power lies. They have lost sight of the human social relationships that have created products for centuries – products that carry within them the dead labor of past workers along with their ideas of the world and themselves. They have little respect for this kind of history because it reveals the root and brevity of their rule and presages the inevitability of their disappearance. To prevent this and to continue to force working people and children to produce for them, stealing their products and returning them to the workers as their private property, to be sold at their chosen prices, requires that they focus all their attention on sophisticated and widespread conditioning. Males suffer a similar threat in that they assume at birth the symbolism given to them by the patriarchy. Their consciousness is distorted by the existing patriarchal relationships and the appearances of male supremacy. Not all males belong to the ruling class so they feel forced to compensate by relating to those below them in the hierarchy as if they were descendants of God-Kings. These can be other races of men as well as women and children. It is at this point we become aware of the sources and processes of racism and sexism.

Black and third world peoples, particularly the women, bear a formidable array of dominating attitudes formalized by legal claims and rationalized by males and the bourgeoisie. One of the most difficult oppressions for women of color to break has been and still is male supremacy because it is so clouded by the exploitation of bourgeois North American and European males. The latter exploitation is primary simply because it destroys our very life-supportive systems. Yet, our lives as women are directly dominated by males who are not in power, and therefore exert enormous human suffering on women and children as a result.

In the last ten years African women, educated by the bourgeoisie for its purposes, but who have chosen to work in the interests of their own sex and people, have researched and attended the ancient practices of female circumcision, excision and infibulation – stages of the mutilation of women's external genital organs, still practiced in Northern and Eastern Africa today. Historical variants have been found in Asia and North America to decrease the pleasure of masturbation. The destruction of the organ that triggers sexual pleasure in women, the cutting of the clitoris, effectively decreases sexual spontaneity. Adhering together the two sides of the vulva obliterates the vaginal opening making intercourse extremely painful for the woman and often pleasurable for the man:

The little girl, entirely nude, is immobilized in the sitting position on a low stool by at least three women. One of them with her arms tightly around the little girl's chest, the other two hold the child's thighs apart by force in order to open wide the vulva. The child's arms are tied behind her back, or immobilized by the other two women guests. The traditional operator says a short prayer. . . . Then she spreads on the floor some offerings to the [God]. Then the old woman takes her razor and excises the clitoris. The infibulation follows: the operator cuts with her razor from top to bottom of the small lip. This nymphectomy and scraping are repeated on the other side of the vulva. The little girl howls and writhes in pain, although strongly held down. The operator wipes the blood from the wound and the mother, as well as the guests, "verify" her work, sometimes putting their fingers in. The amount of scraping of the large lips depends upon the "technical" ability of the operator. The opening left for urine and menstrual blood is miniscule. Then the operator applies a paste and ensures the adhesion of the large lips by means of an acacia thorn, which pierces one lip and passes through the other. She sticks in three or four in this manner down the vulva. These thorns are then held in place either by means of sewing thread, or with horsehair. Paste is again put on the wound. But all this is not sufficient to ensure the coalescence of the large lips; so the little girl is then tied up from her pelvis to her feet; strips of material rolled up into a rope immobilize her legs entirely. Exhausted, the little girl is then dressed and put on a bed. The operation lasts from fifteen to twenty minutes according to the ability of the old woman and the resistance put up by the child.[3]

Chastity belts were brought from the Middle East to Europe

during the Crusades to keep the women chaste, as the men went off for long periods to fight wars against their competitors in other societies. Oriental women were kept "pure" with the insertion of an 8-inch long bamboo stick into the vagina which strapped with a shield and lock. It was similar in construction to the chastity belt but that insertion was of metal.

These traditional customs are considered important aspects of culture and respected by cultural nationalists and bourgeois anthropologists of both sexes because submission to authority is considered correct by them. However, at the base of these practices is a society where men oppress women in order to gain material benefits as well as prestige through the use of women as field cultivators, domestic servants, marketers of products from their own and the children's labor, and as the origin of the future labor force. Work in these rural societies is labor-intensive, as opposed to capital-intensive (use of machines), and requires many hands who must work daily in the gardens and households. Men who now own the land, herds, tools and are looking for profit need a pliable, dependent workforce and women provide both, as well as compensating these men for their powerlessness, vis-à-vis their European and American peers.

Control of women's sexuality, comprehensive throughout society, institutionalized by the state and church is extended to the lower classes who are needed as disciplined workers in the cities and factories. If women's sexuality can be harnessed to the family structure, its threat to capitalist relations and ruling-class profits has been lessened considerably. Women now repress their own sexuality and socialize their daughters to do the same while reproducing the ideology of male supremacy in their sons. They are cut off from the historical roots of their earlier sexual prestige and power, because that history has had to be denied by the capitalist class and those intellectuals who identify with and serve it.

In the United States slavery incorporated a whole people brought from Africa at a stage in their history when males were established rulers over a class structure that could allow "royal women" decision-making power and participation in wars against invading colonialists, an aspect of African culture heavily accentuated by a certain class of African-American men and women. There is no doubt that this phase of capitalist expansion was bitterly resisted by Africans and it took decades to establish. Nevertheless, it meant that Black women would suffer two sexual masters, one white and one Black, here and in Africa. The black slaves under English colonialists were not just private property; both male and female were supervised as if they were domesticated animals. Domination of the male's sexuality was fully as important as regulation of the female's. Black slaves were, after all, very costly "beasts of burden" whose cultural sexual patterns had to be interrupted and broken, forcing them to conform to patterns that would profit the white farmer and plantation owner. Slave labor, though expensive, was essential, since white labor was going West to become independent workers and landowners.

In North America Black women suffered the sexual and economic exploitation of white men and the frustrated rage of Black men. They continued their African roles as planters and caretakers of the household, but now beside the men they had previously served. Black men were dispossesed of their power of privilege that originated from their class position above women. They had been owners of private property, controlled and dispersed the surplus, all three necessary to the origin of capital as well as the power that allows men to be free from working for others. Cut off from their homeland and their accustomed control over Black women and children, Black men experienced themselves as non-men. Tragically for them, their opportunity to move into the capitalist era as capitalists, along with European and North American males, had been stopped cold. There was little possibility of even entering the ruling class.

How have we discovered by intellectual means that bourgeois reason has become nonsense? Better, how have we learned that bourgeois institutions are unjust? As the bourgeoisie is forced to accumulate constantly, they repetitively revolutionize production, throwing millions of us into unemployment and starvation. They bring the world's population closer together in their mad race for cheap labor and more markets. This madness increases as military force and the politics of fascism have to be used to control and organize people. Finally, the other side of this monumental oppression emerges: resistance, rebellion and revolution are the antithesis of repression and exploitation. And in these processes people begin to terret out the roots of their history and cultures, to study and analyze their oppressors in the process of constructing new methods of warfare which include the participation of the entire population; personal relationships change and patriarchal ideas and authority are challenged by women and children; sexual repression is, therefore, lessened and sexuality is freed somewhat to become spiritual and human energy put at the service of changing the world.

Because poor and systematically exploited Black and third world women do not seem to place great emphasis on sexuality in the manner of more comfortable Western women, does not mean our sexual feelings are not important to us. But it should be understood that if you're starving to death along with your children and your men are dead, have migrated or are waging a guerrilla war, sexual pleasure cannot be a primary consideration. True, its expression has been blocked by centuries of cultural and colonial practices to facilitiate a world in men's interests, as well as by a material reality as a surplus labor force and its reproducers. In this kind of world men are utilitarian, assistants to our birthing children who become very important to us emotionally. They are compensation for the rejection of the society which exploits and disparages us and for men who can not love, emotionally restricted as they are by their oppressive conditions. The times of sexual mating serve as a release from stress and body tension that is unending because it is constantly reproduced. Therefore, no amount of orgiastic release allows complete surrender and relaxation. Lovemaking becomes a battlefield where powerless people struggle for power over each other. Through fantasy and romantic yearnings, poor women of color live out sexual desire that cannot be experienced fully.

A black newspaper editor, Mr. Tom Moerane (in South Africa), reports on research undertaken by his daughter among African women. "A significant number of young women regard marriage in an entirely negative manner. They said they did not care about marriage as an institution nor did they think it was of any particular use to them. Some indicated that they desired to bear children and this made it necessary to cohabit with a man, but the 'baby is going to be my baby.' ... The main reason for this attitude seemed to be that young women regarded men as totally irresponsible. I, myself, through my own observations, have to believe that the women in the urban communities are very much more responsible and more practical."[4]

The method of summarizing thousands of years of women's sexual history by emphasizing the larger forces is a method incompatible with the usual bourgeois approach of mounting reams of detail and extracting the larger issues; or indeed forming premises that are limited in their application, if not chauvinistic in attitude. Seeing the whole historical human society, even with its clear gaps, forces the bourgeoisie to face its role as an anti-human force of domination and its place as only a momentary, historical class. It presents to men their relationship to women as a distortion of their humanity and reveals to both the falseness of their feelings of superiority. It does not, however, give us an explanation of how these economic and social formations mold peoples' emotions and, conversely, how these resulting feelings induce ideas and practices that continue the exploitation. How is it that people absorb and propagate ideas directly inimical to their own interests as human beings?

Clues can be found in the historical effects of class society ruled by rich males and in examining the bourgeois method of psychological manipulation. The bourgeois has had to develop psychology, not in a conspiratorial way, but out of its own need to calm its own psyche, rationalizing the contradictions and emotional pain of being human and forced to act inhumanly in order to facilitate the smoother management of its economic and social interests. And, in fact, bourgeois psychology is an ideological construct to keep everyone operating in its interest. It has been somewhat successful in persuading its domestic skilled and professional workforce and seducing upper-class women to serve capitalism as objects. But its philosophy, high cost and general unavailability limits its application to a surplus labor army, domestically and internationally. Here, force, as it always has been historically, is still more effective. For instance, the removal of sources of life, such as housing, health care, education and food, kills off "unneeded" older workers and children within major urban areas, while it removes whole populations geno-cidally in the third world. This reduces an excess labor force that will not be necessary in the future, as the ruling class sees it, because of its plans for cybernating the labor process. Mean-while, it is still important to present surplus workers with a negative reflection of themselves through racism and sexism and to further demoralize them with the inevitability of their inferior position or to constantly bait them psychologically with the hope of instant riches. Religion which is a reflection of the class structure and its ideas is still a potent stabilizing force to keep the poor idolizing those who oppress them. Sexual eroticism and "unlawful" sexuality become a profitable industry, like drugs, and are absorbed and reconstituted as soporifics that dull righteous feelings of rage and rebellion.

These may not be considered specific psychological strategies but they help to provide a context within which particular techniques can be used. For example: under the title, "Strategic Psychological Operations and American Foreign Policy", Robert T. Holt and Robert Van de Velde, professor of political science and a retired US colonel and graduate of the US Intelligence School respectively, establish that one of the most important tactics is what is euphemistically called in general literature "the carrot or the stick". In their more specialized literature they get right to the point: terror and reassurance.

Terror has been used to control the behavior of men since the beginning of history. The effective use of terror is dependent on the use of coercion. Terror is essentially a threat either implicit of explicit. If the threat is to be effective, it must be supported by physical violence – usually the more beastly the more effective the terror. Coercion that is the most effective in instilling widespread terror is that which appears to its victims to be completely capricious. There should be no pattern in its application. Indeed, the history of colonial operations is filled with the systematic use of terror to control native populations. But this is a despicable aspect of colonial history, and we would argue that the use of terror conflicts with democratic values and should not be used in time of peace. Actual war, of course, presents quite a different situation. There are instances in which terror might be the most "humanitarian" tactic available.... An example? Threatening hydrogen bomb usage.[5]

And as to the place of persuasion in the all-embracing technological society, Jacques Ellul suggests in his book, *Propaganda: The Formation of Man's Attitudes*:

When man will be fully adapted to this technological society, when he will end by obeying with enthusiasm, convinced of the excellence of what he is forced to do, the constraint of the organization will no longer be felt by him; the truth is, it will no longer be a constraint, and the police will have nothing to do. The civic and technological goodwill and enthusiasm for the right social myths – both created by propaganda – will finally have solved the problems of men.... In the midst of increasing mechanization and technological organization, propaganda is simply the means used to prevent these things from being felt as too oppressive and to persuade men to submit with good grace.[6]

The basic unit of psychological manipulation is the nuclear family, now isolated from the extended family of the agricultural period and the tribe and clan of earlier times. The human child enters a small, historically derived world rigidified by centuries of sexual repression and necessary to class societies. This small world is still thoroughly conditioned to the rightness of capitalist economic and social relationships and the superiority of men; its members create a climate of entropy and into this enters a lively little child whose sexuality does not include procreation but pleasure. Therefore, it becomes emotionally threatening to parents, rigidly developed by their histories to socialize and produce human bodies and personalities fearful of release and spontaneity, and minds that must see the body as evil and disgusting. Into this basic infantile matrix are inserted the characteristics that limit sexual discharge and with it, rebellious feelings. The tactics are the same as described above but they are not conscious in the parents. Terror and reassurance serve to frighten and terrify the child to the point of submission and reassurance follows for submitting. The force of the child's sexual energy is bottled up and finally repressed. The longing for sexual pleasure is complicated by the need for sexual release under the constant restraints reproduced in the church, school and in the persuasive social relationships of the general society. Sexual feelings appear to be forgotten. Not so; at every opportunity, they manage to release themselves, but in emotionally disturbed and destructive ways.

The mother's role is still as important to the human offspring as it was in early history. She is the central humanizing and controlling factor as well as the sustainer of its life when it is too weak emotionally and physically to defend itself. The human primate's period of infancy is the longest of all the primates and, therefore, the conditioning is long-term, repetitive and deeply invasive of a pliable and open human psyche. Maternal terror, implicit or explicit, threats followed by coercion, are central to sexual repression and the formation of a personality structure filled with impulse control, deadened sensibilities and emotions – rigid bodies that will later be pressed into dull and boring jobs, overseen by authoritarians who continue the role of the parental figures. Emotionally insulated and isolated individuals do not have to be strenuously divided and conquered from above, for the foundation is already there. These kinds of minds and bodies do more than continue the ideas necessary for bourgeois control; they reproduce in others the kind of human psyche corresponding to bourgeois class society and its existing order of domination and submission.

What is important for us to realize is what people have done down through history with what has been done to them. They have primarily submitted and even turned against themselves in the interests of those who have used and oppressed them. But they have also rebelled and these have been brief, historic moments filled with human spiritual ecstasy, closely tied to sexual release and surrender. These experiences facilitated changes in consciousness. Recent revolutions have brought even deeper changes in consciousness and the release of women from some of the more intense patriarchal relationships. Violent revolutions free the body and the mind, bringing great physical and mental strength and new perceptions. Women are increasingly involved in the actual fighting of peoples' wars. And women in the more repressed centers of the world are watching, identifying with them. Their time has not yet come. But they are rebelling in other ways, of which this conference is one small example. (I am sure there is a price that will have to be paid for it.) That will only add to the determination to continue our efforts to demystify and analyze the class and sex which have evolved into their powerful positions over women through exploiting and oppressing the world, basically through the control of female sexuality.

Notes

1 Meek, R.L., *Lectures on Jurisprudence*, Oxford, Clarendon Press, Paris edition.
2 Fitch, Robert, *Nelson Rockefeller: An Anti-Obituary*, Monthly Review

266 *Patricia Murphy Robinson*

Press, vol. 31, no. 2, June 1979.

3 Reported in *Female Circumcision, Excision and Infibulation: The Facts and Proposals for Change*, Rep. no. 47, Minority Rights Group, London, 1980. (See also Abdalla, Raqiya, *Sisters in Affliction: Circumcision and Infibulation of Women in Africa*, Zed Press, London, 1980.)

4 Bernstein, Hilda, *For Their Triumphs and for Their Tears: Women in Apartheid South Africa*, International Defence Fund, 104 Newgate St, London, 1975.

5 Holt and Van deVelde, *Psychological Operations and American Foreign Policy*, University of Chicago Press, 1960.

6 Ellul, Jacques, *Propaganda: The Formation of Men's Attitudes*, Knopf, New York, 1965.

Thinking Sex: Notes for a Radical Theory of the Politics of Sexuality

Gayle Rubin

I The sex wars

Asked his advice, Dr. J. Guerin affirmed that, after all other treatments had failed, he had succeeded in curing young girls affected by the vice of onanism by burning the clitoris with a hot iron. . . . I apply the hot point three times to each of the large labia and another on the clitoris. . . . After the first operation, from forty to fifty times a day, the number of voluptuous spasms was reduced to three or four. . . . We believe, then, that in cases similar to those submitted to your consideration, one should not hesitate to resort to the hot iron, and at an early hour, in order to combat clitoral and vaginal onanism in little girls.

Demetrius Zambaco[1]

The time has come to think about sex. To some, sexuality may seem to be an unimportant topic, a frivolous diversion from the more critical problems of poverty, war, disease, racism, famine, or nuclear annihilation. But it is precisely at times such as these, when we live with the possibility of unthinkable destruction, that people are likely to become dangerously crazy about sexuality. Contemporary conflicts over sexual values and erotic conduct have much in common with the religious disputes of earlier centuries. They acquire immense symbolic weight. Disputes over sexual behavior often become the vehicles for displacing social anxieties, and discharging their attendant emotional intensity. Consequently, sexuality should be treated with special respect in times of great social stress.

The realm of sexuality also has its own internal politics, inequities, and modes of oppression. As with other aspects of human behavior, the concrete institutional forms of sexuality at any given time and place are products of human activity. They are imbued with conflicts of interest and political maneuvering, both deliberate and incidental. In that sense, sex is always political. But there are also historical periods in which sexuality is more sharply contested and more overtly politicized. In such periods, the domain of erotic life is, in effect, renegotiated.

267

In England and the United States, the late nineteenth century was one such era. During that time, powerful social movements focused on "vices" of all sorts. There were educational and political campaigns to encourage chastity, to eliminate prostitution, and to discourage masturbation, especially among the young. Morality crusaders attacked obscene literature, nude paintings, music halls, abortion, birth control information, and public dancing.[2] The consolidation of Victorian morality, and its apparatus of social, medical, and legal enforcement, was the outcome of a long period of struggle whose results have been bitterly contested ever since.

The consequences of these great nineteenth-century moral paroxysms are still with us. They have left a deep imprint on attitudes about sex, medical practice, child-rearing, parental anxieties, police conduct, and sex law.

The idea that masturbation is an unhealthy practice is part of that heritage. During the nineteenth century, it was commonly thought that "premature" interest in sex, sexual excitement, and, above all, sexual release, would impair the health and maturation of a child. Theorists differed on the actual consequences of sexual precocity. Some thought it led to insanity, while others merely predicted stunted growth. To protect the young from premature arousal, parents tied children down at night so they would not touch themselves; doctors excised the clitorises of onanistic little girls.[3] Although the more gruesome techniques have been abandoned, the attitudes that produced them persist. The notion that sex *per se* is harmful to the young has been chiseled into extensive social and legal structures designed to insulate minors from sexual knowledge and experience.

Much of the sex law currently on the books also dates from the nineteenth-century morality crusades. The first federal anti-obscenity law in the United States was passed in 1873. The Comstock Act – named for Anthony Comstock, an ancestral anti-porn activist and the founder of the New York Society for the Suppression of Vice – made it a federal crime to make, advertise, sell, possess, send through the mails, or import books or pictures deemed obscene. The law also banned contraceptive or abortifacient drugs and devices and information about them.[4] In the wake of the federal statute, most states passed their own anti-obscenity laws.

The Supreme Court began to whittle down both federal and state Comstock laws during the 1950s. By 1975, the prohibition of materials used for, and information about, contraception and abortion had been ruled unconstitutional. However, although the obscenity provisions have been modified, their fundamental constitutionality has been upheld. Thus it remains a crime to make, sell, mail, or import material which has no purpose other than sexual arousal.[5]

Although sodomy statutes date from older strata of the law, when elements of canon law were adopted into civil codes, most of the laws used to arrest homosexuals and prostitutes come out of the Victorian campaigns against "white slavery." These campaigns produced myriad prohibitions against solicitation, lewd behavior, loitering for immoral purposes, age offenses, and brothels and bawdy houses.

In her discussion of the British "white slave" scare, historian Judith Walkowitz observes that: "Recent research delineates the vast discrepancy between lurid journalistic accounts and the reality of prostitution. Evidence of widespread entrapment of British girls in London and abroad is slim."[6] However, public furor over this ostensible problem

forced the passage of the Criminal Law Amendment Act of 1885, a particularly nasty and pernicious piece of omnibus legislation. The 1885 Act raised the age of consent for girls from 13 to 16, but it also gave police far greater summary jurisdiction over poor working-class women and children ... it contained a clause making indecent acts between consenting male adults a crime, thus forming the basis of legal prosecution of male homosexuals in Britain until 1967 ... the clauses of the new bill were mainly enforced against working-class women, and regulated adult rather than youthful sexual behaviour.[7]

In the United States, the Mann Act, also known as the White Slave Traffic Act, was passed in 1910. Subsequently, every state in the union passed anti-prostitution legislation.[8]

In the 1950s, in the United States, major shifts in the organization of sexuality took place. Instead of focusing on prostitution or masturbation, the anxieties of the 1950s condensed most specifically around the image of the "homosexual menace" and the dubious specter of the "sex offender." Just before and after World War II, the "sex offender" became an object of public fear and scrutiny. Many states and cities, including Massachusetts, New Hampshire, New Jersey, New York State, New York City and Michigan, launched investigations to gather information about this menace to public safety.[9] The term "sex offender" sometimes applied to rapists, sometimes to "child molesters," and eventually functioned as a code for homosexuals. In its bureaucratic, medical, and popular versions, the sex offender discourse tended to blur distinctions between violent sexual assault and illegal but consensual acts such as sodomy. The criminal justice system incorporated these concepts when an epidemic of sexual psychopath laws swept through state legislatures.[10] These laws gave the psychological professions increased police powers over homosexuals and other sexual "deviants."

From the late 1940s until the early 1960s, erotic communities whose activities did not fit the postwar American dream drew intense persecution. Homosexuals were, along with communists, the objects of federal witch hunts and purges. Congressional investigations, executive orders, and sensational exposés in the media aimed to root out homosexuals employed by the government. Thousands lost their jobs, and restrictions on federal employment of homosexuals persist to this day.[11] The FBI began systematic surveillance and harassment of homosexuals which lasted at least into the 1970s.[12]

Many states and large cities conducted their own investigations, and the federal witch-hunts were reflected in a variety of local crackdowns. In Boise, Idaho, in 1955, a schoolteacher sat down to breakfast with his morning paper and read that the vice-president of the Idaho First National Bank had been arrested on felony sodomy charges; the local prosecutor said that he intended to eliminate all homosexuality from the community. The teacher never finished his breakfast. "He jumped up from his seat, pulled out his suitcases, packed as fast as he could, got into his car, and drove straight to San Francisco. . . . The cold eggs, coffee, and toast remained on his table for two days before someone from his school came by to see what had happened."[13]

In San Francisco, police and media waged war on homosexuals throughout the 1950s. Police raided bars, patrolled cruising areas, conducted street sweeps, and trumpeted their intention of driving the queers out of San Francisco.[14] Crackdowns against gay individuals, bars, and social areas occurred throughout the country. Although anti-homosexual crusades are the best-documented examples of erotic repression in the 1950s, future research should reveal similar patterns of increased harassment against pornographic materials, prostitutes, and erotic deviants of all sorts. Research is needed to determine the full scope of both police persecution and regulatory reform.[15]

The current period bears some uncomfortable similarities to the 1880s and the 1950s. The 1977 campaign to repeal the Dade County, Florida, gay rights ordinance inaugurated a new wave of violence, state persecution, and legal initiatives directed against minority sexual populations and the commercial sex industry. For the last six years, the United States and Canada have undergone an extensive sexual repression in the political, not the psychological, sense. In the spring of 1977, a few weeks before the Dade County vote, the news media were suddenly full of reports of raids on gay cruising areas, arrests for prostitution, and investigations into the manufacture and distribution of pornographic materials. Since then, police activity against the gay community has increased exponentially. The gay press has documented hundreds of arrests, from the libraries of Boston to the streets of Houston and the beaches of San Francisco. Even the large, organized, and relatively powerful urban gay communities have been unable to stop these depredations. Gay bars and bath houses have been busted with alarming frequency, and police have gotten bolder. In one especially dramatic incident, police, in Toronto raided all four of the city's gay baths. They broke into cubicles with crowbars and hauled almost 300 men out into the winter streets, clad in their bath towels. Even "liberated" San Francisco has not been immune. There have been proceedings against several bars, countless arrests in the parks, and, in the fall of 1981, police arrested over 400 people in a series of sweeps of Polk Street, one of the thoroughfares of local gay nightlife. Queerbashing has become a significant recreational activity for young urban males. They come into gay neighborhoods armed with baseball bats and looking for trouble, knowing that the adults in their lives either secretly approve or will look the other way.

The police crackdown has not been limited to homosexuals. Since 1977, enforcement of existing laws against prostitution and obscenity has been stepped up. Moreover, states and municipalities have been passing new and tighter regulations on commercial sex. Restrictive ordinances have been passed, zoning laws altered, licensing and safety codes amended, sentences increased, and evidentiary requirements relaxed. This subtle legal codification of more stringent controls over adult sexual behavior has gone largely unnoticed outside of the gay press.

For over a century, no tactic for stirring up erotic hysteria has been as reliable as the appeal to protect children. The current wave of erotic terror has reached deepest into those areas bordered in some way, if only symbolically, by the sexuality of the young. The motto of the Dade County repeal campaign was "Save Our Children" from alleged homosexual recruitment. In February 1977, shortly before the Dade County vote, a sudden concern with "child pornography" swept the national media. In May, the *Chicago Tribune* ran a lurid four-day series with three-inch headlines, which claimed to expose a national vice ring organized to lure young boys into prostitution and pornography.[16] Newspapers across the country ran similar stories, most of them worthy of the *National Enquirer.* By the end of May, a congressional investigation was underway. Within weeks, the federal government had enacted a sweeping bill against "child pornography" and many of the states followed with bills of their own. These laws have reestablished restrictions on sexual materials that had been relaxed by some of the important

Supreme Court decisions. For instance, the Court ruled that neither nudity nor sexual activity *per se* were obscene. But the child pornography laws define as obscene any depiction of minors who are nude or engaged in sexual activity. This means that photographs of naked children in anthropology textbooks and many of the ethnographic movies shown in college classes are technically illegal in several states. In fact, the instructors are liable to an additional felony charge for showing such images to each student under the age of 18. Although the Supreme Court has also ruled that it is a constitutional right to possess obscene material for private use, the child pornography laws prohibit even the private possession of any sexual material involving minors.

The laws produced by the child porn panic are ill-conceived and misdirected. They represent far-reaching alterations in the regulation of sexual behavior and abrogate important sexual civil liberties. But hardly anyone noticed as they swept through Congress and state legislatures. With the exception of the North American Man/Boy Love Association and the American Civil Liberties Union, no one raised a peep of protest.[17]

A new and even tougher federal child pornography bill has just reached House-Senate conference. It removes any requirement that prosecutors must prove that alleged child pornography was distributed for commercial sale. Once this bill becomes law, a person merely possessing a nude snapshot of a 17-year-old lover or friend may go to jail for fifteen years, and be fined $100,000. This bill passed the House 400 to 1.[18]

The experiences of art photographer Jacqueline Livingston exemplify the climate created by the child porn panic. An assistant professor of photography at Cornell University, Livingston was fired in 1978 after exhibiting pictures of male nudes which included photographs of her seven-year-old son masturbating. *Ms. Magazine, Chrysalis,* and *Art News* all refused to run ads for Livingston's posters of male nudes. At one point, Kodak confiscated some of her film, and for several months, Livingston lived with the threat of prosecution under the child pornography laws. The Tompkins County Department of Social Services investigated her fitness as a parent. Livingston's posters have been collected by the Museum of Modern Art, the Metropolitan, and other major museums. But she has paid a high cost in harassment and anxiety for her efforts to capture on film the uncensored male body at different ages.[19]

It is easy to see someone like Livingston as a victim of the child porn wars. It is harder for most people to sympathize with actual boy-lovers. Like communists and homosexuals in the 1950s, boy-lovers are so stigmatized that it is difficult to find defenders for their civil liberties, let alone for their erotic orientation. Consequently, the police have feasted on them. Local police, the FBI, and watchdog postal inspectors have joined to build a huge apparatus whose sole aim is to wipe out the community of men who love underaged youth. In twenty years or so, when some of the smoke has cleared, it will be much easier to show that these men have been the victims of a savage and undeserved witch-hunt. A lot of people will be embarrassed by their collaboration with this persecution, but it will be too late to do much good for those men who have spent their lives in prison.

While the misery of the boy-lovers affects very few, the other long-term legacy of the Dade County repeal affects almost everyone. The success of the anti-gay campaign ignited long-simmering passions of the American right, and sparked an extensive movement to compress the boundaries of acceptable sexual behavior.

Right-wing ideology linking non-familial sex with communism and political weakness is nothing new. During the McCarthy period, Alfred Kinsey and his Institute for Sex Research were attacked for weakening the moral fiber of Americans and rendering them more vulnerable to communist influence. After congressional investigations and bad publicity, Kinsey's Rockefeller grant was terminated in 1954.[20]

Around 1969, the extreme right discovered the Sex Information and Education Council of the United States (SIECUS). In books and pamphlets, such as *The Sex Education Racket: Pornography in the Schools and SIECUS: Corrupter of Youth*, the right attacked SIECUS and sex education as communist plots to destroy the family and sap the national will.[21] Another pamphlet, *Pavlov's Children (They May Be Yours)*, claims that the United Nations Educational, Scientific and Cultural Organization (UNESCO) is in cahoots with SIECUS to undermine religious taboos, to promote the acceptance of abnormal sexual relations, to downgrade absolute moral standards, and to "destroy racial cohesion," by exposing white people (especially white women) to the alleged "lower" sexual standards of black people.[22]

New Right and neo-conservative ideology has updated these themes, and leans heavily on linking "immoral" sexual behavior to putative declines in American power. In 1977, Norman Podhoretz wrote an essay blaming homosexuals for the alleged inability of the United States to stand up to the Russians.[23] He thus neatly linked "the anti-gay fight in the domestic arena and the anti-communist battles in foreign policy."[24]

Right-wing opposition to sex education, homosexuality, pornography, abortion, and pre-marital sex moved from the extreme fringes to the political center stage after 1977, when right-wing strategists and fundamentalist religious crusaders discovered that these issues had mass appeal. Sexual reaction played a significant role in the right's electoral success in 1980.[25] Organizations like the Moral Majority and Citizens for Decency have acquired mass followings, immense financial resources, and unanticipated clout. The Equal Rights Amendment has been defeated, legislation has been passed that mandates new restrictions on abortion, and funding for programs like Planned Parenthood and sex education has been slashed. Laws and regulations making it more difficult for teenage girls to obtain contraceptives or abortions have been promulgated. Sexual backlash was exploited in successful attacks on the Women's Studies Program at California State University at Long Beach.

The most ambitious right-wing legislative initiative has been the Family Protection Act (FPA), introduced in Congress in 1979. The Family Protection Act is a broad assault on feminism, homosexuals, non-traditional families, and teenage sexual privacy.[26] The Family Protection Act has not and probably will not pass, but conservative members of Congress continue to pursue its agenda in a more piecemeal fashion. Perhaps the most glaring sign of the times is the Adolescent Family Life Program. Also known as the Teen Chastity Program, it gets some 15 million federal dollars to encourage teenagers to refrain from sexual intercourse, and to discourage them from using contraceptives if they do have sex, and from having abortions if they get pregnant. In the last few years, there have been countless local confrontations over gay rights, sex education, abortion rights, adult bookstores, and public school curricula. It is unlikely that the anti-sex backlash is over, or that it has even peaked. Unless something changes dramatically, it is likely that the next few years will bring more of the same.

Periods such as the 1880s in England, and the 1950s in the United States, recodify the relations of sexuality. The struggles that were fought leave a residue in the form of laws, social practices, and ideologies which then affect the way in which sexuality is experienced long after the immediate conflicts have faded. All the signs indicate that the present era is another of those watersheds in the politics of sex. The settlements that emerge from the 1980s will have an impact far into the future. It is therefore imperative to understand what is going on and what is at stake in order to make informed decisions about what policies to support and oppose.

It is difficult to make such decisions in the absence of a coherent and intelligent body of radical thought about sex. Unfortunately, progressive political analysis of sexuality is relatively underdeveloped. Much of what is available from the feminist movement has simply added to the mystification that shrouds the subject. There is an urgent need to develop radical perspectives on sexuality.

Paradoxically, an explosion of exciting scholarship and political writing about sex has been generated in these bleak years. In the 1950s, the early gay rights movement began and prospered while the bars were being raided and anti-gay laws were being passed. In the last six years, new erotic communities, political alliances, and analyses have been developed in the midst of the repression. In this essay, I will propose elements of a descriptive and conceptual framework for thinking about sex and its politics. I hope to contribute to the pressing task of creating an accurate, humane, and genuinely liberatory body of thought about sexuality.

II Sexual thoughts

"You see, Tim," Phillip said suddenly, "your argument isn't reasonable. Suppose I granted your first point that homosexuality is justifiable in certain instances and under certain controls. Then there is the catch: where does justification end and degeneracy begin? Society must condemn to protect. Permit even the intellectual homosexual a place of respect and the first bar is down. Then comes the next and the next until the sadist, the flagellist, the criminally insane demand their places, and society ceases to exist. So I ask again: where is the line drawn? Where does degeneracy begin if not at the beginning of individual freedom in such matters?"

(*Fragment from a discussion between two gay men trying to decide if they may love each other, from a novel published in 1950.*[27]

A radical theory of sex must identify, describe, explain, and denounce erotic injustice and sexual oppression. Such a theory needs refined conceptual tools which can grasp the subject and hold it in view. It must build rich descriptions of sexuality as it exists in society and history. It requires a convincing critical language that can convey the barbarity of sexual persecution.

Several persistent features of thought about sex inhibit the development of such a theory. These assumptions are so pervasive in Western culture that they are rarely questioned. Thus, they tend to reappear in different political contexts, acquiring new rhetorical expressions but reproducing fundamental axioms.

One such axiom is sexual essentialism – the idea that sex is a natural force that exists prior to social life and shapes institutions. Sexual essentialism is embedded in the folk wisdoms of Western societies, which consider sex to be eternally unchanging, asocial, and transhistorical. Dominated for over a century by medicine, psychiatry, and psychology, the academic study of sex has reproduced essentialism. These fields classify sex as a property of individuals. It may reside in their hormones or their psyches. It may be construed as physiological or psychological. But within these ethnoscientific categories, sexuality has no history and no significant social determinants.

During the last five years, a sophisticated historical and theoretical scholarship has challenged sexual essentialism both explicitly and implicitly. Gay history, particularly the work of Jeffrey Weeks, has led this assault by showing that homosexuality as we know it is a relatively modern institutional complex.[28] Many historians have come to see the contemporary institutional forms of heterosexuality as an even more recent development.[29] An important contributor to the new scholarship is Judith Walkowitz, whose research has demonstrated the extent to which prostitution was transformed around the turn of the century. She provides meticulous descriptions of how the interplay of social forces such as ideology, fear, political agitation, legal reform, and medical practice can change the structure of sexual behavior and alter its consequences.[30]

Michel Foucault's *The History of Sexuality* has been the most influential and emblematic text of the new scholarship on sex. Foucault criticizes the traditional understanding of sexuality as a natural libido yearning to break free of social constraint. He argues that desires are not preexisting biological entities, but rather, that they are constituted in the course of historically specific social practices. He emphasizes the generative aspects of the social organization of sex rather than its repressive elements by pointing out that new sexualities are constantly produced. And he points to a major discontinuity between kinship-based systems of sexuality and more modern forms.[31]

The new scholarship on sexual behavior has given sex a history and created a constructivist alternative to sexual essentialism. Underlying this body of work is an assumption that sexuality is constituted in society and history, not biologically ordained.[32] This does not mean the biological capacities are not prerequisites for human sexuality. It does mean that human sexuality is not comprehensible in purely biological terms. Human organisms with human brains are necessary for human cultures, but no examination of the body or its parts can explain the nature and variety of human social systems. The belly's hunger gives no clues as to the complexities of cuisine. The body, the brain, the genitalia, and the capacity for language are all necessary for human sexuality. But they do not determine its content, its experiences, or its institutional forms. Moreover, we never encounter the body unmediated by the meanings that cultures give to it. To paraphrase Lévi-Strauss, my position on the relationship between biology and sexuality is a "Kantianism without a transcendental libido."[33]

It is impossible to think with any clarity about the politics of race or gender as long as these are thought of as biological entities rather than as social constructs. Similarly, sexuality is impervious to political analysis as long as it is primarily conceived as a biological phenomenon or an aspect of individual psychology. Sexuality is as much a human product as are diets, methods of transportation, systems of etiquette, forms of labor, types of entertainment, processes of production, and modes of oppression. Once sex is understood in terms of social analysis and historical understanding, a more realistic politics of sex becomes possible. One may then think of sexual politics in terms of such phenomena as populations, neighborhoods, settlement patterns, migration, urban conflict, epidemiology, and police technology. These are more fruitful categories of thought than the more traditional ones of sin, disease, neurosis, pathology, decadence, pollution, or the decline and fall of empires.

By detailing the relationships between stigmatized erotic populations and the social forces which regulate them, work such as that of Allan Bérubé, John D'Emilio, Jeffrey Weeks, and Judith Walkowitz contains implicit categories of political analysis and criticism. Nevertheless, the constructivist perspective has displayed some political weaknesses. This has been most evident in misconstructions of Foucault's position.

Because of his emphasis on the ways that sexuality is produced, Foucault has been vulnerable to interpretations that deny or minimize the reality of sexual repression in the more political sense. Foucault makes it abundantly clear that he is not denying the existence of sexual repression so much as inscribing it within a large dynamic.[34] Sexuality in Western societies has been structured within an extremely punitive social framework, and has been subjected to very real formal and informal controls. It is neccesary to recognize repressive phenomena without resorting to the essentialist assumptions of the language of libido. It is important to hold repressive sexual practices in focus, even while situating them within a different totality and a more refined terminology.[35]

Most radical thought about sex has been embedded within a model of the instincts and their restraints. Concepts of sexual oppression have been lodged within that more biological understanding of sexuality. It is often easier to fall back on the notion of a natural libido subjected to inhumane repression than to reformulate concepts of sexual injustice within a more constructivist framework. But it is essential that we do so. We need a radical critique of sexual arrangements that has the conceptual elegance of Foucault and the evocative passion of Reich.

The new scholarship on sex has brought a welcome insistence that sexual terms be restricted to their proper historical and social contexts, and a cautionary scepticism towards sweeping generalizations. But it is important to be able to indicate groupings of erotic behavior and general trends within erotic discourse. In addition to sexual essentialism, there are at least five other ideological formations whose grip on sexual thought is so strong that to fail to discuss them is to remain enmeshed within them. These are sex negativity, the fallacy of misplaced scale, the hierarchical valuation of sex acts, the domino theory of sexual peril, and the lack of a concept of benign sexual variation.

Of these five, the most important is sex negativity. Western cultures generally consider sex to be a dangerous, destructive, negative force.[36] Most Christian tradition, following Paul, holds that sex is inherently sinful. It may be redeemed if performed within marriage for procreative purposes and if the pleasurable aspects are not enjoyed too much. In turn, this idea rests on the assumption that the genitalia are an intrinsically inferior part of the body, much lower and less holy than the mind, the "soul," the "heart," or even the upper part of the digestive system (the status of the excretory organs is close to that of the genitalia).[37] Such notions have by now acquired a life of their own and no longer depend solely on religion for their perseverance.

This culture always treats sex with suspicion. It construes and judges almost any sexual practice in terms of its worst possible expression. Sex is presumed guilty until proven innocent. Virtually all erotic behavior is considered bad unless a specific reason to exempt it has been established. The most acceptable excuses are marriage, reproduction, and love. Sometimes scientific curiosity, aesthetic experience, or a long-term intimate relationship may serve. But the exercise of erotic capacity, intelligence, curiosity, or creativity all require pretexts that are unnecessary for other pleasures, such as the enjoyment of food, fiction, or astronomy.

What I call the fallacy of misplaced scale is a corollary of sex negativity. Susan Sontag once commented that since Christianity focused "on sexual behavior as the root of virtue, everything pertaining to sex has been a 'special case' in our culture."[38] Sex law has incorporated the religious attitude that heretical sex is an especially heinous sin that deserves the harshest punishments. Throughout much of European and American history, a single act of consensual anal penetration was grounds for execution. In some states, sodomy still carries twenty-year prison sentences.

Outside the law, sex is also a marked category. Small differences in value or behavior are often experienced as cosmic threats. Although people can be intolerant, silly, or pushy about what constitutes proper diet, differences in menu rarely provoke the kinds of rage, anxiety, and sheer terror that routinely accompany differences in erotic taste. Sexual acts are burdened with an excess of significance.

Modern Western societies appraise sex acts according to a hierarchical system of sexual value. Marital, reproductive heterosexuals are alone at the top of the erotic pyramid. Clamoring below are unmarried monogamous heterosexuals in couples, followed by most other heterosexuals. Solitary sex floats ambiguously. The powerful nineteenth-century stigma on masturbation lingers in less potent, modified forms, such as the idea that masturbation is an irferior substitute for partnered encounters. Stable, long-term lesbian and gay male couples are verging on respectability, but bar dykes and promiscuous gay men are hovering just above the groups at the very bottom of the pyramid. The most despised sexual castes currently include transsexuals, transvestites, fetishists, sadomasochists, sex workers such as prostitutes and porn models, and the lowliest of all, those whose eroticism transgresses generational boundaries.

Individuals whose behavior stands high in this hierarchy are rewarded with certified mental health, respectability, legality, social and physical mobility, institutional support, and material benefits. As sexual behaviors or occupations fall lower on the scale, the individuals who practice them are subjected to a presumption of mental illness, disreputability, criminality, restricted social and physical mobility, loss of institutional support, and economic sanctions.

Extreme and punitive stigma maintains some sexual behaviors as low status and is an effective sanction against those who engage in them. The intensity of this stigma is rooted in Western religious traditions. But most of its contemporary content derives from medical and psychiatric opprobrium.

The old religious taboos were primarily based on kinship forms of social organization. They were meant to deter inappropriate unions and to provide proper kin. Sex laws derived from Biblical pronouncements were aimed at preventing the acquisition of the wrong kinds of affinal partners: consanguineous kin (incest), the same gender (homosexuality), or the wrong species (bestiality). When medicine and psychiatry acquired extensive powers over sexuality, they were less concerned with unsuitable mates than with unfit forms of desire. If taboos against incest best characterized kinship systems of sexual organization, then the shift to an emphasis on taboos against masturbation was more apposite to the newer systems organized around qualities of erotic experience.[39]

Medicine and psychiatry multiplied the categories of sexual misconduct. The section on psychosexual disorders in the *Diagnostic and Statistical Manual of Mental Disorders* (*DSM*) of the American Psychiatric Association (APA) is a fairly reliable map of the current moral hierarchy of sexual activities. The APA list is much more elaborate than the traditional condemnations of whoring, sodomy, and adultery. The most recent edition, *DSM-III*, removed homosexuality from the roster of mental disorders after a long political struggle. But fetishism, sadism, masochism, transsexuality, transvestism, exhibitionism, voyeurism, and pedophilia are quite firmly entrenched as psychological malfunctions.[40] Books are still being written about the genesis, etiology, treatment, and cure of these assorted "pathologies."

Psychiatric condemnation of sexual behaviors invokes concepts of mental and emotional inferiority rather than categories of sexual sin. Low status sex practices are vilified as mental diseases or symptoms of defective personality integration. In addition, psychological terms conflate difficulties of psychodynamic functioning with modes of erotic conduct. They equate sexual masochism with self-destructive personality patterns, sexual sadism with emotional aggression, and homoeroticism with immaturity. These terminological muddles have become powerful stereotypes that are indiscriminately applied to individuals on the basis of their sexual orientations.

Popular culture is permeated with ideas that erotic variety is dangerous, unhealthy, depraved, and a menace to everything from small children to national security. Popular sexual ideology is a noxious stew made up of ideas of sexual sin, concepts of psychological inferiority, anti-communism, mob hysteria, accusations of witchcraft, and xenophobia. The mass media nourish these attitudes with relentless propaganda. I would call this system of erotic stigma the last socially respectable form of prejudice if the old forms did not show such obstinate vitality, and new ones did not continually become apparent.

All these hierarchies of sexual value – religious, psychiatric, and popular – function in much the same ways as do ideological systems of racism, ethnocentrism, and religious chauvinism. They rationalize the well-being of the sexually privileged and the adversity of the sexual rabble.

Figure 1 diagrams a general version of the sexual value system. According to this system, sexuality that is "good," "normal" and "natural" should ideally be heterosexual, marital, monogamous, reproductive, and non-commercial. It should be coupled, relational, within the same generation, and occur at home. It should

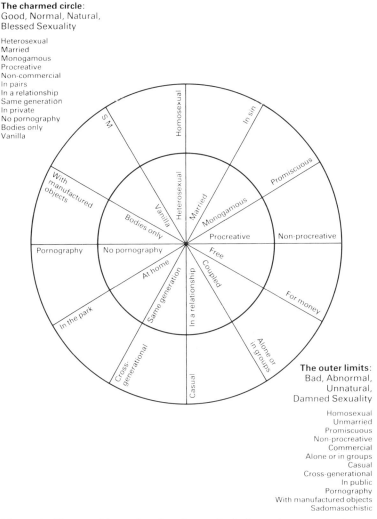

The charmed circle:
Good, Normal, Natural,
Blessed Sexuality

Heterosexual
Married
Monogamous
Procreative
Non-commercial
In pairs
In a relationship
Same generation
In private
No pornography
Bodies only
Vanilla

The outer limits:
Bad, Abnormal,
Unnatural,
Damned Sexuality

Homosexual
Unmarried
Promiscuous
Non-procreative
Commercial
Alone or in groups
Casual
Cross-generational
In public
Pornography
With manufactured objects
Sadomasochistic

Figure 1 The sex hierarchy: the charmed circle vs the outer limits

not involve pornography, fetish objects, sex toys of any sort, or roles other than male and female. Any sex that violates these rules is "bad," "abnormal," or "unnatural." Bad sex may be homosexual, unmarried, promiscuous, non-procreative, or commercial. It may be masturbatory or take place at orgies, may be casual, may cross generational lines, and may take place in "public," or at least in the bushes or the baths. It may involve the use of pornography, fetish objects, sex toys, or unusual roles (see Figure 1).

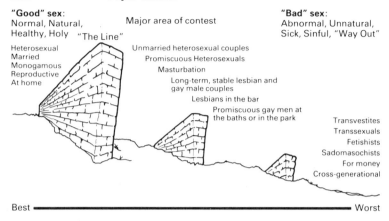

Figure 2   The sex hierarchy: the struggle over where to draw the line

Figure 2 diagrams another aspect of the sexual hierarchy: the need to draw and maintain an imaginary line between good and bad sex. Most of the discourses on sex, be they religious, psychiatric, popular, or political, delimit a very small portion of human sexual capacity as sanctifiable, safe, healthy, mature, legal, or politically correct. The "line" distinguishes these from all other erotic behaviors, which are understood to be the work of the devil, dangerous, psychopathological, infantile, or politically reprehensible. Arguments are then conducted over "where to draw the line," and to determine what other activities, if any, may be permitted to cross over into acceptability.

All these models assume a domino theory of sexual peril. The line appears to stand between sexual order and chaos. It expresses the fear that if anything is permitted to cross this erotic DMZ, the barrier against scary sex will crumble and something unspeakable will skitter across.

Most systems of sexual judgment – religious, psychological, feminist, or socialist – attempt to determine on which side of the line a particular act falls. Only sex acts on the good side of the line are accorded moral complexity. For instance, heterosexual encounters may be sublime or disgusting, free or forced, healing or destructive, romantic or mercenary. As long as it does not violate other rules, heterosexuality is acknowledged to exhibit the full range of human experience. In contrast, all sex acts on the bad side of the line are considered utterly repulsive and devoid of all emotional nuance. The further from the line a sex act is, the more it is depicted as a uniformly bad experience.

As a result of the sex conflicts of the last decade, some behavior near the border is inching across it. Unmarried couples living together, masturbation, and some forms of homosexuality are moving in the direction of respectability (see Figure 2). Most homosexuality is still on the bad side of the line. But if it is coupled and monogamous, the society is beginning to recognize that it includes the full range of human interaction. Promiscuous homosexuality, sadomasochism, fetishism, transsexuality, and cross-generational encounters are still viewed as unmodulated horrors incapable of involving affection, love, free choice, kindness, or transcendence.

This kind of sexual morality has more in common with ideologies of racism than with true ethics. It grants virtue to the dominant groups, and relegates vice to the underprivileged. A democratic morality should judge sexual acts by the way partners treat one another, the level of mutual consideration, the presence or absence of coercion, and the quantity and quality of the pleasures they provide. Whether sex acts are gay or straight, coupled or in groups, naked or in underwear, commercial or free, with or without video, should not be ethical concerns.

It is difficult to develop a pluralistic sexual ethics without a concept of benign sexual variation. Variation is a fundamental property of all life, from the simplest biological organisms to the most complex human social formations. Yet sexuality is supposed to conform to a single standard. One of the most tenacious ideas about sex is that there is one best way to do it, and that everyone should do it that way.

Most people find it difficult to grasp that whatever they like to do sexually will be thoroughly repulsive to someone else, and that whatever repels them sexually will be the most treasured delight of someone, somewhere. One need not like or perform a particular sex act in order to recognize that someone else will, and that this difference does not indicate a lack of good taste, mental health, or intelligence in either party. Most people mistake their sexual preferences for a universal system that will or should work for everyone.

This notion of a single ideal sexuality characterizes most systems of thought about sex. For religion, the ideal is procreative marriage. For psychology, it is mature hetero-sexuality. Although its content varies, the format of a single sexual standard is continually reconstituted within other rhetorical frameworks, including feminism and socialism. It is just as objectionable to insist that everyone should be lesbian, non-monogamous, or kinky, as to believe that everyone should be heterosexual, married, or vanilla – though the latter set of opinions are backed by considerably more coercive power than the former.

Progressives who would be ashamed to display cultural chauvinism in other areas routinely exhibit it towards sexual differences. We have learned to cherish different cultures as unique expressions of human inventiveness rather than as the inferior or disgusting habits of savages. We need a similarly anthropological understanding of different sexual cultures.

Empirical sex research is the one field that does incorporate a positive concept of sexual variation. Alfred Kinsey approached the study of sex with the same uninhibited curiosity he had previously applied to examining a species of wasp. His scientific detachment gave his work a refreshing neutrality that enraged moralists and caused immense controversy.[41] Among Kinsey's successors, John Gagnon and William Simon have pioneered the application of sociological understandings to erotic variety.[42] Even some of the older sexology is useful. Although his work is imbued with unappetizing eugenic beliefs, Havelock Ellis was an acute and sympathetic observer. His monumental *Studies in the Psychology of Sex* is resplendent with detail.[43]

Much political writing on sexuality reveals complete ignorance of both classical sexology and modern sex research. Perhaps this is because so few colleges and universities bother to teach human sexuality, and because so much stigma adheres even to scholarly investigation of sex. Neither sexology nor sex research has been immune to the prevailing sexual value system. Both contain assumptions and information which should not be accepted uncritically. But sexology and sex research provide abundant detail, a welcome posture of calm, and a well developed ability to treat sexual variety as something that exists rather than as something to be exterminated. These fields can provide an empirical grounding for a radical theory of sexuality more useful than the combination of psychoanalysis and feminist first principles to which so many texts resort.

III Sexual transformation

As defined by the ancient civil or canonical codes, sodomy was a category of forbidden acts; their perpetrator was nothing more than the juridical subject of them. The nineteenth-century homosexual became a personage, a past, a case history, and a childhood, in addition to being a type of life, a life form, and a morphology, with an indiscreet anatomy and possibly a mysterious physiology.... The sodomite had been a temporary aberration; the homosexual was now a species.

Michel Foucault[44]

In spite of many continuities with ancestral forms, modern sexual arrangements have a distinctive character which sets them apart from preexisting systems. In Western Europe and the United States, industrialization and urbanization reshaped the traditional rural and peasant populations into a new urban industrial and service workforce. It generated new forms of state apparatus, reorganized family relations, altered gender roles, made possible new forms of identity, produced new varieties of social inequality, and created new formats for political and ideological conflict. It also gave rise to a new sexual system characterized by distinct types of sexual persons, populations, stratification, and political conflict.

The writings of nineteenth-century sexology suggest the appearance of a kind of erotic speciation. However outlandish their explanations, the early sexologists were witnessing the emergence of new kinds of erotic individuals and their aggregation into rudimentary communities. The modern sexual system contains sets of these sexual populations, stratified by the operation of an ideological and social hierarchy. Differences in social value create friction among these groups, who engage in political contests to alter or maintain their place in the ranking. Contemporary sexual politics should be reconceptualized in terms of the emergence and on-going development of this system, its social relations, the ideologies which interpret it, and its characteristic modes of conflict.

Homosexuality is the best example of this process of erotic speciation. Homosexual behavior is always present among humans. But in different societies and epochs it may be rewarded or punished, required or forbidden, a temporary experience or a life-long vocation. In some New Guinea societies, for example, homosexual activities are obligatory for all males. Homosexual acts are considered utterly masculine, roles are based on age, and partners are determined by kinship status.[45] Although these men engage in extensive homosexual and pedophile behavior, they are neither homosexuals nor pederasts.

Nor was the sixteenth-century sodomite a homosexual. In 1631, Mervyn Touchet, Earl of Castlehaven, was tried and executed for sodomy. It is clear from the proceedings that the earl was not understood by himself or anyone else to be a particular kind of sexual individual. "While from the twentieth-century viewpoint Lord Castlehaven obviously suffered from psychosexual problems requiring the services of an analyst, from the seventeenth century viewpoint he had deliberately broken the Law of God and the Laws of England, and required the simpler services of an executioner."[46] The earl did not slip into his tightest doublet and waltz down to the nearest gay tavern to mingle with his fellow sodomists. He stayed in his manor house and buggered his servants. Gay self-awareness, gay pubs, the sense of group commonality, and even the term homosexual were not part of the earl's universe.

The New Guinea bachelor and the sodomite nobleman are only

tangentially related to a modern gay man, who may migrate from rural Colorado to San Francisco in order to live in a gay neighborhood, work in a gay business, and participate in an elaborate experience that includes a self-conscious identity, group solidarity, a literature, a press and a high level of political activity. In modern, Western, industrial societies, homosexuality has acquired much of the institutional structure of an ethnic group.[47]

The relocation of homoeroticism into these quasi-ethnic, nucleated, sexually constituted communities is to some extent a consequence of the transfers of population brought about by industrialization. As laborers migrated to work in cities, there were increased opportunities for voluntary communities to form. Homosexually inclined women and men, who would have been vulnerable and isolated in most pre-industrial villages, began to congregate in small corners of the big cities. Most large nineteenth-century cities in Western Europe and North America had areas where men could cruise for other men. Lesbian communities seem to have coalesced more slowly and on a smaller scale. Nevertheless, by the 1890s, there were several cafes in Paris near the Place Pigalle which catered to a lesbian clientele, and it is likely that there were similar places in the other major capitals of Western Europe.

Areas like these acquired bad reputations, which alerted other interested individuals of their existence and location. In the United States, lesbian and gay male territories were well established in New York, Chicago, San Francisco, and Los Angeles in the 1950s. Sexually motivated migration to places such as Greenwich Village had become a sizable sociological phenomenon. By the late 1970s, sexual migration was occurring on a scale so significant that it began to have a recognizable impact on urban politics in the United States, with San Francisco being the most notable and notorious example.[48]

Prostitution has undergone a similar metamorphosis. Prostitution began to change from a temporary job to a more permanent occupation as a result of nineteenth-century agitation, legal reform, and police persecution. Prostitutes, who had been part of the general working-class population, became increasingly isolated as members of an outcast group.[49] Prostitutes and other sex workers differ from homosexuals and other sexual minorities. Sex work is an occupation, while sexual deviation is an erotic preference. Nevertheless, they share some common features of social organization. Like homosexuals, prostitutes are a criminal sexual population stigmatized on the basis of sexual activity. Prostitutes and male homosexuals are the primary prey of vice police everywhere.[50] Like gay men, prostitutes occupy well demarcated urban territories and battle with police to defend and maintain those territories. The legal persecution of both populations is justified by an elaborate ideology which classifies them as dangerous and inferior undesirables who are not entitled to be left in peace.

Besides organizing homosexuals and prostitutes into localized populations, the "modernization of sex" has generated a system of continual sexual ethnogenesis. Other populations of erotic dissidents – commonly known as the "perversions" or the "paraphilias" – also began to coalesce. Sexualities keep marching out of the *Diagnostic and Statistical Manual* and on to the pages of social history. At present, several other groups are trying to emulate the successes of homosexuals. Bisexuals, sadomasochists, individuals who prefer cross-generational encounters, transsexuals, and transvestites are all in various states of community formation and identity acquisition. The perversions are not proliferating as much as they are attempting to acquire social space, small businesses, political resources, and a measure of relief from the penalties for sexual heresy.

IV Sexual stratification

An entire sub-race was born, different – despite certain kinship ties – from the libertines of the past. From the end of the eighteenth century to our own, they circulated through the pores of society; they were always hounded, but not always by laws; were often locked up, but not always in prisons; were sick perhaps, but scandalous, dangerous victims, prey to a strange evil that also bore the name of vice and sometimes crime. They were children wise beyond their years, precocious little girls, ambiguous schoolboys, dubious servants and educators, cruel or maniacal husbands, solitary collectors, ramblers with bizarre impulses; they haunted the houses of correction, the penal colonies, the tribunals, and the asylums; they carried their infamy to the doctors and their sickness to the judges. This was the numberless family of perverts who were on friendly terms with delinquents and akin to madmen.

Michel Foucault[51]

The industrial transformation of Western Europe and North America brought about new forms of social stratification. The resultant inequalities of class are well known and have been explored in detail by a century of scholarship. The construction of modern systems of racism and ethnic injustice has been well documented and critically assessed. Feminist thought has analyzed the prevailing organization of gender oppression. But although specific erotic groups, such as militant homosexuals and sex workers, have agitated against their own mistreatment, there has been no equivalent attempt to locate particular varieties of sexual persecution within a more general system of sexual stratification. Nevertheless, such a system exists, and in its contemporary form it is a consequence of Western industrialization.

Sex law is the most adamantine instrument of sexual stratification and erotic persecution. The state routinely intervenes in sexual behavior at a level that would not be tolerated in other areas of social life. Most people are unaware of the extent of sex law, the quantity and qualities of illegal sexual behavior, and the punitive character of legal sanctions. Although federal agencies may be involved in obscenity and prostitution cases, most sex laws are enacted at the state and municipal level, and enforcement is largely in the hands of local police. Thus, there is a tremendous amount of variation in the laws applicable to any given locale. Moreover, enforcement of sex laws varies dramatically with the local political climate. In spite of this legal thicket, one can make some tentative and qualified generalizations. My discussion of sex law does not apply to laws against sexual coercion, sexual assault, or rape. It does pertain to the myriad prohibitions on consensual sex and the "status" offenses such as statutory rape.

Sex law is harsh. The penalties for violating sex statutes are universally out of proportion to any social or individual harm. A single act of consensual but illicit sex, such as placing one's lips upon the genitalia of an enthusiastic partner, is punished in most states with more severity than rape, battery, or murder. Each such genital kiss, each lewd caress, is a separate crime. It is therefore painfully easy to commit multiple felonies in the course of a single evening of illegal passion. Once someone is convicted of a sex violation, a second performance of the same act is grounds for prosecution as a repeat offender, in which case penalties will be even more severe. In some states, individuals have become repeat felons for having engaged in homosexual love-making on two separate occasions. Once an erotic activity has been proscribed by sex law, the full power of the state enforces conformity to the values embodied in those laws. Sex laws are notoriously easy to pass, as legislators are loath to be soft on vice. Once on the books, they are extremely difficult to dislodge.

Sex law is not a perfect reflection of the prevailing moral evaluations of sexual conduct. Sexual variation *per se* is more specifically policed by the mental-health professions, popular ideology, and extra-legal social practice. Some of the most detested erotic behaviors, such as fetishism and sadomasochism, are not as closely or completely regulated by the criminal justice system as somewhat less stigmatized practices, such as homosexuality. Areas of sexual behavior come under the purview of the law when they become objects of social concern and political uproar. Each sex scare or morality campaign deposits new regulations as a kind of fossil record of its passage. The legal sediment is thickest – and sex law has its greatest potency – in areas involving obscenity, money, minors, and homosexuality.

Obscenity laws enforce a powerful taboo against direct representation of erotic activities. Current emphasis on the ways in which sexuality has become a focus of social attention should not be misused to undermine a critique of this prohibition. It is one thing to create sexual discourse in the form of psycho-analysis, or in the course of a morality crusade. It is quite another to graphically depict sex acts or genitalia. The first is socially permissible in a way the second is not. Sexual speech is forced into reticence, euphemism, and indirection. Freedom of speech about sex is a glaring exception to the protections of the First Amendment, which is not even considered applicable to purely sexual statements.

The anti-obscenity laws also form part of a group of statutes that make almost all sexual commerce illegal. Sex law incorporates a very strong prohibition against mixing sex and money, except via marriage. In addition to the obscenity statutes, other laws impinging on sexual commerce include anti-prostitution laws, alcoholic beverage regulations, and ordinances governing the location and operation of "adult" businesses. The sex industry and the gay economy have both managed to circumvent some of this legislation, but that process has not been easy or simple. The underlying criminality of sex-oriented business keeps it marginal, underdeveloped, and distorted. Sex businesses can only operate in legal loopholes. This tends to keep investment down and to divert commercial activity towards the goal of staying out of jail rather than the delivery of goods and services. It also renders sex workers more vulnerable to exploitation and bad working conditions. If sex commerce were legal, sex workers would be more able to organize and agitate for higher pay, better conditions, greater control, and less stigma.

Whatever one thinks of the limitations of capitalist commerce, such an extreme exclusion from the market process would hardly be socially acceptable in other areas of activity. Imagine, for example, that the exchange of money for medical care, pharmacological advice, or psychological counseling were illegal. Medical practice would take place in a much less satisfactory fashion if doctors, nurses, druggists, and therapists could be hauled off to jail at the whim of the local "health squad." But that is essentially the situation of prostitutes, sex workers, and sex entrepreneurs.

Marx himself considered the capitalist market a revolutionary, if limited, force. He argued that capitalism was progressive in its dissolution of pre-capitalist superstition, prejudice, and the bonds of traditional modes of life. "Hence the great civilizing influence of capital, its production of a state of society compared with which all earlier stages appear to be merely local progress and idolatry of nature."[52] Keeping sex from realizing the positive effects of the market economy hardly makes it socialist.

The law is especially ferocious in maintaining the boundary between childhood "innocence" and "adult" sexuality. Rather than recognizing the sexuality of the young, and attempting to provide for it in a caring and responsible manner, our culture denies and punishes erotic interest and activity by anyone under the local age of consent. The amount of law devoted to protecting young people from premature exposure to sexuality is breathtaking.

The primary mechanism for insuring the separation of sexual generations is age of consent laws. These laws make no distinction between the most brutal rape and the most gentle romance. A 20-year-old convicted of sexual contact with a 17-year-old will face a severe sentence in virtually every state, regardless of the nature of the relationship.[53] Nor are minors permitted access to "adult" sexuality in other forms. They are forbidden to see books, movies, or television in which sexuality is "too" graphically portrayed. It is legal for young people to see hideous depictions of violence, but not to see explicit pictures of genitalia. Sexually active young people are frequently incarcerated in juvenile homes, or otherwise punished for their "precocity."

Adults who deviate too much from conventional standards of sexual conduct are often denied contact with the young, even their own. Custody laws permit the state to steal the children of anyone whose erotic activities appear questionable to a judge presiding over family court matters. Countless lesbians, gay men, prostitutes, swingers, sex workers, and "promiscuous" women have been declared unfit parents under such provisions. Members of the teaching professions are closely monitored for signs of sexual misconduct. In most states, certification laws require that teachers arrested for sex offenses lose their jobs and credentials. In some cases, a teacher may be fired merely because an unconventional lifestyle becomes known to school officials. Moral turpitude is one of the few legal grounds for revoking academic tenure.[54] The more influence one has over the next generation, the less latitude one is permitted in behavior and opinion. The coercive power of the law ensures the transmission of conservative sexual values with these kinds of controls over parenting and teaching.

The only adult sexual behavior that is legal in every state is the placement of the penis in the vagina in wedlock. Consenting adults statutes ameliorate this situation in fewer than half the states. Most states impose severe criminal penalties on consensual sodomy, homosexual contact short of sodomy, adultery, seduction, and adult incest. Sodomy laws vary a great deal. In some states, they apply equally to homosexual and heterosexual partners and regardless of marital status. Some state courts have ruled that married couples have the right to commit sodomy in private. Only homosexual sodomy is illegal in some states. Some sodomy statutes prohibit both anal sex and oral-genital contact. In other states, sodomy applies only to anal penetration, and oral sex is covered under separate statutes.[55]

Laws like these criminalize sexual behavior that is freely chosen and avidly sought. The ideology embodied in them reflects the value hierarchies discussed above. That is, some sex acts are considered to be so intrinsically vile that no one should be allowed under any circumstance to perform them. The fact that individuals consent to or even prefer them is taken to be additional evidence of depravity. This system of sex law is similar to legalized racism. State prohibition of same sex contact, anal penetration, and oral sex make homosexuals a criminal group denied the privileges of full citizenship. With such laws, prosecution is persecution. Even when they are not strictly enforced, as is usually the case, the members of criminalized sexual communities remain vulnerable to the possibility of arbitrary arrest, or to periods in which they become the objects of social panic. When those occur, the laws are in place and police action is swift. Even sporadic enforcement serves to remind individuals that they are members of a subject population. The occasional arrest for sodomy, lewd behavior, solicitation, or oral sex keeps everyone else afraid, nervous, and circumspect.

The state also upholds the sexual hierarchy through bureaucratic regulation. Immigration policy still prohibits the admission of homosexuals (and other sexual "deviates") into the United States. Military regulations bar homosexuals from serving in the armed forces. The fact that gay people cannot legally marry means that they cannot enjoy the same legal rights as heterosexuals in many matters, including inheritance, taxation, protection from testimony in court, and the acquisition of citizenship for foreign partners. These are but a few of the ways that the state reflects and maintains the social relations of sexuality. The law buttresses structures of power, codes of behavior, and forms of prejudice. At their worst, sex law and sex regulation are simply sexual apartheid.

Although the legal apparatus of sex is staggering, most

everyday social control is extra-legal. Less formal, but very effective social sanctions are imposed on members of "inferior" sexual populations.

In her marvelous ethnographic study of gay life in the 1960s, Esther Newton observed that the homosexual population was divided into what she called the "overts" and the "coverts." "The overts live their *entire* working lives within the context of the [gay] community; the coverts live their entire *nonworking* lives within it."[56] At the time of Newton's study, the gay community provided far fewer jobs than it does now, and the non-gay work world was almost completely intolerant of homosexuality. There were some fortunate individuals who could be openly gay and earn decent salaries. But the vast majority of homosexuals had to choose between honest poverty and the strain of maintaining a false identity.

Though this situation has changed a great deal, discrimination against gay people is still rampant. For the bulk of the gay population, being out on the job is still impossible. Generally, the more important and higher paid the job, the less the society will tolerate overt erotic deviance. If it is difficult for gay people to find employment where they do not have to pretend, it is doubly and triply so for more exotically sexed individuals. Sadomasochists leave their fetish clothes at home, and know that they must be especially careful to conceal their real identities. An exposed pedophile would probably be stoned out of the office. Having to maintain such absolute secrecy is a considerable burden. Even those who are content to be secretive may be exposed by some accidental event. Individuals who are erotically unconventional risk being unemployable or unable to pursue their chosen careers.

Public officials and anyone who occupies a position of social consequence are especially vulnerable. A sex scandal is the surest method for hounding someone out of office or destroying a political career. The fact that important people are expected to conform to the strictest standards of erotic conduct discourages sex perverts of all kinds from seeking such positions. Instead, erotic dissidents are channeled into positions that have less impact on the mainstream of social activity and opinion.

The expansion of the gay economy in the last decade has provided some employment alternatives and some relief from job discrimination against homosexuals. But most of the jobs provided by the gay economy are low-status and low-paying. Bartenders, bathhouse attendants, and disc jockeys are not bank officers or corporate executives. Many of the sexual migrants who flock to places like San Francisco are downwardly mobile. They face intense competition for choice positions. The influx of sexual migrants provides a pool of cheap and exploitable labor for many of the city's businesses, both gay and straight.

Families play a crucial role in enforcing sexual conformity. Much social pressure is brought to bear to deny erotic dissidents the comforts and resources that families provide. Popular ideology holds that families are not supposed to produce or harbor erotic non conformity. Many families respond by trying to reform, punish, or exile sexually offending members. Many sexual migrants have been thrown out by their families, and many others are fleeing from the threat of institutionalization. Any random collection of homosexuals, sex workers, or miscellaneous perverts can provide heart-stopping stories of rejection and mistreatment by horrified families. Christmas is the great family holiday in the United States and consequently it is a time of considerable tension in the gay community. Half the inhabitants go off to their families of origin; many of those who remain in the gay ghettoes cannot do so, and relive their anger and grief.

In addition to economic penalties and strain on family relations, the stigma of erotic dissidence creates friction at all other levels of everyday life. The general public helps to penalize erotic non-conformity when, according to the values they have been taught, landlords refuse housing, neighbors call in the police, and hoodlums commit sanctioned battery. The ideologies of erotic inferiority and sexual danger decrease the power of sex perverts and sex workers in social encounters of all kinds. They have less protection from unscrupulous or criminal behavior, less access to police protection, and less recourse to the courts. Dealings with institutions and bureaucracies – hospitals, police, coroners, banks, public officials – are more difficult.

Sex is a vector of oppression. The system of sexual oppression cuts across other modes of social inequality, sorting out individuals and groups according to its own intrinsic dynamics. It is not reducible to, or understandable in terms of, class, race, ethnicity, or gender. Wealth, white skin, male gender, and ethnic privileges can mitigate the effects of sexual stratification. A rich, white male pervert will generally be less affected than a poor, black, female pervert. But even the most privileged are not immune to sexual oppression. Some of the consequences of the system of sexual hierarchy are mere nuisances. Others are quite grave. In its most serious manifestations, the sexual system is a Kafkaesque nightmare in which unlucky victims become herds of human cattle whose identification, surveillance, apprehension, treatment, incarceration, and punishment produce jobs and self-satisfaction for thousands of vice police, prison officials, psychiatrists, and social workers.[57]

V Sexual conflicts

> The moral panic crystallizes widespread fears and anxieties, and often
> deals with them not by seeking the real causes of the problems and
> conditions which they demonstrate but by displacing them on to 'Folk
> Devils' in an identified social group (often the 'immoral' or 'degenerate').
> Sexuality has had a peculiar centrality in such panics, and sexual
> 'deviants' have been omnipresent scapegoats.
>
> Jeffrey Weeks[58]

The sexual system is not a monolithic, omnipotent structure.
There are continuous battles over the definitions, evaluations,
arrangements, privileges, and costs of sexual behavior. Political
struggle over sex assumes characteristic forms.

Sexual ideology plays a crucial role in sexual experience.
Consequently, definitions and evaluations of sexual conduct are
objects of bitter contest. The confrontations between early gay
liberation and the psychiatric establishment are the best example
of this kind of fight, but there are constant skirmishes. Recurrent
battles take place between the primary producers of sexual
ideology – the churches, the family, the shrinks, and the media –
and the groups whose experience they name, distort, and
endanger.

The legal regulation of sexual conduct is another battleground.
Lysander Spooner dissected the system of state sanctioned moral
coercion over a century ago in a text inspired primarily by the
temperance campaigns. In *Vices Are Not Crimes: A Vindication
of Moral Liberty*, Spooner argued that government should protect
its citizens against crime, but that it is foolish, unjust, and
tyrannical to legislate against vice. He discusses rationalizations
still heard today in defense of legalized moralism – that "vices"
(Spooner is referring to drink, but homosexuality, prostitution, or
recreational drug use may be substituted) lead to crimes, and
should therefore be prevented; that those who practice "vice" are
non compos mentis and should therefore be protected from their
self-destruction by state-accomplished ruin; and that children
must be protected from supposedly harmful knowledge.[59] The
discourse on victimless crimes has not changed much. Legal
struggle over sex law will continue until basic freedoms of sexual
action and expression are guaranteed. This requires the repeal of
all sex laws except those few that deal with actual, not statutory,
coercion; and it entails the abolition of vice squads, whose job it
is to enforce legislated morality.

In addition to the definitional and legal wars, there are less
obvious forms of sexual political conflict which I call the territorial
and border wars. The processes by which erotic minorities form
communities and the forces that seek to inhibit them lead to

struggles over the nature and boundaries of sexual zones. Dissident sexuality is rarer and more closely monitored in small towns and rural areas. Consequently, metropolitan life continually beckons to young perverts. Sexual migration creates concentrated pools of potential partners, friends, and associates. It enables individuals to create adult, kin-like networks in which to live. But there are many barriers which sexual migrants have to overcome.

According to the mainstream media and popular prejudice, the marginal sexual worlds are bleak and dangerous. They are portrayed as impoverished, ugly, and inhabited by psychopaths and criminals. New migrants must be sufficiently motivated to resist the impact of such discouraging images. Attempts to counter negative propaganda with more realistic information generally meet with censorship, and there are continuous ideological struggles over which representations of sexual communities make it into the popular media.

Information on how to find, occupy, and live in the marginal sexual worlds is also suppressed. Navigational guides are scarce and inaccurate. In the past, fragments of rumor, distorted gossip, and bad publicity were the most available clues to the location of underground erotic communities. During the late 1960s and early 1970s, better information became available. Now groups like the Moral Majority want to rebuild the ideological walls around the sexual undergrounds and make transit in and out of them as difficult as possible.

Migration is expensive. Transportation costs, moving expenses, and the necessity of finding new jobs and housing are economic difficulties that sexual migrants must overcome. These are especially imposing barriers to the young, who are often the most desperate to move. There are, however, routes into the erotic communities which mark trails through the propaganda thicket and provide some economic shelter along the way. Higher education can be a route for young people from affluent backgrounds. In spite of serious limitations, the information on sexual behavior at most colleges and universities is better than elsewhere, and most colleges and universities shelter small erotic networks of all sorts.

For poorer kids, the military is often the easiest way to get the hell out of wherever they are. Military prohibitions against homosexuality make this a perilous route. Although young queers continually attempt to use the armed forces to get out of intolerable hometown situations and closer to functional gay communities, they face the hazards of exposure, court martial, and dishonorable discharge.

Once in the cities, erotic populations tend to nucleate and to occupy some regular, visible territory. Churches and other anti-vice forces constantly put pressure on local authorities to contain such areas, reduce their visibility, or to drive their inhabitants out of town. There are periodic crackdowns in which local vice squads are unleashed on the populations they control. Gay men, prostitutes, and sometimes transvestites are sufficiently territorial and numerous to engage in intense battles with the cops over particular streets, parks, and alleys. Such border wars are usually inconclusive, but they result in many casualties.

For most of this century, the sexual underworlds have been marginal and impoverished, their residents subjected to stress and exploitation. The spectacular success of gay entrepreneurs in creating a variegated gay economy has altered the quality of life within the gay ghetto. The level of material comfort and social elaboration achieved by the gay community in the last fifteen years is unprecedented. But it is important to recall what happened to similar miracles. The growth of the black population in New York in the early part of the twentieth century led to the Harlem Renaissance, but that period of creativity was doused by the Depression. The relative prosperity and cultural florescence of the gay ghetto may be equally fragile. Like blacks who fled the South for the metropolitan North, homosexuals may have merely traded rural problems for urban ones.

Gay pioneers occupied neighborhoods that were centrally located but run down. Consequently, they border poor neighborhoods. Gays, especially low-income gays, end up competing with other low-income groups for the limited supply of cheap and moderate housing. In San Francisco, competition for low-cost housing has exacerbated both racism and homophobia, and is one source of the epidemic of street violence against homosexuals. Instead of being isolated and invisible in rural settings, city gays are now numerous and obvious targets for urban frustrations.

In San Francisco, unbridled construction of downtown skyscrapers and high-cost condominiums is causing affordable housing to evaporate. Megabuck construction is creating pressure on all city residents. Poor gay renters are visible in low-income neighborhoods; multimillionaire contracters are not. The specter of the "homosexual invasion" is a convenient scapegoat which deflects attention from the banks, the planning commission, the political establishment, and the big developers. In San Francisco, the well-being of the gay community has become embroiled in the high-stakes politics of urban real estate.

Downtown expansion affects all the territorial erotic underworlds. In both San Francisco and New York, high investment construction and urban renewal have intruded on the main areas of prostitution, pornography, and leather bars. Developers are salivating over Times Square, the Tenderloin, what is left of North Beach, and South of Market. Anti-sex ideology, obscenity law, prostitution regulations, and the alcoholic beverage codes are all being used to dislodge seedy adult businesses, sex workers, and leathermen. Within ten years, most of these areas will have been bulldozed and made safe for convention centers, international hotels, corporate headquarters, and housing for the rich.

The most important and consequential kind of sex conflict is what Jeffrey Weeks has termed the "moral panic." Moral panics are the "political moment" of sex, in which diffuse attitudes are channeled into political action and from there into social change.[60] The white slavery hysteria of the 1880s, the anti-homosexual campaigns of the 1950s, and the child pornography panic of the late 1970s were typical moral panics.

Because sexuality in Western societies is so mystified, the wars over it are often fought at oblique angles, aimed at phony targets, conducted with misplaced passions, and are highly, intensely symbolic. Sexual activities often function as signifiers for personal and social apprehensions to which they have no intrinsic connection. During a moral panic, such fears attach to some unfortunate sexual activity or population. The media become ablaze with indignation, the public behaves like a rabid mob, the police are activated, and the state enacts new laws and regulations. When the furor has passed, some innocent erotic group has been decimated, and the state has extended its power into new areas of erotic behavior.

The system of sexual stratification provides easy victims who lack the power to defend themselves, and a preexisting apparatus for controlling their movements and curtailing their freedoms. The stigma against sexual dissidents renders them morally defenseless. Every moral panic has consequences on two levels. The target population suffers most, but everyone is affected by the social and legal changes.

Moral panics rarely alleviate any real problem, because they are aimed at chimeras and signifiers. They draw on the pre-existing discursive structure which invents victims in order to justify treating "vices" as crimes. The criminalization of innocuous behaviors such as homosexuality, prostitution, obscenity, or recreational drug use, is rationalized by portraying them as menaces to health and safety, women and children, national security, the family, or civilization itself. Even when activity is acknowledged to be harmless, it may be banned because it is alleged to "lead" to something ostensibly worse (another manifestation of the domino theory).[61] Great and mighty edifices have been built on the basis of such phantasms. Generally, the outbreak of a moral panic is preceded by an intensification of such scapegoating.

It is always risky to prophesy. But it does not take much prescience to detect potential moral panics in two current developments: the attacks on sadomasochists by a segment of the feminist movement, and the right's increasing use of AIDS to incite virulent homophobia.

Feminist anti-pornography ideology has always contained an implied, and sometimes overt, indictment of sadomasochism. The pictures of sucking and fucking that comprise the bulk of pornography may be unnerving to those who are not familiar with them. But it is hard to make a convincing case that such images are violent. All of the early anti-porn slide shows used a highly selective sample of S/M imagery to sell a very flimsy analysis. Taken out of context, such images are often shocking. This shock value was mercilessly exploited to scare audiences into accepting the anti-porn perspective.

A great deal of anti-porn propaganda implies that sadomasochism is the underlying and essential "truth" towards which all pornography tends. Porn is thought to lead to S/M porn which in turn is alleged to lead to rape. This is a just-so story that revitalizes the notion that sex perverts commit sex crimes, not normal people. There is no evidence that the readers of S/M erotica or practicing sadomasochists commit a disproportionate number of sex crimes. Anti-porn literature scapegoats an unpopular sexual minority and its reading material for social problems they do not create.

The use of S/M imagery in anti-porn discourse is inflammatory. It implies that the way to make the world safe for women is to get rid of sadomasochism. The use of S/M images in the movie *Not a Love Story* was on a moral par with the use of depictions of black men raping white women, or of drooling old Jews pawing young Aryan girls, to incite racist or anti-Semitic frenzy.

Feminist rhetoric has a distressing tendency to reappear in reactionary contexts. For example, in 1980 and 1981, Pope John Paul II delivered a series of pronouncements reaffirming his commitment to the most conservative and Pauline understandings of human sexuality. In condemning divorce, abortion, trial marriage, pornography, prostitution, birth control, unbridled hedonism, and lust, the pope employed a great deal of feminist rhetoric about sexual objectification. Sounding like lesbian feminist polemicist Julia Penelope, His Holiness explained that "considering anyone in a lustful way makes that person a sexual object rather than a human being worthy of dignity."[62]

The right wing opposes pornography and has already adopted elements of feminist anti-porn rhetoric. The anti-S/M discourse developed in the women's movement could easily become a vehicle for a moral witch hunt. It provides a ready-made defenseless target population. It provides a rationale for the recriminalization of sexual materials which have escaped the reach of current obscenity laws. It would be especially easy to pass laws against S/M erotica resembling the child pornography laws. The ostensible purpose of such laws would be to reduce violence by banning so-called violent porn. A focused campaign against the leather menace might also result in the passage of laws to criminalize S/M behavior that is not currently illegal. The ultimate result of such a moral panic would be the legalized violation of a community of harmless perverts. It is dubious that such a sexual witch-hunt would make any appreciable contribution towards reducing violence against women.

An AIDS panic is even more probable. When fears of incurable disease mingle with sexual terror, the resulting brew is extremely volatile. A century ago, attempts to control syphilis led to the passage of the Contagious Diseases Acts in England. The Acts were based on erroneous medical theories and did nothing to halt the spread of the disease. But they did make life miserable for the hundreds of women who were incarcerated, subjected to forcible vaginal examination, and stigmatized for life as prostitutes.[63]

Whatever happens, AIDS will have far-reaching consequences on sex in general, and on homosexuality in particular. The disease will have a significant impact on the choices gay people make. Fewer will migrate to the gay meccas out of fear of the disease. Those who already reside in the ghettos will avoid situations they fear will expose them. The gay economy, and the political apparatus it supports, may prove to be evanescent. Fear of AIDS has already affected sexual ideology. Just when homosexuals have had some success in throwing off the taint of mental disease, gay people find themselves metaphorically welded to an image of lethal physical deterioration. The syndrome, its peculiar qualities, and its transmissibility are being used to reinforce old fears that sexual activity, homosexuality, and promiscuity led to disease and death.

AIDS is both a personal tragedy for those who contract the syndrome and a calamity for the gay community. Homophobes have gleefully hastened to turn this tragedy against its victims. One columnist has suggested that AIDS has always existed, that the Biblical prohibitions on sodomy were designed to protect people from AIDS, and that AIDS is therefore an appropriate punishment for violating the Levitical codes. Using fear of infection as a rationale, local right-wingers attempted to ban the gay rodeo from Reno, Nevada. A recent issue of the *Moral*

Majority Report featured a picture of a "typical" white family of four wearing surgical masks. The headline read: "AIDS: HOMO-SEXUAL DISEASES THREATEN AMERICAN FAMILIES."[64] Phyllis Schlafly has recently issued a pamphlet arguing that passage of the Equal Rights Amendment would make it impossible to "legally protect ourselves against AIDS and other diseases carried by homosexuals."[65] Current right-wing literature calls for shutting down the gay baths, for a legal ban on homosexual employment in food-handling occupations, and for state-mandated prohibitions on blood donations by gay people. Such policies would require the government to identify all homosexuals and impose easily recognizable legal and social markers on them.

It is bad enough that the gay community must deal with the medical misfortune of having been the population in which a deadly disease first became widespread and visible. It is worse to have to deal with the social consequences as well. Even before the AIDS scare, Greece passed a law that enabled police to arrest suspected homosexuals and force them to submit to an examination for veneral disease. It is likely that until AIDS and its methods of transmission are understood, there will be all sorts of proposals to control it by punishing the gay community and by attacking its institutions. When the cause of Legionnaires' Disease was unknown, there were no calls to quarantine members of the American Legion or to shut down their meeting halls. The Contagious Diseases Acts in England did little to control syphilis, but they caused a great deal of suffering for the women who came under their purview. The history of panic that has accompanied new epidemics, and of the casualties incurred by their scapegoats, should make everyone pause and consider with extreme scepticism any attempts to justify anti-gay policy initiatives on the basis of AIDS.

VI The limits of feminism

We know that in an overwhelmingly large number of cases, sex crime is associated with pornography. We know that sex criminals read it, are clearly influenced by it. I believe that, if we can eliminate the distribution of such items among impressionable children, we shall greatly reduce our frightening sex-crime rate.

                                                                J. Edgar Hoover[66]

In the absence of a more articulated radical theory of sex, most progressives have turned to feminism for guidance. But the relationship between feminism and sex is complex. Because sexuality is a nexus of the relationships between genders, much of the oppression of women is borne by, mediated through, and constituted within, sexuality. Feminism has always been ᵥ interested in sex. But there have been two strains of fen thought on the subject. One tendency has criticized the restrictions on women's sexual behavior and denounced the high costs imposed on women for being sexually active. This tradition of feminist sexual thought has called for a sexual liberation that would work for women as well as for men. The second tendency has considered sexual liberalization to be inherently a mere extension of male privilege. This tradition resonates with conservative, anti-sexual discourse. With the advent of the anti-pornography movement, it achieved temporary hegemony over feminist analysis.

The anti-pornography movement and its texts have been the most extensive expression of this discourse.[67] In addition, proponents of this viewpoint have condemned virtually every variant of sexual expression as anti-feminist. Within this framework, monogamous lesbianism that occurs within long-term, intimate relationships and which does not involve playing with polarized roles, has replaced married, procreative hetero-sexuality at the top of the value hierarchy. Heterosexuality has been demoted to somewhere in the middle. Apart from this change, everything else looks more or less familiar. The lower depths are occupied by the usual groups and behaviors: prostitution, transsexuality, sadomasochism, and cross-generational activities.[68] Most gay male conduct, all casual sex, promiscuity, and lesbian behavior that does involve roles or kink or non-monogamy are also censured.[69] Even sexual fantasy during masturbation is denounced as a phallocentric holdover.[70]

This discourse on sexuality is less a sexology than a demonology. It presents most sexual behavior in the worst possible light. Its descriptions of erotic conduct always use the worst available example as if it were representative. It presents the most disgusting pornography, the most exploited forms of prostitution, and the least palatable or most shocking manifesta-tions of sexual variation. This rhetorical tactic consistently misrepresents human sexuality in all its forms. The picture of human sexuality that emerges from this literature is unremittingly ugly.

In addition, this anti-porn rhetoric is a massive exercise in scapegoating. It criticizes non-routine acts of love rather than routine acts of oppression, exploitation, or violence. This demon sexology directs legitimate anger at women's lack of personal safety against innocent individuals, practices, and communities. Anti-porn propaganda often implies that sexism originates within the commercial sex industry and subsequently infects the rest of society. This is sociologically nonsensical. The sex industry is hardly a feminist utopia. It reflects the sexism that exists in the society as a whole. We need to analyze and oppose the manifestations of gender inequality specific to the sex industry. But this is not the same as attempting to wipe out commercial sex.

Similarly, erotic minorities such as sadomasochists and transsexuals are as likely to exhibit sexist attitudes or behavior as any other politically random social grouping. But to claim that they are inherently anti-feminist is sheer fantasy. A good deal of current feminist literature attributes the oppression of women to graphic representations of sex, prostitution, sex education, sadomasochism, male homosexuality, and transsexualism. Whatever happened to the family, religion, education, child-rearing practices, the media, the state, psychiatry, job discrimination, and unequal pay?

Finally, this so-called feminist discourse recreates a very conservative sexual morality. For over a century, battles have been waged over just how much shame, distress, and punishment should be incurred by sexual activity. The conservative tradition has promoted opposition to pornography, prostitution, homosexuality, all erotic variation, sex education, sex research, abortion, and contraception. The opposing, pro-sex tradition has included individuals like Havelock Ellis, Magnus Hirshfeld, Alfred Kinsey, and Victoria Woodhull, as well as the sex education movement, organizations of militant prostitutes and homosexuals, the reproductive rights movement, and organizations such as the Sexual Reform League of the 1960s. This motley collection of sex reformers, sex educators, and sexual militants has mixed records on both sexual and feminist issues. But surely they are closer to the spirit of modern feminism than are moral crusaders, the social purity movement, and anti-vice organizations. Nevertheless, the current feminist sexual demonology generally elevates the anti-vice crusaders to positions of ancestral honor, while condemning the more liberatory tradition as anti-feminist. In an essay that exemplifies some of these trends, Sheila Jeffreys blames Havelock Ellis, Edward Carpenter, Alexandra Kollantai, "believers in the joy of sex of every possible political persuasion," and the 1929 congress of the World League for Sex Reform for making "a great contribution to the defeat of militant feminism."[71]

The anti-pornography movement and its avatars have claimed to speak for all feminism. Fortunately, they do not. Sexual liberation has been and continues to be a feminist goal. The women's movement may have produced some of the most retrogressive sexual thinking this side of the Vatican. But it has also produced an exciting, innovative, and articulate defense of sexual pleasure and erotic justice. This "pro-sex" feminism has been spearheaded by lesbians whose sexuality does not conform to movement standards of purity (primarily lesbian sadomasochists and butch/femme dykes), by unapologetic heterosexuals, and by women who adhere to classic radical feminism rather than to the revisionist celebrations of femininity which have become so common.[72] Although the anti-porn forces have attempted to weed anyone who disgrees with them out of the movement, the fact remains that feminist thought about sex is profoundly polarized.[73]

Whenever there is polarization, there is an unhappy tendency to think the truth lies somewhere in between. Ellen Willis has commented sarcastically that "the feminist bias is that women are equal to men and the male chauvinist bias is that women are inferior. The unbiased view is that the truth lies somewhere in between."[74] The most recent development in the feminist sex wars is the emergence of a "middle" that seeks to evade the dangers of anti-porn fascism, on the one hand, and a supposed "anything goes" libertarianism, on the other.[75] Although it is hard to criticize a position that is not yet fully formed, I want to draw attention to some incipient problems.

The emergent middle is based on a false characterization of the poles of the debate, construing both sides as equally extremist. According to B. Ruby Rich, "the desire for a language of sexuality has led feminists into locations (pornography, sadomasochism) too narrow or overdetermined for a fruitful discussion. Debate has collapsed into a rumble."[76] True, the fights between Women Against Pornography (WAP) and lesbian sadomasochists have resembled gang warfare. But the responsibility for this lies primarily with the anti-porn movement, and its refusal to engage in principled discussion. S/M lesbians have been forced into a struggle to maintain their membership in the movement, and to defend themselves against slander. No major spokeswoman for lesbian S/M has argued for any kind of S/M supremacy, or advocated that everyone should be a sadomasochist. In addition to self-defense, S/M lesbians have called for appreciation for erotic diversity and more open discussion of sexuality.[77] Trying to find a middle course between WAP and Samois is a bit like saying that the truth about homosexuality lies somewhere between the positions of the Moral Majority and those of the gay movement.

In political life, it is all too easy to marginalize radicals, and to attempt to buy acceptance for a moderate position by portraying others as extremists. Liberals have done this for years to communists. Sexual radicals have opened up the sex debates. It is shameful to deny their contribution, misrepresent their positions, and further their stigmatization.

In contrast to cultural feminists, who simply want to purge sexual dissidents, the sexual moderates are willing to defend the rights of erotic non-conformists to political participation. Yet this defense of political rights is linked to an implicit system of ideological condescension. The argument has two major parts. The first is an accusation that sexual dissidents have not paid close enough attention to the meaning, sources, or historical construction of their sexuality. This emphasis on meaning appears to function in much the same way that the question of etiology has functioned in discussions of homosexuality. That is, homosexuality, sadomasochism, prostitution, or boy-love are taken to be mysterious and problematic in some way that more respectable sexualities are not. The search for a cause is a search for something that could change so that these "problematic" eroticisms would simply not occur. Sexual militants have replied to such exercises that although the question of etiology or cause is of intellectual interest, it is not high on the political agenda and that, moreover, the privileging of such questions is itself a regressive political choice.

The second part of the "moderate" position focuses on questions of consent. Sexual radicals of all varieties have demanded the legal and social legitimation of consenting sexual behavior. Feminists have criticized them for ostensibly finessing questions about "the limits of consent" and "structural constraints" on consent.[78] Although there are deep problems with the political discourse of consent, and although there are certainly structural constraints on sexual choice, this criticism has been consistently misapplied in the sex debates. It does not take into account the very specific semantic content that consent has in sex law and sex practice.

As I mentioned earlier, a great deal of sex law does not distinguish between consensual and coercive behavior. Only rape law contains such a distinction. Rape law is based on the assumption, correct in my view, that heterosexual activity may be freely chosen or forcibly coerced. One has the legal right to engage in heterosexual behavior as long as it does not fall under the purview of other statutes and as long as it is agreeable to both parties.

This is not the case for most other sexual acts. Sodomy laws, as I mentioned above, are based on the assumption that the forbidden acts are an "abominable and detestable crime against nature." Criminality is intrinsic to the acts themselves, no matter what the desires of the participants. "Unlike rape, sodomy or an unnatural or perverted sexual act may be committed between two persons both of whom consent, and, regardless of which is the aggressor, both may be prosecuted."[79] Before the consenting adults statute was passed in California in 1976, lesbian lovers could have been prosecuted for committing oral copulation. If both participants were capable of consent, both were equally guilty.[80]

Adult incest statutes operate in a similar fashion. Contrary to popular mythology, the incest statutes have little to do with protecting children from rape by close relatives. The incest statutes themselves prohibit marriage or sexual intercourse between adults who are closely related. Prosecutions are rare, but two were reported recently. In 1979, a 19-year-old Marine met his 42-year-old mother, from whom he had been separated at birth. The two fell in love and got married. They were charged and found guilty of incest, which under Virginia law carries a maximum ten-year sentence. During their trial, the Marine testified, "I love her very much. I feel that two people who love each other should be able to live together."[81] In another case, a brother and sister who had been raised separately met and decided to get married. They were arrested and pleaded guilty to felony incest in return for probation. A condition of probation was that they not live together as husband and wife. Had they not accepted, they would have faced twenty years in prison.[82]

In a famous S/M case, a man was convicted of aggravated assault for a whipping administered in an S/M scene. There was no complaining victim. The session had been filmed and he was prosecuted on the basis of the film. The man appealed his conviction by arguing that he had been involved in a consensual sexual encounter and had assaulted no one. In rejecting his appeal, the court ruled that one may not consent to an assault or battery "except in a situation involving ordinary physical contact or blows incident to sports such as football, boxing, or wrestling."[83] The court went on to note that the "consent of a person without legal capacity to give consent, such as a child or insane person, is ineffective," and that "It is a matter of common knowledge that a normal person in full possession of his mental faculties does not freely consent to the use, upon himself, of force likely to produce great bodily injury."[84] Therefore, anyone who would consent to a whipping would be presumed *non compos mentis* and legally incapable of consenting. S/M sex generally involves a much lower level of force than the average football game, and results in far fewer injuries than most sports. But the court ruled that football players are sane, whereas masochists are not.

Sodomy laws, adult incest laws, and legal interpretations such as the one above clearly interfere with consensual behavior and impose criminal penalties on it. Within the law, consent is a privilege enjoyed only by those who engage in the highest-status sexual behavior. Those who enjoy low-status sexual behavior do not have the legal right to engage in it. In addition, economic sanctions, family pressures, erotic stigma, social discrimination, negative ideology, and the paucity of information about erotic behavior, all serve to make it difficult for people to make unconventional sexual choices. There certainly are structural constraints that impede free sexual choice, but they hardly operate to coerce anyone into being a pervert. On the contrary, they operate to coerce everyone toward normality.

The "brainwash theory" explains erotic diversity by assuming that some sexual acts are so disgusting that no one would willingly perform them. Therefore, the reasoning goes, anyone who does so must have been forced or fooled. Even constructivist sexual theory has been pressed into the service of explaining away why otherwise rational individuals might engage in variant sexual behavior. Another position that is not yet fully formed uses the ideas of Foucault and Weeks to imply that the "perversions" are an especially unsavory or problematic aspect of the construction of modern sexuality.[85] This is yet another version of the notion that sexual dissidents are victims of the subtle machinations of the social system. Weeks and Foucault would not accept such an interpretation, since they consider all sexuality to be constructed, the conventional no less than the deviant.

Psychology is the last resort of those who refuse to acknowledge that sexual dissidents are as conscious and free as any other group of sexual actors. If deviants are not responding to the manipulations of the social system, then perhaps the source of their incomprehensible choices can be found in a bad childhood, unsuccessful socialization, or inadequate identity formation. In her essay on erotic domination, Jessica Benjamin draws upon psychoanalysis and philosophy to explain why what she calls "sadomasochism" is alienated, distorted, unsatisfactory, numb, purposeless, and an attempt to "relieve an original effort at differentiation that failed."[86] This essay substitutes a psycho-philosophical inferiority for the more usual means of devaluing dissident eroticism. One reviewer has already construed Benjamin's argument as showing that sadomasochism is merely an "obsessive replay of the infant power struggle."[87]

The position which defends the political rights of perverts but which seeks to understand their "alienated" sexuality is certainly preferable to the WAP-style bloodbaths. But for the most part, the sexual moderates have not confronted their discomfort with erotic choices that differ from their own. Erotic chauvinism cannot be redeemed by tarting it up in Marxist drag, sophisticated constructivist theory, or retro-psychobabble.

Whichever feminist position on sexuality – right, left, or center

– eventually attains dominance, the existence of such a rich discussion is evidence that the feminist movement will always be a source of interesting thought about sex. Nevertheless, I want to challenge the assumption that feminism is or should be the privileged site of a theory of sexuality. Feminism is the theory of gender oppression. To automatically assume that this makes it the theory of sexual oppression is to fail to distinguish between gender, on the one hand, and erotic desire, on the other.

In the English language, the word "sex" has two very different meanings. It means gender and gender identity, as in "the female sex" or "the male sex." But sex also refers to sexual activity, lust, intercourse, and arousal, as in "to have sex." This semantic merging reflects a cultural assumption that sexuality is reducible to sexual intercourse and that it is a function of the relations between women and men. The cultural fusion of gender with sexuality has given rise to the idea that a theory of sexuality may be derived directly out of a theory of gender.

In an earlier essay, "The Traffic in Women," I used the concept of a sex/gender system, defined as a "set of arrangements by which a society transforms biological sexuality into products of human activity."[88] I went on to argue that "Sex as we know it – gender identity, sexual desire and fantasy, concepts of childhood – is itself a social product."[89] In that essay, I did not distinguish between lust and gender, treating both as modalities of the same underlying social process.

"The Traffic in Women" was inspired by the literature on kin-based systems of social organization. It appeared to me at the time that gender and desire were systemically intertwined in such social formations. This may or may not be an accurate assessment of the relationship between sex and gender in tribal organizations. But it is surely not an adequate formulation for sexuality in Western industrial societies. As Foucault has pointed out, a system of sexuality has emerged out of earlier kinship forms and has acquired significant autonomy.

Particularly from the eighteenth century onward, Western societies created and deployed a new apparatus which was superimposed on the previous one, and which, without completely supplanting the latter, helped to reduce its importance. I am speaking of the deployment of *sexuality* . . . . For the first [kinship], what is pertinent is the link between partners and definite statutes; the second [sexuality] is concerned with the sensations of the body, the quality of pleasures, and the nature of impressions.[90]

The development of this sexual system has taken place in the context of gender relations. Part of the modern ideology of sex is that lust is the province of men, purity that of women. Women have been to some extent excluded from the modern sexual system. It is no accident that pornography and the perversions have been considered part of the male domain. In the sex industry, women have been excluded from most production and consumption, and allowed to participate primarily as workers. In order to participate in the "perversions," women have had to overcome serious limitations on their social mobility, their economic resources, and their sexual freedoms. Gender affects the operation of the sexual system, and the sexual system has had gender-specific manifestations. But although sex and gender are related, they are not the same thing, and they form the basis of two distinct arenas of social practice.

In contrast to my perspective in "The Traffic in Women," I am now arguing that it is essential to separate gender and sexuality analytically to more accurately reflect their separate social existence. This goes against the grain of much contemporary feminist thought, which treats sexuality as a derivation of gender. For instance, lesbian feminist ideology has mostly analyzed the oppression of lesbians in terms of the oppression of women. However, lesbians are also oppressed as queers and perverts, by the operation of sexual, not gender, stratification. Although it pains many lesbians to think about it, the fact is that lesbians have shared many of the sociological features and suffered from many of the same social penalties as have gay men, sadomasochists, transvestites, and prostitutes.

Catherine MacKinnon has made the most explicit theoretical attempt to subsume sexuality under feminist thought. According to MacKinnon, "Sexuality is to feminism what work is to marxism ... the molding, direction, and expression of sexuality organizes society into two sexes, women and men."[91] This analytic strategy in turn rests on a decision to "use sex and gender relatively interchangeably."[92] It is this definitional fusion that I want to challenge.

There is an instructive analogy in the history of the differentiation of contemporary feminist thought from Marxism. Marxism is probably the most supple and powerful conceptual system extant for analyzing social inequality. But attempts to make Marxism the sole explanatory system for all social inequalities have been dismal exercises. Marxism is most successful in the areas of social life for which it was originally developed – class relations under capitalism.

In the early days of the contemporary women's movement, a theoretical conflict took place over the applicability of Marxism to gender stratification. Since Marxist theory is relatively powerful, it does in fact detect important and interesting aspects of gender oppression. It works best for those issues of gender most closely related to issues of class and the organization of labor. The issues more specific to the social structure of gender were not amenable to Marxist analysis.

The relationship between feminism and a radical theory of sexual oppression is similar. Feminist conceptual tools were developed to detect and analyze gender-based hierarchies. To the extent that these overlap with erotic stratifications, feminist theory has some explanatory power. But as issues become less those of gender and more those of sexuality, feminist analysis becomes irrelevant and often misleading. Feminist thought simply lacks angles of vision which can encompass the social organization of sexuality. The criteria of relevance in feminist thought do not allow it to see or assess critical power relations in the area of sexuality.

In the long run, feminism's critique of gender hierarchy must be incorporated into a radical theory of sex, and the critique of sexual oppression should enrich feminism. But an autonomous theory and politics specific to sexuality must be developed.

It is a mistake to substitute feminism for Marxism as the last word in social theory. Feminism is no more capable than Marxism of being the ultimate and complete account of all social inequality. Nor is feminism the residual theory which can take care of everything to which Marx did not attend. These critical tools were fashioned to handle very specific areas of social activity. Other areas of social life, their forms of power, and their characteristic modes of oppression, need their own conceptual implements. In this essay, I have argued for theoretical as well as sexual pluralism.

VII Conclusion

... these pleasures which we lightly call physical...

Colette[93]

Like gender, sexuality is political. It is organized into systems of power, which reward and encourage some individuals and activities, while punishing and suppressing others. Like the capitalist organization of labor and its distribution of rewards and powers, the modern sexual system has been the object of political struggle since it emerged and as it has evolved. But if the disputes between labor and capital are mystified, sexual conflicts are completely camouflaged.

The legislative restructuring that took place at the end of the nineteenth century and in the early decades of the twentieth was a refracted response to the emergence of the modern erotic system. During that period, new erotic communities formed. It became possible to be a male homosexual or a lesbian in a way it had not been previously. Mass-produced erotica became available, and the possibilities for sexual commerce expanded. The first homosexual rights organizations were formed, and the first analyses of sexual oppression were articulated.[94]

The repression of the 1950s was in part a backlash to the expansion of sexual communities and possibilities which took place during World War II.[95] During the 1950s, gay rights organizations were established, the Kinsey reports were published, and lesbian literature flourished. The 1950s were a formative as well as a repressive era.

The current right-wing sexual counter-offensive is in part a reaction to the sexual liberalization of the 1960s and early 1970s. Moreover, it has brought about a unified and self-conscious coalition of sexual radicals. In one sense, what is now occurring is the emergence of a new sexual movement, aware of new issues and seeking a new theoretical basis. The sex wars out on the streets have been partly responsible for provoking a new intellectual focus on sexuality. The sexual system is shifting once again, and we are seeing many symptoms of its change.

In Western culture, sex is taken all too seriously. A person is not considered immoral, is not sent to prison, and is not expelled from her or his family, for enjoying spicy cuisine. But an individual may go through all this and more for enjoying shoe leather. Ultimately, of what possible social significance is it if a person likes to masturbate over a shoe? It may even be non-consensual, but since we do not ask permission of our shoes to wear them, it hardly seems necessary to obtain dispensation to come on them.

If sex is taken too seriously, sexual persecution is not taken seriously enough. There is systematic mistreatment of individuals and communities on the basis of erotic taste or behavior. There are serious penalties for belonging to the various sexual occupational castes. The sexuality of the young is denied, adult sexuality is often treated like a variety of nuclear waste, and the graphic representation of sex takes place in a mire of legal and social circumlocution. Specific populations bear the brunt of the current system of erotic power, but their persecution upholds a system that affects everyone.

The 1980s have already been a time of great sexual suffering. They have also been a time of ferment and new possibility. It is up to all of us to try to prevent more barbarism and to encourage erotic creativity. Those who consider themselves progressive need to examine their preconceptions, update their sexual educations, and acquaint themselves with the existence and operation of sexual hierarchy. It is time to recognize the political dimensions of erotic life.

Acknowledgments

It is always a treat to get to the point in a paper when I can thank those who contributed to its realization. Many of my ideas about the formation of sexual communities first occurred to me during a course given by Charles Tilly on "The Urbanization of Europe from 1500-1900." Few courses could ever provide as much excitement, stimulation, and conceptual richness as did that one. Daniel Tsang alerted me to the significance of the events of 1977 and taught me to pay attention to sex law. Pat Califia deepened my appreciation for human sexual variety and taught me to respect the much-maligned fields of sex research and sex education. Jeff Escoffier shared his powerful grasp of gay history and sociology, and I have especially benefited from his insights into the gay economy. Allan Bérubé's work in progress on gay history has enabled me to think with more clarity about the dynamics of sexual oppression. Conversations with Ellen Dubois, Amber Hollibaugh, Mary Ryan, Judy Stacey, Kay Trimberger, and Martha Vicinus have influenced the direction of my thinking.

I am very grateful to Cynthia Astuto for advice and research on legal matters, and to David Sachs, book-dealer extraordinaire, for pointing out the right-wing pamphlet literature on sex. I am grateful to Allan Bérubé, Ralph Bruno, Estelle Freedman, Kent Gerard, Barbara Kerr, Michael Shively, Carole Vance, Bill Walker, and Judy Walkowitz for miscellaneous references and factual information. I cannot begin to express my gratitude to those who read and commented on versions of this paper: Jeanne Bergman, Sally Binford, Lynn Eden, Laura Engelstein, Jeff Escoffier, Carole Vance and Ellen Willis. Mark Leger both edited and performed acts of secretarial heroism in preparing the manuscript. Marybeth Nelson provided emergency graphics assistance.

I owe special thanks to two friends whose care mitigated the strains of writing. E.S. kept my back operational and guided me firmly through some monumental bouts of writer's block. Cynthia Astuto's many kindnesses and unwavering support enabled me to keep working at an absurd pace for many weeks.

None of these individuals should be held responsible for my opinions, but I am grateful to them all for inspiration, information, and assistance.

A note on definitions

Throughout this essay, I use terms such as homosexual, sex worker, and pervert. I use "homosexual" to refer to both women and men. If I want to be more specific, I use terms such as "lesbian" or "gay male." "Sex worker" is intended to be more inclusive than "prostitute," in order to encompass the many jobs of the sex industry. Sex worker includes erotic dancers, strippers, porn models, nude women who will talk to a customer via telephone hook-up and can be seen but not touched, phone partners, and the various other employees of sex businesses such as receptionists, janitors, and barkers. Obviously, it also includes prostitutes, hustlers, and "male models." I use the term "pervert" as a shorthand for all the stigmatized sexual orientations. It used to cover male and female homosexuality as well but as these become less disreputable, the term has increasingly referred to the other "deviations." Terms such as "pervert" and "deviant" have, in general use, a connotation of disapproval, disgust, and dislike. I am using these terms in a denotative fashion, and do not intend them to convey any disapproval on my part.

Notes

1 Demetrius Zambaco, "Onanism and Nervous Disorders in Two Little Girls", in François Peraldi (ed.), *Polysexuality, Semiotext(e)*, vol. IV, no. 1, 1981, pp. 31, 36.

2 Linda Gordon and Ellen Dubois, "Seeking Ecstasy on the Battlefield: Danger and Pleasure in Nineteenth Century Feminist Sexual Thought", *Feminist Studies*, vol. 9, no. 1, Spring 1983; Steven Marcus, *The Other Victorians*, New York, New American Library, 1974; Mary Ryan, "The Power of Women's Networks: A Case Study of Female Moral Reform in America", *Feminist Studies*, vol. 5, no. 1, 1979; Judith R. Walkowitz, *Prostitution and Victorian Society*, Cambridge, Cambridge University Press, 1980; Judith R. Walkowitz, "Male Vice and Feminist Virtue: Feminism and the Politics of Prostitution in Nineteenth-Century Britain", *History Workshop Journal*, no. 13, Spring 1982; Jeffrey Weeks, *Sex, Politics and Society: The Regulation of Sexuality Since 1800*, New York, Longman, 1981.

3 G.J. Barker-Benfield, *The Horrors of the Half-Known Life*, New York, Harper Colophon, 1976; Marcus, op. cit.; Weeks, op. cit., especially pages 48-52; Zambaco, op. cit.

4 Sarah Senefield Beserra, Sterling G. Franklin, and Norma Clevenger (eds), *Sex Code of California*, Sacramento, Planned Parenthood Affiliates of California, 1977, p. 113.

5 Ibid., pp. 113-17.

6 Walkowitz, "Male Vice and Feminist Virtue", op. cit., p. 83. Walkowitz's entire discussion of the *Maiden Tribute of Modern Babylon* and its aftermath (pp. 83-5) is illuminating.

7 Walkowitz, "Male Vice and Feminist Virtue", op. cit., p. 85.

8 Beserra et al, op. cit., pp. 106-7.

9 Commonwealth of Massachusetts, *Preliminary Report of the Special Commission Investigating the Prevalence of Sex Crimes*, 1947; State of New Hampshire. *Report of the Interim Commission of the State of*

New Hampshire to Study the Cause and Prevention of Serious Sex Crimes, 1949; City of New York, *Report of the Mayor's Committee for the Study of Sex Offences*, 1939; State of New York, *Report to the Governor on a Study of 102 Sex Offenders at Sing Sing Prison*, 1950; Samuel Hartwell, *A Citizen's Handbook of Sexual Abnormalities and the Mental Hygiene Approach to Their Prevention*, State of Michigan, 1950; State of Michigan, *Report of the Governor's Study Commission on the Deviated Criminal Sex Offender*, 1951. This is merely a sampler.

10 Estelle B. Freedman, " 'Uncontrolled Desire': The Threat of the Sexual Psychopath in America, 1935-1960", paper presented at the Annual Meeting of the American Historical Association, San Francisco, December 1983.

11 Allan Bérubé, "Behind the Spectre of San Francisco", *Body Politic*, April 1981; Allan Bérubé, "Marching to a Different Drummer", *Advocate*, October 15, 1981; John D'Emilio, *Sexual Politics, Sexual Communities: The Making of the Homosexual Minority in the United States, 1940-1970*, Chicago, University of Chicago Press, 1983; Jonathan Katz, *Gay American History*, New York, Thomas Y. Crowell, 1976.

12 D'Emilio, op. cit., pp. 46-7; Allan Bérubé, personal communication.

13 John Gerassi, *The Boys of Boise*, New York, Collier, 1968, p. 14. I am indebted to Allan Bérubé for calling my attention to this incident.

14 Allan Bérubé, personal communication; D'Emilio, op. cit.; John D'Emilio, "Gay Politics, Gay Community: San Francisco's Experience", *Socialist Review*, no. 55, January-February 1981.

15 The following examples suggest avenues for additional research. A local crackdown at the University of Michigan is documented in Daniel Tsang, "Gay Ann Arbor Purges", *Midwest Gay Academic Journal*, vol. 1, no. 1, 1977; and Daniel Tsang, "Ann Arbor Gay Purges", part 2, *Midwest Gay Academic Journal*, vol. 1, no. 2, 1977. At the University of Michigan, the number of faculty dismissed for alleged homosexuality appears to rival the number fired for alleged communist tendencies. It would be interesting to have figures comparing the number of professors who lost their positions during this period due to sexual and political offenses. On regulatory reform, many states passed laws during this period prohibiting the sale of alcoholic beverages to "known sex perverts" or providing that bars which catered to "sex perverts" be closed. Such a law was passed in California in 1955, and declared unconstitutional by the state Supreme Court in 1959 (Allan Bérubé, personal communication). It would be of great interest to know exactly which states passed such statutes, the dates of their enactment, the discussion that preceded them, and how many are still on the books. On the persecution of other erotic populations, evidence indicates that John Willie and Irving Klaw, the two premier producers and distributors of bondage erotica in the United States from the late 1940s through the early 1960s, encountered frequent police harassment and that Klaw, at least, was affected by a congressional investigation conducted by the Kefauver Committee. I am indebted to personal communication from J.B. Rund for

314   *Gayle Rubin*

information on the careers of Willie and Klaw. Published sources are scarce, but see John Willie, *The Adventures of Sweet Gwendoline*, New York, Belier Press, 1974; J.B. Rund, "Preface", *Bizarre Comix*, vol. 8, New York, Belier Press, 1977; J.B. Rund, "Preface", *Bizarre Fotos*, vol. 1, New York, Belier Press, 1978; and J.B. Rund, "Preface", *Bizarre Katalogs*, vol. 1, New York, Belier Press, 1979. It would be useful to have more systematic information on legal shifts and police activity affecting non-gay erotic dissidence.

16 "Chicago is Center of National Child Porno Ring: The Child Predators", "Child Sex: Square in New Town Tells it All", "U.S. Orders Hearings On Child Pornography: Rodino Calls Sex Racket an 'Outrage' ", "Hunt Six Men, Twenty Boys in Crackdown", *Chicago Tribune*, May 16, 1977; "Dentist Seized in Child Sex Raid: Carey to Open Probe", "How Ruses Lure Victims to Child Pornographers", *Chicago Tribune*, May 17, 1977; "Child Pornographers Thrive on Legal Confusion", "U.S. Raids Hit Porn Sellers", *Chicago Tribune*, May 18, 1977.

17 For more information on the "kiddie porn panic" see Pat Califia, "The Great Kiddy Porn Scare of '77 and Its Aftermath", *Advocate*, October 16, 1980; Pat Califia, "A Thorny Issue Splits a Movement", *Advocate*, October 30, 1980; Mitzel, *The Boston Sex Scandal*, Boston, Glad Day Books, 1980; Gayle Rubin, "Sexual Politics, the New Right, and the Sexual Fringe", in Daniel Tsang (ed.), *The Age Taboo*, Boston, Alyson Publications, 1981; on the issue of cross-generational relationships, see also Roger Moody, *Indecent Assault*, London, Word Is Out Press, 1980; Tom O'Carroll, *Paedophilia: The Radical Case*, London, Peter Owen, 1980; Tsang, *The Age Taboo*, op. cit., and Paul Wilson, *The Man They Called A Monster*, New South Wales, Cassell Australia, 1981.

18 "House Passes Tough Bill on Child Porn", *San Francisco Chronicle*, November 15, 1983, p. 14.

19 George Stambolian, "Creating the New Man: A Conversation with Jacqueline Livingston", *Christopher Street*, May 1980; "Jacqueline Livingston", *Clothed With the Sun*, vol. 3, no. 1, May 1983.

20 Paul H. Gebhard, "The Institute", in Martin S. Weinberg (ed.), *Sex Research: Studies from the Kinsey Institute*, New York, Oxford University Press, 1976.

21 Phoebe Courtney, *The Sex Education Racket: Pornography in the Schools (An Exposé)*, New Orleans, Free Men Speak, 1969; Dr Gordon V. Drake, *SIECUS: Corrupter of Youth*, Tulsa, Oklahoma, Christian Crusade Publications, 1969.

22 *Pavlov's Children (They May Be Yours)*, Impact Publishers, Los Angeles, California, 1969.

23 Norman Podhoretz, "The Culture of Appeasement", *Harper's*, October 1977.

24 Alan Wolfe and Jerry Sanders, "Resurgent Cold War Ideology: The Case of the Committee on the Present Danger", in Richard Fagen (ed.), *Capitalism and the State in U.S.-Latin American Relations*, Stanford, Stanford University Press, 1979.

25 Jimmy Breslin, "The Moral Majority in Your Motel Room", *San*

Francisco Chronicle, January 22, 1981, p. 41; Linda Gordon and Allen Hunter, "Sex, Family, and the New Right", *Radical America*, winter 1977-8; Sasha Gregory-Lewis, "The Neo-Right Political Apparatus", *Advocate*, February 8, 1977; Sasha Gregory-Lewis, "Right Wing Finds New Organizing Tactic", *Advocate*, June 23, 1977; Sasha Gregory-Lewis, "Unravelling the Anti-Gay Network", *Advocate*, September 7, 1977; Andrew Kopkind, "America's New Right", *New Times*, September 30, 1977; Rosalind Pollack Petchesky, "Anti-abortion, Anti-feminism, and the Rise of the New Right", *Feminist Studies*, vol. 7, no. 2, summer 1981.

26 Rhonda Brown, "Blueprint for a Moral America", *Nation*, May 23, 1981.

27 James Barr, *Quatrefoil*, New York, Greenberg, 1950, p. 310.

28 This insight was first articulated by Mary McIntosh, "The Homosexual Role", *Social Problems*, vol. 16, no. 2, fall 1968; the idea has been developed in Jeffrey Weeks, *Coming Out: Homosexual Politics in Britain from the Nineteenth Century to the Present*, New York, Quartet, 1977, and in Weeks, *Sex, Politics and Society*, op. cit.; see also D'Emilio, *Sexual Politics, Sexual Communities*, op. cit.; and Gayle Rubin, "Introduction" to Renée Vivien, *A Woman Appeared to Me*, Weatherby Lake, Mo., Naiad Press, 1979.

29 Bert Hansen, "The Historical Construction of Homosexuality", *Radical History Review*, no. 20, Spring/Summer 1979.

30 Walkowitz, *Prostitution and Victorian Society*, op. cit.; and Walkowitz, "Male Vice and Female Virtue", op. cit.

31 Michel Foucault, *The History of Sexuality*, New York, Pantheon, 1978.

32 A very useful discussion of these issues can be found in Robert Padgug, "Sexual Matters: On Conceptualizing Sexuality in History", *Radical History Review*, no. 20, spring/summer 1979.

33 Claude Lévi-Strauss, "A Confrontation", *New Left Review*, no. 62, July-August 1970. In this conversation, Lévi-Strauss calls his position "a Kantianism without a transcendental subject."

34 Foucault, op. cit., p. 11.

35 See the discussion in Weeks, *Sex, Politics and Society*, op. cit., p. 9.

36 See Weeks, *Sex, Politics and Society*, op. cit., p. 22.

37 See, for example, "Pope Praises Couples for Self-Control", *San Francisco Chronicle*, October 13, 1980, p. 5; "Pope Says Sexual Arousal Isn't a Sin If It's Ethical", *San Francisco Chronicle*, November 6, 1980, p. 33; "Pope Condemns 'Carnal Lust' As Abuse of Human Freedom", *San Francisco Chronicle*, January 15, 1981, p. 2; "Pope Again Hits Abortion, Birth Control", *San Francisco Chronicle*, January 16, 1981, p. 13; and "Sexuality, Not Sex in Heaven", *San Francisco Chronicle*, December 3, 1981, p. 50. See also footnote 62 below.

38 Susan Sontag, *Styles of Radical Will*, New York, Farrar, Strauss, & Giroux, 1969, p.46.

39 See Foucault, op. cit., pp. 106-7.

40 American Psychiatric Association, *Diagnostic and Statistical Manual of Mental and Physical Disorders*, 3rd edn, Washington, DC, American Psychiatric Association.

41 Alfred Kinsey, Wardell Pomeroy, and Clyde Martin, *Sexual Behavior in the Human Male*, Philadelphia, W.B. Saunders, 1948; Alfred

Kinsey, Wardell Pomeroy, Clyde Martin, and Paul Gebhard, *Sexual Behavior in the Human Female*, Philadelphia, W.B. Saunders, 1953.

42 John Gagnon and William Simon, *Sexual Deviance*, New York, Harper & Row, 1967; John Gagnon and William Simon, *The Sexual Scene*, Chicago, Transaction Books, Aldine, 1970; John Gagnon, *Human Sexualities*, Glenview, Illinois, Scott, Foresman, 1977.

43 Havelock Ellis, *Studies in the Psychology of Sex* (two volumes), New York, Random House, 1936.

44 Foucault, op. cit., p. 43.

45 Gilbert Herdt, *Guardians of the Flutes*, New York, McGraw-Hill, 1981; Raymond Kelly, "Witchcraft and Sexual Relations", in Paula Brown and Georgeda Buchbinder (eds), *Man and Woman in the New Guinea Highlands*, Washington, DC, American Anthropological Association, 1976; Gayle Rubin, "Coconuts: Aspects of Male/Female Relationships in New Guinea", unpublished ms., 1974; Gayle Rubin, review of *Guardians of the Flutes*, *Advocate*, December 23, 1982; J. Van Baal, *Dema*, The Hague, Nijhoff, 1966; F.E. Williams, *Papuans of the Trans-Fly*, Oxford, Clarendon, 1936.

46 Caroline Bingham, "Seventeenth-Century Attitudes Toward Deviant Sex", *Journal of Interdisciplinary History*, spring 1971, p. 465.

47 Stephen O. Murray, "The Institutional Elaboration of a Quasi-Ethnic Community", *International Review of Modern Sociology*, July-December 1979.

48 For further elaboration of these processes, see: Bérubé, "Behind the Spectre of San Francisco", op. cit.; Bérubé, "Marching to a Different Drummer", op. cit.; D'Emilio, "Gay Politics, Gay Community", op. cit.; D'Emilio, *Sexual Politics, Sexual Communities*, op. cit.; Foucault, op. cit.; Hansen, op. cit.; Katz, op.cit.; Weeks, *Coming Out*, op. cit.; and Weeks, *Sex, Politics and Society*, op. cit.

49 Walkowitz, *Prostitution and Victorian Society*, op. cit.

50 Vice cops also harass all sex businesses, be these gay bars, gay baths, adult book stores, the producers and distributors of commercial erotica, or swing clubs.

51 Foucault, op. cit., p. 40.

52 Karl Marx, in David McLellan (ed.), *The Grundrisse*, New York, Harper & Row, 1971, p. 94.

53 Clark Norton, "Sex in America", *Inquiry*, October 5, 1981. This article is a superb summary of much current sex law and should be required reading for anyone interested in sex.

54 Bessera et al., *op. cit.*, pp. 165-7.

55 Sarah Senefeld Beserra, Nancy M. Jewel, Melody West Matthews, and Elizabeth R. Gatov (eds.), *Sex Code of California*, Public Education and Research Committee of California, 1973, pp. 163-8. This earlier edition of the *Sex Code of California* preceeded the 1976 consenting adults statute and consequently gives a better overview of sodomy laws.

56 Esther Newton, *Mother Camp: Female Impersonators in America*, Englewood Cliffs, New Jersey, Prentice-Hall, 1972, p. 21, emphasis in the original.

57 D'Emilio, *Sexual Politics, Sexual Communities*, op. cit., pp. 40-53, has

an excellent discussion of gay oppression in the 1950s which covers many of the areas I have mentioned. The dynamics he describes, however, are operative in modified forms for other erotic populations, and in other periods. The specific model of gay oppression needs to be generalized to apply, with appropriate modifications, to other sexual groups.

58 Weeks, *Sex, Politics and Society*, op. cit., p. 14.

59 Lysander Spooner, *Vices Are Not Crimes: A Vindication of Moral Liberty*, Cupertino, CA, Tanstaafl Press, 1977.

60 I have adopted this terminology from the very useful discussion in Weeks, *Sex, Politics and Society*, op. cit., pp. 14-15.

61 See Spooner, op. cit., pp. 25-9. Feminist anti-porn discourse fits right into the tradition of justifying attempts at moral control by claiming that such action will protect women and children from violence.

62 "Pope's Talk on Sexual Spontaneity", *San Francisco Chronicle*. November 13, 1980, p. 8; see also footnote 37 above. Julia Penelope argues that "we do not need anything that labels itself purely sexual" and that "fantasy, as an aspect of sexuality, may be a phallocentric 'need' from which we are not yet free." in "And Now For the Really Hard Questions", *Sinister Wisdom*, no. 15, fall 1980, p. 103.

63 See especially Walkowitz, *Prostitution and Victorian Society*, op. cit., and Weeks, *Sex, Politics and Society*, op. cit.

64 *Moral Majority Report*, July 1983. I am indebted to Allan Bérubé for calling my attention to this image.

65 Cited in Larry Bush, "Capitol Report", *Advocate*, December 8, 1983, p. 60.

66 Cited in H. Montgomery Hyde, *A History of Pornography*, New York, Dell, 1965, p. 31.

67 See for example Laura Lederer (ed.), *Take Back the Night*, New York, William Morrow, 1980; Andrea Dworkin, *Pornography*, New York, Perigee, 1981. The *Newspage* of San Francisco's Women Against Violence in Pornography and Media and the *Newsreport* of New York Women Against Pornography are excellent sources.

68 Kathleen Barry, *Female Sexual Slavery*, Englewood Cliffs, New Jersey, Prentice-Hall, 1979; Janice Raymond, *The Transsexual Empire*, Boston, Beacon, 1979; Kathleen Barry, "Sadomasochism: The New Backlash to Feminism", *Trivia*, no. 1, fall 1982; Robin Ruth Linden, Darlene R. Pagano, Diana E. H. Russell, and Susan Leigh Starr (eds), *Against Sadomasochism*, East Palo Alto, CA, Frog in the Well, 1982; and Florence Rush, *The Best Kept Secret*, New York, McGraw-Hill, 1980.

69 Sally Gearhart, "An Open Letter to the Voters in District 5 and San Francisco's Gay Community", 1979; Adrienne Rich, *On Lies, Secrets, and Silence*, New York, W.W. Norton, 1979, p. 225. ("On the other hand, there is homosexual patriarchal culture, a culture created by homosexual men, reflecting such male stereotypes as dominance and submission as modes of relationship, and the separation of sex from emtional involvement – a culture tainted by profound hatred for women. The male 'gay' culture has offered lesbians the imitation role-stereotypes of 'butch' and 'femme', 'active' and 'passive,' cruising, sado-masochism, and the violent, self-destructive world of 'gay'

bars."); Judith Pasternak, "The Strangest Bedfellows: Lesbian Feminism and the Sexual Revolution", *WomanNews*, October 1983; Adrienne Rich, "Compulsory Heterosexuality and Lesbian Existence", in Ann Snitow, Christine Stansell, and Sharon Thompson (eds), *Powers of Desire: The Politics of Sexuality*, New York, Monthly Review Press, 1983.

70 Julia Penlope, op. cit.

71 Sheila Jeffreys, "The Spinster and Her Enemies: Sexuality and the Last Wave of Feminism", *Scarlet Woman*, no. 13, part 2, July 1981, p. 26; a further elaboration of this tendency can be found in Judith Pasternak, op. cit.

72 Pat Califia, "Feminism vs. Sex: A New Conservative Wave", *Advocate*, February 21, 1980; Pat Califia, "Among Us, Against Us – The New Puritans", *Advocate*, April 17, 1980; Califia, "The Great Kiddy Porn Scare of '77 and Its Aftermath", op. cit.; Califia, "A Thorny Issue Splits a Movement", op. cit.; Pat Califia, *Sapphistry*, Tallahassee, Florida, Naiad, 1980; Pat Califia, "What Is Gay Liberation", *Advocate*, June 25, 1981; Pat Califia, "Feminism and Sadomasochism", *Co-Evolution Quarterly*, no. 33, spring 1981; Pat Califia, "Response to Dorchen Leidholdt", *New Women's Times*, October 1982; Pat Califia, "Public Sex", *Advocate*, September 30, 1982; Pat Califia, "Doing It Together: Gay Men, Lesbians, and Sex", *Advocate*, July 7, 1983; Pat Califia, "Gender-Bending", *Advocate*, September 15, 1983; Pat Califia, "The Sex Industry", *Advocate*, October 13, 1983; Deirdre English, Amber Hollibaugh, and Gayle Rubin, "Talking Sex", *Socialist Review*, July-August 1981; "Sex Issue", *Heresies*, no. 12, 1981; Amber Hollibaugh, "The Erotophobic Voice of Women: Building a Movement for the Nineteenth Century", *New York Native*, September 26-October 9, 1983; Maxine Holz, "Porn: Turn On or Put Down, Some Thoughts on Sexuality", *Processed World*, no. 7, spring 1983; Barbara O'Dair, "Sex, Love, and Desire: Feminists Struggle Over the Portrayal of Sex", *Alternative Media*, spring 1983; Lisa Orlando, "Bad Girls and 'Good' Politics", *Village Voice*, Literary Supplement, December 1982; Joanna Russ, "Being Against Pornography", *Thirteenth Moon*, vol. VI, nos 1 and 2, 1982; Samois, *What Color Is Your Handkerchief*, Berkeley, Samois, 1979; Samois, *Coming to Power*, Boston, Alyson, 1982; Deborah Sundahl, "Stripping For a Living", *Advocate*, October 13, 1983; Nancy Wechsler, "Interview with Pat Califia and Gayle Rubin", part I, *Gay Community News*, Book Review, July 18, 1981, and part II, *Gay Community News*, August 15, 1981; Ellen Willis, *Beginning to See the Light*, New York, Knopf, 1981; for an excellent overview of the history of the ideological shifts in feminism which have affected the sex debates, see Alice Echols, "Cultural Feminism: Feminist Capitalism and the Anti-Pornography Movement", *Social Text*, no. 7, spring and summer 1983.

73 Lisa Orlando, "Lust at Last! Spandex Invades the Academy", *Gay Community News*, May 15, 1982; Ellen Willis, "Who Is a Feminist? An Open Letter to Robin Morgan", *Village Voice*, Literary Supplement, December 1982.

74 Ellen Willis, *Beginning to See the Light*, op. cit., p. 146. I am indebted

to Jeanne Bergman for calling my attention to this quote.

75 See, for example, Jessica Benjamin, "Master and Slave: The Fantasy of Erotic Domination", in Snitow et al., op. cit., p. 297; and B. Ruby Rich, review of *Powers of Desire, In These Times*, November 16-22, 1983.

76 B. Ruby Rich, op. cit., p. 76.

77 Samois, *What Color Is Your Handkerchief*, op. cit.; Samois, *Coming To Power*, op. cit.; Pat Califia, "Feminism and Sadomasochism", op. cit.; Pat Califia, *Sapphistry*, op. cit.

78 Lisa Orlando, "Power Plays: Coming To Terms With Lesbian S/M", *Village Voice*, July 26, 1983; Elizabeth Wilson, "*The Context of 'Between Pleasure and Danger': The Barnard Conference on Sexuality*", *Feminist Review*, no. 13, spring 1983, especially pp. 35-41.

79 *Taylor* v. *State*, 214 Md. 156, 165, 133 A. 2d 414, 418. This quote is from a dissenting opinion, but it is a statement of prevailing law.

80 Bessera, Jewel, Matthew·, and Gatov, op. cit., pp. 163-5. See note 55 above.

81 "Marine and Mom Guilty of Incest", *San Francisco Chronicle*, November 16, 1979, p. 16.

82 Norton, op. cit., p. 18.

83 *People* v. *Samuels*, 250 Cal. App. 2d 501, 513, 58 Cal. Rptr. 439, 447 (1967).

84 *People* v. *Samuels*, 250 Cal. App. 2d. at 513-514, 58 Cal. Rptr. at 447.

85 Mariana Valverde, "Feminism Meets Fist-Fucking: Getting Lost in Lesbian S & M", *Body Politic*, February 1980; Wilson, op. cit., p. 38.

86 Benjamin, op. cit. p. 292, but see also pp. 286, 291-7.

87 Barbara Ehrenreich, "What Is This Thing Called Sex", *Nation*, September 24, 1983, p. 247.

88 Gayle Rubin, "The Traffic in Women", in Rayna R. Reiter (ed.), *Toward an Anthropology of Women*, New York, Monthly Review Press, 1975, p. 159.

89 Rubin, "The Traffic in Women", op. cit., p. 166.

90 Foucault, op. cit., p. 106.

91 Catherine MacKinnon, "Feminism, Marxism, Method and the State: An Agenda for Theory", *Signs*, vol. 7, no. 3, spring 1982, pp. 515-16.

92 Catherine MacKinnon, "Feminism, Marxism, Method, and the State: Toward Feminist Jurisprudence", *Signs*, vol. 8, no. 4, summer 1983, p. 635.

93 Colette, *The Ripening Seed*, translated and cited in Hannah Alderfer, Beth Jaker, and Marybeth Nelson, *Diary of a Conference on Sexuality*, New York, Faculty Press, 1982, p. 72.

94 John Lauritsen and David Thorstad, *The Early Homosexual Rights Movement in Germany*, New York, Times Change Press, 1974.

95 D'Emilio, *Sexual Politics, Sexual Communities*, op. cit.; Bérubé "Behind the Spectre of San Francisco", op. cit.; Bérubé, "Marching to a Different Drummer", op. cit.

Histoire d'O
The Construction of a
Female Subject

Kaja Silverman

O, still lying motionless on her back, her loins still aflame, was listening and she had the feeling that by some strange substitution Sir Stephen was speaking for her, in her place. As though he was somehow in her body and could feel the anxiety, the anguish, and the shame, but also the secret pride and harrowing pleasure that she was feeling, especially when she was alone in the street, or when she got into a bus, or when she was at the studio with the models and technicians, and she told herself that any and all of these people she was with, if they should have an accident and have to be laid on the ground or if a doctor had to be called, would keep their secret, even if they were unconscious and naked; but not she: her secret did not depend upon her silence alone, did not depend on her alone.[1]

The heroine of *Histoire d'O*, like some of Freud's more rebellious heroines, knows herself to be constituted in and through a discourse which exceeds her – one which speaks for her, in her "place." That discourse organizes her body in such a way that even prone and silent it is immediately readable by any of the male members of Roissy, the brothel to which O is taken. It equips her with a "secret" which permits her to be fully known and controlled.

Psychoanalysis would tell us that O's condition is synonymous with subjectivity – that since desire is always articulated from the place of the Other, woman (like man) is inevitably spoken through a discourse which anticipates and transcends her.[2] However, as Freud himself acknowledges, the male subject has consistently provided the focus and model for descriptions of subjectivity.[3] The masculine pronoun, with its dual reference to the entire human species and its dominant gender, has facilitated an elision of the problems specific to woman within patriarchal culture. Not even recent psychoanalytic theory has taken account of the quite different constitution of the female subject – of her radical alienation from the discourses which first construct her body, and then supply her with an interiority (variously known as soul, feelings, consciousness, the unconscious) entirely congruent with that bodily construction.

The question of what is specific to female experience has been the starting point for much recent debate. Feminist theoreticians have devoted a good deal of their energy over the past ten years to an investigation of the precise status of "the feminine," attempting to arrive at a satisfactory definition not only of the female subject, but of what precedes subjectivity for woman. The investigation thus proceeds on two fronts, exploring on the one hand what distinguishes female from male subjectivity within the present symbolic order, and on the other what is lost for woman during her entry into that order.

Luce Irigaray, Julia Kristeva and Michèle Montrelay, French psychoanalysts who have all at one time or another labored under the shadow of Lacan, agree that femininity to a large extent not only escapes symbolic structuration, but is capable of subverting it. All three associate woman with ungrammatical or a-logical speech, emphasize for her the importance of the maternal connection, and argue that her relation to her body escapes symbolic mediation. They see the body as a pre-cultural given which plays a determinative role in female existence – as enjoying a privileged relation to her own being, and consequently to jouissance[4] (a pleasure which radically exceeds cultural laws and limits).

Montrelay offers the most elaborate version of this theory, and one whose unusual clarity and coherence demand respect if not acquiescence. Her argument depends heavily upon the maintenance of two sets of oppositions, those between "femininity" and "woman," and "repression" and "censorship." "Femininity" designates a complex of drives which remain outside cultural organization, whereas "woman" refers to the female subject who, like the male subject, is an effect of repression.

Montrelay identifies repression with the operation whereby the phallus is erected within the unconscious as a representation of castration. Since that representation corresponds by analogy with the penis, it is able to stand in for it and, in the process, to organize male sexuality.[5] Censorship, on the contrary, excludes without representing. Since for Montrelay femininity is censored, not repressed, it remains a "dark continent," a real which threatens to submerge not only the female subject but the entire symbolic order.[6]

L'Ombre et le nom cites three reasons why femininity escapes repression. First, because the female genitalia are less visible than the male, the little girl is able to maintain a more private and hence less supervised relation to her body. Second, her precocious sexuality is "concentric," turned in upon itself:

it reflects all psychic movement according to circular and closed schemes, it compromises woman's relation to castration and to law: to absorb, to take, to understand, is to reduce the world to the most archaic instinctual 'laws'. It is a movement opposed to that presupposed by castration: where the *jouissance* of the body loses itself 'for' a discourse which is Other.[7]

Finally, there is a continuity between the little girl's first object choice and the mirror stage which does not obtain for the little boy; she progresses, that is, from love of the mother to love of an image which at least in a certain sense duplicates the mother. The female subject is for this reason less radically alienated from her primordial drives than the male subject, and much likelier to remain confined within the realm of mirror relationships.

This is not to say that within Montrelay's account the female subject does not possess an unconscious; her unconscious, like that of the male subject, is "normally" structured in relation to the paternal signifier, the Name-of-the-Father.[8] However, the paternal signifier does not *represent* her sexuality except in so far as it induces in her an identification with the male position; that signifier determines her cultural existence, but leaves her sexuality intact.

For Montrelay, the representation of sexuality which is currently held out for women – that of a lack or hole – is absolutely alien to femininity. We recall that within Lacanian psychoanalysis the notions of castration and the phallus occupy a problematic double space; castration signifies simultaneously the loss of being which is the "price" of entry into the symbolic order – what Lacan calls the "pound of flesh," and which he equates with the penis – and the female subject's cultural deprivation – her symbolic impotence. Similarly, the phallus signifies both the fullness of being which must be renounced in order to come into the symbolic legacy, and the symbolic legacy itself.[9]

The oft-repeated Lacanian assertion that woman *is* the phallus whereas man *has* the phallus dramatizes the profound ambiguities of that last term. In so far as woman's body is understood as escaping symbolic structuration, she can be described as being the phallus but not having it (i.e. as existing within the real, but being cut off from cultural privilege). And in so far as the male subject is understood as entering into the paternal position through the loss of his being, he can be said no longer to be but to have the phallus (i.e. to have lost the real, but to have gained the symbolic legacy).

By concentrating so exclusively on the first clause in this scenario – that is, on the female subject's continued residence within the real – Montrelay is able to argue that woman lacks nothing, and that her sexuality remains untouched by the endlessly repeated depiction of the feminine as a hole or an abyss. Indeed, Montrelay proposes that the female subject herself promotes such representations in an attempt to escape the repression to which the male subject necessarily succumbs. She mimes or apes the zero with which culture signifies her in order to protect her privileged relation with her body:

a lack is simulated and thereby the loss of some stake – an undertaking all the more easily accomplished precisely because feminine anatomy exhibits a lack – that of the penis. At the same time as being her own phallus, therefore, the woman will disguise herself with this lack, throwing into relief the dimension of castration as *trompe-l'oeil.*

The ways in which this can occur are multiple. One can play on the absence of the penis through silence just as well as through a resounding vanity. One can make it the model of erotic, mystical, neurotic experiences.[10]

Montrelay cites *Histoire d'O* as exemplary of this masquerade. Thus for her, O as prototypical female subject continues to enjoy an unmediated relation with the real behind the drama of castration played out at the cultural level.

However, as other feminist theoreticians have been quick to observe, no one – either female or male – enters the symbolic order and attains the status of subject without experiencing a simultaneous alienation from the phenomenological and biological real. This point has been made by Monique Plaza and Jacqueline Rose among others,[11] but it finds its most extreme expression in the writings of the *m/f* collective.

Not only do the members of this collective – Parveen Adams, Beverly Brown and Elizabeth Cowie – reject unequivocally the notion of any timeless female essence, but they deny that there is any reality prior to or outside of discourse. Consequently, they understand terms like "female" and "body" as highly relativistic, as carrying meaning only within the confines of particular discourses. They also stress the contradictions which separate one discourse from another. For the *m/f* collective, discourses do not overlap to produce a more or less stable social field, with more or less stable subject-positions, but operate autonomously, often without any common basis. The terms "woman" and "female body" are thus reduced to the status of free floating signifiers, signifiers which lack any constant meaning. The *m/f* argument is presented most unambiguously in "The Feminine Body and Feminist Politics":

To use the term 'construction' or 'constructed body' supposes a recognition of the diversity and irreducibility of the ways in which terms such as 'woman' or 'the body' might figure in different discourses and practices .... to state that the body is constructed across a range of discursive practices is to argue that it is impossible to sum discourse in order to produce a knowledge of the body whose precise degree of truth can be assessed....

Many analyses take knowledge of the body to be automatically knowledge of one's own person, and, where this is a sexed body, to be knowledge of oneself as a man or a woman. In arguing that the body is constructed, and constructed in a variety of ways, one is making . . . identification impossible. If the body exists in a number of ways for medical and legal practice . . . then, clearly, there can be no *one* sexed body to bear the burden of individuality. If, further, the *sexed* body exists differently for those practices, then the problem of identification is made even more problematic. The consequence is that neither the individual, nor the sum of individuals, can find a primary location within their bodily definition. Instead, one finds a variety of agents, with varying rights and forms of recognition, and this cannot simply be reduced to a totality of individuals, even a totality of women.[12]

Thus, whereas for Montrelay the female body altogether evades discourse, for the *m/f* collective it is never anything more than a semiotic counter whose valence shifts from discourse to discourse. That body neither pre-dates nor assumes any consistent identity or shape as a consequence of discourse.[13]

In this essay I would like to return to the issue of specificity, to address once again the question of what defines the female body and how that body prefigures a certain subjectivity for women within the present cultural order. It will be my working hypothesis (a hypothesis which will be "tested" through *Histoire d'O*) that while human bodies exist prior to discourse, it is only through discourse that they arrive at the condition of being "male" or "female" – that discourse functions first to territorialize and then to map meaning onto bodies. In other words, I will argue that the female body cannot be seen as existing outside discourse, as Montrelay suggests, since it is precisely with that body that subjectivity begins.

The following remarks will also occupy a theoretical space to one side of the *m/f* position, disputing the notion that the female body can be seen as a signifier which "floats" from discourse to discourse, undergoing in the process radical transformations of meaning which somehow liberate individual women from obligatory residence within an oppressed subject-position. I will attempt to demonstrate that very close links are forged between actual bodies and discourses, and that those links are both durable and mutually reinforcing at all key junctures.

The most helpful concept currently available to us for articulating the relationship between real and constructed bodies is *anaclisis*. "*Anaclisis*" is the name given by Freud to the leaning or propping of the erotic drive upon the self-preservative instincts, a support system whereby the mother, source of nourishment and warmth to the infant child, becomes for that very reason its first object choice.[14] The notion of *anaclisis* is also central to Lacan's theory of the subject, within which desire, a cultural construct, derives sustenance from the drives, last vestige of the real.[15] In an analogous way discursive bodies lean upon real ones – lean both in the sense of finding their physical support in, and of exerting their own pressure upon real bodies. Thus real bodies are tied to, and in the process shaped by, discursive formations. All these varieties of *anaclisis* must be understood as preceding, and indeed making possible, the partitioning off of the unconscious from the pre-conscious, and the subject's psychic alignment with the symbolic order.

What I am suggesting is that the structuration of the female subject begins not with her entry into language, or her subordination to a field of cultural desire, but with the organization of her body. That body is charted, zoned and made to bear meaning, a meaning which proceeds entirely from external relationships, but which is always subsequently apprehended both by the female subject and her "commentators" as an internal condition or essence. It proceeds, that is, from the establishment of a series of equivalences or matches between a material surface, which is isolated from other material surfaces and designated "woman" on the basis of a certain genital configuration, and a wide variety of other objects, ranging from clothing to the penis. Although that genital configuration has neither coherence nor significance outside discourse, the connection between it and "woman" is trans-discursive, i.e. it is maintained by all the discourses which presently constitute the dominant symbolic order in the West. Until there is a genuine rupture in the symbolic order, that connection will remain sufficiently stable, so that even if a new discourse comes into existence, it will provide the terms under which the female subject is defined.

That order can best be challenged not by assigning woman a place outside of it (a place which anyway can never be anything other than a utopia, in the strictest sense of that word), but by altering her relation to discourse. The specificity of the female body and of woman's psychic economy can only be maintained as long as discursive practices are determined by the gender differences which they themselves project.

Within the existing social arena the female subject does not participate in the production of the meaning which organizes her outside and gives her an inside, since she is excluded from what Foucault calls "discursive fellowships."[16] While it is no doubt true that all subjects, male and female, are structured through discourse, and are in that respect passive,[17] men enjoy another kind of discursive association as well, which is not available to women – an "active" or "speaking" association.

Foucault enumerates three sets of rules which he sees as relevant to the operations of discourse: rules of exclusion; rules of classification, ordering and distribution; and rules governing use. The first two sets determine a discursive field (what elements are included, which excluded; what things are privileged, which negatively defined). The last set determines who may use a discourse and under what conditions; helps to disseminate it; and assures its social appropriation (i.e. makes certain that its power is confined to those areas of the social field where power has already been consolidated).[18]

Discourse always requires a speaking position (a position from which power-knowledge is exercised) and a spoken subject (a position brought into existence through the exercise of power-knowledge). For instance, "analyst" indicates a speaking subject, whereas "patient" designates a spoken subject. The analyst can occupy the position of a spoken subject in relationship to himself (indeed, Freud encourages analysts to put aside some time each day for self-analysis). However, the patient can never occupy the position of speaking subject *vis-à-vis* the analyst, and is in fact frequently told that what he or she thinks is of no consequence, that all critical or censoring faculties should be suspended, and that the analyst will decide what is significant.[19]

Each analyst belongs to a psychoanalytic association or fellowship, and he engages in the discourse of which he is a "fellow" only under certain conditions (e.g. the analytic situation). That fellowship and those conditions make certain that the power-knowledge of psychoanalysis is enjoyed only by "experts" or figures of paternal authority. This consolidation of power-knowledge assures the social appropriation of the discourse, and its exercise in the service of an already-existing symbolic order.

By virtue of his gender, the male subject is an automatic candidate for admission to any discursive fellowship for which he has the additional qualifications. This privilege is a limited one, since the rituals involved in using a discourse make certain that it is employed in "orthodox" ways. Nevertheless, the male subject is thus capable of knowing and even of defining himself according to a particular discourse, which means that he is permitted to occupy the positions both of speaking and spoken subject.

The female subject, on the contrary, is, on the basis of her gender, automatically excluded from all current discursive fellowships except those like feminism, which have grown up in opposition to the dominant symbolic order. She is consequently deprived of the power and knowledge which those fellowships imply, and is incapable of occupying anything but the position of a spoken subject – that is, of having anything but a passive relationship to discourse as long as she "plays by the rules."[20] She is known but not knowing; seen but not seeing; represented and signified, but unable to participate in those twin operations. (There is of course always the exception to this general rule: the "unusual" woman who gains admittance to a discursive fellow-ship. However, she is admitted precisely because she is "unusual," thereby confirming through her deviation from the female "norm" the larger rule of exclusion.)

Histoire d'O and the apologetic essays which have accom-panied that novel since its first publication[21] bring these issues into sharp relief. They attest, that is, to the fact that female subjectivity begins with the body, a body which is quite literally written. These texts also make explicit at more than one juncture the exclusion of the female subject from the discourses which produce her.

These assorted pieces of writing belong of course to the discourse of pornography – a discourse that dramatizes with unusual clarity the disjunction between the speaking (male) subject and the spoken (female) subject. The fellowship whose members have the right to use this discourse is represented within the novel by Roissy, but it has extra-diegetic members as well – most notably Jean Paulhan and André Pieyre de Mandiargues, writers of the two apologetic essays. The only "unusual" woman is Anne-Marie. She is not a club member, but she enjoys certain discursive rights. All the other women, including the imaginary author,[22] are refused membership in the club of Roissy, although its male members have unlimited access to them.

The members of the Roissy fellowship exercise their discursive power through the relentless alignment of the female body with other surfaces. In the scene from which the introductory quot-ation is taken, O lies among the photographs of another woman, while René and Sir Stephen discuss both of them. The heat of the sun has partially dissolved the photographs, so that O has become "stuck" to them. Her body repeatedly becomes attached to other objects – clothes, chains, rings, dildos, the male sex organ – although usually through a much more painstaking and premeditated articulation. On each occasion some sort of transmission is effected – O's body has meaning imprinted upon it by the object with which it is connected, and is in the process re-constituted. Over the course of the two novels the network of relationships which creates and sustains O's body becomes increasingly complex and extended.

The same obsessive delineation of equivalences characterizes the translator's note in the English edition of Histoire d'O, as well as the critical essays which "introduce" that edition. The translator, a certain Sabine d'Estrée, speaks of herself as a perfect "match" for the author – as someone capable of subordinating herself to an almost mechanical functionalism. What permits the smooth alignment of translator and author is their shared sexual identity (or rather what is posited as their shared sexual identity):

Story of O, written by a woman, demands a woman translator, one who will humble herself before the work and be satisfied simply to render it, as faithfully as possible, without unwanted interruption or unwanted elaboration. Faced with a work such as *O*, male pride, male superiority . . . will, I am certain, intrude. Like O, therefore, I have tried to humble myself, to remain as faithful as possible . . . to the intent and style of the author. (p. xii)

As this passage makes clear, within the discourse of pornography one term is always subordinated to the other. Significantly, this is the only occasion on which Réage emerges as the dominant partner; in the situations described by Paulhan and Mandiargues "she" is always cast as a slave.

Those two commentators bring into existence a quite elaborate network, one which implicates not only Réage, but her reader. Mandiargues identifies Réage with her heroine in what is unquestionably the most compact of all the interpenetrations effected by the novels and their critical apparatus, an identification which is made to seem spontaneous and voluntary:

Proud Réage . . . has a way of involving herself, of slipping, at the worst possible moments, into the skin of her heroine, which is enough to make one feel a certain tenderness for her. The way one would feel toward a brave bull who has fought well. (p. xviii)

And having attached the Roissy ring to the ring-finger of Réage's left hand, he uses that "marriage" as the basis from which to project a series of literary affiliations:

Shall we one day see on the finger of some woman the formidable ring which strips the person wearing it of her freedom, since she places her body at the disposal of those who are able to read the insignia engraved in the setting? And, what is especially important, shall we be able to tell which one is Pauline Réage? Probably not. But already Baudelaire is offering his hand to her, the Portuguese Nun is approaching a bit timidly, the Nun of Dulman is ready to open her arms to her, and she is about to enter the small circle of blessed and accursed creatures which constitutes the only aristocracy which one considers today with any degree of respect. (p. x)

The pronoun "we" seems to locate both Baudelaire and the writer in "that small circle of blessed and accursed creatures." However, several other details indicate that they belong instead to the fellowship of Roissy, the members of whom are always sharply differentiated from the female inmates. First, the passage contains many of the trademarks of one who belongs to a discursive fellowship, and is entrusted with the safeguarding of its power-knowledge: the will to truth (a truth which finds its guarantee in the iron ring),[23] the need to effect closure ("that small circle"), and the careful distinction which is drawn between the speaking and knowing subject (the one who "considers") and the spoken and known subject (the one who is considered).

Second, whereas the women enumerated by Mandiargues are visualized as approaching and embracing Réage, Baudelaire is content with extending his hand to her – a "masterly" gesture associated with both René and Sir Stephen (pp. 66-7). By means of these details Mandiargues meticulously maintains the separation between the subject who belongs to a discursive fellowship, and the one whose only privilege is to be constituted through its discourse.

Paulhan much more openly disassociates himself from this false aristocracy. In fact, he claims to have nothing to do with their "blessed and accursed" plight. He begins his prefatory essay with an account of a revolt by two hundred blacks against a master who liberated them – a revolt, in short, against freedom and for enslavement. Paulhan uses this story to "prove" that subjugation is entirely a matter between an individual (black or female) and his or her psychic/biological needs; that enslavement is always self-enslavement, a "truth" he finds particularly compelling in O's case:

in the *Story of O*, there is no lack of tortures. However, René refuses to inflict any, and although Sir Stephen consents to them, it is as if he is performing a duty. As far as we can tell, they do not enjoy themselves. There is nothing sadistic about them. It all happens as though it were O alone, who, from the very outset, demanded to be chastised, forced in her retreats. (p. xxix)

Paulhan thus denies that O's subjectivity is constituted for her by the discourse of pornography, as well as his own participation in the operations of that discourse.

Paulhan extends his discursive network even further than Mandiargues, creating not only Pauline Réage but the entire female gender in the image of O. He cites various details from the first novel which "a man would never have thought of, or at least would never have dared to express," and which he consequently finds irrefutable evidence of female authorship. He also produces a "strange lover letter" from the supposed author in which "she" asks to be treated in an identical manner to O. However, Paulhan is not content to stop with this equation; he makes O's story a kind of true confession of the masochistic bases of female desire, universalizing that desire by connecting it with woman's "blood" or nature. In other words, he posits an essence of woman which conforms in every respect to the spoken subject of pornography:

At last a woman who admits it! Who admits what? Something that women have always refused till now to admit (and today more than ever before). Something that men have always reproached them with: that they never cease obeying their nature, the call of their blood, that everything in them, even their minds, is sex. That they have constantly to be nourished, constantly washed and made up, constantly beaten. That all they need is a good master, one who is not too lax or kind. . . . In short, that we must, when we go to see them, take a whip along. (p. xxv)

However, despite all his attempts to locate the masochistic imperative in a pre-discursive essence of woman, and despite his refusal to admit his own complicity in the power-relations that create masochism, Paulhan no sooner concludes that the entire female gender wants to be beaten than he discloses the source of that desire. ("Rare is the man who has not dreamed of possessing Justine.")

Paulhan and Mandiargues are not just members of the discursive fellowship of pornography; they are its commentators. Their function as commentators, to which they painstakingly conform, is to repeat *ad infinitum* the same discourse, to "say finally what has been articulated deep down" in some earlier, more "original" and "sacred" text – a text which is of course here supplied by *Histoire d'O*.[24] One of the chief ways in which they both repeat and circumscribe the contents of that text is by insisting that it is the confession of a woman author. Paulhan and Mandiargues present the terms "male" and "female" as a timeless and universal set of power-relations which under the will to truth will always necessarily duplicate themselves, and which are ideally concentrated in the figures of Sir Stephen and O.

The woman who steps into a cab at the beginning of *Histoire d'O* seems to have so limited a range of discursive relations that she can be described in two sentences, sentences that merely itemize her clothing:

She is dressed as she always is: high heels, a suit with a pleated skirt, a silk blouse and no hat. But long gloves come up over the sleeves of her jacket, and in her leather handbag she has her identification papers, her compact, and her lipstick. (p. 3)

She is reduced to the status of a completely undifferentiated instrumentality by severing her connection with these garments and accessories, a severence which is partially effected by René when he obliges her to remove her undergarments and cuts her bra straps, but which is finalized inside Roissy, where the remaining items are eliminated. René tells her immediately before she enters that house: "You're merely the girl I'm furnishing."

However, over the course of *Histoire d'O* signification invades ever more microscopic and highly organized portions of her body. That invasion occurs through the obsessive matching up of O's anatomy with clothing, apparatuses of torture, designated rooms or parts of rooms, penises, and more abstract and metaphysical constructions like "guilt" and a "soul." O is produced through an exercise of power which excludes her from certain architectural spaces, but associates her with others; which denies her access to language, but insists that she scream and moan; which obliges her to eliminate particular items of clothing from her wardrobe, but requires her to add others; and which prevents her from looking at male faces, but compels her to gaze at their sexual organs.

Before turning to an examination of the discursive relations which constitute O, I would like to clarify those elements which are admitted into the discursive field of the novel as designating "woman" – the limits of her "reality," or to state it differently, the female "potentiality" which can be realized through "development." O is above all an exterior with various recesses or depressions, what Deleuze and Guattari would call "a body with organs" (mouth, vagina, anus).[25] These organs or orifices are not so much portals into the world as entry-points through which multiple penetrations occur. They have no linguistic or generative function, and movement in relation to them is always from without.

Thus O's vagina is depicted not as a hole, but as an opening. Because within *Histoire d'O* women are desired and looked at precisely for their openings, new ones are constantly constructed; O's mouth, anus and the lacerations in the surface of her skin all provide additional points of entry, and so code her more fully as "woman." At Roissy she, like the other female inmates, usually wears her skirt either rolled up in front or behind, in part to reveal the marks from her most recent whipping, but even more importantly so as to expose to the male gaze one of her two lower orifices.[26] During the first novel these openings become more and more visible; her anus is enlarged, and a double ring with a medallion is attached to her labia.

O manifests no sense of her body except in response to acts of aggression against it. She never experiences hunger, sleepiness, poor health or discomfort of any sort except in so far as it is induced by her captors. Her physical sensibility is at moments of aggression quite acute, however; she gags during oral intercourse, burns after vaginal intercourse, and is "rent" during anal intercourse. Penetration is depicted as a tearing, lacerating activity, which not only enlarges but in effect creates O's organs. It is no exaggeration to say that her body is constituted through the regimen to which it is subjected – that it is the consequence of a specific discursive operation.

She also has no independent thoughts at any point during the two novels, and virtually no thoughts whatever for the first thirty pages of *Histoire d'O.* What little cognitive activity is associated with her during the cab ride, or her initiation into life at Roissy is no more than a response to tactile stimuli, or to remarks which pertain in some way to her body.

Yet midway through her initial stay at Roissy, O arrives not only at a constant awareness of her body, but at something approximating an inner life – the inner life of a mystic or a saint:

> That she should have been ennobled and gained in dignity through being prostituted was a source of surprise, and yet dignity was indeed the right term. She was illuminated by it, as though from within, and her bearing bespoke calm, while on her face could be detected the serenity and imperceptible smile that one surmises rather than actually sees in the eyes of hermits. (p. 44)

However, the qualification "as though from within" conveys a certain dubiousness about the autonomy of O's consciousness, suggesting that if it is appropriate to speak of her as having an inside, that inside is the consequence of something external to her, of the multiple whippings and penetrations which have been performed upon her body.

It is in fact by means of the constant violation of her body that O comes to have whatever interiority she ever enjoys. We are told, for instance, that O is most exposed or open when she is "covered" with marks. This seeming paradox alerts us to the fact that the whip-lashes which criss-cross her body construct her as an object to be maltreated. By asserting O's compliance with abuse, the marks bring that compliance into existence. In other words, the secret they purport to reveal is a consequence of the revelation. O herself notes a few lines later that her "secret" did not depend on her alone. Actually, the situation is even more extreme; her "secret" does not depend on her at all, but on the discourse by means of which she is first inscribed, and then read.[27]

Since that discourse is architecturally bounded – since, that is, particular physical spaces form the perimeters within which significant alignments are established between the surfaces of O's body and assorted other objects – I will organize the remainder of this discussion around the four major locations within which the story of O unfolds: Roissy, the apartment in the Ile St Louis, Sir Stephen's apartment, and Anne-Marie's house.

The enclosure of the Sadean site . . . forms the basis of a social autarchy. Once shut in, the libertines, their assistants, and their subjects form a total society, endowed with an economy, a morality, a language, and a time articulated into schedules, labors and celebrations. Here, as elsewhere, the enclosure permits the system.[28]

The various houses and apartments in *Histoire d'O* serve a similar function to the enclosure in the Sadean text. They project a closed society, and effect an absolute regimentation both of bodily and mental activities. Their closure is the pre-requisite not only for that regimentation, but for the meaning it carries.[29] At the same time, each area abuts onto other areas, just as the discourse of pornography abuts onto other discourses. The different architectural spaces join together to form the larger discursive order within which all the smaller signifying events are "lodged."

Roissy

Roissy and Anne-Marie's residences constitute the two most highly differentiated spaces. For this reason they also offer the most highly refined cultures. Located in a residential neighborhood near Paris, Roissy looks like an ordinary dwelling from the exterior, but the interior bears no relation to the houses around it. Only part of that interior emerges with any clarity in *Histoire d'O* – the part which the sequel, *Retour à Roissy*, associates with the main enclosures, and which could be said to be specific to the discourse of pornography.

Almost directly inside the front door is a bedroom, devoid of furniture, but carpeted and lined with closets. A mirrored bathroom with hair-dressing equipment adjoins this room. Together they represent a transitional territory between the outside and the rest of the house; in them O is stripped of the remainder of her street clothing, bathed, and made up by two women dressed as chambermaids.

Each of these operations defines O's body in some way. Because she is not permitted to wash herself, her body is linked to hands other than her own. And because she is obliged to remain on a reclining chair with her knees spread while her hair dries, the mouth of her vagina is exposed to the anonymous gaze of the mirrors. These mirrors inaugurate pornography's scopic regime, a regime which is from the very outset "objectively" conceived – i.e. located within an architectural system which transcends any individual male gaze, but within which that gaze participates.

The subsequent application of cosmetics to O's body is extremely elaborate, and represents the first stage in its obsessive territorialization. Because her mouth is the only part of her face which will ever be brought into any contact with meaning, it is made up, while the rest remains undefined – indeed invisible. Considerably more attention is lavished on her breasts, which are in the process divided into three zones: tip, halo and cleavage. Perfume delineates a series of other hollows or openings – the anus, the arm-pits, the vagina and the palms of the hands. Finally, a metaphoric relationship is established between her mouth and her vagina by rouging the labia. The other portions of O's body remain, at least for the moment, outside meaning.

O is then moved further inside the chateau, to a red and black room. She is seated on an ottoman, in front of another set of mirrors. For the first time the male principle makes itself felt, both through the entrance of a valet, and through the implied gaze of one of the masters. This room mediates between the one immediately beyond the entrance, which would appear to be the exclusive territory of the female inhabitants who wash and make up O, and the more privileged inner rooms, which are occupied by Roissy's membership. The valets mediate in a similar fashion between O and the other women on the one hand, and the masters on the other.

The valet who enters wears clothes which conceal everything but his penis, and which give prominence to the whip he carries. Even his head is masked, although once O has learned to keep her eyes lowered the mask is no longer necessary. He is thus signified entirely in terms of phallic power, as are all the men who stay at Roissy, regardless of class. One of them explains the dress code to O at the outset of her residence there:

If the costume we wear in the evening – the one I am now wearing – leaves our sex exposed, it is not for the sake of convenience, for it would be just as convenient the other way, but for the sake of insolence, so that your eyes will be directed there upon it and nowhere else, so that you may learn that there resides your master, for whom, above all else, your lips are intended. (p. 16)

The club members wear street clothes during the day, but life at Roissy derives its value from what occurs at night. Besides, once a particular anatomical configuration has been internalized by O as signifying "maleness," it scarcely matters what her captors wear since all she will ever "see" is a collective penis. Sir Stephen, for instance, later dresses according to the most conservative standards of Paris, yet O never for a moment fails to identify him with the phallus.

Male identity is thus assumed to be quite stable; not only is it keyed to a single rather to a variety of bodily zones, but it is finally more an "idea" than an organ. (This conceptualization corresponds precisely to Lacan's assertion that the phallus is not the penis, but rather a signifier of the privileges that accompany the penis in patriarchal culture.)[30] The female body, on the contrary, is at all points literalized.

Constraining devices play a central role in this literalization. The valet supervises the measurement of O's cheek neck and wrists for the leather collar and bracelets which she will thereafter wear, assuring an exact match. These items represent that condition of perfect instrumentality which is O's destiny. (When Sir Stephen looks at her carefully for the first time she feels herself "being measured and weighed as the instrument she [knows] full well she [is]."(p. 66) Not only do they align her with that fate, but they provide the means by which she can be linked with other apparatuses, such as whipping posts, walls, or beds, and the means by which her arms are rendered powerless by being hooked together behind her back. They are the relay between O and a larger discursive field.

After eating dinner in a small cabin, O is taken to the library. This is the most privileged room in the chateau, both because it is the sole domain of the masters, and because it is the most public area of torture and sexual abuse. Here a blindfolded and handcuffed O is subjected to a much more violent territorialization than that effected earlier. The zones previously marked through cosmetics and perfumes as potential openings (mouth, anus, vagina) are now in fact opened. These penetrations occur in that part of the room most coded for male relaxation – by the fire, within a circle of leather chairs. O's body is then chained to a gallery inserted in one of the walls, and ritually whipped.

On this occasion, O is not blindfolded the way she will thereafter be during the torture sessions at Roissy. Her victimizers tell her that they want her to see herself being whipped, presumably so that she will subsequently visualize her body in terms of that activity, as "to-be-whipped." Indeed, that phrase is written on the back of a publicity photograph of O in *Retour à Roissy*, and functions as a command to the men who prostitute her there.

During her first stay at Roissy, O is whipped only between the waist and thighs. This area is mapped out as receptive to abuse even before she enters the building, since it is the part of her body undressed by René. The events leading up to this first torture establish a pattern which is thereafter scrupulously observed during the first half of O's stay: her body is washed and prepared, then penetrated, and finally beaten. On the nights when O is not taken to the library, one of the valets whips her.

This physical territorialization is accompanied by a verbal

colonization which brings O's body into alignment with a whole network of rules and prohibitions. She is told by the men sitting around the fire that she is there to serve her masters, to whom her body entirely belongs:

> Your hands are not your own, nor are your breasts, nor, most especially, any of your bodily orifices, which we may explore or penetrate at will. ... you have lost all right to privacy or concealment, and ... will never close your lips completely, or cross your legs, or press your knees together. ... You will never touch your breasts in our presence and ... when requested you will open your clothes, and then close them again when we have finished with you. (p. 16)

O's body is, by means of these multiple violations and legal restraints, brought within the discourse of pornography. Not only do they constitute her as a body with organs, but they determine the precise function of those organs; O is defined in terms of phallic meaning.

Once she has been thus territorialized and defined, O is dressed in the costume she will thereafter wear in the afternoons and evenings. That wasp-waisted dress shapes her body in accord with its new responsibilities, exposing her breasts and orifices, and sharply constricting the "useless" area between those privileged zones. It also serves as an apparatus of constraint and discipline, training the body to be erect (to stand up straight, to project breasts, buttocks, stomach), and assisting in the larger task of transforming female flesh into pure instrumentality. In the days that follow O's anus is also widened with the aid of the dildo, making it more receptive to future penetrations. This operation extends control over her anal muscles.

Indeed, control is extended over all her bodily activities. She is obliged to lift her skirt whenever she sits so that her naked buttocks touch the surface of the chair; her food is selected and prepared for her, and she eats it under restricted conditions (silence, solitude, nudity); she is bathed, dressed and made up by others; high-heeled mules impede her progress when she walks, and alert her captors to her approach; and her excretory activities are overseen either by one of the valets or several of the other female inmates. At night chains attached to her bracelets and collar not only confine her to the bed, but determine the position of her body. Deprived of the use of her hands, and unable to bring any of her limbs together, she is incapable of feeling (and hence of thinking about) anything but the implements that organize her body.

Finally, and perhaps most importantly, O is obliged to listen in silence to whatever her captors say to her. She is at no point permitted to participate in the production of meaning; instead, she supplies the passive surface upon which meaning is inscribed. She is also compelled to keep her eyes lowered in the presence not only of the masters, but the valets. This injunction serves two purposes: it confines O's vision to the sexual organ which charts and penetrates her body, and it dramatizes her exclusion from and subservience to the enunciating gaze of the sadistic subject.[31]

During the second half of O's stay at Roissy she is kept in solitary confinement, chained to the wall of a primitive cell. She is fed only fruit, bread and water, and is violated and beaten around the clock by men whose identity remains so indeterminate that she loses all track of their number. Because she never leaves this room, and because she remains unclothed, the only operative differentiations during this period of time are those between penetration and non-penetration, whipping and its surcease.

The whipping of O serves a very precise and important signifying function (more so, it should be noted, than penetration, which leaves behind only temporary traces): it constitutes her body as "readable" through a system of writing. The signifiers "trace" and "mark" are used so frequently in relation to the whipping of O that they become virtually synonymous with that activity. Whenever Pierre, O's "special" valet, whips her, he is careful to leave intervals (syntagmatic distances) between each lash so that all the abrasions will be visible, and after a recent beating O is always required to wear her skirt rolled up so that the marks can be "read."

The meaning which is thereby produced bears no relation to O's feelings or thoughts, or even to the signals of pain which she involuntarily emits; her captors tell her that they judge the result of their torture not by her screams or tears, but by "the size and color of the welts" raised by the whips (p. 12). The abrasions thus function as signifiers for a power imposed on O from outside, rather than as indicators of her pain.

However, while never ceasing for a moment to signify the sadistic subject who has inflicted them, the marks simultaneously signify O as the masochistic subject who not only receives but wants them. Because it is imperative that these two signifieds be posed in opposition to each other – that the subject-position implied by the donor of pain be held at the greatest possible remove from that implied by the receiver of pain – a very different strategy of reading is proposed for the latter than for the former. Instead of reading "outward," as we are encouraged to do in the case of the signifying complex "donor of welt/sadistic subject," we are told to read "inward," to locate the masochistic subject within an interior space. Although the reading operation invariably begins at the body's surface ("bearing," "face," "smile"), it always moves in the direction of a spiritual abstraction ("dignity," "calm," "illumination," "serenity," "ennoblement").

The duplicity of this signifying operation becomes even clearer when we realize that while the discourse which structures O's body and attributes to her a matching consciousness unquestionably transcends her, it also requires her as a writing surface. Even O understands that she is a necessary element in the discourse of Roissy, and that René's status as a speaking subject of pornography depends entirely upon his position within a larger discursive network. She also knows that through "the medium of her body" René and Sir Stephen arrive at something "more acute, more intense than an amorous communion" (p. 102).

O functions as the effect or distillate of the power exercised upon her body. It is only through her (or one of the other female inmates of Roissy) that this power can be exercised, and that those who exercise it can produce themselves as speaking subject. The extent of that power (and hence the potency of its exerciser) is keyed the surfaces of the female body – both to the ever more microscopic segmentation of its surfaces, and to the graduating intensity of its pain.

O notes René's inability personally to whip her, or to sodomize her in their apartment in the Ile St Louis. However, by surrendering O to the general use of the Roissy membership, René achieves discursive adequacy, and participates in a power which would otherwise elude him. He thereby becomes "the hand that blindfolds her, the whip wielded by the valet Pierre . . . the chain above her head, the unknown man who [comes] down on her, and all the voices which [give] her orders."[43]

O plays an equally vital role in the relationship of René and Sir Stephen, a relationship predicated not so much on identification as on desire. Sir Stephen accommodates himself with ease to pornography's sadistic speaking position, never wavering in the exercise of its power. Implicit in René's discursive impotence is the wish to receive pain rather than to inflict it – to be had by rather than to be Sir Stephen. He gratifies that (homosexual) desire through O, whose body gives him erotic access to the other man:

Each time she emerged from Sir Stephen's arms, René looked for the mark of a god upon her. . . . impressed and overwhelmed, he gazed for a long time at the thin body marked by thick, purple welts like so many ropes spanning the shoulders, the back, the buttocks, the belly, and the breasts, welts which sometimes overlapped and criss-crossed. Here and there a little blood still oozed.

"Oh, how I love you," he murmured. (p. 106)

The end of O's period of solitary confinement marks the completion of the first stage of her structuration. Her body has been made a receptive surface for discipline and punishment, and she already gives evidence of a corresponding interiority. O returns with René to the apartment in the Ile St Louis for a period of preparation before the much more severe regime imposed by Sir Stephen.

The apartment in the Ile St Louis

The apartment over which René presides is characterized by a much less rigorous articulation of space than are any of the other architectural enclosures in *Histoire d'O*. Although O and René have separate bedrooms, as befits their different status within the discourse of pornography, the third main room lacks any functional specificity; it is by turns a study, a living room and a spare bedroom. René's inability to deploy space with the absolute precision of Roissy is symptomatic of his larger discursive impotence.

When O takes up residence once again in the Ile St Louis, René obliges her to surrender all her underwear, and all outer garments which deny easy access to her body. In their place he puts a uniform of close-fitting sweaters and pleated skirts. Apart from this, René uses no physical constraint. However, O never ceases for a moment to be a distillate of the power that has been exercised upon her, even in complete solitude. When she gazes in the mirror she still sees herself as an inmate of Roissy:

> She was no longer wearing either a collar or leather bracelet, and she was alone, her sole spectator. And yet never had she felt more totally committed to a will which was not her own, more totally a slave, and more content to be so. (p. 58)

This passage indicates that what Paulhan and Mandiargues call O's "soul" is nothing other than a psychic registration of the power relations by means of which her body has been mapped and defined – the relations, that is, between her wrists and their manacles; her neck and its collar; her feet and their high-heeled mules; her breasts, waist and buttocks and the dress which has molded them; her thighs and the whips which have lashed them; her mouth, anus and vagina and the penises which have penetrated them; her eyes and the enslavement reflected back at them by the mirrors of Roissy; and her body as a "whole" and the architectural spaces which have contained it. The "case" of O shows as clearly as the Panopticon that the subject can be made to oppress herself by internalizing the external structure within which her body is organized, and that this oppression can have a terrifying relentlessness.

He who is subjected to a field of visibility, and who knows it, assumes responsibility for the constraints of power; he makes them play spontaneously upon himself; he inscribes in himself the power relations in which he simultaneously plays both roles; he becomes the principle of his own subjection. By this very fact, the external power may throw off its physical weight; it tends towards the non-corporeal; and, the more it approaches this limit, the more constant, profound and permanent are its effects; it is a perpetual victory that avoids any physical confrontation and which is always decided in advance.[33]

However, O has not yet reached the limit described by Foucault. Her identity is still so dependent upon physical pain and subjugation that in their absence she feels dazed and directionless. She is an instrument without a function, a slave without a master, a "Christian" without a "God" (p. 94). O's desires are satisfied by the figure responsible for their creation: Sir Stephen.

Sir Stephen's apartment

The transfer of O from René to Sir Stephen occurs within the confines of yet another architectural space, an apartment on the rue de Poitiers. The rooms of this two-floor apartment are "laid out in a straight line," without the confusing complexity of Roissy. The most public of its spaces, the living room, provides the scene of the actual exchange, as well as Sir Stephen's initial violation of O. She is also whipped in that room, after being chained to a chandelier.

O spends this first night at Sir Stephen's apartment, but is excluded from his bedroom; she is housed instead in a small adjoining room. The other space which structures her relationship with Sir Stephen, at least in its subsequent stages, is his study. The latter is situated directly above the living room, thereby reiterating the organizing principle of the "straight line." This architectural paradigm admits only of unequivocal horizontal or vertical movement, a movement in keeping with the rigors of Sir Stephen's regime. Here everything is always out in the open, from his feelings for O (he tells her that he doesn't love her, but that she will nevertheless obey him) to her desire for subjugation.

For the first time O can not only be trusted to speak, but is obliged to do so. Under Sir Stephen's rule she is aligned with certain linguistic formulae which in turn equip her with the baggage of masochistic desire. She is thus brought even more fully within discursive control. René and Sir Stephen insist that O give a verbal consent to her own involvement in a scenario which has not yet been revealed to her – that she acknowledge verbally what the marks on her body imply, i.e. that with her "anything goes."

It is thus only rather late in her history, long after she has been constructed as a pliant and docile body, that O emerges as a subject in the Lacanian sense of that word – that she accedes to the language of the Other, a language which pre-exists and coerces her, but through which she acquires a consciousness of self. This access to language is portrayed by the novel as the translation of set phrases from the second to the first person. In the course of this grammar lesson O succumbs not only to the language but to the desires of the Other.

The speaking of masochistic desires through O organizes her inner space in ways which provide new occasions for discipline and punishment. This interiority is no sooner constructed than it is found to contain guilt – a guilt whose origins must be traced, explored and defined. O is thus required to confess to desires which become shameful the moment they are annexed to her.

The strategy whereby taboo desires are imposed upon the cultural subject from without is by no means specific to the discourse of pornography. As Deleuze and Guattari point out, that imposition is virtually synonymous with Oedipal structuration, a structuration which punishes the infantile subject for the very dreams it inaugurates, thereby binding that subject to the family both through desire and guilt.[34]

Significantly, as soon as O has finished transposing all the formulae with which she has been provided, she recalls a print she saw years ago entitled "Family Punishment," in which the theme of guilt occupied a conspicuous place:

the woman was kneeling, as she was, before an armchair. The floor was of tile, and in one corner a dog and child were playing. The woman's skirts were raised, and standing close beside her was a man brandishing a handful of switches, ready to whip her. They were all dressed in sixteenth-century clothes. (p. 77)

The semiotic complexities of this passage warrant careful examination, because they throw a more general light on the terms under which the female subject lives out her Oedipal desires. First, O recalls the image of female subjugation as something which belongs to a moment long ago not only in her own history, but in that of her culture (i.e. as a crisis which began centuries ago, and which will always be anterior to any experiences she might have). Second, it is available to her only in the most elaborately mediated ways; it is not only a memory, but a memory of a picture. The image of female subjugation is thus the product of two levels of representation, the initial model of which is not recoverable. This doubly mediated representation structures and gives meaning to an event in the present – the whipping of O by Sir Stephen. However, the so-called memory comes into existence only as a consequence of the later event, one of whose functions would precisely seem to be to equip O with an Oedipal past. (Sir Stephen subsequently provides O with a uniform which casts her in the role of daughter, thereby ensuring a daily re-enactment of the familial romance.)

After this episode, O devotes herself to an intense and entirely new self-scrutiny, a search for the origins of the "sin" Sir Stephen has detected in her – wantonness. She "recalls" her involvement in two heavily over-determined scenarios of female guilt, in both of which she assumes a position which the novel marks out as legitimately belonging only to the male subject: the scenarios of the *femme fatale* and the lesbian adventuress. In the first of these she usurps the sadistic position, relegating numerous men to the masochistic position, while in the second she plays the part of aggressor and mistress-of-ceremonies, supervising the linguistic, visual and erotic transactions into which she enters with other women:

She, and she alone, set the rules and directed the proceedings (something she never did with men, or only in the most oblique manner). She initiated the discussions and set the *rendez-vous*, the kisses came from her too. . . . As much as she was in a hurry to behold her girl friend naked, she was equally quick to find excuses why she herself should not undress. (pp. 96-7)

Sir Stephen thus effects a complete psychic structuration of O. He links her not only to the rhetorical formulae of confession, and to the self-destructive desires of the masochistic subject, but to a guilty past and a future of punishment and expiation.

Sir Stephen increases the territory over which power may be exercised in other ways as well, annexing her professional to her private life. Not only must O now go to work dressed in a manner which leaves her body completely accessible to anyone who knows her "secret," but she is commissioned with the task of recruiting one of her models for Roissy. Moreover, things which had previously occurred only in private retreats, and under the cover of darkness, now go on in the middle of Paris in broad daylight. This last transition is negotiated when Sir Stephen appears at O's apartment in the Ile St Louis for the first time, and issues commands she is accustomed to hearing only in his apartment. The place and hour force her to be even more "open" about herself, to "confess" even more fully to her shameful desires:

[her] self-consciousness was made all the more apparent to her because it was not taking place in some specific spot to which she had to repair in order to submit to it, and not at night, thereby partaking of a dream or of some clandestine existence in relation to the length of her life with René. The bright light of a May day turned the clandestine into something public: henceforth the reality of the night and the reality of the day would be one and the same. Henceforth – and O was thinking: at last. . . . Henceforth, there would be no hiatuses, no dead time, no remission. (p. 108)

By inducing O to assume certain desires as her own through confessing them, and by organizing her working life as well as her entire physical economy in relation to them, Sir Stephen constitutes for her a reality within which she is entirely contained, and beyond which it would be impossible to stray.

Anne-Marie's house

Anne-Marie's house, both in its secluded location and architectural design, resembles Roissy more than any of the novel's other living spaces. It is situated at the end of the Fontainebleau Forest, next to an enclosed garden. The house contains a number of bedrooms on the second floor for its "guests," as well as one on the ground floor for the most recent arrival. However, the most privileged areas are Anne-Marie's bedroom, into which she takes one of the other women every night, and the directly adjoining music room. The former might best be characterized as the scene of erotic exercise, and the latter as the staging-ground for discipline and punishment.

Anne-Marie's bedroom is only briefly decribed (we are told that it is a large white room without mirrors). Considerably more attention is lavished on the music room, where daily rituals of torture occur. Although it does in fact contain a stereo and radio, its central feature is a raised rotunda with two columns. It also has cork-lined doors, which trap the victims' screams.

Anne-Marie stages her rituals of torture on the raised rotunda. An elaborate contraption suspends the victim's buttocks and spread legs in the air, exposing the most sensitive region of her body to the torturer's whip, and permitting the on-lookers to "read" the marks left behind. Each day's victim is chosen through a draw, as is the torturer. A third draw determines whether the victim will be whipped, or merely suspended for three hours on the dais. These events structure the entire waking existence of the inmates.

The women suspended on the dais at Anne-Marie's house are

visible only as buttocks and spread thighs; their faces cannot even be seen. They are "open" simultaneously to penetration and pain, and they feel themselves to be under constant surveillance, even when no one else is in the room. This single apparatus is so efficient that it replaces all of Roissy's complex and bulky machinery. As a consequence, there are virtually no house rules at Anne-Marie's. Indeed, the only two requirements function to divest rather than to encumber: the first dictates absolute idleness for O and her companions, and the second obliges them to go without clothing. Only Anne-Marie and her servants are permitted to cover their bodies, and in Anne-Marie's case the exception indicates privilege.

Anne-Marie is the only woman in *Histoire d'O* who is allowed to participate in even a restricted way in the discursive fellowship of Roissy. However, far from qualifying the larger rule of exclusion, the limited powers given to Anne-Marie help to naturalize the condition of O and the other inmates. Because these women are subjected to an even more relentless discipline and punishment in her "gynocracy" than they are in the patriarchal environment of Roissy, they are encouraged to believe that their passivity and pain are an integral part of themselves, rather than the products of male discourse:

[Anne-Marie] was bent on proving to every girl who came into her house, and who was fated to live in a totally feminine universe, that her condition as a woman should not be minimized or degraded by the fact that she was in contact only with other women, but that, on the contrary, it should be heightened and intensified. (pp. 152-3)

Under this regime an entirely new part of O's body – her inner thighs – is exposed to and marked by pain, and her waist undergoes a much more extreme constriction (at the end of her stay, that portion of O's body between the "useful" breasts and thighs has been reduced to the radius of ten fingers). She is also engaged in an even fuller complicity with her own suffering, since Anne-Marie extracts from O a "thank-you" after each whipping.

However, by far the most important discursive events in this section of the novel – events marking the completion of O's subjectivity – are the piercing of her labia and the branding of her buttocks. The first of these operations makes possible the insertion into O's labia of a double ring engraved with her name, Sir Stephen's name, a crossed whip and a riding crop. The second of these operations scars Sir Stephen's initials on each side of O's buttocks. These two inscriptions constitute O fully and finally as an object to be penetrated; the piercing of her labia creates a new opening in that part of the female anatomy already most coded as a "hole," while the branding iron leaves behind several recesses half an inch deep.

The rings attached to O's labia and the initials burned into her rear have a different semiotic status from the whip-marks that cover her stomach and thighs. All three have an existential relation to O's body, but whereas the whip-marks are simply traces of abuse, giving no clue to the identity of the abuser, the rings and brand introduce onto the surface of that body a privileged and "secondary" signifier – the paternal signature or phallus.

That signature gives the lie to Montrelay's notion that because the phallus does not represent the female body in the way that it represents the penis, her body remains a "dark continent," beyond structuration. Montrelay's formulation rests upon the assumption that in order for structuration to occur, the relation between real and discursive bodies must be one of analogy. However, the initials branded onto O's buttocks suggest that no such relation need exist between the phallus and an actual body for the former to exercise an organizing effect upon the latter. That inscription is certainly not "motivated" by O's real body, and yet it shapes that body, gives it meaning.

Histoire d'O thus suggests a much more intimate connection between real and discursive bodies than the *m/f* collective would be willing to grant, providing an account of female subjectivity as much at odds with theirs as with Montrelay's. It indicates, that is, that the discourse of pornography leans so hard upon real bodies that it transfers to them its structure and significance, a structure and significance which are then internalized in the guise of a complementary consciousness and set of desires. The "case" of O points to the *anaclitic* relation between real and discursive bodies – to the way in which meaning shapes the materiality which supports it, rather than imitating a pre-existing pattern. As Heath observes, "The question of representation . . . is not initially that of the represented . . . but that of the subjective effect produced, the point of the action of the representation, of its represented."[35]

There are, as the *m/f* collective has pointed out, important points of non-coincidence between the female bodies projected by various discourses. These divergences remind us that female subjectivity is a construction, and that it is consequently open to change. They also provide a potential challenge to the illusory coherence of the symbolic order, and should be maximized until that potential is realized.

However, it would also seem imperative to confront the ways in which female subjectivity is over-determined – to acknowledge the points of coincidence between different constructions of "the feminine." There is ultimately an alarming consensus as to what woman is and wants, and that consensus has been produced through shared assumptions about the female body. This discursive "surplus" assures the stability of traditional definitions of the female subject. It also exerts intense pressure upon what might be called the "brute materiality" of real bodies. The powerful hold which discourse exerts upon the female subject's corporeal existence is suggested by a striking image from *Histoire d'O*: as Sir Stephen takes possession of O for the first time, she feels herself "frozen to the sofa like a butterfly impaled upon a pin, a long pin composed of words and looks which pierced the middle of her body." (p. 71) Finally, it would seem important to acknowledge the determining effect which the female subject's corporeal structuration has upon her psychic existence – to explore the relevance for woman of Freud's observation that the ego is "first and foremost a bodily ego ... the projection of a surface."[36]

Histoire d'O is more than O's story. It is the history of the female subject – of the territorialization and inscription of a body whose involuntary internalization of a corresponding set of desires facilitates its complex exploitation. That history will never read otherwise until the female subject alters her relation to discourse – until she succeeds not only in exercising discursive power, but in exercising it differently.

Notes

A version of this paper appeared in *enclitic*, vol. 7, no. 2, 1984.

1 Pauline Réage, *Story of O*, trans. Sabine d'Estrée, New York, Grove, 1965, p. 113. All future citations from the novel will be taken from this edition.

2 In "Analysis and Truth or the Closure of the Unconscious", Jacques Lacan writes:

it is in the space of the Other that the subject sees himself, and the point from which he looks at himself is also in that space. Now this is also the point from which he speaks, since in so far as he speaks, it is in the locus of the other that he begins to constitute that truthful lie by which is initiated that which participates in desire at the level of the unconscious. (*Four Fundamental Concepts of Psychoanalysis*, trans. Alan Sheridan, New York, Norton, 1978, p. 114)

3 Sigmund Freud, "Some Psychical Consequences of the Anatomical Distinctions Between the Sexes", *The Standard Edition of the Complete Psychological Works*, trans. James Strachey, London, Hogarth, 1958, vol. XIX, p. 249.

4 Luce Irigaray argues, in *Ce Sexe qui n'en est pas un*, Paris, Minuit, 1977, that woman enjoys a continuous and extra-cultural auto-eroticism, and that her discourse escapes the codes which govern

male discourse. Julia Kristeva advances a similar claim through her consistent association of woman with the "semiotic" rather than the "symbolic." That equation finds perhaps its most extreme formulation in "Motherhood According to Giovanni Bellini", an essay which treats childbirth as the triumph of female instinct over male culture:

By giving birth, the woman enters into contact with her mother; she becomes, she is, her own mother; they are the same continuity differentiating itself. She thus actualizes the homo-sexual fact of motherhood, through which a woman is simultaneously close to her instinctual memory, more open to her own psychosis, and consequently, more negatory of the social, symbolic bond.

(*Polylogue*, Paris, Seuil, 1977, pp. 409-35; English version *Desire in Language: A Semiotic Approach to Literature and Art*, trans. Thomas Gora, Alice Jardine and Leon S. Roudiez, New York, Columbia University Press, 1980, pp. 237-70; see also Claire Pajaczkowska's partial translation of and extremely helpful introduction to this essay in *m/f* no. 5/6, 1981, pp. 149-63.)

5 See Michèle Montrelay, *L'Ombre et le nom: sur la feminité*, Paris, Minuit, 1977, pp. 55-81; English version "Inquiry into Femininity", trans. Parveen Adams, *m/f*, no. 1, 1978, pp. 83-101.
6 Montrelay, "Inquiry into Femininity", op. cit., p. 90.
7 Montrelay, "Inquiry into Femininity", op. cit., p. 91.
8 In "Parole de femme sur le transfert de l'hystérie", an earlier chapter of *L'Ombre et le nom*, Montrelay defines hysteria as the refusal on the part of the female subject to be so unconsciously structured.
9 This is a point which Stephen Heath also makes in "Difference", *Screen*, vol. xviii, no. 3, 1979, p. 88:

The difficulty in [Lacan's] theory is that castration is the term both of the division of the subject in the movement of symbolic difference and of a sexual difference that differentiates individual subjects as between male and female; it crosses, in other words, from universal function to effective realisation without doubt, with the latter thus becoming the constant form of the former and, in fact, its nature.

10 Montrelay, "Inquiry into Femininity", op. cit., pp. 91-3.
11 See Monique Plaza, " 'Phallomorphic Power' and the Psychology of 'Woman'", trans. Miriam David and Jilly Hodges, *Ideology and Consciousness*, vol. 4, 1978, pp. 5-36, and Jacqueline Rose, "'Dora' – Fragment of an Analysis", *m/f*, no. 2, 1978, pp. 5-21.
12 Beverly Brown and Parveen Adams, "The Feminine Body and Feminist Politics", *m/f*, no. 3, 1979, p. 43. A nearly identical position is maintained by Parveen Adams and Jeff Minson in "The 'Subject' of Feminism", *m/f* no. 2, 1978, pp. 43-61; by Parveen Adams in "A Note on Sexual Division and Sexual Differences", *m/f*, no. 3, 1979, pp. 51-7; and by Beverly Brown, "A Feminist Interest in Pornography – Some Modest Proposals", *m/f*, no. 5/6, 1981, pp. 5-18.
13 Since it dispenses with the notion of an oppressed group, this formulation would render inoperative any classical form of political struggle.
14 See Sigmund Freud, "On Narcissism", *The Standard Edition of the Complete Psychological Works*, op. cit., vol. XIV, pp. 73-102.
15 In "Direction of Treatment and Principles of its Power", Lacan

described desire as borrowing "its heavy soul from the hardy shoots of the wounded drive" (*Ecrits*, trans. Alan Sheridan, New York, Norton, 1977, p. 265).

16 See Michel Foucault, *The Archaeology of Knowledge and the Discourse on Language*, trans. A. M. Sheridan, London, Tavistock, 1972, pp. 225-6.

17 I have discussed this issue at length in "Masochism and Subjectivity", *Framework*, vol. 12, 1980, pp. 2-9; "The Celestial Suture: It's A Wonderful Life", *Framework, vol. 14, 1981, pp. 16-22; and "Changing the Fantasmatic Scene"*, *Framework*, vol. 20, 1983, pp. 27-36. It should perhaps be noted here that the present essay was written in 1981, prior to "Changing the Fantasmatic Scene".

18 These rules can be found in Foucault, op. cit., pp. 215-37.

19 Sigmund Freud, *Interpretation of Dreams, The Standard Edition of the Complete Psychological Works*, op. cit., vol. IV, pp. 100-2.

20 I discuss some of the ways in which the female subject can transform her relation to discourse by employing it in unorthodox ways in "Helke Sander and the Will to Change" (*Discourse* no. 6, Fall 1983).

21 Paulhan's essay accompanies *Histoire d'O* in both the French and the English versions. Mandiargues's essay appears in the English version of *Histoire d'O*, but the French version of *Retour à Roissy*.

22 I do not intend to enter here into the general speculation about the identity of Pauline Réage. To some degree that speculation is irrelevant, since regardless of who actually wrote the novel, the subjectivity designated by the name "Paule Réage" is a pornographic construction.

23 In *The Archaeology of Knowledge and the Discourse on Language*, Foucault describes the "will to truth" as a discursive mechanism for directing all investigation toward a pre-determined goal (pp. 218-19).

24 Foucault, op. cit., pp. 220-1.

25 This is a bodily construction which Gilles Deleuze and Felix Guattari associate with Oedipalization, and against which they argue at length in *Anti-Oedipus: Capitalism and Schizophrenia*, trans. Robert Hurley, Mark Seem and Helen R. Lane, New York, Viking, 1977.

26 In "Photography/Pornography/Art/Pornography", *Screen*, vol. xxi, no. 1, 1980, p. 203, John Ellis argues that

> The availability of vaginal imagery in recent pornography can be said to have a directly educative effect for both men and women, as well as tending to dispel the aura of strangeness produced by the centuries of concealment of the vagina in Western representations.

However, *Histoire d'O* shows that pornography does not so much reveal as construct. In his response to Ellis's article, Paul Willemen theorizes about the display of female genitalia in ways which are much more pertinent to the present discussion:

> In the vast majority of porn, women are the space on which male pleasure is inscribed. This can take different forms: through the disposition of the body so as to grant maximum access to the look; through the imprinting on woman of the traces of male pleasure, i.e., the dispersal of "seminal signifers".... Even when a woman is shown to be deriving pleasure from masturbation, her body is always arranged in relation to the accessibility of her genitalia to the look.

("Letter to John", *Screen*, vol. xxi, no. 2, 1980, p. 60.)

27 In Michel Foucault, *A History of Sexuality*, trans. Robert Hurley, New York, Pantheon, 1978, Foucault suggests that confession functions as an invisible form of coercion: "The obligation to confess is . . . relayed through so many different points, is so deeply ingrained in us, that we no longer perceive it as the effect of a power that constrains us." (p. 60)

28 Roland Barthes, *Sade/Fourier/Loyola*, trans. Richard Miller, New York, Hill & Wang, 1976, p. 17.

29 Dennis Giles remarks in "Pornographic Space: The Other Place", *Film: Historical-Theoretical Speculations: The 1977 Film Studies Annual: Part 2*, Pleasantville, New York, Docent, 1977, that in pornographic films the central female character is frequently enclosed within an isolated space, much like the heroine of the "woman's film" (p. 57).

30 For Lacan the phallus is the signifier *par excellence*, the signifying unit most central to subjectivity and the symbolic order. He is particularly clear on this point in "Desire and the Interpretation of Desire in *Hamlet*", trans. James Hulbert, *Yale French Studies*, vol. 55/56, 1977, p. 8.

31 Heath comments on the impossibility within classic narrative and representational schemas of woman ever participating in authoritative vision:

If the woman looks, the spectacle provokes, castration is in the air, the Medusa's head is not far off; thus, she must not look, is absorbed on the side of the seen, seeing herself seeing herself, Lacan's femininity. ("Difference", op. cit., p. 92)

Significantly, O is a fashion photographer, and she returns briefly to her profession after her stay at Roissy. However, the photographs she takes all contain images of female passivity and bondage, suggesting O's inability to see anything but the subjectivity which has been conferred upon her. Since, moreover, René and Sir Stephen canvas the photographs for possible new victims, authority is invested in their gaze, not O's.

32 Claire Pajaczkowska proposes in "The Heterosexual Presumption: A Contribution to the Debate on Pornography", *Screen*, vol. xxii, no. 2, 1981, pp. 79-84, that dominant pornography always effects this displacement – that its fetishizing mechanisms make "'woman' adequate as a sexual object" in order to enable "the homosexual manoeuvre to be successfully and completely enacted, thus providing a partial defence against homosexuality."

33 Michel Foucault, *Discipline and Punish: The Birth of the Prison*, trans. Alan Sheridan, New York, Vintage, 1979, pp. 202-3.

34 Deleuze and Guattari, op. cit., pp. 54-6.

35 Stephen Heath, "The Turn of the Subject", *Ciné-Tracts*, vol. 7/8, 1979, p. 44.

36 Sigmund Freud, *The Ego and the Id, The Standard Edition of the Complete Psychological Works*, op. cit., vol. XIX, p. 27.

Search for Tomorrow: On Feminism and the Reconstruction of Teen Romance

Sharon Thompson

The sexual life of maturing youth is almost entirely restricted to indulging in phantasies.

Sigmund Freud[1]

As soon as their children are old enough to understand sex, they send them to the *ghotul*, a dormitory for adolescents. . . . Sleeping partners are rotated so no one will be "ruined by love."

Verrier Elwin[2]

1 The texts

Several years ago, I embarked on what turned out to be an impossible project: a book of interviews with pubescents about puberty. If there are more reluctant interview subjects, I have never encountered them. Puberty, like pregnancy, is a secret the body cannot keep forever, but to the extent that language constructs physical experiences – makes them real, gives them shape, limits, and significance – pubescents exercise their right to remain vague, amorphous, unshaped and unlimited by words, concealed: if not to repress, then to keep private, personal, their own. Their silence struck me as an act of self-possession, and I admired it, but I was nevertheless convinced at the time that liberation lay in the public direction: in sharing secrets and in shaping them rather than, through silence, accepting pre-existing molds. French historian Michel Foucault would argue, no doubt, that I was but another dupe of the system that enthralls by causing one and all to obsess and confess *ad infinitum* about the subject on which so much attention from the right and the left is focused.[3] I see his point now, although my agreement is halfhearted. At the time, however, my point of view was not even shaded by Foucault. I was out to be a missionary of sex. Besides, I had to finish the book.

I proceeded by raising and then raising again (and in the case of boys raising yet again) the age of the young people I interviewed on the theory that teenagers might be more willing and able to talk about puberty after they had made it to the other side of the sexual divide but before they had time to forget what had happened. (The fogs of adolescent amnesia are notorious, particularly in regard to the aspect of puberty I most wanted to talk about, the subjective.)[4] By the end of the project, I was reduced to interviewing twenty-five-year-old boys, who told me, in tones suggesting that they were baring their chests for the good of the project, pubertal anecdotes revolving mainly around early heterosexual play or disconnected homosexual episodes like circle jerks. Upon being questioned about puberty, girls of fifteen and sixteen, on the other hand, rushed into fullblown narratives about sexual and romantic life.[5] As a fiction writer, I was stunned to realize that almost every girl over fifteen could tell, in virtually one three- or four-hour breath, a story of her own that was imbued with the discoveries, anguish, and elation of intimate relations. It was as if every teenage girl I spoke with revealed herself to be a Colette, a Rhys, a Sagan, a teller if not a writer of a romantic fable whose moral or example was meant to be passed on to prepare the way for others – to warn and guide sister neophytes on the path of love.

The stories had a polished quality, and I think this was because they were rehearsed. These were the stories that teenage girls spend hundreds of hours telling each other, going over and over detail and possibility as part of the process of constructing and reconstructing sexual and existential meaning for themselves. At the same time, the stories were lived in the telling. Girls wept and glowed in the course of single interviews, which often lasted, with very little prodding, four or five hours. Contradictions within single interviews made explicit an implication that has to be acknowledged: that the interviews present a *version* of the self, one edited for myriad conscious and unconscious purposes. In particular, these narrators tend to present the self as innocent, well-intentioned, chastened by experience, victim rather than victor or co-operator even when the facts they recount may suggest a different interpretation. Because these are told stories, it is also important to acknowledge that the narrators probably edited their remarks for the listener: a woman in her thirties, asking personal questions and carrying a tape recorder.[6]

For all my mixed feelings and second thoughts about the interviews in retrospect, I came away from each with the sense that I had been entrusted with something as valuable, as telling and prophetic, as a first love when the lover reads it, like an omen, for the future. Gathering the narratives has become something of an addiction with me, not unlike my own addiction to romance (it's suspicious, I know, that I tend to collect these interviews in the spring), but this is not because they tell the story I want to hear, the story I would tell if left to my own devices: teenage sexual pleasure without repercussion, won, in part, by second-wave feminism. But neither have I heard with any frequency the tale the anti-pornography movement insists is the sexual story for all women, that of coercion, exploitation, and violence.[7] Anguish suffuses many of the interviews. There are many stories of psychological danger. In too many cases, teenage girls gamble away their chances for economic and intellectual autonomy; but while the imbalance in power relations between men and women, the double standard, and the two-sphere system underlie many of the sexual losses that figure painfully in these stories, actual or feared exploitation or violence come up relatively infrequently. This is an important point. Most teenage girls' lives are "ruined by love," in Elwin's phrase – to the extent they are ruined, shortcircuited, or pared down – not by the pleasures and dangers associated with sex and not by promiscuity, but by a propensity to stake precious time and lose heart at the gaming table of romance.[8]

The chief promise I made when I elicited these stories was that I would let the stories tell their own tales. Together, however, they tell larger tales, and this paper is a beginning toward sorting those out, particularly regarding their implications for feminism. I focus here chiefly on heterosexual, white, working-class teenagers, because the themes developed in this essay – regarding the chasm between expectation and likelihood, wish and possibility – are particularly dramatic in this group. This is so partly, I think, because so much depends on intimate life when little is expected from work, but also because of the traditional expectations about the stability of intimate life developed in this group over the last few generations. While many of the observations in this paper apply to teenagers of color, others do not, and the differences are sometimes marked, and sometimes subtle. I restrict these comments to white teenagers, because my interviewing is not yet extensive enough for me to describe these differences with any certainty. I am not emphasizing lesbian teenagers, because their sexuality places them in a different historical relation to ideas about, for example, the likely permanence of true love, although some of the concepts arise in lesbian narratives as well. Here and there I will compare working-class sexual experience to middle-class sexual experience, which may appear to more nearly match feminist standards as they are popularly understood. This occurs partly because of the middle-class origin of many feminist assumptions, and also because the ethos of, say, *Our Bodies, Ourselves* seems to have permeated the liberal middle-class to a greater extent than it has other groups. But this does not mean that middle-class teenage sexual life is trouble-free and raises no questions for feminists. Finally, the references here to class are not meant to indicate that differences of education, race, geography, or ethnicity as well as the subtle, but less commonly enumerated differences of familial and peer sexual histories and traditions are not also telling and suggestive. I work here with the category of class, fairly loosely applied, because it clarifies some problems of adolescent sexuality feminism must address if it is not to be lost once again in the generation gap.

The concept of a generation gap has to be raised warily. As social historian John Gillis has shown, the idea of a generation gap has often served to mask other crucial differences, particularly those of class. Within a given class, there is continuity between generations; within a generation, there are differences among classes, and these differences also have a continuity. Such traditions as misrule, for example, are raveled into peer group and gender socialization, passed down from senior to sophomore, parent to child.[9] But social movements that have not taken root in these traditions are highly vulnerable to generation gap rhetoric, which dismisses the achievements and aspirations of a previous generation with adjectives more generally reserved for old hats.

Feminism failed to cross the generation gap in the 1920s, and it is in danger of failing again now.[10] We have taken root to some extent, and we can rely on the influence of reproductive autonomy and labor force participation to bring another generation of women somewhat independently to a feminist understanding. But the failure of feminism to reach effectively across the boundaries of class and race – and the related tendency to define the feminist lifestyle in rigid and moralistic terms – is currently being compounded by generational differences, and it will work against our capacity to win a battle that may ultimately prove as crucial as the fight against the right wing: the battle against being cut off from the future, against being labeled and dismissed as old history. It would be an ironic fate for those who have understood so keenly how much we are a part of the past to fail because we did not manage to make ourselves a part of the future. To avoid it, as Amber Hollibaugh argues eloquently in another connection, we must learn to apprehend and speak through differences. Silence no more obliterates the divisions of history than those of class and race. Those who go unmentioned assume with some reason that their interest lies elsewhere.[11]

The following remarks are based on approximately fifty life histories. In all, I have interviewed over 150 adolescents from 1978-83. Although the teenagers constitute a sample of convenience rather than a demographically representative group, I have spoken with teenagers of different class, race, and ethnic backgrounds. Whenever possible, I used a snowball technique.

While this technique conveyed some sense of the way in which a peer group or a clique constituted itself a sexual community, with its own rules and attitudes about sex and gender, it had the disadvantage of exclusivity: rarely did a subject introduce someone whose views and experiences she disapproved. To reach those who thought or felt differently, I had to begin again, through another source or by interviewing at random in a public place, which was not always feasible. This qualification is not intended to suggest that I believe a larger statistical study would bear more fruit in considering such complex dynamics of people's experience of sex and gender. These matters do not easily lend themselves to closed-ended interview schedules, large numbers, and multivariate analysis. It is corrective, in this regard, to recall that Zelnik, Kantner, and Ford conclude their massive 1971-9 study of adolescent sex and pregnancy with the admission that, "For the most part we have not been very successful in explaining the various aspects of behavior we have subjected to analysis."[12]

2   The quest-romance

In contemporary teenage life, if not in medieval literary tradition, the quest-romance is the female adventure, the primary vocation for girls who live dangerously.

One of our culture's most intense myths [points out literary critic Ann Snitow], the ideal of an individual who is brave and complete in isolation is for men only. Women are grounded, enmeshed in civilization, in social connection, in family, and in love ... while all our culture's rich myths of individualism are essentially closed to them. Their one acceptable moment of transcendence is romance.[13]

That sex and romance are primary connecting threads in girls' tradition is evident in the narratives of teenage girls, which make it clear that in the current period, at least, sex and romance are the organizing principles, the fundamental projects in many, many teenage girls' lives.

What is the relation between sex and romance for teenage girls? And what is the function of romance? "Romance is a show they'll never close," contends a recent rock song. Is this the case? Or is romance an atavism rapidly dying of its own dead weight? Is it false consciousness? Survival strategy?

Romance and sex are snarled in teenage girls' discourse, if not inextricably, at least sufficiently so that taking them together and apart is essential to understanding the train of thought. Romance, for example, figures in teenage conversation as a euphemism or metaphor for sex; as an introductory code word signaling permission for a discussion of sex; as a wholly separate category; or as an amalgam of relationship, passion, sex, and desire. It is easier to point out the fusion than to try to take the terms apart.

Romance is what the narratives begin to be about – the mysterious chemistry of attraction and the ensuing chain reaction: I wanted him, he wanted me, we, he, then I, then she, her and me. Like the murder in a detective novel, sex makes it a story worth telling. Sex makes it adult, real. Romance is the quest for sexual destiny, the search for a partner custom-made by the stars, the genes, or by so many random, subtle, and exquisitely specific factors that the process may as well be ascribed to magic. It is the search for the one or the ones who will recognize and validate by loving or having sex with the seeker, the one waiting to be found. The archetype of romance, claims critic Northrop Frye, is in dream, "the search of the libido or desiring self for a fulfillment that will deliver it from the anxieties of fertility over the wasteland."[14]

Romance is suspense, the tale. Sex is detail, the proof. Sex is also the turning point, the climax, the culmination, the end. Romance begins with the turn-on. It makes the clock start ticking. Sex is the test, the apotheosis of romance, the transubstantiation of romance into the body. In Frye's terms, sex is fulfillment, as pregnancy is fertility. Sex is validation, affirmation, the response of the body that, like the pea under the mattress, the battle with the dragon, is thought to make it impossible to lie about two crucial issues: identity (worthiness) and desire. Romance is the promise, the hope, the contract in draft, unsigned.

For a few teenage girls, the quest-romance takes the light form extolled by magazines like *Self* and *Cosmopolitan*, that of a cheerful sexual adventurousness, a compounding of the self through sexual accumulation, intermixed with episodes of coupledom. A teenage girl intercepted in a shopping mall, for example, responded to questioning about romance with this comment:

"Oh, I love romance. I do, I do. I love a lot of things about love. . . . You know, you get that special feeling. That feels good. I'm going to meet somebody now. . . . The other ones are just lust, you know. You just like to be with them but this one I love. I know I do."

But for most, and certainly for most white, working-class, heterosexual girls, the quest is highly serious. It is goal-directed promiscuity, and the omnipresent grail remains love: true, monogamous, permanent, one-man, one-woman couple love.

It is a sign of how integral this ideal is to the understanding of what makes life worth living that neither feminism nor the changing imperatives of labor force participation on which feminism increasingly places such reliance have affected teenage girls' dedication to it more than slightly. Most girls expect to work in their adult lives, but overall not even middle-class girls seem to expect that richness and meaning will come to them through work, although in the wake of an unhappy love affair, a teenager may allude to a career on which she is at least temporarily placing her fragile hopes:

"My idea of what I want to do right now is to get a career that I love, like being a legal secretary or something so that I can be totally independent of a guy. Whereas, if I marry somebody or even live with somebody and they leave me, I won't have anything to worry about because I'll be totally independent. That's definitely what I want to do. There's no question about it."

Work is on the teenage girl's agenda, generally, for pragmatic reasons. The possible death of passion is now as practical a consideration as the death of a provider. Even assuming the most optimistic curve for her economic and romantic future – a partner who stays in love, employed, and alive – it is unlikely that one partner will be able to earn enough to take care of a family throughout its span. These are the reasons to prepare for work. They are not inspirational except in so far as they concern financing love.

When teenagers like the one above talk about putting their hopes, or some of their hopes, on work, generally there is a swift return to the idea of relationship and love. In the instance given, this occurred in the next sentence: "Second of all, I want the ideal relationship with a guy. I guess I want somebody to love me and care about me as much as I do them. I think I deserve that."

Whether the measure is compatibility or obsession, fulfillment or fertility, accommodation or surrender, for teenage girls romance is, at bottom, the quest for life after separation. Separation is a major issue in adolescence. The feminist understanding of this complicated process begins with Freud who observed that girls had only to separate enough to avoid frigidity, while boys had to separate more thoroughly because society needed them to establish "higher social units" and could not afford to have them "swallowed up by the family."[15] Freud's observation provoked the feminist recognition of the centrality of separation for girls, and feminist theorists responded that both genders had to, as Chodorow has phrased it, "give up . . . incestuous love objects . . . in favor of other primary objects . . . to go out into the nonfamilial relational world."[16] Changing economic and social conditions have made this theoretical argument material necessity for many girls, compounding the psycho-analytic issues of separation with historical ones. Separation of this magnitude represents a considerable shift in girls' tradition, and the close identification between mother and daughter and the continuing cultural pressure toward domesticity and femininity make this a wrenching, disorienting experience for girls in the current period.[17]

In this context, romance can serve as a halfway house on the road to autonomy and separation. When romantic expectations and possibilities are in relative accord, when the body is assuaged and diverted with pleasure, romance and sex can make separation much easier, exchanging sensuality and sexuality for parental comfort and embraces; reversing and at the same time continuing the process of making the unconscious, a process of fascination and illumination. As an enticement to leave the family behind, to commence the odyssey of discovery, romance is essential to the path that leads toward autonomy and also to the path that leads to modes of collectivity other than the familial. But the difficulty of combining love and work, the tendency to, rather, exchange one for the other, can make romance instead a dead-end. And when romance goes badly, it adds to the anxiety of separation. It is like being abandoned by a lover the day one's parents die. In this period, particularly, romance is a profoundly heroic if still hypnotic discipline, one of risk and instruction; a matter less of momentary pleasures, honeyed soporific words, and the ensuing chains of love, than of bitter pills and empty arms. For increasingly, as we will see, romance is an isolate's path, the brave and lonely search for women's booty, a perilous journey on which one risks the self.

3   Teenage girls and second-wave feminists: parallels, distinctions

To understand the sexual and romantic dilemma of teenage girls in the 1980s, it is necessary to acknowledge a historical distinction between second-wave feminists, who came of age for the most part of the 1960s, and teenagers in the 1980s. This distinction may seem labored – obviously time has passed – but it has to be drawn, because some of the best feminist work on teenagers rests on an assumption that sprang initially from the fact that many feminists were barely out of their teens when they made the nearby opening bids of second-wave discourse. The assumption is that teenage girls and adult feminists have the same interests – whether for protection or liberation – and the same history. This assumption continues for many subtle reasons. It may reflect, for example a tendency to think of adolescence not as a mutable developmental stage open to economic and cultural influences, but as fixed by biology. It may stem from the habit of universalizing experience. "I was a teenager," we think, "and so I know how it is," forgetting that time, as well as many other differences, may have made that experience specific. Perhaps it also signals a residual tendency to think of women as children.[18] More influential, I suspect, is the increasing similarity between adolescent and adult sexual lifestyles. While adolescents are now, like adults, sexually active, adults follow a seemingly perpetual courtship pattern that places them on common ground – and sometimes in actual competition – with teenage girls.[19] The equation of adulthood with the thirty-year marriage is a deep one in our culture, but so is the equation of sexual activity with adulthood, with the result that we tend to think of sexually active adolescents as adults and of sexually active unmarried adults as adolescents.

On the whole, the identification of second-wave feminists with teenage girls has had healthy consequences for practice. While those who conflate adolescence with childhood have tended to argue, in the name of protection, for imprisoning teenage girls in the asexual preserve of innocence, those who have identified with – as? – teenagers have staunchly defended the outer boundaries of teenage sexual freedom and reproductive rights on the conviction that teenage girls, like all women, have the right to control their own bodies. Without these rights, no autonomous teenage culture incorporating a liberated (that is, not taboo) sexuality can take shape. But at the same time identification with teenage girls has led feminists to overlook the extent to which sexual and reproductive conditions have changed with the result that second-wave discourse no longer resonates for teenage girls as it once did.

Before the 1970s, sex itself probably constituted the greatest risk connected with romance for girls. The throw-of-the-dice probability of pregnancy was everpresent. In addition, the female teenage sexual adventurer ran a high risk of being declared a sexual outlaw. Most girls institutionalized in the study Gisela Konopka recorded in *The Adolescent Girl in Conflict* (1966) were reported as having "some problems in relation to sex." These problems included simply being sexually active. Miscegenation was cited frequently, and lesbianism and out-of-wedlock pregnancy were clear grounds for institutionalization.[20] Institutionalization may have been an extreme or chiefly class-bound practice, but the rules of sex and gender harshly affected many teenage girls more generally. Many had illegal abortions as teenagers or bore children they would not have had under other circumstances. Girls "in trouble" – a euphemism for pregnant – were shunted off to homes for unwed mothers or married to lovers whom they would more gladly have never seen again had there been another way out. The protocol of popularity and the strictures of the double standard constituted more subtle, but nevertheless rigid, forms of sexual control.

In the 1970s, conditions shifted significantly. In 1972 in *Eisenstadt* v. *Baird*, the Supreme Court held that single as well as married people had a right to contraception; in 1973 in *Roe* v. *Wade* the Court found abortion a matter of privacy between a woman and her doctor. The right of a minor to purchase over-the-counter contraception was not established until 1977. The political exposure to feminist sexual theory was very important to the shifts in sexual opinion as well. Institutionalization became less common, although some teenage girls, particularly those living with single mothers, may still be placed in institutions as persons in need of supervision (PINS). With the inception of the lesbian and gay movements, the social context for lesbian teenagers changed also.[21]

The familial context has changed as well. The sexual politic of women's liberation took shape in the context of rhetoric of domestic isolationism and nuclearity.[22] For teenage girls in the current period, the illusion of nuclear-family security has given way to a rising sense that intimate divisions are a statistical probability and that men cannot be depended upon for commitment or provision. One recent study indicated that of children born in the 1968-9 cohort, 15 per cent had experienced a family break-up by age one, and almost 40 per cent by age thirteen. As the divorce rate was higher in the 1970s than the 1960s, the researchers hypothesized that "the number who would not reside with both . . . parents throughout childhood could reach half the population." In addition, almost 40 per cent of those living with a single mother either had had no communication with the father in the past five years or didn't even know if he was living.[23] It is not necessary to participate in the neo-conservative lament about the decline of the patriarchal family to recognize that this is a very different picture from that of the protectionist crucible that shaped second-wave feminist conclusions about what had to be won from life and what was likely to be lost.[24]

Overall these changes had enormous significance for young women, and they are key to understanding teenage sexual and romantic experience in the 1980s. For second-wave feminists the quest was for freedom – for example, for the right to have or not to have sex as a matter of individual choice. Independence, for example, could be vaunted in second-wave discourse partly because it seemed impossible to achieve. The family was perceived, whatever may have been the reality, as inescapably smothering. In contrast, for teenage girls in the 1980s – some of whom played "women's lib" instead of "house" in childhood –

independence appears inescapable, and this is particularly so for those who pin their hopes on men. Relative freedom seems to loom in all its threat and possibility.

As insubstantial and transitory as this freedom may be in view of the persistent right-wing siege against teenage sexual privacy and freedom, it has nevertheless lasted a lifetime for girls coming of sexual age in the 1980s: It seems the given, not the goal. The disbelief with which teenagers greeted the Squeal Law indicated how much teenage sexual rights are already taken for granted. Dealing with the expansion, however limited, of sexual freedom is already a part of peer tradition. Older sisters tell war stories about the problems of sexual freedom. Thus, although some teenage girls still have to stuggle within the family or within their narrow communities for the space and time to be autonomous in any terms, by and large the quest is less for freedom than to win something, to make something out of freedom. The problem is what and how – and is it possible.

The task is to reconstruct the relation between permanence and liberty, adventure and security. To an extent, teenage girls are struggling with the problem nineteenth-century feminists predicted when they argued against breaking the connection between sex and reproduction on the grounds that it constituted the only way women had to persuade men to commit themselves to relationship.[25] But it is, finally, not a problem of enforcement but of vision. It demands facing the deconstruction of sex, romance, and intimacy and renegotiating the bargain between the genders. Under the strain of this task, teenage girls often try to retreat, as this paper will begin to show, into traps that feminism recently sprang at least partly free of: compulsory monogamy and premarital chastity; the double standard; the flypaper dreams of motherhood, the nuclear family; true and eternal love, whether lesbian or heterosexual. But at the same time, many find themselves moving, or choosing to move, beyond the magnetic field of nineteenth- and earlier twentieth-century taboo, taking for themselves romantic and sexual agency, and moving onto relatively uncharted ground, at least for adolescents in our period, reinvesting romance with Oedipal material, taking psychological and economic risks rather than enduring meaninglessness or the chasm of perpetual separation. It is important to note that retreat by no means describes the full range of teenage girls' sexual and romantic choice.

Below I will describe the salient details of heterosexual working-class teenage sex and romance in the 1980s in order to establish a context for discussing a painful, organizing sexual experience for many teenage girls in this period as they address the new sexual provisos. Finally, I will suggest some of the implications of this material for feminist practice.

4 First love

In the texts, romance begins with desiring or being desired, with liking or being liked, or with the onset of romantic longing.

"So one day Don passed by in his truck when I was in a car with Shelly. He pulled up to my side, and I'm sitting there like, 'Oh my God,' and he's looking at me and saying, 'Who's that blonde? Who's that blonde? I've got to meet that girl. I love that girl.' So he told Shelly he wanted to meet me but I knew he was dating this girl Julie in this other town and I said, 'Well, everybody's telling me, don't get involved with him. He's the wrong guy to get involved with because he dates too many girls.' "

Or:

"But like I was walking to meet her, and he was there, and then I met him, and I said, 'Hi.' and all this, but then right after that, the next day, I think I liked him."

Or:

"If something is going to happen, then I'll daydream. If we're going to have a test or something like that ... like if I meet a boy, like what will happen in the future or something.... It just comes and goes ... happy sometimes, exciting, just different feelings."

Or, in contrast, a lesbian:

"It was a mostly black school. There were some white kids in the school but not many, and then this gorgeous, beautiful Hispanic girl did not join in the teasing. She told them to lay off. Less than a week later, we discovered that we lived sort of in the same neighborhood, and we started taking the bus home together. Then we discovered we didn't want to take the bus home together. We wanted to walk because it meant more time talking. Both of us had our own ideas about the world.... We'd start out talking about school, and we'd end up talking about the situation in China ... and within three months, I was so in love with the girl. It was amazing."

Women, it has been said, can romanticize anyone, while men romanticize women on the basis of their appearance.[26] There is a good deal of evidence for this in the descriptions girls give of the boys and men with whom they have found themselves – or made themselves – enchanted; for example:

"He was a slob. I mean, in everything else, he was so nice, but he was such a slob. He'd wear his clothes for like a week at a time. Never take a bath. It stunk sometimes. Really. He's got a pudge nose ... sandy blond hair. It's more brown now, but it's like ... he used to get these big globs of knots. I mean like a nest, and he wouldn't cut them out. Like you would try and comb them out.... One day I had him, and I was pulling them out, and he was screaming . . . and it was this big bump. It was disgusting really. Now he's got short hair . . . but it doesn't really go anywhere. It's so straight and stringy. I mean, he ain't good looking. No way."[27]

Although the bodily stakes have changed somewhat and the ante is up – that is, each sexual stage probably takes place somewhat earlier than it used to, although not so much earlier as the sensationalist accounts would have it – the early stages of romance are still differentiated by gender.[28] He: Will she let me? She: Does he care for me? It is extremely rare for a teenage girl to tell a story about wanting to go farther sexually than her partner (although she may wish for more pleasure) and this has never arisen in an interview with a white working-class girl. The classic story of sexual progress is the same old story.

"They'll pressure a girl. They'll tell her they love her so much, and they don't want to leave her. They'll say anything. . . . When I was little the big things were just little things – like, if he wanted to put his hand up your shirt or something. You know. 'My God, should I let him?' That was the big thing, you know. Come on. Then as you got older, you figured out, 'What the hell. It's nothing.' Then . . . it was like, 'I want to get down.' They'd come right out and say it. I'd go, 'You know, I can't believe you're saying that.' And they'd go, 'Come on, now, what's the matter with it,' and you'd get into this big, long discussion."

Descriptions of pre-coital sexual experience, like the one above, raise the question of what has changed in teenage non-coital or pre-coital sex. This is difficult to judge. Tales of conquest or successful sexual negotiation generally relate non-coital sex to coital. The idea that non-coital sex may constitute an episode in its own right, a story with a proper ending, has virtually no standing, except among certain cultural feminists who eschew penetration and for whom non-coital sex therefore constitutes the only acceptable sexual episode.[29] In contrast, the language of negotiation and conquest is highly articulated throughout most of the culture, and it is an integral part of the fabric of most sexual tales. Pull out this thread and it seems there is no story at all. This is partly because, particularly for girls, centering a story around pleasure itself is taboo in the extreme. It is far less forbidden to say, "I had sex," than to say, "I had pleasure."

Taboo is not the only reason such statements are rare. Another reason may be that there is less petting in adolescence than in other periods. At least, in comparison with the documentation on petting in other periods compiled by contemporary historians as well as with the findings of Kinsey and others, there seems a striking absence of petting in the life histories. Petting constituted the chief sexual activity for the young after the end of the disciplined sexual forms of bundling and night-courting and before the rise of non-marital teenage sexual intercourse. Historians Christine Stansell and Kathy Peiss have offered evidence that petting became common practice among working girls in the mid-nineteenth century, and historian Paula Fass indicates that there was a very developed cuture of petting in the 1920s.[30] Kinsey also documented an extensive culture of petting in the late 1930s through the 1940s, noting that:

many girls attend dances or other social activities where they may become involved in petting with several different males in a single evening. In many cases the petting is limited to simple kisses and caresses; in other cases it quickly turns to those techniques which are specifically calculated to bring sexual arousal and possibly orgasm.

Kinsey's cohort research indicated that petting to orgasm had increased since the turn of the century.[31]

In contrast to Kinsey's description or orgasmic sexual play with a number of partners, the life histories seem to describe a flat sexual landscape – one of few partners, a limited repertoire of sexual activities, and relatively little pleasure, particularly orgasmic pleasure. With the lifting of the injunction against teenage coitus, it seems, coitus became the new rule. The life histories contain very few descriptions of non-coital petting, and most of these are early pubertal descriptions of exploratory sexual games or mock dates, which do not include references to desire or sexual feeling. Because the double standard continues to hold sway – in fact, teenage girls rely on it to give them a modicum of sexual power in their negotiations with boys to a troubling degree – this apparent coitalization has been accompanied by a rule of monogamous true love. Girls attempt to extend the rule of true love to boys but on the whole it is girls who practice monogamy, however serially. The shift away from forepleasure is probably temporary. There is no reason to believe that where intercourse is permitted, forepleasure and seduction must fall by the wayside. On the contrary, we know, for example, that among adults of all classes forepleasure and other once primarily aristocratic nonreproductive sexual modes have been increasingly practiced since the nineteenth century.[32] The likelihood is rather that coitalization and the apparent reduction in the range of sexual activities is a function of the relatively recent taboo on adolescent coitus and will shift as that taboo fades farther into the past. The association of monogamy – however serial – with adolescent intercourse seems more entrenched, however, and it raises serious questions. Monogamy is a protection against the depredations of sexual exploitation but it exacts a high price in rigidifying and narrowing the range of sexual exploration, and of social interaction.

In the 1920s, if one may trust F. Scott Fitzgerald, a first kiss constituted the divide between the innocence of childhood and the beginning of sexual life. The primary dividing line for teenage girls in the 1980s is virginity, and this is so whether a girl resolves the issues of sexual initiation in relative autonomy or under intense external pressure, in a state of desire aroused by forepleasure or with the desire solely to meet the challenge. The idea of waiting until marriage or true love or at least until someone proves he or she cares prevails as a theoretical ideal among teenage girls in almost every group. In heterosexual practice it is hard to arrange since teenage boys, in the throes of the male version of separation, seem equally set on proving to themselves that they can get under the skin of a woman without feeling a thing, without ceding a single fresh cell of memory, without crossing a single synapse back toward infancy, without losing an iota of self, of manhood.[33]

There are a number of reasons for the widely held significance of virginity in teenage sexual and romantic life. It is a central theme in some of the most ancient and reverberating stories in western culture. The hymen is Sleeping Beauty's wall of thorns; it is the beleaguered castle. It is stigma and emblem; protection and inhibition; trial and proof. The idea that a hero must be scorched by passion, pricked to bleeding by conscience and desire, and that the heroine must be sexually asleep in a latency trance so strong that she is virtually in a coma, is learned almost as early as speech by almost every girl child in the country.[34]

Far from being something that teenage girls take lightly, then, as the media and the new right would have it, first intercourse is loaded down with expectations and symbolic weight. It is as if in the world view of teenage girls, the whole sex/gender system – those arrangements by which, to cite anthropologist Gayle Rubin's useful definition, "the biological raw material of human sex and procreation is shaped by human, social intervention, and satisfied in a conventional manner" – depends now on the initiation of heterosexual intercourse.[35]

In this light, the intensity of the bargaining over virginity can be understood as deriving from the belief, or suspicion, that first intercourse is an absolute test of the chances for a committed relationship and a test of sexual worth. To get an accurate reading on these questions, one must do more than bargain: one must give it up. For the real question is, Will he be enthralled by me? Am I in the possession of the power of sex? Here is the paradox: these questions can only be addressed by having sex.

Yet in having sex a girl risks what she thinks may be the only thing she has to gamble. And the refrain still runs in the back of her head: once he gets what he wants. . . .

Sex is the spin of the coin. There are only two possible answers: yes or no. With so much at stake, you want to play when the time is right, when the moon is full, when the tides of the body are so strong that they must surely sweep the two of you into the future. As to her desire, it is postponed. The most cynical, sophisticated teenage girl hopes at least for a moment to remember that he will remember too. Like contraception, her desire awaits a "closer relationship."[36]

How does first intercourse stack up against these expectations?

It is fortunate, perhaps, that the expectations are not directed toward the notion of erotic pleasure, for again, contrary to the propaganda, this aspect of teenage sex and romance is very seldom about unearthing the hidden, buccaneer treasure of the body.

"He was very gentle with me. Very. He couldn't have been more gentle and just the way he talked with me – aw. But it felt like there was a knife going through me. It really hurt a lot. The pain was like I couldn't take it."

"I was dying. I was so scared. . . . It was all right."

For comparison, a middle-class narrative:

"Well, I had tripped the night before. I was very exhausted, and I was supposed to be going up to his house to talk it out because I felt really shitty about the whole thing. Instead of talking it out, we had ended up kissing, and it was a very cold day. It was in October. It was very cold, and we were on the floor in his room. And I said, "This is very uncomfortable. Can we go up in your loft?" So I guess he assumed that I wanted to screw, and I had never done that, and I just really didn't assume that. But after we started kissing and touching and everything like that, I didn't really feel uncomfortable about screwing. I just felt fine about it until *during*. I mean, during wasn't so great. During felt like, Why was this happening to me? This was so horrible. It wasn't horrible. It was just not great. It wasn't . . . I was expecting it to be much nicer than it felt. It didn't hurt or anything. It just didn't feel really good."

Lesbian narratives about sexual initiation have a very different texture, probably largely because they do not usually include defloration. The lesbian equivalent of "giving it up" may be the first sexual experience with a woman that is perceived as lesbian – that is, that involves giving up the sense of oneself as heterosexual, as straight. Only sometimes is this the first lesbian experience *per se*. In general, lesbian narratives about early sexual experience – as opposed to initiation, which is probably not a fair comparison because of the variable of defloration – more often include references to pleasure and less often include references to discomfort. Frequently, they recount the guilt one partner may feel for having initiated another. (Guilt may appear in a heterosexual history as well, but generally the girl feels guilty, not for having initiated the boy but for having had sex herself.) Here is one lesbian report. The narrator is a black college student, recalling her high-school initiation. In another section of the history, she recounted having read hundreds of Harlequin and other heterosexual romance novels without any sense of discrepancy between heterosexual romance plots and her own experience and desire. She also told of having begun to feel sexual tension among her girlfriends during the religious retreats they attended as a group.[37]

"It was a particularly tense evening. Oh, Jeanie was spending the night. We were both staying at my sister's. She and I had been sort of becoming very tense, and it seemed as if we had known that sort of thing was going to happen. I don't think that anything at all provoked it but . . . oh, for some reason my sister wasn't there. I think she had gone to see a movie with her roommate or something. All that was involved at that point was kissing and petting and things like that, and my sister came in and that sort of broke it up abruptly. I think that we both sort of expected it to start just because that was the way the conversations had been going. I guess there were things about, 'Well, what do gay people do?' And, 'Why would anyone be interested in someone of the same sex?' And things like that. That same night we resumed things later on and Jeanie was extremely upset about it. She kept a bottle of, I don't know, Darvon. She was so upset at having 'led me astray,' quote unquote, that she threatened to take the entire bottle. She was very dramatic."

Q: "How did you feel about it?"

A: "Pretty adventurous. . . . I was very conscious of the romantic or that I was supposed to feel swept away. I really didn't have a clue of what I was supposed to have been doing, but I was very conscious of what I was supposed to have been feeling and sort of felt that way. Looking back, I don't think that was necessarily true arousal, but it was perceived to be."

The question that the heterosexual passages raise, particularly in conjunction with the paucity of foreplay, is why so little pleasure? Is it simply that defloration is necessarily painful? Why then are the descriptions of the early experiences following initiation generally also lacking in pleasure? One possibility is that the lovers are new, and sexual pleasure is both skill and an acquired taste. A girl who waits passively for a male peer to pleasure her may have a long wait. Another possibility – one that is supported by the lack of any mention of pre-coital desire in the texts – is that many girls are having sex before they are ready, that is, before desire is aroused, before, as the Central Indian tribe, the Muria, described by Elwin, express it, "the falling of the waters."[38] Girls may choose to have sex perhaps because they are giving in to sexual pressure but also out of sexual curiosity and a desire to take on the challenge of sex, as a trial or a *rite de passage*. The absence of desire need not be developmental, however, but may be rather a function of the lack of foreplay and the lack of a belief that a girl contemplating sex has a right to desire. Indeed, a girl may view her own desire as counter-productive in sexual negotiations, for reasons explored below.

The absence of pleasure, as well as that of desire, arises from other sources as well. It seems likely that many teenage girls are so entrenched in the good-girl socialization described by Webster and Gilbert in *Bound by Love* that they never think of pleasure, and it is fairly clear that issues of strategy are also involved: that girls are working not on a pleasure principle, but attempting to pull off the old bargain on slender contemporary grounds: as I let you take me bit by bit, you must commit yourself to me in equal measure. Trading pleasure for pleasure largely undercuts that sort of bargain; that is, if it is recognized that a girl enjoys sex as a boy does, and the boy considers his pleasure enough – all he wants from sex – how can she persuade him to pay for sex in the coin of intimacy?

Finally, as Dinnerstein argues in *The Mermaid and the Minotaur*, giving up pleasure may be the penalty girls pay to make up for disloyalty to the mother in transferring erotic ties to the male. (This may partially explain why teenage lesbians talk more about pleasure than heterosexual teenagers.) Dinnerstein eloquently describes the cost of these manoeuvers when she argues that the double standard that permits pleasure for men and not women injures

the animal center of self-respect: the brute sense of bodily prerogative, of having a right to one's bodily feelings. A conviction that physical urges which one cannot help having are unjustified, undignified, presumptuous, undercuts the deepest, oldest basis for a sense of worth; it contaminates the original wellspring of subjective autonomy.[39]

On the most pragmatic grounds, it is a bad bargain as well: the girl who trades off pleasure for permanence is giving up one modest good she might be able to get for something she is highly unlikely to win.

A rare interview with a middle-class teenager who had the good fortune to have a first lover with whom she had oral sex but not intercourse (an extremely unusual instance) and a second lover who was remarkable for reasons having to do with his alternative, liberal upbringing and education, suggests how differently first intercourse might come about:

"Like he said, 'Do you want to sleep over?' and I said, 'Yeah,' and he said – he'd always say – 'Do you want to have sex?' and I'd say, 'Yeah, I really do. I want to have sex with you, but when the time is right, you know.' And he'd say, 'Okay, okay,' and he'd never force it on me or anything. And that night when we had sex, you know, he said 'Do you want to?' and I said, 'Yeah, I do, but just be really careful.' He was really, really good. I mean, really good about it. Really nice. He made me feel really good and like . . . it didn't hurt a lot. I mean, of course, it hurt a little bit but it didn't really hurt as much as I had expected because I heard from . . . two of my best friends, 'Oh, it killed, it killed. I really was going to tell him to stop, but I just figured I'd go through with it.' They made it sound like such a heavy, hurtful thing. So I was surprised because he made me feel so comfortable . . . and the next day, and I had told him, 'You were really sweet to me, and it was really nice.' He would just say, 'Relax, don't worry about it. I won't hurt you. Tell me if I'm hurting you,' and stuff like that. And then we started having sex all the time."

Having sex all the time is rarely the aftermath of first sexual intercourse for teenage girls, particularly not for teenagers who start sexual activity before age fifteen, for whom the interval between first and second intercourse is more than four times longer than for women who begin sexual relations at seventeen or over. One reason may be simply that it is not an experience they want to repeat, since it isn't pleasurable particularly, and probably also doesn't inspire sacred devotion in their lover.[40] To the extent that first intercourse constituted a challenge, a rite of passage, it is behind them. Why repeat the experience until desire presses? The decision not to repeat it is relatively easy to live with. It involves the exercise of autonomy. So, too, does deciding to continue a relationship that is valuable in some sense. But the third scenario has a jagged edge. It's the old story line from *True Romance*: girl gives in, girl gets dumped.

The common explanation is another old one: He only wanted one thing. But why does he only want one thing? The classic feminist explanation inherited from social purity is that men are lusting beasts, and we have a lingering tendency to think of teenage boys as being possessed by a variety of wander-lust that drives them from girl to girl led by a magic sword with a mind of its own. And so it may be. But it seems as likely that teenage sex is deeply unnerving to boys, much as they desire and seek it, because of the disjuncture between what sex is really like and what coming of sexual age as a man is thought to be. Becoming a man is a matter of arming oreself in a muscled body, becoming impermeable (unlike permeable women), being immovable, a super-man, a man of steel, while actually going to bed with a woman involves taking off one's clothes, becoming naked and to some extent dependent, and going out of control: returning, in other words, to the wild, helpless, luxurious state of infancy. To be naked and fondled by a woman is to be a baby not a man – particularly if one ejaculates prematurely. Nothing in culture and nothing in gender socialization prepares a boy for this experience, and under the circumstances it doesn't seem surprising if he turns his face from his first lovers as he must, as a male, from his mother, in order to sever his connection with women and thereby declare himself a man. Lastly, there are economic factors operating as well. The job picture may look as bleak to boys as the romantic picture looks to girls. A boy who foresees an adulthood of unemployment may imagine himself totally swallowed up in domestic life, an abhorrent fate to one socialized for autonomy and separation. The work of historian Ellen Ross on working-class domestic life in nineteenth-century England is suggestive here in its indication that when economic conditions do not enable men to become husband-providers, they may conceive of themselves in other roles, for example, as lovers, as dandy, as miscellaneous man about town.[41]

But whether a boy acts out of beastliness, terror, or depressed economic expectations, the experience of breaking up soon after beginning to have sexual intercourse is none the less agonizing for the girl, and this may be so even when she requests or consciously brings about the break-up.

5   Breaking up is hard to do. . . .

To understand the pain of breaking up, it is necessary to remember what is at stake and how little is won. To a great extent, it is a problem of expectation, of too much riding on a bet made with the worst kind of odds. Sex, intimacy, and permanence are fused. It is an all-or-nothing ideal. Virginity is seen as perhaps the most valuable possession one will ever be able to exchange for love. Exposing sexuality is equated with making the deepest self vulnerable. (Again, biology is invested with significance it need not have for want of any other system of meaning.) Adolescent sex is not seen, as dating mainly was, as a practice game, but as, if not the real thing, then the same as the real thing will be.

Sexuality is perceived as the link with the future. She who is found worthy thinks herself assured of a future of esteem and caresses as well as financial help, if not unflagging support. But she who imagines that she has not been proven worthy foresees a lonely and dull future, a humiliating abyss, or – more statistically probable – a frantic life of single motherhood, a life leeched by low wages, a thousand responsibilities, and few gratifications but those of obligation and maternal sublimation.[42]

Before she has sex, a teenager may imagine that for her it will be different. Her mother, or the older women around her, were fools. They didn't know what was important or they didn't have what it took to get what was important and keep it. Secure in adolescent omnipotence, she is at once arrogant and innocent. Yet she also knows there is reason for fear. When her presumption is thrown into doubt by experience, she enters a period of existential terror. The cold glories of omnipotence give way to the hot muck of obsession and despair.

The monogamization that – for girls, at any rate – has accompanied the coitalization of adolescent sexuality heightens the pain and the sense of danger that teenage girls feel when a break-up occurs on the heels of first intercourse. On the most pragmatic level, the problem is simply that the girl probably doesn't have any other boyfriends. Very likely, she hasn't lined up any on the sidelines either, because to do so would be to evidence a lack of faith in the "true love" that makes it all right to have sex. It seems to be considered bad faith, also, to rapidly search out a replacement. The pre-coital waiting period and the post-coital period of mourning are an integral part of the symbolic proof that love was "true" – that is, not transient, not impermanent, not a form of vagrancy. While these waiting periods are essential to self-respect, they also undermine self-respect, because they increase the sense of isolation, the sense that one will never be loved.

The loss of sex itself may also contribute to the pain of breaking up. For all that first coitus does not generally reverberate with pleasure, it is probably the first recapture of infantile sexuality. This recapture takes place under the transformed circumstances of the post-pubescent body and it includes reciprocal enjoyment (however minimal for the girl). Mature sexuality is not the same as infantile sexuality but it is so very like that it raises a dual terror: first, the terror that one is returning to the helplessness and dependency of infancy. Second, that the accompanying voluptuousness will be lost and forbidden again: that it will never return, or that one will have to wait another decade-and-a-half – in adolescent terms another lifetime (that is, as long as one has waited this time around) for the next dip into the naked and reciprocal pleasures. Just because the pleasures may fail on the first few tries does not mean that the body has no intuition, sparked by memory, nurtured by culture, that they may well forth.[43] (A rare sign that teenage girls realize sex can become pleasurable for girls is suggested by the frequent remark, "I'm not one of those that can't live without it," which suggests that another reason for evading sexual pleasure is that sex is perceived to be an addiction that may lead to further and further degradation at the hands of the pushers of sex.

This is hardly a paradise of sexual freedom. The archetypal quest-romance is more on target: the hero risks ritual death.[44] Two examples:

"I was hysterical. He told me this over a phone, and if he told me in person, I would have killed him. I would have killed him."

"It's really had an effect on me. I've become very quiet. That is not me. I am not a quiet girl. I go to parties, and I'll go to clubs with my friends. I didn't stop living. I still go out. But I find that I can't talk to guys. I'll sit there and I won't say a word. I'll sit there all night with my drink in my hand. I'll have my cigarettes. I'll laugh with my friends a little maybe. But I am not the same person. I'm very inactive. I'm eating a lot. I'm gaining weight because of him. But that's only little parts of it. I can't even begin to explain how I feel inside. I almost killed myself over him. I was taking somebody home and I was thinking about him and I was really depressed. I was thinking I really didn't want to live anymore. I was making a u-turn. You know how you look in your rear view mirror and somebody's coming right alongside and you don't see them? I didn't even think to look over to the side. I just smashed right into him and this guy said if I didn't jump out of the way just in time, I could have had my legs crushed. That was all over him."

In this state of depression, girls who previously did well in school may begin to fail. They cut classes. They drop out. And often they confront the reality of pregnancy as well.[45]

6 Sexual retreats

One common reaction is to try to go backwards, to reconstruct not only the old world of limits and permissions, taboos and guarantees, but even to reconstruct the body. One teenager, for example, in describing her first experience of intercourse, declared at the end: "But it was nothing. Like he didn't even have an orgasm inside of me. I couldn't really consider it making love to him. Not really. I kept pushing him off." She went on to reconstruct her previously held declaration of sexual limits:

"No one's ever going to hurt me that way again and I'll make sure of it. I'm not saying I'll never be hurt again but I'll try my hardest to avoid it. My idea right now is that I don't think I'm ever going to let a guy touch me again until I'm engaged or married. Until I'm sure that guy means it. I'm not saying that he's going to stay with me for the rest of his life, but until I'm sure that relationship means as much to him as it does to me and until I'm positively proven that it does, there's going to be no way that guy is going to lay a hand on me. That's my attitude right now and that's the way it's going to stay."

But it didn't. And another: "I guess we had the right love at the wrong time. . . . I won't let no one else touch me. Never again. It's either Lenny or nobody." These retreats back into pseudo-virginity, into an ideal of chastity, partly explain the statistics showing a delay between first and second intercourse. But second intercourse occurs generally, and at that point, teenage girls seem to feel compelled to come up with another set of limits. Oral sex is frequently placed off-limits by teenage girls, and this seems more prevalent among working-class than middle-class girls although it is by no means an exclusively working-class reaction.[46] Generally, the subject of oral sex comes up in the course of a teenager making a distinction between herself and another girl; for example –

"That girl has a very bad reputation. Like she used to give guys, uhm, blowjobs? Once Joey asked me for a blowjob. I couldn't believe he asked me that, and he said, 'Well, you hang out with her.' "

And a teenager from a relatively better-off suburb, largely Catholic, in a big city:

"She was really possessive. Really kiss ass. She went to his house every day. After work, she was there. And if he wasn't there, she'd sit and have coffee with his mom. She called him every day at work. She made herself available to him whenever he wanted her. She called him four or five times a day. She really kissed his ass, and I didn't even do that. And she did like oral sex and stuff like that. I never really got into that, you know. Everything was new to me. I never felt that way in my *life* about anybody besides him."

It is important to note that not all discriminations about what is or is not acceptable are so traditional. These discriminations can take "bizarre forms."[47] For example, a working-class punk teenager from an industrial area described her sexual life with a man she lived with when she was sixteen as follows:

"I'm not sadomasochistic. I mean, in a way, I am, but I mean I'm not going to pull a machete on somebody and go, 'Whoa, fuck me or I'll kill you.' I haven't gotten to that point yet. I mean, like that guy I was living with during the summer. . . . He wasn't that bad, but he was pretty s-s-s-adistic or whatever. . . . He'd have spikes on, like here. He always had them on. Always. And he'd just be, he was also like into self-inflicted cuts and shit, and he always had like cuts and swastikas cut into his legs and shit and the part about it that I really couldn't say anything was that he wasn't really fucked up on drugs. I mean, he'd do drugs and trip, but he wasn't really fucked up on them to the point where he didn't know what he was doing. He did know what he was doing, and he was intelligent, but he was just so pissed off. I think if you're intelligent, you get madder because you really know what's going on. . . . He would like push me around and shit but he'd never like, uh, sit down and beat the hell out of me and say, 'If you don't do this because I'm a guy and I'm stronger.' He never came to that toward anything. . . ."

Q: "Then what was the violence?"

A. "I guess just like sexually itself, just the way we were. We weren't like two submissive little kids – ahh, I'm really in love and blushing and all that shit. Violence is sexually exciting to a certain point. If there's a gun to your head, I don't think that's sexually exciting. Or he beats the hell out of you with a lead pipe. Like there's certain points . . . where it's like, forget it, you know. It just depends on the person. . . . I remember he was like into handcuffs and all that bullshit and stuff like that, but nothing that would like break my arms or anything. Nothing that – I mean, I'd have black and blue marks and shit but nothing would bother me. Black and blue marks never bothered me. Like I go slamdancing and I come home black and blue, but it doesn't bother me."

The sexual line drawn by this teenager – and drawn firmly and rigidly – placed lesbianism absolutely out of bounds.

"I've been in that situation where I was hanging around with one of my friends and he was with his girlfriend and she went after me and I just freaked out on her. I said, 'Get away from me. Just get away from me,' and I started freaking out."

"There is a fine line," she said in a slightly different context, "between everything."

Others may have sex only with girls (the intention here may be to save their heterosexual virginity for marriage) or refuse to associate with anyone who has sex with both genders (that is, the line is against bisexuality). Still others may have sex only if "he" or "she" cares. The variations are not limitless but any available set of yes and no sexual definitions may be seized for the purpose. Like computer hardware, adolescent sexuality tends toward the binary.

But to what purpose? Of what possible use is it to permit s&m but not lesbianism, or to permit intercourse but not oral sex? To permit lesbianism but save intercourse for marriage? To permit lesbianism or heterosexuality but not bisexuality? To permit premarital or nonmarital pregnancy but not promiscuity or lesbianism?

A flippant but not altogether superficial answer is that these limits are meant to serve many of the same purposes compulsory legalized heterosexual monogamy serves: they provide mechanisms to order sexual exploration and rationalize sexual retreat; they explicate and establish sexual value; they put some brakes on. They shape sex. They describe sexual identity, no small matter in a culture that advertises sexuality as comprising the essence of self. They also offer rationalizations for sexual losses (for instance, the teenager who has never given a blowjob may salve her sexual ego with the knowledge that she did not play every card in her hand, after all). But whereas getting married involves signing on to a pre-written contract, the process of setting limits described here is comparatively original, inventive.

In effect, these seemingly miscellaneous rules for sex and romance constitute local and individual erotic systems which teenage girls are fashioning out of the scraps and relics of Victorianism, romanticism, modernism, and feminism. This effort requires at once acts of fantasy and recognition, creation and acceptance, rebellion and accommodation. The task is to make what is needed out of what is, or might be, or has been. It requires a goal, a system of meaning, a set of rules, and a method of enforcement. The first three requirements are easy enough to fill, but the last, at present, must depend on the failing powers of guilt and love. Maintaining an individual or local erotic system is, in other words, a largely futile project because no small group of girls nor individuals can effectively enforce a system of this sort without the complicity of material conditions, the greater culture, and the deep pulls of the unconscious. At the least, the individual has to stick by her own system and – if she is to have an intimate relationship – convince at least one other person to go along too. But chances are she herself will not stick by it. These systems are more ritual than reality, more promise than fulfillment, more guideline than rule.

7 Feminism and teen romance

From a feminist perspective, the efforts of teenage girls to shape their sexual lives are striking in the degree to which they involve an attempt to exercise sexual power, particularly given how poor a bargaining position many feel they are in and how desperately they want to make the bargain of sex for love. But there are clearly problems here, both for teenage girls and for feminism.

At the least, many teenage girls seem in dire need of some of the basics of feminist advice. The pain and frustration that many heterosexual teenage girls feel stems, largely, from the futility of trying to blindly strike the old bargain of sex for love under changed material and social conditions. They need to know that it is not because there is something wrong with them that the old bargain no longer works. They need to know what some possible terms of new bargains might be and have some broader understanding of the different ways in which adolescent sexual experience might be – or has been – shaped and explicated.

They need to know more about pleasure – that they have a right to pleasure and how to get it. They need to have a more objective understanding of what is going on in male sexual decision-making.

Feminism has not very effectively communicated its understanding of the sexual and romantic dialectic to teenage girls, although it has had liberating and clarifying significance for the lives of teenage girls in its defense of teenage sexual and reproductive freedom and its support of teenage girls' right to know the facts about their bodies and about sexuality. Those who have dispensed feminist advice to teenagers in the recent past have fallen, with notable, mostly health-oriented exceptions, into the traps of protectionism and euphemism. One wing of the feminist movement talks solely in terms of rape, incest, molestation, and exploitation. There is unquestionably a place in feminism for this work. But in not acknowledging the limits of a politics that deals with only sexual violence and not with other sexual and romantic themes, and in conflating violence with sexuality, this work often fails to describe, or leave space for, the breadth of teenage girls' experience. The feminist relationship to romance has also taken a toll. Feminism has generally derogated romance. The rationalist tradition that feminism is heir to viewed romance as a variety of superstition that would vanish in the light of reason and free love, and nineteenth- and twentieth-century feminists alike have distrusted romance as one of the chief ways that woman "do it" to themselves, that is, dupe and enchain themselves. Romance, we have said, is a trap too charged with misogyny and domination for women to risk. But can a field so magnetized with Oedipal material be simply written off? And if not, how much can it be moved around, played with, redesigned, resocialized, so that it enriches but does not kill. At the least, there are strategic reasons not to defer to romance but to acknowledge its power.[48]

In contrast to the angry tone of the work that equates sex with violence, another strain of the discourse has been cheerful, characterized by such guidelines as "just be yourself" or "do what you want to do, what will make you happy," notions that rest on some of the most prevalent assumptions of the 1960s;[49] for example, that feelings are simple, linear, trustworthy, and unambiguous; that they are a natural base for morality and spring forth of their own spontaneous energy after the removal of restraints, conventions, and coercion. There are other simplicities here as well. In place of romance, this work has urged healthy peer sex and/or masturbation. The belief that peer sex is naturally pure and equal is naive at best. The emphasis on masturbation is important for its emphasis on the pedagogy of orgasm and for the extent to which it has represented an opposition to the taboo on female sexual autonomy. But the enthusiasm for masturbation as a replacement for other forms of sexual experience raises some questions as well. Is it, perhaps, a way of keeping sex clean, out of the mess of passion and exudation? A way of encouraging girls to turn, as usual, inward? Other pieces of this literature advertise feminism as a solution to the problem of contemporary relationship. Teenage girls are cynical about this material, because it makes light of their experience and it does not work. There are few panaceas for romantic and sexual problems. Feminism can offer a diagnosis regarding the sources of these problems in gender socialization and inequity and a number of long-term strategies for change. It can suggest the path of autonomy, but we have no magic words, no love potions. In the most recent past, a conservation hue about "too much, too soon" has arisen in some feminist quarters, which argue for rulemaking.[50] This position misdiagnoses the key structural problem. Teenage girls are not having too much, too soon. They have too little – too little pleasure, too few options, not enough sexual power. Even if rulemaking were an effective parental option, it would not be so for feminism. Only a return to the primal rule – the shotgun connection of sex, reproduction, and marriage – can make the old bargain of sex for permanent love work. Unless we are prepared to rule out feminism, we must look to a different strategy. We can no more run backwards to the taboos of the past because we see that change brings disorientation and suffering than revolutionaries could voluntarily reinstate a tyrant.

The feminist task in regard to adolescent sexuality is limited and strategic. Feminism can not make romance simple, easy, painless. "There is," as Ellen Willis said, "an irreducible risk in loving," and there are risks in freedom as well.[51] For feminism the chief goal is not finally to protect young girls from the sexual reality but to protect and expand the possibilities for women's liberation – that is, for equalizing the genders and expanding women's opportunities for knowledge, pleasure, and work – for lives rich with personal and collective meaning. We cannot retreat from alienation into the illusory shelter of the past. "There is only one way left to escape the alienation of present day society," as Barthes suggested, *"to retreat ahead of it,"* toward a more supple and various integration of sex, romance, love, and work, the collective and the individual, the shared and the personal.[52]

In regard to theory, there are many open questions. We need to reconsider, for example, the psychoanalytic discourse about latency and separation in connection with sexual experience, and we need to think about ways to enhance patterns of socialization that would lead to a more probable integration of sex and work for girls. The divergence in gender socialization for peer sexual relations also raises some thorny questions. While the gender gap has lessened in some respects, in others it seems to be dangerously widening, as some teenage girls flee to motherhood and boys to anomie. The monogamization of teenage sex also raises serious questions. Is this an expansion of possibility and experience or a reduction?[53]

The feminist relationship to romance also calls for reconsideration. Effective feminist work with teenagers must speak to the magnetism and concerns of sex and romance not dismiss them. Feminism, like romance, must be a dance as well as a march, must admit the pull of the body and of fantasy as well as of conscience, must be a seduction as well as an obligation, appeasement as well as demand, must be a struggle not only for justice and equality, but for the accommodation of these with the web of promise and possibility that winds back through the centuries and will lead toward the future. In practice, this means that feminists must defend the sexual autonomy without which no new culture of adolescent sex and romance can take shape. We must also protect teenagers' reproductive health. These are givens, but in addition feminists must take up again the task of connecting with personal experience. Consciousness raising at puberty could be very important to young girls coming of age sexually because it is precisely at this point that many take on femininity like stigma. Projects focusing on romantic disappointment could speak directly to the concerns of teenage girls (a Heartbreak Hotline? Romantics Anonymous?). We must acknowledge and explicate the difficulty of transforming the relation between the genders and speak to why that transformation is worth the pain of change. We must level with teenage girls and give them an opening to level with feminism – so that feminism becomes theirs as it has been ours. There is no rationale here for false optimism, condescending dogmatism. Adolescents have a notoriously keen distaste for hypocrisy, patronage, condescension, and autocratic invasions of privacy and freedom. Finally, because in the throes of romance, many girls drop out of school or fall behind in their work, feminists must struggle to ensure that those programs that permit students to catch up educationally or return to school after an absence are not cut out of existence as they are currently being, but rather expanded.

In the long run, a strategy consonant with feminism – that is, consonant with the equality of women – must work toward increasing pleasure and decreasing frustration; disentangling sex, intimacy, and romance at least sufficiently so that their difference becomes perceptible; narrowing the distance between the genders; integrating growth, separation, and sensuality; and transforming sexual and reproductive freedom for women into what it has been traditionally – if mythically – for men: a source of comfort, pleasure, and excitement, a sequence, as the quest-romance depicts it, of "marvelous adventures."[54]

But we cannot pretend that sexual and romantic life is a series of marvelous adventures for most teenage girls today. To construct the future, we must acknowledge the painful realities of the present as well as its advantages (which are also, it is important to recall, tangible and significant). We must do this not solely because we want to organize teenagers in defense of feminism, as necessary as that is, but also because if we do not, we leave teenage girls out on the jagged cutting edge created by the separation of sex from reproduction. We leave adolescence for girls, in other words, in perhaps a worse condition than we found it when we were ourselves taken with the fervor of feminism, and that is a grave betrayal not only of feminism, but of women.

Acknowledgments

This piece could not have been written without the provocation of those who are trying to think anew about sex, many of whom are represented in this volume. I am particularly grateful to Ann Snitow and Christine Stansell for their rigor and support; to Anne Hart, whose questions about puberty initiated this exploration; and to Carole Vance whose encouragement has bolstered me through several drafts and whose criticisms have so thoroughly shaded and honed the text that I despaired of citing her contributions individually. And finally, of course, I thank the teenagers who taught me much more than I asked to learn.

Notes

1 Sigmund Freud, *Three Essays on the Theory of Sexuality*, New York, Basic, 1962, p. 92.
2 Verrier Elwin, *The Kingdom of the Young*, Oxford, Oxford University Press, 1947, pp. 45-7.
3 Michel Foucault, *The History of Sexuality*, vol. 1, New York, Vintage, Random House, 1980.
4 See, for example, Peter Blos, *On Adolescence: A Psychoanalytic Interpretation*, New York, Free Press, Macmillan, 1962, p. 189.
5 It seems relevant in this regard that the average age of first intercourse for girls is reported to have leveled off at 15.5 years for blacks and 16.4 years for whites. For girls, having sex – or at least beginning the sequence of romantic adventure, first fully desiring or

being desired or desiring to be desired – is evidently perceived as equivalent to beginning to have a story worth telling. (See Melvin Zelnik and John F. Kantner, "Sexual Activity, Contraceptive Use and Pregnancy Among Metropolitan-Area Teenagers: 1971-1979", *Family Planning Perspectives*, vol. 12, no. 5, September/October, p. 230.

6 For an analysis of the way that life histories are shaped in the telling, see Gelya Frank and L.L. Langness, *Lives: An Anthropological Approach to Biography*, Novato, California, Chandler & Sharp, 1981. Regarding the question of how the tales were shaped for the interviewer, Carole Vance has suggested that these are tales told to someone's mother. Perhaps, but while I am easily old enough to be the mother of a teenager, it does not necessarily follow that the life histories were censored on my behalf. My line of questioning and tape recorder evoked, I think, not a prudish mother but some combination of high-school sex ed teacher, family planning clinic counselor, Nancy Friday, and Helen Gurley Brown. It is not my sense either that a peer would have elicited more accurate stories, although they might have heard different ones. Many girls have acknowledged falsifying their experience in conversations with peers. Another likely source of distortion is the literary and popular tradition of romance. This is too complex a matter to more than mention here but it is important to note that these influences are far from linear, as the Harlequin-inspired lesbian initiation cited later in this article suggests. In any case, I am convinced that the greatest distortions came not from the sense of audience but from the narrators' belief that their stories had to cohere and that the narrator had to appear to have unified character and to be in the right.

7 See, for example, Andrea Dworkin, *Pornography: Men Possessing Women*, New York, Perigee, G.P. Putnam's Sons, 1981.

8 I am, of course, indebted to Kristin Luker for the concept of risk-taking that runs through this text. See Luker, *Taking Chances: Abortion and the Decision Not to Contracept*, Berkeley, University of California Press, 1975.

9 John Gillis, *Youth and History: Tradition and Change in European Age Relations, 1770 – Present*, New York, Academic, 1981, pp. 214-15.

10 Rayna Rapp and Ellen Ross, "It Seems We've Stood. . . ", *Ms.*, vol. 11, no. 10, April 1983, pp. 54-6.

11 Amber Hollibaugh, "Desire for the Future: Radical Hope in Passion and Pleasure", this volume, pp. 401 10.

12 Melvin Zelnik, John F. Kantner, and Kathleen Ford, *Sex and Pregnancy in Adolescence*, Beverly Hills, California, Sage, 1981, as cited in Anne R. Pebley, "Teenage Sex", *Family Planning Perspectives*, vol. 14, no. 4, July/August 1982, p. 232. The narrow focus of these studies on coitus and pregnancy compounds researchers' inability to illuminate their subject; for example, pregnancy cannot be understood without reference to romance and relationship. The heterocentric bias of researchers also causes them to miss a great deal, as does their odd tendency to take obviously contradictory replies at face value.

13 Ann Barr Snitow, "Mass Market Romance: Pornography for Women is

Different", *Radical History Review*, vol. 20, Spring/Summer 1979, p. 150.
14 Northrop Frye, *Anatomy of Criticism*, New York, Atheneum, 1966, p. 193.
15 Freud, op. cit., pp. 91, 93.
16 Nancy Chodorow, *The Reproduction of Mothering: Psychoanalysis and the Sociology of Gender*, Berkeley, University of California Press, 1978, p. 134. Chodorow also discusses how difficult this process is for adolescent girls.
17 For discussions of the implications of the mother-daughter relationship in such matters, see Chodorow, op. cit., and Dorothy Dinnerstein, *The Mermaid and the Minotaur: Sexual Arrangements and Human Malaise*, New York, Harper & Row, 1977.
18 Shulamith Firestone, *The Dialectic of Sex: The Case for Feminist Revolution*, New York, Bantam, 1970, p. 72: "Women and children are always mentioned in the same breath."
19 See Ellen Ross, " 'The Love Crisis': Couples Advice Books of the Late 1970s", *Signs*, vol. 7, no. 2, Autumn 1980, pp. 206-46, for a discussion of shifting courtship patterns in adulthood.
20 Gisela Konopka, *The Adolescent Girl in Conflict*, Englewood Cliffs, New Jersey, Prentice-Hall, 1966, p. 4, *passim*. Also see Linda Gordon and Ellen DuBois, "Seeking Ecstasy on the Battlefield: Danger and Pleasure in Nineteenth-Century Feminist Sexual Thought", in this volume, pp. 31-49.
21 *Eisenstadt* v. *Baird* 405 US 438 (1972); *Roe* v.*Wade* 410 US 113 (1973). On current practices of institutionalization, see *Family Court Disposition Study*, Vera Institute of Justice, 1981, pp. 423-95.
22 For a description of this rhetoric, see Betty Friedan, *The Feminine Mystique*, New York, Dell, 1963.
23 Frank F. Furstenberg, Jr. and Christine Winquist Nord, "The Life Course of Children of Divorce: Marital Disruption and Parental Contact", paper presented at the annual meeting of the Population Association of America, San Diego, April 29-May 1, 1982, as reported in *Family Planning Perspectives*, vol. 14, no. 4, July/August 1982, pp. 211-12.
24 For responses to the neo-conservative discourse about the family, see Michelle Barrett and Mary McIntosh, *The Anti-Social Family*, London, Verso, 1982; Barrie Thorne with Marilyn Yalom (eds), *Rethinking the Family: Some Feminist Questions*, New York and London, Longman, 1981; and Barbara Ehrenreich, *The Hearts of Men*, New York, Doubleday, 1983.
25 For a discussion of nineteenth-century feminist views on this issue, see Linda Gordon, *Woman's Body, Woman's Right*, Harmondsworth, Penguin, 1977, pp. 95-115.
26 Private communication, Ann Barr Snitow, 1983.
27 A good deal more could be said about this quotation as well as about this topic – e.g., the question of who and how women romanticize is probably also connected with attractiveness and how that affects power in a relationship, and there are also psychological issues regarding eroticization.

28 To what extent more sex now takes place at earlier ages than it did a
few decades ago is open to question. With the exception of Kinsey,
the most reliable researchers have concentrated on coitus as a
measure of sexual activity, so that we have virtually no trustworthy
statistics on non-coital or pre-coital sexuality in adolescence after
1949. Moreover, pre-1970, post-Kinsey studies are fairly contradictory. Briefly, some studies indicate that the percentage of
teenagers having sexual intercourse rose steeply from the 1930s to
the early 1970s, while others show percentages that are lower than
Kinsey's data for the late 1930s and 1940s. Kinsey's interviews, which
took place between 1934 and 1949, showed that 3 percent of
adolescent females fifteen and under and 20 percent of women
between sixteen and twenty-five had experienced coitus or reported
that they had. The Zelnik, Kantner, and Ford studies are probably the
most reliable point of comparison for Kinsey's data, on the basis of
sample size and continuity. Their work shows a fairly steady rise in
the number of teenage girls who have had what they designate as
"premarital" intercourse, from 30 percent in 1971 to 43 percent in
1976 and 50 percent in 1979, a rise accounted for almost entirely by
an increase in nonmarital intercourse among never-married white
girls. It is important to note that approximately 12 percent of the sexually active cited in the 1976 and 1979 studies had had intercourse only
once, and that 44 percent of the sexually active surveyed by Zabin
and Clark reported periods of sexual abstinence of four months or
more. See J. Roy Hopkins, "Sexual Behavior in Adolescence", *Journal
of Social Issues*, vol. 33, no. 2, 1977, pp. 67-85 for a review of pre-1972
studies of adolescent sexuality; see Alfred C. Kinsey et al., *Sexual
Behavior in the Human Female*, Philadelphia and London, W.B.
Saunders, 1953, pp. 282-345; Zelnik, Kantner, and Ford, op. cit., pp.
230-7; Laurie Schwab Zabin and Samuel D. Clark, "Why They Delay",
Family Planning Perspectives, vol. 13, no. 5, September/October 1981,
p. 211.

29 Alice Echols, "The Taming of the Id: Feminist Sexual Politics, 1968-
83", this volume, pp. 50-72.

30 For discussions of bundling and night-courting, see, for example,
Ellen Ross and Rayna Rapp, "Sex and Society: A Research Note from
Social History and Anthropology", in Ann Snitow, Christine Stansell,
and Sharon Thompson (eds), *Powers of Desire: The Politics of
Sexuality*, New York, Monthly Review Press, 1983, pp. 51-73; H R
Styles, *Bundling: Its Origins, Progress and Decline in America*,
Albany, Joel Munsell, 1869; and Lawrence Stone, *The Family, Sex and
Marriage in England*, London, Weidenfeld & Nicolson, 1977, p. 606.
On nineteenth-century working-class girls and sexuality, see Kathy
Peiss, "'Charity Girls' and City Pleasures: Historical Notes on
Working-Class Sexuality, 1880-1920", in Snitow et al., *Powers of
Desire*, op. cit., pp. 74-87, and Christine Stansell, "Eroticized Terrain:
The Sexual Landscape of Early Nineteenth Century New York City",
unpublished paper, delivered at the History of Sexuality Series, SUNY
Buffalo, March 1983. On the 1920s, see Paula Fass, *The Damned and
the Beautiful*, New York, Oxford University Press, 1977, pp. 260-89.

31 Kinsey, op. cit., p. 243. Also, F. Scott Fitzgerald recorded a reduction
in the number of suitors a girl was likely to have as the courtship
became increasingly sexualized. In *This Side of Paradise*, he noted
that

> The "belle" had become the "flirt", and "flirt" had become the "baby vamp."
> The "belle" had five or six callers every afternoon. If the P.D. [Popular
> Daughter] has two, it is made pretty uncomfortable for the one who hasn't a
> date with her. (F. Scott Fitzgerald, *This Side of Paradise*, New York, Charles
> Scribner's Sons, 1920, p. 59.)

32 Stansell, "Eroticized Terrain", op. cit.
33 For example, Gloria Gilbert, in *The Beautiful and the Damned*, begins
the record of her life with her first kiss and writes "FINIS" to it with
marriage. Between the beginning and the end of her narrative sense
of self, she kisses so many that one suitor bemoans having to think of
her as a "public drinking glass." (F. Scott Fitzgerald, *The Beautiful
and the Damned*, New York, Charles Scribner's Sons, 1922, pp. 147-8
and 182.)
34 For discussions of the culture and psychology of manhood, see, for
example, Dinnerstein, op. cit.; Ehrenreich, op. cit.; Jessica Benjamin,
"Master and Slave: The Fantasy of Erotic Domination", in Snitow et al.,
Powers of Desire, op. cit., pp. 280-99; and the spate of texts by men
about being masculine published in the last decade, including
Leonard Kriegel, *On Men and Manhood*, New York, Hawthorn, 1979,
and Joe L. Dubbert, *A man's place: masculinity in transition*,
Englewood Cliffs, New Jersey, Prentice-Hall, 1979. The text on
virginity is a liberal rendering of Frye, op. cit., p. 193.
35 Gayle Rubin, "The Traffic in Women", in Rayna Reiter (ed.), *Toward
an Anthropology of Women*, New York, Monthly Review Press, 1975,
p. 165. Rubin refers in this definition to the macro-systems that
effectively shape sex and reproduction. Teenage girls are cognizant
rather of the micro-sex/gender system that they both shape and are
shaped by. As one teenager explained the limits of her system: "I'm
not speaking for the whole country or anything or the whole United
States. I'm just saying that I know just a little part of the world, just a
little place."
36 Zabin and Clark, op. cit., p. 213: 36.7 percent of respondents cited
"have a closer relationship with partner," as a contributing reason for
seeking contraception.
37 For lesbian and gay teenage reports of early sexual experience, see
Ann Heron (ed.), *One Teenager in Ten*, Boston, Alyson, 1983.
38 Elwin, op. cit., p. 128.
39 Dinnerstein, op. cit., p. 73; Paula Webster and Lucy Gilbert, *Bound by
Love: The Sweet Trap of Daughterhood*, Boston, Beacon, 1982.
40 This suggests that as sporadic sexual intercourse is correlated with
unplanned pregnancy, pleasure might reduce the unplanned pregnancy rate. Unfortunately, there is only a slim statistical hint to go on
here, and that is complicated by a number of other implications
embedded in the same material. Zabin and Clark, op. cit., p. 213,
reported that "having sex more often lately" was the fourth most
frequently cited "most important reason" for visiting a family planning
clinic while "expect to have sex more often" was the sixth. "Afraid

might be pregnant" and "just started to have sex" were, respectively, the two most frequently cited reasons. Statistics on teenagers who have had intercourse before age fifteen may be found in Michael A. Koenig and Melvin Zelnik, "The Risk of Premarital First Pregnancy Among Metropolitan-Area Teenagers: 1976 and 1979", *Family Planning Perspectives*, vol. 14, no. 5, September/October 1982, pp. 239-47. That report contains other confounding statistics; for example, that for white teenagers beginning intercourse before age fifteen is highly correlated with the risk of pregnancy throughout the teenage years.

41 The description of male sexual experience owes a great deal to Dinnerstein, op. cit. For a discussion of social purity themes and feminism, see Gordon, *Woman's Body*, op. cit., pp. 116-35 and Snitow et al., *Powers of Desire*, op. cit., as well as Judith R. Walkowitz, *Prostitution and Victorian Society: Women, Class and the State*, New York, Cambridge University Press, 1980, pp. 242-5.

42 On the economics of single motherhood, see Barbara Ehrenreich and Karin Stallard, "The Feminization of Poverty", *Mother Jones*, July/August 1982, pp. 217-24.

43 Dinnerstein, op. cit., *passim*.

44 Frye, op. cit., p. 187.

45 The relationship between pregnancy and the issues discussed here is not altogether simple, and pregnancy itself is an extremely complicated issue. Space limitations make it impossible to do the matter critical justice, but it does seem necessary to mention the obvious: that pregnancy does arise in the narratives and plays a role – actually, a number of roles – in sexual negotiations.

46 For a discussion of adult working-class women's attitudes toward oral sex, see Lilian Breslow Rubin, *Worlds of Pain: Life in the Working-Class Family*, New York, Basic, 1976, pp. 138-41. For attitudes regarding oral sex in the 1940s, see Kinsey, op. cit., p. 257.

47 Gayle Rubin, op. cit., p. 165.

48 In comparison, the popular forms that appeal to teenage girls – soap operas and romances, for example – seem profoundly, if opportunistically, relevant to teenage experience. Romances go straight to the point: they tantalize with the brass ring of true love; they play out the Oedipal drama. In the end, they proffer a happy Freudian resolution (not frigid but not precisely separated either); but at least the genre makes it clear. The happy ending is fiction. Soap operas touch on separation, on the connection between male and female, on the problem of continuity itself. The lure of the soaps is not happiness but suspense. Like a rigid sex and gender system, they guarantee tomorrow. For discussions of nineteenth-century feminist ideas regarding rationality, sex, and romance, see, for example, William Leach, *True Love and Perfect Union: The Feminist Reform of Sex and Society*, New York, Basic, 1980, and Linda Gordon's review of that volume, "The Women's Dream of Perfect Harmony", *In These Times*, April 8-14, 1981, p. 20. For another discussion of romance, see Shulamith Firestone, op. cit., pp. 146-55.

49 The best-known example is Andrea Eagan's *Why am I so Miserable*

If These Are the Best Years of My Life?, New York, Pyramid, 1977, a book whose easy optimism belies its title; see Chapter 1, pp. 19-31, and p. 109. It is important to acknowledge that Eagan was one of the first to recognize that time was separating teenagers and feminists and to attempt to talk feminism and sex to teenage girls. Within the limitations of its terms and genre, the book does its best to have a bearing on real life. Unfortunately, real life turns out to be more complicated and difficult than the genre can reflect.

50 *Ms.*, July 1983, cover and pp. 37-43.

51 Ellen Willis, *Beginning to See the Light*, New York, Random House, 1981, p. 145.

52 Roland Barthes, *The Pleasure of the Text*, New York, Hill & Wang, 1975, p. 40.

53 My instinct here is that strategies that emphasize pressuring boys into the adolescent equivalent of companionate marriage are doomed to failure, and they are not necessarily good for girls. Although there are important cultural differences in these matters, it seems generally the case that boys currently flee the more, the greater the pressure toward intimacy. Adolescence may be at once too soon and too late to resolve the problem of male socialization. Engaging boys in nurturant activities may be a good idea, but irrevocable nuclearity is another issue. And while romantic affirmation may be a tonic for many girls, and while some girls find in pregnancy and early marriage a reason to save their own lives, this may also constitute another way of being "swallowed up by the family."

54 Frye, op. cit., p. 192.

The Forbidden:
Eroticism and Taboo

Paula Webster

A truly radical feature of feminism has been the permission we
have given each other to speak. We understand that through
speech we could discover who women were and how we had
been constructed; talk and the analysis that followed were the
first steps toward change. And so we spoke. We shared our
doubts and disappointments, rages and fears; we nurtured the
strengths we discovered and the insights that had been
unappreciated for so long. We talked about our mothers, our
fathers, our lovers or the ones we wanted to have. We sought
through the comfort of words to articulate in a collective effort at
clarity what had been vague, confusing, debilitating and painful.
We spoke the unspeakable; we broke the taboo on silence.

Looking back to that time now, it remains quite curious that
given our commitment to explorations of the mundane and the
marvelous, we devoted so little time to open and direct
discussion of sexual pleasure. While we spent many meetings
talking about our bodies and their particularities, the erotic
contours of our imaginations remained buried in layers of
propriety and ambivalence. Face to face, when it came to
describing our desires, we were strangely mute. Our discussions
of sex were barely audible.

In print, however, we were brave. There was the vaunted
rediscovery of the clitoris and its many pleasures. With the full
force of feminist analysis to support us, we declared with relief
and then authority that vaginal orgasms were a myth, that our
fears of being inadequate women were groundless. From its
lowly position as a second-rate alternative to partner-sex,
masturbation rose in our collective esteem and consciousness to
a political epiphany. Even if we never went to Betty Dodson's
workshops, or answered Shere Hite's questionnaires, most of us
felt better knowing that we were like other women and other
women were like us. Masturbation became the symbol of
autonomous feminist sexuality, a logical reconciliation of our
bodies and our lives, and a necessary foundation for knowing
what was erotically satisfying.[1]

Reassurance from the printed page enabled women to revise
or reinvent a relationship with their own bodies, but when it came

to sex with others, an unwritten orthodoxy prevailed. It felt taboo to talk about what we liked and the partner we liked to do it with. As we collectively and individually sought consistency among our beliefs, world views and actions, whatever and whomever didn't comfortably fit with our new selves was left out of the discussion. We feared contradicting what we said we wanted, and began to lie or tell only half-truths, keeping secrets that might reveal our deviance to members of our movement, community or preference group. We committed ourselves to correctness and its false but familiar bindings, deleting our mistakes, denying desires that had not gotten group approval. The sexual domain in general had become less taboo but some wishes, some thoughts, some acts and some partners were as off-limits as before. Feminist orthodoxy, which we created, observed and enforced with righteousness, prevailed.

As we rallied to denounce media depictions of feminine desire and desirability, asserting that women did not want to look like *that* or be treated like *that*, it appeared that we were on the verge of suggesting what in fact we did want. But instead, our list of taboos marked off more and more unacceptable terrain. "Perverse" pleasures, like voyeurism, bondage, s/m, fetishism, pornography, promiscuity, and intergenerational, group, interracial, public or phone sex were presented as incomprehensible. As we disclaimed any identification with, or interest in, these fantasies and activities, that part of the pedestal, supposed to protect our innocence and insure our purity, was rebuilt. Could we admit that we liked to look, when we denigrated those who liked to look at us? What kind of women would we be, if we desired to break any of the taboos that domesticated our sexuality, leaving us deprived but safe? Even daring to speak about what we might like seemed dangerous. Could we be thinking unfeminist thoughts?

The idea that sex between women was ideal, equal, perfect and perfectly feminist became a barrier to lesbians who wanted to speak explicitly about their sexual lives. Speaking honestly involves admitting that you have problems, anxiety, ambivalence and conflict, issues that were given little room. Now that the taboo on lesbianism had moved a fraction, for a moment, in this restricted radius of the radical women's movement, lesbians were asked to carry the banner of "good sex" and leave their more complex feelings at the door. After all, we needed Amazons with no problems, and we needed some vision of utopian eroticism.

The *ancien régime* was heterosexuality, with its inequality, inefficient and selfish male partners, and millennia of suppression. If heterosexual women could find anything to talk about that was positive, it was suspect. Heterosexual couplings were dismal, and women who could reveal the depth of their dissatisfaction were given some sympathy, but "sleeping with the enemy" was not seen as interesting, or liberatory sex. In public, heterosexual desires that were the least bit unconventional were dismissed as heterosexist indoctrination. Fearful of being labeled in this way, straight women grappled privately with the meaning of false consciousness as did their lesbian friends. For some yet to be discovered reason, we reduced our convoluted relationships with eroticism to issues of preference and purity, alienating ourselves from each other with stereotypes that eliminated contradictions and betrayed our real feelings. Lesbians couldn't have bad sex and heterosexuals couldn't have good sex. Anything that would have proved this untrue was suppressed, in a misdirected effort at unity.

This stereotyping of eroticism led to deep ambivalence among women who had been able to compare and contrast so many other important zones of their experience. Equating preference with the possibilities for pleasure left lesbians and straight women constricted and ashamed to talk of their "deviance." New alliances around desire might have emerged then, but instead respect for old taboos and new feminist taboos was strengthened. Surrounded by silence, we pretended to talk.

The lack of information we had then and have now about our own and other women's sexual lives leaves us anxious to know where we stand in relation to our peers – to women. If we knew how far from or near the "average" our wishes are, we think we might feel *more* normal, more acceptable and lovable – more "feminine." But we also fear finding out where we stand because we might feel *less* acceptable, normal, or lovable. When we finally hear about the sexual practices of women who are unlike us, we are never indifferent. First we may wonder what is wrong with them, desiring such "bizarre things," but quickly we turn the question back . . . what is wrong with me? We weave in and out between contempt and curiosity wondering who should be placed beyond the pale. We say that we can't believe that they like what they like or act by choice. Of course, they couldn't be feminists! Or could they? Could it be that these women, who have more sexuality in their lives and have traveled to more exotic places with it, are better than us? Our curiosity is tinged with envy and confusion. Could I do such a thing? Would I want to? Do I want to? How will I know myself when it is done? Am I a nymphomaniac or am I repressed? Is there a category for me – where do I belong?

Like strangers in a strange land, we ask ourselves these poignant questions when we admit our confusions to consciousness. The responsibility of creating a sexual life congruent with our often mute desires seems awesome and very likely impossible. How many women do we know (including ourselves) who almost defiantly say they have *no* fantasies, or no *need* to act them out? How many times have we resisted knowing what it is that might give us erotic pleasure? How many women do we know who "just couldn't" have an affair with a married man, enjoy two lovers, buy pornography, flirt with someone she liked, call up someone for a date, use sex toys? Going beyond the erotic territory that is familiar feels forbidden; we stop even our imaginings when confronted with taboo. Our hearts race; the world seems fragmented and threatening; we say "no" over and over again, convincing ourselves that to act or even to dream of new pleasure would be devastating. We meet the taboo head-on, and we are immobilized.

I remember when my reflections on the nature of erotic taboo were made startlingly clear and concrete by the chance conversation with a stranger, Martin, who called one day to ask my thoughts on the future of feminism. He said that he had been very impressed by an article I wrote in the "Sex Issue" of *Heresies*,[2] and wanted to know if I believed that women were getting more powerful, assertive. What an intriguing opener! "Yes," I said proudly, "that is quite true." There was a tense silence. I wondered if he was speaking in code, trying to "tell me something." Earlier I had received a call from a man who had read an article on matriarchy that I had written,[3] and he wanted to know if women were going to be as *dominant* as they had been in the mother-right past. That time I got frightened and hung up on him. I didn't like the way he sounded; he wanted somebody to dominate him, I was sure. I protected myself with moral indignation, because it made me feel very vulnerable to have this complete stranger insinuating that because I wrote about matriarchy I might be looking to dominate men.

Martin, however, did not frighten me; it was he who seemed vulnerable, with his agitated hesitations and unsuccessful subterfuge. I wanted to hear him out. I was curious.

He led up to "it" very slowly, interspersing his questions with compliments to "all feminists," especially those who wrote about sex. He assured me that he was sincere, just a regular guy who worked in an office and carried a briefcase. That is why he had to make this call from a phone booth. And then – "Don't you think that there are feminists who would like to make a man more feminine, more like a woman?" Did he mean smash gender? I doubted it. "Yes." I thought he had a point. There must be. "They could make men act much nicer." That's for sure. "Don't you think that there are some men who would rather be women?" Is this what he wanted to tell me, that he was a transsexual? Would it be cruel to let him go on, was that nice? There was a subtle change in my understanding of our power dynamic. Suddenly I realized that I could choose to understand what he meant, or I could make him suffer by my incomprehension.

He finally pleaded his case. "Don't you want to give orders to a man? Don't you ever have the fantasy of making a man do exactly what you want, like making him clean your house, wash your clothes, or pick up your laundry?" Was that all, a cleaning service? Of course, he assumed that since I was a woman I might have cleaned many a boyfriend's apartment, and naturally would be interested in altering the division of labor. But I realized that this is not what he was getting at; we were not talking about the radical redistribution of housework, but a sexual scene in which I would run the show.

He assured me that *it* would be easy. I would just have to yell at him when he made mistakes, humiliating him for his incompetence, reducing him to tears and pitiable entreaties for my forgiveness. Curtly I told him that *I* was a *feminist*, perhaps he hadn't understood, and I believed in equality, not in replicating the oppressive power relations of patriarchy. He apologized and said of course he had understood, but since he was willing to pay for my "services," the relationship would be equal. For some perverse reason I told him to let me think about it. He promised to call again.

In our next conversation I asked what he intended to pay for such an afternoon devoted to *his* pleasure. Meekly, he said he thought that $50 was a reasonable amount. I became indignant, surprising myself. That was too little for such demanding work. He asked me to suggest a just price and without hesitating I demanded $250, considering the time and effort involved. I now realize that this was no abstract calculation, but a poor woman's notion of the value of such tabooed behavior. He said he would think about it and call me again.

In our next conversation I had to withdraw my offer since I had realized that this whole thing was not a game, and more frightening than satisfying. The fantasies I tried to conjure up did not turn me on. I had thought seriously about his offer, tossing it around, trying to see if there was anything there that appealed to me. I must admit that I also thought about the newspaper headlines crying my shame, and the neighbors listening at my door, ready to have me evicted. In truth, what really stopped me was an unnamed and perhaps unnameable fear. I was disappointed that I wouldn't have this experience, this opportunity to see if I could really dominate a man, but I was more relieved. What if I liked it? What if I could get into it?

Each conversation with Martin had become more friendly and

inevitably frank, tinged with the intimacy one can have with a stranger. I was struck by his sense of humor, his honesty and the specificity of his desires. I was sympathetic to his commitment to find a woman who was truly interested instead of what he called a "cold professional." I was flattered by his impulse to call a feminist and find out if she shared his desires. Given his limited reading of feminist literature, he thought that feminism was unequivocally in favor of sexual liberation. He was sure that he had come to the right place. "Isn't there one feminist in New York who wants to humiliate a man and get reimbursed for it?" He was amazed and, I think, unconvinced when I told him I didn't know anybody who would take his offer seriously. He was puzzled that my own taboo desires could not be shared. "Do feminists have fantasies?" he inquired. I answered, "Of course."

We said goodbye and wished each other good luck with our respective sexual desires and their eventual fulfillment. Martin would have to find someone, most likely a professional, to let him dress as a woman, to command him as Marta, to allow him to act out his fantasy of being a woman in a sexist society. I would have to. . . .

I thought about my Martin/Marta talks for a long time, marveling at both the urgency and specificity of his desires and the diffuse and lackadaisical quality of mine. Would I have responded differently if he had intuited one of my lazy, unformed wishes; if he could have assured me of total safety and reciprocity; if he had been a friend or lover instead of a stranger? Would I still have found something to stop me from acting out my forbidden wishes for erotic pleasure?

Martin made me think of the limits I put on my sexual longings and my inordinate respect for the conventions of erotic taboo. Our conversations encouraged me to think about what was operating to restrict and deny my research into this area of my life which I had constructed to be free of ambiguity, experimentation and the forbidden.

It is in the nature of taboo that territories are marked off from one another, the known separated from the unknown, the inside/private from the outside/public, the good from the bad, the sacred from the profane, the acceptable from the forbidden. Crossing the boundaries that are supposed to maintain order and predictability is like entering an uncharted space. It feels dangerous. We are not sure how to orient ourselves; we don't know the rules. Embedded in all domains of culture are rules about what behavior is permissible, with whom, when, where, under what conditions and with what accouterments. These rules, internalized and thought to be "natural," are reflected in our understanding of what sexuality is and what different desires and acts mean. For each of us the area marked TABOO is similtaneously personal, cultural, political and social. No matter how "wild" or "conventional" we think our sexual thoughts and practices are, contained in what we think is erotically possible for us, as women, are a myriad of zones thought impossible to explore. For example, at the workshop on this topic for the Barnard Conference, women spoke of what was taboo for them.[4]

"I want to have sex without love."

"I want to buy a strap-on dildo."

"I want to have sex with my student."

"Patriarchal men turn me on."

"I want to be able to say what I want."

"I like sucking cock."

"I want to get married and have children."

"I want to rape a woman."

"I want instant gratification . . . why don't women have glory holes?"

"I want to sleep with a young girl/boy."

"I want to be watched but not touched."

"I want more than one lover."

"I want to look sexy on the street."

"I would like to be able to flirt."

"I want to fuck my husband in the ass."

"I want to sexually caress my child."

"I would like to have sex with my brother/sister/father/mother."

"I would like to have sex with my best friend."

"I want to have vaginal orgasms, if there is such a thing."

"I want to go to the limits."

"I want to discover what I want."

"I want to be able to be turned on to my long term relationship."

"I want to fantasize about being a porn star."

"I want to really like my body."

"I want to be fucked into insensibility, everywhich way."

"I want to talk dirty in private."[5]

Women's relationship to erotic taboo is complex. For some, playing with the distance from or proximity to the forbidden is a tension-filled turn-on. Without taboo sex might not feel so delicious. Naughty feels nice, and just "bad" enough to be intensely pleasurable. Taboo thoughts about taboo people, acts, situations and words are often nurtured, honed and elaborated to heighten our fantasies, again and again. Yet, over time, some taboos are assimilated, domesticated and drained of their charge. Others disappear the first time we try something new and are not ashamed. Sexual sophistication, like the sophistication of aesthetic and intellectual tastes, is inevitable, though it is often marked by some vague sense of regret for a past state of innocence (or ignorance). In this way we develop over our lifetime a varied sexual repertoire and, if we are lucky, new sources of erotic pleasure. Personal and historical change reveals the exaggeration of fears and guilt. But how many of us have been able to pursue what fascinates us, or ask for what we want, or take risks with our sexual identities molded by the constraints of femininity? Many of us still stand at the borders of our desires, hesitating, complaining, berating ourselves and/or our lovers for the sexual deprivation we live with and feel helpless to change.

When we imagine traveling into the territory of the forbidden we are obsessed with fears of loss. We have been told, by those who are said to care most about us, that social status drops dangerously low for the woman who seeks pleasure. The very thought of acting on our desires conjures up an unappetizing picture of a creature who is driven and out of control, at odds with how we would like to be seen. We imagine that our fantasies will topple the order of the universe, depriving us of the esteem of parents, friends, lovers or children. If we threaten the privilege supposedly accorded respectable women, we are convinced we will not survive. Afraid that we will be rejected, humiliated and expelled from the feminist world, lesbian and heterosexual, we cling tighter and longer to what has always been safe. Consumed by baroque visions of our own voraciousness, we affirm a domino theory of sexual appetite, in which one step will lead to excesses worthy of Bocaccio. The world will have to visit us in the bedroom or wherever we think our sexual haunts will be; we will stop feeding our children, sending birthday cards to Mom, miss all of our meetings, and pack the typewriter away for good. In this apocalyptic future our hedonism will take over – we will do anything with anyone. Our good name will be tarnished, we will be stigmatized, we will destroy our support systems and be isolated. If we don't follow the rules so deeply embedded in our feminine unconscious, we fear a terrible retaliation. And so we continue to observe the taboos for our gender, remaining reluctant to even know what could turn us on.

Being interested in sex is a primary taboo for women. Perhaps this is why Women Against Pornography could attract so many women ready to swear that they find none of that sleazy, pornographic sex interesting. Denying their curiosity like the Oedipal daughter, they insist that they could never do anything like that or want anything like that. They assume that women who like talking dirty, anal sex, voyeurism, or even vibrators are suspect, certainly not feminists. But women are feminism's constituency. How do we understand the differences between ourselves and the women who send their photos to *Hustler*, or write letters to *Penthouse Forum*, or buy sex toys, split-crotch panties, and dream of being dominated or becoming domin-atrixes? We cannot remain indifferent to the sexual texts and subtexts of women's lives if we are to create a feminist discourse on female sexuality that will replace the familiar one of commiseration.

When women discuss eroticism in private, the content of the dialogue is depressingly predictable. Starting with a complaint filled with disappointment or even rage, it moves to fantasies of a more pleasurable sex life but ends with the imponderable – is it her/him or me? Is it possible to get what I want? Am I asking too much? Maybe it is not really that important to be sexually fulfilled? While the rejection of deprivation in other areas of women's lives has been the agenda of the feminist movement, sexual deprivation has not been theorized to any great degree. Instead, in midnight phone calls, private talks on private walks, women have told each other how sexually unsatisfied they are and how hopeless and helpless they feel about their situation. It feels dangerous to describe the wounds this absence causes and the passivity that overwhelms us even when we know we want more.

Wrapped in romanticism, we say we will change partners, or wait for the One who will do it for us, turn us on, make us feel sexual. Acting in a self-directed way, to know our sexual wishes and to act on them feels selfish, unfeminine, not nice. Like frustrated children who must wait to have their needs attended to by protective adults, the ones who initiate and act, women wait for permission to respond, but we are afraid to insist on pleasure as our right. To get what we want (once we know what it is) is a taboo that needs to be broken.

Our dissatisfaction, however, creates a potential source of action. Accepting our deprivation may be painful at first, but it is a first step toward defining the nature of our sexual appetite. Erotic scarcity has served to debilitate our most constructive efforts to undo the damage of patriarchal repression. There may be more "good sex" available once we know what we like and what we have to do to put it in our lives. We may fear a deluge of sexual feelings that have been denied and suppressed, but in our attempts to be conscious of our choices, the real ambivalence can be exposed and worked through. Breaking some of our own taboos, imposed by patriarchal culture on all women, assented to by feminism and given legitimacy by each of us, could give us a new sense of ourselves and our possibilities. When shame is replaced by curiosity and fear by self-knowledge gained through experience lived in the world rather than in our heads, dogmatism will no longer be so appealing, and deprivation will not seem "normal." Experimentation, however, is never all or nothing. If we don't see stars the first time, if it isn't perfect, we often conclude that this is bad or boring and should never be done again. Actually it may take several tries to learn the social as well as the sexual skills, the techniques and responses necessary to enjoy something. Remember what your mother told you about olives; forget what she said about sex.

Our mothers, to whom we often dedicate our movement if not our lives, were either bizarrely matter-of-fact when they told us about sex, or bitter and resentful. Either your father wanted too much or too little, and she had to put up with "it". Needless to say, she never told you *if* she masturbated (or how, when or where) or *how* she felt about it. Nor did she tell you if she liked rough or gentle sex, being on top or bottom, whether she read pornography, or had fantasies about the milkman, her brother-in-law, her best girlfriend or her own children. Sexually mute and mysterious, our mothers observed the taboo imposed by motherhood, and presented us with little or no knowledge of what women's sexuality was like or could be. We have no documented erotic heritage, and the exploration is made even more difficult by our mother's sacrifices. We may feel that we betray her when we want more than she had.

We know as little about our feminist foremothers as the women who birthed us; and in both cases it seems an act of deep impropriety to wonder what kind of sex they liked. Yet it feels irresistible to ponder de Beauvoir's demands on Sartre, or the fantasies that fueled Virginia Woolf's longings or whether Willa Cather was butch in bed. Our contemporaries are as silent as the dead. Sara, Kathy, Nancy and Pat won't talk because it is too personal, and we don't push. If we knew what they were doing, we might feel competitive, jealous or defeated; we might wonder how their politics were being influenced by their practices. We are ambivalent about knowing; what if we find out something that makes us uncomfortable? Often with a mixture of relief and disappointment we change the topic, divert the attention from ourselves, cite taboos on privacy and integrity, and retreat from comparing their lives to our own, their pleasures to ours.

Some conclude from the quiescent sexual state women find themselves in that women's sexuality is like that – calm, passive, romantic, and other–directed. We are seen and come to see ourselves as tame and easily satisfied, more interested in giving than getting pleasure. While feminism has helped us to know ourselves as struggling with complex contradictions on many fronts, it has encouraged us all to postpone the exploration of sexual subjectivity by fanning our fears of exclusion from the universal sisterhood we have sought to create. By making sex an ideological battleground where the forces of good and evil fight to the death, complex questions of pleasure, power and feminine desire have been reduced to simple-minded answers.

My desire to encourage women to break taboos, rebel against prohibitions and rally around pleasure in fantasy and action is tempered by a note of caution (not admonition). To break private erotic taboos without being conscious of our unique sexual values would leave us feeling troubled and disoriented. In all new ventures, we need to be aware of our limits, the levels of novelty we can tolerate, the anxiety we can comfortably endure. Women's attachment to magical thinking (for example, men are lustful, women are not; my lover controls my sex life; I have no desires that are not nice; if I am very attractive, I will have good sex) is supported by irrational fears and major denials. Yet these won't wither away or be rooted out by platitudes of support or a new version of correct-lining. To name these inhibitions as in large part self-imposed, childish, or effective but ultimately destructive defenses against autonomy and pleasure will not usher any of us into the Golden Age of Gratification. We have had enough experience to prove that naming, while crucial, is never sufficient. We also need to explore the hesitations women feel when pleasure is realizable and imminently available. When we have come to terms, privately and collectively, with our demons and judges, our sexual shame and guilt, our desires to take and renounce responsibility for our happiness, we may be ready to talk honestly about our erotic particularities, and from there create a politics of sexuality worthy of our best efforts.

We do not need to wait for a feminist or any other type of revolution to explore our sexuality. There are a number of things we can do right now. We can begin to speak of what we were afraid to say in those years of consciousness raising. We can form new groups to have long and intimate conversations with women we know will not be offended, judgmental, or discouraging. We can support each other to learn by doing – starting slow and building on what we learn and what feels good. We could team up with women who have similar questions, or those who have been called "perverts" by the movement, to get guided tours of places that fascinate us, zones that are definitely off our usual maps: porn shops, sex parties, gay bars. With friends, we

The paragraphs

might get the support to treat ourselves well and take this work seriously. There are books to be read, attitudes to upset, time to be carved out of our "busy" schedules, skills to learn, and moments to integrate the novelty of being a self-directed sexual actor. If we use our friends merely to mirror our dissatisfaction (she won't fuck me in the ass, he won't go down on me), then we stay stuck, affirming for one another that nothing can be done until They, whomever they may be, change and give us what we say we want.

The collective project of creating an erotic culture for women should not be postponed by concluding that the distance from here to there is too far or too difficult to travel. Our friends can alert us to the dangers, both real and imagined, and help us distinguish one from the other. Some fears are appropriate and some merely resistance to change. If we can create a counter-chorus to the vast organization of repression we confront as women, we will be better able to experiment with confidence and a realistic sense of self-preservation. The spaces, rules, protections, information, projects, and productions that will emerge from this collective effort are yet to be imagined. The work is largely ahead of us, but, as we can see, it has begun.

In preparation we have the task of naming ourselves desiring creatures, with important passions, aversions, and prejudices. We experience a mix of desires for power and powerlessness, love and revenge, submission and control, monogamy and promiscuity, sadism and masochism. Once we are able to acknowledge our own complete relationships to these feelings, we will be less likely to submit to pressures to punish our sisters who have dared to speak, act, and write about the taboos they have broken and the forbidden territories they have explored.

Although the fear is potent and real, we will not perish if we challenge the taboos that domesticate our sexual desires. The more we know about the dimensions of our hungers, their finite limits and requirements, the more entitled we may feel to speak of our own wishes and listen with compassion to our friends. In recognizing our sexual appetites as "normal," we might lose our sense of ourselves as the victims of sex, unable to reject deprivation and erotic underdevelopment by acting in our own interests for pleasure. For many of us, this image of sexual autonomy is as frightening as our fantasies of loss and chaos. We have no models for "good" women who want and get "bad" sex. And who would we be if we got what we wanted? If we said "yes" instead of "no," "I'll try" instead of "I could never," would we still be women? From those women who have tried, the message is very encouraging – changing the quality of sex immediately improves the quality of the rest of one's life.[6]

There are no guarantees that an expanded sexual style can be slipped on like some chemise from Paris. There will be moments of panic and paralysis. There will be threats from the outside world as well as internal agitation. But we have experienced, withstood, and mastered conflict before, moving closer to ourselves. By re-creating feminism in this century, a movement that gave us the very important permission to collectively analyze, challenge, and change our situation, we tapped unpredictable energies to transform our lives. The women's movement gave us courage. It is time to return that gift and share it with each other.

Acknowledgments

I would like to thank the women who participated in my workshop for their intelligence and honesty in discussing this topic and tell them, if belatedly, how much I appreciated what they had to say. In addition, I would like to thank Carole Vance, Robert Roth, and Pat Califia for editorial comments. The wisps, wafts and whacks of conversations with friends and lovers, past and present, carried me along.

Notes

Portions of this article were previously published in "Going all the Way...to Pleasure", *Ms. Magazine*, vol. XI, nos 1 and 2, "The Anniversary Issue", pp. 260-3.

1 Remember those golden oldies, Shere Hite, *The Hite Report: A Nationwide Study of Female Sexuality*, New York, Dell, 1976; and Betty Dodson's slim volume replete with cunt drawings, *Liberating Masturbation: A Meditation on Self-Love*, New York, Bodysex Designs, 1974?

2 It was ironic and perhaps inevitable that the "Sex Issue" of *Heresies: A Feminist Publication on Art and Politics*, New York, Heresies Collective, 1981, was conceived of and in part realized by some of the same women who worked collectively on the earlier *Heresies* issue on "Women and Violence".

3 This article, "Matriarchy: A Vision of Power", appeared in Rayna Reiter (ed.), *Towards an Anthropology of Women*, New York, Monthly Review Press, 1975, pp. 141-56. Because it questioned certain orthodoxies within anthropology, I was introduced to the reactions of those who felt I was treading on something sacred. Clearly I had bumped against a taboo.

4 Approximately forty women in the workshop received small pieces of paper on which they were asked to write something erotic that was taboo for them. The pieces were shuffled and redistributed. Each woman read another's forbidden fantasy. It felt taboo for me to be speaking about "these things" in an academic institution dedicated to the education of young women; I felt powerful and sexual, but

exposed and uncertain how far to go. Will I be an outcast or a heroine? We spoke directly to each other, and if only for that moment, it felt somewhat safe.

5 When I asked my good friend, Robert Roth, a radical thinker on sex and a writer of great power, if he thought what had been said was tame, he quoted me a line from his own work which was quite useful: "Timid expressions often feel like ferocious assertions to the person who makes them. The effort is often extreme and brave." I agree.

6 In order not to create more pressure on ourselves, it is important to be realistic about how much change is possible in one lifetime. If we can understand how difficult personal change is, how anxious we feel about any change, and how loaded the sexual arena has been and may continue to be, we will be able to applaud even our tiny, baby steps, knowing pleasure is possible.

Suggested reading

Angela Carter, *The Sadeian Woman*, New York, Pantheon, 1978.

Betty Dodson, *Liberating Masturbation: A Meditation on Self-Love*, New York, Bodysex Designs, 1974.

Mary Douglas, *Purity and Danger*, New York, Praeger, 1966.

Mary Douglas (ed.), *Rules and Meanings*, New York, Penguin, 1973.

Lucy Gilbert and Paula Webster, *Bound by Love*, Boston, Beacon, 1982.

Shere Hite, *The Hite Report: A Nationwide Study of Female Sexuality*, New York, Dell, 1976.

Juliet Mitchell and Jacqueline Rose (eds), *Feminine Sexuality: Jacques Lacan and the Ecole Freudienne*, New York, Pantheon, 1983.

Paula Webster, "Pornography and Pleasure", *Heresies Sex Issue #12*, vol. 3, no. 4, 1981, pp. 48-51.

CLOSING
SESSION

Desire for the Future: Radical Hope in Passion and Pleasure

Amber Hollibaugh

When I was ten, I found a set of Xeroxed pages showing 236 positions for sexual intercourse. Later that day I met three of my girlfriends in the field behind my house and stared at those pictures. It was a solemn, but hysterical occasion. We studied those images, desperately trying to understand how anyone could enjoy doing what those pictures suggested. Looking first at a picture, then down at our adolescent bodies, we asked, "Do you suppose he really puts it in there?" We were in that field till late afternoon and when everyone else left, I got sick. I threw up for fifteen minutes. Sex and penetration were horrifying ideas. I knew that one day some man would expect me to be the woman in those pictures. I swore I wouldn't be.

Every time I see pornography or hear a woman describe something she enjoys sexually that I can't imagine liking, I feel myself slipping back to that field to stare at those Xeroxed pages again, and I am struck by the extraordinary price women must pay to explore their own sexual questions, upbringings, and experiences.

Women in this culture live with sexual fear like an extra skin. Each of us wears it differently depending on our race, class, sexual preference and community, but from birth we have all been taught our lessons well.

Sexuality is dangerous. It is frightening, unexplored, and threatening. The ways that women enter a discussion of sexuality are different from each other. The histories and experiences are different, the ways we express those differences (and define them politically) are extremely varied.

Many of us became feminists because of our feelings about sex: because we were dykes or we weren't; because we wanted to do it or we didn't; because we were afraid we liked sex too much or that we didn't enjoy it enough; because we had never been told that desire was something for ourselves before it was an enticement for a partner; because defining our own sexual direction as women was a radical notion.

But in all our talking about sex, we have continuously focused on that part of our sexuality where we were victims. Our rage, which had given us the courage to examine the terrible penalties attached to being female in this culture, had now trapped us into a singularly victimized perspective. Our horror of what had happened to us made it impossible to acknowledge any response other than fury at the images and acts of sexuality surrounding us.

It is painful to admit that the main focus of our feminist sexual theory has been aimed primarily at pornography, as easy to justify as it is deeply feminine. "Good" women have always been incensed at smut. Our reaction went far beyond disgust at pornography's misogyny or racism; we were also shocked at the very idea of explicit sexual imagery. At heart, our horror at pornography is often horror at sex itself and reflects a lesson all women carry from their earliest childhoods: sex is filthy.

But looking at the danger and damage done us is only a part of coming to terms with sex. We should also begin to look at sexuality itself and at what we mean by words like desire, passion, craving and need.

Do we think that sex is socially constructed? Is there any element of biology influencing or defining aspects of desire? If we think of sexuality as a combination of language, consciousness, symbolism, pleasure and motion, then how does that fit with our real lives as sexual women? What do we share in common; why are we each sexually different from one another? Should we attempt to wipe the sexual slate clean and begin again? Could we if we wished to? Do we desire what is forbidden? If the forbidden is connected to taboo, how can we resist oppression without destroying our means to excitement? What is the connection between the erotic and danger, the erotic and comfort? What creates the need to "fuse" temporarily with a partner during sex? What are the options created by imagining a separation between sex and gender; what are the dangers? Is there "feminist" sex? Should there be?

It is important to keep in mind that we're not discussing sexual abstraction, but creating the atmosphere and opportunities for ourselves in bed. Our theories affect the way we *feel* sex today and shape what we consider talking about with each other as well as what we will go home and try. This discussion will change the sensation of our orgasms as well as the way that women in the future will experience their own sexual feelings. The way each of us was raised lies close to the surface of sexual desires and the explanations we explore today will have the same effect on the women who follow us.

We will never open up women's futures if we censor the dangerous material of this debate before we have begun. We are in grave peril if we edit out of our analysis all women whose sexual histories do not correspond to a "correct" notion of feminist sex. At this moment, we have gone further than just remove experiences and people who don't fit comfortably within our picture of the sexual universe; we have also attempted to slander and quiet those women whose intellectual ideas disagree or challenge the prevailing attitudes in the women's movement about sex. Those of us who have helped create a feminist movement in order to resist not only sexual violence against women, but also sexual stigma, censorship and repression, who fought to expand more sexual options for women have found ourselves outside "feminist standards, political integrity and moral authority"[1] and have grown silent in our meetings, CR groups, and feminist journals and papers.

How have we gotten to this point? Do we, as feminists, truly believe that pornography is the major issue facing all women at this time? Do we believe that if we managed to wipe it out, many other aspects of our oppression would crumble as well? In the struggle against pornography, are we creating new definitions of sexual sickness and deviance?

Who are all the women who don't come gently and don't want to; don't know yet what they like but intend to find out; are the lovers of butch or femme women; who like fucking with men; practice consensual s/m; feel more like faggots than dykes; love dildoes, penetration, costumes; like to sweat, talk dirty, see expressions of need sweep across their lovers' faces; are confused and need to experiment with their own tentative ideas of passion; think gay male porn is hot; are into power? Are we creating a political movement that we can no longer belong to if we don't feel our desires fit a model of proper feminist sex?

Feminism has always had trouble expressing the radically different ways that oppressions bear on women, just as it has a terrible time facing the idea of sexual differences among women, straight or gay, working-class, Jewish, third world, young, old or physically different. It is easy, for example, to speak of the double or triple oppression of working-class and/or women of color but another to reckon with the actual realities of working life. It may make much more sense to spend eight hours stripping than working in a dry cleaning plant, or as an LPN (Licensed Practical Nurse) or office worker taking home $132.00 a week. Sex industry work may offer a woman not only more money but a greater sense of power. Contrary to popular middle-class beliefs, working in a peep show is not the end of the world. The sex industry and its surrounding communities are often more socially and economically desirable than the jobs or groups of people that form the alternative.

I have always been more ashamed of having been a dancer in night clubs when I've talked about it in feminist circles than I ever felt in my hometown, working-class community. There are many assumptions at work behind feminist expressions of surprise and horror: I must be stupid or I could have done something better than that; I must have been forced against my will or I was just too young to know better; I have prefeminist consciousness; I had a terrible family life; I must have hated it; I was trash and this proved it; and finally, wasn't I glad I'd been saved?

I hear these sentiments endlessly in the feminist movement, distinctions which confuse the reasons for making different choices and what they mean in women's lives. Sex is not the same for all of us, and a movement that is primarily white and middle-class (or includes women who aspire to middle-class values) cannot afford to decide who or how women are made victims in a sexual system built on class and race mythologies equally as damaging and vicious as sexist ones. "The Man" has many different faces, some of them female and white, and our alliances are not automatic or clear-cut.

Unfortunately, the idea that sexual variation, that *difference*, could be the key to analyzing sexuality and desire, a way of untying the stubborn knots of a bitterly heterosexist culture, has yet to appear distinctly enough in our theorizing about sexuality. As simple an action as patting somebody's ass may have wildly different meanings depending on family, culture, time, race and expectations. When a woman looks at a picture of a man and a woman fucking, doesn't it matter if she is straight or gay, likes cocks or thinks they're awful, was raised a Catholic in a small town in Minnesota or was the only gypsy child in her community? Doesn't that have a deep and radical impact on what a woman considers pornographic and what she considers sexy? Or are we to believe that there is a "natural" reaction which all women have to sexually explicit images which warns us immediately if and when those images cross the line to lewd?

People fuck differently, feel differently when they do it (or don't) and want sex differently when they feel passion. We live out our class, race, and sex preferences within our desire and map out our unique passions through our varied histories. These are the differences that move the skin, that explode the need inside a cunt and make sex possible.

Women are always made to pay on either side of the sexual dialectic. We live terrified of harassment or attack on the street and in our homes and we live terrified that other people will discover our secret sexual desires. Much is forbidden even to women's imaginations. We are deprived of the most elementary right to create our images of sex. It is a hard truth that far too many women come up blank when they are asked what their sexual fantasies look like. Sexual fantasies are the rightful property of men, romance the solid female terrain. Yet most of our ability to act on our desires rests in the possibility of imagining the feel and smell of the sex we want.

When I was younger, I tried to control my imagination more strictly than my sex life; my mind scared me much more than the actual things I was doing in bed. No one had ever told me that I could explore fantasy without ever going further than dreaming. I really believed that if an image rested at the corners of my mind, giving it center stage would inevitably lead to doing it. So, every time I dreamed of fucking fur, not flesh, I was horrified. I worried I might still dream of fucking a man, that I would betray both lesbianism and feminism by dreams of penetration, power, and of being overwhelmed. And I panicked when I thought of my mother (and of this desire for her as my lover) or of the multilayered worlds full of desert islands, baby bottles, whips, pleading voices singing for the right to seduce me, winds that whistled between my thighs.

At heart, I was much less afraid of how men might imagine me in a pornographic picture than I was terrified of how *I* might paint myself inside a sexual drama. In my mind, at least, I wanted, needed, to try everything I could think up, needed to see where my own sexual imaginings would take me, and needed to read and experiment with images and materials that excited or alarmed me. Instead, my terror of the unconscious in my own sexual fantasy life was unremitting. I spent too many years struggling against what I was afraid would surface if I let myself go. It was a deeper closet than the one I had been in before I had come out as a lesbian.

It is a bitter irony to me that I was in my mid-thirties before someone explained to me that I was not what I dreamed, that fantasies had a reality of their own and did not necessarily lead anywhere but back to themselves. I had never understood that I might be deeply fascinated by an idea but not enjoy it at all if I actually tried it, that fantasy could give me a way to picture different aspects of my own growing sexual consciousness (or explore my lover's) without going any further. It would also allow me a freedom unhindered by the limits of my body or the boundaries of my conscience. In my life I need monogamy, but I am free to experiment with an army of lovers in my fantasy. In reality I am limited to a certain number of orgasms done in a particular sequence, but in my mind I am capable of infinite climaxes and paths to satisfaction.

I am often shocked by my own sexual world. It is much denser and more forbidden than I knew. But it is also richer and has helped me find the beginnings of the words that might make sex of the body as complex and satisfying as my dreams of it. It has begun to give me back sensation in my body that had been lost for years.

By providing a distinction between love and sex, fantasy also allowed me to begin breaking my addiction to romance. As a child, I often dreamed about sex, about being pushed down a hill beside our house, tied to a tree, captured by deep-voiced lovers. (My lovers, as children, often dreamed another thread of this theme, being the girls who grew penises, who became Errol Flynn, the pirate taking the women he desired.) As I began to fear these fantasies, I also began to work with feverish energy to rearrange my sexual dreams into a romantic scenario, the rightful arena of sex for a woman. I did it well. I was "swept of my feet," not captured; held closely to a devoted lover, not bound to her bed; and properly married to anyone I fucked (or at least you could hear their begging for my hand in the background). I filled my dreams with men, trying desperately to organize my fantasies correctly.

I was on the run from my own desires. I was angry and afraid of the feelings that were alive in my body. I felt driven between my wish to be a decent, reasonable woman and an equally powerful wish to throw all my beliefs and upbringing away and explode into my own sexual raving. I thought I would go mad with it. Like women in centuries before me, I feared sexual insanity, feeling that my lusts would lead me further and further from the communities I wished would accept me – middle-class intellectuals, Marxists, and, later, feminists – and into the underworld of passion which would envelop me.

By the time I was 17, I had begun to seek out these unnamed cravings. Against all precaution, I drove myself into crazier and crazier sexual situations, the more forbidden the better. I was burning up. There has never been a time when I was in more sexual danger than then, a time when I sought to forget my desire and act on it at the same moment.

But it is always dangerous to refuse the knowledge of your own acts and wishes, to create a sexual amnesia, to deny how and who you desire, allowing others the power to name it, be its engine or its brake. As long as I lived afraid of what I would discover about my own sexuality and my fantasies, I had always to wait for another person to discover and "give" me the material of my own desires.

Every time we have been afraid of our own desires, we have robbed ourselves of the ability to act. Our collective fear of the dangers of sexuality has forced us into a position where we have created a theory from the body of damage done us. We have marked out a smaller and smaller space for feminists to be sexual in and fewer actual ways for physical feelings to be considered "correct." By recognizing the dangers of our circumstances, we have said, "There is no way to be a woman in this culture and be sexual too. I will live first with the anger and then hope we can change enough about the world that the woman after me may be safe enough to fuck. For now, it will have to be enough." But this isn't enough, and we know it. We have settled for an easy way out of the terrible problem we face. We have accepted a diminished set of alternatives and become paralyzed by the fear.

But there is another way, a way that's more difficult and demands we take a riskier stance to define and act on our desires. We can begin to reclaim our rights to fight, to experiment, to demand knowledge and education about sex. We can begin in another spot, saying that there is too much we don't know yet to close any doors that a woman enters to try and capture her sexual feelings. We can say that our sexuality is more complex than the things that have been done to us and that we gain power through our refusal to accept less than we deserve. We can dare to create outrageous visions.

The borders are shrinking and fewer women feel that they can reconcile their sexual desires with their political beliefs. We must live with the danger of our real desires, give them credit and airing. We must demand better contraception, self-defense classes, decent, non-judgmental sex education, the right to control our bodies and set new boundaries of female experimentation and self-knowledge. Feminism should be seen as a critical edge in the struggle to allow women more room to confront the dangers of desire, not less. By selecting our truths, we have censored the roots of our own future as sexual people. Every history of desire that we have refused to acknowledge has removed us a step in an attempt to unravel and reclaim the daring of our sexual selves. Each judgment has scaled down our own ability to fuck, and our desperate need to explore why we feel the desires we each call our own.

The truth is that our current state of feminist affairs has demanded that women live outside power in sex. We seem to have decided that power in sex is male, because it leads to dominance and submission, which are in turn defined as exclusively masculine. Much of our theorizing has suggested that any arousal from power felt by women is simply false consciousness. In real life this forces many feminists to give up sex as they enjoy it, and forces an even larger group to go underground with their dreams. For many women who have no idea what they might eventually want, it means silencing and fearing the unknown aspects of their passions as they begin surfacing. Silence, hiding, fear, shame – these have always been imposed on women so that we would have no knowledge, let alone control, of what we want. Will we now impose these on ourselves?

The assumption that women don't need fantasy is just as devastating to a woman's sense of power and pleasure in sex as assumptions that we don't "need" sex really, only men do. And the idea that the fantasies of women are the same as, or merely derivative or in the service of male values, only serves to belittle our already shaky beliefs about our own sexual importance.

No matter how sex is played out or with what gender, power is the heart, not just the beast, of all sexual inquiry.

It is the undertow of desire between my lover and myself that propels me through all the "good" reasons I can invent to stop myself from wanting sex. It is erotic tension that ignites the wildness of my imagination and the daring to figure out how to make my desires feel against the skin as I imagined them beforehand. With these, I let go, finally, to another woman's direction and sexual need for me, and find ways to crack through my lover's defenses and push her further. I want to be unafraid to be the erotic person I created in my own fantasies as a 12-year-old girl, dreaming that someone would at last make me scream because it felt so fine. I want to let go, to compel my desires into an experience of my body that awakens me, satisfies me, finally, and doesn't leave me angry and bitter that yet another woman was too afraid of her own passion to push against mine and see how far we could have gone.

Sometimes I want to play, resist, fight against another woman sexually; sometimes I want to surrender. I can't imagine sex without this. In the end, I don't want to do away with power in sex like a part of the feminist movement; I want to redistribute that power and knowledge so I can use it (and use it better) for myself and my partner. I think there is a way to confront the sexism and racism within sex without erasing the sources and intensity of our pleasures. Doing it side by side doesn't guarantee that sex is free of any fantasy of power, and refusing to experiment with elements of our desires leaves us all the more terrified of our right to sex and satisfaction.

We must say we want sex and set our own terms. We must build a movement that validates the right for a woman to say yes instead of no; a movement that thinks we haven't heard enough about sex rather than too much, and which reclaims an eroticism not defined by a simple political perspective or narrow vision which insists on excluding women to sustain its standards. We are searching for ways to examine sexuality, consent and power. We want to expand what we understand about sexuality so that more of us can live the desires we envision. We must start from where we are right now, from the real bodies we live in, the real desires we feel.

There are four prerequisites for that possibility:

1 The right to discuss openly the shapes and images of our own desires, recognizing how class, race and sexual preference influence the scope of the discussion and our conclusions.

2 The right to take sexual risks without also risking our right to a secure place within the feminist community.

3 The need to educate ourselves with the best available information about all aspects of human sexuality and have that material available in our own institutions, bookstores and community centers.

4 The obligation to use, then go beyond, personal insights and histories to create a body of sexual theories as complex as each one of us.

Feminists must enter the fight again, angrily, passionately. Feminism cannot be the new voice of morality and virtue, leaving behind everyone whose class, race, and desires never fit comfortably into a straight, white, male (or female) world. We cannot afford to build a political movement that engraves the sexual reactions of nineteenth-century bourgeois women onto a twentieth-century struggle.

Instead of pushing our movement further to the right, we should be attempting to create a viable sexual future and a movement powerful enough to defend us simultaneously against sexual abuse. We must demand that our pleasure and need for sexual exploration not be pitted against our need for safety. Feminism is a liberation movement; it needs to fight with that recognition at its center. We cannot build a movement that silences women or attempts to fight sexual abuse isolated from every other aspect of our oppression. And we can never afford to build a movement in which a woman can "lose her reputation." Feminism must be an angry, uncompromising movement that is just as insistent about our right to fuck, our right to the beauty of our individual female desires, as it is concerned with the images and structures that distort it. This goal is not an end in itself but a means which will ultimately determine the future and direction of our desires. As feminists, we should seek to create a society limited only by those desires themselves.

Acknowledgments and notes

Special thanks to Dorothy Allison, John D'Emilio, Jeff Escoffier, Barbara Kerr, Joan Nestle, Marcia Pally, Gayle Rubin, Ann Snitow, Carole Vance, and my lover, Esther Newton, whom I met through this conference and who never wavered in her support of this work or myself.

A version of this paper appeared in *New York Native*, issue no. 7, September 25, 1983.

1 Amber Hollibaugh, "The Erotophobic Voice of Women," *New York Native*, issue no. 7, September 25, 1983, p. 33.

is it true what they say about colored pussy?

hattie gossett

hey
is it really true what they say about colored pussy?
come on now
dont be trying to act like you dont know what i am talking about
you have heard those stories about colored pussy so stop pretending
you havent
you have heard how black and latina pussies are hot and uncontrollable
and i know you know the one about asian pussies and how they go from
side to side instead of up and down
and everybody knows about squaw pussies and how once a whiteman
got him some of that he wasnt never no more good
now at first i thought the logical answer to these stories is that they are
ignorant racist myths
but this i thought: what about all the weird colored stories about colored
pussy?
cuz you know colored pussies werent always treated with the highest
regard we deserve in the various colored worlds prior to our
discovery by the european talentscout/explorers
and we still arent
so now why is it that colored pussies have had to suffer so much
oppression and bad press from so many divergent sources?
is it cuz we really are evil and nasty and queer looking and smelly and
ugly like they say?
or
is it cuz we possess some secret strength which we take for granted but
which is a terrible threat to the various forces which are trying to
suppress us?
i mean just look at what black pussies have been subjected to alone
starting with ancient feudal rape and polygamy and clitoridectomy and
forced child marriages and continuing right on through colonial
industrial neocolonial rape and forced sterilization and experimental
surgery
and when i put all that stuff about black pussies together with the stories
i hear from other colored pussies about what they have had to go
through i am even more convinced
we must have some secret powers!
this must be why so many people have spent so much time vilifying
abusing hating and fearing colored pussy
and you know that usually the ones who be doing all this vilifying
abusing hating and fearing of colored pussy are the main ones who
just cant leave colored pussy alone dont you

411

they make all kinds of laws and restrictions to apartheid-ize colored
   pussy and then as soon as the sun goes down guess who is seen
   sneaking out back to the cabins?
and guess who cant do without colored pussy in their kitchens and fields
   and factories and offices?
then theres the people who use colored pussy as a badge of certification
   to ensure entry into certain circles
finally when i think about what would happen if all the colored pussies
   went on strike even for a day
look out!
(especially if the together white pussies staged a same day sympathy
   strike)

the pimps say colored pussy is an untapped goldmine
well they got it wrong
colored pussies aint goldmines untapped
colored pussies are yet un-named energies whose power for lighting up
   the world is beyond all known measure

yo daddy! – an 80s version of the dozens

hattie gossett

1

yo daddy
yo daddys daddy
his daddy
his great granddaddys great great granddaddys daddy
yo daddy look like death ridin radar waves
yo daddy walk like a broke dick dog
yo daddy dips snuff wears a bowler hat and walks pintoed with a cane
yo daddys breath smell like chemical fallout and industrial waste and
  hes always up in somebodys face
yo daddys uncles brotherinlaw is havin a middleage crisis and is makin
  a fool outta hisself over young girls and his wife got tired of his shit
  and put him out
yo daddys daddys daddys daddy was the slave who stayed behind
  when everybody else escaped to freedom talkin bout i aint gonna
  leave ma massa cuz he been so good to me

2

the employer who wants to pinch my ass and pay me less money than he
  would a man? his daddy
the wifebeaters daddy
the rapists daddy
the childmolesters daddy
the socialworkers and judges who say lesbians aint fit mothers? their
  daddies
the slumlords daddy
the industrial polluters? their daddies
the committee in charge of cutting back social services? their daddies
the stepup nuclear power production committee? their daddies
all the other bigtime capitalists daddies
and their smalltime neocolonial overseers daddies too
like the chastity belt daddy
and the drawing & quartering bonebreaking burning at the stake daddy
and the madonna on the cross in a crisscross daddy
and the polygamy daddy
and the cliterectomy daddy
and the foot bindin daddy
and the child bride daddy
and the chador and veil daddy

413

3

i dont haul no coal daddy
i dont want nothin black but a cadillac daddy
makin babies for the revolution he doesnt take care of daddy
the womans position in the revolution is prone daddy
speakin out about womens oppression in public but insistin on his
    patriarchal privileges in private daddy
no foreplay daddy
all technique and no feelins daddy
yes i enjoy oral sex but i think cunnilingus is abhorrent and repulsive
    daddy
yeah i want some head and naw i aint gonna eat no pussy daddy
no stayin power daddy
if i give you some money and some coke can i watch you and your
    girlfriend freak off daddy
do you want to tie me up and beat me daddy
can i tie you up and beat you daddy
no technique daddy
no warmth sensitivity gentleness tenderness either daddy
roll over and go to sleep daddy

4

if a woman is not a profit to me shes a pain in the ass daddy
a woman is like a pipe you gotta break em in daddy
a menstruating lactating woman cant touch food enter holy places sleep
    in the house with or touch men daddy
women are childlike sickly neurotic helpless incapable of serious
    thought son they will throw lye and cocacola on you while you sleep
    take yo money and make a fool outta you barbeque yo clothes slash
    yo tires put things in yo food bleed every month blow yo mind live
    longer than you daddy
shes cute when shes mad daddy
little girls should wear bouncy curls play passively with pinkpastyfaced
    dolls and with all their hearts and souls hope to die shonuff cross yo
    heart and open yo legs love their daddies daddy
yo daddy
my daddy
they all got little bitty peanut dicks

One Hour Mama[1]

Porter Grainger

I've always heard that haste makes waste,
So I believe in takin my time.
The highest mountain can't be raced,
It's something you must slowly climb.

I want a slow and easy man;
He needn't ever take the lead,
Cause I work on that long time plan
And I ain't alookin for no speed.

I'm a one hour mama, so no one minute papa
Ain't the kind of man for me.
Set your alarm clock papa, one hour that's proper,
Then love me like I like to be.

I don't want no lame excuses,
Bout my lovin being so good,
That you couldn't wait no longer
Now I hope I'm understood.

I'm a one hour mama, so no one minute papa
Ain't the kind of man for me.

I can't stand no greenhorn lover
Like a rookie goin to war
With a load of big artillery
But don't know what it's for

He's got to bring me reference
With a great long pedigree
And must prove he's got endurance
Or he don't mean snap to me.

I can't stand no crowing rooster
What just likes a hit or two.
Action is the only booster
Of just what my man can do.

I don't want no imitation.
My requirements ain't no joke
Cause I got pure indignation
For a guy what's lost his stroke.

I'm a one hour mama, so no one minute papa
Ain't the kind of man for me.
Set your alarm clock papa, one hour that's proper,
Then love me like I like to be.

I may want love for one hour
Then decide to make it two,
Takes an hour fore I get started
Maybe three fore I'm through.

I'm a one hour mama, so no one minute papa
Ain't the kind of man for me!

Notes

1 These lyrics come from a song sung by Ida Cox. Although the original
record was never produced (too fresh, perhaps), the test pressing has
been retrieved and can be found on the album *Mean Mothers,
Independent Women's Blues, Volume 1*, Rosetta Records 1300.

Ida Cox was one of the super singers of the 1920's, a very big star, and is the
woman who gave us "Wild Women Don't Have the Blues".... She was 43 and
very independent when she sang this and has lived fully and seen plenty – how
else could she be so straightforward and clear? (liner notes).

For additional information about Ida Cox and other blues singers, see
Rosetta Reitz, *Mean Mothers Shout the Blues* (forthcoming).

La Dulce Culpa[1]

Cherríe Moraga

What kind of lover have you made me, mother
who drew me into bed with you at six/at sixteen
oh, even at sixty-six you do still
lifting up the blanket with one arm
lining out the space for my body with the other

    as if our bodies still beat
    inside the same skin
    as if you never noticed
    when they cut me
    out
    from you.

What kind of lover have you made me, mother
who took belts to wipe this memory from me

    the memory of your passion
    dark & starving, spilling
    out of rooms, driving
    into my skin, cracking
    & cussing in spanish

    the thick dark *f* sounds
    hard *c's* splitting
    the air like blows

    you would get a rise out of me
    you knew it in our blood
    the vision, of my rebellion

What kind of lover have you made me, mother
who put your passion on a plate for me
nearly digestible. Still trying to swallow
the fact that we lived most of our lives
with the death of a man
whose touch ran
across the surface of your skin
never landing nightly
where you begged it
to fall

    to hold your desire
    in the palm of his hand

for you to rest there
for you to continue.

What kind of lover have you made me, mother
so in love
with what is left
unrequited.

Notes

1 This poem and the following four poems by Cherríe Moraga are
copyright © Cherríe Moraga, 1983. From *Loving in the War Years: Lo
que Nunca Pasó por Sus Labios* (Boston, South End Press), 1983.

What is Left

Cherríe Moraga

Mamá
I use you
like the belt
pressed inside your grip
seething for contact

I take
what I know
from you and want
to whip this world
into shape
      the damage
has defined me
as the space you provide
for me in your bed

. . . .

I was not to raise an arm against you

But today
I promise you
I *will* fight back

Strip the belt from your hands

and take you

into
my arms.

Loving in the War Years

Cherríe Moraga

Loving you is like living
in the war years
I *do* think of Bogart & Bergman
not clear who's who
but still singin a long smoky
mood into the piano bar
drinks straight up
the last bottle in the house
while bombs split
outside, a broken
world.

A world war going on
but you and I still insisting
in each our own heads
still thinkin how
if I could only make some contact
with that woman across the keyboard
we size each other up
    yes...
Loving you has this kind of desperation
to it, like do or die, I
having eyed you from the first
time you made the decision to move
from your stool
to live dangerously.

All on the hunch
that in our exchange of photos
of old girlfriends, names
of cities and memories
back in the states
the fronts we've manned
out here on the continent
all this on the hunch
that *this* time there'll be
no need for resistance.

Loving in the war years
calls for this kind of risking
without a home to call our own

I've got to take you as you come
to me, each time like a stranger
all over again. Not knowing
what deaths you saw today
I've got to take you
as you come, battle bruised
refusing our enemy, fear.

We're all we've got. You and I

maintaining
this war time morality
where being queer
and female is as rude
as we can get.

Passage

Cherríe Moraga

on the edge of the war near the bonfire
we taste knowledge[1]

there is a very old wound in me
between my legs
where I have bled, not to birth
pueblos or revolutionary
concepts or simple
sucking children

but a memory
of some ancient
betrayal.

so that when you touch me
and I long to freeze, not feel
what hungry longing I used to know
nor taste in you a want
I fear will burn
my fingers to their roots
it is out of my control.

your mouth opens, I long for dryness.
The desert, untouched.
Sands swept without sweat.

Atzlán.[2]

Pero, es un sueño. This safety
of the desert.
My country was not like that.
Neither was yours.

We have always bled
with our veins
and legs
open
to forces
beyond our control.

Notes

1 *Stephen Berg, Nothing in the Word. Versions of Aztec Poetry,* New York, Grossman, 1972.
2 The mythical/historical place, in the area of present-day northern New Mexico, from where the Aztecs were to have migrated before settling in what is now Mexico City. It is the mythical homeland of the present-day Chicano people.

The Slow Dance

Cherríe Moraga

Thinking of Elena, Susan – watching them dance together. The images return to me, hold me, stir me, prompt me to want *something*.

Elena moving Susan around the floor, so in control of the knowledge: how to handle this woman, while I fumbled around them. When Elena and I kissed, just once, I forgot and let too much want show, closing my eyes, all the eyes around me seeing me close my eyes. I am a girl wanting so much to kiss a woman. She sees this too, cutting the kiss short.

But not with Susan, Susan's arm around Elena's neck. Elena's body all leaning into the center of her pelvis. *This is the way she enters a room*, leaning into the body of a woman.

The two of them, like grown-ups, like women. The women I silently longed for. Still, I remember after years of wanting and getting and loving, still I remember the desire to be that *in sync* with another woman's body.

And I move women around the floor, too – women I think enamored with me. My mother's words rising up from inside me – "A *real* man, when he dances with you, you'll know he's a *real* man by how he holds you in the back." I think, *yes*, someone who can guide you around a dance floor and so, I do. Moving these women kindly, surely, even superior. *I can handle these women.* They want this. And I do too.

Thinking of my father, how so timidly he used to take my mother onto the small square of carpet we reserved for dancing, pulling back the chairs. She really leading the step, him learning to cooperate so it *looked* like a male lead. I noticed his hand, how it lingered awkwardly about my mother's small back, his thin fingers never really getting a hold on her.

I remember this as I take a woman in my arms, my hand moving up under her shoulder blade, speaking to her from there. It is from *this* spot, the dance is directed. From *this* place. I tenderly, with each fingertip, move her.

423

I am my mother's lover. The partner she's been waiting for. I can handle whatever you got hidden. I can provide for you.

But when I put this provider up against the likes of Elena, *I* am the one following/falling into her. Like Susan, taken up in the arms of this woman. *I want this.*

Catching the music shift; the beat softens, slows down. I search for Elena – the bodies, the faces. *I am ready for you now.* I want age, knowledge. *Your body that still, after years, withholds and surrenders – keeps me there, waiting wishing.* I push through the bodies, looking for her. Willing. Willing to feel *this time* what disrupts in me. Girl. Woman. Child. Boy. Willing to embody what I will in the space of her arms. Looking for Elena. I'm willing, wanting.

And I find you dancing with this other woman. My body both hers and yours in the flash of a glance.

I can handle this.

I am used to being an observer.

I am used to not getting what I want.

I am used to imagining what it must be like.

Sex Without Love

Sharon Olds

How do they do it, the ones who make love
without love? Beautiful as dancers,
gliding over each other like ice-skaters
over the ice, fingers hooked
inside each other's bodies, faces
red as steak, wine, wet as the
children at birth whose mothers are going to
give them away. How do they come to the
come to the come to the God come to the
still waters, and not love
the one who came there with them, light
rising slowly as steam off their joined
skin? These are the true religious,
the purists, the pros, the ones who will not
accept a false Messiah, love the
priest instead of the God. They do not
mistake the lover for their own pleasure,
they are like great runners: they know they are alone
with the road surface, the cold, the wind,
the fit of their shoes, their over-all cardio-
vascular health – just factors, like the partner
in the bed, and not the truth, which is the
single body alone in the universe
against its own best time.

Bestiary[1]

Sharon Olds

Nostrils flared, ears pricked,
Gabriel asks me if people can mate with
animals. I say it hardly
ever happens. He frowns, fur and
skin and hooves and slits and pricks and
teeth and tails whirling in his brain.
You *could* do it, he says, not wanting the
world to be closed to him in any
form. We talk about elephants
and parakeets, until we are rolling on the
floor, laughing like hyenas. Too late,
I remember love – I backtrack
and try to slip it in, but that is
not what he means. Seven years old,
he is into hydraulics, pulleys, doors which
fly open in the side of the body,
entrances, exits. Flushed, panting,
hot for physics, he thinks about lynxes,
eagles, pythons, mosquitoes, girls,
casting a glittering eye of use
over creation, wanting to know
exactly how the world was made to receive him.

Note

1 "Bestiary" first appeared in *Poetry Northwest*, summer 1980, vol. xxi, no. 2.

The Sisters of Sexual Treasure

Sharon Olds

As soon as my sister and I got out of our
mother's house, all we wanted to
do was fuck, obliterate
her tiny sparrow body and narrow
grasshopper legs. The men's bodies
were like our father's body! The massive
hocks, flanks, thighs, elegant
knees, long tapered calves –
we could have him there, the steep forbidden
buttocks, backs of the knees, the cock
in our mouth, ah the cock in our mouth.
      Like explorers who
discover a lost city, we went
nuts with joy, undressed the men
slowly and carefully, as if
uncovering buried artifacts that
proved our theory of the lost culture:
that if Mother said it wasn't there,
it was there.

Outside the Operating Room of the Sex-Change Doctor

Sharon Olds

Outside the operating room of the sex-change doctor, a tray of penises.
There is no blood. This is not Vietnam, Chile, Buchenwald.
They were surgically removed, under anesthetic. They lie there neatly, each with a small space around it.
The anesthetic is wearing off now. The chopped-off sexes lie on the silver tray.
One says *I am a weapon thrown down. Let there be no more killing.*
Another says *I am a thumb lost in the threshing machine. Gold straw fills the air. I will never have to work again.*
The third says *I am a caul removed from his eyes. Now he can see.*
The fourth says *I want to be painted by Géricault, a still life with a bust of Apollo, a drape of purple velvet, and a vine of ivy leaves.*
The fifth says *I was a dirty little dog, I knew he'd have me put to sleep.*
The sixth says *I am safe. Now no one can hurt me.*
Only one is unhappy. He lies there weeping in terrible grief, crying out *Father, Father!*

The Partisans and the S.S.

Sharon Olds

When the men and women went into the woods
they knew what would happen if the others caught
    them.
They knew their bodies would be undone,
their sexual organs dismantled as if to
break the mold so the human could not be
made anymore. They knew what the others
went for,
the center of the body,
and not just for the exquisite pain but to
send them crudely barren into death,
throwing those bodies down in the village at dawn to
show that all was ended, the genitals
themselves gone –
            and the young kept
going into the woods. Each time
the others dumped a body in the square,
raw blackness between its legs,
ten more people took to the woods, springing
up there on the loam dark as the
corpse's wound, as if they were its children.

The Solution

Sharon Olds

Finally they got the Singles problem under control, they made it scientific. They opened huge sex centers – you could simply go and state what you want and they would find you someone who wanted that too. You would stand under a sign saying *I Like To Be Touched And Held* and when someone came and stood under the sign saying *I Like To Touch And Hold* they would send the two of you off together.

At first it went great. A steady stream of people under the sign *I Like To Give Pain* paired up with the steady stream of people from under *I Like To Receive Pain. Foreplay Only – No Orgasm* found its adherents, and *Orgasm Only – No Foreplay* matched up its believers. A loyal Berkeley, California policeman stood under the sign *Married Adults, Lights Out, Face To Face, Under A Sheet* because that's the only way it was legal in Berkeley – but he stood there a long time in his lonely blue law coat. And the man under *I Like To Be Sung To While Bread Is Kneaded On My Stomach* had been there weeks without a reply.

Things began to get strange. The *Love Only – No Sex* was doing fine; the *Sex Only – No Love* was doing really well, pair after pair walking out together like wooden animals off a child's ark, but the line for *38 D Or Bigger* was getting unruly, shouting insults at the line for *8 Inches Or Longer*, and odd isolated signs were springing up everywhere, *Retired Schoolteacher And Parakeet – No Leather, One Rm/No Bath/View Of Sausage Factory.*

The din rose in the vast room. The line under *I Want To Be Fucked Senseless* was so long that portable toilets had to be added and a minister brought in for deaths, births, and marriages on the line. Over under *I Want To Fuck Senseless* – no one, a pile of guns. A hollow roaring filled the enormous gym. More and more people began to move over to *Want To Be Fucked Senseless.* The line snaked around the gym, the stadium, the whole town, out into the fields. More and more people joined it, until *Fucked Senseless* stretched across the nation in a huge wide belt like the Milky Way and since they had to name it they named it, they called it the American Way.

Epilogue

Carole S. Vance

The controversy surrounding the Barnard conference represents in microcosm some of the larger issues which the conference sought to address: the diversity in women's sexual experience; the gap between what is said and what is done; the inadequacy of our language to describe women's experience; the complex meaning of sexual images; the terror aroused by sexuality. As Academic Coordinator of the conference, I report these events[1] not to exacerbate conflicts further, but because I believe them to be emblematic of our larger difficulty. Most prominent is the volatility of sexuality, which arouses more intense reaction than almost any other issue of equal seriousness. In the face of the evident power of the fear of difference and the relentless operation of the system of sexual hierarchy, feminists need to begin the discussion of sexuality by admitting, as Dorothy Allison says, "that for each one of us desire is unique and necessary and simply terrifying."[2]

In the week preceding the conference, women identifying themselves as members of anti-pornography groups made telephone calls to metropolitan area feminists and to Barnard College denouncing the conference organizers for inviting proponents of "anti-feminist" sexuality to participate. They criticized the conference for promoting patriarchal values antithetical to the basic tenets of feminism, and they objected to particular participants by name, reportedly portraying them as sexual deviants.[3] Because the conference was designed to open up feminist dialogue about sex, these women characterized it as dominated by sexual nonconformists, who were in fact only part of the wide spectrum of opinion represented there. Anti-pornography critics rightly perceived the planning committee's attempt to redress the balance between sexual pleasure and sexual danger as an intellectual and political intervention in the discussion which they had recently dominated. But they wrongly concluded that an analysis of sexual danger had been excluded from the conference. They objected, in truth, to their loss of control over the discourse.

Two days before the conference, the Barnard College administration reacted by confiscating 1500 copies of the conference's major text, the *Diary of a Conference on Sexuality*. The *Diary*, a seventy-two page handbook prepared for distribution to regist-

431

rants on the day of the conference, was a unique document designed by talented feminist artists. Illustrated by witty and evocative sexual images, the *Diary* contained minutes and bibliographies from planning committee discussions; personal statements from committee members; the conference concept paper; and abstracts and suggested readings from workshops.[4] Juxtaposing text and image, the *Diary* invited readers to consider their inter-relationship. Knowing that the conference raised more questions than it could possibly answer, planners viewed the *Diary* as a way to share these questions and the planning process more fully with registrants.

College officials had raised no objection to the conference program and content during the months of planning. One can only conclude that these telephone calls were instrumental in triggering administration panic which led to the hasty *Diary* seizure. Members of the planning committee were informed of the confiscation less than twenty-four hours before the conference. At the time, staff from the Women's Center, under pressure from the administration, presented the seizure as their own decision. The *Diary*, it was feared, would jeopardize conference funding,[5] interfere with other fundraising, and offend readers outside the feminist community who might not understand the text and images presented therein. It soon became apparent that the decision to confiscate the *Diary* had been made by the college President herself, who later stated that the appearance of Barnard's name in the publication implied endorsement of particular points of view – inappropriate for a college.[6] The administration proposed to reprint the *Diary* only if references to the college, the women's center, and the funding source were deleted. This plan was, in President Ellen Futter's words, "designed to minimize the college's role in the *Diary*."[7] The excised *Diary* was to be distributed by mail after the conference. The confiscation left planning committee members stunned and outraged. The *Diary's* designers (who held copyright) considered the seizure to border on theft. Ironically, in trying to avert what they anticipated as a public relations problem, college administrators caused a major controversy about censorship, thus adding more fuel to the fire of how we represent sexuality.

The reaction to the *Diary* and the images it contained makes clear how problematic representation remains. "The graphics . . . appear to be at the center of the controversy," noted the *Barnard Bulletin*.[8] (Nor were objections directed solely at sexual images, since objections were voiced to a photo appearing to ridicule Jeane J. Kirkpatrick, then chief United States delegate to the United Nations and a Barnard alumna.[9]) But the sexual image in particular remains potent, disturbing, often taken as a literal endorsement of the idea it attempts to represent. Such a simplistic view rules out irony, humor, and ambiguity for both creator and viewer. In fact, the conference emphasized the written word, with only the *Diary* and a small number of presentations analyzing sexual images and representations; in this respect, it followed academic convention, in which the text is privileged.[10] Yet even the conference's small efforts to examine images and consider their complex meanings foundered on visual illiteracy and literal-minded overreaction. Unless we advance in this area, we will be consigned to the public display of the most homogenized "positive" images and to sexual representations that are the counterpart of socialist realist art. As we learned during the planning process, sexual images cut a wide swathe. To examine images and the diverse responses they arouse is a salutory experience, which gave rise to Vance's One-Third Rule: show any personally favored erotic image to a group of women, and one-third will find it disgusting, one-third will find it ridiculous, and one-third will find it hot.

The difficult position of the Women's Center in this incident raises troubling questions about the status of women's centers in the university, especially in a period of backlash against feminist thought that affects institutions.[11] Often not enjoying the status of full-fledged departments and staffed by scholars without tenure, women's centers are vulnerable to administrative pressure via threats to fire staff and to reduce funding. Caught in this bind, feminist efforts to accommodate and to be reasonable often fail, since they are based on the erroneous tactic that women who are powerless and "nice" will be protected. It is ironic that women's centers find themselves in the position of seeking protection from mainstream, often male, institutions, since the conference explicitly examined the limitations of protection in the female sphere. We've learned that protection comes at a price.

On the day of the conference, anti-pornography protesters attended wearing t-shirts bearing the logo "For a Feminist Sexuality" on the front and "Against S/M" on the back. They leafleted arriving participants with a two-page handout signed by Women Against Pornography, Women Against Violence Against Women, and New York Radical Feminists, although the last two groups appear to have taken a minor role, if any, in drafting it.[12] The leaflet criticized the conference's "promotion of one perspective on sexuality and its silencing of a major portion of the feminist movement."[13] In their view, conference organizers had "shut out a major part of the feminist movement and thrown their support to the very sexual institutions and values that oppress all women"[14] and endorsed "a tiny offshoot of the women's movement that is part of the backlash against radical feminism."[15] The unavailability of the *Diary* to registrants on that day made the conference's purpose more vulnerable to distortion. Leaflets were handed out before any papers or presentations were made, and registrants' perceptions of what occurred were colored by the leaflet's inflammatory and sensational charges. The leaflet was a masterpeice of misinformation, as the politics of feminist groups were misrepresented and women were accused of promoting pornography.

The leaflet, along with the rumors and distorted newspaper reporting it inspired, depicted a phantom conference, restricted to but a few issues which matched the anti-pornographers' tunnel vision concerns about sexuality. Like the phone calls, the leaflet attacked individual women by name and accused them of unconventional sexual opinions, practices, and fantasies. The leaflet further blurred the boundary between thought and practice,[16] as defenders of other feminists' right to speak were crudely transformed into advocates or practitioners of stigmatized sexual acts. As the petition organized by supporters of the conference noted: "The leaflet contributed significantly to an atmosphere in which the diversity of the conference and the broad issues it raised were obscured."[17] That such diversity of thought and experience should be reduced to pornography, S/M, and butch/femme – the anti-pornographer's counterpart to the New Right's unholy trinity of sex, drugs, and rock 'n' roll – is an example of the effective use of symbols to instigate a sex panic.

The attack on the conference had several consequences beyond the *Diary* seizure and the distortion of the conference. The Rubinstein Foundation cancelled funding for the 1983 Conference.[18] And although Barnard College sponsored the tenth Scholar and Feminist Conference entirely at its own expense, the content was more closely restricted, and supervised by the administration.[19] The women's center was reported to be subject to increasing supervision by college administration.[20] The *Diary* was eventually reprinted and distributed, but not without the intervention of a lawyer, and plans for a 1983 conference handbook were scuttled.[21] Chief victims of the leaflet included individual women – feminists – who were subjected to scurrilous attacks, with consequent damage to their names and livelihoods.[22] "Friends" and colleagues decided they were too controversial to associate with; anonymous calls were made to their employers; they were disinvited to feminist panels and conferences; projects in which they were even marginally involved were blacklisted. Personal attacks made at the conference disrupted their lives for months.

The events surrounding the conference illustrate the operation of a sex panic in which irrational fears about sexuality are mobilized by the effective use of alarming symbols. Women's colleges have been notoriously subject to sex panics since their founding in the nineteenth century, when their all-female student bodies were vulnerable to charges of lax supervision, immorality, and lesbianism, all supposed results of women's departure from the "natural" female sphere. A powerful piece of folk knowledge among women's college staff is that articles in the *New York Times* and *Harpers* alleging lesbianism at women's colleges caused enrolments at these colleges to drop for several years.[23] The aftermath of the Barnard conference shows that feminists are as subject to sex panics as administrators of women's colleges, and that in this case, panics in separate spheres fed each other.

In order to operate, sex panics mobilize fears of pollution in an attempt to draw firm boundaries between legitimate and deviant forms of sexuality and individuals. The polluting elements, drawn from the "sexual lower orders," are given enormous power: present in even small quantities, they threaten to engulf and contaminate all. In this regard, there is no such thing as "a little bit of S/M" in the current feminist discussion, no more than there could be just a little bit of homosexuality twenty years ago in the US State Department's purges of homosexuals during the Cold War.[24] Moreover, those who do not immediately agree to eliminate sexual pollution, or who acquiesce in its continued existence, or who defend proponents' right to be heard are themselves assumed to be highly questionable, sexual fellow-travelers. The only method of averting attack, then, is to see that polluting subjects are not discussed, never placed on the agenda.

In the face of sex panics, feminists are caught in a conservative impulse. We recognize, rightly, that sex is one of the most dangerous grounds on which to be attacked. We sometimes seek to protect ourselves by disowning "deviant" elements, wishing to seem reasonble and not extreme to critics. But critics are not satisfied until all elements of nonconformity have been eliminated or silenced. Thus, accusations of sexual deviance remain powerful: if we cede ground, the margin of what is considered acceptable shrinks daily.

Charges of sexual deviance have changed in regard to content. Within feminism, sex panics in mainstream institutions were instigated by charges of lesbianism, for example, in the late 1960s NOW purges, whereas now they are instigated by charges of sadomasochism. Sex panics create a public relations problem for those women who are concerned with protecting the public face of feminism. Feminists learned, however, that an attack on lesbians was an attack on all women, whether lesbian or heterosexual. Successful attacks diminished all women's options and posed a powerful threat to feminism, since any un-feminine behavior could be labeled "lesbian" and thus controlled. At that time, feminists discovered that the only suitable response in the face of a sex panic was to stop denying the presence of devalued persons and acts, an endless and defensive task, and to insist, "Yes, we are everywhere." We would do well to remember this lesson now.

Sex panics, conducted over a brief time, sometimes leave enduring legacies. The legacy of this conference is a mixed one. Women's centers may now find it more difficult to sponsor conferences on sexuality, believing themselves liable to attacks by reactionary administrations as well as anti-pornography feminists. Individuals may think twice before they speak in defense of sexual minorities or admit membership in such groups, or even venture to speak at all.

On the other hand, the conference succeeded in expanding the terms of feminist discourse. It provided an opportunity for diverse views to emerge, in spite of efforts to censor discussion. It marked a divide by posing new questions and by suggesting that feminists could begin to provide a safe space in which women can talk about sexuality in all its complexity. Moreover, many feminists recognized and supported this effort, as the signers of the petition indicate:

Feminist discussion about sexuality cannot be carried on if one segment of the feminist movement uses McCarthyite tactics to silence other voices. We reaffirm the importance and complexity of the questions feminists are now beginning to ask about sexuality and endorse the Barnard conference for this effort to explore new territory. In an age of reaction, we believe it is important for feminists to resist the impulse to censor ourselves, as strongly as we resist the efforts of others to censor us.[25]

We lack a safe space to talk about sex. In the university, feminists often censor ourselves before even presenting our first drafts. Conference titles are adjusted, speakers are rejected, and themes are reformulated in an attempt to appear reasonable, mainstream, and acceptable. Some of the people feminists seek to please are uncomfortable even putting "sex" and "women" together. We tame ourselves in anticipation of their nervousness, lest the topic seem too visceral, too personal, too powerful.

Where is a safe space to talk about sex? Perhaps the women's movement could be that place. It remains true, however, as Dorothy Allison says, that in regard to sex, "none of us is safe, because we have never made each other safe."[26] Safety requires curiosity, good will, the suspension of judgment, and belief that our diverse sexualities both require acknowledgment and visibility. It would be ironic if in our zeal to create sexual safety for women, we came to police and silence ourselves just as we

accuse men of wishing to do. It would be tragic if such a program
is taken up in the name of feminism.

But we are at the beginning of a long exploration, and we have
succeeded in taking some steps forward. I remain optimistic that
women will continue to explore and expand the bounds of sexual
discourse, envisioning a world in which women can be sexual
and safe, a world which makes possible sexual autonomy and
choice.

The lesson of the conference is simple: there is no safe space
unless we make one.

Notes

Thanks are due to the women, too many to name individually, who
suffered the aftermath of the conference and persevered. This epilogue
attempts to record these events, in the belief that a better understanding
of sex panics will enable us to more effectively resist them.

Thanks to Julie Abraham, Meryl Altman, Jan Boney, Pat Califia, Lisa
Duggan, Kate Ellis, Diane Harriford, Jonathan Katz, Barbara Kerr, Rayna
Rapp, Ann Snitow, Paula Webster, and Jeff Weinstein for reading and
commenting on early drafts of the epilogue, although I remain
responsible for the opinions expressed.

1 Fuller accounts of controversies surrounding the conference and the
   seizure of the *Diary* by Barnard College can be found in: Marcia Pally,
   "The Fireworks at the Sexuality Conference: Whom Should Feminists
   Fuck?", *New York Native*, May 24-June 6, 1982, pp. 14-16; Lisa
   Orlando, "Lust at Last, Or Spandex Invades the Academy", *Gay
   Community News*, May 15, 1982, pp. 8-9; *Barnard Bulletin* special
   edition, vol. 79, no. 13, May 12, 1982, which contains the following
   articles about the conference: Mary Witherell, "Futter Cites Inaccur-
   ate Portrayal for Confiscation", pp. 1-2, 4; Jessica McVay and Mary
   Witherell, "President Comments on Confiscation", pp. 1-4; and Jessica
   McVay, "Whose Point of View is it Anyway?", p. 3. Also, Elizabeth
   Wilson, "The Context of 'Between Pleasure and Danger': The Barnard
   Conference on Sexuality", *Feminist Review*, no. 13, February 1983, pp.
   35-41; "Notes and Letters", *Feminist Studies*, vol. 9, no. 1, Spring 1983,
   pp. 177-82, which includes the petition by conference organizers and
   supporters protesting the leafleting at Barnard. In vol. 9, no. 3, Fall
   1982, pp. 589-602, the editors of *Feminist Studies*, Carole S. Vance,
   Brett Harvey, Ellen Willis, Pat Califia, and Gayle Rubin comment on
   the leaflet; also included is a statement by the Lesbian Sex Mafia
   (LSM). See also the conference bibliography, this volume, pp. 449-50.
2 Dorothy Allison, "Public Silence, Private Terror", this volume, pp.
   103-14.
3 Orlando, op. cit., p. 8; Pally, op. cit., p. 16.
4 Hannah Alderfer, Beth Jaker, Marybeth Nelson (eds), *Diary of a
   Conference on Sexuality*, New York, Faculty Press, 1982. Available
   from Diary, 299 Riverside Drive, No. 9B, New York, NY 10025. The
   special issue of the *Barnard Bulletin*, op. cit., contains the most

detailed accounts of the seizure. For reviews of the *Diary*, see: Lisa
Orlando, "Bad Girls and 'Good' Politics", *Voice Literary Supplement*,
no. 13, December 1982, pp. 1, 16-19; Judith Butler, *"Diary of a
Conference on Sexuality"*, *Gay Community News*, book review
section, December 4, 1982, pp. 1 and 6; Sue Golding, "Dear Diary:
How Do We Learn to 'Speak Sex'?", *The Body Politic*, May 1983, p. 37.
5 Witherell, op. cit., p. 2.
6 McVay and Witherell, op. cit.; Witherell, op. cit.
7 Witherell, op. cit., p. 2.
8 Ibid., p. 1.
9 See Alderfer, Jaker, and Nelson (eds), op. cit., p. 57 for a photo of
Kirkpatrick accompanying the workshop description for "Class,
Cultural and Historical Influences on Sexual Identity in the Psychotherapeutic Relationship". A year later, Barnard trustees selected Mrs
Kirkpatrick to receive the Barnard Medal of Distinction at commence-
ment. Students and faculty, opposed to interventionist government
foreign policies, protested the award, which Mrs Kirkpatrick
eventually declined. See *New York Times*, May 1, 1983, p. 48 and
May 18, 1983, p. B1.
10 Personal communication, Frances Doughty and Barbara Kruger.
11 See "Notes and Letters: Political Attacks on Women's Studies
Programs and Women's Centers", *Feminist Studies*, vol. 9, no. 3, Fall
1983, pp. 603-5; Martha Nelson and Lisa Master, "Witch-hunt Knocks
Out Women's Studies Program", *Ms.*, vol. 11, no. 8, February 1983.
12 Lisa Orlando, for example, is puzzled at the endorsement by New
York Radical Feminists, "which, as a former member, I thought no
longer existed" and calls the "Coalition for a Feminist Sexuality"
which coordinated the leaflet "a WAP Front" ("Lust at Last", op. cit.,
p. 16). Reportedly, Los Angeles WAVAW agreed to cosign the leaflet
sight unseen, assured that the leaflet was a statement about S/M and
not an attack on individuals. See Pat Califia, "In Response to Dorchen
Leidholdt's 'Lesbian S/M: Radicalism or Reaction' ", *New Women's
Times*, October 1982, p. 13. For general accounts of the leafleting, see
Pally, op. cit., p. 16; or Orlando, "Lust at Last", op. cit., p. 8, and "Bad
Girls and 'Good' Politics", op. cit., p. 16; Barbara O'Dair, "Sex, Love,
Desire: Feminists Struggle over the Portrayal of Sex", *Alternative
Media*, Spring 1983, pp. 12-16.
13 "Notes and Letters", *Feminist Studies*, vol. 9, no. 1, op. cit., p. 180.
14 Ibid., p. 182.
15 Ibid., p. 180.
16 Thus, feminists who hold diverse views are lumped together in novel,
if absurd, groupings. Gayle Rubin notes that

> the anti-porn movement has invented a new boogeyman which I have come to
> call the "S/M continuum".... The S/M continuum functions as a dark, mirror
> opposite of the "lesbian continuum." ... The S/M continuum lumps together
> a few actual sex perverts, a lot of projected terrors, pornography, rape, men,
> the left, the Nazi party, the Barnard Sex Conference, butch/femme lesbians,
> and everyone who writes for the *Village Voice*. (*Feminist Studies*, vol. 9, no. 3,
> op. cit., p. 600.)

17 Petition in Support of the Scholar and the Feminist IX Conference, in

this volume, pp. 465-7. The petition was circulated by conference organizers and was endorsed by approximately 200 signators.

18 Orlando, "Bad Girls and 'Good' Politics", op. cit., p. 16; Peg Byron, "More Punishment for Barnard Sexuality Conference", *Womanews*, July-August 1982, p. 5; Ellen Willis, "Who is a Feminist? A Letter to Robin Morgan", *Voice Literary Supplement*, no. 13, Dec. 1982, pp. 16-17; Wilson, op. cit., p. 39; Jessica McVay, "Diary Reprinted and Mailed, But . . . ", *Barnard Bulletin*, vol. 80, no. 2, September 7, 1982, pp. 1, 4.

19 Peg Byron, "Barnard Scholar/Feminist Conference", *Gay Community News*, June 4, 1983, p. 3; McVay, "Diary Reprinted and Mailed, But . . .", op. cit., p. 4.

20 Orlando, "Bad Girls and 'Good' Politics", op. cit., p. 16 and "Lust at Last", op. cit., p. 8; Willis, op. cit., p. 17; Wilson, op. cit., p. 39; O'Dair, op. cit., p. 16.

21 Jessica McVay, "Diary Reprinted and Mailed, But . . . ", op. cit.; Byron, "Barnard Scholar/Feminist Conference", op. cit.

22 *Feminist Studies*, vol. 9, no. 3, op. cit.

23 Ann Roiphe, "The Trouble at Sarah Lawrence", *New York Times*, sec. 6, March 20, 1977, pp. 21-2, 30, 33, 34, 37-8, 40; Barbara Grizzuti Harrison, "What Do Women Want? A Look at Smith College and the Future of Feminism", *Harpers*, October 1981, pp. 39-58.

24 Evelyn Torton Beck notes that unconventional or previously invisible topics have a similarly engulfing quality in the classroom:

It has been my experience that any mention of lesbianism, no matter how brief, in a heterosexual environment seems to expand until it takes up all the space. Students are so unused to this taboo topic, that once they hear about "it," all else seems to recede into the background. "Teaching about Jewish Lesbians in Literature: From 'Zeitl and Rickel' to *The Tree of the Begas*", in Margaret Cruikshank (ed.), *Lesbian Studies*, Old Westbury, Feminist Press, 1982, p. 85.

Thanks to Julie Abraham for bringing this reference to my attention.

25 Petition in Support of the Scholar and the Feminist IX Conference, in this volume, pp. 465-7.

26 Allison, op. cit., pp. 103-14.

ADDENDA:
THE SCHOLAR AND
THE FEMINIST IX
CONFERENCE

The concept paper outlined the major themes and questions which the conference wished to address. It summarized and distilled ongoing discussions of the planning committee from September 1981–January 1982 and guided speakers and workshop leaders in regard to the perspective of the conference. The conference program indicates scheduled events on April 24, 1982. The bibliography includes reports, discussion, and commentary in response to the conference.

Concept Paper

The ninth The Scholar and the Feminist conference will address women's sexual pleasure, choice, and autonomy, acknowledging that sexuality is simultaneously a domain of restriction, repression, and danger, as well as a domain of exploration, pleasure, and agency. This dual focus is important, we think, for to speak only of pleasure and gratification ignores the patriarchal structure in which women act, yet to talk only of sexual violence and oppression ignores women's experience with sexual agency and choice and unwittingly increases the sexual terror and despair in which women live.

This moment is a critical one for feminists to reconsider our understanding of sexuality and its political consequences. On the one hand, the feminist community has been engaged by intense discussion about sexuality. The debate has moved from women's right to have sexual pleasure detached from reproduction to sexual violence and victimization. Most recent issues include: the meaning and effect of pornography; sexual safety versus sexual adventure; the significance of sexual styles, for example, butch/femme; male and female sexual nature; and politically correct and incorrect sexual positions. On the other hand, the Right-Wing attack on feminists' recent gains attempts to reinstate traditional sexual arrangements and the inexorable link between reproduction and sexuality. In doing so, the Right offers a comprehensive plan for sexual practice which resonates in part with women's apprehension about immorality and sexual danger. To respond convincingly, as feminists we cannot abandon our radical insights into sexual theory and practice but must deepen and expand them, so that more women are encouraged to identify and act in their sexual self-interest.

Behind feminist debates and the Right Wing's focus on sexuality, we think, are social and political changes wrought by capitalist transformations and the women's movement during the nineteenth and twentieth centuries, most notably the breakdown in the traditional bargain women made, and were forced to make, with men: if women were "good" (sexually circumspect), men would protect them; if they were "bad," men would violate and punish them. As parties to this system, "good" women had an interest in restraining male sexual impulse, a source of danger to women, as well as their own sexuality which might incite men to act. Nineteenth-century feminists elaborated asexuality as an option for "good" women, using female passionlessness and male

443

sexual restraint to challenge male sexual prerogatives and the characterization of women as intrinsically sexual. Recent gains in the second wave of feminism call for increased sexual autonomy for women and decreased male "protection," still within a patriarchal framework. Amid this flux, women feel more visible and sexually vulnerable. The old bargain, which opposed sexual safety and sexual freedom, is breaking down, but women's fear of reprisal and punishment for sexual activity has not abated. For this reason, the sexual problematic has commanded the attention of feminist theorists in both centuries.

Feminist work on sexuality starts from the premise that sex is a social construction which articulates at many points with the economic, social, and political structures of the material world. Sex is not simply a "natural" fact. Although we can name specific physical actions (heterosexual or homosexual intercourse, masturbation) which occurred at various times and places, it is clear that the social and personal meaning attached to these acts in terms of sexual identity and sexual community has varied historically. In light of a wealth of material, we restrict our analysis to nineteenth- and twentieth-century America, while retaining the notion of historical and cultural construction of sexuality. Without denying the body, we note the body and its actions are understood according to prevailing codes of meaning. Believing that biological sex is conditionable, we return to the question "What do women want?" – a question we can entertain now that it is *we* who are asking it.

Sexuality poses a challenge to feminist scholarship, since it is an intersection of the political, social, economic, historical, personal, and experiential, linking behavior and thought, fantasy and action. For the individual, it is the intersection of past, current, and future experience in her own life. That these domains intersect does not mean they are identical, as the danger of developing a feminist sexual politics based on personal experience alone illustrates. We need sophisticated methodologies and analyses that permit the recognition of each discrete domain as well as their multiple intersections. Despite the many interrelationships of sexuality and gender, we do not believe that sexuality is a sub-part of gender, a residual category, nor are theories of gender fully adequate, at present, to account for sexuality.

Feminist work on sexuality confronts three problems: (1) multiple levels of analysis, (2) limited data about women's experience, (3) overdeveloped theory, in light of limited data.

(1) We talk as if information about sexuality comes from a single source, but in fact it comes from many sources: for example, sexual behavior and acts; inner, psychological ex-

perience; the public presentation of our sexual selves; sexual style; images and representations available in the culture; the place of sexuality in the discourse of the political community to which we belong; sexual ideology. When we compare the sexual situation between and within groups of women, it is important to remember that no conclusions can be drawn by comparing only one layer of sexual information without considering the others.

Within feminism, we find it easier and more politically correct to talk about sexual differences between women than sexual similarities. This is understandable, given our wish to acknowledge real diversity of experience and to insist on our visibility through *difference* from dominant groups, the same difference causing our long invisibility. We think it is important to simultaneously discuss women's similarities and differences, questioning whether the acquisition of femininity and the conditions for its reproduction affect all women in a distinct way, cutting across sexual preference, sexual object, and specific behavior.

(2) We base our theories on limited information about ourselves and, at best, a small number of other women. Given the complex grid of class, race, sexual preference, age, generation, and ethnicity, our personal experience can speak to but a small part of the sexual universe. Yet we wish to develop a framework inclusive of all women's experience. (Sexuality must not be a code word for heterosexuality, or women a code word for white women.) To do so we must make a renewed effort to talk with each other, agreeing to break the taboo that denies us access to information that lies beyond the boundaries of our lived sexual experience. Such is the only way to remedy our ignorance and avoid a sexual theory circumscribed by the boundaries of individual lives and idiosyncracies.

(3) We find it easy to say publicly: "Women want...," "Women hate...," "Women are turned on by...," "Women are afraid of...," "Women like...." However, we find it excruciating to say publicly: "I want...," "I hate...," "I am turned on by...," "I am afraid of...," "I like...." Clearly, our hesitation to make the private and personal become public and potentially political has significant implications. Our theory, as it stands, is based on limited facts marshalled by overdeveloped preconceptions. It is also clear that any discussion of sexuality touches areas of unconscious conflict and fear. Feminists have been remiss in failing to address the power of unconscious sexual prohibitions and the appeal of primitive myths and metaphors about the Child, The Good Girl, the Man and the Family. Unarticulated, irrational reactions wreak havoc in our own movement and at the same time are cleverly used against us by the Right.

Sexuality is a bread and butter issue, not a luxury, not a frill. Women experience sexual pleasure and displeasure in their daily lives, even as women in different communities and different situations may articulate and organize around these experiences in different ways. Sexuality cannot wait until other, more "legitimate" issues are resolved. The division between socio-economic and sexual issues is false; we reaffirm their intimate connection in domesticity, reproductive politics, and the split between public and private, fantasy and action, male and female. We cannot pospone the consideration of sexual issues until after the "revolution." Such a tactic implies a belief in a natural, unfettered sexuality which will emerge after more basic issues of production and redistribution are resolved. Feminists who oppose the biologized woman or man cannot put their faith in a biologized sexuality.

We see the conference not as providing definitive answers, but as setting up a more useful framework within which feminist thought may proceed, an opportunity for participants to question some of their understandings and consider anew the complexity of the sexual situation. Our goal is to allow more information about the diversity of women's experiences to emerge. In morning papers and afternoon workshops, participants will consider the question: what is the status of sexual pleasure – in feminist theory and analysis and in the social world in which women live? and by so doing, inform and advance the current debate.

Much has been written about women giving and receiving pleasure; the conference is a step toward women taking pleasure and a contribution to envisioning a world which makes possible women's sexual autonomy and sexual choice.

Carole S. Vance
Academic Coordinator

Conference Program

Opening Session

Welcoming Remarks by Ellen V. Futter, President, Barnard

Introductory Remarks by Carole S. Vance, Academic Coordinator, Columbia University

"How Feminists Thought About Sex: Our Complex Legacy," Ellen Carol DuBois, SUNY, Buffalo, and Linda Gordon, University of Massachusetts, Boston

"Interstices: A Small Drama of Words," Hortense Spillers, Haverford College

"The Taming of the Id: Feminist Sexual Politics 1965–1981," Alice Echols, University of Michigan

Afternoon workshops

"Power, Sexuality and the Organization of Vision," Mary Anne Doane, Brown University, and Barbara Kruger, artist

"Lacan: Language and Desire," Maire Kurrik, Barnard College

"Political Organizing Around Sexual Issues," Cheryl Adams, Lesbian Feminist Liberation; Noreen Connell, New York City Planned Parenthood; and Brett Harvey, No More Nice Girls

"Pornography and the Construction of a Female Subject," Bette Gordon, Hofstra University, and Kaja Silverman, Simon Fraser University

"Teen Romance: The Sexual Politics of Age Relations," Camille Bristow, The Center for Public Advocacy Research, and Sharon Thompson, The Center for Open Education

"Everything They Always Wanted You to Know: Popular Sex Literature," Meryl Altman, Columbia University

"Beyond the Gay/Straight Split: Do Sexual 'Roles' (Butch/Femme) Transcend Sexual Preference?", Esther Newton, SUNY, Purchase, and Shirley Walton, Djuna Books

"Sexuality and Creativity – A Theatre Workshop," Shirley Kaplan, Barnard College

"Aggression, Selfhood and Female Sexuality: Rethinking Psychoanalysis," Dale Bernstein, psychotherapist, and Elsa First, psychotherapist

"Class, Cultural and Historical Influences on Sexual Identity in the Psychotherapeutic Relationsip," Oliva Espín, Boston University, and Pat Robinson, clinical social worker

"Beyond Politics: Understanding the Sexuality of Infancy and Childhood," Mary S. Calderone, MD, Sex Information and Education Council of the US (SIECUS), and Kate Millett, writer

"The Defense of Sexual Restriction by Anti-Abortion Activists," Faye Ginsburg, Graduate Center-CUNY, and Susan Hill, National Women's Health Organization

"Politically Correct, Politically Incorrect Sexuality," Dorothy Allison, *Conditions*; Muriel Dimen, Lehman College-CUNY; Mirtha N. Quintanales, Ohio State University; and Joan Nestle, Lesbian Herstory Archives

"The Myth of the Perfect Body: Age, Weight, and Disability," Roberta Galler, Postgraduate Center for Mental Health, and Carol Munter, Council on Eating Problems

"The Forbidden: Eroticism and Taboo," Paula Webster, Institute for the Study of Sex in Society and History

"Sexual Purity: Maintaining Class and Race Boundaries," Diane Harriford, SUNY, Stony Brook

"Concepts for a Radical Politics of Sex," Gayle Rubin, University of Michigan

"Sex and Money," Arlene Carmen, Judson Memorial Church

Closing session

"Desire for the Future: Radical Hope in Passion and Pleasure," Amber Hollibaugh, *Socialist Review*

Poetry readings by hattie gossett, Cherríe Moraga and Sharon Olds

Bibliography

Hannah Alderfer, Beth Jaker, and Marybeth Nelson (eds), *Diary of a Conference on Sexuality*, New York, Faculty Press, 1982. Available from Diary, 299 Riverside Drive (9B), New York, NY 10025.

Angela Bonavoglia, "Tempers Flare Over Sexuality Conference," *New Directions for Women*, July/August 1982, p. 15.

Judith Butler, "Diary of a Conference on Sexuality," *Gay Community News Book Review Section*, December 4, 1982, pp. 1, 6.

Peg Byron, "Barnard Scholar/Feminist," *Gay Community News*, June 4, 1983, p. 3.

Peg Byron, "More Punishment for Barnard Sexuality Conference," *Womanews*, July–August 1982, p. 5.

Peg Byron, "Sex Spurs Censorship," *Womanews*, May 1982, p. 4.

"Feminists Split on 'Correct' Sex," *Body Politic*, July/August 1982, p. 16.

Jackie Forster, "Jackie Forster Has Just Hit New York," London *Gay News*, no. 241, May 5–June 9, 1982, p. 31.

Sue Golding, "Dear Diary: How Do We Learn to 'Speak Sex'?", *Body Politic*, May 1983, p. 37.

"Letters," *Off Our Backs*, vol. XII, no. 8, September 1982, pp. 32-6. Includes Claudette Charbonneau's response to her critics and letters from Ellen Willis, Joan Nestle, Barbara Grier, Pauline Bart, Juana Maria Paz, and others, commenting on *OOB's* conference coverage.

"Letters," *Off Our Backs*, November 1982, p. 26. Includes letters from Samois, Women Against Violence in Pornography and the Media (WAVPM), and Cleveland Women Against Violence Against Women (WAVAW).

"Letters and Responses," *Off Our Backs*, vol. XII, no. 7, July 1982, pp. 23-7. Includes responses to *OOB* coverage of the conference by Cherrie Moraga, Gayle Rubin, Amber Hollibaugh, Shirley Walton, and Frances Doughty; and the post-conference petition protesting the leafleting.

"Letters: WAP vs. Willis: Body Politics," *Village Voice*, January 4, 1983, pp. 10, 12. Letters from Elizabeth Dworan and Dorchen Leidholdt and a response from Ellen Willis.

Jessica McVay, "Diary Reprinted and Mailed, But . . . ," *Barnard Bulletin*, vol. 80, no. 2, September 7, 1982, pp. 1, 4.

Jessica McVay, "Whose Point of View is it Anyway?", *Barnard Bulletin*, special edition, vol. 79, no. 13, May 12, 1982.

Jessica McVay and Mary Witherell, "President Comments on Confiscation," *Barnard Bulletin*, special edition, vol. 79, no. 13, May 12, 1982.

"Notes and Letters," *Feminist Studies*, vol. 9, no. 3, Fall 1983, pp. 589-602. Includes a statement by the editors; letters from Carole S. Vance, Brett

Harvey, Ellen Willis, Pat Califia, Gayle Rubin; and a statement from the Lesbian Sex Mafia (LSM).

"Notes and Letters: The Barnard Conference," *Feminist Studies*, vol. 9, no. 1, Spring 1983, pp. 177-82.

Barbara O'Dair, "Sex, Love, Desire: Feminists Struggle Over the Portrayal of Sex," *Alternative Media*, Spring 1983, pp. 12-16.

Lisa Orlando, "Bad Girls and 'Good' Politics," *Voice Literary Supplement*, no. 13, December 1982, pp. 1, 16-19.

Lisa Orlando, "Lust at Last, Or Spandex Invades the Academy," *Gay Community News*, May 15, 1982, pp. 8-9.

Marcia Pally, "The Fireworks at the Sexuality Conference: Whom Should Feminists Fuck?" *New York Native*, May 24–June 6, 1982, pp. 14-16.

"Towards a Politics of Sexuality: Barnard College's Ninth Scholar and the Feminist Conference," *Off Our Backs*, vol. XII, no. 6, June 1982, pp. 2-5, 19-25, 29. Conference coverage includes articles by Carol Anne Douglas, Alice Henry, Tacie Dejanikus, Fran Moira, and a letter by Claudette Charbonneau.

Ellen Willis, "Who is a Feminist? A Letter to Robin Morgan," *Voice Literary Supplement*, no. 13, December 1982, pp. 16-17.

Elizabeth Wilson, "The Context of 'Between Pleasure and Danger': The Barnard Conference on Sexuality," *Feminist Review*, no. 13, February 1983, pp. 35-41.

Mary Witherell, "Futter Cites Inaccurate Portrayal for Confiscation," *Barnard Bulletin*, special edition, vol. 79, no. 13, May 12, 1982.

Petition in Support of the Scholar and Feminist IX Conference

On 24 April 1982, the women's center at Barnard College held this year's Scholar and the Feminist Conference, entitled "Towards a Politics of Sexualty." The aim of the conference was to address women's sexual autonomy, choice, and pleasure, acknowledging that sexuality is simultaneously a domain of restriction, repression, and danger, as well as exploration, pleasure, and agency. The organizers were concerned that a premature orthodoxy had come to dominate feminist discussion. Feminists have focused on sexual violence, but have paid relatively little attention to sexuality per se. Given our limited knowledge about sexuality, the organizers believed that intellectual curiosity and exploration were necessary to advance feminist theory and politics and they wanted a conference that would critically examine theories of sexuality, both within and outside the women's movement. To this end, the women's center and a planning committee of feminist scholars, writers, students, and activists invited about forty women, representing a wide range of disciplines and perspectives, to speak and lead workshops on sexuality and feminism. Their diverse subject matter included such issues as feminist thinking about sex in the nineteenth century, debates about sexuality within the present movement, childhood and adolescent sexuality, eroticism and taboo, the relation of sexuality to class and race, and the question of whether there is such a thing as a "politically correct" feminist sexuality. The conference drew eight hundred registrants, the largest audience ever to attend the Scholar and the Feminist series.

The signers of this letter, many of whom were actively involved in the conference as planners, speakers, or participants, regard it as an important, although difficult, intellectual and political moment, a breakthrough for feminism. Though sexuality is crucial to an analysis of women's oppression, it remains an intensely emotional, often anxiety-producing subject for all of us. These reactions, however, must be distinguished from a series of overt, political attacks on the conference designed to control and confine feminist inquiry about sexuality, in particular:

1 In the days preceding the conference, individuals associated with a coalition organized by Women Against Pornography, Women Against Violence Against Women, and New York Radical Feminists called prominent feminists to denounce the conference for inviting proponents of "anti-feminist" sexuality to participate. Because the conference was designed to open up feminist dialogue about sex, it was portrayed as dominated by sexual nonconformists, who were part of the wide spectrum of opinion represented there.

451

2 The Barnard College administration also seems to have been alerted, and reacted by confiscating fifteen hundred copies of the conference diary, a sixty-page booklet which included planning committee minutes, workshop abstracts, bibliographies, and graphics. The seizure of the diary eliminated an important source of information about the conference's planning process and scope and rendered the conference vulnerable to confusion or distortion.

3 At the conference, a coalition leaflet was distributed which singled out and misrepresented some individual participants. They, and the groups to which they belonged, were attacked by name as morally unacceptable and beyond the feminist pale. The effect was to stigmatize individuals identified with controversial sexual views or practices, such as butch-femme roles, sadomasochism, or criticism of the antipornography movement. The leaflet contributed significantly to an atmosphere in which the diversity of the conference and the broad issues it raised were obscured.

4 Meanwhile, the Helena Rubinstein Foundation has withdrawn financial support for the Scholar and the Feminist series.

5 There remains a very real possibility that the Barnard administration will limit the autonomy of the Barnard women's center and curtail its ability to work with and serve the New York feminist community.

We are signing this letter to protest these and all such attempts to inhibit feminist dialogue on sexuality. Feminist discussion about sexuality cannot be carried on if one segment of the feminist movement uses McCarthyite tactics to silence other voices. We reaffirm the importance and complexity of the questions feminists are now beginning to ask about sexuality and endorse the Barnard conference for its effort to explore new territory. In an age of reaction, we believe it is important for feminists to resist the impulse to censor ourselves, as strongly as we resist the efforts of others to censor us.

Henry Abelove, Julie Abraham, Hannah Alderfer, John Allec, Dorothy Allison, Dennis Altman, Janet Altman, Meryl Altman, Marguerite Anbenstein, Marilyn B. Arthur, Carol Ascher, Carl Auld, Brett Averill, J. Badagliacco, Bev Balliett, Linda Bamber, Barbara Baracks, Victoria Bardawill, Robin Z. Bartlett, Mae Bauner, Ros Baxandall, Chris Bearchell, Richard Debout, Marjorie Bellis, Bonnie Bellow, Janet Bellwether, Marshall Berman, Joan E. Biren, Bettine Birge, Gwenda Blair, Debbie Bloomfield, Audrey S. Blumberg, Pamela Bolen, Wini Breines, Camille Bristow, Gene Brown, Nancy Brown, Elly Bulkin, Judith Butler, Pat Califia, Roz Calvert, Arlene Carmen, Jan Clausen, Terry Collins, Susan Contratto, Betsy Crowell, Dale Davis, Regina Davis, Camilla Decarnin, Marianne DeKoven, Samuel R. Delaney, Gary Delgado, Meg Dellenbaugh, John D'Emilio, Muriel Dimen, Mary Ann Doane, Betty Dodson, Frances Doughty, Martin B. Duberman, Ellen DuBois, John E. Duggan, Carol Duncan, Rachel Blau DuPlessis, Caroline Dutton, Alice Echols, Deborah Edel, Lynn Eden, Sherry Edwards, Diane Ehrensaft, Zillah Eisenstein, Kate Ellis, Barbara Epstein, Jeff Escoffier, Bruce Eves, Patricia S. Faunce, Maxine Feldman, Geoffrey T. Ferguson, Louise Fishman, Ann Fitzgerald, Phillip Fotheringham, Susan Fraiman, Estelle Freedman, Bob Gallagher, M. Colette Gallion, Darlaine C. Gardetto, Terry A. Garey, David Gibson, Lucy Gilbert, Faye Ginsburg, Kristin Glen, Sue Golding, Jill Goldstein, Jewelle L. Gomez, Hattie Gossett, Bette Gordon, Sarah Grace, Jeremy Grainger, Vikki Grant, Barbara Grier, Linda Grishman, Daphne Groos, Moonyean Grosch, Larry Gross, Atina Grossman, Marilyn Hacker, John Hammond, Gerald Hannon, Bert Hansen, Donna Haraway,

Susan Harding, Brett Harvey, Linda Hoagland, Eve Hochwald, Amber Hollibaugh, Janis Butler Holm, June Howard, Candace Howes, Allen Hunter, Joseph Interrante, Ed Jackson, Beth Jaker, Katherine Jensen, Kathryn Johnson, Lauren R. Joichin, Suad Joseph, E. Ann Kaplan, Marilyn Kaggen, Jonathan Katz, Rochelle Kern, Barbara Kerr, Alice Kessler-Harris, Joel Kovel, Grenouille LaBlau, Jane Lazarre, Sally Lelong, Mary Clare Lennon, Judith Levine, Kathryn London, Margaret A. Lourie, Anne Lovell, Doris Lunden, Sandra Lundy, Meg Luxton, Phyllis Lyon, Ruth Mahancy, Del Martin, Lisa Master, Donna J. McBride, Tim McCaskell, Marci McCaulay, John McClure, Carol McCurk, Susan J. McKinstry, Jane Melnick, Linda Metcalf, Robin Metcalf, Sybil Meyer, Ruth Milkman, Alan V. Miller, Juliana Milroy, Honor Moore, Cherrie Moraga, David Morris, Marybeth Nelson, Joan Nestle, Esther Newton, Judith Newton, R.J. Nocera, Molly Nolan, Cathy Nonas, Fran Now, Brian O'Dell, Harriet Older, Alix Olson, Susan O'Malley, Lisa Orlando, Bobbye Ortiz, Sherry B. Ortner, Susan Osborn, Robert A. Padgug, Marcia Pally, Cynthia Palmer, Pam Parker, Jean Pauline, Sue Pearlgut, Jami Peelle, John Perreault, Stacey Pies, David Plotke, Ken Popert, Minnie Bruce Pratt, Deborah Proos, Roslyn Pulitzer, Mirtha Quintanales, Nancy Rabinowitz, Paula Rabinowitz, Nina Raff, Corinne Rafferty, Victoria Ramstetter, Rayna Rapp, Johanna Reimoldt, Caren Renee, Claire Riley, Patricia M. Robinson, Ere M. Rommel, Deborah Rosenfelt, Carole Rosenthal, Pam Rosenthal, Robert Roth, Debra Rothberg, Gayle Rubin, Sara Ruddick, Joanna Russ, Mary P. Ryan, Arnold Sachar, Victoria Sanders, Lynda Schor, Herbert Schreier, Chris Sciabarra, Tom Schoenherr, Eve Kosofsky Sedgwick, Marsha Seeley, Kate Sefton, Mab Segrest, Patricia Sharpe, Martha Shelley, Charley Shively, Sandra Silberstein, Kaja Silverman, Frank Sirianni, Sue Skope, Sky, Barbara Smith, Nina J. Smith, Ralph K. Smith, Ann Snitow, Kathleen Snow, Natalie Sokoloff, Judith Stacey, Robert Stanford, Tommy Steele, Laurie Stone, Nadine Taub, Meredith Tax, Sheila Ortiz Taylor, Aron Teel, Sharon Thompson, Gregg Thompson, Pat Thornton, Virginia Tiger, Susan Thames, David Thorstad, Kay Trimberger, Laura Tow, Gaye Tuchman, Scott Tucker, Ellen Turner, Peter Vallas, John Van Hoewyk, Carole Vance, David Varas, Martha Vicinus, Paul Volpe, Sonny Wainwright, Daniel J. Walkowitz, Judith R. Walkowitz, Shirley Walton, Ann Wallace, Mary Ruth Warner, Paula Webster, Marilyn Wedenoja, Jeff Weinstein, Sandra Whisler, Eileen Willenborg, Ellen Willis, Alexander Wilson, Peter Wilson, Howard Winant, Shebar Windstone, Charlene Wrobel, Patsy Yaeger, and Marilyn B. Young.

Index

Hollibaugh, Amber, 353; "What We're
Rolling Around in Bed With", 243
homosexuals, 2, 63, 71n., 257, 273, 279,
282-3, 284, 288-9, 302, 304; AIDS and,
299-300; arrests of, 270-1;
communities of, 286; cultural
feminists and, 61; differing attitudes
to, 285; Earl of Castlehaven, 285;
expansion of gay economy, 242-3,
296; FBI and, 270; gay rights
movement, 275; history of, 276;
"homosexual menace", 269; hs. as an
ethnic group, 286; immigration policy
and, 291; laws against, 269, 291;
migration of, 286-7, 292-3, 295-7;
militant hs., 287; military regulations
and, 291, 295; need for secrecy, 292;
in New Guinea, 285; persecution of,
270-1, 297, 313, 317; promiscuous hs.,
279, 283; queerbashing, 4, 271; s/m
hs., 244; treatment in sex manuals,
124; *see also* lesbians
Human Life Amendment, 207
Hustler, 5

impotence, 131
incest, 1, 3, 6, 34, 63, 142, 279, 305;
father/daughter i., 217, 221-2;
society's reaction to i., 218
individualism, 63
infancy, 22
infibulation, 259
intercourse, 8, 59, 243, 363, 364-9, 370,
371-2
Irigaray, Luce, 321

"J": *The Sensuous Woman*, 117, 120-1,
123
Jeffreys, Sheila, 302

Kinsey, A.C., 11, 135, 273, 284, 310, 362,
363
kissing, 8, 363
Koedt, Anne, 55
Kollantai, Alexandra, 302
Konopka, Gisela: *The Adolescent Girl
in Conflict*, 358
Kreps, Bonnie, 50
Kristeva, Julia, 321, 347n.

Lacan, Jacques, 321, 322, 324-5, 335,
341, 349n.
Lesbian Sex Mafia, 111-12
lesbianism/lesbians, 2, 4, 8, 10, 14,
48-9n., 142-3, 248, 279, 308, 435, 439n.;
androgynous ls., 236; bar dykes, 279;

Buffalo Lesbian community, 240n.;
Daughters of Bilitis, 248; "dykes",
249, 279, 402; feminists and, 19, 111,
232; Hispanic ls., 158; insecurity of,
108, 113-14; law and, 304-5; l.
communities, 286; l. cultural
feminists, 61-2; ls'. fears, 103-14; l.
feminists, 247, 248; l. separatists,
55-6; Lesbian Sex Mafia, 111-12;
monogamous ls., 301; need for
communication, 108; "pro-sex"
feminism, 302-3; rehabilitation of, 22;
repression of, 125; *Sapphistry*, 105;
sexual lives of, 386; s/m. l. feminists,
72, 303; struggle for recognition,
54-5; teenagers and, 358, 359, 365-6;
threat of, 55; treatment in sex
manuals, 124-5; West Coast Lesbian
Feminist Conference, 59; *see also*
butch/femme relationships
Lessing, Jill, 167-8
Levin, Robert, J.: *see* Masters and
Johnson
Livingston, Jacqueline, 272
Luker, Kristin: *Taking Chances*, 184-5

"M": *The Sensuous Man*, 122, 126
m/f collective, 323-4, 345
Mandiargues, André Pieyre de, 327,
328, 329, 330, 339
Mann Act, 269
marriage, 3, 118-19, 181, 184, 278, 279
Marx, Karl, 7, 82, 88, 308
masochism, 280
Masters, W.H. and Johnson, V.E. with
R.L. Levin, 11, 70n.; *The Pleasure
Bond*, 117-18, 121; sex within
marriage, 118-19
masturbation, 8, 9, 41, 104, 136, 219, 220,
259, 267, 268, 269, 279, 282, 301,
375-6, 385
men, 1; aggression of, 2; attacks
against male sexual privileges, 36;
cultural feminists and, 59-60;
patriarchal society, 258; power of,
251, 258
Millett, Kate: *Sexual Politics*, 81
Montrelay, Michèle: *L'Ombre et le
nom*, 321-3, 324
Moraga, Cherrie, 110; *La Dulce Culpa*,
417-18; *Loving in the War Years*,
420-1; *Passage*, 422; *The Slow
Dance*, 423-4; *What is
Left*, 419
Moral Majority, 43, 274, 295; *Moral
Majority Report*, 300